MW00757180

TENNESSEE
WILLIAMS

Biography

Honky Tonk Parade: New Yorker Profiles of Show People
The Diaries of Kenneth Tynan (editor)
Show and Tell: New Yorker Profiles
Sinatra: The Artist and the Man
Dame Edna Everage and the Rise of Western Civilisation:
Backstage with Barry Humphries
The Orton Diaries (editor)
Coward the Playwright
Prick Up Your Ears: The Biography of Joe Orton
Notes on a Cowardly Lion: The Biography of Bert Lahr

Criticism

Light Fantastic: Adventures in Theatre
Life-Show: How to See Theater in Life and Life in Theater (with Jonathan Price)
Astonish Me: Adventures in Contemporary Theater
Acting-Out America: Essays on Modern Theatre
Up Against the Fourth Wall: Essays on Modern Theater
A Casebook on Harold Pinter's The Homecoming (edited with Anthea Lahr)

Novels

Hot to Trot
The Autograph Hound

Plays

Elaine Stritch at Liberty (with Elaine Stritch)
The Manchurian Candidate (adaptation)
The Bluebird of Unhappiness: A Woody Allen Revue (adaptation)
Diary of a Somebody (adaptation)
Accidental Death of an Anarchist (adaptation)

Jour. Bent House
Taos, N.M.

Lagu. Calif.

T. L. Williams
42 Aberdeen Pl.
St. Louis, Mo.

T. L. williams
722 Toulouse St. between Dauphine &
new Orleans, L.a.

Bourbon

1431 Duncan
Key West

811 E. New Jersey
Hawthorne, California

New Orleans

" I, too, am beginning to feel an immense
need to become a savage and
create a new world"
Strindberg to Gauguin

Hotel Lutetia
Bld. Raspail
Paris, France

W. 63rd St.
N.Y.C.

Tenn. Williams
15 E. 37 - N.Y.C.
June 1940

Tennessee Williams
Mens Residence Club
34th Street
New York City

T. Williams
Via Aurora 7 45

TENNESSEE WILLIAMS

Mad Pilgrimage of the Flesh

JOHN LAHR

W. W. NORTON & COMPANY

NEW YORK • LONDON

FRONTISPIECE: Front endpaper of Williams's copy of *The Collected Poems of Hart Crane* (1933), which traveled with him.

For information about special discounts for bulk purchases, please contact W. W. Norton Special Sales at specialsales@wwnorton.com or 800-233-4830

Photo Research Editor: Ann Schneider

Manufacturing by Courier Westford
Book design by JAMdesign
Production manager: Julia Druskin

Library of Congress Cataloging-in-Publication Data

Lahr, John, 1941– author.
Tennessee Williams : mad pilgrimage of
the flesh / John Lahr. — First edition.
    pages cm.
Includes bibliographical references and index.
ISBN 978-0-393-02124-0 hardcover
1. Williams, Tennessee, 1911–1983. 2. Dramatists,
American—20th century—Biography. I. Title.
PS3545.I5365Z7326 2014
812'.54—dc23
[B]
                              2014022281

W. W. Norton & Company, Inc.
500 Fifth Avenue, New York, N.Y. 10110
www.wwnorton.com

W. W. Norton & Company Ltd.
Castle House, 75/76 Wells Street, London W1T 3QT

1 2 3 4 5 6 7 8 9 0

To

Connie Booth

Deborah Treisman

Georges Borchardt

&

Martha Ruby Lahr

My luck

Art to me is an anecdote of the spirit.

—MARK ROTHKO

Contents

Preface

"The one duty we owe to history is to rewrite it," Oscar Wilde said. The story of Tennessee Williams's life and work, it seems to me, is a case in point. Since his death, in 1983, more than forty books have been written about him. Much is gossip, much is self-serving, much is academic tracery, almost none of it risks an interpretation, which is the job of criticism. Amid this enormous posthumous production, however, a few volumes stand out: *Tom* by Lyle Leverich provides invaluable, previously unknown details of Williams's childhood; two volumes of *Selected Letters* (scrupulously edited by Albert J. Devlin and Nancy M. Tischler) show Williams to be an epistolary, as well as a theatrical, star, though they take his voluminous correspondence only up to 1957; and *Notebooks* (edited by Margaret Bradham Thornton) brings between hard covers Williams's scattershot but riveting personal diaries from 1936 to 1981—a calendar of pain that charts his "bulldog battle" to claim his freedom, his sanity, and his talent. *Five O'Clock Angel: Letters of Tennessee Williams to Maria St. Just, 1948–1982*, disingenuously edited by the recipient, nonetheless contains Williams's high-spirited, intimate, and detailed account of many of the highs and lows of their long acquaintanceship. Taken together (along with his youthful letters to Donald Windham, which were published during his lifetime), these books form a kind of global positioning device for the geography of Williams's roiling interior. The news they bring makes it possible, and imperative, to construct a new map of the man and his work.

As early as 1939, having just acquired an agent, a Rockefeller grant, and a career path, Williams vowed to write plays that were "a picture of my own heart." Over the decades, as that outcrying heart opened, faltered, and atrophied, Williams stuck to his game plan: "to be simple direct and terrible . . . I will speak truth as I see it . . . without concealment or evasion and with a fearless unashamed frontal assault upon life." The plays are his emotional autobiography, snapshots of his heart's mutation. So, to tell the story of the plays is to tell the story of the man, and vice versa. But how to track him?

"The real fact is that no one means a great deal to me," Williams said in his first-ever, unguarded interview, with the *New York Times*, on April 22, 1945. He went on, "I'm gregarious and like to be around people, but almost anybody will do. . . . I prefer people who can help me in some way or another, and most of my friendships are accidental." Williams is at his most alert, eloquent, humorous, vulnerable, and forthright when talking about the one pure thing in his life: his work. In my attempt to bushwhack through his vertiginous paper trail, my goal has been to stick closely, though not exclusively, to the people who meant the most to his theatrical adventure and to whom he spoke his heart: Audrey Wood, James Laughlin, Elia Kazan, Cheryl Crawford, Brooks Atkinson, Donald Windham, Paul Bowles, Paul Bigelow, and Lady Maria St. Just. To create a sense of the immediacy and the drama in his connections to these people and to create a mosaic of quotation and interpretation, rather like that of a *New Yorker* profile, I have intentionally let their voices butt up against one another on the page.

This biography has a strange history. In 1983, primarily on the basis of the success of my recent biography of the playwright Joe Orton, *Prick Up Your Ears*, I was contacted by representatives of the Williams Estate, who asked that I write Williams's authorized biography and force off the field a tyro by the name of Lyle Leverich, a San Francisco theater producer who had never written a book but whom Williams had, nonetheless, twice authorized, in writing, to tell his story. If the Williams Estate could announce me as the official biographer, the thinking went, the theatricals would refuse to cooperate with this carpetbagger. I had a seven-year-old son and an English wife, and we were living in London: I declined.

In 1994, now the senior drama critic of *The New Yorker*, I was approached by Lyle Leverich and Andreas Brown, of Gotham Book Mart, who were hoping that I could help liberate *Tom*, Leverich's completed first volume, from a five-year stranglehold inflicted on it by Williams's soi-disant literary executor, Maria St. Just. I ended up writing a *New Yorker* profile on the estate's shenanigans. (Parts of that profile, "The Lady and Tennessee," appear in an abridged form in this biography.) Through the long process of reporting and the final victorious result, Lyle and I became friends. He asked me if, should anything happen to him, I would finish the job. We may not have held the same views about the psychology of the Williams family or about biography, but we shared a belief in Williams's greatness and in a mission "to report his cause aright." So I said yes.

A few years later, on a trip to San Francisco to review a play, I learned that Lyle had died. He had indeed put me in his will; and I was now ready to do the book. But although the biography started out as the second volume of Lyle's enterprise—I inherited seven FedEx boxes of files and seventy untranscribed tapes (which were, for my critical purposes, largely useless)—it didn't end that way. In order to reinterpret the plays and the life, I needed to revisit Williams's childhood and to take a different tack from Lyle's encyclopedic chronological approach. For this stylistic reason, W. W. Norton has chosen to publish *Tennessee Williams: Mad Pilgrimage of the Flesh* as a stand-alone biography.

TENNESSEE
WILLIAMS

CHAPTER 1

Blood-Hot and Personal

Into this scene comes the man of truth—awkward, timid, inept, even with an almost idiotic side. But he is the bringer of truth, the man from whom progress grows. He creates or destroys, there is no middle ground or compromise in him.

—CLIFFORD ODETS,
The Time Is Ripe: The 1940 Journal of Clifford Odets

I suspect my only influences were Chekhov, D.H. Lawrence—and my life. —TENNESSEE WILLIAMS

On March 31, 1945, at the Playhouse Theatre on Forty-Eighth Street, on the unfashionable side of Broadway, in New York City, the curtain rose on the sold-out opening night of *The Glass Menagerie* ten minutes late, at 8:50 P.M. Tennessee Williams, the show's thirty-four-year-old playwright, sat in the aisle seat on the left side of the sixth row. Wearing a gray flannel suit with a button missing, a water-green shirt, and a pale conservative tie, he seemed, according to one paper, "like a farm boy in his Sunday best." Beside him was his friend, and cruising sidekick, Donald Windham, with whom he was collaborating on the romantic comedy *You Touched Me!* A few seats away in the same row, his chic, diminutive agent, Audrey Wood, sat clutching the hand of the renowned set designer Robert Edmond Jones, her escort for the evening. At the clumsy dress rehearsal the day before, an aphorism of William Liebling, her husband and business partner, kept playing through her mind—"You're only as good as the night they catch you." At the dress rehearsal, as the cast got their notes, the play's tyro producer Louis Singer slid beside her. "Tell me—you are supposed to know a great deal about theater—is this or is it not the worst dress rehearsal you've seen in your life?" he said. Words, for once, failed Wood. She nodded a vigorous yes.

Wood fiercely believed in Williams and in her own instincts. Her father, William Wood, a theater manager, had exposed her at a young age to the art and business of vaudeville and theater; the agency that she founded with Liebling in 1937 would come to represent some of the most influential theatricals in the industry: William Inge, Carson McCullers, Robert Anderson, Marlon Brando, Montgomery Clift, Paul Newman, Audrey Hepburn, Elizabeth Taylor, Natalie Wood, Elia Kazan, and Joshua Logan among them. But Williams, her client of six years, had not yet known success. On April Fool's Day, 1939, tipped off to his talent, Wood had written the unknown author, "It seems to me, from what I've heard about you, that you may be exactly the kind of author whom I might help." She judged him "not a finished dramatist" but "highly promising." By May of that year, Williams had joined forces with Wood, who promptly sold one of his short stories to *Story* magazine. "You are playing a very long shot when you take an interest in my work," Williams wrote her. So it had proved. More than anyone in the Broadway audience that opening night, Wood understood the precariousness of his situation. "I'd reached the very, very bottom," Williams said, recalling his state of mind. "I couldn't have gone on with these hand-to-mouth jobs, these jobs for which I had no aptitude, like waiting on tables, running elevators, and even being a teletype operator. . . . I couldn't have made it for another year, I don't think."

Eddie Dowling, a jug-eared fifty-one-year-old actor, was improbably cast as Tom Wingfield, the play's young narrator. He was also the show's co-director and co-producer. Standing in front of set designer Jo Mielziner's transparent fourth wall—a see-through scrim that evoked the delicate moods of the play by allowing the exterior of the alley and the fire escape to be lit both separately and simultaneously with the shabby genteel interior of the Wingfield apartment, Dowling went into the opening speech. "Yes, I have tricks in my pocket, I have things up my sleeve," the Narrator said, brazenly announcing Williams's visionary powers. "But I

William Liebling and Audrey Wood, 1942

am the opposite of a stage magician. He gives you illusion that has the appearance of truth. I give you the truth in the pleasant disguise of illusion. To begin with I turn back time."

As the lights faded out on Dowling, they faded in on Laurette Taylor as Amanda, the matriarch of the hapless Wingfield family, entering upstage into the apartment's dining room. The reception for Taylor, who had made her Broadway debut in 1903 at the age of sixteen and had been a full-fledged star for more than thirty years, was deafening. On the eve of her sixty-first birthday, she was returning to Broadway after a five-year hiatus. Her rustication was the aftermath of an Actors' Equity suspension for drunkenly disrupting and closing a play. The death of her playwright husband, Hartley Manners, in 1928, had sent Taylor "on the longest wake in history," as she liked to joke. "She'd closed many a show on opening night. The managers despised her, and they thought I was crazy entirely to have anything to do with her," Dowling said. Management might have been wary of Taylor—"the alcoholic of alcoholics," as she was known on the Rialto—but the public's loyalty was rock solid. "Nothing like this we'd ever heard before. And so it thwarted the action a little bit, and it threw her. It really threw her," Dowling recalled about the barrage of applause that greeted Taylor. To fill the stage time and to settle the audience, Taylor brushed the hair out of her eyes and talked into the telephone. "It's Amanda," she said, holding the receiver in her hand—vamping until the applause died down—"It's Amanda. And I've got to talk to you." Finally the audience grew quiet. "This was just about the time I came through the door and said, 'Ma, I've got good news for you,'" Dowling recalled. "Instead of giving me the right answer, she took me into the second act."

WOOD HAD ASKED Dowling to direct *The Glass Menagerie* because of his success staging William Saroyan's delicate and poetic *The Time of Your Life* in 1939. When she rushed him the slender, fifty-page script, Dowling was two weeks into casting a play called *The Passionate Congressman*. "Audrey I love the play that you sent me and I'll buy it," he told her. "Buy it for what?" Wood asked. "I said, 'We'll do it as a play.' She said, 'Will you put a curtain raiser in front of it? It's too short.' I said, 'We'll do no such thing. We'll make it 'long enough.'" Dowling added: "Send the boy around."

Dowling met "a sick, tormented boy" profoundly wary of Broadway and those swamis of box-office wisdom, "the Broadway crowd." "He couldn't believe. He sat and watched. He'd been through the wringer so much. I don't think he even heard half of what I was talking about," Dowling recalled. "He was far away. He was arriving at a decision within himself." "He said, 'Do you really mean that this will go into a Broadway theatre?' I said, 'Well, I wouldn't be wasting your time or my own, and I wouldn't be spending this money if I didn't think so. The Broadway theatre is the only theatre I know.' Without much ado, he left, not too excited. He didn't say much of anything."

"Success is like a shy mouse—he won't come out while you're watching," Williams had written; he certainly didn't see *The Glass Menagerie*'s potential. Dismissing it as "a nauseous thing" and "an act of *compulsion not love*," he scrawled his displeasure on the title pages of the various drafts: "a rather tiresome play," "the ruins of a play," "a lyric play," and, on the final submitted manuscript, "a gentle play." To this last comment Williams appended a note: "The purposes of this play are very modest. The hurdles are lowered to give the awkward runner an exercise in grace and lightness of movement. No stronger effect is called for than that evoked by a light but tender poem."

But the cloud that seemed to hang over Williams's view of the play didn't obscure its shine for Dowling. He broke his contract for *The Passionate Congressman*. "I gave up a sure $25,000 to do it, and I didn't have twenty-five cents when I did it. I was always just ahead of the sheriff," he said. The producers were furious, but Dowling's enthusiasm for his new property was so infectious that he persuaded one of them, Louis Singer, to put up $50,000 without ever having read it. The no-read condition was only part of the tough deal Dowling cut with Singer, who balked at first. "I said, 'Make up your mind.' He hesitated, and I thought I was going to lose him," Dowling recalled. "I said, 'I'll tell you what I'll do. You know what the usual deal is on the Street. The money gets 50% and the producer gets 50%, but the money gets their investment back before the other fellow gets a cent and then they divide dollar for dollar.' He said, 'That's right. Is that what you're proposing?' I said, 'No. That's the deal you've got now. You bring in an agreement where you're not to read the play, you're not to attend any rehearsals, you're not to have anything to do with this. You keep completely away, until we're getting ready to open, and until everything is paid for and all the bills are up. If you do this, I'll give you an extra 25%. You get 75% and I get 25%.' And that was the deal."

Dowling could turn his attention now to casting the four-hander, whose biggest challenge was Amanda Wingfield, the embattled bundle of Southern decorum and Puritan denial. At the suggestion of George Jean Nathan, an influential critic and the model of the waspish Addison DeWitt in the film *All About Eve*, Dowling went to see Laurette Taylor, who lived above the Copacabana at the top of Hotel 14 on East Sixtieth

Street, where, as Dowling said, "she'd been hibernating with a gin bottle for twelve years." "She was a long time allowing me up," Dowling recalled. When she opened the door, the sight of her frightened him. "She was in her bare feet, with an old beaten[-up] kimono around her, and her hair all scraggly. It was a pitiful kind of thing," he said. He gave her the pitch and the play. "Is your telephone on here?" Taylor asked, and shut the door.

Not acting had left Taylor in a "jam about money." To keep going and to keep her brain from ossifying in the loneliness of her handsome apartment, Taylor wrote short stories and articles for *Vogue* and *Town and Country*. She also completed a novel, which she tried, unsuccessfully, to sell to the movies. But "no play has come my way all winter, which is indeed very discouraging," she wrote to her son. "I am, of course, desperately let down in my courage for a bit and certainly let down in my finances."

Taylor immediately sat down to read the play. "Between two and three in the morning, after I finished reading 'The Glass Menagerie', I thought a lot about the mother in the story," Taylor said later. In Amanda Wingfield's misguided endurance, Taylor recognized both the comedy and the tragedy of a grief that she herself was still living through. "I could look back and see her as a girl. Pretty, but not very intelligent, with plenty of beaux. Not seventeen of them, of course. She says seventeen in the play, but she's lying. I know why her husband left her. She talked and talked until he couldn't stand it. She nags her children to pull them out of their poverty. She loves them. For them, she has strength and tenacity." During the war years, Taylor had been sent scripts with only "tobacco-spitting mammas, horrible old harridans—crude disgusting roles," as she put it. Now, she knew that "the absolutely right part had come along."

The next day, Taylor called Dowling and asked him back up to her apartment. Taylor met him at the door with the play under her arm. "She'd spruced up a little bit," Dowling recalled. "Do you think Broadway, this bastardly place, will buy this lovely, delicate fragile little thing?"

OPPOSITE PAGE: Eddie Dowling as the Narrator in *The Glass Menagerie*

Taylor asked. "This is what I'm betting on," Dowling replied. "That's the kind of talk I like to hear," Taylor said, adding "but you can't get a theatre with me." Dowling pooh-poohed Taylor's worry and told her that was his concern. "Can we talk business. Can you tell me what you want?" Dowling said.

"Right this minute? You know what I'd like better than anything else in the world? I'd like a martini," Taylor replied.

"Would you like me to take you out and get you a martini?" Dowling said.

Taylor did a little twirl around the room and lifted her leg. "She said, 'I can't go out. Look,'" Dowling recalled. "She said, 'Look at those nylon stockings. There's a war on, you know that. I don't have a pair of stockings to my name.' I said, 'I could order some things for you.'" Taylor continued, "You're a big shot, head of the USO [United Service Organizations]. You have a lot of influence. Could you get me a few pairs of nylon stockings?"

"I can get you all the stockings you want. I have to get them for the troupes we send abroad. I'll get them for you today," Dowling said.

"All right," Taylor said. "You've got your actress. I'll play that Southerner."

Dowling was thrilled to have his star; but Tennessee Williams, after hearing her first tentative reading at Hotel 14, was not. When he and Dowling got outside, Dowling remembered, Williams stood beside a row of garbage cans, beseeching him, "Oh, Mr. Dowling, you've got to get rid of that woman who's doin' a Negress. My mother ain't a Negress. My mother's a lady." "Young man," Dowling told him. "You'll live to eat those words." He went on: "You wait till the curtain goes up on it. You just wait."

ON DECEMBER 16, 1944, the day the company was to catch the train to Chicago, where the play was trying out, Williams almost didn't make it to Grand Central. The night before, he'd gone on the town with Dowling, Louis Singer, George Jean Nathan, and Nathan's girlfriend, Julie Haydon, who played Laura Wingfield, Amanda's daughter. Margo Jones, whom Williams called "the Texas Tornado" and whom he had lobbied to be the play's co-director, an agreement that rankled Dowling, who referred to her as "my assistant," also joined the party. They were having seasonal drinks at a French café when Dowling proposed a toast to Williams. "Wouldn't it be great, George, a fine Christmas present, if the curtain went up and the next day the Chicago papers gave our boy a hit?" Dowling said. "Just a minute before you drink that toast," Nathan cut in. "You're asking a whole lot, Dowling. I don't think there's going to be anything like that unless this young man takes out a lot of the delicatessen that's in there. I know it's still stunk up with a lot of Limburger he's got to get out of there. If he doesn't, you'll be back before New Year's, and we'll have a New Year's drink at the Algonquin."

With that, Nathan told Haydon to get her things, and got up to leave. "As Tiny Tim said," he remarked to the assembled. "Bless you merry gentlemen, let nothing you dismay, even the wisdom of the acidulous Nathan." The famous critic was hardly out the door before Singer started to cry. "I knew it. I knew it," he sobbed. "What did you know?" Dowling said. "Ilka Chase told me. Laurence Stallings told me. The president of City College, my dear friend. A lot of my broker friends. They all told me what a silly ass I was to put up all this money. I don't want to go to Chicago. I knew everything that Mr. Nathan said." "Oh, you did? How did you find this out?" Dowling challenged him. "You left a copy of the play on the desk one day and I read it," Singer replied.

Williams was stung by the scene, but most of all by Nathan. "He doesn't mean to hurt you," Dowling told him later in the night. "Don't think that he dislikes you or that there's anything personal about this. . . . He's disappointed in me that I haven't had more influence with you." Dowling added: "Go home and don't try to sleep. Take a bottle of gin home with you. Have a damn good night. Stagger onto the train, but get on it and come out there." Williams didn't say whether he would or wouldn't be on the train. But later, after he'd left, Margo Jones took Dowling's arm. "Thank you, Eddie. He'll be on the train," she said. And the next morning, he was.

Setting off for Chicago, Williams didn't know what to expect. "It's just in the lap of the gods," he wrote to his friend the publisher James Laughlin, whom he frequently addressed as "Jay." "Too many incalculables—

Julie Haydon and Laurette Taylor as Laura and Amanda in *The Glass Menagerie*

the brain-cells of an old woman, a cold-blooded banker's reckoning of chances, enigmas of audiences and critics. It is really a glass menagerie that we are taking on the road and God only knows how much of it will survive the journey."

The troupe had a mere fifteen days in Chicago to get their show to opening night. "Well, it looks bad, baby," Williams noted in his diary after an early rehearsal. In the narrow, carpeted Chicago rehearsal hall, Williams was perplexed by Taylor's flat, ungiving performance and her ad-libbing. "My God, what corn!" Williams screamed over the footlights after Taylor "made one of her little insertions." Williams wrote Windham about the encounter. "She screamed back that I was a fool and all playwrights made her sick that she had not only been a star for forty years, but had made a living as a writer which was better than I had done."

"What was she working toward in that terrifyingly quiet and hidden laboratory of her work in progress?" he wrote, several years later, recalling his mounting despair at her muted presentation. "There she sat, a small round woman with amazingly bright eyes usually shielded by a wide-crowned hat that came down level with her eyebrows. I say 'sat' advisedly for she did not often rise to her feet and when she did, she made such indefinite, shuffling movements that you wondered if she realized she was actually standing up! What was she thinking? What was she doing? What was going on? Only the eyes seemed much alive to the progress of rehearsals. How they darted and shone as if they possessed some brilliant life of their own! Watching inwardly, outwardly! But what? And the speech—God help us! She usually seemed to have difficulty forming words with her tongue and sometimes the words were indistinguishable, they were only vague mutterings. . . . Sometimes she would not bother to get to her feet and perform a cross in the playing area. Rather she would mention it verbally. 'Now I get up,' she would say, 'and I go over there.' She would point a bit indefinitely, sometimes more at the ceiling than the floor, and you wondered if she intended to walk up the side of a flat like a human fly. 'When I get over there,' she would continue, hesitantly, 'I open my pocketbook and take out a handkerchief and sniff a little. No, I don't,' she would suddenly amend. 'I sit right there like I'm sitting and I don't do a thing!' And she would look up with blazing eyes at this heaven-sent inspiration, not at all troubled by the blank look that she got from the rest of us in the dim room. I was keeping a journal at the time. I don't have it with me but I can quote from memory this line. 'Poor Laurette! She mumbles and fumbles! Seems hopelessly lost!' "

Williams found himself in a full-court press of production concerns. Dowling condescended to him—he called him "laddie"—and badgered him for rewrites. "Mr. Dowling . . . is trying (in vain) to get the author to write more (God knows he talks forever more!) in his part," Taylor wrote to her son. "Tennessee is Southern, thirty [*sic*], and very obstinate when they call him 'an ungrateful little squirt.' " (Williams's response to Dowling had been to drawl, "I can't find the tranquility in Chicago to write.")

Singer, fearing economic catastrophe and refusing even to pay twenty-five dollars for a new dress for Laura, demanded a happy ending. At one crucial production meeting, Singer said he wanted Laura and the Gentleman Caller—Tom's workmate whom Tom is pressured to invite to dinner as a potential suitor for his sister—to get together at the finale. Williams was being steamrolled. Knowing the limitations of his shy, awkward personality, Margo Jones put her foot down. "Tennessee, don't change that ending," she said, slamming her fist into her palm. Part of Jones's job description was to run interference for Williams; she then leveled her husky voice at the producer: "Mr. Singer, if you make Tennessee change the play the way you want it, so help me I'll go around to every critic in town and tell them about the kind of wire-pulling that's going on here." Williams's ending stayed.

The opening night performance of *The Glass Menagerie* in Chicago was on the snowy day after Christmas in 1944. "It was a strange night," Dowling said. "There was no applause for anybody, no applause on entrances, nothing. It was bitter cold. The audience, it seemed to me in the first part of it, were all huddled like people trying to get close to each other to try to keep warm." Although subsequent ads for the play dubbed it "the greatest play in fifty years," the first-night audience, according to Audrey Wood, "was respectful but hardly ecstatic. The reviews were good, especially that of Claudia Cassidy, the drama critic of the Chicago

Tribune. She and Ashton Stevens, another respected critic took it upon themselves to campaign for the survival of 'The Glass Menagerie,'" Wood recalled. However, there were no advance ticket sales and the box-office takings for the first fortnight were a meager $11,530. "For eight weeks, we starved. We were losing four and five thousand a week," Dowling recalled. For a production capitalized at $75,000, the writing was on the fourth wall. For most of its ten-week run, *The Glass Menagerie* was on the verge of closing.

The play's commercial future may have been in doubt, but the amperage of Laurette Taylor's star never was. The reviews heaped lavish praise on her, with the *Chicago Tribune* even comparing her to the legendary Eleanora Duse. Show-biz cognoscenti began converging on Illinois to see what the excitement was about—among them, Spencer Tracy, Katharine Hepburn, Raymond Massey, Maxwell Anderson, Luther Adler, Gregory Peck, and Ruth Gordon. (After seeing the play twice, Gordon sent Taylor three-dozen roses with a poem that read, "When Miss Taylor plays in 'The Menagerie of Glass' / She makes all other actresses seem a pain in the ass.")

Despite all the ballyhoo, only at the last minute did the production find a Broadway theater. By that time, Williams was in the doghouse. After he'd published a snippy letter to the editor in the *Chicago Herald-American* lamenting "the distortions that have taken place since businessmen and gamblers discovered that theater could be made part of their empire," Dowling and Singer, furious, struck his name from all pre-Broadway publicity. "Pandemonium back-stage!" Williams wrote to James Laughlin, with less than three weeks to go before Broadway. "Intrigues, counter-intrigues, rages, smashed door-panes—quelle menagerie!" He added: "Things are so tense all the time you never know when the whole company will just blow up and vanish! Actors are just not believable—so fantastic! Especially the good ones."

The Glass Menagerie opened on Broadway on the warmest March 31 on record. "We arrived in New York a week before our opening. I rehearsed them all week because I was worried about Miss Taylor. The minute she found out in Chicago that the odds were against us in getting a theater in New York and we might close there, she began to sneak a little martini or two. Nothing I couldn't handle, but I was frightened stiff." Even on opening night, Dowling had rehearsed the company until five in the afternoon, then called the cast back onstage at seven for "a quick run-through." "It seemed incredible to us that by curtain time Laurette would have the strength left to give a performance," Tony Ross, who played the Gentleman Caller, said. "All the company were on me, but I knew very well what I was up to," Dowling said.

The day was muggy; the trees in Central Park had begun to bud. Williams, accompanied by Donald Windham, spent the afternoon rummaging through junk shops on Second and Third Avenue in search of a lampshade for the show's second act. He dropped by a bookstore in Penn Station to tell his friend, the actor-turned-playwright Horton Foote, about the opening. Foote, who was eight years younger than Williams, thought of him as "artistically my big brother." Both men were young playwrights trying to forge a new, emotionally truthful American theater. Foote, who had read early versions of the play, had received permission to stage the Gentleman Caller scene at his Neighborhood Playhouse acting class. He was keen to be at opening night. Williams explained that he had ceded to his agent all but two tickets, with which he was taking Windham. He told Foote that he'd try to slip him in.

At about five-thirty, as Dowling and his wife, Ray, reached their hotel near the theater to change clothes and get some dinner, there was, as Dowling recalled it, "a torrential downpour." "Oh, it was frightful," he said. "And this was our opening night. Of course it didn't mean anything so far as tickets were concerned, but it meant a whole lot in performance, because when you bring in an audience soaking, wringing wet from head to foot, with all this sort of stuff, it's an uncomfortable audience. Well, it was just an ominous kind of thing to happen at that particular time." When they came out on the street again, at quarter to seven, the rain had stopped. "The most beautiful rainbow that I've ever seen in my life was right across the sky encompassing the whole Playhouse Theatre, the sign, the sidewalk, everything," Dowling said. "It was almost like daylight. It was so gorgeous— this beautiful rainbow. And she and I stood and looked up at it. We were two very, very happy people." They strolled to the theater, "thanking all of the gods that we ever heard about, and just feeling so reassured."

As the Dowlings turned into the alley leading to the Playhouse's stage door, they saw Laurette Taylor. She was slumped on the steps, with the rain dripping from the roof onto her. She was drunk and "soaking, wringing wet, like a cat that's been locked out all night," Dowling said. They got her to her feet. "Hel-lo, Ray. Hel-lo, Eddie. It's the rain. Nothing wrong with me. Just the rain," she said. Curtain time was ninety minutes away. Dowling and his wife walked Taylor around, feeding her black coffee and stewed tomatoes from a can. Finally, an hour later, they got her into her dressing room, where she took a shower. "We could hear the buzzing of a great crowd outside," Dowling recalled. The beaming producers were backstage full of news of the celebrities in attendance. "I said nothing to anybody about her," Dowling recalled.

Fifteen minutes before curtain, Williams, with Horton Foote in tow, found Dowling smoking a cigarette in the alley. "Eddie, can you get him a seat for tonight?" Williams asked.

"Laddie, it's all sold out," Dowling said, turning to Foote. "Would you mind standing?"

"No, sir."

Dowling disappeared inside the stage door for a few minutes.

Because of Foote's warmth and bushy-tailed ingenuousness, Williams referred to him behind his back as "a pineapple ice cream soda"; however, the same earnest qualities had kept Foote in Williams's mind as possible casting for either the Gentleman Caller or Tom.

Dowling pushed open the stage door. "Tennessee, tell them in front to let him in. He's to stand," Dowling said.

"Thank you, sir," Foote said.

"Let's hurry," Williams said to Foote. They bustled off down the alley to the front of house.

Inside, as Williams rushed to his seat, Margo Jones worked the aisles, glad-handing friends. "Darlin', we gonna change the whole theater I'm tellin' you, we gonna do it. Honey, we gonna bring you along with us," she gushed to Foote just before the lights dimmed.

Arguing with Dowling outside Taylor's apartment after her inept first reading, Williams had invoked his first monumental Broadway-bound failure, *Battle of Angels*, a theatrical dream that had gone up in smoke. "Oh, my God, our fate will be worse with this thing in Chicago than 'Battle of Angels' in Boston," he said.

Williams had begun writing *Battle of Angels* in late 1939, almost a year after the day, December 26, 1938, that he, a recent graduate from the University of Iowa drama school, had mailed a batch of plays from his grandparents' house in Memphis to a Group Theatre competition and set off for New Orleans to claim his literary and sexual destiny. Williams wagered everything on his imagination. "Know Your Opportunity—Seize It" was the family motto, and Williams did just that. In an attempt to disguise the three years that he'd shaved off his age to meet the competition requirement, Tom Williams had signed himself "Tennessee" for the first time. In one of the scripts he submitted—*Not About Nightingales*—the hero, about to attempt a prison escape at the finale, announces, "Now is the time for unexpected things, for miracles, for wild adventures like in the storybooks! . . . Almost a chance! I've heard of people winning on a long shot." Williams was taking a similar leap of faith, and the bet paid off. The judges at the Group Theatre, the most innovative and influential theater company of the thirties, had awarded him one hundred dollars. They had also steered him to Audrey Wood.

Battle of Angels, which Williams began under the working title "Shadow of My Passion," was, according to its author, "a huge advance over its predecessors." "I am packing into it practically all that I have felt about life," he wrote. Williams's first full-scale attempt "to fuse lyricism and realism," the play represented "the country of [his] childhood." "Onto it I projected the violent symbols of my adolescence. It was a synthesis of the two parts of my life already passed through. And so the history of the play begins anterior to the impulse to write it. It begins as far back as I remember, in the mysterious landscape of the Delta country, the smoky quality of light in the late afternoons when I, as a child, accompanied my grandfather, an Episcopal clergyman, on seemingly endless rounds of rural parishioners," he said.

Working on *Battle of Angels*

The play was a personal, opaque, overwrought, somewhat absurd parable about a dying, penny-pinching ogre of a husband (Jabe), a dutiful,
desolate wife (Myra), trapped by economic circumstance into a humiliating, loveless marriage, and a free-spirited young bundle of sexual cha-

risma (Val), whose exciting presence rattles the cage of propriety in the pious, hidebound rural community of Two Rivers, Mississippi.

In the character of Val, Williams made a myth of his remodeled self. He imbued the wanderer with his overheated imagination ("one of my biggest troubles," Val says), his fictionalized age (twenty-five), his own former eccentric work habits (selling shoes while writing poems on shoeboxes), his haunted promiscuity (Val is dogged by the mysterious Woman from Waco), his literary aspirations (Val is writing a book—"When people read it, they're going to be frightened. They'll say it's crazy because it tells the truth!"), and a surname, Xavier, that sounded like "Savior," and resembled Sevier, a distinguished name in the Williams genealogy, which linked the family to the first governor of Tennessee. In fact, before settling on "Tennessee" as his literary persona, Williams had considered using "Valentine Sevier" as his own pseudonym. In choosing the name "Tennessee," Williams had styled himself as a kind of pioneer. Val Xavier is cut from a similarly intrepid mythic mold: he is a pilgrim soul of sorts—"Says he's exploring the world an' ev'rything in it!" according to one local gossip—who offers the community of Two Rivers a new kind of transcendence. For the shy Williams, who claimed to "always feel that I bore people and that I'm too ugly," Val was a totem of Williams's newfound instinctual liberation and a transparent piece of autoerotic wish-fulfillment. "I, too, am beginning to feel an immense need to become a savage and to create a new world," the play's epigram, words from August Strindberg to Paul Gauguin, reads.

Answering to the nickname "Snakeskin" (he wears a snakeskin jacket), Val is an agent of change. Newly arrived in town, he wanders into a dry-goods store looking for work. Soon he has called life out of the store's joyless proprietress, Myra, and the other local womenfolk. "Decent is something that's scared like a little rabbit," he tells Myra. "I'll give you a better word, Myra. . . . Love." Val's vagabond swagger captures the women's imagination: they ogle him, they are confounded by him, they fantasize about him, they pursue him. His presence broadcasts the primacy of passion over reason; in Two Rivers, it makes him an almost immediate subject of scandal and concern. "Passion is something to be proud of," the town's wild child and cynic, Cassandra ("Sandra") Whiteside, tells him, one fugitive kind to another. "It's the only one of the little alphabet blocks they give us to play with that seems to stand for anything of importance." While the women of the town project their longing onto Val, the threatened men set out to drive Val's free spirit away and finally to destroy it.

The battle of the play's title is the clash of the romantic life force versus the philistine death force: a simulacrum of Williams's own battle to shake off the constrictions of his repressed upbringing and to redefine himself both as a man and as an artist. "We of the artistic world are the little gray foxes and all the rest are the hounds," he wrote from Mexico, where he had gone to write in 1940. "The butcher, the baker, the candle-stick maker—also the typewriter rent man and the landlord, Etc.—are our natural enemies. We expect no quarter from them and are determined to give them none. It is a fight to the death, never mistake about that."

There's no question into what camp Myra belongs when she makes her second entrance into the mercantile store; she's dressed in "shiny black satin with large scarlet poppies"—symbols of sleep and death, which align her with her dying husband, Jabe, as "an enemy of light." Her talk percolates with resignation. "You heard me cussing when I come downstairs? Inside I cuss like that all the time," she tells Val. "I hate ev'ry body; I wish this town would be bombarded tomorrow and everyone daid. Because—I got to live in it when I'd rather be daid in it—an' buried." Over time, Val opens Myra up to her sexual nature and to love. Through passion, she is reborn.

Battle of Angels bore witness to Williams's quest for spiritual transformation, for "new patterns," as an antidote to "this welter of broken pieces, wreckage, that floats on the surface of life." "I have spent so many years making myself over in such a way as to get along with bastards, cultivating a tough skin, rejecting my tender responses before they are rejected," he said. The regenerative power of the primitive—the shedding of psychological skin—is signaled by Val's snakeskin jacket, "a shameless, flaunting symbol of the Beast Untamed!" and an emblem of both his protean metamorphosis and his wild, feral nature. After Val is lynched,

Christ-like, by an angry mob of townsmen, the snakeskin is the only part of him that remains. Hung up by the Conjure Man on the back wall of the dry-goods store in the play's last moment, the jacket glows in a shaft of sunlight—a radiance that clearly suggested the sacramental. The Conjure Man, the final stage direction reads, "seems to make a slight obeisance before it. The religious chant from across the wide cotton fields now swells in exaltation as the curtain falls." The moment announces Williams's romantic credo: instead of dedicating himself to God, he made a god of the self.

A TELEGRAM CALLING Williams back to Broadway in the winter of 1940 found him in Acapulco:

> BETTER RETURN AT ONCE. WE ARE CASTING YOUR PLAY FOR IMMEDIATE PRODUCTION.
>
> —*Theresa Helburn, Theatre Guild, New York.*

Since the late twenties, Eugene O'Neill had been the Theatre Guild's star playwright and its claim to fame. Although the Guild was on a winning streak, with five hits in a row, including *The Philadelphia Story*, with Katharine Hepburn, by 1940 it was looking for a new literary star to hitch its wagon to. For the Guild and for Williams, the choice of *Battle of Angels* was a big roll of the dice.

Flushed with a sense of both victory and age, Williams was suddenly overwhelmed with elegiac memories of the raffish life he'd only just begun to live. "I am becoming more and more a complete hedonist," Williams wrote to a friend about his sensual education south of the border, around the time that the Theatre Guild summoned him back to the United States. In a Mexican cantina, he sat down in a wicker chair and recorded some of the most vivid moments of his "twenty-six years of living":

> I remembered particularly the *Vieux Carré* of New Orleans where I first learned how a poor artist lives. I remembered the Quarter Rats, as we were called. The prostitute Irene who painted the marvelous pic-

tures and disappeared, Helen who entered my life through a search for a lost black cat, the jobless merchant seaman, Joe, who wrote sea-stories more exciting than Conrad's which were destroyed when the house he lived in burned. . . . The sunlight rich as egg-yolk in the narrow streets, great, flat banana leaves, and the slow, slow rain. The fog coming up from the river, swallowing Andrew Jackson on his big iron horse. . . . Life getting bigger and plainer and uglier and more beautiful all the time. I remembered thumbing a ride from Santa Monica to San Francisco to see William Saroyan and the Golden Gate Exposition. Saroyan wasn't there but the fair was marvelous. . . . I remembered days of slightly glorified beach-combing in Southern California. Picking squabs and dropping one feather for each bird in a bottle and collecting afterwards two cents for each feather. Selling shoes across from the M-G-M lot in Culver City and spending lunch hour watching for Greta Garbo. Never with any success. Taking care of a small ranch up Canyon Road in Laguna Beach. And the sound of dogs barking a long way off at night when the moon started rising. . . . School-days in Mississippi. Walking along aimless country roads through a delicate spring rain with the fields, flat, and wide, and dark, ending at the levee and at the cypress brakes, and the buzzards wheeling leisurely a long way up. Dark life. Confused, tormented, uncomprehendable and fabulously rich and beautiful.

When Williams got up, he noticed the American journalist and bon vivant Lucius Beebe sitting at a rival cantina in a crisp white linen suit. He crossed the plaza to share his news. Beebe thrust out his hand in congratulation and asked Williams how he felt in this triumphant, life-changing moment. "Old," Williams said, adding, "The irresponsible days of my youth are over." There was a silence, then Beebe smiled and said, "Has it occurred to you that the play might be a failure?" "No," Williams said. "I hadn't thought of that." "You'd better think of it, Son," Beebe said.

Williams's emergence on the theatrical scene in the winter of 1940 was poised to fill a peculiar vacuum in the field. By 1940, William Saroyan had gone from being Broadway's great white hope to a figure of fun. "Will Saroyan ever write a great play?" Rodgers and Hart joked in "Zip," the show-stopping striptease in *Pal Joey* that sent up Gypsy Rose Lee's intellectual pretensions. After the failure of Clifford Odets's 1940 *Night Music*, the Group Theatre, which over the decade had fought the good fight to broaden the expressiveness and seriousness of American theater, was in the process of collapsing. (It officially disbanded in 1941.) Odets had been the Group's literary star and its meal ticket. In plays such as *Waiting for Lefty, Awake and Sing!, Golden Boy,* and *Rocket to the Moon*—full of lament and liveliness—he had captured since the mid-thirties the heartbreak of the American soul under capitalism. The disappointment of *Night Music* and the collapse of the Group sent Odets into semipermanent theatrical retirement in Hollywood. In the public mind, Odets had replaced Eugene O'Neill as the great American dramatist. By the time the Group began mounting Odets's plays, O'Neill himself, disdaining Broadway's "show shop," had retired from commercial theater to work on a nine-play cycle. (He finished only two.) Although Williams was pessimistic about his chances in the contemporary commercial theater—"What can we produce from the tall silk hat of our esoteric fancy to cast a spell upon this sweating rabble?" Williams wrote to his friend Paul Bigelow—he arrived on the scene just at the time everything in American life, including the stage, was about to change.

"We were deceived by the maturity of the play into misjudging the immaturity of the author," the director Margaret Webster said. Williams later admitted as much. "Probably no man has ever written for the theatre with less foreknowledge of it," he wrote. He had no experience with casting, interfering producers, petulant actors, backstage politics, or, crucially, rewriting under pressure. *Battle of Angels* was written "before I knew what a proscenium arch was," Williams said. The Guild, however, was planning a four-star production. The play was submitted to Joan Crawford, who thought it "low and common"; to Tallulah Bankhead ("It's impossible, darling," she told Williams); and, finally, to Miriam Hopkins, a talented but temperamental film star looking to revive her flagging career. Hopkins was tempted to star and, in order to have more control over the final product, to invest in the show. "HOPKINS MAY PLAY HILLBILLY'S 'ANGELS,'" *Variety* announced in its October 30 issue.

The play was set to open in Boston, a famously puritanical community. To Williams's agent, Audrey Wood, the decision signaled "a deep collective death wish." The producers also chose an opening night that clashed with the first night of *Lady in the Dark*, the musical collaboration of Moss Hart, Ira Gershwin, and Kurt Weill, starring Gertrude Lawrence. The first-string critics would inevitably cover the all-star production, leaving the rest—"a bunch of prissy old maids," according to Williams—for *Battle of Angels*.

To his first meeting with Miriam Hopkins, over a champagne supper at her elegant apartment in the Ambassador Hotel in New York, Williams wore a corduroy jacket and riding boots, which he cavalierly propped up on her yellow satin chaise longue. Hopkins, he wrote to his family, "raised the roof about her part in the play." He added, "I think she wants to do a solo performance." For most of the meeting, according to Webster, who was also present, Williams didn't "seem much interested; once, when Miriam became a little vehement, he prefaced his reply with 'As far as I can gather from all this hysteria,'" Webster recalled, adding, "This is known in the language of *Variety* as 'a stoperoo.'" However, it didn't stop Hopkins from jumping up, at one point, and shrieking, "'I am old, I am tired, I am getting lines under my eyes!'" Williams, who admired Hopkins's beauty and intelligence onstage, judged her "the most temperamental person I have ever met, a regular hellion."

By the time *Battle of Angels* opened, Hopkins had lived up to Williams's judgment. She had fired three different Vals. Seriously concerned about the script, toward the end of the rehearsals she protested to Williams, "For heaven's sake, do something, something!" "How it wrung my heart that I could do nothing for her," Williams wrote. "She had staked so much on this play. It was to mark her triumphal return to the stage, where her talent as a dramatic actress could operate without the bonds that bad screen vehicles had recently put on her. . . . Oh, if only my head would clear up a little—if I could only find some lucid interval in this dervish frenzy that was sweeping us all unprepared into Boston and disaster!"

MIRIAM HOPKINS, who will appear in the Theater Guild's production of Tennessee Williams' new play, "Battle of Angels," at the Wilbur Theater for two weeks beginning a week from tonight.

Miriam Hopkins, star of *Battle of Angels*

Battle of Angels had had only one day's rehearsal in the theater before it opened. Added to "a not very satisfactory cast," according to Webster, were the technical glitches of a complex production—the most bedeviling of which was the apocalyptic blaze at the finale, in which the dry-goods store is torched. Williams's script only suggested, with the flourishing of a blowtorch, the conflagration that razed the store—the fire played as a representation of both mob violence and romantic purification. The Boston premiere, however, required the illusion of an actual blaze. At the technical rehearsal, at the last moment, when Val and Sandra exchange their final lines of dialogue before being consumed by the flames, there was a mere whiff of smoke. "The store would not, it absolutely would not, catch fire," Webster recalled, adding, "After the final dress rehearsal the technical staff took solemn oaths on Bibles that it absolutely should catch fire, even if it meant self-immolation."

According to Williams's account of the opening night, things went fairly well for the play until it became clear that a character, Vee, a mystic and painter, had portrayed Val as Jesus in one of her visionary canvasses. "Up and down the aisles the ladies and gentlemen began to converse with sibilant whispers," Williams said. "Subdued hissings and clucking were punctuated now and then by the banging up of a seat." At the finale, the over-primed smoke pots began to fill the stage with "great sulphurous billows" that "coiled over the footlights." "Outraged squawks, gabbling, sputtering spread through all the front rows of the theatre," Williams said. The torching of the store became "like the burning of Rome."

"To an already antagonistic audience this was sufficient to excite something in the way of pandemonium," Williams said. The first six rows were filled with acrid smoke. Theater-goers fainted, panicked, and bolted for the exits "like heavy heedless cattle." "Nothing that happened on the stage from then on was of any importance," Williams said. The last poetic moments of catharsis between Val and Sandra went unheard. At the curtain call, according to Williams, Hopkins, "gallantly smiling and waving away the smoke with her delicate hand," took her bow to the backs of the bolting audience. After the orchestra had emptied, Williams recalled some scattered applause issuing from the balcony.

If ever the professional debut of a major playwright was a greater fiasco, history does not record it. *Battle of Angels* set a kind of high-water mark for disaster. "The bright angels were pretty badly beaten in Boston," Williams wrote to a friend. Even the audience in St. Petersburg, Russia, in 1896, which booed Anton Chekhov's *The Seagull* so loudly that the actors could not hear themselves speak, stayed to the finale to vent its hate. Williams left his opening night stunned and speechless, according to his friend, the poet William Jay Smith. "He appeared so suicidal that I could not leave him alone," Smith recalled. Back at the hotel, Smith read the poems of John Donne to the disconsolate author for several hours.

The next morning, Williams and Wood, already well aware of their public humiliation in the press—"The play gives the audience the sensation of having been dunked in mire" (*Boston Globe*)—crossed the Boston Common for a postmortem at the Ritz-Carlton with the producers and the production team. A young boy, brandishing a cap pistol, jumped into their path and fired at them. There was a sudden pop, "which seemed to us the roar of a cannon," Wood recalled. Instinctively, Wood and Williams recoiled and clutched each other. "It's the Guild. They're after me!" Williams said. "We both rocked with laughter because we knew in a few minutes it was all about to begin and there wasn't time for anything other than laughter," Wood recalled.

At the meeting, the producers demanded major cuts; Williams handed them a rewrite of the final scene. "I will crawl on my belly through brimstone if you'll substitute this," he said. The Theatre Guild panjandrums, however, were not in the mood for promises. Lawrence Langner, one of the Guild's directors, rambled on about the Guild being an art institution. "If we were not," he said, "we would all be sunning ourselves in Florida . . . but since we continue to be art producers we are struggling in Boston with an unknown playwright." Williams looked at Wood and giggled. Langner caught him at it. "At that moment," Wood later wrote to Williams, "I realized whatever would befall you in the future you would hold your own and 'whether the cup with sweet or bitter run' you would stand up and take it. And by God you have—and do and will—continue."

But there was still more "bitter" for Williams to endure. The outraged word of mouth of Theatre Guild subscribers was that the play was dirty, a view that was reinforced by some of the newspaper critics. A member of the Boston City Council called the play "putrid" and demanded its closure, adding, "The police should arrest the persons responsible for bringing shows of this type to Boston." The police commissioner demanded changes in the dialogue, which was thought to be "improper and indecent"; the assistant city censor, arguing that "too many of the lines have double meanings," also threw his weight against the play. The odium around *Battle of Angels* reached as far afield as Williams's hometown Mississippi newspaper, the *Clarksdale Register*, which slapped down its native son for writing "DIRT" and giving a false picture of the Delta.

"Tennessee was completely taken by surprise and greatly shaken," Webster said. "It seemed to me that if 'Battle of Angels' was nothing else it was certainly clean, certainly idealistic," Williams told her. For about half the play's run, according to Williams, "censors sat out front and demanded excision from the script of practically all that made it intelligible, let alone moving." To counter the City Council furor and to speak up for the beleaguered playwright, Miriam Hopkins held a press conference in which she addressed the accusations of "dirtiness," which she called "an insult to the fine young man who wrote the show." "You can tell them for me that I haven't gotten to the point where I have to appear in dirty plays," she said, adding that "dirt" was in the eyes of the beholder. "MIRIAM HOPKINS SAYS BOSTON COUNCIL SHOULD BE THROWN IN HARBOR WITH TEA," bannered one of the Boston papers the next day.

A few days later, at another production meeting, Williams was told that *Battle of Angels* would close in Boston without transferring to Broadway. "You don't seem to see that I put my heart into this play," Williams retorted. "You must not wear your heart on your sleeve for daws to peck at," Webster told him. "At least you are not out of pocket," Theresa Helburn chimed in. Recalling the moment, Williams said, "I don't think I had any answer for that one, any more than I had anything in my pocket to be out of." After a two-week capacity engagement, *Battle of Angels* closed, in Williams's words, "for recasting, re-writing, re-everything." Williams, who had expected to make eight hundred dollars for the run, ended up with two hundred. "What a failure!" he wrote to James Laughlin.

"Nothing whatever in this whole experience could have encouraged the author to go on writing for the stage," Webster said. "And it was that which troubled me most." The Guild sent out an unprecedented and defensive newsletter to its subscribers, explaining that "the play was more a disappointment to us than to you"; it concluded, "'Battle of Angels' turned out badly but who knows whether the next one by the same author may not prove a success." "I am right smack behind the eight-ball. And it

Margaret Webster, the British director of *Battle of Angels*

is going to take plenty of luck to keep me out of the pocket," Williams wrote to Langner from Key West, where he had gone to lick his wounds and rewrite his play. "A few weeks ago I was a bright possibility. Now I'm just a bubble that burst in Boston!" He added, "You all know that I'm something more than that. But nobody else knows it."

———————

WHILE UNDER SIEGE in Boston, Williams had written "Speech from the Stairs," a poem that seemed to acknowledge a change in the geography of his interior.

> O lonely man,
>
> the long, long rope of blood,
>
> the belly's rope that swung you from your mother,
>
> that dark trapeze your flesh descended from
>
> unwillingly and with too much travail,
>
> has now at last been broken lastingly—
>
> You must turn for parentage toward the stars . . .

Romantic idealism—the notion of beauty and sensation as a means of redemption—would be the guide and inspiration for his young adult self. "That is the one ineluctable gift of the artist, to project himself beyond time and space through grasp and communion with eternal values," Williams wrote to his friend Joseph Hazan in 1940, invoking Van Gogh, D. H. Lawrence, and Katherine Mansfield. He went on, "Isn't there beauty in the fact of their passion, so much of which is replete with the purest compassion. . . . Let us both have the courage to believe in it—though people may call us 'esthetes,' 'romantics,' 'escapists'—let's cling tenaciously to our conviction that this world is the only reality worth our devotion."

In "the days AB—After Boston," as he referred to the debacle in his diary, Williams could still take hopeful stock of himself. He was young, fresh, "capable of passion and tenderness—my mind—vague, dreamy, but sincere and thoughtful and with a wealth of experience—my heart still with a purity, after all this time." He added, "The past—the future—a continuing stream—something will save me from utter ruin no matter what comes." Those impecunious days—he had as little as five dollars in his pocket and even had to briefly pawn his typewriter for food—were filled mostly with work and wonder at what lay ahead. Williams had everything to play for and a bracing resilience to survive his disappointments. "This is a one-way street I have chosen, and I have to follow it through with all the confidence and courage that necessity gives you," he wrote to Wood. The adventure of his writing, his travels, and his sexuality filled him with expectation and a kind of optimism. On the day in 1941 when he recorded the final rejection of *Battle of Angels* in his diary, Williams also noted, "I have diverted myself with the most extraordinary amount of sexual license I have ever indulged in. New lover every night barely missing one." It was, he wrote, "a rich and exciting period sexually—the most active of my life. But I wasn't happy—neither was I unhappy."

In the years that followed the failure of *Battle of Angels*, Wood steered Williams to important theater connections, to grant-giving agencies, even to Hollywood, where for five months in 1943 he worked haphazardly on a Lana Turner movie for MGM—"a celluloid brassiere," he called it— making the studio minimum of $250 a week. (During that time, Williams also wrote a screen treatment for a play he had titled "The Gentleman Caller," which he would rework over the next two years into *The Glass Menagerie*.) With her formal eloquence and her starchy bearing, Wood was a kind of empowering mother whom Williams saw as his salvation. ("Dear Child of God," he began one letter to her.) In these early years, her messianic belief in his talent was almost all that sustained him. In his voluminous correspondence with Wood, he poured out his deepest longings. "I want an *audience*," he wrote in early September 1942. "If I get *that*, I am satisfied, for then I can throw up in their faces the things they won't take till they know me, all the little, helpless, unspoken-for crowd of sheep-like creatures I seem to find in the world and wish quixotically to be the equally little and helpless voice of."

Williams's theatrical world and his lyrical voice seemed swamped in the tumult of the World War. "I cannot see ahead nor can anyone," he confided to his diary, adding, "I suspect it will be especially hard for us who are not made to be warriors. Our little works may be lost." To a friend, he wrote, "The things that I have to sell in my work—what little I can give to the world in the way of poetic truth—is going rapidly down on the wartime market, and lies and manic laughter and nationalistic hoopla are soaring dizzily up!" He went on, "Who can we speak to, who can we write for—what can we *say*—Nothing but GOD BLESS AMERICA!"

But, in a way, the war provided Williams with the spiritual challenge he needed. In his 1942 diary, he hectored the fragile side of himself, which could so easily lose heart: "I must be able to be a post-war artist. Keep awake—alive—new. Perform the paradox of being hard and yet soft. Survive without calcification of the tender membranes." It was during this time that Williams began to dream of "a new form, non-realistic," which he called "sculptural drama." "The three-act play . . . is probably on its way out anyhow," he wrote. "This form, this method, is for the play of short cumulative scenes which I think is on its way in." He imagined "something resembling a restrained type of dance with motions honed down to the essential and the significant. Playing with cigarettes, toying with glasses—the myriad little nervous businesses of realistic drama will be out. The pure line, the strongly chiseled profile will at once point and restrain the emotional impact of drama . . . . Apocalypse without delirium."

In 1941, Williams's vision of a new theatrical climate was pie in the sky. "I think there is going to be a vast hunger for life after all this death— and for light after all this eclipse," he wrote to William Saroyan. "People will want to read, see, feel the living truth and they will revolt against the sing-song Mother Goose book of lies that are being fed to them." By 1943, however, this vague hope of change had become a full-blown conviction. "We must remember that a new theatre is coming after the war with a completely new criticism, thank God," he told Horton Foote. He went on, "Keep your ear to the ground and concentrate on honesty till you know what else is coming! All these people are going, going—GONE!" He added, "Maybe we are, too, but—*En Avant!*"

In a world turned upside down by calamity, Williams lost perspective on his own work. After re-reading an early one-act version of *The Glass Menagerie*, in 1943 he wrote in his diary, "It is appalling. Something has definitely gone wrong—that I was able to write such shit. Hysterical and empty." He worked slowly, with "no overwhelming interest," as he wrote to Windham in July 1943: "It lacks the violence that excites me, so I piddle around with it." "I have been horribly worried over 'The Gentleman Caller,'" Williams wrote to his champion Margo Jones in August 1943. "Loving the story and characters, but doubting the audience-appeal and strength of the plot." Williams confessed to Jones that writing the play had been "hell." "Everybody has liked the script so far, the first time this has happened with any of my plays, and it surprises me," Williams said, adding, "I guess it's a sign that the theatre *is* changing." By August 1944, Williams had completed the play, but his doubts remained. "Have finished 'The Caller,'" he wrote to Windham. "No doubt it goes in my reservoir of noble efforts. It is the *last* I will try to write for the *now* existing theatre."

The thunderous applause of *The Glass Menagerie*'s Broadway first-nighters, which greeted Laurette Taylor on her first entrance, sent Taylor so far off course that she jumped into the second act; it also gave Dowling, now onstage as her son, Tom, time to guide her back on track. "I said, 'Ma, c'mon, now,'" Dowling recalled. "She came back like a little terrier." A bucket had been placed in the wings for Taylor. "The few minutes she had between scenes, she was leaning over and retching horribly," Tony Ross recalled. "She played almost through a fog," Dowling said. When they weren't on stage, the cast, at once amazed at Taylor's performance and aghast at her offstage vomiting, clustered in the wings to watch her. "There was nothing left inside of her, poor thing, but on stage—good God!" Ross recalled. Even Williams from his sixth-row seat soon realized that he was present at a special occasion. He was struck by Taylor's "supernatural quality on stage." "I had never seen a performance like it in my whole life. It was something like out of another world," he said. Later on, he would recollect, "Laurette's basic tragedy was not in herself but in the shabby microcosm of the commercial theatre. It had nothing to offer her that corresponded to what she had to give. Her talent was like a chandelier, all glittering crystal and gold, that was hung incongruously in a kitchen." But now, miraculously, even for the critics in the audience, something rarely, if ever, experienced was happening before their eyes: illumination and revelation coalesced in Taylor as Amanda worried about her children and invoked her long-lost life of youth and hope. "There is an inexplicable rightness, moment by moment, phrase by phrase, endlessly varied in the transitions," Stark Young would later write in the *New Republic*. "Technique, which is always composed of skill and instinct working together, is in this case, so overlaid with warmth, tenderness, and wit, that any analysis is completely baffled. Only a trained theater eye and ear can see what is happening, and then only at times." At intermission, Wood had to be disabused of her high anxiety. "Stop all this hand clasping and stop digging your elbow into my side," Robert Edmond Jones told her. "You have absolutely nothing to worry about—any longer."

The Glass Menagerie began with Amanda calling Tom to the dinner table. "We can't say grace until you come back to the table," she said to her dreamy son. As they intuited from Taylor's weird radiance, Williams and the enthralled audience were in the presence of it. Taylor seemed to inhabit and to transform into light the punishing suffocation and loss of his "haunted household."

Throughout his life, Williams, who was the most autobiographical of American playwrights, always approached his typewriter in the same way: "I begin with a character in a situation—a vague one. If I have a problem, I invent people in parallel circumstances, create parallel tensions. It is my way of working out problems." Writing was good, he said, "in exact ratio to the degree of emotional tension which is released in it." By the end of each writing day—he wrote for up to eight hours at a time—manuscript pages were scattered across his desk and at his feet. This disarray made a larger symbolic point: his mess was now outside him. For Williams, writing was a kind of cleansing. "There are only two times in this world when I am happy and selfless and pure," he said. "One is when I jack off on paper and the other when I empty all the fretfulness of desire on a young male body."

The pulse behind Williams's unique voice—as he told Brooks Atkinson, the legendary drama critic at the *New York Times*—was desperation: "that thing that makes me write like a screaming banshee, when under this impulse to scream all the time is a deep, deep longing to call out softly with love." On stage and off it, hysteria was Williams's idiom. "I have a vast traumatic eye / set in my forehead center / that tortures to its own design / all images that enter," Williams wrote. His plays put those images on stage and made a spectacle of his haunted interior—which he once characterized as "sixteen cylinders inside a jalopy." Each play, he felt, registered "the climate of my interior world at the time in which [it was] written." "I took to the theatre with the impetus of a compulsion," Williams explained, describing the immediate charm of representation—re-presentation—of his dimly understood but persecuting internal world, a sump of confounding and conflicting projections ("the siege of all that is not I," he called them).

"The turbulent business of my nerves demanded something more animate than written language could be," he said. "It seemed to me that even the giants of literature, such as Chekhov, when writing narratives were only describing dramas. And they were altogether dependent on the sensitivity of their readers. Nothing lived of what they had created unless the reader had the stage inside him, or the screen, on which their images could be visibly projected. However with a play, a play on the stage—let any fool come to it! It is there, it is really and truly there—whether the audience understands it or not!" Williams had begun to feel, he said, "a frustrating lack of vitality in words alone. I wanted a plastic medium. I conceived things visually, in sound and color and movement." He added, "Suddenly I found that I had a stage inside me: actors appeared out of nowhere . . . and took the stage over."

At the time of his conversion to drama, in his early twenties, Williams had never been backstage and, he said, "had not seen more than two or three professional productions: touring companies that passed through the South and Middle West. My conversion to theatre arrived as mysteriously as those impulses that enter the flesh at puberty." For two decades, however, he'd had a ringside seat at some unforgettable and indigestible family scenes. Williams's childhood was not happy, but it was noisy. He was born into a hate-filled parental drama—a theater of war in which the children were stunned witnesses. In "Portrait of a Girl in Glass," the short story that was the basis for *The Glass Menagerie*, the Narrator says, "In five years' time I had nearly forgotten home. I had to forget it, I couldn't carry it with me."

For Williams, however, his family was never far from his mind. In a sort of séance with the ghosts of his past, their narratives and their voices were perpetually reworked into his cast of characters. His closest relatives—his benevolent grandparents, the Reverend Walter Dakin and Rosina Dakin, known as "Grand," in whose various Southern Episcopal rectories Williams had spent his early life; his feared and frequently absent traveling-salesman father, Cornelius Coffin ("CC") Williams; his prim and protective mother, "Miss Edwina"; his younger brother, Dakin; and his older blighted sister, Rose, who at the age of thirty-three was given one of the first prefrontal lobotomies in America—along with Williams himself, with his own "irreconcilably divided" nature, formed what the novelist and man of letters Gore Vidal astutely called "his basic repertory company." Williams's romance with the theater allowed him to get his insides out and to act out the warring fragments of family madness to which he had been an understudy all his life. To put feelings into the audience and to watch its startled response was also reassuring; it allowed Williams to reenter childhood innocence and to be known for himself as he never was in the family.

According to Vidal, who on occasion wrote in the same room as Williams, the playwright entered entirely into his imaginary world while working; he was "so absorbed that, as he was typing, he was acting out what his characters were doing." The pinched world of *The Glass Menagerie*, with its alley and fire escape, its secondhand furniture, is a poetic, if not literal, representation of the Williams family's existence in St. Louis—where the family moved in 1918 when Williams was seven so that CC could accept a management position with the International Shoe Company, then the biggest shoe company in the world, after working four years as a traveling salesman for them. In 1943, while he was staying at his parents' house and working on *The Glass Menagerie*, Williams wrote "Cortege," a poem that evoked the suffocating trauma his displaced family had experienced in St. Louis: "Nowhere was ease / You lost belief in everything but loss."

In fact, although Williams claimed that his life before St. Louis "was completely unshadowed by fear," he was already no stranger to loss. Between the ages of four and six, he had lost the use of his legs (probably a case of diphtheria, which kept him an invalid for two years); his beloved black nanny, Ozzie, who disappeared without explanation; and, to all extents and purposes, his father, who, like the absent patriarch in *Menagerie*, "had fallen in love with long distances" and returned only occasionally to the rectory for fractious reunions with the family.

In St. Louis, Williams hung onto his mother's skirts and her every word. He also absorbed Edwina's voluble displeasure about her husband and her home. "His winter breath / made tears impossible for her," he wrote in "Cortege." Soon after the move, Williams's depressions—"the blue devils" that would plague him for the rest of his life—began. In his mind, the title *The Glass Menagerie* summoned up the idea of the family's fragility in the face of a new urban brutality:

When my family first moved to St. Louis from the South, we were forced to live in a congested apartment neighborhood. It was a shocking change for my sister and myself accustomed to spacious yards, porches, and big shade trees. The apartment we lived in was about as cheerful as an Arctic winter. There were outside windows only in the front room and kitchen. The rooms had windows that opened upon a narrow alley way that was virtually sunless and which we grimly named "Death Alley" for a reason which is amusing only in retrospect. There were a great many alley cats in the neighborhood which were constantly fighting the dogs. Every now and then some unwary young cat would allow itself to be pursued into this alley way which had only one opening. The end of the cul-de-sac was directly beneath my sister's bedroom window and it was here that the cats would have to turn around to face their pursuers in mortal combat. My sister would be awakened in the night by the struggle and in the morning the hideously mangled victim would be lying by her window. The side of the alley way had become so odious to her, for this reason that she kept the shade constantly drawn so that the interior of her bedroom had a perpetual twilight atmosphere. Something had to be done to relieve the gloom. So my sister and I painted all her furniture white; she put white

With father, Cornelius ("CC")

curtains at the window and on the shelves around the room she collected a large assortment of little glass articles of which she was particularly fond. Eventually the room took on a light and delicate appearance, in spite of the lack of outside illumination. When I left home a number of years later, it was this room that I recalled most vividly and poignantly when looking back on our home life. They were mostly little glass animals. By poetic association they came to represent, in my memory, all the softest emotions that belong to recollection of things past. They stood for the small and tender things that relieve the austere pattern of life and make it endurable to the Sensitive. The alley way where the cats were torn to pieces was one thing—my sister's white curtains and tiny menageries were another. Somewhere between them was the world that we lived in.

The Williams family's impoverishment was as much emotional as material. As Edwina pointed out in her memoir *Remember Me to Tom*, their first apartment "was no tenement." "We could not afford to buy a house in an exclusive neighborhood so we kept trying to find roomier apartments, and houses for rent," she wrote. Over the subsequent decade, the family moved nine times, shifting the façade of bourgeois comfort with them—a piano in the parlor, a record player, a car, a membership to the local country club, and, latterly, a cook. In the rural calm of Clarksdale, Mississippi, the Williamses had been part of a minister's household, a patrician bulwark of the local community. St. Louis dislocated them not just from place but also from prestige. The abrasions of anonymity in middle-class city dwelling were unsettling for everyone, but especially unconscionable for a snob like Edwina, who was an active member of the Daughters of the American Revolution (she was born in Ohio but adopted the style and manners of a Southern belle) and whose head had been turned by the raffish CC Williams partly because he came from one of the first families of Tennessee. CC's mother, Isabel Coffin, had a pedigree that stretched back to the Virginia settlers; his father, Thomas Lanier Williams II—for whom Tennessee was named—was a well-known politician with an illustrious family tree. But, with CC, a pedestrian salesman, the heroic lineage of the clan seemed to have come to a halt.

Williams saw his literary endeavor both as revenge against his father's stalled life and as rebirth of his ancestors' legacy of daring. "The Williamses had fought the Indians for Tennessee," he wrote. "And I had already discovered that the life of a young writer was going to be something similar to the defense of a stockade against a band of savages." In an early

With mother, Edwina

stab at the material of *The Glass Menagerie*—a verse drama entitled "The Wingfields of America"—Williams invoked the still water on which the family destiny seemed to have floundered. "In the beginning there was high adventure for the Wingfields, and they were equal to it," the Narrator of "The Wingfields" begins. He goes on:

> The contents of the Americas were baptized in their blood.
> They were the pioneers. . . .
> They were the ones
> That took the trail westward again,
> for the lands that were known
> were not large enough to contain them

The introduction to the poem concludes:

> Dimly and under the surface of their lives, the Wingfields
> wondered where the excitement had gone, what had become of the first
> wonderful something
>> With which they had come
>>> Through the mists of morning and through the
>>> mountain pines with horses and barges and guns—
>>> *To make a new world!*
>>> What had they made? A world!
>> But was it actually new?
>>> That is what the Wingfields dimly wondered.

Williams, who called CC "the saddest man I ever knew," wrote, "He was not a man capable of examining his behavior toward his family, or capable of changing it." When CC was five, his mother died of tuberculosis. Her early death, as Williams wrote in his memoir, left CC without "the emollient influence of a mother," or, as it happened, without the containing influence of a father. In four unsuccessful bids to become the governor of Tennessee, Thomas Lanier Williams II had squandered much of the family fortune. CC was shunted off to a series of oppressive and inferior boarding schools, where he quickly acquired a reputation for hell-raising. Finally, he was sent to military school, where his "fierce blood" inevitably played itself out in a series of disciplinary misadventures. He was rebellious and restless. He flirted with the notion of becoming a lawyer, and even studied for two years at the College of Law at the University of Tennessee before volunteering to fight in the Spanish-American War. But both the law and the military were too authoritarian for CC's bumptious, wayward spirit. For a time CC worked as the regional manager of a telephone company before becoming a drummer for a Knoxville men's clothing firm. As a traveling salesman he could live by his own rules and by the laws of motion. In Williams's early play *The Spinning Song*, the father admits a need for "continual excitement"; if CC didn't have a destiny or a solid emotional core, the road, at least, provided a kind of direction. For CC movement was an antidote to anxiety; over time, his peripatetic writer-son—known to his friends as "Bird"—would adopt the same defensive strategy. "I have an instinct for self-destruction," Williams has a character say in *Battle of Angels*. "I'm running away from it all the time."

CC and Edwina were victims of their hidebound times. In both their lives something remained hidden. CC drew an iron curtain around his feelings, refusing ever to discuss his own parents or his childhood, which made his volatility all the more arbitrary and bewildering. Likewise, Edwina never acknowledged or understood the secret in her own family between her convent-educated mother—"the least demonstrative person I've known," she said—and her doting father, who was "not the most masculine of men," as Williams described him. Despite his lifelong show of rectitude, according to Gore Vidal, who knew him, the civilized Reverend Dakin had an interest in the "Grecian vice." Although Williams alluded to a certain caprice in Reverend Dakin's nature—"he is humble and affectionate but incurably set upon satisfying his own impulses whatever they may be"—he left it for others to read the sexual implications in the ferocity of Reverend Dakin's denial during one crucial incident of his old age.

One day in 1934, in Memphis, when the Reverend was living on a retirement pension of eighty-five dollars a month, two men came to the door. The Reverend handed over most of his wife's savings—cashing in five thousand out of seventy-five hundred dollars' worth of government bonds. "She said 'Why, Walter?' Again and again, till finally he said, 'Rose, don't question me any more because if you do, I will go away by myself and you'll never hear from me again!'" Williams wrote. "At that point she moved from the wicker chair to the porch swing. . . . As my grandmother swung gently back and forth and evening closed about them in their spent silence . . . I felt without quite understanding, something that all their lives had been approaching, even half knowingly, a slow and terrible facing of something between them. 'Why, Walter?' The following morning my grandfather was very busy and my grandmother was totally silent. He went into the tiny attic of the bungalow and took out of a metal filing case a great, great, great pile of cardboard folders containing all his old sermons. He went into the back yard of the bungalow with this load, taking several trips . . . and then he started a fire and fifty-five years of hand-written sermons went up in smoke. . . . What I most remember more than that blaze, was the silent white blaze of my grandmother's face as she stood over the washtub . . . not once even glancing out of the window where the old gentleman, past eighty, was performing this auto-da-fé as an act of purification. 'Why, Walter?' Nobody knows! Nobody but my grandfather who has kept the secret into this his ninety-sixth spring."

"The Bird told me that he thought that his grandfather had been blackmailed because of an encounter with a boy," Gore Vidal wrote. The Reverend Dakin's last words were "I want to go to Key West"—a homosexual watering hole he frequently visited with Williams, who bought a house there in 1950. "You'd think, being an Episcopal Minister, he'd have wanted to go to Heaven," Dakin Williams told the press, missing the point that to a man of Reverend Dakin's likely closeted inclinations, Key West *was* Heaven.

Williams, who often complained of feeling "like a ghost," grew up in not one but two haunted households where secrets and the unsayable suffused daily life with a sense of masquerade, creating an emptiness as palpable, elusive, and corrosive as it was to the Wingfields. The blown-up "ineluctably smiling" photo of Amanda's decamped husband "facing the audience" on the living room wall allows a sense of the spectral to hover ironically at the edge of *The Glass Menagerie*'s theatrical experience, at once an immanence and homage to the presence of absence in the fabric of the Williams family life. To their children and to themselves, CC and Edwina were ghostly figures, both unknowable and unknowing. Never having experienced much love or ease, CC inevitably chose a partner who could provide him with neither. Edwina's personality, according to Williams, was marked by a "gross lack of sensitivity." CC was a dashing twenty-seven when he met Edwina, who thought herself over the hill at twenty-three. He knew—as salesmen must—how to persuade; he had liveliness, humor, and a gift of the gab. "One thing your father had plenty of—was charm!" Amanda says in *The Glass Menagerie*, echoing Edwina's familiar mantra of disenchantment. "Before we arrived in St. Louis, I saw only the charming, gallant, cheerful side of Cornelius," Edwina wrote (omitting to mention that, in those early days, CC had seen only the seductive, playful side of her). "I never could understand how Cornelius and Edwina ever got together," Margaret Brownlow, a well-born Knoxville friend of the family, said. "To Edwina, there was no fun in life at all. To Cornelius, everything was fun. He drank. He danced. He smoked. He just did everything. Edwina just frowned on that. She just wasn't raised that way and she didn't like it." She added, "She rather fancied herself."

When Edwina set up house in St. Louis, she was thirty-four. She had been married to CC for eleven years; it was the first time that the family lived under one roof away from her parents. It was also the first time that Edwina had to cook. When CC had asked for Edwina's hand in marriage, the Reverend Dakin told him, "Edwina can't sew. And she can't cook. There's nothing she can do but be a social butterfly." CC replied, "Mr. Dakin, I am not looking for a cook." By her own admission, Edwina was a spoiled only child; her domestic ignorance was a badge of aristocratic honor. But in St. Louis, deprived of her parents and her privilege, she was thrown back on herself and on the limitations of her and her husband's Victorian rigidities. For different reasons, both members of the couple were soon disappointed and furious. CC took refuge from his hurt in excessive drink; Edwina, a teetotaler, showed her umbrage through excessive propriety. The result was war. Whereas Williams's maternal grandparents were for him an inspirational model of intimacy—"Baucis and Philemon . . . that's what they were like. . . . I thank God that I have seen exemplified in my grandmother and grandfather the possibility of two people being so lovingly close as they were that they were almost like a tree"—his parents were "split violently apart and tore the children apart through division and conflict." Edwina claimed with much justification to be terrorized by her husband, who, Williams wrote, always entered "the house as though he were entering it with the intention of tearing it down from inside." CC, who made a good salary, withheld money; Edwina, who was some kind of emotional terrorist herself, withheld affection.

The beautiful, pious chatterbox who had sworn her devotion to CC was now devoted exclusively to her children. (CC never handled the news of his own paternity well. On hearing that his wife was pregnant with their first child, Rose, he was stunned. "It was as though a thunderclap had broken," Edwina said. After Tom was born, CC remarked to Rose within earshot of Edwina, "We don't think much of that new baby, do we?" And when Edwina informed him that she was pregnant with their third child, Dakin, CC responded, "Then it isn't mine!") CC felt increasingly unloved and unappreciated by his household; for her part, Edwina used her children as a kind of fortress against what she perceived as CC's cruelty and betrayal. The children got the full measure of her concern and her intelligence; CC got the full measure of her prudery and her tongue. After Dakin's birth in 1919, CC was banished from the marital bed. Edwina wanted nothing to do with sex; CC, as Dakin Williams recalled, "was eager to get as much as he could, wherever he could get it."

In *The Spinning Song*, Williams dramatized the double bind of his parents' standoff—which *The Glass Menagerie* reimagines in rather more positive terms, turning his father into a poetic symbol of absence rather than acrimony, and his mother into a figure of "great but confused vitality" instead of a scold. In one scene of *The Spinning Song*, a small boy is crying at the foot of a Christmas tree as his father glowers over him; the mother takes the father to task for bringing his "turbulence" into their home and declares, "Our marriage was a mistake." The father, in response, displaces his anger at his wife onto the child, whom he hectors about properly picking up his toy blocks—"Your mother's made you a sissy!" The boy "stares at him with helpless fear," then "runs to his mother for protection." The scene continues:

MOTHER: You've frightened him! . . .
FATHER: That's right. Turn the children against me.
MOTHER: They don't know you. You're a stranger almost. And it

would be better for you to stay one than come home on holidays to shock them. . . .

(*Ariadne enters clutching a doll. Stands frightened, staring . . .*)

FATHER: They're my children.

MOTHER: You've disowned them already.

FATHER: I've been cut off.

MOTHER: Yes, but you did the cutting!

FATHER: Laura, let's don't quarrel, not today!

MOTHER: (*crying out*) Look at poor Ariadne! Ariadne come here! You've terrified her with your drunken shouting. (*The girl runs to her.*) . . . See what you've done? You've spoiled their Christmas for them. They're not like other children. They're more easily bruised, they have to be sheltered more. . . .

FATHER: I love the children.

MOTHER: You show it very strangely.

FATHER: I love you, Laura.

MOTHER: You show that strangely, too.

(*He grasps her rigid figure in an embrace.*)

FATHER: Find some way to quiet me, keep me still!

MOTHER: It's too late!

CC was blinkered and belligerent; as he aged, his body began to bear signs of these traits. He had sight in only one eye; part of one ear had been bitten off in a poker fight. (His ear was repaired by plastic surgery, but nothing could mend his reputation within the International Shoe Company.) Full of rages and resentments, he was aloof, dismissive, quick-tempered, and frequently terrifying. "Most of the time, life with him held either spoken or unspoken terror," Edwina wrote. "In my mind, my husband became 'the man of wrath.'" Williams, like Edwina, gave CC a wide berth. The home was a hothouse of violence. "Come out of there. I'm going to kill you," CC shouted to Edwina when he was liquored up. According to her, he threatened abandonment on an almost monthly basis. "Take the children and go. Just get out," CC brayed. Williams wrote of his father's gruff booming voice, "You wanted to shrink away from it, to hide yourself."

At seven in the morning on New Year's Day, 1933, for instance,

Edwina was preparing breakfast for the children when CC arrived home after an all-night bender. "I made the mistake of protesting, not realizing how much under the influence of liquor he was," she wrote in her diary. "He flew into a rage and threatened me. I locked my door and tried to reason with him through the closed door. 'Open that door or I'll bust it in!' Before I could obey the command he had suited the action to the word, the lock broke, the door flew open striking me in the nose and knocking me to the floor where I lay dazed. Meanwhile Rose wakens, hears the commotion, sees me lying on the floor with nose bleeding and rushes into the hall screaming, 'Help, he is killing her!'" In *Battle of Angels*, Williams captured something of the toxic marriage. "And I—I had to endure him!" Myra tells Val about her husband. "Ahh, my flesh always crawled when he touched me."

Edwina liked to say that CC loved only "two breathing things: Dakin and the dog in the house." (Edwina's nickname for CC was "Neal," which was also the name of one of their dogs.) CC took Dakin with him to Cardinals baseball games and to Ruggeri's steak house for a seventy-five-cent T-bone. To Rose, however, he could be withering. Once, after she danced for him, CC remarked, "Just like a moo-cow." And to his un-athletic, morbidly shy, and effeminate first son—the first male to replace him in Edwina's affections—CC could be annihilating. He ridiculed him as "Miss Nancy"; when Williams flunked ROTC, in his third year at the University of Missouri—an insult to the military heritage of the Williams family—CC took the draconian measure of withdrawing him from the university and putting him to work at the International Shoe Company—a job that Williams characterized as "designed for insanity . . . a living death." Despite his son's complaints and subsequent breakdown, the hard-nosed CC contended that Tom's sixty-five dollars a month was "a whole lot more than he was worth." "Dad resented any money Mother spent on Tom, and violent arguments were precipitated by bills Mother incurred at Famous-Barr for clothes for Tom," Dakin recalled.

OPPOSITE PAGE: Rose Williams as a teenager

Williams never sought or got much approval from CC. "Off and on he would make abortive efforts to show affection, would ask me to go downtown to the movies with him," he wrote to the critic Kenneth Tynan of their childhood relationship. "I would go but would be frozen stiff with fear of him and, being defeated repeatedly, he gave up." "I think he loved me," Williams said of his father, but he was never quite sure. His reaction to CC's fiats was not titanic fury but "desolation," he recalled. "[Tom] did not defy his father. I can only guess what this must have cost him psychically," Edwina said. "I had begun to regard Dad's edicts as being—as far as I was concerned—too incomprehensibly and incontestably Jovian to feel about them anything but what a dead-tired animal feels when it's whipped on further," Williams said. "Of course, under this hopeless non-resistance there must have been an unconscious rage, not just at Dad but my own cowardice and impotent submission. This I realize because as I have grown older I have discovered a big underground rebellion that was there all along, just waiting for a way out."

Well into his adulthood, Williams continued to see his combustible father through the lens of his mother's disillusionment. "It was like walking on eggs every minute of the day and night," Edwina said of her marriage. "Cold, cold, cold / was the merciless blood of your father," Williams's poem "Cortege" begins. It continues, "She passed him and crept sidewise / down the stairs, / loathing the touch / of the doorknob he had clasped, / hating the napkin / he had used at the table." While working on *The Glass Menagerie* in St. Louis in 1943, Williams wrote to Windham, "The old man has just now left the house on his long anticipated trip to the West Coast. We hope he never comes back, but nothing returns more certainly than evil." The "evil" and the "we" announced both Williams's bias and his collusion in his mother's version of events. (Another sign of his internal alliance was Williams's distinctive drawl; CC had no Southern accent, his mother did.) For most of his adult life, Williams dreaded his visits home. "My father—how to meet him again—will I be able to do it?" he wrote in his 1942 journal. "Or will I run away again?—And cheat my poor Mother who goes without a servant to keep me going?" In 1943, he wrote, "We made talk alone for the first time in probably ten or fifteen years. A pathetic old man but capable of being a devil." He went on: "It's like a Chekhov play, only much wilder and sadder." By this time, the fractious family was so polarized that CC ate alone at a first sitting, and Edwina and her parents ate second.

"What a dark and bewildering thing it is, this family group," Williams wrote to Windham. "I can only feel one thing, the necessity for strength and the pettiness of all other considerations. I guess that is what I came home for. Because I can't give them any help." "Does nothing but stay home and drink," Williams wrote to Wood about his father. "When sufficiently drunk I think he is dangerous. Mother says that he talks threateningly and abusively to my grandfather." By the time of his last visit home, in early March 1945, before the opening of *The Glass Menagerie*, Williams could no longer spend time in the house. For the entire week he felt compelled to stay away from five in the afternoon until two in the morning—"Any excuse just to get away and escape talk and questioning!" he confided to Laughlin. He continued, "Tonight I came in at ten—the earliest—and was greeted by a flood of tears and reproaches—and how could I explain or excuse myself except by saying—Yes, it's true, I can't stand it here, not even one night out of one week out of one year!"

Williams's eloquence, like his neurotic nature, was part of his family inheritance. While the family's violence shaped his personality, its fluency shaped his prose. The Dakins, Ottes, and Williamses, who comprised his family tree, were well educated and well spoken. Williams grew up saturated in the rich linguistic brew of biblical imperative, Puritan platitude, classical allusion, patrician punctilio, and Negro homily. His beloved grandfather, the Reverend Dakin, who was the formative male figure of his early years, had a mellifluous voice and enjoyed reading aloud. ("He could recite poetry by the yard," Edwina said. "I'm sure Tom got some of his love of books from Father.") The Reverend was also something of a ham in the pulpit. Delivering his sermons, which were written out in a hand as limpid and florid as his speech, he spoke with particular dramatic flair. "Pitch now your tents toward Heaven and the Sure Rising," he intoned, in a sermon first given in 1901, a decade before

With grandmother and grandfather, Rosina Dakin ("Grand") and the Reverend Dakin

Williams was born, and last delivered in 1920, by which time Williams
was in the habit of clinging to his grandfather's every metaphor-laden
word. "As the storm of sin rages fiercely about you and within you, as the
horizon of the world grows darker with new and ever new forms of evil,

learn to shelter yourself more and more closely in the Rock of Ages till the storm shall cease and the blackened sky pierced by radiant rays of glory from the Son of Righteousness who will come to you with healings in his Wings."

Edwina was as wordy as her father, though her proselytizing was of a different kind. "Is my mother a lung lady?" Williams asked, in one of his earliest recorded childhood sentences. Although Edwina chose to construe this as a comical malaprop for "young lady," the answer to her toddler's question was an unequivocal yes. Edwina was all lungs. "She was always talking," Dakin said. "There was never any silence. You would step in the room, and she immediately started." He went on, "She liked to focus the attention on herself by talking. She wouldn't pay any attention to anyone but herself. It was like water dripping—tip, tip, tip."

Edwina wasn't just a talker: she was a narrative event, a torrent of vivid, cadenced, florid, and confounding speech that could not be denied. Eloquence was a show of power amid her powerlessness. As a child, she had dreamed of being an opera singer; in adulthood her operatics were exhibited through bouts of feinting, rowing, and talking—performances that made a manipulative spectacle of her un-boundaried feeling. With the fine filigree of her language, as Dakin pointed out, "she was trying to gain the stage." ("Miss Edwina will still be talking for at least an hour after she's laid to rest," Williams wrote in his essay "Let It All Hang Out.") In her verbal fights with CC, according to Williams, Edwina was "rarely if ever bested."

A large word horde was part of a Southern belle's arsenal of seduction, the sugar to swat the fly. "It wasn't enough for a girl to be possessed of a pretty face and a graceful figure," Amanda tells Tom in *The Glass Menagerie*, as she launches into a story about her legendary gentleman callers. "She also needed to have a nimble wit and a tongue to meet all occasions. . . . Never anything coarse or common or vulgar." As Amanda preached it and Edwina lived it, talk was a tool, an exhibition, and an assertion. In Edwina's case, speech renovated reality; it imposed a sense of coherence on the emotional chaos of her life, diverting her hostility away from herself and making her unknowable. "I always like to forget the unpleasant," Edwina wrote, adding, "I often pretended to feel gay when I was in anguish. I did not think it fair of parents to take out their feelings on children. . . . I believe it would have been far more grim had I not pretended things weren't as bad as they seemed. All of us are actors to the degree that we must be to survive." For Edwina's children to survive her and to get the emotional support they needed, they had both to indulge and to join her narrative. At the beginning of *The Glass Menagerie*, as Amanda is about to launch into a reverie about her past, Williams demonstrated this complicity:

> TOM: I know what's coming!
> LAURA: Yes. But let her tell it.
> TOM: Again?
> LAURA: She loves to tell it.
> (*Amanda returns with bowl of dessert.*)
> AMANDA: One Sunday afternoon in Blue Mountain—your mother received—seventeen!—gentleman callers! . . .
> TOM: I bet you could talk.
> AMANDA: Girls in those days knew how to talk, I can tell you.

Edwina's wall of words was designed to keep the world at attention and at bay. Speech was a sort of confidence trick: that is, her words were intended to give confidence both to others and to herself. "You couldn't sit with Edwina without wanting to imitate her," Gore Vidal said. "She had this rather grim face, a very long upper lip. I used to call her the good Gray Goose. Tennessee thought that terribly funny." Williams, whom Edwina claimed "was exceptionally observant as a child," was a good audience for his mother, a fact to which *The Glass Menagerie* bears witness—a retelling of the saga of her upbringing as a Southern belle, her suitors, her God-fearing piety, her husband's abandonment, and her gallant support of her fragile brood. All Edwina's homilies, aphorisms, and idioms, with their particular quality of denial, were absorbed by Williams and reenacted by Amanda. When Edwina first saw herself re-created on stage, as she sat with her son at the Chicago opening, Williams recalled, she "looked like a horse eating briars. She was touching her throat and clasping her hands and quite unable to look at me." Later, backstage,

Laurette Taylor asked her, "Well, Mrs. Williams, how did you like yourself?" "Myself?" Edwina said grandly, rising above what she saw as Taylor's impertinence.

Edwina was, as Williams politely characterized her in his memoir, "a moderately controlled hysteric." And, like many hysterics, she had trouble with her body; she was frigid. "She used to scream every time she had sex with my father," Williams said. "And we children were terrified. We'd run out in the streets and the neighbors would take us in." Dakin, who joked about his mother being "president of the anti-sex league," said, "She didn't believe in sex, she avoided it completely." Edwina described her love to her children, rather than demonstrating it. Kissing and hugging—the ordinary tactile expressions of maternal affection—were not in her repertoire. "She just didn't touch you," Dakin said. "She didn't react well to anything physical. We never had it, and didn't expect it."

Amanda, like Edwina, avoids the physical. In the course of the play, the stage directions indicate, she touches her son only three times. "Don't quote instinct to me!" she snaps at Tom, upbraiding him for his defense of human passion. "Instinct is something that people have got away from! It belongs to animals! Christian adults don't want it!" For Edwina, spiritual self-sacrifice took the place of passion, a substitution that made her, in Williams's eyes, "an almost criminally foolish woman." With her "monolithic Puritanism," as Williams called it, Edwina embodied "all the errors and mistakes and misunderstandings that her time and background could produce. She is so full of them that she is virtually a monument of them, nor has she outgrown a single one of them," he wrote in 1946. He added, "*Society* should be *scourged* for producing such 'Christian martyrs'!—such monuments of misapprehension!" In the hope that her hapless daughter, who had never graduated from high school or held a job, might become a secretary, Edwina had Rose practice typing such self-improving homilies as:

> Achievement, of whatever kind, is the crown of effort, the diadem of thought. By the aid of self-control, resolution, purity, righteousness and well-directed thought a man ascends; by the aid of animality, indolence, impurity, corruption, and confusion of thought a man descends.

Like all hysterics, Edwina was adept at transmitting her inner state to others. Her martyred look, which is preserved in *The Glass Menagerie*'s second scene, could pierce even CC's bow-wow façade. Recalling an evening when his father came late and drunk to the dinner table, Williams wrote, "She fixes on him her look of silent suffering like a bird dog drawing a bead on a covey of quail in the bushes." Edwina's performance could draw out of CC an almost "maniacal fury." In the case of her children, who most needed her emotional support, that fury turned inward.

Thanks to the dread of the physical that Edwina "imposed," Tennessee, Rose, and Dakin were strangers to their own bodies. Dakin remained sexually inexperienced until his marriage at the age of thirty-seven; Rose, whose first signs of madness, according to a 1937 Farmington State Hospital report, were a "reaction to delusions of sexual immorality of family," died a virgin; and, by his own admission, Williams didn't masturbate until he was twenty-six, "and then not with my hands but by rubbing my groin against my bed-sheets while recalling the incredible grace and beauty of a boy-diver plunging naked from the high board in the swimming-pool of Washington U. in St. Louis."

In *The Glass Menagerie*, Laura's desire—for her gentleman caller, Jim O'Connor, on whom she had a secret high-school crush—paralyzes her; she literally can't bring herself to stand and to answer the front door. In the Williams family, the fear of showing desire made the "highly sexed" Rose hunch her narrow shoulders in the presence of the opposite sex and "talk with an almost hysterical animation which few young men knew how to take." "She made no positive motion toward the world but stood at the edge of the water, so to speak, with feet that anticipated too much cold to move," Williams writes in "Portrait of a Girl in Glass," his first portrayal of Laura, whose gimp leg stands in for Rose's psychological disability. Williams had his own form of morbid shyness. Having begun early on "to associate the sensual with the impure, an error that tortured me during and after pubescence," he found it "almost entirely impossible . . . to speak aloud in class." Anything that promised exposure both excited and confounded him. "Almost without remission for the next four or five years, I would blush whenever a pair of human eyes, male or female (but mostly female since my life was spent mostly among members of that gender) would meet mine," he wrote in his memoir. It was a shyness that persisted for years. "What taunts me worst is my inability to make contact with the people, the world," Williams wrote in a 1942 diary entry. "I remain one and separate among them. My tongue is locked. I float among them in a private dream and shyness forbids speech and union."

Edwina, who once boasted that "the only psychiatrist in whom I believe is our Lord," was, according to Williams, "essentially more psychotic than my sister Rose." "Like a force of nature, she seemed to be directed blindly," Williams said. Her paranoia and her terror lodged in her children, modifying their behavior and keeping them at once overly suggestible and under wraps. Like Amanda, she used her children as vessels into which she emptied the desires and the fears of her frustrated heart. "You're my right-hand bower! Don't fall down, don't fail!" Amanda exhorts her idealized son. For a long time, Williams and Rose struggled to maintain their image as dutiful, well-mannered representations of their mother's hopes. Rose, in Edwina's romantic fantasy, was a Southern belle and wife-to-be. Likewise, in the first beats of *The Glass Menagerie*, Amanda orders the crippled dateless Laura to sit: "Resume your seat, little sister—I want you to stay fresh and pretty—for gentleman callers!" "I'm not expecting any gentleman callers," Laura says, who knows her disability debars her from a normal life. "But Mother—," she says. "I'm—crippled!" Amanda refuses to acknowledge even the most glaring fact of Laura's damage. "Nonsense! Laura, I've told you never, never to use that word. Why, you're not crippled, you just have a little defect—hardly noticeable, even!" she says. Before Laura's eyes and ours, Amanda fictionalizes the world and insists that her children deny the truth of their very essence.

> AMANDA: It's almost time for our gentleman callers to start arriving. (*She flounces girlishly toward the kitchenette.*) How many do you suppose we're going to entertain this afternoon? . . .
> LAURA: (*alone in the dining room*) I don't believe we're going to receive any, Mother.
> AMANDA: (*reappearing, airily*) What? No one—not one? You must be joking!
> (*LAURA nervously echoes her laugh. . . .*)

For her first-born son, Edwina's desires were especially strong. "My mother was extremely, overly I would say, affectionate toward my brother," Dakin Williams said. With CC permanently struck from her emotional map, Edwina formed a marriage of sorts with young Tom. "Her husband had deserted her shortly after S. was born," Williams wrote in the short story that preceded the 1945 play *Stairs to the Roof*. "She was determined the boy should not escape from her too." From the day she bought her chronically shy twelve-year-old son a ten-dollar typewriter, Williams was, in her mind, "mah writin' son," joined to her apron strings by a shared fantasy of self, a sort of grandiose co-production that became his destiny. "Within a few months," Williams wrote to Elia Kazan, writing "became the center of my life . . . then all of a sudden one day when I sat down at the second-hand (maroon-colored) Underwood portable that I had received for Xmas . . . it suddenly occurred to me: this is my life, this is my love! What will I do if I LOSE it? —And the thought struck such terror in my heart, that for—I forget the exact intervals of time—days, weeks!—I was not able to write. I was a blocked artist!"

In a real sense, Williams the writer was dreamed up by the disappointed Edwina. Writing strengthened his bond with his mother at the same time that it provided Edwina with yet another soldier in her battle against the disdained and disdainful CC, who, as Dakin said, "thought writers were complete zeroes who would never amount to anything, i.e. make money." "I feel uncomfortable in the house with Dad, when I know he thinks I'm a hopeless loafer," Williams wrote. As Cornelius spurned Tom's efforts, Edwina "doubled her support," Lyle Leverich writes in *Tom*. "Whether intentionally or not, she had fashioned a vengeful weapon that served as a permanent wedge between father and son." For Williams, storytelling became a kind of collusion, an attempt to live up to his mother's vivacity, her way of imagining, and her sense of him. The burden of the roles the children inhabited finally became insupportable.

Unacknowledged by CC and reconstituted by Edwina—the unspoken family message was "you cannot have the feelings you have"—the children struggled to make a place in their lives for their own emotional reality. The combination of CC's violence and Edwina's repression was at the root of Williams's various physical complaints, and of his breakdown

With father and mother

at the International Shoe Company in 1935. "I was a sweet child. Child murdered," he wrote in his journals. The horrible family atmosphere was also a recipe for madness. According to Williams, Rose had "the same precarious balance of nerves that I have to live with" but no outlet for them; gradually, and inexorably, she descended into her own unreachable world. One of her reported "delusions," she told one of her doctors, was that "all of the family were mentally deranged." After Rose's first break-down, Williams recalled her walking into his tiny room "like a somnam-bulist" and announcing "we must all die together." A psychiatrist told CC, "Rose is liable to go down and get a butcher knife one night and cut your throat." "Tragedy. I write that word knowing the full meaning of it," Williams wrote in his journal on January 25, 1937. "We have had no deaths in our family but slowly by degrees something was happening much uglier and more terrible than death."

When the disoriented and delusional Rose was first admitted to the Farmington State Hospital, at the age of twenty-eight, the psychiatrist who debriefed her observed, "Insight was entirely absent although she at times states that she is mentally ill as a result of her family's troubles." In Williams's eyes, Rose's lobotomy was, to some degree, a result of Edwina's sexual hysteria, an enforcement of radical innocence through the surgical removal of the part of the brain that remembers. "Mother chose to have Rose's lobotomy done. My father didn't want it. In fact he cried. It's the only time I saw him cry," Williams said. "Why was the operation performed? Well, Miss Rose expressed herself with great eloquence, but she said things that shocked Mother. Rose loved to shock Mother." He went on, "Rose said, 'Mother, you know we girls at All Saints College, we used to abuse ourselves with altar candles we stole from the Chapel.' And Mother screamed like a peacock! She rushed to the head doctor, and she said, 'Do anything, *anything* to shut her up.'" The lobotomy was a family tragedy; it finally and forever fit Rose into Edwina's version of life. Rose, as Edwina wrote, "now lived in a world where she remembers only the good things."

Where Rose was forced to comply, Williams escaped, mostly into his writing, in which he was able to turn himself and the torture of his family into an event of a different kind. In playwriting, he found a strategy both to hide himself away and to vent his murderous feelings. On the stage, he could exorcise his anger. Writing, he said, was an act of "outer oblivion and inner violence." He likened his lyrical impulses—what he called his "sidewalk histrionics"—to the performance of a little Southern girl he once saw, decked out in "cast-off finery," who screamed to her indifferent friends, "Look at me, look at me, look at me!" until she fell over in "a great howling tangle of soiled white satin and torn pink net. And still nobody looked at her." (Williams's first story, "Isolated"—published in *Junior Life* at five cents a copy—was a three-paragraph fantasy about a flood that leaves him marooned and invisible until he is saved by a search party that is "reclaiming dead bodies.") Rose, who had no symbolic release for her rage, took it out on herself and her family. The lobotomy was the reverse of her brother's solution: outer violence and inner oblivion. According to her psychiatric report prior to the lobotomy, Rose suffered from "somatic delusions: felt her heart was as big as her chest; thought that her body had disappeared from her bed." The lobotomy transformed her literally into a ghost of her former self.

That ghostliness is built into *The Glass Menagerie*, in which shards of memory play out the Narrator's internal drama. By standing outside the scene, the Narrator suggests both his and Williams's detachment, which verges on the spectral. Absence dominates the play. A specially lit photograph of the Wingfields' missing father in his First World War uniform stands on the Wingfield mantelpiece, serving as a reminder—as if one were needed—of the omnipresent weight of CC's abandonment: the grief that punished and unhinged the Williams family. Tom Wingfield— like the young Williams, whose depressions he described as "interior storms that show remarkably little from the outside" and which created "a deep chasm between myself and all other people"—feels himself to be, if not a ghost, then not exactly alive. "You know it don't take much intelligence to get yourself into a nailed-up coffin," he says. Tom's habitual moviegoing, which so mystifies Amanda, is no mystery to him. "People go to the movies instead of moving!" he explains. Psychic survival is linked to make-believe.

At the finale, the Narrator stands before the audience as a haunted man, hounded by figments of his internal world. "I traveled around a great deal," he says. "The cities swept about me like dead leaves, leaves that were brightly colored but torn away from the branches. I would have stopped, but I was pursued by something[. . . .] Then all at once my sister touches my shoulder. I turn around and look into her eyes . . . Oh, Laura, Laura, I tried to leave you behind me, but I am more faithful than I intended to be!" The Narrator stands in a spotlight, bathed in white light—the light of the imagination.

In the first moment of the play, the Narrator announces the "tricks up his sleeve"; in the last beats, he shows how, through the act of storytelling and artifice, he has taken command of himself. The stage becomes "almost dancelike," a hallucinatory tableau vivant in which Williams transforms what he called "my doomed family" into a form of glory. The panoply of his recollected misery becomes a dumb show—an "interior pantomime," the stage directions call it: "The interior scene is played as though viewed through soundproof glass. Amanda appears to be making a comforting speech to Laura who is huddled upon the sofa. Now that we cannot hear the mother's speech, her silliness is gone and she has dignity and tragic beauty. Laura's dark hair hides her face until at the end of the speech she lifts it to smile at her mother. . . . Amanda's gestures are slow and graceful . . . as she comforts the daughter." Instead of being overwhelmed by the memories of family madness, the Narrator is now in control of his own internal turmoil. "Blow out your candles, Laura—and so good-bye," he says, in the last line of the play. Laura does as she's told. The silent final gesture demonstrates the Narrator's dramatic prowess; it also broadcasts Williams's dramatic goal—to redeem life, through beauty, from the humiliation of grief.

W hen the final curtain came down on the Broadway opening of *The Glass Menagerie*, the audience knew that some kind of theater history had been made. "Never before in my experience or never since and perhaps never again in my life will there be anything like it," Eddie Dowling said. "It was really a thunderous, thunderous thing." The cast took twenty-four curtain calls. Laurette Taylor, "holding out the ruffles of the ancient blue taffeta as though she might break again into the waltz of her girlhood," was crying. "All the people backstage were crying," recalled the actress Betsy Blair, who was Julie Haydon's understudy. For the first time that year, a Broadway audience rose to its feet shouting, "Author, Author!" The calls persisted until Williams was coaxed out of his seat. With a helping hand from Dowling, he climbed up onto the stage. The audience experienced Williams's childhood just as he had—startled, bewildered, terrified, and excited. Now, as he stood before the boisterous crowd, he even seemed jejune. Slight, his hair closely cropped, his jacket button missing, the blushing author bowed awkwardly to the actors; in so doing, he showed his backside to the audience.

After the curtain came down for the last time, Taylor threw her arms around Dowling. "Eddie, I can't remember anything," she said. "Does it look like a success?"

I said, "Well, Laurette, you must have left your hearing aids home because there's never been such . . . "

She said, "Well, I never pay attention to applause. But the quiet during the performance, Eddie. What is the quiet?"

"We learned from thirteen or fourteen weeks in Chicago, Laurette, about the quiet."

"But," she said, "New York isn't Chicago. They're intelligent in New York."

I said, "Laurette, this isn't a matter of intelligence. These are basic emotions, my dear girl, and haven't you caught on yet to the kind of play we're doing?"

She said, "Oh, don't give me all that nonsense." She said, "Why wasn't there some reaction to my funny lines? I didn't get one so-and-so."

I said, "Well, you'll find out very soon."

The number of people who came backstage to see the actors was so large that the Playhouse's safety curtain had to be lifted to allow the euphoric spillover crowd to loiter onstage. "It was like after a World Series game when they come down out of the stands. That's what it was," Dowling said. He continued, "We went on for a long time after. . . . I don't suppose there's been a hit since like it. Certainly no actress before or since has ever made the impression this woman made. She's a legend along with Bernhardt and Duse, and all out of that little play."

To the sharp eye of the *New Republic*'s Stark Young, who wrote the most evocative and informed response to the play, Taylor was "the real and first talent of them all." "Here is naturalistic acting of the most profound, spontaneous, unbroken continuity and moving life," he wrote. In later years, Williams would recall the rest of the cast as "pretty run-of-the-mill," but his memory of Taylor's peerless performance never lost its luster. "Her talent was luminous in a way that exceeded the natural. There was a rightness about her that you could not see beyond," he wrote after she died in 1946. "Once in a while, only once in a while and not long, the confusion and dimness about us so thickly is penetrated by a clarity, an illumination of this kind, which makes it still possible to believe that the tunnel in which we move is not closed at both ends."

Afterward, the first-nighters filed off to a party in Williams's honor that Wood was hosting at the Royalton. Williams was too stunned to socialize. He and Windham disappeared into the balmy night. They walked the city for hours and forgot about the party. "I don't remember feeling a great sense of triumph," Williams said. "In fact, I don't remember it very well at all. It should have been one of the happiest nights of my life. . . . I'd spent so much of my energy on the climb to success that when I'd made it and my play was the hottest ticket in town, I felt almost no satisfaction." Williams's word for this moment in his life was "providential"—"suddenly, providentially, 'The Glass Menagerie' made it when I was thirty-four." As if to underscore the inexplicable nature of the play's good fortune, he kept in his scrapbook a published astrological chart showing "a planetary tie-up" the night of the premiere "that is amazing."

To the young playwright Arthur Miller, *The Glass Menagerie* augured what he called "a revolution" in New York theater. "In one stroke," Miller wrote, "'The Glass Menagerie' lifted lyricism to its highest level in our theatre's history. . . . In [Williams], American theatre found, perhaps for the first time, an eloquence and amplitude of feeling." "It seems to me that your glass menagerie began a renaissance of our theatre . . . the climate of creation was invigorated," his friend Carson McCullers wrote years later, assessing the seismic impact of the play.

It was not only the American theater that was reborn. Edwina Williams, to whom her dutiful son gave half his royalties—*The Glass Menagerie* would run for 563 performances—was also reborn, liber-

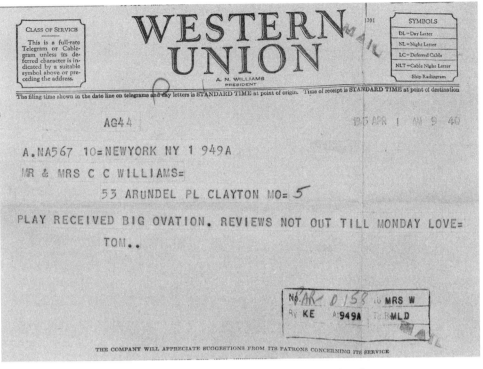

Telegram to parents about the Broadway opening night of *The Glass Menagerie*

ated by her new wealth to leave her disastrous marriage. "I was happy to have my freedom," she said. "The walls of the house had resounded with wrath for too many years and now there was peace at long last." Laurette Taylor was reborn as a legend in her time. "The postman can ring twice," she said. "From here on I'm just kicking the clouds around." And overnight, in the public's mind, Tom Williams was reborn as Tennessee Williams, playwright. The day after the opening, according to the front page of the *New York Times*, "there was a feeling of release— release from a hard winter and a promise of release, soon, from at least some of the cares of war." The day was Easter Sunday, 1945.

The news of Williams's reversal of fortune arrived at his parents' household by telegram a few days after the opening:

REVIEWS ALL RAVE. INDICATE SMASH HIT. LINE BLOCK LONG AT BOX OFFICE. LOVE, TOM.

Well, not quite all raves. The *New York Times*, not for the first time, missed the point, and the boat. Lewis Nichols, in his review, dismissed *The Glass Menagerie* as "snatches of talk about the war, bits of psychology, occasional moments of rather flowery writing." Stark Young fired back in the *New Republic*: "Such a response and attitude as that Mr. Nichols expresses helps to tie our theatre down. What we need in the theatre is a sense of language, a sense of texture in speech, vibration and impulse in speech. Behind the Southern speech in the mother's part is the echo of great literature, or at least a respect for it. There is the sense in it of her having been born out of a tradition, not out of a box." Although, in public, Taylor was fond of telling the press that "in playing Amanda you're riding on the audience's shoulders," in private, she knew it was the playwright's shoulders the character rode on. "The whole week has been fantastic: such bravos! Such notices!! Such raves!!!" she wrote to her son on April 8. "The play and that remarkable fellow Tennessee Williams have (as you can see) come under the wire, and no matter how marvelous the actress—The Play's the Thing."

WITHIN A MONTH of the play's opening, V-E day brought an end to the war in Europe, and President Franklin Delano Roosevelt died. Fueled by longing and by loss, the republic, which had deferred its dreams through fifteen years of Depression and five years of war, assumed, seemingly overnight, a new momentum, a glorious and guilt-ridden race for its own survival. Recalling this time as "the greatest moment of collective inebriation in American history" in his novel *American Pastoral*, Philip Roth wrote, "Sacrifice and constraint were over. . . . The lid was off." In the next decade, American per-capita income would triple, the greatest growth of wealth in the history of Western civilization. Inevitably, given such enormous social and economic change, the American consciousness also underwent a sort of mutation. "Everything was up for grabs," Arthur Miller said. "They were all for Number One. The death of Roosevelt was a major blow to the psyche of the country. The father was dead. It meant that the axis of concentration turned violently and very quickly away from the society to the self." He added, "It was a difference in the idea of the individual." Over the next decade, this cultural journey to the interior was manifested in the shift from social realism to Abstract Expressionism, from Marxism to Freudianism, from theatrical naturalism to Williams's "personal lyricism." It is not insignificant that Arthur Miller's *Death of a Salesman*, one of the iconic expressions of postwar America, was originally titled *The Inside of His Head*.

"There is no dynamic in life or art without form," Clifford Odets wrote in his journal in 1940. "So what is to be the new dynamic of democracy?" *The Glass Menagerie* answered that question. With its combination of exhaustion and exhilaration, the play looked both backward and forward in time, both outward and inward. Its romantic posture, its debate between self-sacrifice and self-interest perfectly captured the nation's mood. The characters in *The Glass Menagerie* are born out of the scarcity and the stasis of the prewar thirties, not the buoyant postwar forties. But through its resilient Narrator, hell-bent on seizing his life and finding his personal fulfillment, the play pointed toward accidental but transcendent survival. "Overcome selfishness!" Amanda hectors Tom, who, in the end, embraces it. The garish sexual, emotional, and spiritual struggles of the individual, what Walt Whitman called "the destiny of me," were the focus of Williams's concern. The self-involvement that made Williams's plays inaccessible to a wartime audience now in peacetime made them resonant.

Out of the depredations of his childhood, Williams set about remodeling his own character. "I build a tottering pillar of my blood / . . . against the siege of all that is not I," he wrote in "The Siege." His early diaries and letters strained under the pressure of his self-invention; at times, in their urgency, they took on an almost religious tone. During his apprentice years—"that long upward haul as a professional writer, that desperate, stumbling climb"—he prayed to Hart Crane, whose poems he carried in his jacket pocket: "I am thy frail ghost-brother. Thy equal wanderer. Guide me," he wrote in his diary. Sometimes, he beseeched Anton Chekhov too: "Breathe into me a little of thy life!" he pleaded. He lit votive candles for his own success and succor. "I will burn one for you and for me . . . a *ten-cent one!*" he wrote to a friend. "We will be purified and redeemed!—I work hard these days. For me there is either success or destruction sooner or not so sooner & so I *work*."

Williams re-created himself on the grandiose plan of Artist, a "Homo Emancipatus—the Completely Free Man." "The poet, the dreamer . . . fights a solitary battle against the world's dullness—the others, conscious of no such enemy in the field think him a mad man who is struggling with phantoms," Williams wrote inside his volume of Hart Crane. But there was a price to be paid along the way to his hard-won freedom, a price in torment and loneliness. "When will the cool white time of healing arrive?" he prayed in his 1940s diary. "When will the fingers of peace be laid on my forehead? Oh, days ahead—give me a sign! Give me a candle to walk by! Oh it's so bewildering, uncertain where I stand. Courage, my lad—en avant." The heaven he sought was his own individuality. "Am I still looking for God? No, just for my self," he said.

In *The Glass Menagerie*, Amanda's first full sentence is about grace. "We can't say grace until you come to the table," she calls to Tom. Grace is again invoked as the Gentleman Caller sits down to break bread with Laura and the rest of the family. "I think we may—have grace—now," Amanda says. But grace is granted at the finale only to the Narrator, Tom Wingfield. Haunted, restless, guilt-ridden, searching for a truth that keeps him in perpetual motion, he is released by the luck of talent into the world, no longer earthbound but airborne by his imagination. Through his literary ability—as the interior pantomime of Amanda and Laura at the finale demonstrates—Williams's storytelling is the act of grace, redeeming his life and the lives of others with a meaning and a beauty that feels like blessing.

With the success of *The Glass Menagerie*, that long-delayed something that Williams lived for—"the time when I would first catch and hold an audience's attention"—had arrived. He recognized it now for what it was: a simulacrum of the child's longing to be held. "We come to each other, gradually, but with love," Williams wrote in the play's introduction. "It is the short reach of my arms that hinders, not the length and multiplicity of theirs. With love and with honesty, the embrace is inevitable."

The hubbub of Williams's new life began almost immediately. He was photographed by *Vogue* in broody profile with a raincoat over his shoulder; he was interviewed in *The New Yorker*'s Talk of the Town section;

within a week—with his royalties estimated at a thousand dollars a week—he was complaining to the *Times* about the burdens of the American tax system. "I guess I'm getting spoiled," he told the reporter. "That's the second time in my life I've ordered room service." Embossed invitations went out, inviting Williams's newfound society to meet "Mrs. Edwina Williams, Miss Laurette Taylor, and The Reverend Walter Dakin" over "tea and cocktails" at Sherry's. "This is the twilight of an era in the theatre," Williams had written a friend in 1943. "God knows what's coming next." The answer, as it turned out, was him.

CHAPTER 2

The Heart Can't Wait

What do I want? I want love and creative power!—*Eh bien!*
Get it!   —TENNESSEE WILLIAMS,
Notebooks, 1938

"May God be merciful to me and open some door, some avenue of escape," Williams had prayed in an early diary; now, with the success of *The Glass Menagerie*, mercy rained down on him. The play won every major theatrical prize except the Pulitzer. In September 1945, Williams's romantic comedy *You Touched Me!*—"a last, desperate throw of the literary dice in the direction of Broadway" is how he described it in 1942—opened at the Booth Theatre, with Montgomery Clift in the lead. Williams's "drizzle puss self" seemed to evaporate. Although subsequent editions of *The Glass Menagerie* appended his famous 1947 essay, "The Catastrophe of Success," which made a legend of the "spiritual dislocation" that accompanied his sudden good fortune, in the early months of his renown Williams was caught up in the rollicking velocity of his fame.

The playwright, who only a "few years earlier had confessed to his diary that he didn't have enough money to eat, now dined cavalierly from room service. "Once I ordered a sirloin steak and a chocolate sundae, but everything was so cunningly disguised on the table that I mistook the chocolate sauce for gravy and poured it over the sirloin steak," he recalled. He also bought himself $125 suit to match the deluxe company he was keeping: Eugene O'Neill; the actress Katharine Cornell, who wanted him to write a play for her; and the director and producer Guthrie McClintic, who promised to give him the names of well-connected people to look up on his spring trip to Mexico. The last time he was there, Williams told McClintic, "I nearly went crazy the first few days—from loneliness—and . . . got embroiled in situations from which I barely escaped with my life. So it would be lucky to have a few of the non-throat-cutting variety." He got his introductions, and along with them the discovery that in the aristocracy of success there are no strangers. "I have met the following here," he wrote to Audrey Wood from Mexico City, "Leonard Bernstein, Dolores Del Rio, Rosa Covarrubias, Norman Foster (now directing Mexican films), Romney Brent's sister, Balanchine, Chavez and many lesser notables of the International Set (!) all of whom have invited me places."

Just before the New Year, Williams moved back to the French Quarter of New Orleans, where he'd begun his artistic adventure in December 1938. Then, Tom Williams had signed himself into a rooming house on Rue Toulouse as "Tennessee Williams, Writer." Now, his name needed no explanation. "About an hour after my arrival," he wrote to Wood, "the hotel owner rushed out of his office and seized my hand and exclaimed: 'Mr. Williams, this is indeed an honor! We saw your play in New York.'" Although he met with three reporters and gave a radio interview soon after his arrival, Williams promised Wood that in New Orleans he was going to have "no telephone and if necessary an assumed name." He added, "I'm going to be a very serious, hard-working boy again—all else is vanity." A month later, he wrote to Wood again: "I am switching back and forth between two long plays, the one about the sisters started in Chicago and one about a Spinster begun in New York. Right now I am doing more with the sisters, it is now set in New Orleans and is called 'A Street-car Named Desire'—there is one by that title that runs close by my apartment, and proceeding in the other direction down the next street is one called 'Cemeteries.' In spite of this I am not really in a very morbid state of mind, as this might suggest." Williams had surrendered to the flesh; his new plays dramatized this capitulation. The ensuing twenty-four-month period would be the most fecund of his writing life.

The year 1946, in particular, would be a watershed—one in which Williams first glimpsed both his greatness and his downfall. For most of the year, he had two productions on Broadway. A road company of *The Glass Menagerie* was crisscrossing America. His first book of short plays,

27 Wagons Full of Cotton: And Other One-Act Plays, was in bookstores. He seemed finally to have achieved his heart's desire. A certain confidence and expansiveness had seeped into his manner and his metabolism. "I was not a young man who would turn many heads on the street," he said. But fame had invested him with a glamour that gave his small torso fresh allure; he was experiencing the refreshing rush of visibility. "I never put on a shirt, just a leather jacket," he told Wood. "I go unshaven for days and nobody says, Look at that bum, they say, That is the fellow who wrote 'The Glass Menagerie'! Droit de Seigneur, Noblesse Oblige and Honi Soit Qui Mal Y Pense, all rolled into one!"

Williams grew a mustache, and he began to go out into New Orleans society. But success also meant that Williams didn't need to go out to the world; the world came to him. Women began to set their hats at the famous author. "I am going through quite an experience with this young lady," he wrote to James Laughlin, unnerved by the tenacity of a woman called Sylvia who had "more or less forcibly" got him on a train to Washington, D.C., for a command performance of *The Glass Menagerie* on January 27, 1946, which was part of FDR's sixty-third birthday celebration. "She is one of these people with a passion for lost causes, is beautiful enough to have anybody she wanted but is apparently attracted only by the line of most resistance. So she came down here from New York and so far the most complete and graphic candor on my part has not convinced her that propinquity will not conquer all. I have always been more or less overlooked by good-looking women and once upon a time I sometimes suffered acutely from the fact, so the novelty of the situation makes it all the more impossible to cope with."

To Laughlin, Williams added, "No, I don't want to be 'saved.' I don't think anyone has ever been happier with his external circumstances." The louche byways of New Orleans were, he said, his "particular milieu." He found the hedonistic city "more restful" than Manhattan. "If you can imagine how a cat would feel in a cream-puff factory you can imagine my joy at being back in the Quarter," he wrote to Wood. Williams spelled out the delights of New Orleans in more specific camp detail to his friend and erstwhile cruising companion Oliver Evans, whom he addressed as "my dear Daughter." "The streets are teeming with ambulatory vistas," he wrote in a letter urging Evans to visit. "The small dark kind that are barely contained by their buttons and while I know you will grieve for the Sisters left behind you, I have no doubt that certain errands of piety and mercy may draw you occasionally out upon the streets." Evans wasn't tempted. Writing to "my sainted Mother," he replied, "Your prolonged absence from this and other places of worship (Gregory's Bar, Pink Elephant, 1-2-3 Club and Times Square Baths, to mention only a few) has aroused considerable comment among the more pious elite, who are beginning to fear you may have been taken in by one of those strange Southern cults." Evans preferred, he said, to "linger yet awhile in the Holy innocence of my present chaste existence, surrounded by the pious Sisters of our beloved Order of St. Vaseline."

There was another pleasurable difference between Williams's life in New York and his new life in New Orleans: he had money. "I am purring with gratitude," he wrote to Laughlin. He could afford a high-ceilinged apartment at 710 Orleans Street, with twelve-foot shuttered windows and a balcony that looked out at the back of the St. Louis Cathedral. The apartment stood, Williams said, "across the street from a Negro Convent that has the funniest cornerstone. . . . It reads 'Convent of the Sisters of St Joseph . . . Sisters of the Holy Family Laid October 13, 1885, by Arch-face.' What a boy Archbishop Pontiface must have been!"

lliams's hectic sexual wayfaring seemed to have reached d happy resolution. For the first time in his life, he found ed down with someone: the muscular, volatile Amado "Pan-uez y Gonzalez whose tall Mexican good looks—"dark of hair, dark of eyes"—gave Williams the mistaken first impres-cho was a bullfighter rather than a receptionist at the Pontchartrain Apartment Hotel in New Orleans. (Pancho called Williams "Torito.") "I wish I had a lovely little clown for a friend," Williams had confided to his diary in 1943. "One that had sorrows but made me sunny. I want to be friends with some wild thing." In the shape of the hard-drinking and combustible Pancho—"rambunctious" was Elia Kazan's word for him—even this wish was granted.

"Companionship was not a familiar or easy thing," Williams wrote of the "unprecedented duration" of their relationship, when he came to rec-

ollect it in the autobiographical story "Rubio y Morena," whose narrator
"had lately become what is called a Name." The narrator's lover is Amada,
a woman whom the narrator at first "took to be a man"; in fact, Amada
was a man, transposed from Pancho whose first name was Amado. "I
have been having quite a hectic time of it—living with a little Mexican
full of tricks, for about two months," Williams wrote to Paul Bigelow on
February 27. "I didn't mind her bringing in trade as long as she saved a
little of her energy for my own entertainment but recently she started
falling asleep as soon as her trade departed. So I kicked her out of bed
and sent her out on the streets. She is a pretty thing—She took refuge
with a Creole belle who had wanted her badly while she was staying with
me but was considerably disconcerted to have her altogether on his
hands." Williams went on, "I wrote her a mildly affectionate note of farewell which she mistakenly interpreted as a plea to return. So back she
came tonight with her 2 shirts, alarm clock and perfume. . . . These Mex-
icans are charming little things—if you can live through them!"

As Williams was surviving so sensationally, his family's fate, by comparison, seemed ever more parlous. His father had retired from the shoe
company and retreated to "his bedroom with the bottle," as Williams told
Wood. He "does nothing but stay home and drink," he wrote. After Williams's beloved "Grand" suffered a lung hemorrhage while playing the
piano and died two years earlier, the Reverend Dakin had taken up residence in his daughter's home—in what proved to be a sort of
grace-and-disfavor arrangement. "Conditions at home must be worse
than terrible," Williams wrote to Wood on January 3, 1946. "My father
. . . is at home all the time so poor grandfather has to stay in his room. . . .
They can't stand the sight of each other!" Rose, who had been lobotomized in 1943, was beyond memory or desire. As for Edwina, she bustled
dutifully between the enemy camps of her fractious family, alone with
the story of her grievances and her God.

"In spite of basic damnation, I am incorrigibly lucky," Williams wrote.
"I feel that God should walk into this mellow kitchen of mine with drawn
sword and just wordlessly chop my head off because I have been too for-
tunate compared with the female members of my doomed house." For
the moment, Williams had achieved a sort of equipoise in his life and in

his work, a seismic internal shift that had been foreshadowed in *The Glass Menagerie*. "I am waking up," Tom says, broadcasting vague intimations of transformation. Jim, the gentleman caller, sees no signs of the awakening and says so. "The signs are interior," Tom replies. "I'm planning to change."

"IT TAKES FIVE or six years to use something out of life," Williams once told *Time*. "It's lurking in the unconscious—it finds its meaning there." In 1939, Williams had vowed to make his plays "a picture of my own heart . . . myself without concealment." Now, six or seven years later, working in New Orleans under "ideal conditions" and with prodigious energy, he looked back on the landscape of abdications that had forestalled his coming of age and kept him from knowing his own heart for so long. His writing became both a conscious and an unconscious attempt to chart the unlearning of repression.

"He had no idea of what his real desires were," Williams wrote of Anthony Burns, the timid thirty-year-old hero of "Desire and the Black Masseur," his short story that was completed in April 1946. Burns, like Williams at that age, "by virtue of so much protection . . . still had in his face and body the unformed look of a child and he moved like a child in the presence of critical elders. In every move of his body and every inflection of speech and cast of expression there was a timid apology going out to the world for the little space that he had been somehow elected to occupy in it." "His desires, or rather his basic desire," Williams wrote of Burns, "was so much too big for him that it swallowed him up as a coat that should have been cut into ten smaller sizes, or rather there should have been that much more of Burns to make it fit him."

But, whereas Burns's unexamined desires lead him to annihilation—he is ultimately, and literally, devoured by sexuality, embodied by the black masseur—Williams's own exploration of the sensual led to a sort of liberation. In "Chart of Anatomy"—the second play he'd mentioned to Wood, the one about the spinster (later retitled *Summer and Smoke*), about a prim, dutiful, Southern virgin called Alma Winemiller—Williams replayed his own shift from the spiritual to the carnal. "Miss Alma grew up in the shadow of the rectory, and so did I," Williams said.

She "is my favorite because I came out so late and so did Alma, and she had the greatest struggle." The play is both a dissection of his suffocating family and homage to the climate of fretful desire out of which he had finally emerged.

WILLIAMS'S OWN TRANSITION from timid virgin to florid gay man was his defining struggle. He had grown up in a hothouse of thwarted desire. Edwina's hysteria had infected everything and everyone around her. "Please be sure that no single copy of anything falls into [my parents'] hands," Williams instructed Wood in 1941. "My mother wrote me the other day that the plays in 'American Scenes' were 'ugly details about indecent people' and a disgrace to the kinfolk mentioned in the preface. I am afraid she would burn them in order to save my reputation." Edwina's perfervid vigilance reflected an asceticism that was based on her father's preaching. "By the flesh is meant that corrupt nature which we inherit from our first parents; and 'to live after the flesh' is to follow the devices and desires of our own hearts without any restraint on Christian principle," the Reverend Dakin said, in a sermon first preached on the eighth Sunday after Trinity in 1896. He went on, "People are apt to plead the weakness of the 'flesh' as an excuse for yielding to temptation. They forget that to *yield* is a sin; that every victory over self aids in another conflict, that we are placed here to conquer ourselves, 'to fight the good fight.'"

Edwina, like her father, became expert at replacing carnal arousal with spiritual arousal—a sort of psychic jujitsu in which sacrifice became passion. Through his mother's exhortations and the books that his grandfather pressed on him—*The Ascent of the Soul* was one—the righteous message was brought home to Williams. "Character is the man—the *whole* man—the seen, the unseen, the known, and the unknown—the whole including all the hurts," the Reverend Dakin preached. "Character is the product of daily, hourly actions and words and thoughts . . . struggles against temptation, submissiveness under trial." Williams's sense of character was forged along these hair-shirted lines. "I had begun to associate the sensual with the impure, an error that tortured me during and after pubescence," he wrote. "Or did I, and this seems most likely now, say to myself, Yes, Tom, you're a monster!"

In *You Touched Me!*—a sort of prolegomenon to passion—a pious forty-year-old English spinster, Emmie, who is "the proud proprietress of a virgin mind," rules a household that includes Emmie's brother Cornelius, the bibulous and long-suffering former sea captain, and his daughter, the timid Matilda, who is in her early twenties. Cornelius has also adopted Hadrian, "a youth of twenty-one," who returns to this landlocked household in rural England after spending years in the Air Force and brings a sense of the world into an airtight environment whose grace and beauty, the stage directions point out, "nevertheless are not in vital contact with the world." As the acting edition explains, the story is about overcoming "the fears and reticences that have been instilled in the boy and girl" by Emmie, who represents "not predatory maternity but aggressive sterility."

The play's claustrophobic, twilight environment—"like being under water," Matilda says—mirrors Williams's own toxic family milieu. "The Victorian actually prevailed until the beginning of the 20's and is still prevailing in large middle and upper middle class sections of the South at least," Williams wrote to Wood in 1942. "I grew up, for instance, among just such characters as Emmie and Matilda. In fact Mother and her friends around Columbus, Port Gibson and Natchez would probably consider Emmie a little 'advanced.' *You all* forget how old-fashioned *the provinces remain.* . . . the fear of the world, the fight to face it and not run away, is the realest thing in all experience to *me,* and when I use it in my work, I am always surprised that it does not communicate clearly to others."

You Touched Me! dramatizes both the violent innocence of virginity—a state in which people make themselves strangers to the world and to their own desires—and, in the character of Hadrian, the liberation of those desires through knowledge of the flesh. "Virginity is mostly the consequence of bad environment and unfavorable social conditions," Cornelius says. He goes on, "Emmie's is congenital. . . . Matilda's case is acquired. Exposed to a virulent case of it like Emmie's, the healthiest constitution would be infected."

In his letter to Wood, Williams explained Matilda this way: "Without intervention, she would drift into that complete split with reality which is schizophrenic." Williams saw in Matilda's confusion a parallel to Rose, "who found it too much and escaped as Matilda is in danger of escaping."

(Rose's lobotomy erased all memory of desire and inhibition.) Williams, like Hadrian, was saved by his willingness to give in to his own sexuality. "I doubt that anything ever did me more good as a writer than the many years of loneliness, of 'cruising around,' making sudden and deep acquaintances one after another, each one leaving a new and fresh print on me," he wrote in 1950.

You Touched Me! first voiced Williams's revelation. As Hadrian

Rehearsing *You Touched Me!*, 1945

"catches her fingers and holds her from flight," he spells out to Matilda his carnal discoveries. "New wonders, new thrills, new excitements!" He continues, "I whisper to you because it is—still a secret." Hadrian, whom the script describes as "the opposite of the closed house," is an embodiment of the sensual. He is also emblematic of sexuality's role in tearing apart the parent-child relationship. At the finale, as he carries Matilda out of the house in his arms, Emmie says, "Where are you going?" "Forward!" Hadrian calls back over his shoulder. "Forward's the way—for an old man's daughter to go," the Captain concludes.

FOR WILLIAMS, THIS embrace of the sensual world was hard won and relatively recent. His evolution into genital sexuality—the transformation essential for male adulthood—had been woefully postponed. He described his youthful self as "the little puritan." He didn't masturbate until he was twenty-six. "I didn't know what such a thing *was*. Well, I'd heard of it, but it never occurred to me to practice it," Williams said. Except for his one hapless heterosexual coupling at the University of Iowa, he remained celibate until the age of twenty-seven. In the most prescient autobiographical passage of *You Touched Me!* the orphan Hadrian links sexual appetite with a child's need to be fed, and connects his own physical obsession to the absence of a mother's touch:

> HADRIAN: . . . I grew up reaching for something that wasn't there any more—maybe the breast of my mother.
> EMMIE: (*Disgustedly*) Uhhhhh!
> HADRIAN: Something warm and able to give me comfort—I guess that's what I'm still reaching for. To be warmed—touched—loved! . . . After I left here I learned the ways that you get along in the world—working hard and facing things straight—but still I had that longing, not satisfied yet. To be touched. Now I feel that need more than ever. *That's* why I came back here for a second try.

Edwina's children inevitably inherited her fear of the flesh. Her puritan hectoring echoes through Williams's plays: "Don't hang back with the beasts." "To me—well, that is the secret, the principle of existence—the everlasting struggle and aspiration for more than our human limits have placed within our reach." "Don't quote instinct to me! Instinct is something that people have got away from! It belongs to the animals. Christian adults don't want it!" For a long time, Williams allowed his instinctual life to be ruled by his mother's dicta. By refusing to acknowledge his own sexuality, he elected to remain a child well into his twenties. He had no clear sexual identity, no sexual body, and, by virtue of the fact that he had no meaningful connection to CC, he did not disengage from his father. Living with his embattled parents and his grandparents, he also had no model of couples nourishing each other sexually.

Rose had been driven mad by the taboo around sex and by its disruptive power; Edwina had become a frigid virago; CC, a drunken, furious absence, forced to carouse with whores; and even the Reverend Dakin was made a stranger to himself. When Williams was a young adult, the mere touch of another's flesh on his own eroticized body—the "body electric," as he sometimes called it, invoking Whitman—could give him a spontaneous orgasm, itself a defense against the forbidden sexual act. Recalling his first female love, Hazel Kramer, Williams said, "She was frigid. She'd make me count to ten before she'd let me kiss her; we were both 11 when we met and we were sweethearts until she was in college. She said, 'Tom, we're much too young to think about these things.' But I constantly thought about sex. In fact, the first time I had a spontaneous ejaculation was when I put my arm around Hazel on a river boat in St. Louis. She had on a sleeveless dress and I put my arm about her and stroked her bare shoulder and I had on white flannel pants and I *came,* and we couldn't go on dancing." Later, in college at the University of Iowa, Williams recalled being "deeply in love with my roommate 'Green Eyes' but neither of us knew what to do about it." He continued, "If he came to my bed, I'd say, 'What do you want?' I was so puritanical I wouldn't permit him to kiss me. But he could just touch my arm and I'd come. Nothing planned, just spontaneous orgasms."

During those university years, Williams's self-assessments still echoed the annihilating judgment of his father. "Faults—I am egocentric, introspective, morbid, sensual, irreligious, lazy, timid, cowardly—But if I were God I would feel a little bit sorry for Tom Williams once in a while—he doesn't have a very ~~gay~~ easy time of it and he does have guts of a sort even though he is a stinking sissy!" he wrote in his diary in 1937. Williams felt "stunted"; he complained of his puerile nature: "Only my longings and my critical faculty, my sense of my own unfitness, has any dignity." In social spheres, Williams frequently felt hapless, unable to make himself either felt or seen. "Why do women ignore me so consistently these days," he wrote. "Sometimes they look at me as though I weren't there—I believe it's mostly because I'm so damned short—and then I'm too lazy to be interesting when I'm out among people I don't know well."

When Williams was finally initiated into heterosexual sex by a big-chested University of Iowa student, Bette Reitz—a "genuine nympho," according to Williams, who took pity on his timorous longing, which touched "a maternal chord"—he vomited and failed the challenge. The following night, however, he was successful. "I was . . . terribly impressed with myself," he said. Returning to his fraternity house after midnight and standing at the latrine beside an Alpha Tau Omega brother, he recalled saying, "'I fucked a girl tonight.' 'Yea, yea, how was it?' 'Oh, it was like fucking the Suez Canal,' I said and felt like a man full grown." By the next summer, according to his memoir, he was "finally fully persuaded that I was 'queer' but had no idea what to do about it."

In *Summer and Smoke*, in front of an anatomy chart, Alma Winemiller and John Buchanan debate inhibition and transgression. "This part down here is the sex," Buchanan points out to Alma. "I've fed . . . as much as I wanted—You've fed none—nothing." The battle between these forces was one that Williams fought in the presence of his own anatomy. "I must get my mind off my body and onto other things," he wrote in his diary in 1937. Two years later, after a New Year's Eve spree had introduced him "to the artistic and Bohemian life of the Quarter with a bang," Williams was still hard at work scourging himself of desire. "Am I all animal, all willful, blind, stupid *beast*?" he wrote (echoing one of his grandfather's sermons)—"How much better is man with all his advantages than the beast? . . . What does he *do* to cultivate the spiritual, to feed the spiritual? Is there another part that is *not* an accomplice in this mad pilgrimage of the flesh?" Williams asked himself.

In New Orleans, Williams said, he first "discovered a certain flexibility in my nature." However, it remained to be seen just how flexible Williams was. When he finally had his first homosexual experience—or, at least, the one first mentioned explicitly in his diary—on June 11, 1939, Williams reacted as he had to his first heterosexual intercourse: he vomited. "Rather horrible night with a picked up acquaintance Doug whose amorous advances made me sick at the stomach," he wrote. "Purity!—Oh God—it is dangerous to have ideals."

A few days later, in his next notebook entry, he continued in the same vein: "I had the experience Sat. night which confused and upset me and left me with a feeling of spiritual nausea," he wrote. "I don't fit in with the careless young extroverts of the world—people of my own kind are so difficult to find and one is always being disillusioned & disappointed—Oh, Hell!—I must learn to be lonely and *like* it—at least there is something clean about being lonely—not cluttered up and smeared over with cheap, filthy personalities who take everything out of you that is decent and give you nothing but self-disgust! But oh, God, it's so hard." On June 25, he wrote in his notebook, "I seem to be my *normal* self again—full of neurotic fears, a sense of doom, a dreadful lifeless weight on my heart and body. Oh, of course, that isn't *quite* my normal condition."

Williams had traveled West for the first time in February 1939, with a young heterosexual teacher-turned-clarinet-player named James Parrott, who wanted to try his luck in Hollywood as an actor and a musician. "It is good for me to have somebody around that I can feel an unselfish affection for," Williams wrote. Nonetheless when Parrott dropped Williams off at the Los Angeles Y on March 6, Williams noted an explosion of sudden feeling: "I felt like I was going to cry—could scarcely control my voice. . . . I was completely *lost*." Not for the first time, he was unmanned by what he called "appalling loneliness." "If only tomorrow I'll meet somebody who'll help me somehow!—at least be kind to me and relieve my loneliness."

On July 6, Williams described meeting "a delightful personality," a salesman who drove him from Santa Monica to Berkeley. The salesman, he said, "had an extraordinarily sensitive and philosophical mind—we talked quite beautifully for hours and it left a very nice taste in my mouth after the many hurts and loneliness of the recent period. Strange experience to delve so deep into another lonely human heart just in the course of a few hours." Williams was struck by the nonphysical charm of the encounter, which he found "perfect and complete." "I might have looked him up afterwards," he wrote, but he decided against it, because continuance "might have detracted from that perfection." Platonic friendships kept carnality out of the equation; they kept life from being, as he wrote, "Chaotic! (Messy)." "I want something straight and clean and perfect," he wrote. "Why can't I make it with my art?"

When Williams met up with Parrott again later that summer, though, things were far from perfect. Despite Parrott's generosity and patience with Williams, the two friends were not happy together. Williams put the tension between them down to his off-putting emotional neediness. "I demand so much, I *give* so much in a relationship—So there is a desert between us," he wrote. "My loneliness makes me grow like a vine about people who are kind to me—then it is hard to loosen the vine when the time has come for separation." He went on, "All my deep loves & friendships have hurt me finally. I mean have caused me *pain*, because I have felt so much more than the other person could feel. Then I am so pursued by blue devils—No wonder I cling for salvation to whomsoever passes by."

The particular barrenness of Williams's life in this period—a spectacular deprivation that is mirrored in *Summer and Smoke* by Alma's housebound social and emotional imprisonment—led him to a kind of living death of resignation, "enduring for the sake of endurance," as Alma puts it. Faced with his own solitude and his sexual starvation, in a direct echo of Alma's words, Williams vowed, "Now I must make a positive religion of the simple act of *endurance*—I must endure & endure & *still endure*." Williams, by his own admission, was "an expert at graceful retreat but at vigorous assault I'm rather pathetically unskilled."

Like Alma, who suffers from all kinds of psychosomatic symptoms—heart trouble, insomnia, nervousness, ennui—Williams was plagued by a series of complaints that signaled his quiet desperation. The aridity of life reduced him to "a strange trance-like existence" and pushed him to a numbed point where, as he wrote, "the heart forgets to feel even sorrow after a while." "The dreadful heavy slipping by of the days like oxen on a hot dusty road toward some possible spring—dreadfully athirst but not knowing where the water is hidden," he wrote. "Oh strange and dreadful caravan of tired cattle—Quo Vadis?—Where? Why?—What!!" Alma "was caging in something that was really quite different from her spinsterish, puritanical nature," Williams said in 1961; so was he. His 1939 notebook is full of longing but no courage to act on it. "I need somebody to envelop me, embrace me, pull me by sheer force out of this neurotic shell of fear I've built around myself lately," he wrote. "I feel all but annihilated. Yes, something *does* have to break and damn soon or I *will*."

Williams had to unlearn repression; this meant doing battle with the congenital shyness that prevented him from showing or knowing his feelings. "What taunts me most is my inability to make contact with the people, the world," he wrote in his diary. "I remain one and separate among them. My tongue is locked. I float among them in a private dream and shyness forbids speech and union. This is not always so. A sudden touch will release me. Once out, I am free and approachable. I need the solvent." Williams had grown up on a confounding diet of rejection and idealization, which had left him unconfident about the allure of his essential nature. "I am so used to being a worm," he wrote in 1937. Later, he explained, "I've never had any feeling of sexual security." "I'm only attracted to androgynous males. . . . I find women much more interesting than men, but I'm afraid to try to fuck women now. . . . Because women aren't as likely as the androgynous male to give you sexual reassurance. With a boy who has the androgynous quality in spirit, like a poet, the thing is more spiritual. I need that." (As late as 1943, despite the fact that he was a produced playwright and a contract writer for MGM, he still wondered to his diary why someone like the publisher of New Directions, Jay Laughlin, would seek him out and want to be friends. "It is so easy to ignore a squirt like me.") Experience had taught him, he said, that "to know me is not to love me." "I am a problem to anybody who cares anything about me—Most of all to myself who am, of course, my only ardent lover (though a spiteful and a cruel one!)"

Eventually, Williams, like Alma, found release in male pickups and a life of profligacy. At first, however, Williams struggled in vain against his homosexual nature. "I am as pure as I ever was—in fact purer—essentially—Ah, well . . . " At the end of 1939, he noted, "Thank god I've gotten bitch-proof."

By February 1940, alternately thrilled and appalled, Williams had joined the sexual merry-go-round. "My first real encounter was in New Orleans at a New Year's Eve party during World War Two," Williams recalled. "A very handsome paratrooper climbed up to my grilled veranda and said, 'Come down to my place' and I did, and he said, Would you like a sunlamp treatment? And I said, Fine, and I got under one and he proceeded to do me. That was my coming out and I enjoyed it." He had said good-bye to the ascetic aspect of his prolonged adolescence, but the hello to his adult sexual instincts took some adjustment. "Ashes hauled," he wrote in his diary. "Somehow pretty sick of it." Two weeks later, noticing in the mirror that his boy self was evaporating, he wrote, "Oh, Lord, I don't know what to make of this life I'm living. Things *happen* but they don't add up to much. . . . I'm getting ugly though. My face looks so heavy and coarse these days. I feel that my youth is nearly gone. Now when I need it most!" With sex, Williams noted, "the restless beast in the jungle under the skin, comes out for a little air."

Williams had liberated his desire, only to be lumbered by appetite. "I ache with desires that never are quite satisfied," he wrote. "This promiscuity is appalling really. One night stands. Nobody seems to care particularly for an encore." He added, "Still waiting for the big thing to come along." Sex, he was learning, was a way of discharging aggression. Love didn't enter into the equation. "The big emotional business is still on the other side of tomorrow," he wrote. "That's why I'm restless. Maybe tropical sunlight—or moonlight—would stir something up that I'm in need of. Shit." By mid-1940, "this awful searching-business of our lives" was no easier for Williams. "My emotional life has been a series of rather spectacular failures," he wrote in his diary. "Last night was the grand anti-climax—Ah, l'amour, la guerre et la vie!! When will it happen—and how?" He added, "Haggard, tired, jittery, fretful, bored—that is what lack of a reciprocal love object does to a man. Let us hope it spurs his creative impulse—there should be *some* compensation for this hell of loneliness. Makes me act, think, *be* like an idiot—whining, trivial, tire-

Williams in the flesh, 1943

some." He scrawled in his notebook, "*You* coming toward me—*please* make *haste! J'ai soif! Je meurs de soif!*"

Williams soon took to his new lifestyle like a bass to a top-water lure. Once he was fortified by a few drinks, his congenital shyness evaporated. "His practice in a room of half a dozen more or less presentable males was to make a pass at the one he found most attractive and then, if it was not successful, to go on down the line," Windham recalled. Windham continued, "If none of these approaches was successful, there were still the showers and steam rooms at the Y." Williams recalled cruising Times Square with Windham. "He would dispatch me to street corners where sailors or GIs were grouped, to make very abrupt and candid overtures, phrased so bluntly that it's a wonder they didn't slaughter me on the spot," Williams wrote. "Sometimes they mistook me for a pimp soliciting for female prostitutes and would respond 'Sure, where's the girls?'—and I would have to explain that they were my cruising partner and myself. Then, for some reason, they would stare at me for a moment in astonishment, burst into laughter, huddle for a brief conference, and, as often as not, would accept this solicitation, going to my partner's Village pad or to my room at the Y." According to Windham, during these early wolfish years, Williams's "quotidian goal was to end up in bed with a partner at least once before the twenty-four hours was over."

In less than fifteen months, Williams went from prude to lewd. "I was just terribly over sexed, baby, and terribly repressed," Williams told *Playboy.* "I'm getting horny as a jack-rabbit," he wrote to Windham in October 1940, from the arid confines of the family home, where, ironically, his mother and grandmother—"the most uncompromising of southern Puritans . . . seem to believe it my sacred and peculiar mission to eliminate sex from the modern theatre." He went on, "So line up some of that Forty-second Street trade for me when I get back!" Once in New York, in his diaries, the image of satyr alternated with that of a sad sack. From a man-child unwilling even to touch himself, he had progressed to "deviant Satyriasis," as he referred to his sexual rampage. "Sexuality is an emanation, as much in the human being as the animal," he said. "Animals have a season for it. But for me it was a round-the-calendar thing."

"I went out cruising last night and brought home something with a marvelous body," he wrote to Paul Bigelow. "It was animated Greek marble and turned over even. It asked for money and I said, Dear, would I be living in circumstances like this if I had any money?" Sometimes, Williams's lovers were startled by the beating of Williams's own hungry heart. "I am always alarming bed partners by having palpitations," he wrote. "Tonight my pulse was taken by the alarmed guest and it was counted 'over 100.' Considerably over I guess. I am so used to it it doesn't disturb me except when it makes me breathless. Well, tonight was worth palpitations. An almost ideal concurrence of circumstances and a record for me of 5 times perfectly reciprocal pleasure."

"As the world grows worse it seems more necessary to grasp what pleasure you can, to be selfish and blind, except in your work," he wrote to Windham. In his romantic imagination, this was a belief that would develop into something like a full-blown religion. "I'd like to live a simple life—with epic fornications," he wrote in 1942. "I think for a good summer fuck you should cover the bed with a large white piece of oil-cloth," he wrote the same year. "The bodies of the sexual partners ought to be thoroughly, even superfluously rubbed over with mineral oil or cold cream. It should be in the afternoon, preferably soon after lunch when the brain is dull. . . . It should be a bright, hot day, not far from the railroad depot and the scene of the fornication should be a Victorian bedroom at the top of the house with a skylight letting the sun directly down on the bed. . . . If the sexual partner is a southern belle with intellectual pretensions and a beautiful ass, it must be plainly told where the charm is concentrated and urged to keep the loftier cerebral processes out of the picture at least till after the first ejaculation. This little item is from my Mother's Recipe Book, on the page for meat dishes."

However, whenever Williams's lecherous smile was met with cold teeth, he grew dispirited. "I cruised with 3 flaming belles for a while on Canal Street and around the Quarter," he wrote in 1941. "They bored and disgusted me so I quit and left Saturday night to its own vulgar, noisy devices." Sometimes, Williams met not with pleasure but with violence. "Tonight ran into some 'dirt' at the Polynesian bar—for the first time in my life I was struck—not hard enough to hurt anything but my spirit," he wrote. "Close shave. Returned to the safety of 'James' Bar' where I met the companion of last night and we resumed our cruising—again fruitless for me."

IN *YOU TOUCHED ME!* Williams wrote of "unspent tenderness" growing and growing "until it gets to be something enormous. Then finally there is so much of it. It explodes inside them—and they go to pieces." He knew the feeling. "When I now appear in public, the children are called indoors and the dogs pushed out!" he wrote to a friend in 1941. "My cumulated sexual potency is sufficient to blast the Atlantic fleet out of Brooklyn. . . . I have never felt quite so rape-lusty." In a sense Williams's promiscuity served as a sort of powerful antidepressant; it provided a sense of external adventure to a life that seemed to him internally stalled. In his poem "The Siege," written in the early forties, Williams, who did not like or trust his body, described his blood as mercury, an unstable element that can't hold its shape and needs to be contained:

> Sometimes I feel the island of my self
> a silver mercury that slips and runs
> revolving frantic mirrors in itself
> beneath the pressure of a million thumbs.
>
> Then I must that night go in search of one
> unknown before but recognized on sight
> whose touch, expedient or miracle,
> stays panic in me and arrests my flight.

As the poem suggests, Williams didn't seem to know just what was inside him—and he needed to be inside someone else in order to piece together his fragmented self. "I always want my member to enter the body of the sexual partner," Williams said. "I'm an aggressive person, I want to give, and I think it should be reciprocal." His sexual delirium had about it a sense of both panic and primness. "In his room, amid the disordered contents of his suitcase and footlocker trunk, he kept, besides a jar of Vaseline, a bottle of Cuprex, against crabs, and a tube of prophylactic salve, against gonorrhea. A small drawstring bag, like the bags cigarette tobacco was sold in then, accompanied the tube of salve, to tie around his genitals and protect his clothing when he dressed after the salve was applied," Windham wrote of Williams during his prowling days at the Y. He added, "When he was not on the make and trying to charm, his behavior frequently suggested that he had never been part of any family, and certainly never under the supervision of a punctilious mother who was a Regent of the D.A.R.—Daughters of the American Revolution." On the contrary, like Williams's habit of sucking his teeth, licking his lips, and eating when he pleased—"I think I have gone as far toward release from dogmatic strictures as anyone goes," he confided to his diary—promiscuity was another way of forgetting home and its deadly climate of repression.

Williams, who often complained of feeling like a ghost, had himself become a denizen of the night. The night eroticized his sense of absence, that oppressive emptiness he had carried with him since childhood. "Evening is the normal adult's time for home—the family," he observed in his diary in 1942, already aligning himself with the sexual renegades. "For us it is the time to search for something to satisfy that empty space that home fills in the normal adult's life. It isn't so bad, really. Usually we go home with nothing. Now and then we succeed." Cruising was some dream-like odyssey of reclamation, as Tom says in *The Glass Menagerie*, "to find in motion what was lost in space." A large part of its addictive thrill was in being chosen; it gave an emotional lift to Williams's deflated self. He began to see sex as "spiritual champagne," and the Rx for his blues.

The excitement of pickups—"the asking look in his eyes"—turned tables on his hunger. ("*You* coming toward me—*please* make *haste!* . . . (You—you—is *this* you?—'Coming toward me?')") By being desired, Williams was emptied of need; the stranger became the needy one. In that sense, Williams's cruising held the promise of another kind of emotional relief—each time it succeeded, he had been chosen, he had been taken in, he knew he was real. Having rejected his mother's Puritan strictures, his Christian faith, his "normal" self, he embraced homosexuality's "rebellious hell," and with it, he claimed his animality. "I know myself to be a dog, but—animal nature no longer appears embarrassing in one's self," he wrote. "It has become so universally apparent in others." "I wonder, sometimes, how much of the cruising was for the pleasure of my cruising partner's companionship and for the sport of pursuit and how much was actually for the pretty repetitive and superficial satisfactions of the act itself," Williams wrote of this period. "I know that I had yet to experience in the 'gay world' the emotion of love, which transfigures the act to something beyond it."

IN JUNE 1940, "at the nadir of my resources, physical, mental, spiritual," Williams took himself off to the artsy enclave of Provincetown, Massachusetts—"P-Town," as it was called, an abbreviation that to Williams stood for "pilgrimage" in "mad pilgrimage of the flesh." To his friends, he reported that life there was "beautiful and serene"; the result of a regimen that included "taking free conga lessons, working on a long, narrative poem, swimming every day, drinking every day, and fucking every night." On one of those days, in a two-story shack on Captain Jack's Wharf, which sat on stilts above the ebb and flow of the tide, Williams caught a glimpse of Kip Kiernan, to whom he would dedicate his first book of stories and whose pictures he would carry in his wallet until it was lost in the sixties. Kiernan, born Bernard Dubowsky, was a Canadian draft dodger who had invented a new name for himself and a new life in art. He and his roommate, Joe Hazan, who would become a confidant of Williams, had ambitions to be dancers; both took beginners' classes at the Duval School of Ballet and then switched on partial scholarships to the American School of Ballet in Provincetown. "Neither of us had any talent at all in ballet," Hazan said, adding of Kip, "He just didn't have it. He wasn't meant to be a dancer. He'd studied sculpture some place before."

To Williams, Kip *was* sculpture. His well-proportioned muscular torso may have made him top-heavy as a dancer, but it made him perfect as an erotic ideal. "My good eye was hooked like a fish," Williams wrote. (He had a cataract in one eye at the time.) "I will never forget the first look I had at him, standing with his back to me at the two-burner stove, the wide and powerful shoulders and the callipygian ass such as I'd never seen before! He didn't talk much. I think he felt my vibes and was intimidated by my intensity." Among the accessories to this splendid body were, according to Williams, "slightly slanted lettuce-green eyes, high cheekbones, and a lovely mouth." "When he turned from the stove, I might have thought, had I been but a little bit crazier, that I was looking at the young Nijinsky," Williams wrote; the Nijinsky parallel was one that Kip himself drew later "with Narcissan pride." A few days later, Williams moved into Kiernan and Hazan's clapboard bungalow on Captain Jack's Wharf, sleeping on cots downstairs with Hazan while Kip slept upstairs in the single bedroom. "He had Southern charms, and Kip had a lot of charm," Hazan remembered. "So it was easy to be friends with him. . . . The experience I had with Kip was that that he had been successful sexually with girls. I never had any indication of homosexuality, not the slightest in any way."

One July night soon afterward, Williams declared his passion. His "crazed eloquence" silenced Kip for a few moments. Finally, Kip said, "Tom, let's go up to my bedroom." In a letter to Windham, Williams set down a unique account of his ravished surrender.

> We wake up two or three times in the night and start all over again like a pair of goats. The ceiling is very high like the loft of a barn and the tide is lapping under the wharf. The sky amazingly brilliant with stars. The wind blows the door wide open, the gulls are crying. Oh, Christ. I call him baby . . . though when I lie on top of him I feel like I was polishing the Statue of Liberty or something. He is so enormous. A great bronze statue of antique Greece come to life. But with a little boy's face. A funny up-turned nose, slanting eyes, and underlip that sticks out and hair that comes to a point in the middle of his forehead. I lean over him in the night and memorize the geography of his body with my hands—he arches his throat and makes a soft, purring sound. His skin is steaming hot like the hide of a horse that's been galloping. It has a warm, rich odor. The odor of life. He lies very still for a while, then his breath comes fast and his body begins to lunge. Great rhythmic plunging motion with panting breath and his hands working over my body. Then sudden release—and he moans like a little baby. I rest with my head on his stomach. Sometimes fall asleep that way. We doze for a while. And then I whisper "Turn over." He does. We use brilliantine. The first time I come in three seconds, as soon as I get inside. The next time is better, slower, the bed seems to be enormous. Pacific, Atlantic, the North American continent . . . And now we're so tired we can't move. After a long while he whispers, "I like you, Tenny."—hoarse—embarrassed—ashamed of such intimate speech! And I laugh for I know that he loves me!—That nobody ever loved me before so completely. I feel the truth in his body. I call him baby—and tell him to go to sleep. After a while he does, his breathing is deep and even, and his great deep chest is like a continent moving slowly, warmly beneath me. The world grows dim, the world grows warm and tremendous. Then everything's gone and when I wake up it is daylight, the bed is empty.—Kip is gone out.—He is dancing.—Or

posing naked for artists. Nobody knows our secret but him and me.
And now *you*, Donnie—because you can understand. Please keep this
letter and be very careful with it. It's only for people like us who have
gone beyond shame!

In Williams's description, Kip's large size is associated with the female
(the Statue of Liberty); Williams's smallness places him in the position of
an infant with his gargantuan mother. It's a connection that Williams
makes instinctively—moving directly from the account of Kip's huge
sculpted body to the image of his "little boy's face." For Williams, the
experience was a movement of both men between the roles of mother
and child, culminating in Kip's surrender to Williams and Williams's
pleasure. "Last night you made me know what is meant by beautiful

The dancer Kip Kiernan, his first love

pain," Kip told Williams the day after their first night together, as they walked on the dunes. "I know Kip loved me," Williams wrote. Williams's restless heart had found its object of desire. "I also know it couldn't have been very easy to be waked up four or five times a night for repeated service of my desire. One morning he said: 'Tenn, I'm too little and you're too big.' Well I was not 'too big'—just sort of parlor-size as they put it in those days—but Kip did have an exceptionally small anal entrance and to be entered that way each night, well, it's a wonder he didn't come down with a fistula."

In the midst of this emotional whirlwind, Williams's old habit of blushing returned, tormenting his days, which he spent translating his riotous emotions—"ecstasy one moment—O dapple faun!—and consummate despair the next"—into the verse drama *The Purification*. After a while, according to his autobiography *Memoirs*, "Kip turned oddly moody. . . . We would go places together and he would suddenly not be there, and when he came to bed, after an absence of some hours, he'd explain gently, 'I had a headache, Tenn.'" After a chamber music concert one night, Kip rushed off by himself. "Moves me to find someone afflicted as I am with mental conflicts," Williams wrote in his diary. "Still it troubles me—this is so much what I need, what I want, what I have been looking for the past few months so feverishly. Seems miraculous. It is too good to be true." He continued, "I fear his being lost to me already . . . oh, what an ache of emptiness I would have to endure—for now, for the first time in my life, I feel I am near to the great *real* thing that can make my life complete. Oh, K.—don't stay away very long.—I'm lonely tonight." Despite his fears about Kip—"Will it be all gone, will it still be there," he wrote of Kip's love on his way back to Provincetown from a quick trip to New York—Williams put on a braggadocio face. "I am being courted by a musician and a dancing instructor and a language professor, one of them has a big new Buick and drives us all over the Cape," he wrote at the end of July. "They all want Kip but hope to English off me or something since he is apparently less accessible than me—an unmistakable bitch—I think love has made me young again, or maybe it's the blue dungarees."

In mid-August, according to Williams, "a girl"—Shirley Brimberg, who as Shirley Clarke later became a famous documentary filmmaker —"entered the scene." Williams was on the dunes with a group of artists that included another still-unknown cultural star, Jackson Pollock, when a solemn-looking Kiernan appeared with his bike. "Tenn, I have to talk to you," he said. With Kip perched on the handlebars, Williams rode into Provincetown. "On the way in, with great care and gentleness, he told me that the girl who had intruded upon the scene had warned him that I was in the process of turning him homosexual and that he had seen enough of that world to know that he had to resist it, that it violated his being in a way that was unacceptable to him." One morning soon afterward, upstairs in Kip's room, Williams "made a horrible ass of myself—insulting a stupid little girl" (he hurled a riding boot at Brimberg, "missing her, but not intentionally") "because she had been instrumental in my unhappiness. Felt quite unnerved, almost hysterical—silly! The whole mess has got to end *now*—"

It did. "*C'est fini*," Williams wrote in his diary on August 15. He was overcome by a despair that echoed down the decades to the annihilating impotence of his solitary childhood. "I can't save myself. Somebody has got to save me," he wrote. "I shall have to go through the world giving myself to people until somebody will take me." The loss, he wrote, "threatens to wreck me completely." Deracinated and embattled, he prayed to God: "You whoever you are—who takes care of those beyond caring for themselves—please make some little charitable provision for the next few days of Tennessee." Back in Manhattan, he frequently spoke Kip's name to his diary: "Oh, K.—if only—only—*only*." "K.—dear K.—I love you with all my heart. Goodnight." He saved his parting shot for his only written letter to Kip: "I hereby formally bequeath you to the female vagina, which vortex will inevitably receive you with or without my permission."

"Do you think I am making too much of Kip?" Williams asked the reader in a rhetorical line that was cut from *Memoirs*. "Well, you never saw him." In a sense, Williams never stopped seeing Kip. At the time of their breakup, he wrote, "K., if you ever come back, I'll never let you go. I'll bind you to me with every chain that ingenuity of mortal love can devise!" Kip never came back (he married, then died of a brain tumor, in

1944, at the age of twenty-six); but through the alchemy of Williams's stagecraft, in a sense, he also never went away.

"Tennessee could not possess his own life until he had written about it," Gore Vidal observed. "To start with, there would be, let us say, a sexual desire for someone. Consummated or not, the desire . . . would produce reveries. In turn, the reveries would be written down as a story. But should the desire still remain unfulfilled, he would make a play of the story and then—and this is why he was so compulsive a working playwright—he would have the play produced so he could, at relative leisure, like God, rearrange his original experience into something that was no longer God's and unpossessable but *his*." Vidal continued: "The sandy encounters with his first real love, a dancer on the beach at Provincetown, and the dancer's later death ('an awful flower grew in his brain'), instead of being forever lost, were forever his once they had been translated to the stage."

"For love I make characters," William said. As well as being the subject of *Something Cloudy, Something Clear* (1981), Kip's muscular outline informed the proportions and the sexual presence of many of the subsequent steamy male heroes that Williams called into the world. Val in *Battle of Angels* "has a fresh and primitive quality, a virile grace and freedom of body and a strong physical appeal"; John Buchanan in *Summer and Smoke* has the "fresh and shining look of an epic hero"; Alvaro in *The Rose Tattoo* "is one of those Mediterranean types that resemble glossy young bulls . . . has a massively sculptural torso"; Brick in *Cat on a Hot Tin Roof* is "still slim and firm as a boy"; and Stanley Kowalski in *A Streetcar Named Desire*, of course, needs no description—he *is* "the body electric" that Williams indirectly invoked in his farewell letter to Kip: "I love you (with a robust manly love, as Whitman would call it) as much as I love anybody." Writing closed the circle of desire.

ON THE REBOUND from Kip, Williams went on a sexual binge. In Mexico, he was raped by a handsome, powerful Mexican beach boy who swam out to his raft and later ravished him in his beach shack. "I screamed like a banshee and couldn't sit down for a week," he said. Back in Provincetown, there were rent-party orgies; and during his five-month stint at

MGM, there were the blacked-out bushes on Santa Monica's Ocean Avenue, near where Williams was living. "I have just had an orgy with a
Ganymede of 15 years exactly, met on the Palisades," he wrote to Windham. "Moaned like a wounded bird pierced twice by the arrow of love,
and I have just sent him home to get ahead of Mama who works on the
swing-shift. If Saint Oscar wasn't working with me this summer I would
wind up not in Mexico but San Quentin."

On his sexual rounds that year, 1943, Williams was beaten up by sailors he'd taken to a room at the Hotel St. George. "Why do they strike us?
What is our offence?" he wrote in his diary. But even this violence
informed his heart. "Not that I like being struck," he recorded a few days
after the incident. "I hated it, but the keenness of the emotional situation,
the material for art."

Sexuality brought Williams down to earth and into life. "What do you
expect to get from this sort of life?" Stanley asks Blanche about her promiscuity, in the first version of *Streetcar*. "Just life," she says. Sexuality also
called all absolutes into question. "The truth of the matter is that all human
ideals have been hats too big for the human head," Williams wrote in his
diary in 1942. "Chivalry—democracy—christianity—The Hellenic ideal
of Intellectual purity (the one I find most appealing)—all too big a hat!"

Desire brought Williams to a new place and to a new sense of his own
literary power. *Summer and Smoke* and *Streetcar* picked up the story of
Williams's psychic evolution where *The Glass Menagerie* left off. (*The
Glass Menagerie* broadcast William's invented romantic self—a seeker of
truth and "companions." In the opening speech, the adult Tom Wingfield
boasts that he has "tricks in my pocket"; though the play only hints at it,
sex is clearly one of them.) Through the characters of Alma and then
Blanche—who in an early draft is "charged with plenty of that blue juice
which is the doves of Aphrodite's or anyone's car!"—Williams brought his
own promiscuity and the forces that drove it into the center of the drama.
"She tries to explain her life to him but he can see only the details of
promiscuity, not the underlying panic and need for protection which had
forced this upon her," Williams wrote of Blanche, in his first description
of the play to Audrey Wood on March 23, 1945.

In 1941, Williams was shocked to hear Oliver Evans, a poet and professor of English whom he'd met in Provincetown and who would become one of his lifelong friends and traveling companions, say, "We ought to be exterminated for the good of society." Williams reported the "sad but poignant" episode to his diary. "If you think we are dangerous, why do you act as you do? Why do you not isolate yourself?" he asked Evans. "Because I am rotten," Evans replied. "How many of us feel that way, I wonder?" Williams wrote. "Bear this intolerable burden of guilt? To feel some humiliation and a great deal of sorrow at times is inevitable. But feeling guilty is foolish. I am a deeper and warmer and kinder man for my deviation. More conscious of need in others, and what power I have to express the human heart must be in large part due to this circumstance."

In his writing, Williams defended himself against Evans's kind of guilt and shame by turning sexuality into a kind of theology. Even as he was embarking on his discipleship to the carnal, in 1942, he intuited that the experience of war would force Americans to find a new faith beyond self-sacrifice. "What are we doing, we people who put words together, who project our shadows on stages," he wrote to the acclaimed German director Erwin Piscator, whose first playwriting seminar at the New School Williams had attended. "But trying to create a new and solid myth—or *faith*—or *religion*—in place of the old and desiccated and *fruitless* one of 'simple endurance'?" The self-aggrandizement that Piscator had criticized in *Battle of Angels* when he and Williams met for the second time in 1942—"Mr. Williams, you have written a Fascist play—all of your characters are selfishly pursuing their little personal ends and aims in life with a ruthless disregard for the wrongs and sufferings of the world around them"—was actually a portrait of Williams's "underground devils" and of the "naked and savage kinds of creation" required to trap them onstage. The "vast hunger for life after all this death" that Williams had predicted to William Saroyan in 1941 had taken hold; Williams invested the "long fingers" of desire with a sense of the divine. He referred to his own sexual spree as a "daemon," a divinity. Williams's characters, too, embodied the gospel of the flesh; in the process, devils became angels.

In *Battle of Angels*, his first attempt to set out the tenets of his new romantic gospel, Val, who is "too selfish for love," is burned to death for his sexuality, which nonetheless revives the community of Two Rivers, Mississippi. As Williams began to question the old myth of salvation—the epigram to *Summer and Smoke* is from Rilke: "Who, if I were to cry out, would hear me / among the angelic orders?"—he replaced it with a new one in which salvation is based on the unlearning of Christian principle. His plays function in a world where the credo is libido. "Probably the greatest difference in the world is the difference between being fucked and well-fucked," he wrote in 1943.

In *Summer and Smoke*, John Buchanan, the little devil of the prologue, grows up to be a big one, but one "unmarked by the dissipations in which he relieves his demoniac unrest." Gambling, drinking, womanizing, the young doctor Buchanan is all romantic excess, elevating the ungovernable and the unconscious to the level of heroism: "a Promethean figure, brilliantly and restlessly alive in a stagnant society." Buchanan, who refers to prayer as "worn-out magic," tells the pious Alma, "It's yet to be proven that anyone on this earth is crowned with so much glory as the one that uses his senses to get all he can in the way of—satisfaction." "Self-satisfaction?" she asks. Buchanan replies, "What other kind is there." Alma, of course, embodies Christian self-sacrifice and has all the attendant faith in transcendence—"the everlasting struggle and aspiration for more than our human limits have placed in our reach." To her, Buchanan has been blessed with "all the gifts of the gods . . . but all he cares about is indulging his senses!" Waste, it turns out, is an issue both for her and for him. "I should have been *castrated*!" Buchanan says at one low point, admitting to Alma later, "I'm more afraid of your soul than you're afraid of my body."

Williams resolves the situation with a reversal of manners. The repressed Alma eventually gives herself over to the spontaneous and the ungovernable in her own nature—she finds a place for wildness in her life—while Buchanan, who becomes dedicated to his medical calling, is converted to Alma's spiritual rigor. "I came here to tell you that being a gentleman, doesn't seem so important to me any more, but you're telling me I've got to remain a lady," she says, laughing "rather violently." "The tables have turned with a vengeance."

The argument between indulgence and commitment, sensuality and

Alma Winemiller (Margaret Phillips) giving a valedictory salute in the
1948 Broadway premiere of *Summer and Smoke*

soul is precisely the argument Williams was having with himself during these years. Sex was disruptive; the pull toward pleasure—a state demonstrated by Stella's "narcotized tranquility" in *Streetcar*—was a push away from refinement and mission. Sexuality, Williams knew, could disrupt the mind and derail the will. "I cannot create," he wrote in his diary. "I am mentally torpid. And I do not seem to care very much. Perhaps it is the excessive sexual activity. Perhaps I have really burned my daemon out." He added, "I must find purity again. A whole undivided heart. Something simple and straight. A passionate calm. . . . Am I still looking for God? No—just for myself." In a letter to Hazan, he wrote, "I pray for the strength to be separate, to be austere. That is the best future for me— asceticism and consecrated work. But remember what an animal I am!" He went on, "I have started off on a rather disciplinary regime. Only one or two drinks a day, when very low, and a calm endurance of moods instead of a mad flight into intoxication and social distraction. When I feel like writing a little poem, instead I sit down and labor away on a long play. It is tedious to me for some reason . . . the animal in me rebels against it and wants to do little, diverting things, such as sentimental lyrics or things about sex. But I see now that to grow or even to survive I must practice more discipline with myself and I am resolved to do this."

Alma Winemiller's spiritual turnabout is a simulacrum of Williams's own. Alma, like Williams, had engineered an escape from "the cage of Puritanism." Once she has cast off her parents and the rectory, the serenity she finds is not the peace of heaven but the bliss of pickups and pills. "The prescription number is 96814," she says at the finale. "I think of it as the telephone number of God!" In Williams's renovated consciousness, revelation is gratification. The body is spiritualized: offering the promise of a communion that brings resurrection in the flesh, not the afterlife. "And still our blood is sacred," he wrote in "Iron Is the Winter." "To the mouth / the tongue of the beloved is holy bread."

By the time Williams returned to New Orleans at the end of 1945— "I need a soft climate and softer people," he wrote in his diary—his sexual landscape had become as dramatic as his interior one. "N.Y. holds me only by the balls, but that is sometimes a hard hold to break. There is so much sex there," he wrote to Donald Windham. "I was running quite a little establishment at the Shelton, what with Oliver's raids on the steam room and the bar and my own chicken run. That part was hard to relinquish for I—alas—am not yet ready to forswear all fleshly attachments. However N.O.L.A. is not strictly celibate."

Still, his promiscuity quickly dissipated in favor of a relationship, with his new partner, Pancho Rodriguez. "Our friendship was more spiritual than sexual," Rodriguez recalled. "It was like two broken down people trying to survive and help each other." Pancho was "the rare and beautiful stranger" for whom Williams had longed since the breakup with Kip. "I don't think he was disappointed," Rodriguez said. "I was very handsome then. . . . I had a lot of charm then and a lot of charisma." He added, "My behavior was very good socially, up to the point that I would drink so much. But I always had the intelligence of walking out of a place before I would be criticized. Nobody saw me drunk after midnight."

Like Williams, Pancho was something of a vagabond and a lost soul. "I was a casualty of war," Rodriguez said. "I had wanderlust in me." He served for four years with the Army Corps, some of that time in the South Pacific. "Right in the thick of it," Williams told Margo Jones. "Then he was let out of the army without an honorable discharge simply because he had a spell of confusion and talked too trustingly to an officer about it. So he has nothing to show for what he went through, and none of the G.I. compensations, which I think is an outrage." Rodriguez's oldest sister played the piano in her band at the La Luna Night Club—a Spanish watering hole—in New Orleans; when she promised to find him work, he moved there. Not long after he arrived, Pancho ran into Williams. "It was not until I met him that I sort of settled down," Rodriguez said. "I had a sense of irresponsibility to myself. I wanted to do something very constructive, but something kept me from doing it."

Contending with Pancho kept Williams from being overwhelmed by his own craziness. When drunk, Pancho could be violent; but he also made Williams's life exciting, bringing out, as Williams said, "the bright side of myself." A cardboard record they made in New Orleans preserved their affectionate playfulness:

> Tennessee: This is Vanilla Williams interviewing Princess Rodriguez who just arrived here from Monterey. . . . Have you gotten around much yet?
>
> Pancho: Ah, yes I have, Vanilla. I have gotten around. I've been cruising on Canal Street, you know.
>
> Tennessee: Oh, honey, get off Canal Street. Miss Canal Street is no good. You should get on Miss Royal or Miss Bourbon. You should get to Personality Bar. That's the place for new girls.
>
> Pancho: The Personality Bar?
>
> Tennessee: Yes, ma'am. . . . Princess Rodriguez, you get your ass up to the Personality Bar. That's where the queens all carry little ladies— twenty-two pistols to protect themselves against dirt.
>
> Pancho: I know, but I have a personality already. I don't want to go there.
>
> Tennessee: Well, honey, you'll shine there. That's the place for you.
>
> Pancho: How about L'Affiche?
>
> Tennessee: L'Affiche is elegant, honey. That's piss-elegant. That's this elegant business. Now, you don't want to be this elegant business, do you?

"Well bred people find it difficult to break out of their shell of good-breeding. They live constantly under wraps," Williams said. Pancho embodied Williams's deliberate regression. By the standards of Williams's refined upbringing, Pancho was trash. Williams had aligned himself with the pagan and the redemption of the instinctual, which, like the cool water Alma mentions at the finale of *Summer and Smoke*, "comes from deep underground." Decades later Williams told Studs Terkel that Alma "was willing—when she gave up her great love—she was finally willing to settle for an attractive salesman." Williams was also speaking of himself.

Pancho *was* his attractive salesman. A man-child of twenty-five, Pancho was sensual, explosive, jealous, unlettered, and primitive. Pancho's frequent and fantastic misdoings filled Williams's life with sensational melodrama. "All of my nights with Pancho, and many of my days, in those days when he was so fond of fire-water, were inclined toward a great deal of wildness," Williams wrote in the original manuscript of *Memoirs*, changing Pancho to "Santo" in the published version because he was "sort of an off-beat saint." "At first I entertained him in my apartment only two

With Pancho Rodriguez

or three evenings a week but he decided to move in and in he moved and that was the end of my social success in New Orleans."

"My deportment wasn't too exemplary at that time of my life," Pancho said. When he was on his bad behavior, Pancho could empty a room in a heartbeat, and he did. "The scenes he created scared respectable society away," Williams wrote. "I received no more invitations to debut parties in the Garden District." Their relationship propelled Williams even faster toward the horizon of his desires and even further into Bohemia. "He could not explain this thing to himself and yet he did not regret it," Williams wrote in his short story "Rubio y Morena," a meditation on their relationship. Like the narrator, Williams "had never been able to believe that anybody sincerely cared much about him." Pancho's uncomplicated ardor "restored his male dominance. In his heart he knew this and was grateful."

Williams also had written Pancho into the schematic emotional equation of "Chart of Anatomy." On the page, he was the rapacious, fiery Mexican Rosa Gonzales, "some loud tacky thing with a Z in her name!" Pancho's sister's club—La Luna—became the Moon Lake Casino, "where anything goes" and which is, Alma says, "gay, very gay." Pancho was representative of Williams's extravagant new romantic reordering of existence. He was a package of paganism, through whom Williams found the redemption of the instinctual. Rosa's irresistible, insidious hold on the prodigiously gifted Dr. Buchanan reimagined Pancho's subterranean pull on Williams—something he both craved and feared. "Did anyone ever slide downhill as fast as I have this summer? . . . Like a greased pig," Buchanan tells Rosa, to whom he is briefly and improbably engaged. Rosa does for Buchanan what Pancho did for Williams. As a catalyst of his undoing, Pancho "widened the latitude of his experience . . . the circus-trapeze of longing on which he had kicked himself senselessly back and forth." Pancho didn't know much, didn't think much, didn't have much to say: nevertheless, his presence reprieved Williams from his isolation, his sense of being "sentenced to solitary confinement inside our own skins." "Of all the people I have known you have the greatest and warmest heart," Williams wrote to Pancho; like the narrator in "Rubio y Morena," quite to his surprise, Williams "had grown to love" him.

In late April 1946, hoping to escape muggy New Orleans and to refresh himself for the grind of completing "Chart of Anatomy," Williams decided to take off for a few months to Taos, New Mexico, "to breathe the fine air between those two ranges of mountains, the Lobos and the Sangre de Christo." He set out in his new car, a convertible Packard Roadster christened "Skatterbolt" by the family, making a stopover in St. Louis. Pancho, who worked at a department store, told Williams he would rendezvous with him in New Mexico after he gave notice. "I have learned how to use an hydraulic jack and a lug-wrench which is really a milestone in my life!" Williams wrote to Audrey Wood from the road. By the time he reached St. Louis, both his radiator and his heterosexual masquerade to the family had been blown.

"When I got home I found a telegram—opened and read by the family—which stated that he had quit his job and was leaving for Taos and would I please wire him some money to live on till I arrived there," Williams wrote Donald Windham. "I need not tell you the reception this wire had in the bosom of the family. They have cross-examined me about Pancho and the wire ever since I got here. He has called me long-distance a couple of times, with Mother scuttling downstairs to grab up the phone so she could listen in on the conversation. Naturally I would have to practically hang up on the poor kid, especially when he burst into tears and begged me to leave here at once as he was lonely and hungry in the middle of the desert!" Williams added, "I guess the cat is all but out of the bag, although I have covered up as well as I can—you know how well that is!"

"I'm sorry I couldn't talk to you much on the phone," he wrote to Pancho, promising to wire money. "We have two phones, one upstairs and one down and Mother usually listens at the other phone. I was terrified that you would say something." He continued, "I wish you would write me immediately but please be extremely careful what you put in any communication addressed here. Make the letter very casual but tell me where you are staying in Taos, how you like it—do you think you'll be happy there? . . . Staying with me you would not need much money but knowing you, I am afraid you will be restless without something in the way of an occupation. I shall be writing awfully hard during the days and there is not society of the sort in New Orleans—although I consider that to be an advantage. However the important thing is that I shall see you very soon!"

The first day on the road from St. Louis to Taos, Williams's car and his body began to break down. He felt stabbing pains in his abdomen. "Jack in Black had come out of the bushes," Williams wrote. As he continued west, both he and the car grew worse. In Missouri, his pain was diagnosed as cramps and nerves; in Kansas, as low-grade appendicitis; in Oklahoma, as kidney stones. After Williams abandoned his car in Oklahoma and got himself by bus to Taos, the Sisters of Nazareth at the Holy Cross Hospital told him that because he had a fever and a white blood cell count of 18,000, his appendix might have burst and therefore he required immediate surgery.

"The altitude affected my heart, and I did not think I'd pull through," he wrote Audrey Wood. "Pancho sat in the hospital with me and I made out my last will and testament while the young doctors shaved my groin for surgery," Williams wrote. "I had nothing to leave but the playscript of 'Battle of Angels' and I left it to Pancho." Pancho took the will and tore it to pieces. "He always had moments of great style, and this was one of them," Williams said. As Williams breathed in the anesthesia, he experienced "a sensation of death." "Claustrophobia, feeling of suffocation are my greatest dreads," he explained later about the moment. As he went under, Williams's last words were, "I'm dying! I'm dying!"

When Williams came to, "Dios Mio!"—Spanish for "My God!"—were his first words. "I don't know why I said it in Spanish," Williams told Audrey Wood. "Probably the strong influence of Hispanic culture!" The doctors told him that instead of finding a ruptured appendix, they discovered that he had Meckel's diverticulitis, "a rare intestinal problem." To his close friends—Audrey Wood, James Laughlin, Paul Bigelow, Donald Windham—Williams wrote extended accounts of the traumatic event. Even ten years later, reimagining the operation for the critic Kenneth Tynan, the word picture of his torment remained remarkably the same.

As he lay recuperating from the surgery, one of the sisters bustling through her chores remarked to Williams, "Well, you're all right now. Of course you're probably going to get something like this again in a few years, but we all have to go sometime, or other, don't we?" Williams received her statement almost like a curse. "One of the good sisters of the Holy Cross came into my room and advised me to make my peace with the Lord as whatever improvement I showed would only be temporary," he told James Laughlin. Nothing the doctors said would disabuse Williams of his opinion—formed on the basis of the sister's coded words and his own analysis of the decayed parts of his intestine—that he had pancreatic cancer. "I don't know what you got and I don't care what you got, it's nothing to me," the dressed-down sister told him, returning to hiss her fury while he was still taking plasma.

"Since then, and despite the assurances of the doctors, I have been expecting to die, which is something I have never really looked forward to at all," he wrote to Laughlin. Williams's life had acquired both a sense of urgency and a sense of an ending. Still recovering at the hospital three days later, he wrote to Donald Windham, "I am sitting up here smoking and writing, but feel profoundly changed in some way. I did not know life was so precious to me or death so unalluring." The incident proved to be a watershed. "This was when the desperate time started," he told Kenneth Tynan. The moment marked the beginning of a three-year period when he thought he was "a dying man and a still young one."

In an attempt to shed his sense of doom, Williams left Taos to lose himself in work and in the recuperative delights of a Nantucket summer. He rented a gray clapboard house at 31 Pine Street and invited a number of friends to distract him. "As everyone remarked, the house seemed just like the Wingfield apartment except there was more light," Williams wrote to Margo Jones. "But after the first week there were no clean sheets or towels and the atmosphere of southern degeneracy had completely triumphed over the brisk New England climate."

The first to arrive that summer was a stranger, Carson McCullers, to whom Williams had written praising her novel *The Member of the Wedding* and suggesting they meet up before his imminent death. "She was a crashing bore, but Tennessee found her sort of tragic and interesting," Gore Vidal said. "The minute I met her she seemed like one of my oldest and best friends!" Williams confessed to James Laughlin. He went on, "We are planning to collaborate on a dramatization of her last book soon as I get my present play finished. I think this play will be my last effort to write for Broadway. From now on I shall write for a nonexistent art-theatre."

McCullers, like Williams, was lion-hearted. Her poem "Love and the Rind of Time" addressed "Those who find it a little harder to live / And therefore live a little harder." She was Southern; she had battled ill health, alcoholism, insecurity, and her own wayward sexual desires. Williams called McCullers his "sister." In later years, she would keep a writing room in her Nyack house for Williams. "I feel that once I can be with you nothing will frighten me and I can rest safe," she wrote him. "My self-confidence—about health, and work, and realization of my inward self—are dependent on you: sometimes it disturbs me to realize how much. But not really—I know nothing but good can come of our alliance."

Williams cherished the memory of that summer—"the last good year before her stroke"—including his first sighting of McCullers disembarking the ferry: a tall girl in slacks and baseball cap, flashing a radiant snaggle-toothed grin. None of the passengers seemed to fit her description, so Williams and Pancho started up the gangplank to see if anyone else was still on board. Just then, her two battered suitcases in hand, McCullers came toward them. "Are you Tennessee or Pancho?" she asked. Williams identified himself. He suggested they go for a swim; Pancho, already drunk at midday, joined them. They changed at the bathhouse. Outside was a patio with a long row of rocking chairs overlooking the water; in each chair sat an old lady. "For some reason Pancho did not like the way they looked and he turned his rage upon them," Williams recalled. "At the top of his voice, addressing these very proper old ladies, he shouted, 'What are you looking at? You're nothing but a bunch of old cock-suckers!'"

"Tennessee, honey, that boy is wonderful, you are lucky to have him with you!" McCullers said.

Williams was, he said, "by no means convinced of this"; in time, neither was McCullers. Nonetheless, "they went home and set up housekeeping." McCullers cooked "spuds Carson"—olives and onions mashed with the potatoes—and pea soup with hot dogs. At night, she played Bach and Schubert on the upright piano in the living room. Sometimes

With Carson McCullers, 1946

she and Williams listened to Sousa marches on a windup Victrola or read Hart Crane to each other. During the day, they sat at opposite ends of a long table and wrote together—he finishing *Summer and Smoke*, she beginning the stage adaptation of *The Member of the Wedding*. For his part, Williams said, "Carson is the only person I've ever been able to stand in the same room with me when I'm working." McCullers was equally grateful and gracious. "I feel you are a true collaborator in this work," she wrote to him when it was finished two years later, "and the credit should be acknowledged."

"Pancho was subdued for a while," Williams said. Inevitably, however, the intimacy Williams and McCullers found between them—their reading, their writing, their shared Southern associations—inspired envy. Pancho began to throw spoiling scenes. "My friend Pancho has been cooking and keeping the house for me which has been a saving," Williams wrote to Audrey Wood in the autumn. "But he is now in a mysterious Mexican rage and has packed his trunk intending to leave for Mexico. I think it is partly because of Carson's presence. He resents the fact that we have long literary conversations which he does not understand. This situation is also upsetting. Carson is so vague that she does not appear to notice it." Williams did; in a letter to Pancho he tried to reason him out of his unreasonableness:

1) As you ought to know, I have no one else in my emotional life and have no desire for anyone else.

2) I have never thought of you as being *employed* by me. That is all an invention of your own. If we were man and woman, it would be very clear and simple, we would be married and simply sharing our lives and whatever we have with each other. That is what I had thought we were actually doing. When I say "Pancho is doing the cooking and the house-work" I am only saying that Pancho is being kind enough to help me, and knowing me as you do, you should realize that that is the only way in which I could possibly mean it.

3) This is a dark, uncertain period we are passing through and a time when we ought to stand beside each other with faith and courage and the belief that we have the power in us to come back out in the light.

4) I love you as I have never loved anyone else in my life.

5) You are not only my love but also my luck. For 3 months I have lived in a dark world of anxiety, inexpressible even to you, which has made me seem different—You may not have guessed this, but you are about the only thing that has kept me above the water.

Over the next year, as part of Williams's strategy of pacification, Pancho was brought into increasing contact with the A-list to which Williams was a new fixture. "When Tennessee would mention, 'I want you to meet my friend Pancho Rodriguez,' they expected a little Mexican boy with a sombrero," Pancho recalled, who saw himself as "very proud, I thought I knew everything." His efforts to appease Pancho's insecurity bought Williams anything but an easy life. Pancho's arrogance and fragility were a toxic combination. When Pancho went with Williams and McCullers to tea with Katharine Cornell and her director husband Guthrie McClintic, who were expecting "Chart of Anatomy" to be a vehicle for her, McClintic took "a violent dislike" to him. Among these distinguished theatricals, Pancho became a subject of scandal and concern, "the Mexican problem," as Williams himself was finally forced to concede to Margo Jones. McCullers smelled a gold digger and an impediment to Williams's creative life. "Don't, for God's sake, be unhinged by Pancho. You must protect yourself," she wrote him. Paul Bigelow reported her high anxiety to his companion Jordan Massie, who was McCullers's distant cousin. "Carson says that Ten's Mexican has imported his whole family from Texas into Louisiana and they are all living in New Orleans in the greatest *gemutlicheit!*" Bigelow added, "Tennessee has not only acquired an old man of the sea, he has acquired the old man's descendants, and I know that class of Mexican, especially of the border region, is wily and shrewd and almost impossible to be rid of."

Even Dakin Williams, when he came to visit Williams in 1946, got a taste of Pancho's transgressive behavior. As he was undressing for the night, Pancho—Dakin claimed—had come into his bedroom. "I had peeled down to my jockey shorts," he said. "Seating himself on my bed, immediately next to me, he draped his arm over my shoulder, giving me a friendly pinch on the nipple. 'Dakin, I want you to sleep with me tonight.'" "Dakin stayed up all night shaking and being very nervous and saying the rosary," Pancho recalled. "He was afraid I would do something, I guess." After the visit, Dakin wrote Williams about Pancho. He was not, he said, "an asset to you socially" and "has all the attributes of . . . well . . . you know what." The letter, in which Dakin asked, "How can you do this to me and to our family?" earned a blistering reply from Williams; according to Dakin, it "had the predictable effect of terminating the warm brotherly relationship that had once existed between us."

As reports of Williams's ill health and his struggle with "Chart of Anatomy" began to reach her, Audrey Wood became increasingly paranoid about Pancho's insidious influence. She gave credence to rumors that Pancho was poisoning her client. "No amount of reassurance on my part can quite remove the fear that Tenn may actually be in some sort of danger," wrote Bigelow, whom the Liebling-Wood agency had asked to go to New Orleans to winkle out the dark truth. "She resented me," Rodriguez said. "She was afraid I might destroy Williams through my behavior."

At the end of the summer, after checking himself into Manhattan's St. Luke's Hospital in a vain search for pancreatic cancer, Williams included Pancho in his professional meetings with Audrey Wood, which outraged her. In October, according to Rodriguez, the shy Williams asked him to raise the issue of foreign royalties over dinner. "'Audrey, what happened to the money from the royalties,'" Rodriguez said with characteristic bluntness. "She looked at me and said, 'Why are you asking me that?' Audrey never forgot that again. She was very wary of me." Rodriguez continued, "From then on there was a campaign to get rid of me." Wood saw Pancho as a threat to both Tennessee's livelihood and her own.

"Audrey wanted to ask my advice again as to whether she should lecture Tennessee about his folly in insisting on allowing Pancho to be present at all interviews and to take him out of the country, just now when the moving picture arrangements are just being defined," Bigelow wrote to Massie regarding the long drawn-out film negotiations for *The Glass Menagerie*, about which Pancho had high-handedly criticized Wood for dawdling. Certainly, Pancho was familiarizing himself with Williams's deals and dollars. Although the gossip columnist Louella Parsons broke the news to the nation about the half-million-dollar sale of *The Glass Menagerie* to Hollywood, it was Pancho on a cardboard record cut in New Orleans on October 17, 1946, who proudly broadcast the terms of the actual contract. "A deal has been completed by Charles [Feldman] for the film rights to 'The Glass Menagerie'. It was done yesterday. The four character play, written by Tennessee Williams, the Broadway playwright, will bring $400,000 against 8 and 2/3 percent of the feature's net profits, plus 1 and 1/3 percent of the $400,000. One half of the $400,000 advanced payment is to be paid when the contract is signed and the remainder next January 16."

Whatever the exact figures—the price was the highest yet paid for a Broadway play—Williams was suddenly a rich man. Wood feared that Pancho might exploit Williams's loyalty to him and seize his literary interests out from under her. "It was an error of incalculable magnitude for Tenn to let Audrey know in such a way that she had to acknowledge it, his relationship with Pancho," Bigelow wrote to Massie. He went on, "Liebling feels that if Audrey goes there she will immediately arouse Pancho's suspicions and perhaps cause the removal of Tenn's entire work from that agency. . . . I know Audrey is disturbed because Tenn is producing no work. She told me at breakfast a week ago . . . that the new play is only a sketch for a play and that it is all Tenn has written in two years. For a careful intellectual writer, that would not be surprising or alarming, for Tenn it is catastrophic, for it means that his great impulse toward written expression is either weakening or may die, or that he is so deeply troubled and un-channeled by emotional conflict that no expression of any sort is possible for him. . . . Naturally I am worried about these accounts of Tenn and Pancho."

"I was jealous of all of them," Rodriguez said. "I didn't want for him to get close to anybody else. I suspected everybody wanted to take him away from me." Whenever Pancho felt his access to Williams blocked, he lashed out. One night in Nantucket, after an argument with Williams, he returned home drunk. The front door was locked. From the upstairs light, he could tell that Williams was in bed reading. "He didn't answer my call to open the door," Rodriguez said. Finally, Pancho found his keys. "I walked in, and I started to break all the light bulbs in the house." Williams, who had provoked the incident, subsequently used it as a detail of passion in *A Streetcar Named Desire*.

However, Williams waited until *Memoirs* to dramatize the collateral damage of another of Pancho's scenes in May 1947. "You take your friends out of here before I throw them out," Pancho told Williams, who was entertaining Donald Windham and his partner the actor Sandy Campbell in their room at the Royalton in New York. Instead of returning after thirty minutes as he'd promised, two hours later Williams was still drinking with his friends in the lobby of the Algonquin. Pancho loudly approached them. Williams asked for the check; Pancho shouted for the waiter to bring everyone's check separately. "We're the sugar daddies!" Pancho said, turning to Windham. "Well, did you get another three hundred dollars out of Mr. Williams?" "Pancho, you aren't jealous of me, are you?" Windham said. "Jealous of you!" Pancho shouted. "I think you and Sandy are two of the biggest whores who ever appeared on Broadway!"

According to Windham, "Tenn . . . disappeared behind a screen at the end of the lobby, while Pancho continued about how low I was and how Tennessee supported everyone. When the waiter arrived Tenn appeared and paid the check, left a dollar in change for the tip, and fled. Pancho, without ceasing his monologue, dumped the change from the tray onto the table. 'Is this for me?' the waiter asked. 'No, this is for you,' Pancho said, pushing over a quarter and pocketing seventy-five cents." During the scene Pancho taunted Williams and Windham. "You ought to see your room now, Mr. Williams. Maybe you two ought to go over and see it together. You're both writers, maybe you can make a story out of it."

The Royalton room and most of Williams's possessions had been trashed. "A portable typewriter borrowed from Audrey had been smashed," Williams wrote to Windham, enclosing Pancho's first-ever note of apology. "A new suit and hat torn to shreds, all my books torn up, vase and glasses smashed. For some reason he neglected to attack my manuscripts. Of course if he had I would have thrown him in jail and perhaps he knew it. Altogether about one hundred and fifty dollars worth of damages! I am taking it out of his allowance—gradually." He added, "When you analyze his behavior, it becomes so pitiful it makes you more tearful than angry. He has never had any security or comfort or affection and he thinks that the way to hold it is by standing over it with tooth and claw like a wild-cat!"

In the grueling last months of 1946, as Williams wrestled "Chart of Anatomy" into shape, Pancho's most potent rival was Williams's work. Like Amada in "Rubio y Morena," Pancho seemed to exist for Williams "on the other side of a center which was his writing. Everything outside of that existed in a penumbra as shadowy forms on the further side of a flame." Pancho didn't deal well with Williams's self-absorption. Williams had quiet days to write; however, the evenings brought "the always turbulent return of Pancho from his day's work at the clothing store."

"SITUATION OF MY psyche remains nightmarish," Williams confided to his diary in November. He added, "The iron jaws of a trap seem to hold me here in a little corner, backing away from panic. I cling to little palliative devices—the swimming pool-the sleeping tablets-reading in bed-sometimes movies-the familiarity of Pancho." The sense of collapse that beset Williams signaled anxiety about his play and about Pancho. Williams stopped having sex, or wanting it, which worried him. "The nightingales can't sing anymore. They just died on the branches. And it's all a bit useless here." Even though the doctors whom he consulted during these months continued to tell him that he did not have cancer, in his weakness, burning stomach, and abdominal twinges, his body seemed to act out his dread. "Nausea persists," he wrote in his December diary. "Dr. Sullivan seems bored and impatient and offers no suggestion except that I see a psychiatrist." In his own self-analysis, Williams admitted to Audrey Wood, "Undoubtedly a lot of my symptoms are what is called 'psychosomatic.' I get depressed about my work or something and feel as if I were about to give up the ghost." He added, "Miss Alma has been an ordeal. I have gotten so tired of her."

On November 1, Williams finished an early draft of the play. He wired Wood on November 11:

STILL DISSATISFIED WITH SCRIPT. SHOW GUTHRIE IF HE WISHES BUT NO ONE ELSE TILL I PREPARE FINAL VERSION.

"I agree with Guthrie that I don't think this is for Cornell, primarily because I don't think Cornell physically can ever fit herself into this play. I find it extremely hard to envision Cornell as a woman who is under the domination of her mother, father, church, and finally a man she loves but who doesn't love her. On the other hand, I could believe a woman like Helen Hayes or a younger version of her in this predicament." On December 1, Williams confided to his diary: "Still here, still working on 'Chart'. Sometimes it seems just a grade or two superior to a radio soap-opera. I have committed some astonishing lapses of taste in this play." He added, "This week coming—Margo will visit here one night on her way to Dallas. I'll finish up this 3rd draft before she gets here and let her read it. If she is encouraging it will help."

On December 7, Laurette Taylor died suddenly. To Williams, her death was another augury of his decline. During this grief-stricken week, Williams read "Chart" aloud to a friend. "He kept yawning as I read," Williams wrote. "And so I read badly and when I finished, he made this devastating remark: 'How could the author of "The Glass Menagerie" write such a bad play as this.'" "Maurice's negative reaction and Margo's unexpressed but suspected disappointment took whatever was left of the wind from my sails and I don't even feel like sending the ms. off," he wrote on December 16. (In fact, Jones liked *Summer and Smoke* and agreed to direct it at her Dallas Theatre.) He was failing at art and at life. "Quarreled with Pancho last night," he wrote in his diary. "He brought his brother home with him for the second consecutive night which would be alright if I were well but I don't want anyone around when I'm sick. Is it possible that I *am* losing my mind?" Nonetheless, on December 19, "feeling pretty desolate," Williams sent off the final draft of "Chart of Anatomy" to Audrey Wood, then feeling unwell he went to bed "with newspaper and Crane and Hemingway. Two of the best bed-partners a sick old bitch can have." He judged "Chart" incomplete. "Somehow or other, for a complex of psychological reasons, I did not do as well with 'Chart' as I should have," he wrote to Wood, adding, "My interest has shifted to the other long play which may turn out to be stronger."

"I haven't caught sight of my old guardian angel in a long time," Williams confided to his diary in mid-December. "Where are you Angelo mio? Can't you hear my little cries of distress? If I were well, I feel that I would be writing my best work now. *If!*" Williams added, "One of Mr. O'Neill's pipe dreams." On Christmas Eve, however, Williams recorded a rare moment of contentment. "Pancho is home with me and preparing a nice supper. There are clean sheets on the bed. I read, write, smoke and am tolerably peaceful." He had begun to rework "The Poker Night." "I . . . find it surprisingly close to completion," he wrote. "All in all I think it's better than 'Chart'. Simpler and straighter & therefore more forceful. The ending is not yet right. May continue working on that tomorrow." The new play posed a set of totally different dramatic problems. It was relatively short (ninety-four pages) and structurally compact; it had, Williams told Wood, about six characters and was "rather harsh, violent and melodramatic with some pretty rough characters: a relief after the rectory."

After welcoming in 1947 with a New Year's Eve party, Williams began working "desultorily" on "The Poker Night." Reverend Dakin was on his way to visit him, but even the cheering anticipation of his grandfather seemed unable to lift Williams's spirits. Audrey Wood had not responded about "Chart"; Williams feared the worst. "She is probably disgusted with it. So was I," he wrote. "Oh, how dull I am!" In his battle against depression—"this huge, dreadful game of fox and hounds with neurosis," Williams called it—action was often the antidote to anomie. "Thinking of driving down into Florida if I remain well," he noted in his diary for January 2. A couple of weeks later, he and his nearly ninety-year-old grandfather were on the road from New Orleans to Key West in a newly purchased secondhand white Pontiac.

"Grandfather was a wonderful traveling companion," Williams said. "Everything pleased him. He pretended to see clearly despite his cataracts and in those days you could shout to him and he'd hear you." They took up residence in a two-room suite on the top floor of the La Concha Hotel that offered a view "over a clean sweep of the sea that covers the bones of [Hart] Crane." Williams worked in the morning; they spent the afternoons at the beach. His grandfather had purchased a pith helmet and a pair of swimming trunks decorated with palm trees. "You cannot imagine what a fantastic sight he is! Everyone smiles at us on the street, we are such an odd looking couple, I suppose," Williams wrote to Pancho. "Yesterday he walked in a fruit-store and said, 'I want a dozen *California*

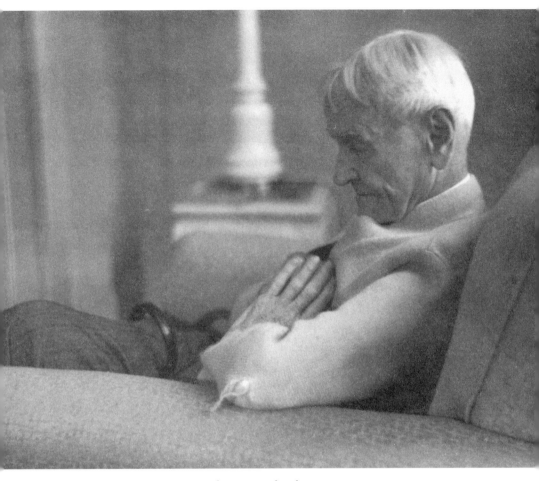

The Reverend Dakin

oranges'!" Williams continued, "It takes him half an hour to order a meal because he really wants everything on the menu. I have to read it to him all the way through several times shouting like a circus-barker. But he is enjoying himself and that is really the object of the trip."

"By the calendar I am somewhat younger than you, but only by the calendar which is an unimportant thing," Williams had written his grandfather a few months earlier. "You are one of the youngest people I have ever known, and incidentally one of the two people I have most loved and admired in this world. You know who the other one was and still is." Williams's enduring love was reciprocated; Reverend Dakin's un-judgmental pleasure in his grandson and in his writing grounded Williams and strengthened him. (Williams subsequently repaid this allegiance by leaving all his royalties to Sewanee, his grandfather's alma mater.) "Just being with him renewed my own pleasure in the fact of existence," Williams recalled. It also renewed his confidence. "I think the change was good for me, physically, but I miss being with you all the time," Williams wrote to Pancho. As it turned out, even the distance from Pancho, and from the destructive aspects of their relationship, proved to be some kind of psychological stimulus. In the benign Florida atmosphere, with its dramatic absence of abrasion, when Williams turned back to the tormented and tempestuous world of "The Poker Night," to his surprise the characters seemed to flow powerfully onto the page. "It went like a house on fire, due to my happiness with Grandfather," he recalled.

In the first-draft scenes of "The Poker Night," with muscular, terse dialogue undecorated by the fine filigree of his lyricism, Williams set out the lineaments of need in each of his main characters: Blanche's hysteria over the loss of both the family home and the husband who "loved me with everything but one part of his body"; her baby sister Stella's bed sweetness with her virile uncouth husband Ralph. In these notional scenes, sex and survival were already the stakes of play. Williams imagined Blanche's breakdown but not the cause of it. He had not yet situated the story in the specific steamy locale of New Orleans or imposed a patina of symbolism on Stella's address—Elysian Fields—a name that held out the promise of eternal delight. At first, Stella appeared to Blanche to have settled merely in "an awful city wilderness." Before her husband entered, Stella described him as "a different species." Ralph, whose name Williams instructed to be changed to "Stanley" when the first draft was typed up, was a mutant breed, a person who had successfully adapted to this vacant, barbarous habitat, someone willed beyond the dimensions of cultivated behavior: in other words, a primitive.

In the simple situation—desperate visiting sister intrudes on sensual paradise of sibling—Williams did what he could not do in "Chart of Anatomy"—he dramatized desire instead of talking about it. He put psychology into behavior. In Blanche's airs and graces, her ablutions, her romantic persiflage, her insistence on illusion—"the soft people have got to—shimmer and glow—put a—paper lantern over the light"—the hysteric's masquerade was incarnated. She used her wound as lure. She made a spectacle of the broken connection between herself and her own desires. By contrast, Stanley was comfortable in his skin—"Be comfortable is my motto," he says. He was clear about his needs and about how to satisfy them. Here, where life was reduced to the creaturely taking and giving of pleasure, to the expression of passion however violent and craven, impulse, not idealism, ruled. Williams's characters acted out yet another deliberate regression that "Chart of Anatomy" merely indicated. When Blanche suggests to Stella that she should get out of the hovel she's living in, she replies "slowly and emphatically," "I'm not in anything I want to get out of."

As Williams pored over the rewrite, he turned Stanley and Stella's railroad flat into a battleground that externalized his own internal war. Pancho's capricious intrusiveness, the absence of calm, the lunatic sense of his own collapse, the bouts of sexual pleasure, the compulsion to cling to the temperamental and abusive love object, the memory of the deadly family home, the need to endure—all these warring personal issues became the pigments that brought Williams's characters to life. "Nobody sees anybody *truly*," Williams wrote a few months later to Elia Kazan, in an attempt to entice him to direct the play by explaining it. "Vanity, fear, desire, competition—all such distortions within our own egos—condition our vision of those in relation to us." He went on, "Add to those distortions in our *own* egos, the corresponding distortions in the egos of the *others*—and you see how cloudy the glass must become through which we look at each other." This drama of misperception required that the audience understand in each character both the public face and the unconscious desire it hid. Williams built up this complex contradictoriness, the division in each character that Kazan would characterize in his notebook as "Masks" and "Spines":

| Damsel in Distress | BLANCHE | find protection |
| The King of Ball and Jane | STANLEY | Keep things his way (B antagonist) |

Housewife:	STELLA	Hold onto Stanley (B and
narcotized asleep		herself the CAPTIVE,
		Glazed always day
		dreaming
He man-Mama's Boy	MITCH	Get away from his mother
		(B the lever)

Long after he had done *Streetcar*, Elia Kazan wrote, "I kept puzzling over the play—which must be a measure of its size—and about the author. The more I thought about the play, the more mysterious the play appeared." He continued, "It was certainly not what it seemed to be, a moral fable of the brutalization of a sensitive soul by a sadistic bully. Then what was it? Something far more personal." Where Alma was preserved in the aspic of Victorian America, in Blanche the vestiges of the Victorian world—the refinements of mind and manners—were brought into fierce conflict with the modern spirit of self-aggrandizement. This clash of worlds and wills called out of Williams the most accurate coordinates of the split in his own internal geography, those life and death forces contending within him.

WHEN WILLIAMS SAT down to complete the play, his postoperative sense of renewed life was at odds with the sense of doom that had plagued him through the fall. A *froideur* had begun to creep into his relationship with Pancho. Williams wrote in late March 1947 that Pancho had "threatened to leave several times lately" and "I have twice bought him railroad tickets which he has subsequently cashed in and remained." Williams added, "I am not sure how I would feel if he left. . . . Lately, I have been philandering a bit, here and there. I think it is an excellent thing for a relationship to have little side-dishes now and then but not everybody can see it that way. However, I intend to suit myself in the matter." Williams's restlessness had returned and with it a familiar loneliness. "Somehow in my life I have not succeeded in winning and holding the love of any person," he wrote in his diary. "I have misjudged and made wrong choices in my relations and wind up now with no one capable of feeling anything much for me. Maybe I have been too cool and reserved—only my work held my heart. And I've had a way of evading emotional responsibility with people. The times they might have loved me I've slipped away."

When the rewritten Blanche first enters Stella and Stanley's louche New Orleans world, she brings with her a strung-out sense of collapse and a neediness that the character shared with her author. When she gets off the streetcar, Blanche is literally and figuratively at the end of the line, "a desperate driven creature"—Williams explained to Kazan—"backed into a last corner to make a last desperate stand." Her life has been a series of abdications; she is exhausted by the masquerade of gentility. Williams knew the panic-struck feeling. "To breathe quietly—how sweet!" he wrote at the time. "Oh, how sweet it would be to exist altogether without this tired old fabrication of flesh—such a mess of impurities and disintegrations—such a pitiful mess. But where is existence except in this ruin."

Blanche, like Williams, longs for the safety of embrace and for release from terrible loneliness, "a cleft in the rock of the world that I could hide in," as she famously says. Her turmoil—the promiscuity, the drinking, the fear behind the display of erudite charm—is a veiled admission of Williams's own delirium. She believes, we learn, that her words have inadvertently caused the suicide of her beloved husband, just as Williams feared that his had precipitated his sister's descent into madness. "It was because—on the dance-floor—unable to stop myself—I'd suddenly said—'I saw! I know! You disgust me,'" Blanche says, haunted by the unforgivable outburst at her homosexual husband, who rushes from her and blows his brains out. Blanche exposed her husband's sexuality; Williams exposed his sister's fragility. In one way or another, for both "the searchlight which had been turned on the world was turned off again."

To get to Elysian Fields, Blanche takes two streetcars: one named "Desire," the other "Cemeteries." The destinations of the streetcars suggest the parameters of Blanche's self-destructive journey. As the story unfolds, her legend of loss turns out to be more than her first momentary loss of composure: she has lost her husband, her home, her good name, her purity, and, in the end, her sanity. Her airs and graces cover her self-loathing. Her conscious mind sees marriage as her salvation—

"Sometimes—there's God—so quickly," she says when Mitch, Stanley's poker-playing buddy, takes a shine to her.

But the play traps another unconscious wish: to find someone to kill her. In the brutish Stanley, who in the original version sold "mortuary equipment and appliances," Blanche recognizes a death dealer. "The first time I laid eyes on him I thought to myself, that man is my executioner! That man will destroy me," she tells Mitch. In scene 4, when Stanley enters and overhears Blanche telling Stella, "He's *common*! . . . There's something downright—*bestial*—about him!" Blanche unwittingly seals her fate, calling out the violence and envy that lie just beneath Stanley's ruthless hedonism. In his production script, beside Blanche's lines about his brutishness, Kazan wrote, "This Stanley never forgets. He's common. He's common! He'll make her common as shit. He'll fuck her and rape her. He'll degrade her utterly. That's his only answer." From the earliest sketches of the play to the final draft, Stanley made his entrance carrying dead meat. Stanley is all about flesh and feast, both of which require killing (even the stage directions point out that the package is "red-stained"). "We've had this date with each other from the beginning," he says just before he rapes her. And so he has. "I'll put it to you plainly," Kazan said, whose collaboration with Williams would become one of the century's great theatrical partnerships, "Tennessee Williams equals Blanche. He is Blanche. And Blanche is torn between a desire to preserve her tradition, which is her entity, her being, and her attraction to what is going to destroy her traditions."

In "Chart of Anatomy," the character of Alma had been easy to write. "She simply seemed to exist somewhere in my being," Williams said, who considered her one of his best female characters. "However, Johnny Buchanan, the boy she was in love with all her youth, never seemed real to me but always a cardboard figure." In "The Poker Night," Stanley, a personification of Williams's erotic ideal, had a priapic vividness that Buchanan never did. In the original stage directions, Stanley's carnal charisma was self-evident:

> He is a man of thirty-two or three who moves slowly not out of
> apathy but from extreme male assurance. He is of medium height,

about five feet eight or nine, and strongly, compactly built. He is eminently pleased with his body and all its functions and this pleasure, this animal joy in his own being, is implicit in all his movements and attitudes. For the past fifteen years the center of his life has been pleasure with women, the giving and taking of it, not with weak indulgence, uxoriously or dependently, but with the power and pride of a richly feathered male bird among hens. Branching out from this complete and satisfying center are all the auxiliary channels and interests of his life, such as his success as a salesman and his easy, close friendship with men, his appreciation of rough humor, his love of good drink and food, his enjoyment of games, his car, his radio, everything that is his, that bears his emblem of the gaudy seed-bearer. He is contemptuous of weak men, he doesn't understand weakness. He is not even interested in his son and won't be until the boy is big enough to fight him.

For his study of unruly, self-centered testosterone, Williams kept a model close at hand. "Sometimes my violence scared the hell out of him," Pancho Rodriguez said about the mad scenes he played out with Williams. His dramatic explosions may have been scary, but they served Williams in a strategic literary way. On a personal level, they allowed Williams's emotional neediness to be in Pancho, not in himself. "I felt that he was exploiting me," Rodriguez said. "He used me as an inspiration for his work, to put me in positions where he wanted to see how I would react to certain situations, and out of those situations, write his own version of it." Rodriguez added, "Tennessee told me one day much later that the poetic quality in me had brought out his desire to continue and finish 'A Streetcar Named Desire.'" Certainly, like Blanche taunting Stanley, Williams pushed Pancho near to murder.

One night in the spring of 1947, staying in a rented cottage near Provincetown that they had christened "Rancho Pancho," Williams and Pancho drove to hear the jazz singer Stella Brooks at a local auberge called Atlantic House. "I had a great fondness for her, which was not pleasing to Pancho," Williams recalled. "He shouted some obscenities at her during her act and rushed off somewhere." Williams wandered out on the porch and began talking to a handsome, well-built young man with whom he ended up on the dunes. "I have never regarded sand as an ideal or even desirable surface on which to worship the little god," Williams said. However, that moonless night, Williams said, "the little god was given such devout service that he must still be smiling."

While an exhausted Williams was wandering through the fog of Provincetown, Pancho returned to the Atlantic House and retrieved their car. Assuming Williams had gone to Stella Brooks's place, he went there first. "Pancho gave her a clout in the eye, and he left her place a shambles," Williams recalled. As Williams made his way home on foot, trudging up a steep hill toward North Truro, he spotted a pair of headlights of a wildly careening car coming down the hill toward him. "With that protective instinct of mine, I somehow surmised that the driver of this car was Pancho," Williams said, who stepped off the road as it approached. "Pancho drove the car into the field of marsh grass with what seemed the intention of running me down," Williams wrote. As Williams bolted across the marshes toward the ocean, Pancho, shouting obscenities in Spanish and English, gave chase. When Williams reached the ocean, he clambered out onto a wooden pier and "suspended myself from its under structure, just above water level. I remained there till Pancho, not being a bloodhound, lost track of me and had gone screaming off in some other direction." The incident would lead to the first of many banishments of Pancho from Williams's world.

On the day he completed "The Poker Night"—March 16, 1947—Williams wrote in his diary, "It looks like P and I may have reached the hour of parting—He has been increasingly temperamental. Has quit his job. Is crazily capricious. I still care for him but right now I hunger for peace above all else." The play rated higher marks than his relationship. "A relative success," he wrote in his diary on the same day. "Not pleasant but well-done. I think it will make good theatre, though its success is far from assured." He sent it off to Audrey Wood. "It makes me shiver and shake to deposit in a post-office slot the first draft of a new play addressed to Miss Audrey Wood, and till she gives a report on her reaction, which may be two or three weeks after I mailed it, the shakes and shivers continue and steadily increase." Over the previous year, Wood had dawdled over *Summer and Smoke* and been curt about

Camino Real. "She said something like this: 'Darling, promise me you won't show this to anyone yet,'" Williams recalled years later.

But to his new play Wood's response was immediate and passionate. "Tennessee's script was as close to the finished play which opened in New York as anything he's ever written, before or since," Wood said. When Williams mentioned Margo Jones's commitment to doing *Summer and Smoke* in Dallas, Wood was adamant: "Don't think about this until you finish rewrite on 'Poker Night.' That comes first. We are both anxiously waiting the changes."

By March 25, Williams had sent off the revisions; Wood's only quibble now was with the play's title, which to her ear smacked of a Western action novel. Williams suggested an earlier notion. Before sending "The Poker Night" to the typist, Wood crossed out the title and scrawled across the manuscript's front page the more poetic and tantalizing "A Streetcar Named Desire." "Do you think anything will be done about 'Poker Night' this summer?" Williams wrote her a few days later. "I want to take a very active part in it, particularly casting, and I am wondering whether that would be done on the East or West Coast. This sounds as though I were quite certain it *will* be produced. Actually I am only hoping so, very strongly." He added, "Please do advise me about where to go!"

By April 8, Williams had his answer; he was to go to Charleston, South Carolina—halfway between New York and New Orleans—to meet Wood, Liebling, and a would-be producer, Irene Selznick—a name unknown to him—whom they felt would be "safe" and give the play "an all-out" production. Williams wired Wood:

MY TRAIN LEAVES 5:30 WEDNESDAY EVENING ARRIVES 8:15 THURSDAY EVENING. THIS WOMAN HAD BETTER BE GOOD.

As swift and strategic as Wood had been about finding Williams a potential producer, she was equally dictatorial about Pancho. "Audrey repeated twice on the phone that I should come *alone!*" he wrote to Windham, en route to the assignation with Selznick. He added, "She is supposed to have sixteen million dollars *and* good taste. I am dubious." Pancho, whom Williams sometimes dubbed "the Princess" in his letters, had been a keen reader of movie magazines since childhood and knew that this putative producer was kin to two of Hollywood's most famous powerhouses: the daughter of MGM studio head Louis B. Mayer, then the highest-paid man in the United States, and the estranged wife of producer David O. Selznick. "I did not know that Mrs. Selznick existed but the Princess even knew that her first name was Irene!" Pancho was furious at being left behind. "In fact she left me at the station with the baleful threat that she might not be there when I got back," he wrote to Windham, adding, "The Princess was inconsolable."

"I HAVE ALWAYS proceeded on the theory that as an agent I must cast the producer for a play as carefully as one would eventually cast the director, and the performers," Audrey Wood said. By that criterion, Wood had done only moderately well for her beloved client. Lawrence Langner, who co-produced the botched *Battle of Angels* for the Theatre Guild, ended up something of a joke to Williams, who teased his pretentiousness by referring to him as "Lawrence Stanislavsky Langner." He was equally cynical of his *Glass Menagerie* producers, Louis Singer and Eddie Dowling. Singer was a novice and a bully. Williams no longer "wanted any part of Singer (except his millions, which I can't get)." He was also "deeply indignant" about what he considered Dowling's mismanagement of the national company.

At the time Wood called on her, Selznick was forty and in the process of divorcing. Besides nursing a broken heart, she was nursing *Heartsong*, dying a slow death out of town. "My heart was with the playwright," Selznick said. Even before Wood set her cap at Selznick, the news of Selznick's literary zeal had gotten back to her. Selznick may not have had deep knowledge of theater, but she had something more important: deep ambition, deep connections, and deep pockets. "I wanted to find someone with money enough to keep a play out of town for as long as I thought it should be there, and also enough funds to cast the play perfectly, and to engage the right director for it," Wood said. Wood called Selznick twice; on her third try, she finally got her on the other end of the line: "Third and last call, my girl. Have you lost your manners?" Wood said, in her royal, starchy manner. Wood wouldn't talk specifics on the phone but proposed a tête-à-tête that afternoon. Wood's combination of formality and urgency hooked Selznick. At their meeting, Wood expertly reeled in her prospect. "Why me?" Selznick asked, "dazed with disbelief" at being offered Williams's new play. "Find me someone else," Wood said.

Selznick read the play overnight. She tried to turn it down, but Wood pressed her to take a few days to think it over. "The play was bigger than I wanted, earlier than I wanted," Selznick wrote. "I couldn't swallow it, and I couldn't spit it out. If I didn't do it, I was washed up; take my marbles and go home; fraidy-cat." In a letter written after their first meeting, still on "Mrs. Selznick" terms, Wood began by praising her—"I have a distinct feeling that you have the kind of approach, sustaining endurance and the right sense of humor and that all these virtues will help enormously toward making you a successful New York producer"—then neatly finessed Selznick's natural qualms by playing the gender card. "The other day you seemed to have only a list of Godfathers. After all, there is another sex and with your permission I am appointing myself 'Godmother No. 1.'" (Over time, Wood's godmotherly role gave the neophyte producer a place in theatrical history; it also gave Wood and her husband 4 percent of the show's profits for their $10,000 investment.)

Wood's first godmotherly gesture was to deliver Tennessee Williams to the Hotel Fort Sumter in Charleston. "Feeling like a marriage broker," Wood sent Selznick and Williams off for an hour's walk. She had prepared Selznick for Williams's shyness and for his disconcerting habit of looking away when others spoke. Selznick remembered the stroll as perfunctory. "I walked looking straight ahead," she recalled. "The closest we came to contact was at the crossings, when, as a Southern gentleman, he took my arm. Neither the play itself nor my relation to it was mentioned, so I could hardly hold forth, although he did ask if I liked the original title 'Poker Night.'"

At dinner, with still no mention of her status with the production, conversation strayed to possible directors. "The only time he seemed impressed was when he found out John Huston was a friend of mine," Selznick said. "I couldn't tell how I was doing, because he *did* turn away whenever I spoke to him." Then, according to Selznick, as coffee was being served, Williams abruptly said, "Enough. This is a waste of time.

Come on, Audrey." He pushed away from the table. Selznick sat "mortified." Wood turned back to her and said, "Come on, Irene." As they moved out of the dining room, Selznick heard Williams say to Wood, "Let's get this over with." Wood produced the contract—it was finalized on April 19, 1947—and Williams signed. Then, looking up, Williams fixed his eyes on Selznick and smiled at the woman who not twenty-four hours before he had referred to as "a Female Moneybags from Hollywood." "I was prepared for anything but this," Selznick said, who produced glasses from the bathroom and toasted the new alliance with a bottle of whisky. That night Selznick sent a coded telegram to her office:

BLANCHE HAS COME TO LIVE WITH US. HOORAY AND LOVE.

Wood had chosen Charleston for the rendezvous in order to cauterize theatrical gossip and to prevent the inevitable leaks to the press. When the news finally broke, the panjandrums of the Rialto were incensed. Kermit Bloomgarden proclaimed himself "shocked." Cheryl Crawford, the only seasoned female producer on Broadway, was "seething." "I think it's wrong that a new producer was handed our best playwright on a golden platter," she scolded Wood. "I hear 'Streetcar' was offered to no one else. I wouldn't be angry if it had gone to others who have earned the right. Some of us have stuck with the theatre all of our working lives, taken great chances, done the first plays of many authors, taken the failures, kept going." "There was a hysteria of snobbery along Broadway's inner circles," Kazan wrote. "I'm embarrassed to say that I was part of it; snobbery comes quickly to the successful on our street." Kazan and his powerful Broadway lawyer Bill Fitelson at first refused to take Selznick's calls. Fitelson went one step further; according to Kazan, he swaggered that "none of his clients would ever work for her." To the nabobs of commercial theater it seemed that one of the most promising new playwrights had been poached by a Hollywood interloper with only a flop and a famous family to her name.

With Wood and Selznick riding shotgun, Williams traveled straight to New York from Charleston to choose a director. "Irene is nice but overwhelmingly energetic and a real slave driver," Williams wrote to Pancho, with an apology for the detour North. He went on, "This is a tough job, baby, but a great deal—in fact, everything—depends on it. I just hope the old Toro will stand up under the pressure!" Joshua Logan, John Huston, Margo Jones, Tyrone Guthrie, and Kazan were on the short list; but once Williams saw Kazan's production of Arthur Miller's *All My Sons*, the Broadway hit of the season, he recognized the "strong but fastidious director" he'd been hoping to find. *All My Sons* exuded what Williams called Kazan's "peculiar vitality." Williams wanted Kazan, and only him.

"The cloudy dreamy type, which I admit to being, needs the complementary eye of the more objective and dynamic worker," Williams wrote Kazan, by way of special pleading to direct his play. "I believe you are also a dreamer. There are dreamy touches in your direction which are vastly provocative but you have the dynamism my work needs." Selznick rushed the script to Kazan, but the thirty-eight-year-old director didn't rush to read it. However, his wife, Molly Day Thacher, who had championed Williams for the Group Theatre prize he had won in 1938, read his copy. She considered *Streetcar* a masterpiece. When Williams called the house wanting to know her husband's reaction, she told him so. "Gadg likes a thesis," Williams said to her. "I haven't made up my mind what the thesis of this play is." Thacher hounded her husband to read it. When he did, Kazan had "reservations." "I wasn't sure Williams and I were the same kind of theatre animal," he said.

Williams was shy, standoffish, and fragile; Kazan, on the other hand, was brash, extroverted, and powerful. Williams was discombobulated; Kazan was a fixer, known to his colleagues as "Gadg"—short for "gadget"—a remnant from his stagehand days and his ability to make himself useful. He was all sinew and sensibility; he exuded a sure-footed, ruthless vigor. A notorious philanderer who wrapped himself in the charisma of his prowess, Kazan bustled through his days with an irresistible appetite for life. Although their temperaments dramatically differed, both Williams and Kazan were pathfinders who wanted to change the shape of American theater. In acting, Kazan was pioneering the same unflinching interior exploration of the self that Williams's plays were attempting on the page. "What our stage does is put a strong light on a person, on the inner life, the feelings of a person. These become monumental things," he explained. As an actor with the Group Theatre in the 1930s, Kazan had the distinction of shouting, "Strike! Strike! Strike!"— the rabble-rousing theatrical mantra of the decade—in Clifford Odets's iconic *Waiting for Lefty* (1935). Kazan earned the soubriquet "Proletarian Thunderbolt." "I was intense, an intensity that came from pent-up anger in me," he said. "I was like an instrument with only three or four very strong notes."

As a director of actors, however, Kazan had an almost symphonic ability to draw out and to orchestrate the tones and textures of his cast. "The best actors' director of any I've worked for," Marlon Brando said. "The only one who ever really stimulated me, got into a part with me. . . . He was an arch-manipulator of actors' feelings." (In 1947, two months before *A Streetcar Named Desire* opened on Broadway, Kazan co-founded The Actors Studio, a systematic elaboration of instinct and impulse that changed the look and naturalistic feel of modern performing, a way of making the hard look easy and the easy look interesting.) Kazan admired Williams's "emotionalism." On the page, Williams oversaw his characters in exactly the same complex way Kazan attended to physical detail on the stage. "All his characters are felt for. No one is a heavy," Kazan said. "He doesn't tend to clean things up, clear them up, straighten them out, oversimplify, or the rest of that kind of dramatic claptrap."

After their first meeting, Kazan was disarmed of his theatrical doubts. "His modesty took me by surprise," he said of Williams. "We had a plain talk and liked each other immediately." Both Kazan and Williams were sexual and social rebels. "We were both freaks," Kazan wrote. "He was, as I was, a disappearer." They shared a profound curiosity about the vagaries of the human heart; in Kazan's case, since Williams was the first homosexual to whom Kazan had ever been close, this included the two of them going on double dates and sharing the same hotel bedroom for their homosexual/heterosexual couplings—after which, Kazan wrote, "My curiosity was satisfied."

In Williams's eyes, he and Kazan made "a perfect team." "Our union, immediate on first encounter, was close but unarticulated," Kazan said. "It endured for the rest of his life." Both Williams and Kazan were roman-tic individualists who shared a faith in the instinctual and in excellence; each in their own way aspired to "burst the soul's sleep." They both also insisted on working as artists in the commercial theater. "I read the play again last night with no phones ringing and I felt close to you," Kazan wrote Williams after their first meeting. "I'll do everything possible to do your play. But I work best in single collaboration with the author. I'll never go back to working for a producer when it means consulting with him (her) on every point as well as with administrators, executives, pro-duction committees, agents, backers and various and sundry personal associates." He added, "All meetings on 'All My Sons' were between two people, Miller and me; that is the best way."

Kazan was preparing Williams for his putsch of the system of Ameri-can theatrical production. "I believed that those same powers over aspects of a production belonged to the director, that he, not the producer, should be the overlord of a production," Kazan wrote. In other words, using a great play as leverage, Kazan was proposing that the workers take over the means of production and that the masters take an executive backseat. The show's unique above-the-title billing—"Elia Kazan's Production of"— announced this silent revolution in theatrical command. For the first time ever in American theater history, the production would be controlled by the artists who made it, not the producers who paid for it.

Before this formulation was arrived at, a great deal of blood had to pass under the bridge. Kazan's asking price was, according to Williams, "pretty stiff." Besides the usual directing fees and percentage of the ticket sales, Kazan wanted a 20 percent share of the profit and billing as co-producer. "Considering that I felt our producer was a beginner, for whom I would have to do much of the work of production, I thought (and do now think) this protective billing was fair enough," Kazan wrote in his autobiography. Williams and Selznick were not of the same opinion. Kazan's demands sent them both into a momentary flop sweat. Nobody was thinking too clearly. Seeing no way out of the rancorous stalemate, Williams suggested "an alternative which I think is even *preferable*." He put himself and Margo Jones forward as possible co-directors. "In writing

Elia Kazan

a play I see each scene, in fact every movement and inflection, as vividly as if it were occurring right in front of me," he naively wrote Selznick, who, in turn, was hurt and outraged at what was perceived as Kazan's greedy high-handedness. The proposed arrangement would relegate the producer to being an observer with little part in the making of the show, a special affront to the Selznick hands-on producing tradition. Rather than agree to Kazan's terms, Selznick offered to step aside. "I was not going to knuckle under, no good would come of it," she said. "In time she would," Kazan said, who knew Williams wanted only him to direct, "because she had to."

Although Kazan would come to respect Selznick, during the rehearsal period he kept her at arm's length. "I was rude," he wrote. "I sometimes handled the lady with unnecessary crudeness." Nonetheless, Selznick staunchly persevered. She hired Jo Mielziner to do the set design. "Tennessee went off his noodle with joy," she wrote in a memo to her business partner. After two disappointing readings in New York with Margaret Sullavan and Pamela Brown, Selznick brought Williams to Los Angeles with Pancho in tow to see Jessica Tandy perform Williams's first sketch of a doomed hysteric, "Miss Lucretia Collins," in his one-act *Portrait of a Madonna*. Kazan was also in town putting the finishing touches to *Gentleman's Agreement*. "We all went to the show," Kazan wrote of the Actors' Lab production, which had been arranged by Tandy's actor-husband Hume Cronyn. "And we were completely . . . taken with Jessie. She'd solved our most difficult problem in a flash." Selznick was also quick to solve Williams's personal problem. She parked Williams and Pancho on the estate of director George Cukor. "It has been a pretty fabulous time out here," Williams wrote Windham, with no mention of his casting woes. "Have gone to some of the biggest parties and met all the big stars and Pancho says, 'It's like a dream come true!'" Williams went on, "It has put him in a wonderful humor and we have both gained about ten pounds so that we look like the big pig and the little pig."

But, as the Southern folk saying goes, the fattenin' hog ain't in luck. That summer, the Selznick office leaked to the press the big news that thirty-four-year-old John Garfield, one of the few sexy Hollywood stars with a proletarian pedigree, had signed on to play Stanley. The contract was drawn up on July 19, 1947, but it was never signed. The following two months of negotiations with Garfield would be, as Williams wrote to Audrey Wood, "about the biggest headache I've had in my theatrical experience—outside of Boston." Garfield wanted a four-month limited-engagement run and a percentage of the play—an unprecedented demand at that time—as well as a guarantee of being cast in the film role, and certain artistic controls, including how many and where the curtains were to be and approval of the last-scene rewrite. Although Kazan claimed in his memoir not to be that keen on Garfield, who was a Group Theatre alumnus and his friend, Selznick's memos indicate "much pressure from Greek headquarters." "Kazan tried to persuade me to give it to him on the basis that I had plenty of money and all I wanted was a hit," Selznick wrote to her business manager.

Since she'd given Kazan such a large percentage of the manager's share of the profit, Selznick offered to match any share of Kazan's percentage he was willing to give up to secure Garfield. He declined. "I therefore had a final luncheon with Garfield either for a long-shot chance or a decent burial," Selznick said. "He made me a sporting proposition." She continued, "Garfield offered to take $1,500 a week against 10% of the gross for a brief period in order to prove his sincerity and at the same time to demonstrate to me his drawing power and the extent of his dramatic and artistic contribution to the show. He felt that after eight weeks in New York I would be willing to renegotiate the contract at terms more advantageous to him." So the negotiations continued into August. With each passing day Williams grew more agitated. "I entered the agreement with Selznick because we were led to believe that we would have what we wanted in every respect and that there were great advantages to be derived from her management in casting due to her Hollywood connections," he complained to Audrey Wood in August. "These advantages have not materialized." He added, "It was bad management that announced Garfield in the papers before he was signed."

As the negotiations with Garfield reached crisis point, Selznick's office was woefully aware of their deplorable position. In a five-page telegram to Selznick, her business manager Irving Schneider told her, "To lose him now means loss of prestige, difficult position with Music Box, bookings, Guild, and theater parties. To overcome these need replace him with name of similar caliber. The show can survive and come through without him but the immediate and near future effects are severely damning. If none of the above plans work . . . then must bring in Tennessee, Lieblings, Kazan to make the vital decision of whether to forego Garfield and face the consequences. Among those consequences incidentally is finding another good Stanley. We must close our eyes for the moment to the insult and injuries and reversals, avoid rehashing, take a deep breath, kiss the mezuzah and plunge." Schneider added, "*Gevalt* seems too tame."

In the end, Garfield came up with yet another demand: if for any reason Kazan were to leave the show, he too would leave. "The Kazan clause" broke the camel's back. On August 18, the deal collapsed. Selznick, feeling "low as a snake," immediately starting turning over other Hollywood options. Richard Conte, Dane Clark, Cameron Mitchell, Gregory Peck, and Burt Lancaster were mooted. Signing "Pollyanna," she wired Schneider:

I HAVE GARFIELD-ITIS IN CHEST AND THROAT. OIVAY

Then, on August 29, a name that didn't appear on any of her extensive casting lists was being wired to Selznick at her Summit Avenue home in Beverly Hills: Marlon Brando.

Brando, who was twenty-three years old, had appeared without much critical attention in five Broadway plays. He was a beautiful, brooding specimen: mercurial, rebellious, and rampant. Like Stanley, he was a ruthless man-child with reservoirs of tenderness and violence. A year before on Broadway in Maxwell Anderson's *Truckline Café*, which Kazan co-produced and Harold Clurman directed, Brando stopped the show with a five-minute "murder monologue." After his speech, the audience applauded for a full minute. "A minute on the stage is a long, long time," Clurman, who had "never seen anything like it," said. He added, "I don't think he ever did anything better"—a judgment that could hardly be contradicted since *Truckline Café* lasted only thirteen performances. Nonetheless, another witness to Brando's memorable ferocious psychic explosion, the critic Pauline Kael, thought to herself, "That boy's having a convulsion! Then I realized he was acting." Brando wasn't trying to act, at least not in the hidebound acting tradition hitherto practiced on the American stage. "There was nothing you could do with Brando that touched what he could do with himself," Kazan said. "In those days he was a genius. His own preparation for a scene, his own personality, armament, memories and desires were so deep that there was very little you had to do, except tell him what the scene was about."

Brando's acting style was the performing equivalent of jazz. The notes were there, but Brando played them in a way that was uniquely personal to him. In his ability to call out of dialogue a heightened sense of emotional truth, the freedom of his stage behavior was mesmerizing and revolutionary. Instead of making everything learned and clear, Brando let the lines play on him and rode his emotions wherever they led him. "He even listened experientially," Kazan said. "It's as if you were playing on something. He didn't look at you, and he hardly acknowledged what you were saying. He was tuned in to you without listening to you intellectually or mentally. It was a mysterious process. . . . There was always an element of surprise in what he did." By turns charming, witty, wounded, cruel—Brando presented the public with an immediacy that seemed un-worked out; his reliance on impulse made him unpredictable and therefore dangerous. For both actor and audience the experience was a submersion in emotional contradiction. "There are no 'good' or 'bad' people," Williams wrote to Kazan when negotiations with Selznick seemed to have broken down. "Nobody sees anybody *truly*, but all through the flaws of their own ego." Brando incarnated this ambivalence and made it sensational.

Over the years, as the legend of his performance as Stanley grew from its initial mixed critical response to what the *New York Times* in his obituary called "epochal," many theatricals took credit for casting him. Audrey Wood claimed it was her husband William Liebling; with more justification, Kazan maintained it was him; Brando insisted that Harold Clurman planted the idea in Kazan's head. "Gadg and Irene both said I was probably too young, and she was especially unenthusiastic about me," Brando recalled in his autobiography. After pondering the script for a few days, even Brando called Kazan to decline the role. The part, he felt, was "a size too large." "The line was busy," Brando recalled later. "Had I spoken to him at that moment, I'm certain I wouldn't have played the role. I decided to let it rest for a while and the next day he called me and said: 'Well, what is it—yes or no?' I gulped and said 'Yes.'" To Kazan, Brando was "a shot in the dark": now only Williams needed convincing. Kazan called Williams, gave Brando twenty dollars, and sent him up to Provincetown to read. "That's all I said," Kazan recalled. "I waited. No return call. After three days I called Tennessee and asked him what he'd thought of the actor I'd sent him. 'What actor?' he asked. No one had showed up, so I figured I'd lost twenty bucks and began to look elsewhere."

Brando, who was broke, had decided to hitchhike with his girlfriend to Provincetown. When he finally arrived at Rancho Pancho around dusk in the last week of August, Brando walked into a scene of "domestic cataclysm," according to Williams. The kitchen floor was flooded, the toilets were blocked, and the light fuse had blown. Like the blackout during the Wingfields' supper, Williams and his houseguests were plunged "into everlasting darkness." "It was all too much for Pancho," Williams said. "He packed up and said he was going back to Eagle Pass. However he changed his mind, as usual." To Williams, Brando was a spectacle of both beauty—"He was just about the best-looking young man I've ever seen"—and prowess. Brando fixed the lights, then unblocked the pipes. "You'd think he had spent his entire antecedent life repairing drains," Williams said.

An hour later, Brando finally got around to reading. He dismissed his girlfriend and sat in the corner of the clapboard house with Margo Jones, her friend Joanna Albus, and Williams, who cued him as Blanche. According to Williams, Brando read the script aloud "just as he played it." "I was the antithesis of Stanley Kowalski," Brando said. "I was sensitive by nature and he was coarse, a man with unerring animal instincts and intuition. . . . He was a compendium of my imagination, based on the lines of the play. I created him from Tennessee's words." Letting Williams's words take him where they would and exuding the freedom of this approach, Brando was only ten minutes into his audition when Jones bolted from her chair with a whoop of delight. "Get Kazan on the phone! This is the greatest reading I've ever heard, in or outside of Texas!" she shouted. "A new value came out of Brando's reading," Williams wrote to Wood. "He seemed to have already created a dimensional character, of the sort that the war has produced among young veterans." He added, "Please use all your influence to oppose any move on the part of Irene's office to reconsider or delay signing the boy, in case she doesn't take to him."

On the evening Brando read, after he had kvelled about him over the phone to Kazan, Williams recalled that Brando "smiled a little but didn't show any particular elation." Later, after dinner, Williams read some poetry, then they retired for the evening. "Things were so badly arranged that Margo and Brando had to sleep in the same room—on twin cots," Williams wrote to Audrey Wood on August 29. "I believe they behaved themselves—the fools!" To Williams, Brando was "God-sent." Brando seemed also to sense the immanence of some big thing. A great actor had met the great writer whose lyric power would release his genius. "When an actor has as good a play under him as *Streetcar,* he doesn't have to do much," Brando said. "His job is to get out of the way and let the part play itself." This powerful alchemy produced in Brando a peculiar shyness when he was around the author. The morning after his audition Brando insisted that Williams walk up the beach with him. "And so we did—in silence," Williams wrote. "And then we walked back—in silence."

BUT FOR PANCHO and Williams the rest of the summer was clamorous. The excitement of a new play was enough to exacerbate Pancho's envy. The arrival into their world of a ravishing powerhouse like Brando, who would make a myth of a petulance that Pancho knew owed its inspiration to him, pushed him over the edge. Even before Pancho tried to run his "Torito" down, Williams sensed trouble brewing. "I am hoping he will go home, at least to New Orleans, until December," he wrote to Wood at the end of August. "He is not a calm person. In spite of his temperamental difficulties he is very lovable and I have grown to depend on his affection and companionship but he is too capricious and excitable for New York especially when I have a play in rehearsal." After the car incident, however, Pancho was sent packing—at least for a while. "It took some doing to get Pancho to leave," Williams recalled. "Probably this phenomenal accomplishment was handled by Irene Selznick who has seldom found herself in a situation with which she couldn't cope, not even the situation of releasing me from Pancho."

Williams returned—"quite gratefully so," he wrote—to Manhattan on September 14 to work on rewrites prior to the beginning of rehearsals at the New Amsterdam Roof on October 6. Although there were over a hundred line changes during the rehearsal period, the most substantive revision was the ending and the final beats after Blanche is carted off to the madhouse. "There is still something too cut-and-dried in the necessary exposition between [Eunice and Stella]," Williams wrote to Selznick on September 8. In the original "Poker Night," Stanley settles back down to a game of cards; outside, according to the stage directions, in front of the building "dim white against the fading dusk," Stella rises from the steps and "elevates the child in her arms as if she were offering it to the tenderness of the sky. Then she draws it close to her and bows her head until her face is hidden by the child's blanket."

In the final version, rewritten during the painful ructions with Pancho between September and October, Stella's original isolated gesture of survival is turned into a much more powerful and ambivalent image—a sort of Renaissance pictorial grouping in which Stanley kneels at the feet of Stella, who holds their child on the stairway and sobs as his fingers open her blouse. "Now, now, love," Stanley coos. "Now, love . . ." The scene demonstrates the couple's preserving lie. In *Streetcar*, Stanley and Stella collude about Blanche's rape. For the Kowalski family to continue, Blanche must be sacrificed. In Williams's story, Pancho also had to be sacrificed so Williams's life—his work, which was his baby—could go on. The aim of the play, he wrote to Kazan, was "fidelity"—a fidelity as much to his own heart as to his characters. "After this experience, I saw every play and every film I worked on as a confession, veiled or partly exposed, but always its author's self revelation," Kazan said. "Probably I would want him back," Williams wrote to Donald Windham in March 1947, in a typical rationalization. "When we are alone he is usually sweet and amenable." Williams spun the notion of Pancho into an acceptable fiction. "He needed me as much as I needed him," Pancho said. "He knew that if we stayed together, we would destroy each other."

In October, while he was hymning the joys of the rehearsals to Margo Jones—"I cannot find words to tell you how wonderful Jessica and Gadg are, and what a superb combination their talents appear to be"—Williams was confiding loneliness to his notebooks. "Today I am particularly aware of missing Pancho." He couldn't be with Pancho, and he couldn't let him go. "I wish I could write you an equally amusing letter but I don't have any little nephews to supply me with comic material," he wrote Pancho in October. "I feel very sober and dull. And when I get home at night, after a day at the disposal of the Selznick company and the Liebling-Wood Corporation, I barely have the strength to hit the typewriter keys. You must try and forgive me for being so stupid and do write me whenever you can. It does me good to hear about your peaceful family life in New

Orleans where I would much prefer to be." Williams ended on a maternal note: "Take care of yourself. Be good, be good, be good! And take your nephews to the zoo."

Around noon in mid-October, Williams's writing was interrupted by a fierce pounding at his apartment door. "Reisito, Torito," the voice outside shouted. Pancho was back. As usual he brought tumult with him. "Unable to break down the door, he jumped onto the cement sills of the gable windows," Williams wrote in *Memoirs*. "I got to them just in time to lock them. A big crowd had gathered outside the brownstone by this time. Pancho was on the sill, hammering at the window until the glass split. Then a policeman intervened. He did not arrest Pancho but he ordered him away." Williams went on, "Pancho looked back at me. His face was covered with tears. I started crying, too, a thing I very seldom do."

The tears spoke both of Williams's love and of his regret. "I am terribly troubled. I don't think I am acting kindly, and that is what I hate above all else," he wrote Margo Jones about "the Mexican Problem." To separate from Pancho meant losing a lover, a child, a family, and a sense of parental goodness. "He was like a father and brother to me," Rodriguez said; in fact, on the evidence, Williams was more like a mother, trying to coax Pancho "to take a man's place in the world." Edwina Williams's scolding voice was moralistic, manipulative, martyred; Williams didn't like it and he didn't want it around him. He tried to talk Edwina out of coming to the *Streetcar* opening. "This play is hardly your dish," he wrote her, with the suggestion that she come to *Summer and Smoke* instead the following season. In the end Edwina would not be denied. Williams bowed to her wishes, but he warned her: "I shall not listen to any moral homilies and dissertations so please leave them at home."

In his dealings with Pancho, however, Williams's maternal performance—liberal, measured, un-intrusive, forgiving—allowed Pancho to have the mother he never had. "Life is hard," Williams wrote to Pancho in November 1947. "As Amanda said, 'It calls for Spartan endurance.' But more than that, it calls for understanding, one person understanding another person, and for some measure of sacrifice, too." He went on, "I feel concerned for you, worried over your lack of purpose. You have so much more than I have in so many ways. Your youth, your health and energy, your many social graces which I do not have. Life can hold a great deal for you, it can be very rich and abundant if you are willing to make some effort and to stop thinking and acting altogether selfishly. In this world the key to happiness is giving, more than getting." The paternal voice was harder for Williams to muster; he didn't know how to be properly assertive or how to lay down the law. After the hurly-burly of Pancho's rambunctious reentry into his life, Williams claimed in *Memoirs* that he took refuge in a hotel, where he stayed until Pancho "had been persuaded that I could not be induced to resume residence with him or willingly see him again." In fact, Williams couldn't bring himself to break so cleanly. For a while, Pancho moved back in with him.

By the time Williams saw his rewritten last scene mounted for the first time in rehearsal, he was once again, like his characters, colluding in the preserving lie of relationship. "My feeling for P. has more or less definitely fallen from desire to custom though my affection is not lost," he wrote on October 27 in his notebook. "I don't think it was time or repetition. It was partly that but other things, a spiritual disappointment, was the more important factor." Williams continued, "He is incapable of reason. Violence belongs to his nature as completely as it is abhorrent to mine. Most of all, I want and now must have—simple peace. The problem is to act kindly and still strongly; for now I know that my manhood is sacrificed in submitting to such a relationship. Oh well—it will work out somehow."

On October 30, at *Streetcar*'s first-night tryout in New Haven, far from being Williams's "ex-valiant ex-companion," Pancho had the seat of honor beside Williams in a row that included Kazan, Selznick, Cole Porter, and Thornton Wilder. Later, at a party, Wilder complained that an aristocrat like Stella would never have fallen for a vulgarian like Stanley. "I thought, privately, this character has never had a good lay," Williams said. Wilder also opined that Blanche was too complex. "But people are complex, Thorn," Williams said.

For sexual and emotional complexity, nothing on stage approached Williams and Pancho off it. At the New Haven opening, the crowd adored Brando—"a performance miracle in the making," according to Kazan.

Flanked by Irene Selznick and Elia Kazan on the set of *A Streetcar Named Desire*

His characterization of Stanley was so strong that it threatened to over-power Tandy and to throw the play off kilter. "Because it was out of bal-ance, people laughed at me at several points in the play, turning Blanche into a foolish character," Brando recalled. "I didn't try to make Stanley funny. People simply laughed, and Jessica was furious because of this, so angry that she asked Gadg to fix it somehow, which he never did. I saw a flash of resentment in her every time the audience laughed at me. She really disliked me for it." Kazan was worried. "I looked to my authority, Tennessee," he said. "He was no help, he seemed enraptured by the boy. 'The son of a bitch is riding a crush,' I said to myself."

"If Tennessee was Blanche, Pancho was Stanley," Kazan said. He went on, "Wasn't he attracted to the Stanleys of the world? Sailors? Rough trade? Danger itself? Yes, and wilder. The violence in that boy, always on a trigger edge, attracted Williams at the very time it frightened him." In Kazan's analysis, Blanche "is attracted to a murderer, Stanley. . . . That's the source of ambivalence in the play. Blanche wants the very thing that's going to crush her. The only way she can deal with this threatening force is to give herself to it. . . . That's the way Williams was. He was attracted to trash—rough, male homosexuals who were threatening him. . . . Part of the sexuality that Williams wrote into the play is the menace of it."

Even as Kazan worked to get this sense of sexual menace on stage; off it, he saw Williams living the threat. In Boston, during the tryout between November 3 and 15, Kazan and Williams stayed at the Ritz-Carlton on the same floor. One night, coming from Williams's room, Kazan heard a "fearsome commotion . . . curses in Spanish, threats to kill, the sound of breaking china (a large vase smashed) and a crash (the ornamental light fixture in the center of the room torn down)." Kazan continued, "As I rushed out into the corridor, Tennessee burst through his door, looking terrified, and dashed into my room. Pancho followed, but when I blocked my door, he turned to the elevator, still cursing, and was gone. Tennessee slept on the twin bed in my room that night. The next morning . . . we heard Pancho returning, and Williams went back into his suite. He didn't look frightened, dismayed or disapproving, but happy that Pancho was back and eager to see the man who'd made such a terrible scene the night before."

"I left New York two or three weeks before the play opened," Rodriguez recalled, whose hotel escapade proved the last straw. "Tennessee felt that I would be better at home. We would get together after the play opened. He promised me that, but he never came back." Even though Pancho had packed many bags and made many dramatic exits—"I used to try and hurt him by telling him that he was uncouth and unmannered, and that he should be with Rose in an institution," Pancho said—gratitude dominated regret in Williams's final elegiac farewell:

> . . . I have never said an untrue thing to you all the times that I have been with you except in those few blind panicky moments when it seemed, perhaps unreasonably, that you had never cared for me at all and that I had been just a matter of convenience for whom you held contempt. To explain those things you have to go back through the entire history of a life, all its loneliness, its disappointments, its hunger for understanding and love. No, there is no point in talking about it any further. I don't ask anything of you, Pancho, this is not to ask anything, not even your pardon. I only want to tell you that I am your friend and will remain so regardless of how you may feel toward me. I offered you more of my heart than I have anybody in the last five years, which you may not have wanted and may now despise but believe me it is still full of the truest affection for you. Wherever you are I want you to have happiness.—salud amor y pesados!

To the end of his days, Rodriguez clung to a sentence from Williams's valedictory note. "I knew that he loved me as much as I loved him," Rodriguez said. "He wrote me a letter saying that 'no one suffers alone'." Williams's letter tried to see both of them clearly; it imposed the kind of humane detachment with which he'd written *Streetcar*, "as if a ghost sat over the affairs of men and made a true record." "When you see that someone needs peace more than anything else, needs quietness and a sense of security, you cannot expect to involve that person in continual turmoil and tension and anxiety and still have him cherishing your companionship all the time," Williams wrote Pancho, cutting him loose. He continued, "No, for his own protection if he wishes to go on living and working, he must withdraw sometime from these exhausting conditions. One does not suffer alone. It is nearly always two who suffer, but sometimes one places all the blame on the other. . . . You know that my affection for you and my loyalty to you as a friend remain unalterable and that while I am alive you will have my true friendship always with you."

———————

BY THE TIME *Streetcar* moved to Philadelphia and its last out-of-town tryout, most of the hurdles that had caused Kazan initial anxiety had been cleared. Tandy had risen to the challenge of Brando's performance; Brando had deepened his role as much from his observation of the director—his posture, his glances, his swagger—as from his notes. He had psyched out Kazan, who in his *Streetcar* journal at least noted a parallel in their psyches: "Stanley (M.B.) like E.K. is self absorbed to the point of fascination." Even Kim Hunter, who played Stella and who Williams worried was "the lame duck in the line-up," raised her game. Selznick, despite her occasional jejune gesture, like handing Kazan pages of single-spaced typewritten notes, over time won his grudging affection. Privately, Kazan told Williams that the show smelled like a hit; to the cast and crew, however, he played down the buzz. "What we've got here is oysters. Not everyone has a taste for oysters. Just do the play and hope for the best," Kazan told his cast before the New York opening. In his first-night telegram to Brando, Williams began:

RIDE OUT BOY AND SEND IT SOLID . . .

"Streetcar opened last night to tumultuous approval," Williams wrote to his publisher James Laughlin on December 4, 1947. "Never witnessed such an exciting evening. So much better than New Haven you wouldn't believe it; N.H. was just a reading of the play. Much more warmth, range, intelligence, interpretation, etc.—a lot of it because of better details in direction, timing." Williams gushed on, "Packed house, of the usual first-night decorations—Cecil Beaton, Valentina, D. Parker, the Selznicks, the others and so on—and with a slow warm-up for first act, and comments like 'Well, of course, it isn't a *play*,' the second act (it's in 3 now) sent the audience zowing to mad heights, and the final one left them—and me—wilted, gasping, weak, befoozled, drained (see reviews for more words) and then an uproar of applause which went on and on. Almost no one rose from a seat till many curtains went up on the whole cast, the 4 principles, then Tandy, who was greeted by a great howl of 'Bravo!' from truly all over the house. Then repeat of the whole curtain schedule to Tandy again and finally . . . . 10 Wms crept on stage, after calls for Author! and took bows with Tandy. All was great, *great*, GREAT!"

Streetcar, as Arthur Miller said, planted "the flag of beauty on the shores of commercial theatre." Miller added, "The play cannot be disparaged." Nonetheless, in the first wave of reviews, some tried. George Jean Nathan, for instance, dubbed Williams a "Southern genital-man." "The play might well have been titled 'The Glans Menagerie,'" he quipped in his review. Among the play's many narrative sensations was the first sighting on the American stage of a sexual male. "In 1947, when Marlon Brando appeared on stage in a torn sweaty T-shirt, there was an earthquake," Gore Vidal wrote. Vidal also contended that "Stanley Kowalski changed the concept of sex in America. Before him, no male was considered erotic. Some were handsomer than others, some had charm. A man was essentially a suit, he wasn't a body." Vidal went on, "Johnny Weissmuller would have been the closest thing, and he was basically sort of androgynous looking. His body had no sex attached to it, whereas Marlon played with his cock onstage and that excited people. The mutation was the Williams effect. The male is his obsession, and male sexuality the benchmark. Females are principal characters in his plays because it's through them that you're going to view the male, which is the playwright's objective."

Part of Stanley's sexual charge is the wallop of his selfishness, which registered the spiritual shift after America's return to normalcy. "He builds a hedonistic life, and fights to the death to defend it," Kazan wrote about him in his notebooks. Liberated from duty, from sacrifice, from class restrictions—all the emotional baggage that Blanche brings with her, represented by the loss of the family plantation, the well-named Belle Reve—each character pursues his own creaturely self-interest. When Stanley roars to his wife and to his intruding, neurasthenic sister-in-law, "I am the king around here," that kingdom of self is, in a way, what all three are trying to claim. In their stage-managed battle

OPPOSITE PAGE: Marlon Brando and Jessica Tandy, the rape scene from *A Streetcar Named Desire*

Embracing Marlon Brando at the "bad notice" party, 1948

Williams found a perfect metaphor of the era's dynamic survival and of his own "divided nature."

Streetcar's success made Williams some kind of king. At the play's opening-night party at the 21 Club, after the reviews had been read out and Williams had run the gauntlet of congratulations, Audrey Wood approached him. "Tenn, are you really happy?" she said.

Williams looked surprised. "Of course I am," he said.

"Are you a completely fulfilled young man?"

"Completely," Williams said. "Why do you ask me?"

"I just wanted to hear you say it," Wood said.

From that moment on, for better or worse, Williams was on a first-name basis with the world. Everyone seemed to be at his table. He rarely signed

OPPOSITE PAGE: Jessica Tandy and Elia Kazan backstage

himself "Tom"; he was "Tenn" or "10." In May 1948, Williams won the Pulitzer Prize; in October, Margo Jones's production of *Summer and Smoke* arrived on Broadway. After it was rumbled by most of the critics, Williams gave the failure the royal brush-off. He threw a catered "bad notice" party to which he invited "the critics who gave us the two worst notices." "The party was really swell," he wrote to Donald Windham.

At one point in the evening, Williams stole away to ride with Marlon Brando on his new motorcycle. Here, at the zenith of the century's promise, in the time of their defining triumph, the greatest actor and the greatest playwright of their era sped around Manhattan feeling the exhilarating surge of power underneath them. Williams had embraced his sexuality and his talent; now he was embracing his new momentum. "I enjoyed the ride, clamping his buttocks between my knees as we flew across the East River and along the river drive with the cold wind whistling and a moon," he said. Williams added, "My closest friends remained after the party—Jane, Tony, Sandy, Joanna, and the boy living with me named Frankie Merlo—Merlo means blackbird—and he is a Sicilian from New Jersey."

CHAPTER 3

The Erotics of Absence

The desiring fingers enclose a phantom object, the hungering lips are pressed to a ghostly mouth.

—TENNESSEE WILLIAMS,
The Roman Spring of Mrs. Stone

My writing dealt with you. I lamented there only what I could not lament on your breast. It was an intentionally long farewell—which you forced out of me, but which I shaped . . .

—FRANZ KAFKA,
Letter to His Father

On December 30, 1947—four weeks after the clamorous opening of *Streetcar*—Tennessee Williams sailed for Europe on the SS *America*. It was his first transatlantic trip abroad as an adult, and he was going solo. "I don't intend to get seriously involved with anyone ever again," he said. *Streetcar* had set off a seismic shift in American theater. It had also triggered a shift in the playwright himself. For Williams, who was now earning two thousand dollars a week in royalties, austerity and anonymity were things of the past. He was a first-class passenger. And no matter how far afield he traveled, the spotlight would always somehow find him. "My nights have been wild and wonderful in Manhattan, lasting always till five in the morning, seldom getting more than four or five hours sleep," he wrote to Margo Jones once he was en route.

On the day of his departure, the attention that the other grandees of the theater lavished on Williams signaled his new power. Jessica Tandy,

Kim Hunter, and Montgomery Clift showed up at the disorganized play-wright's apartment for "a packing-bee." Elia Kazan arrived with cham-pagne. Later, crowded into his stateroom, the group presented him with a dozen white shirts, a cashmere sweater, and a bottle of scotch. Clift brought with him a portable Hermes Baby typewriter—a gift from Margo Jones and a reminder, if Williams needed one, that it was time to get back to work on the rewrites for the upcoming Broadway production of *Summer and Smoke*.

In Europe the parade of celebrities continued: Greta Garbo recom-mended his Paris hotel; Louis Jouvet, Jean-Louis Barrault, and Jean Cocteau—the nabobs of the French theater—turned up to dine with him. (When Williams threw a cocktail party for his famous Parisian friends, he noted dryly, "Sartre did not show up, although reported to be in the neighborhood.") Paris, however, was a disappointment—"cold, bad food, no satisfactory company, no milk for my coffee." Williams gave press interviews in his hotel bathtub—the water was warmer than the radiators. "I found nothing very good about Paris but the quality of the whores," Williams wrote to Kazan. "You can fuck almost anything you lay your eyes on for the price of a black-market dollar." He added, "There is no atmosphere of social unrest in Europe that I am able to sense. You feel no spark of any kind except the stubborn will to survive and you feel that they will support whichever party or doctrine offers them a chance to eat."

When Williams fell ill during his first two weeks abroad, the editor of the fashion magazine *Elle*—a Madame Lazareff, whose husband owned *Paris Jour* and *Paris Soir*—packed him off for a week of rest and relax-ation at the Colombe d'Or, in St.-Paul-de-Vence, where the dining room was a walled terrace garden dominated by a Léger frieze. It rained almost continuously. His first exposure to the sun was on the day he boarded the train in Nice and headed for Rome ("The *sun*—glorious sun—is on my face, in my eyes, and I love it").

BY THE TIME Williams arrived in the Eternal City, fascism and the Sec-ond World War had more or less sealed it off as a destination point for the American traveler. Even in its ravaged, recuperative state, the city quickly became for Williams "the capitol of my heart." "Here in Italy, this place of soft weather and golden light and of great bunches of violets and carnations sold on every corner and the Greek ideal surviving so tangibly in the grace and beauty of the people and the antique sculpture as well," Williams wrote to Carson McCullers soon after arriving. "I cannot write coherently about Rome as I love it so much!"

For Williams, Rome was a "soft city," tender and emollient in the blue transparency of its light, the skyline reminiscent to him of the eternal female: "domes of ancient churches, swelling above the angular roofs like the breasts of giant recumbent women, still bathed in gold light." The warmth of the city extended to its people. "They do not hate Americans at all," he wrote to Brooks Atkinson. "In fact the whole time I've been here I haven't had an unfriendly word or look from any of them."

After less than a month abroad, Williams wrote to Kazan, "I haven't the slightest idea what I am doing over here, but if I were in the States I would probably be a lot more confused." By the third month, however, his uncertainty had turned to impasse. He had fallen, he said later, "under the moon of pause." "Sometimes the lamp burns very low indeed," he confided to McCullers. "For the past five or six days I have been battering my head against a wall of creative impotence." Sex, "the trapeze of the flesh," as he called it, was his antidepressant; it swung him away from his writer's block and into life. "You can't walk a block without being accosted by someone you would spend a whole evening trying vainly to make in the New York bars," he wrote to Windham, adding, "You may wonder how I ever get any work done here. The answer is I don't get much." Williams binged on boys.

Cruising, with its drama of enticement and evasion, of appearance and disappearance, was particularly thrilling in Rome. "In the evenings, very late, after midnight, I like to drive out the old Appian Way and park the car at the side of the road and listen to the crickets among the old tombs," he wrote. "Sometimes a figure appears among them which is not a ghost but a Roman boy in the flesh!" "The nightingales busted their larynx!" he wrote to Oliver Evans, in a letter about a dark-haired Neapolitan lightweight boxer with an "imperial torso," whom he had picked up. "I wish I could tell you more about this boxer, details, positions, amiabilities—but this pale blue paper would blush!" After throwing a few big parties that "turned into orgies," Williams found himself an unwitting set piece in the local homosexual scene. "I remind myself of that lady who Oscar Wilde said had tried to establish a salon but only succeeded in opening a saloon," he told Windham.

When Williams tried to characterize for James Laughlin the extraordinary Roman social whirl—which included new friendships with such expatriate Americans as the novelist Frederic Prokosch and "that unhappy young egotist Gore Vidal"—he spoke of "the ephemeral bird-like Italians, sweet but immaterial, like cotton-candy." The excitement, for him, he explained, lay in savoring their immateriality, their ghostliness, their ability to vanish. "I shall remember all of them like one person who was very pleasant, sometimes even delightful, but like a figure in a dream,

With Gore Vidal and Truman Capote, 1948

insubstantial, not even leaving behind the memory of a conversation: the intimacies somehow less enduring than the memory of a conversation, at least seeming that way now, but possibly later invested with more reality: ghosts in the present: afterwards putting on flesh, unlike the usual way."

WILLIAMS HAD INTENDED his European sojourn as a way of shaking off the self-consciousness of his new celebrity, of getting "back under the dining-room table with a child's beautifully clear eyes," as John Updike described the purpose of travel for the successful writer. But the experience of Rome left him more wide-eyed than clear-eyed. "Italy has been a real experience, a psychic adventure of a rather profound sort which I shall be able to define in retrospect only," he wrote to Laughlin. "I also have a feeling it is a real caesura: pause: parenthesis in my life: that it marks a division between two very different parts which I leave behind me with trepidation."

Williams was no longer a one-hit wonder. The dimension of his success had left him stunned, struggling to retain the long-cherished notion of himself as fugitive outsider and to come to terms with the imperatives of celebrity. "Being successful and famous makes such demands!" he wrote to Audrey Wood. "I wanted it and still want it, with one part of me, but that isn't the part of me that is important or creative." Before his success, Williams had everything to fight for; now he had everything to defend. He had a public name and a public posture. "You know, then, that the public Somebody you are when you 'have a name' is a fiction created with mirrors and that the only somebody worth being is the solitary and unseen you that existed from your first breath and which is the sum of your actions and so is constantly in a state of becoming," he wrote in the essay "On a Streetcar Named Success." "The continual procession"—the visitors, the side trips, the rent boys—only magnified what Williams referred to as his "spiritual dislocation."

By June 1948, when he went north for the English debut of *The Glass Menagerie*, he felt distracted and "as nervous as a cat." "I am quite forlorn here. In spite of almost continual society," he wrote to Windham from the Savoy Hotel in London. Britain's drabness and snobbery sank his spirits. "To really appreciate Italy fully you should come to London first," he wrote to Windham. "Christ, what a dull town and what stuffy people! I have actually been compelled to start working again, which is a sign of real ennui."

In his free time, Williams hobnobbed with Christopher Isherwood, E. M. Forster, and Gore Vidal. On the clock, however, at Brighton's Theatre Royal, where the play was in tryout before its London opening, he had to contend with "the First Lady of the American Theater," Helen Hayes, who was playing Amanda, and with John Gielgud, the play's director. Hayes informed him that the show was in trouble, and Gielgud asked him not to take a bow at the curtain call. "I don't want the beautiful effect of this play diminished by a perspiring little author with a wrinkled shirt and a messy dinner jacket coming up on stage," Gielgud said. Williams had been skeptical of Gielgud from the beginning. "He is too English, too stylish, too removed from the subject and spirit of the script," he had told Wood. As it turned out, Gielgud was also too removed from Williams, who described the director after their first meeting as a "frightfully nervous high-handed prima donna type of person." On matters concerning the original Broadway production, Gielgud chose to consult with the American director Josh Logan, who happened to be passing through town, rather than with Williams, who sat each day a few rows behind him in the theater. Williams repaid the indifference with insolence, referring to Gielgud as "the Old One," and vowed to defy him at the opening on July 28. "John G. says I should *not* take a bow and just out of perversity, now, I am resolved to do so if there is even the faintest whisper of 'Author' in the house," he said to his newest English friend, Maria Britneva, a pert, high-spirited actress of White Russian origin whom he had met at a party in London.

In the end, Williams went one better: he bowed out entirely. His fear of the play's failure, compounded by the prospect of a reunion with Miss Edwina, who traveled to London with Dakin for the first night, proved too much, and Williams fled to Paris. When Helen Hayes met Edwina backstage, she glimpsed the hostility beneath Edwina's show of Southern charm. Introducing Hayes to Dakin, Edwina announced, "I want everybody to see that I have one son who's a gentleman." "She was everything I disliked in an ageing Southern belle," Hayes recalled, "but in the play she was portrayed in a soft-focus of compassion." Edwina denied her connection with Amanda, but in later years she would come to imitate her.

"She's spearing a shrimp, bringing it halfway to her lips, putting it down, going into a long passage from 'The Glass Menagerie,'" Vidal said, recalling one occasion in Florida in the 1950s. "Finally, Tennessee, coughing, says, 'Mother, would you eat that shrimp.' 'Why do you have that funny little cough?' she said. Tennessee said, 'Mother, when you destroy someone's life, you must expect certain debilities.'"

Two days after the London opening, Williams sent Hayes a note of apology. "I do not altogether understand myself how I happened not to manage to make it," he wrote. "You may put this down to my 'pixy behavior' and nobody knows better than I do that I have carried it much, much, much too far! I had looked forward to it intensely for such a long time: then the last few days I became enveloped in a cloud. Overwork. Nerves. A sort of paralysis." On the same day, he also sent a note of thanks to Britneva, whom he called one of the "compensations" of his dire British excursion. "In fact, it is the afternoons with you, the walks, the teas, the companionship—the ability to talk to somebody—that I remember most happily about the English adventure," he wrote.

Britneva exerted an almost immediate power over Williams. A tiny person—about five feet tall—with a mane of brown hair, huge gray-brown eyes, and a beaky nose that she turned up at the world, Britneva had an audacity and a frenetic energy that made her a kind of event. With a bluff, bow-wow manner, she faced down the world. "She scared people," Vidal said. Williams spoke of "her spectacular velocity through time." By sheer force of personality, she found a way to scale the English aristocracy and its talentocracy. "She was extraordinary about weaving her way into people's lives," her friend, the actress Paula Laurence said. "Before you knew it, you were entirely surrounded. But it was done with tremendous affection, the most flattering kind of interest, outrageous presents, and loving attention. How could you not want that?" Britneva was alternately funny, bold, and ferocious; she had, as Kazan said, a "desperate grip on what she valued in life." She was adamant about living up to her dreams—a hard thing to accomplish at any time, and especially so in threadbare postwar Britain. "She is full of a good kind of mischief," Williams said. "Most women hate her and few men know what to think of her."

Certainly the distracted and disorganized Tennessee Williams found

Britneva a godsend. Just before she came into his life, he moaned to Wood, "I am quite incapable of learning the relative values of all these crazy coins, bobs, half crowns, ten shillings, quids, Etc. When Margo [Jones] deserts me"—she had been responsible for getting Williams from Rome to London in June—"I shall be in total chaos!" Almost immediately, Britneva made herself indispensable: clipping the British reviews for Williams as he hunkered down in Paris, sending him gifts, doing his laundry, advising him on presents to send to Helen Hayes and where to buy them, and dispensing a lot of crisp straight talk. "Somehow I cannot make plans or decisions about things like that so I will leave it to you to decide for me, if you will," he wrote to her, having run out of shirts, on July 30. "What do you think we should do? I have great faith in your ability to solve this enormous problem! (Or ignore it!)"

Britneva's loyalty to Williams was almost maternal. In fact, she resembled Edwina both physically and psychically. Both bossy women had the same petite physical outline, brusque emotional attitude, and, as it turned out, a nostalgia for a vanished aristocratic heritage that was largely a grandiose fantasy. In Britneva's life story, Williams recognized his own desperate struggle for survival. He was touched by Britneva's spirit and her circumstances. She was born on July 6, 1921, in St. Petersburg, Russia; thirteen months later, as she told it, under the threat of famine, she escaped to England with her mother, Mary, and her older brother, Vladimir, leaving her father, Dr. Alexander Britnev, apparently to the hands of the murderous Bolsheviks. She arrived in England with rickets, as well as a more lasting malady, a combination of sadness and terror, which her mother brought to their new life and was a large part of Britneva's inheritance. Inevitably, the family aspirations were at odds with the family finances. In order to send her children to good schools, Mary Britneva gave lessons in French and Russian and did line translations of Chekhov's works. She was ambitious for her daughter, shuttling Maria to and from ballet lessons, which Maria attacked with characteristic single-mindedness. When, in 1933, a young dancer with Monte Carlo's Ballets Russes was found to be under the statutory age of twelve, Maria stepped in. After three seasons, she had to give up dance because of foot trouble and, she later told the director Richard Eyre, because "my bosom was too big." She transferred her desire for stardom to the theater and got herself into Michel Saint Denis's acting school.

Almost everyone around Britneva, including Williams, was seduced by her moving portrait of her family of noble White Russians—the paternal grandfather who was the physician to "Dowager Empress Maria Fedorovna at Tsarskoe Selo," and the father who had been "shot by the Soviets." KGB files and government papers, however, show that most of this was revised or fabricated history. Maria's mother was born an English citizen, and she was partly educated in England; Maria's maternal grandfather, Charles Herbert Bucknall, was English. The Britnevs hadn't actually been refugees from the marauding Bolsheviks; they'd had English papers. Britneva's father's family line was made up of *raznochinsti*—intelligentsia descended from petit-bourgeois merchants in Kronshtadt, where they'd owned tugboats and diving equipment and public baths. There was no record of Britneva's grandfather's association with the tsarina. As for Britneva's father, far from being executed by the Bolsheviks, he served in the Red Army. All of which put paid to Maria's claim to be a White Russian, or even an Off-White Russian.

However, Britneva's associations with the rich and the famous gave credibility to her story and to her aura of artistic entitlement. With Williams, she played the devoted, adorable (and needy) girl; he was the benevolent sugar daddy, always ready to spring for vacations, hotels, loans, jewelry, even the occasional dress or fur. "I feel sorry for Maria," he wrote to Windham. "She detests London and has fallen out completely with the Beaumont office"—Hugh (Binkie) Beaumont was the panjandrum of H. M. Tennent's, the powerful West End management company—"so she has no prospect of work. . . . Seems to have no interesting friends here, nobody she likes much and her family is quite poor, except for an aunt who treats her rather coolly. Poor child." "I felt I was in a state of grace when I was with him," Britneva later said, and she was—protected by the big magic of Williams's talent and renown from a world that, for her, had a habit of collapsing.

To win favor, Britneva was capable of acts of enormous rashness. Of a 1946 production in which she was elevated from understudy to walk-on, Gielgud said, "When Edith Evans, as the consumptive wife in

'Crime and Punishment,' coughed too constantly during one of my best scenes, Maria pushed her face in a cushion to keep her quiet. This, as you can imagine, was not well received by the Dame." Maria had won a place forever in Sir John's heart but lost herself a toehold in the mainstream of English theater. Beaumont, the producer of the play, canceled Maria's contract. "She wasn't a good actress," the British drama critic Milton Shulman, who was a neighbor of Britneva's, said. "She was too much a fantasist offstage to be a fantasist onstage." Britneva had neither the conventional looks nor the reserve for the clipped English drawing-room comedy-drama that was the staple of the West End from the mid-forties to the mid-fifties. She had an artistic temperament, but she couldn't produce art. Then she met Williams and hitched her wagon to his star.

The romance of the Williams-Britneva friendship was built on the cornerstone of their first meeting. In her version of the story, Maria cast herself as an ingenue of "eighteen or nineteen." (She was just shy of twenty-seven.) She and Williams met at a dinner at Gielgud's London home on June 11, 1948—a couple of weeks after *Streetcar* was awarded the Pulitzer Prize. "I was invited to this wonderful party. Noël Coward playing the piano. Vivien Leigh, Larry Olivier, the most wonderful people. . . . I suddenly saw in the corner this crumpled little man, very alone—one red sock and one blue sock. I thought he must be another understudy," Britneva later told Dick Cavett on his talk show. It's hardly likely that Williams, already a much-heralded award-winning playwright, went unnoticed at the party. But there were a few things that assuredly did go unnoticed by Britneva. The Oliviers were not there: according to their biographers, they were in Australia most of that year. And it must have been the blithe spirit of Noël Coward who was tinkling the ivories, since Coward himself was in New York, meeting with his publishers, and didn't arrive back in England until nearly two weeks later.

Gore Vidal believed that the two must have actually met several weeks later at a party given by Binkie Beaumont. Wherever the meeting took place, it made boon companions of Britneva, Vidal, and Williams. Vidal recalled the three of them walking along the Strand: "Maria ate and ate. She and her mother were poor. They were still on ration books. She had

With Maria Britneva

some toffees, and she gave me one. I had a pivot tooth—a false tooth—which immediately came out. Riotous laughter from Maria. Could've killed her. The three us became friends. And then she attached herself."

Britneva paid back Williams's generosity with allegiance and excitement. Over the decades, she would become Williams's "five o'clock angel," as he dubbed Britneva. Exhausted after a day's writing, he could always find her waiting at the other end of the phone to fill up his emptiness with plans and amusing badinage. Britneva was variously friend, court jester, dogsbody, confidante, cheerleader, keeper of the flame, and finally, in his Last Will and Testament, legal guardian of his sister (a post that she negotiated well and parlayed into the unofficial but nonetheless influential title of literary executor of his estate). She had a talent for stirring things up. "Word has reached here that Maria B is on her way," Truman Capote wrote to friends in March 1949. "She writes 10"—Tennessee—"almost every day. Tell her please that . . . if she sees me to stay clear as I will slap her in the tits and kick her down the Spanish steps: you should see the things she has written 10 about me! Quel bitch. I mean this, you tell her. She is a dreadful liar." As a playwright, Williams found Britneva's provocations amusing, even dramatically useful. (She would later be the model for Maggie in *Cat on a Hot Tin Roof.*) As a person, he found her recklessness—her "savagely mordant sense of humor," as she called it— both a thrill and a caution. "You seem to say all the things that discreet people only think," he wrote her within the first year of their meeting. "Oh, that tongue of yours! As one who was, and perhaps still is, inclined to like so much of the rest of you, including what I optimistically assume to be your heart, I do most earnestly advise and beseech you to curb it, like the fancy little dogs on Fifth Avenue."

IN EARLY SEPTEMBER 1948, Williams returned to New York to attend the rehearsal period of *Summer and Smoke*. Britneva followed soon after him to minister her particular astringent brand of concern and caprice, and to be his date for the Broadway opening. The day Britneva arrived on the *Queen Mary*, Williams met the boat and took her to see *Streetcar*, where she complained about Brando's mumbling. "Tennessee, with a glint of malice in his eye, said, 'Why don't you go backstage and tell him?'" Britneva recalled. "Which I did. Brando was absolutely delighted and took me to the Russian Tea Room immediately."

During the bumpy Broadway rehearsals for *Summer and Smoke*, Williams's faith in Margo Jones declined; Britneva's place in his affections grew. Britneva's adoration was a happy contrast to Jones's exasperation. "We were fighting," Williams later told Brooks Atkinson, explaining what he saw as Jones's failure of imagination with the play. Jones had used Atkinson's glowing notice in the *Times* of her theater-in-the-round production in Dallas to sell Williams on the idea of her both producing and directing the play on Broadway. "Total autonomy between the two of us," she told him. But as early as April, Williams was voicing doubts about her as director. "If you want to (*dare* to) bring up the subject of Kazan directing, do so," he counseled Wood, "but I doubt that you will get anywhere with it as our girl Jones unquestionably regards herself as the American

Stanislavsky which it is still faintly possible that she may be however much we may doubt it." Although Wood doubted Jones's abilities and her toughness—"I expressed my doubts to Tennessee but he merely shrugged them off," she wrote—Williams "did, as usual, the gentlemanly thing. He'd promised her she could be his director, and that was that."

Jones could certainly talk the talk. ("She was the con of cons," the actor Ray Walston, who made his Broadway debut in *Summer and Smoke*, said.) As Williams learned to his cost, however, she couldn't walk the walk. "The tragedy is that her performance rarely lives up to her passion. Like a lover so anxious, so frightened of his desire, that he can't carry it through," he told Atkinson. Jones's theatrical vision was greater than her technical prowess. Among the many miscalculations surrounding the Broadway production of *Summer and Smoke*—its transfer from a theater-in-the-round to a more removed proscenium, its set, which was too big for the stage—the most fundamental was Jones's inability to communicate with actors. A week into the rehearsals, Williams "began to have depressing premonitions about the venture," he said. "An actor or actress would approach the ecstatic Margo with a question such as 'How do you want me to play this bit, Miss Jones?' '*Play* it? Honey, don't play it, *feel* it.'"

Later, after the production had closed, Capote told Williams a story he had heard from Anne Jackson, who played Nellie in the Broadway production: that Jones had attempted to gee-up the cast by telling them that the play was "the work of a dying man." The story so outraged Williams that he turned over a table in Capote's lap. ("I had been ill at the time, but 'dying' was the furthest thing from my intention, then or any time since, and anyway it struck me as an irrelevant or false and certainly not helpful sort of 'appeal'," Williams explained to Atkinson. "Actors *always* do their best, and the real or imaginary sickness of an author doesn't and shouldn't, couldn't, alter their contribution to the production.") "In my opinion Margo Jones should have confined herself to a regional theatre, preferably in the executive and fund-raising departments," Williams wrote in *Memoirs*. "I think it was there that her genius lay not in the direction of actors or of delicate plays." In his frustration, at one point during rehearsals, Williams bounded up from the stalls to show the actors what he wanted. "I was onstage playing the scene," Walston recalled. "Margo screamed from the audience, jumped up on the stage, threw her script down and said to Tennessee, 'I am directing this play! You get off the stage and get out of the theater!'"

Several days before the opening, at the Music Box Theatre on October 6, Williams and Wood sat together on the steps leading down to the lounge and listened to "Margo Jones's Farewell Address to the Troops," as Wood called it. "She told her cast that without doubt Tennessee Williams was the most important playwright of our times, 'Summer and Smoke' was the best play he'd ever written, the play simply had to succeed here in New York, it was up to them to give a performance worthy of the work," Wood recalled. Finally, Jones looked over to Williams. "Is there anything you'd like to say, Tenn?" she asked. "There's nothing *left* to say, is there?" Williams said, glancing at Wood and smiling.

The almost uniformly dismissive reviews—"A pretentious and amateurish bore" (*New York Herald Tribune*); "mawkish, murky, maudlin and monotonous" (*New York Daily News*)—confirmed Williams's assessment of Jones's "mediocre job." "Not inspired, not vital, as Kazan would have been and as the play so dreadfully needed," he wrote to Windham.

IF THE REVIEWS to *Summer and Smoke* took the shine off Williams's public glory, his private life had taken on a welcome new luster with the reemergence of Frank Merlo. One night, soon after returning from Europe, while walking down Lexington Avenue around midnight, Williams spotted Merlo in a delicatessen. He hadn't seen him since their passionate one-night stand on the Provincetown dunes a year before. Merlo was with a Navy friend. Williams invited them both back to his place on East Fifty-Eighth Street to picnic with their roast-beef sandwiches and potato salad. When Merlo's Navy buddy left to catch a bus back to New Jersey, Merlo stayed on. "Something started or something stopped / and there I was and there was he / . . . For it was late and I was lost," Williams wrote in his plaintive poem "Little Horse"—a nickname given to Merlo by Britneva because of his large front teeth.

There was nothing lost about the pragmatic Merlo, who was twenty-seven when he reconnected with Williams. "He was enthusiastic about everything, extremely positive," said the theater historian Mary

Henderson, who lived around the corner from Merlo when he was growing up in Peterstown, the Italian section of Elizabeth, New Jersey, and
once dated him. "He was a stick of dynamite, and he remained that way
for the rest of his life—voluble, funny." Merlo, whom Williams described
in a poem as "fleshed in a god's perfection," was muscular and handsome
with thick black hair and a swarthy complexion.

Merlo had been a "change-of-life baby," the fifth child of Rosalie and
Mike Merlo, who was a fishmonger in America but had been, according
to Henderson, "an important man in Italy." Throughout his growing up,
Merlo was known as "Fishy"; nonetheless, he carried himself with a distinctive swagger. He had ambitions to be a writer and was something of
an autodidact. "Frank felt very keenly his lack of education," Henderson
said. ("He was far better read than Tennessee," according to Vidal.) In
1941, forging the date on his birth certificate, Merlo dropped out of
Thomas Jefferson High School in his senior year to join the Navy. Despite
his diminutive stature—he was five foot three—he ended up serving
with the Marines. War was his university; the Marines was his fraternity.
"I damn near got to know a whole battalion of men, including officers, of
whom, I may add, I've made some lasting friendships," he wrote.

As a pharmacist mate first class attached to the Marine Corps's First
Division, Merlo saw action in the Pacific Theater. To his best friend Frank
Gionataiso, who had enlisted with him, Merlo recounted coming under
fire in a fierce three-day battle at Guadalcanal while he was carrying a
sixty-five-pound pack on his back and six grenades in his pockets. "I had
just witnessed a Jap .25 cal bullet tearing through the pack of a boy ahead
of me and was sure the Japs could spot my pack. To me it seemed as if the
god-damned thing stuck at least a mile in the air." In front of him, he
spotted a sergeant who had been mortally wounded. Merlo ordered four
men forward to retrieve his body on a stretcher. He continued:

> The path was very narrow, he weighed at least 180 pounds, it was very
> very hot, we had no water, even for him, it was steep climbing and alto-
> gether rotten going. At one point, we were standing on a ridge, and
> although we should have known better, were sky-lined. . . . I stepped
> ahead and just at that moment the air was splintered with the sharp stac-

cato of Jap machine gun fire. The bullets were kicking up the corral rock around us. I inched down below the ridge and looked around. The four men I had just ordered to man the stretcher had dropped their burden. Three of them were hit, two fatally and the other mortally hit. I crawled up, sized up the situation and began to administer aid to the one who was still alive. . . . I gave him some morphine and he died a short while after.

From the calm of the dispensary at the Naval Hospital in Alameda, California, where he served out his tour of duty, the high-spirited Merlo wrote Gionataiso about his widening horizons. He was reading Salvador Dalí's *My Secret Life*. ("It's a very well set up book and profusely illustrated with his work. It costs six dollars and I think well worth the price even if one doesn't care for Dali. He doesn't omit any details and even includes a chapter called 'My Intra-Uterine Memories, or Life in the Womb.' Mad!!!") He was going "high brow," he said. "Every symphony that has come to San Francisco, I've went and seen. Last Saturday I went to see Claudio Arrau, a Brazilian pianist play one of Schumann's Concerto's for piano and orchestra and enjoyed myself immensely. I just see you there, while reading the letter, shaking your head wondering 'what the hell does he want to waste his time going there for?' That same afternoon I 'worked' at a restaurant across the street from the Opera House, which some very good friends of mine own. The whole family was down with the flu and there was just the waitress there to run the place. They were very busy because of the concert and I volunteered to help. I met a lot of nice girls that way. Intelligent besides being good-looking. Saturday night I went to bed with a girl I called 'Red.' Her real name was Freda."

The spectacle of death had fired Merlo's appetite for life. He dreamed of coming east ("When I do, watch out cousin, look out. I have lined up places—Meadowbrook, Blue Room, El Morocco, Hotel Taft, Hotel Pennsylvania, Harlem! Savoy Ballroom, Leon and Eddie's and all of 52nd Street and Yorkville-86th St.") and of traveling ("In regards to travelling after the war, I do intend to go to Samoa, but I shall also, if possible, go to Europe"). He was also considering marriage. "I had intentions of marrying Lena when I first came back," he wrote to Gionataiso on February 3, 1943. "But after thinking it over awhile decided not to, although I

haven't had a change of heart yet. Just leery, I guess." But when he imagined the future, the good times were associated with the company of
women—especially Lena, "who may soon be my future wife (and bed
companion, to be crude about it!)." "Tomorrow I have liberty from eight
in the morning till eight Monday morning," he wrote on February 27,
1943. "I have nothing planned, but shall probably take Lena dancing over
at Sweets, a ballroom along the lines of the Roseland, which features big
name bands occasionally. The last time we went dancing there, Freddie
Slack was playing and when we started to dance, the floor slowly but
surely cleared of dancers and before we knew it, Lena and I were dancing
alone, for the benefit and I dare-say delight, of the admiring crowd. It
always happens no matter where we go. Of course, I love it all and I
always throw a very grateful smile at the dear public; a smile usually so
full of teeth I look like a Jap after blowing up the Panama Canal. By the
way, can you tell me where the Panama Canal is??"

After the war, Merlo returned to Elizabeth, New Jersey, where the
only decent paying job he could find was in construction. But his appetite
for adventure and for the arts drew him inevitably to Manhattan and to
the fringes of bohemia. "He got a job in New York with a ballet company,"
Henderson said. "He was not gay then. . . . If he had been, he would have
been destroyed by those kids." In fact, during the war, Merlo had been
outspoken on the subject of homosexuality. "My tongue, of late, has
become as caustic as any acid," he wrote to Gionataiso in 1943. "I am
attached to Fleet Air Wing #8 which I call 'Fruit Air Wing #8.' Yes, sad
fact, that is the case. Alas, my most horrible nightmare has come to life.
There are so many weak-wrists around here, we don't ever need to worry
about the lack of fans if a hot spell comes. The boys (or should I say girls)
do enough waving to keep the hottest air in circulation. The sad part of it
is, that for the few reserves that are that way, the rest of us have to suffer."

Merlo's sexual volte-face was his ticket to ride into the world of culture. By the time he hooked up with Williams in New York, he had
already been the lover of the Washington columnist Joseph Alsop and the
Broadway lyricist and composer John La Touche. He had also had a flut-
ter in the movies. Between 1940 and 1947, Merlo had walk-on parts in
ten B-action movies, including *Buzzy Rides the Range* (1940), *Lawless*

Frank Merlo on Navy leave in San Francisco, 1943

Clan (1946), *Jack Armstrong* (1946), and *The Vigilante: Fighting Hero of the West* (1947). Polite and well spoken, Merlo was almost exactly the opposite of the quixotic, unlettered Pancho, the mere news of whom sent a frisson of dread through the Williams camp. "Pancho is in town. Need I say more?" Wood once wrote to Irene Selznick. Pancho was unpredictable and violent; Merlo was resolute and generous. Pancho had been dishonorably discharged from the Army; Merlo was a war hero. Pancho created havoc around Williams; Merlo created order. "I thought you knew about Frankie," Oliver Evans wrote to a mutual friend about Merlo. "He's Pancho's successor, more intelligent by far, if not so handsome. There are some who say he's irresistible; I am not one of them." Among Williams's inner circle, however, Evans was in a distinct minority. "Frank was a warm, decent man with a strong native intelligence and a sense of honor," Paul Bigelow said. "Tenn . . . needed someone to look after the ordinary logical structure of everyday life. And with great love, this is what Frank did." Pancho had been a social impediment—"It is a small world with Pancho in it!" Williams wrote to Carson McCullers in 1948. The gregarious Merlo, by contrast, knew how to generate community and to expand the world around Williams.

Williams appointed Merlo his personal secretary and factotum; Merlo, however, was clear-eyed about his function. When he and Williams went to Hollywood in the summer of 1949, after almost a year together, so that Williams could lend a hand to the screenplay of *The Glass Menagerie*, the Hollywood mogul Jack Warner asked Merlo, "What do you do?" "I sleep with Mr. Williams," Merlo replied. He also ran social interference for the shy playwright. Williams's hysterical outbursts, his paranoia, his hypochondria, his infuriating vagueness were nothing compared to the mayhem of the real battles that Merlo had lived through. "He gave me the connection to the day-to-day and night-to-night living," Williams said. "He tied me down to earth." "He kept his wig on—that is, he was a man who kept cool, even when he and Tennessee were exposed to the most appalling pressures of social and professional life," Christopher Isherwood said of Merlo. "He was no goody-goody. He was just plain good." Merlo was "the cleft in the rock," the safe harbor for which Williams had prayed both onstage and off.

Paul Bowles

On December 1, 1948, Merlo, Williams, and Paul Bowles boarded the steamer SS *Vulcania*, bound for Gibraltar and a two-week stay in Morocco with Bowles and his wife, the novelist Jane Bowles. Britneva, who decided to remain in New York, accompanied the threesome to the dock. At the time, the bond between Williams and Merlo was just form-ing. "My sexual feeling for the boy was inordinate," Williams wrote. "Every evening I would cross to his bunk in the stateroom. Aware of my sexual intemperance and what its consequences could be, I began to entertain a suspicion that something was going on between Frankie and Paul Bowles. Nothing was, of course, except friendship."

Despite the companionship of close friends and the pleasures of "the most charming ship I've ever voyaged upon," Williams found himself sinking into a depression that the hectic merry-go-round of rehearsals, productions, and celebrity had kept at bay for the previous year. Britneva was the apparent cause. In her intemperate way, she had confided to Laughlin that she thought Williams was "Finit." "She meant as an artist," Williams wrote in his logbook of the journey. "She said that I had exhausted my material, my old material, and that my life, particularly my circle of friends and 'contacts,' was too narrow and special for me to discover new or more significant subjects. . . . That I associated so much with special cases or freaks that men like Arthur Miller—for whom I had expressed a great admiration—did not feel at ease with me and could make no vital contact: that I was building a barrier between myself and the real world and its citizens." Williams continued, "I felt it was honestly meant and there was a grain of truth in her warning. . . . The fault, the danger which she had partially correctly foreseen, lies in the over-working of a vein: loneliness, eroticism, repression, undefined spiritual longings: the intimate material of my own psyche is what I have filled my work with, and perhaps built it on, and now I have got to include, perhaps predominantly, some other things, and what are they? There is a dilemma, but I am not refusing to face it, and this Cassandra is a little bit premature in her cries of Doom!" Nonetheless, for nearly two months, Williams cold-shouldered Britneva.

With Merlo in tow, Williams shuttled from Morocco to Rome, then to Sicily to meet Merlo's relatives, before returning to the United States ten months later. Williams's wanderings matched his aimless spirit. Almost immediately after Williams arrived for his second extended stay in Rome, an un-mooring entropy, a sort of emotional fog, settled over him. "The simple truth is that I haven't known where to go since 'Streetcar,'" Williams wrote to Kazan and his wife, Molly, from Rome in mid-July 1949, summarizing the first half of his embattled year. "Everything that isn't an arbitrary, and consequently uninspired experiment, seems to be only an echo." When he re-read "The Big Time Operators," the rough sketch of what he considered the theatrical project with the most potential, Williams heard the unmistakable tropes of his old work and his old self. He had tapped into his memories of his father and their Oedipal struggle and shoehorned them into an intended political melodrama about the oil industry:

GLADYS: Your son misses you, Pere.
PERE: That's likely.
GLADYS: In your mind you have branded him a sissy, and that's what's come between you.
PERE: Does he still have on them little velvet knee britches?

GLADYS: He's an adorable little fellow. You mustn't hold that against him. But you do. You resent the fact that he—resembles his mother.

As Williams rightly saw, the play was "a ghost of an idea." "It doesn't seem very like me," he said. "It seems forced, outside my real sphere of interest and aptitude." Williams couldn't make himself care about the characters or find any verve in the writing. However, "The Big Time Operators" did have something new to it: in a rudimentary way, it raised the issue of moral attrition, of a sense of spiritual atrophy, which was an altogether new strain of regret in the theatrical conversation that Williams had with himself. "You are really washed up," one character tells another. "You can't break into the world of glamour and now it's too late for you to become a normal, ordinary person which you should have been satisfied to be in the first place. No, it's too late now. You're too spoiled. You're ruined." The dialogue was haphazard; the fear behind it wasn't.

"The trouble is that I am being bullied and intimidated by my own success and the fame that surrounds it and what people expect of me and their demands on me," Williams wrote. "They are forcing me out of my natural position as an artist so that I am in peril of ceasing to be an artist at all." But who was doing the forcing? The Liebling-Woods took the hit, but Williams himself was the culprit. Attention and glory, with their attendant "little prides and conceits," had changed him. He likened the spiritual effect to sunstroke—"the baleful sun of success"—which causes the brain to lose blood, and leaves the mind and the will unable to mesh. "Talent died in me from over-exposure," he wrote. "I'm not going to hit another jack-pot anytime soon. Until the heart finds a new song and the power to sing it."

Williams understood that he needed to make a change; he also knew that a change of content and of style amounted to a change of metabolism in him, and that took time. "The trouble is that you can't make any real philosophical progress in a couple of years," he wrote to Brooks Atkinson in June 1949. "The scope of understanding enlarges quite slowly, if it enlarges at all, and the scope of interest seems to wait upon understanding. In the meantime there is only continued observation, and variations on what you've already observed." He continued, "I have noticed that painters and poets, and in fact all artists who work from the inside out, have all the same problem: they cannot make sudden arbitrary changes of matter and treatment until the inner man is ripe for it. . . . The great challenge is keeping alive and growing as much as you can; and let the chips fall where they may!"

During these distracted months in Rome, he felt himself a sleepwalker, floating in an unreality like "gauze hung over gauze," as he wrote in his poem "The Soft City." Part of his ennui was due to the narcotic pleasures of Rome. In the afternoons, after a frustrating day at the typewriter, Williams steered his red Buick, nicknamed "Desiderio," through the narrow back streets, "slowly with great pomp and everybody shouts 'Que Bella Macchina!' and only Tyrone Power cuts a more important figure here," he wrote to Wood. The Roman skies were clear—"one long blue and gold ribbon always unwinding and giving you an illusion of permanence"; however, his literary vista was overcast.

For the best part of the year, Williams was driven by an *idée fixe*: "The fear that I am repeating myself, now, have totally exploited my area of sensibility and ought to retire, at least publicly, from the field." "There is no point in hiding from the stark fact that the fire is missing in almost everything I try to do right now," he wrote in May. "Is it Italy? Is it age? Who knows. Perhaps it is just the lack of any more deep need of expression, but I have no satisfactory existence without it. Without it, I have nothing but the animal life that is so routine and weary, except for the moments with F. when we seem close."

In addition to his anxiety over the idea of being written out, Williams had a new anxiety: the idea of being outwritten. "I received today five complete sets of Arthur Miller notices, more than I ever received for any play of my own," he wrote to Wood in February 1949, about *Death of a Salesman*. "Everybody seemed most anxious that I should know how thoroughly great was his triumph." Throughout the spring, with the Broadway disappointment of *Summer and Smoke* just behind him and, looming ahead, the Hollywood fiasco of *The Glass Menagerie*, which was being systematically mangled by Warner Brothers' screenwriters—"the cornball department," as he called them—Williams felt un-stimulated and stuck. Instead of having gold and glory to look forward to, Williams saw only the prospect of ignominy. He was cast down in a "ridiculous state of gloom."

Even his bond with Merlo, which had seemed so promising, had begun to fray. At first, things were jolly enough. In public, Merlo was alert, buoyant, and generally full of fun. He had a natural warmth that drew people to him. That year, the New Jersey boy who had dreamed of being in the cultural swim, found himself on location with Luchino Visconti, at dinner with Roberto Rossellini and Ingrid Bergman, and on a first-name basis with Anna Magnani, W. H. Auden, and Truman Capote. The Italian press referred to Merlo as Williams's "interpreter"; Williams called him "my little secretary," and, as early as February, he was trying to negotiate a permanent place for him in his life and his budget. "I do hope that I can manage, however, to accumulate enough money to bring me in a good monthly income, say, four or five hundred a month," he wrote to Wood, "on which I could keep myself and a small Secretary and a big car."

But by the end of March, Williams's moodiness had created trouble in paradise. He was, he said, "a sorry companion." "I am not alone, but in a way I am lonelier than if I were," he confided to McCullers. "Do you understand what I mean? Yes, I know you do." Capote, writing from Ischia, where he and his partner, Jack Dunphy, were staying in late March, noted that Williams and Merlo had "latched onto us like barnacles" and dished the noticeable strain in their relationship. "Taken in tiny doses I'm really very fond of them both, but darling I can't tell you what it's been like," Capote wrote. "Frankie nags T.W. all day and night, and T.W. I have discovered is a genuine paranoid."

THE STRAIN OF being a factotum by day and an intimate by night also took its toll. Merlo soon found himself oppressed by the imperialism of his doting friend's fame. Williams had the name, the calling, and the money. He was the ticket; Merlo was the passenger. "He hates the dependence involved in our relations," Williams wrote in March. Being the object of desire didn't protect Merlo from the little stings of humiliation that came with the job. "Frankie's passion is clothes and this week we have been on a haberdashery kick," Williams noted in April. "This evening Frank said he needed a dozen suits of underwear. Then I blew up and I said, Honey, you should have married Harry Truman before he went into politics. And he is now looking quite sheepish and has washed his old jockey shorts and hung them all over the bathroom to dry."

By May, cracks appeared in the relationship. "Picked up Frank who had a temperamental fit of some kind—disappeared from the supper table and is still at large," Williams noted on May 23. Almost two weeks later, the accumulated tension of the previous months finally led to an explosion, which Williams described in his journal:

> Violent (verbally) scene on the streets, with shouts of four-letter words a bit reminiscent of the late unlamented ordeal by Pancho, but we talked it out and though I guess the basic tension is still there, indissolubly, I now feel better for the explosion. . . . I suspect that we are only temporizing. I've never made a go of it for very long. The loneliness is rooted too deep in me. And F's a member of a darker race. To admit to myself that I can never be loved? Is that a necessity? Perhaps only a woman could love me, but I can't love a woman. Not now. It's too late. The wise thing now is to draw my heart slowly back into my cage of ribs. Is it? Watch for a while, wait. *Stai tranquillo!* A lot of this may be only the strain of work—without the satisfaction of knowing the work is good. Perhaps you're only imagining F. matters that much.

In a poem written around this time, "Faint as Leaf Shadow," Williams evoked Merlo's slow withdrawal:

> Faint as leaf shadow does he fade
> and do you fade in touching him.
> And as you fade, the afternoon
> fades with you and is cool and dim . . .
>
> And then you softly say his name
> as though his name upon your tongue
> a wall could lift against the drift
> of shadow that he fades among . . .

"When I see him enjoy so much more the company of others . . . it is naturally a bit hard on me, since I believe that I love him," Williams confided to Windham about Merlo. But if Williams was able to hide his jealousy for the most part, Merlo was capable of shows of stroppy displeasure when other lesser lights, like Britneva, who joined them on holiday that summer, claimed his lover's allegiance. "Frank is possessive and destructive of every relationship Tenn has, which is bad, for an artist [like] Tenn needs some impetus—happiness or unhappiness—not just the nervous reactions of a horse," Britneva wrote in a competitive snit in her July diary. She also noted a change in her friend. "There is a curious listlessness and lack of spark in him," Britneva wrote in her diary that June, referring to Williams as "a fish on ice." "His eyes are puffy and tired tired tired. He said he felt 'a hundred years old.'" She continued, "He seems very detached somehow, like something that is running down, unwinding itself."

Uncertain of the success of his heart or his art, Williams worked fitfully on two projects: a short story and a play titled "Stornello," an "Italian name for a type of dramatic-narrative song," Williams explained in his outline for Wood, which was "usually in dialogue form between a male and female singer." But he put the play on the back burner. "This may turn out to be foolish," he wrote to his publisher, "but I don't seem to have any choice in the matter." In the story, adapted from a discarded play and expanded between March and June into a novella, which he intended as a film vehicle for Greta Garbo, Williams faced up to his own emotional and artistic impasse. The tentative title, later re-titled *The Roman Spring of Mrs. Stone*, was "Moon of Pause." His heroine, Karen Stone—a widow and once-renowned actress—is caught up in the expatriate entropy that Williams dubbed "the drift." In a petulant and mercurial gigolo named Paolo she sees a last chance to reclaim her own desires. Mrs. Stone was modeled on the writer and artist Elizabeth Eyre de Lanux, Williams's occasional traveling companion for whom he had posed that year for a large fresco. (After the story was published, she reportedly destroyed the painting.) "Eyre de Lanux is a woman who was a *great* beauty, is now about 45," Williams wrote to Laughlin, underestimating her age by a decade. "I think she has recently had her face lifted while she was mysteriously away in Paris. She has a young Italian lover, a

With coffee at work

boy of 25, startlingly beautiful and the only real rascal that I have met in
Italy. Her blind adoration of him is shocking!" He went on, "Eyre's boy-
friend, Paolo, recently brought her a two-year-old infant that he claims to
be his bastard child and wants her to take care of him. It has no resemblance to him. It is obviously a trick of some kind."

Onto the facts of Eyre de Lanux's situation Williams projected his
own psychic reality. Mrs. Stone, who has retired from the stage and who
has hit the unnerving milestone of fifty (Williams was approaching
forty), is acutely aware of loss—loss of beauty, talent, career, and direction. She feels "stopped" and finds herself taking refuge in the consoling
beauty of Rome, "leading an almost posthumous existence." She, like
Williams, is obsessed with the diminution of her magic: "Mrs. Stone
knew it. She did not fail to discover this creeping attrition and to do
everything in her power to compensate for it by increased exercise of
skill." When she is buttonholed by a bossy American female friend who
is appalled by her promiscuous ways and who tells her that "you can't
retire from an art," Mrs. Stone replies, "You can when you finally dis-

cover you had no talent for it." Like Williams, who referred to himself that winter as a "wounded gladiator," Mrs. Stone saw her career as a perpetual battle, a competitive slog driven by the infantile desire to be "King On The Mountain":

> Scrambling, pushing, kicking and scratching had been replaced by ostensibly civilized tactics. But Mrs. Stone's arrival at the height of her profession, and her heroic tenacity with which she held that position against all besieging elements or persons, with the sole exception of time, could not fail to impress Mrs. Stone as having a parallel to the childhood game on the terrace. At certain unguarded moments, those moments when the cultivated adult self . . . receives a transmission from its original, natural being, she had intercepted the inner whisper of these exultant words: *I am still King On The Mountain!*

Mrs. Stone's surname indicated the gravity of her retreat from that battle. "Security is a kind of death," Williams had written in 1947. A theatrical workhorse who has put herself out to pasture, she finds herself with financial freedom, thanks to her late husband, but no purpose. "Being purposeless was like being drunk," Williams writes. "She was free to drift for hours in no particular direction." Deprived of output and acclaim—the hubbub of success that once surrounded her—Mrs. Stone is overwhelmed by intimations of emptiness.

> She had been continually occupied with more things than a single existence seemed sufficient to hold, and for that reason, the way that centrifugal force prevents a whirling object from falling inward from its orbit, Mrs. Stone was removed for a long time from the void she circled. . . . Mrs. Stone knew, in her heart, that she was turning boldly inward from the now slackened orbit, turning inward and beginning now, to enter the space enclosed by the path of passionate flight. . . . And being a person of remarkable audacity, she moved inward with her violet eyes wide open, asking herself, in her heart, what she would find as she moved? Was it simply a void, or did it contain some immaterial force that still might save as well as it might destroy her?

Paolo, the perfectly formed young Italian hustler who picks up Mrs. Stone, is for her a kind of unexplored territory. Seeing him undressed and sunning himself on a cot beside her, Mrs. Stone "could not bear to look at him. He was too lustrous." Her marriage with the late Mr. Stone was essentially asexual: "Their marriage, in its beginning, had come very close to disaster because of sexual coldness, amounting to aversion, on her part, and a sexual awkwardness, amounting to impotence, on his," Williams writes, describing how the marriage would have broken up had not Mr. Stone broken down and "wept on her breast like a baby, and in this way transferred his position from that of unsuccessful master to that of pathetic dependent." Williams goes on, "Through his inadequacy Mr. Stone had allowed them both to discover what both really wanted, she an adult child, and he a living and young and adorable mother."

The fillip of emotional substitution lent longevity to the Stones' marriage; it also invested the relationship with a ghostly quality— desires were unspoken and loneliness was disguised behind a performance of civility, in which "they exchanged their eagerly denying smiles at each other and their reassuring light speeches." Until her Roman spring—a time that coincides with her menopause—Mrs. Stone enacted seduction onstage; her sexuality, however, was dormant. (In the tentative play outline on which the novella was based, Williams wrote, "Her effort to express a tenderness is . . . difficult. For scenes like this she always has lines memorized!") Like Edwina Williams, with her Puritan terror of the flesh, Mrs. Stone associated sex with dread; menopause puts an end to that:

> What she felt, now, was desire without the old, implicit distraction of danger. Nothing could happen, now, but desire, and its possible gratification. . . . It had been the secret dread in her, the unconscious will *not* to bear. That dread was now withdrawn.

This sudden liberty accounts for her "emotional anarchy" with Paolo. In the game of cat and mouse that she and Paolo play, Mrs. Stone refuses to be the aggressor; she is flirtatious but not active. "Mrs. Stone knew, as well as Paolo knew it, that to become the aggressor in a relationship is to forsake an advantage," Williams writes. "She, too, had once held the trump card of beauty. . . . Her social manner and procedure were still based upon its possession. She showed as plainly as Paolo that she was more used to receive than to offer courtship." Paolo's fecklessness is intentionally confounding: "I will call you in the morning, he would say, or 'I will pick you up for cocktails.' Rarely anything at a fixed point on the clock. Sometimes he failed to appear at all." Nonetheless, the mercurial behavior inspired Mrs. Stone's "incontinent longings," an auto-erotic thrill in which absence created the currency of desire.

Mrs. Stone's pining for the elusive Paolo offered Williams a fictional situation onto which he could project his own agitated emotions. Mrs. Stone's complaint about Paolo was also Williams's about Merlo: "When we're alone together you're so lazy and sulky that you'll barely talk, but the moment you find yourself in front of a crowd, you light up." Merlo's temperamental scenes—his walk-outs, his walkabouts, his vituperative rants—as well as his occasional good moods, were duly noted in Williams's diary. "Frankie and I have been happy lately in Rome," Williams noted on May 30. "I am particularly glad that *he* is." The jealousy, the frustration, the adoration, the lust, even the peace offerings of Williams's relationship found their way into Mrs. Stone's story. "*Stai tranquillo*"— the words with which Mrs. Stone calmed herself after Paolo's bad behavior—were the same words Williams addressed to himself when exasperated with Merlo. He wrote in his notebook on May 29:

> I love F.—deeply, tenderly, unconditionally. I think I love with every bit of my heart, not with the wild, disorderly, terrified passion I had for K[ip] that brilliant little summer of 1940. But doesn't this finally add up to more? If it doesn't it is only because of the mutations— time—in me.
>
> But it is amazing that I who've become so calm and contained about other matters could feel as much as I do when F. is sleeping beside me. If only I could give F. something beside clothes and travel— something that would add to the content of heart and life, make a dif- ference in his state of being. If he left me, and perhaps he will, I would go on living and enduring and I suppose turn him into a poem as I've

done with others. But the poem is already there in his actual presence—
Enough. I said to Paul [Bowles] "I am afraid it will end badly."—Will
it? The best way is to let everything alone—as it is—accept—and
give—*stai tranquillo*.

For both Williams and his fictional alter ego, a world without love was
a dark, vacant place, but also a probability. Throughout Mrs. Stone's passionate pursuit of Paolo, she herself is stalked—by a man who vaguely
resembles him. (He is "somewhat taller than Paolo, but of the same general type.") At the opening of the story, the man is just a handsome,
threadbare, stealthy figure standing hunched near the Spanish Steps,
looking up at Mrs. Stone's palazzo terrace, who seems "to be waiting to
receive a signal of some kind." Over the course of the story, the shadowy
figure takes on an aura of menace. Staring into a shop window, Mrs. Stone
sees his reflection and hears him peeing behind her. Later, in another
chance encounter, the anonymous man exposes himself to her. A predatory figure, an apparition of anonymity and the negative, he at first causes
Mrs. Stone to flee. However, by the end of the story, after she has violently
broken off her affair with Paolo, Mrs. Stone wanders alone in her large
apartment, overwhelmed by the imminence of nothingness—"Nothing
could not be allowed to go on and on and on like this!" she thinks.

Action is the antidote to angst; Mrs. Stone, for the first time, becomes
an agent of her own desire. On the terrace of her apartment, she feels
something stir inside her. "It was nothing that she had planned or wanted
to happen, and yet she was making it happen," Williams writes. Her
stalker—the man waiting for a signal outside—now receives one. Mrs.
Stone wraps her apartment keys in a handkerchief and throws them down
to him. The gesture is a semaphore of absence: emptiness beckoning non-
entity. With this histrionic gesture, the tale also becomes a parable of
"the occult reasons" of Williams's heart, the knowing that "does not need
to be conscious knowing." The figure, who stoops to pick up the keys, is
not described as a person; he is an "it" rather than a "he." "It looked up at
her," Williams writes, "with a single quick jerk of the head, and even now
it was moving out of sight, not away from her but towards her."

The story leaves Mrs. Stone on the brink of an embrace. "Yes, in a few minutes now, the nothingness would be interrupted, the awful vacancy would be entered by something," she says, in the penultimate paragraph. In seizing the moment, Mrs. Stone is also reclaiming the fantasy of her lost love. The encounter holds out the prospect of both emotional survival and self-destruction. *"Look, I've stopped the drift!"* she says in the story's ambiguous last line. By throwing the keys down to a menacing, anonymous figure, she does what Williams did from the stage: she shares herself—puts herself at risk—with her audience by inviting it in. "I don't ask for your pity, but just for your understanding—not even that—no. Just for your recognition of me in you," Williams's spokesman Chance Wayne says to the audience in the final lines of *Sweet Bird of Youth* (1959). A decade earlier, Mrs. Stone asked for the same thing.

ON JUNE 21, 1949, with a draft of his novella finished, Williams sent Wood an eight-page outline for "Stornello." It was a project into which he'd "wandered," he told Kazan and his wife, "simply because it seemed to demand so much less of me." Like *Mrs. Stone*, the landscape of "Stornello" was defined by loss. The heroine, Pepina, a widowed Sicilian seamstress, "idolizes" her late husband, Rosario. Her house is "practically his shrine." To drive home Rosario's absence, the family Parrott frequently calls out Pepina's name "in the voice of the dead husband." The synopsis goes on: "Pepina wishes the Parrott would die . . . it never forgets how Rosario used to call." Neither does Pepina, who for eight years has not "felt the coarse fingers of a man on her matronly flesh." Her house has become an extension of her own petrified puritanical will, a sort of barricade around her desires. Just as she has locked herself away, Pepina has incarcerated her daughter, Rose, in order to protect the lovelorn teenager from the sailor with whom she's infatuated. ("To say she is fallen in love is an understatement," Williams writes. "She is transported with 'the awakening ardors of adolescence!'") Rose ends the standoff and wins her release by threatening to kill herself with a butcher's knife.

Into this arena of hysterical repression comes Umberto, "a young bull of a man: swarthy, powerful—Dionysian!" Like Rosario, Umberto is a truck driver, a brawler; even his build resembles Rosario's. He is, in other words, Rosario's double. At first sight, Pepina "blinks at him with an incredulous gaze," as if she had seen a ghost. For all extents and purposes, she has. Umberto literally and figuratively steps into Rosario's shoes. Like the figure who resembled Paolo in *The Roman Spring of Mrs. Stone*, Umberto is a stand-in for the woman's real object of desire. Briefly, he holds the promise of some kind of emotional salvation. He finds Pepina "molto simpatico." He is warm, "tremendously understanding," and immediately at home. Eager to be helpful, he unwittingly subverts Pepina's closed-off world. He is an agent first of disenchantment (he confirms a rumor of Rosario's infidelity), then of disruption. After a night with Pepina, he drunkenly comes upon Rose asleep on the living-room sofa and gropes her. Nothing survives the emotional chaos of that clownish encounter. Umberto is driven out; Rose rushes to her romantic destiny with the sailor; Pepina batters the Parrott cage. Disabused of everything but the sure knowledge of her unfathomable desire, she is left alone. At the finale, she "crawls sobbing to the Madonna: as the light fades, her prayer becomes audible."

Neither Pepina nor Williams seemed able to find a path beyond endurance to grace, a failing that disappointed Kazan and his wife when they read Williams's synopsis in July. "My efforts to make it sound lively made it sound cheap," Williams wrote them, "but in the character of Pepina there was a lostness which I could feel and write about with reality, and would have, if I wrote it." Although Williams valued ruthless criticism—"Honesty about failure is the only help for it"—the negative response sent him into a tailspin. In his diary, the same day, he wrote:

Approaching a crisis.

Kazan's letter—the dissolution of play project—

Nerves—the fear of talking—society almost intolerable.

Nervous impotence,

Concern over F.

Bodily weakness—fatigue—sloth.

Tonight barely strength to hold this pencil.

Merlo continued to be as capricious in life as Williams's "illogical phantoms" were on the page. The night of his near collapse, Williams wrote,

"Left F. at theatre with 'his gang.' Came home alone under influence (waning) of a seconal taken right after supper. Something has to break soon.—Hope not me." A few days later, he confided to his diary, "Saw Frank only in morning—He disappeared before I got back tonight—first time we haven't dined together in Rome." He added, "Nerves quieter but the trauma is there. And work remains useless." Still, there were nights, duly noted, when "the nightingales sang very sweetly for Frank and I."

While Williams worried about the outcome of his relationship, Hollywood was worrying about the outcome of *The Glass Menagerie*. Warner Brothers sent for Williams. "They say they don't want a fairy-tale ending but there is evidence of double-talk," Williams wrote ruefully to Laughlin on August 17. He went on, "At least I should learn something more about the technique of film-making which I can use creatively on some other assignment perhaps over here. I am on excellent terms with Rossellini and De Sica and Visconti and would enjoy working with any one of them. Last week had supper with Ingrid Bergman and Rossellini. Their 'Fuck you' attitude toward the outraged women's clubs and sob-columnists is very beautiful and should have a salutary affect on discrediting those infantile moralists that make it so hard for anyone to do honest work and live honestly in the States."

Before leaving Rome in late August 1949, for emotional and literary luck Williams threw coins into the Trevi Fountain. His departure from Europe was full of the anxiety of failure; his return to America was full of the excitement of success. In New York, Wood greeted him with the news that Hollywood had agreed in principle to a lush deal for the screen rights to *A Streetcar Named Desire*. At a time when the average yearly income was $2,100, Williams would get half a million dollars, plus a percentage of the film's profits.

Almost instantly, Williams's drift was transformed into direction. In the first week of September, he and Merlo rolled into Hollywood and into its carefully orchestrated world of blandishments and ballyhoo. As a preemptive measure, to bolster her skittish client during the *Menagerie* script conferences, Wood had written ahead to the director George

Cukor to ask that he show Williams some hospitality. "I always feel Tennessee is bound to be in a happier, safer frame of mind if you have your good eye on him," she said. "I think you will find him in the Bel-Air. If not he will be at the Beverly Hills hotel. If he isn't in either place, call me and we will search America together." Wood needn't have worried. Warner Brothers escorted Williams around Los Angeles like the goose who had laid a Fabergé egg.

Amid the low-hanging sycamores and the bougainvillea of the Hotel Bel-Air, he lounged in a three-room Spanish-style bungalow, with a pool just outside his front door. A rented Buick convertible was at his disposal. And Warner Brothers threw him an A-list black-tie party at the swank Chaunticlair—"like a wet dream of Louella Parsons's," Williams joked to Kazan. Williams and Merlo had arrived early, in rented white dinner jackets that made them look more like waiters than grandees. The maître d' barred them from entering. Charles Feldman—the film producer of *The Glass Menagerie* and *A Streetcar Named Desire*—"who was arranging place cards . . . rushed over to make amends," Wood recalled. She added, "Everyone who was anyone in Hollywood of the forties was there that night. Dear Hedda and dear Louella, David Selznick, Sam Goldwyn, Jack Warner, phalanxes of leading men and ladies." Williams was given his first solid-gold cigarette case, lovingly inscribed by management. With a mixture of amusement and awe, he moved through the surreal spectacle among large ice statues of animals, which melted and flooded the floor. He saw his name in blue letters inside an illuminated block of ice. "The deeper you go into this dream-kingdom, the more fantastic it becomes," Williams told Kazan. "I expect to meet the Red Duchess or the Dormouse and the Mad Hatter at any moment."

In time, Williams would find Hollywood anathema to his freedom of expression; in the glamour and the glory of the moment, however, he looked on the glitterati with benign detachment. "They are all very nice, like children, but the games that they are playing do not seem to make any sense," he said. "I think [Clifford] Odets must have approached them from the wrong angle. That is the trouble with an angry social attitude, an outraged premise, you see all the ugly things but not the often-delightful humor and fantasy of it, and the pathos."

Hollywood's charm offensive may have been comically transparent, but it was potent. Williams was bedazzled. Flush with faith in the studio and in the *Menagerie* screenplay, he wrote to his family, "The vulgarities have been eliminated. I have re-written the whole thing according to my own ideas. I now think it has a chance to be a very successful picture." Williams saw the screen test of Gertrude Lawrence, who had finally been chosen to play Amanda. Although he would later call her casting a "dismal error," at the time, under the heady spell of Hollywood, he pronounced her "amazingly good." (Williams arrived twenty minutes late to his first meeting with Lawrence. "I brought her a corsage, and she threw it right in the sink," Williams said.)

The studio's solicitousness was, in part, an attempt to coax Williams into turning *Menagerie*'s vague, problematic ending into a climax with Hollywood uplift. Even before his visit to California, Williams had agreed to give Laura a ray of hope at the film's finale, but it was a difficult task for him, because, as he told the film's director, Irving Rapper, "in my heart the ending as it exists in the play was the artistically inevitable ending." Williams proposed a minor adjustment. "I think it is all right to suggest the possibility of 'someone else coming,'" he wrote to Rapper. "And that 'someone else,' remaining as insubstantial as an approaching shadow in the alley which appears in conjunction with the narrative line 'The long delayed but always expected something that we live for'—it strikes me as constituting a sufficiently hopeful possibility for the future, symbolically and even literally, which is as much as the essential character of the story will admit without violation."

Warner Brothers, however, wanted Williams's poetic sorrow turned into heartwarming salvation. Even while glad-handing Williams at the Chaunticlair, the studio swamis were plotting to betray him and his original vision. Unbeknownst to Williams, they had instructed Peter Berneis, the film's other screenwriter, to come up with his own upbeat ending. Berneis wanted Laura to offer a moral—"a bitter experience can prepare a soul for a new life." As he put it, "If we don't show that Laura changes after the unicorn is broken, if we don't have a basis in her for an eventual open heart and an open mind to receive a man, then we might as well stick to Williams's original tragedy."

Berneis didn't limit himself to suggesting the immanence of a second beau for Laura; he gave her a fellah with a physique and a name: Richard Henderson. To the studio moneymen, this second Gentleman Caller was magic. "We have tagged on the ending for Laura and Tom that was written by Peter Berneis. Williams knows nothing about this. His ending is used in *addition* to the scene between Laura and Tom. . . . My over-all feeling is that this last version is a tremendous improvement over the other scripts. The role of Tom has been built up considerably, Laura's role has much more sympathy piled on it," the film's co-producer, Jerry Wald, who was partly the inspiration for Sammy Glick in Budd Schulberg's 1941 novel *What Makes Sammy Run?*, wrote in a memo to Charles Feldman. Wald continued, "The addition of the new scene with the Gentleman Caller is well worth all the efforts that you went to in getting Williams out here."

At a private screening the following year, with Merlo and Marlon Brando present, Williams saw the final cut. The ending outraged him; it destroyed, he said, the "quality of poetic mystery and beauty which the picture badly needs in its final moments." The film received the bad reviews that Williams had predicted. ("Life isn't a bust just because you've got a bum gam," *Variety* said. The *New York Times*, under the subhead " 'The Glass Menagerie' Reaches the Screen in Somewhat Battered Condition," was not so flippant: "The Glass Menagerie," it said, "comes perilously close to sheer buffoonery in some of its most fragile scenes.") Williams denounced the film as a "travesty." Jack Warner, who had rolled out the red carpet for Williams in September, promptly rolled it up. "Am surprised at Tennessee," he wired Warner Brothers' New York representative Mort Blumenstock. "These temperamental derelicts who get rich on the efforts of others after they create something should offer prayers of thanks instead of finding fault with producers, studios, directors, cameramen. Am not interested in any form shape or manner with his being indignant." But Charles Feldman was. "I can't impress upon you too much the wisdom of cautioning Tennessee not to make any adverse comments to anyone," he wrote Wood, demanding later that Williams say "something very complimentary about the picture that we can use." Williams bowed to pressure and worked up some appropriate weasel words. "In the picture there is less darkness and more light, more humor and less tragedy," he said after *The Glass Menagerie* was released on September 7, 1950.

WILLIAMS WAS MORE apt to be positive about his life than about the botched film. Bored and soured by their Hollywood junket, he and Merlo had made their way to the bohemian outpost of Key West in November 1949. On Duncan Street, at the edge of the town's old section, Williams rented what he called "a sort of Tom Thumb mansion": a snow-white Bahama-style house with a white picket fence, pink shutters, and light-green patio furniture. There, he and Merlo were joined for the winter by Williams's ninety-two-year-old grandfather, Reverend Walter Dakin, who occupied the ground floor. Next door, two Rhode Island red hens and a white leghorn rooster scuttled around an "improvised poultry yard." A "magnificent black goat with big yellow eyes, surely one of God's most beautiful creatures, always straining at his rope as if he had an important errand to run if he could get loose," completed the piquancy of the scene. "Life here is as dull as paradise must be," Williams wrote to Laughlin when he first arrived in Key West.

The following year, for $22,500, Williams bought the house. Over the decades, he improved on his paradise: screw pines, coconut trees, clustering palms, orchids, begonia, and hibiscus were among the many plantings that in time turned his domain into a shady, luxuriant Eden. For the rest of his life, no matter how far afield Williams wandered, 1431 Duncan Street would be his official residence and his only home. He loved, he said, "the water, the eternal turquoise and foam of the sea and the sky." He also loved the house, which he associated with something even rarer than the sun-dappled landscape: harmony. "Frank is now happy here," Williams confided to Bigelow after the first few weeks of Key West living.

Back on native ground, Merlo found himself with full days; he was in charge of the house, the food, and the eccentric Reverend Dakin. "Grandfather is having the time of his life," Williams wrote to Margo Jones. "He's crazy about Frankie who drives him around everywhere that he takes a notion to go, and he usually has a notion to go somewhere." In St. Louis, where he lived in a room in Edwina's house, the

Reverend felt confused and marginalized. (Insisting that her father was only "pretending to be deaf," Edwina refused to repeat anything that he didn't hear.) In his makeshift Key West family, Reverend Dakin was an honored guest, at the center of things. "Tom is so good to me," he wrote to Wood. "I love him." While Merlo and the Reverend ventured out by car most mornings, Williams typed away at the dining-room table, gradually converting the strangulated "Stornello" into the rich comic lyricism of *The Rose Tattoo*. In the afternoons, the ménage decamped to the beach. "A girl makes her best contacts in the afternoon when she can see what she's doing," Williams joked.

"I feel somewhat rejuvenated and moderately at peace for the first time in perhaps three years," he wrote to Jones in the first days of the new

With Merlo outside Key West house, 1957

decade. Even his alcohol intake was down to "five drinks a day," he crowed
to the bibulous Carson McCullers. When Merlo went north for Christmas, intending, among many other treats, to visit Carson McCullers and
see her Broadway hit *The Member of the Wedding*, Williams wrote ahead
to her. "He will bring you good-luck as he has me," he said. Merlo returned
on January 5, 1950, bearing Christmas presents for Williams—records,
cologne, and a gold snake ring with little diamond chips, "the nicest piece
of jewelry I have owned." "Frankie had lost weight at home and seemed
glad to be back in our peaceful little world," Williams said. It was true: for
Merlo, too, these gracious days felt like a blessing. "We shall all be together
again soon in the house we love so much," Merlo wrote later to the Reverend Dakin, from Rome, in July 1950. "God has been very good to us this
year, dear friend, when we think how much happiness and good fortune
these past few months (and coming ones, too) contained."

By December 4, 1949, Williams had completed a "kitchen sink version" of *The Rose Tattoo*. The story celebrated his deliverance from a
creative and emotional stalemate. Inevitably, as Williams's bond with
Merlo solidified, the landscape of his play took on deeper coloration; he
compared it to a "dark, blood-red translucent stone that is twisted this
way and that, to give off its somber rich light." When he submitted the
play to Kazan in June 1950, the light-dark theme was a defining part of
his pitch. "During the past two years I have been, for the first time in my
life, happy and at home with someone and I think of this play as a monument to that happiness, a house built of images and words for that happiness to live in," he wrote. "But in that happiness there is the long,
inescapable heritage of the painful and the perplexed like the dark corners of a big room."

For *The Rose Tattoo*, Umberto, the improbable figure who lures the
widow away from her ascetic resignation and back into life, was rechristened Alvaro Mangiacavallo ("eat a horse"), a surname that incorporated
Williams's nickname for Merlo and made him central to the widow's
erotic excitement, just as "Little Horse" was central to Williams's own
yearning. When Alvaro makes a phone call, on behalf of the widow, to
identify Rosario's inamorata, he says, "Well, this is your little friend,
Alvaro Merlo, speaking!" Alvaro was constructed more or less to Mer-

lo's proportions: "one of those Mediterranean types that resemble glossy young bulls . . . short in stature, has a massively sculptural torso. . . . There is a startling, improvised air about him," the stage directions read. The plump and hysterical widow is a medley of vulnerabilities and vainglories—"the Baronessa," as the community teasingly nicknames her—an outline into which Williams could insert his own porous, crying-out heart. The struggle she faces—between the pleasures of renunciation and of connection—was also dramatized in "Humble Star," a poem Williams wrote just after completing the first draft of *Rose Tattoo* and dedicated to Merlo:

> Death is high.
>
> It is where the green-pointed things are.
> I know, for I left on the wings of it.
>
> While you slept, breathlessness took me
> to a green-pointed star.
>
> I was exalted but not at ease
> in the space.
> Beneath me your breathing face
> cried out, Return, return!
>
> Return, you called while you slept.
> And desperately back I crept
> against the vertical fall.
>
> It was not easy to crawl
> against those unending torrents
> of light, all bending one way,
>
> And only your voice calling, Stay!
> But my longing was great
> to be comforted and warmed

Once more by your sleeping form,
to remain, yet a while, no higher
than where you are,

Little room, warm love, humble star!

Williams honored Merlo's inspiration in another significant way: he gave him a percentage of the play. "I want him to feel some independence," Williams told Wood in March. "His position with me now lacks the security and dignity that his character calls for." Intimacy required equality; the money went some way to ensuring it. *The Rose Tattoo* was also dedicated to Merlo "in return for Sicily"; the exchange to which the play was a testament, however, was as much psychological as geographical. Even before Williams had written about Sicily or visited it, his identification with the place and with Merlo's stories about it signaled a hysteric's desire to merge with the alluring personality of his friend. Merlo regaled Williams with tales of his parents, originally from Ribera, and their large, noisy, bumptious first-generation Sicilian-American family. According to Merlo, sometimes after a family blowup, his mother would take umbrage in the garden and climb into a fig tree to sulk. "I remember Frankie telling us that after one particularly blinding row, she refused to come down," Maria Britneva recalled. "Having shouted at her, and pleaded with her, her sons eventually took an axe to the tree and brought the whole thing down, with her in it." Britneva went on, "Tennessee and I . . . were whimpering with laughter. Frankie was livid."

Merlo's tales of his Sicilian community—with its aggressions and repressions, its emotional extravagance—excited Williams's imagination and suited his rhythm. "My approach to my work is hysterical," he told Kazan. "It is infatuated and sometimes downright silly. I don't know what it is to take anything calmly." The Sicilian response to life was also histrionic; it turned feeling into event. "Have I ever told you that I like Italians?" Williams wrote to Britneva from Rome in 1949. "They are the last of the beautiful young comedians of the world." He went on, "The Young Horse . . . has returned from Sicily where he had a case of galloping dysentery. . . . He said it was the goat's milk that did it. They brought the goat right into his bedroom and milked it beside the bed and handed him the milk and would not take no for an answer as the goat was a great prize. Soon as he has recovered sufficiently, and he is showing some signs of recovery now, we are going back down there together in the Buick. As I am too fat, the goat will do me no harm, and the reports of social life down there are fantastic. The girls are not allowed to speak to the boys till after marriage: a kiss has the same consequences as a pregnancy used to have in the backward communities of the South, and they must still have dowries, no matter how pretty." (A goat appears in *The Rose Tattoo* as an emblem of the play's lyric spirit—"the Dionysian element in human life, its mystery, its beauty, its significance.")

The Rose Tattoo's Sicilian-American locale "somewhere along the Gulf Coast" also strategically allowed Williams to depart from the familiar topography of the South, as well as from the tropes of Southern character, caste, and speech that threatened to stereotype his work. A "giant step forward," Wood called *The Rose Tattoo*, even before she approved of the play. But Williams's personal breakthrough was even more significant than his stylistic one: his guarded self had surrendered to another. *The Rose Tattoo* tried to capture the perplexity of this connection—"the baffled look, the stammered speech, the incomplete gesture, the wild rush of beings past and among each other."

HAVING LABORED SO fiercely to finish *The Rose Tattoo* and to get it to Wood before the New Year, Williams found her silence deafening. By the end of January, feeling "tentative and mixed," afraid even to re-read his play, he finally cabled Wood for a response. Wood immediately wired back that she was "very optimistic and thought it had the making of a great commercial vehicle." Williams saw through her well-chosen words, which made him feel "that the script might be something to pretend had not happened like public vomiting."

Meanwhile, word of the play was leaking out. On January 22, Irene Selznick called Key West asking to read it. "I said I was still too nervous," Williams told Wood. To Bigelow, he worried as he awaited more word from Wood: "The play is probably too subjective, an attempt to externalize an experience which was too much my own." To Gore Vidal, he bitched, "Audrey is sitting on the new script like an old hen."

In late February, Williams finally got an enthusiastic response from

Kazan, who was already in pre-production with the screen version of *A Streetcar Named Desire.* "It is a kind of comic-grotesque Mass said in praise of the Male Force," Kazan wrote—a description so apt that Williams himself later adopted it. "Your letter about the play makes it possible for me to go on with it," Williams replied. "I think you see the play more clearly than I did. I have this creative will tearing and fighting to get out and sometimes the violence of it makes its own block. I don't stop to analyze much. I guess I don't dare to. I am afraid it would go up in smoke. So I just attack, attack, like the goat—but with less arrogance and power!" He went on, "You have a passion for organization, for seeing things in sharp focus which I don't have and which makes our combination a good one."

By his own admission, Kazan was then the most powerful director in America. He had successfully mounted the mid-century's three most important Broadway plays—Thornton Wilder's *The Skin of Our Teeth*, Williams's *A Streetcar Named Desire*, and Miller's *Death of a Salesman*; his second film, *Gentleman's Agreement*, had earned him an Academy Award. "Kazan, Kazan / The miracle man / Call him in / As soon as you can" went a bit of Broadway doggerel about his extraordinary prowess.

Gadg, Kazan's benign nickname, invoked his expertise as a handyman, which extended to tinkering with the construction of plots. He had a forensic sense of dramatic structure and how to fix or to finesse those parts of a story that weren't working. In the case of *The Rose Tattoo*, he saw exactly Williams's intention; he also saw his failures. "I do not think the material is organized properly," he wrote. "It is, at any rate, not ready to produce, or to show."

To trap the ineffable, Williams cast a wide, sprawling net. With un-collated pages scattered around him on the floor, from the outside, Williams's way of working *looked* a mess; his early drafts *were* a mess. "Sometimes I can make a virtue of my disorganization by keeping closer to the cloudy outlines of life which somehow gets lost when everything is too precisely stated," he told Kazan, adding, "Thesis and antithesis must have a synthesis in a work of art but I don't think all of the synthesis must occur on the stage, perhaps about 40% of it can be left to occur in the minds of the audience. MYSTERY MUST BE KEPT! But I must not confuse it with sloppy writing which is probably what I have done a good deal of in Rose Tattoo."

Clotted with exasperating Sicilian speech, opaque symbolism, and a main character, Rosario—the womanizing but idealized husband—who didn't do enough to make Pepina's dramatic trajectory either properly comic or compelling, the kitchen-sink version was more morass than mystery. Pepina sounded hectoring, "like a radio turned up too loud," Molly Day Thacher told Williams. Using the outlines of Williams's cumbersome tale, Kazan sketched a new theatrical picture, providing Williams with a way to reconstruct the play that Williams would carry out almost to the letter:

> I think if you start much later in the story and present a woman who is (as they used to say in the twenties) a frozen asset . . . with every hint in the world of the volcanic energy boiling towards freedom within her—why then you will have real suspense to see it break forth. I'd cut out Rosario. He is much more forceful as a memory, as a legend, something she speaks of, and in name of whom she rejects all other men, not only for herself but for her daughter. . . . This way Pepina will have the meaning of a broader idea. All women have within them a volcanic force, and we (civilization) have done everything possible to seal it off, and tame it. . . . In other words I would concentrate, if I were you, on these two very "moral" people: a woman who is apparently just a neighborhood seamstress and a man who is devoting his life to the traditional Italian (and Greek) virtue of supporting his helpless relatives. . . . And this woman, with her urn and the cachet of dynamite below her belt, and how that dynamite is exploded, darn near against her will. . . . And start much later: possibly with the graduation, and an introduction of Pepina as a very proper Seamstress that all the neighboring women . . . look up to. Then you have somewhere to go. . . . There is and should be something COMIC (in the biggest sense of that word: optimistic and healthy and uncontrollable) about the setting, the characters, the appertinences (I don't know how to spell that word) and the effects.

"Consider Gadg's approach with great care—it has certain virtues—it presents certain grave problems to my way of thinking but maybe one can have one's Alvaro and yet eat the memory of Rosario at the same time," Wood counseled Williams in her first full response to the play. In fact, by keeping Rosario an offstage character, Kazan instinctively repositioned the story so that it tapped more deeply into the sense of absence and yearning that was the emotional core of Williams's lyricism.

Although it took Williams half a year to rebuild his story along Kazan's lines, the director's notes laid down a narrative track that Williams immediately found liberating. By the last week of March, he was reporting exciting new discoveries. "I have just now completed what I think is the best scene in any of my long plays, the first scene between Pepina and Alvaro. It suddenly came out of the bushes!" he wrote to Kazan and his wife. "I feel now that I will be able to do what I want to do with this play, that it is only a matter of patience." But in the next few months such moments of composure were rare. The upheavals of Williams's plot were as extreme as his mood swings. "The most violent see-saw of my life!" he wrote to Wood in early April. "For a few days I will be in a state of euphoria, then I will suddenly hit bottom."

On April 11, Williams felt sufficiently upbeat about the rewrites to send the play to "Dame Selznick." "When I think about Irene I don't even ask myself if I like her or don't like her—although I am pretty sure that I do—I just know—without thinking about it—that the woman has demonstrated one of the most extraordinary powers of will, or drive, or vitality—or whatever you call it—that I've ever seen," he wrote to Wood, who had soured on the imperious, bullying producer whom she had once called "Woman of the Year." Williams went on, "That's what I lack and what the rest of us don't have time for and what is, above everything else, most needed to give a delicate play the fortification and care it must have."

Selznick had kept vigilant watch over *Streetcar* in New York. (She owned 12½ percent of it.) She had cosseted the Williams family by sending letters to Edwina and candy to Reverend Dakin. In London, as Williams's emissary on all literary *Streetcar* matters—"I place it, like Pilate, in your hands," Williams wrote to her—she'd kept a beady eye on Laurence Olivier in his lackluster but successful British-debut production. In Williams's mind the question wasn't whether Selznick should produce *The Rose Tattoo* so much as whether the play should be produced at all. On the other hand, Selznick was looking for product. "I simply had to have a play for the 1950 fall season," she recalled in her memoir. In his cover letter, Williams asked Selznick to "be as devastatingly candid as you please. There is no 'icon' left to be 'clastic'!" he joked.

FIVE DAYS LATER, Selznick did as she was told and lowered the boom. "Just hope with me that I am dead wrong, slightly for my sake—and overwhelmingly for yours," she wrote. For Selznick the work that she had waited so eagerly to read was dead on arrival. In fact, *The Rose Tattoo* seemed to defy diagnosis; Selznick wasn't even sure what to call it. "To me, this is not a play but rather a libretto—far more than either, it is a ballet. As presently conceived, it cries out to be danced or sung, or both, in its entirety. It could be painted, but not played. It is all mood and movement—a violent, colorful pattern *for* emotion and lustfulness." Then there was the issue of his new idiom. "The dialogue is at a penalizing minimum (by *you*, a master of words!) and further reduced by the excessive use of Italian." She also felt let down by the characters: "I keep seeking more which is revealing of the leading characters. I do not 'know' them (beyond their passion and Pepina's grief) and I *must*, if I am to be caught up and feel."

"Your letter knocked the goddam bottom . . . and almost the top off me!" Williams told her. Had that thing, Williams wondered, that "eventually happens to most lyric talents, the candle is burned or blown out and there's no more matches," now happened to him? After a dark twenty-four hours of introspection, he went from self-doubt to self-affirmation. "For the first time since this draft was completed, I liked what I had done and felt that I had done just exactly what I had meant to do in all but a few short passages, that in the play, as a whole, I had said precisely what I had wanted to say as well as it could be said, and the play existed," he wrote Selznick, adding, "For the first time in my life I knew that I must take a solitary position of self-belief."

In *The Rose Tattoo*, Williams used behavior and imagery to express a hysterical hauntedness, an internal drama that Selznick couldn't fathom. "Were I to see rather than read the play, I fear I would be at a loss to understand the sources of sustained crisis under which Pepina labors," she had written. Williams argued that the crisis was "fully documented and justified." He was aware, he said, of the "high pitch of emotion in the characters," which "might make exhausting demands on everybody concerned." It was because of this that he had kept his scenes deliberately low-key, so that the expressive burden was borne as much as possible by the visual, instead of the lines. "The great advance I have made in this play—technically, as a theatre-craftsman—is what you call its 'penalizing minimum' of dialogue and the effects which you seem to think are extraneous ornamentation," he wrote.

Even as Selznick was reading *The Rose Tattoo* onboard ship to London for the British premiere of *Streetcar*, Cheryl Crawford, a seasoned producer, was writing to Kazan to ask that he put in a good word for her as a producer for the play. "I don't know if you realize what it would mean to me to do a play by a writer like Ten," Crawford wrote. "Regardless of Irene's having produced 'Streetcar,' I can say, on record, and without being egotistical, that she has never contributed her life and guts to the theatre as I have. She, or her millions, had a wonderful break, but I don't see that that entitles her to another." Crawford continued, "I feel that the matter of my getting the play is such a toss up that if, without prejudice to Irene's character or ability, you could simply tell Tenn that you like to work with me (you do, don't you?) and point out the justice of my statements, THAT IT WOULD HAVE A STRONG EFFECT." She signed off, "Yours, kind of despondently." As it turned out, Crawford was pushing at an open door. With Selznick out of the running and Wood shrewdly greasing the wheels, Crawford was assured the role of Williams's producer. The real problem turned out to be Kazan himself.

J ust before Williams and Merlo sailed for Europe on May 20, 1950, because of film projects with John Steinbeck (*Viva Zapata!*) and Arthur Miller (*The Hook*), Kazan let Williams know that he probably would not be able to fit *The Rose Tattoo* into his directing schedule. On the same day, Molly Day Thacher told Williams what she thought of the play: *The Rose Tattoo*, Thacher said, represented a departure from the human into formalism; the only character she could understand and feel close to in the play was the daughter. Williams replied to Kazan, dating his letter "All-At-Sea, May, 1950." "It is a bad thing that there is only one American director who appears equipped to handle plays in a non-conventional form," he wrote. "I think it is far more important to the theatre to train directors than actors. Now there is you, Danny Mann, [Harold] Clurman and Bobby Lewis and you are the only one of the group that I would feel safe with." On foreign soil, Williams was still at sea. In Paris, he lost his passport; at the last minute, he balked at the plan to travel to England to attend the premiere of *Streetcar* with Vivien Leigh playing Blanche. By his own account, seized by "a grim, nihilistic mood," he "plunged into the anarchistic nightlife that the city has to offer." He also fired off another plaintive letter to Kazan:

> . . . I have never been anything with you but completely honest and completely loyal in thought, word, and deed, and . . . you are the only person in my professional world for whom I have a very deep liking as well as an artistic affinity and the sort of respect that I have only given once or twice before in my life. The rejection by Irene hurt my pride and my confidence but yours goes deeper than that. I know, you haven't worded it like a rejection but that's what it adds up to. I understand about Zapata. The script is finished, it is ready to shoot. In August or September you will do Streetcar. But now you talk about a commitment to a movie-script which is not finished, "not right yet but on the way." Now I think I know Art Miller well enough to know that he would not demand that this film take precedence over my play. Both of us are terribly serious about our work, Art and I, desperately serious about it and we both have a true respect for each other and I don't think he would anymore stand in my way than I in his in making demands on your time. An uncompleted film-script can be scheduled at any time in the future, that is, the shooting of it. The period in which a play can go into production is definitely restricted. So I wish you had not mentioned that as one of the reasons you can't do "Tattoo." It makes it appear that the real reason is somewhere between the lines, which is evasive and not like you at all. I wish we could talk to each other for then I feel, in fact know, that you would make things clearer.

In mid-June, Kazan wrote to reassure Williams and to reiterate his interest in *The Rose Tattoo*. He had instructed Crawford not to engage another director, a bit of encouragement to which Williams was "clutching . . . for all it is worth." Kazan's letter brought tears to Williams's eyes. "Not very manly of me, but still in character, since I have never pretended to have much hair on my chest," he wrote back. "The moisture came from relief, for your letter removed the doubt I had felt about your continued interest in my work and myself. I have too much reserve with people, as a rule, too much doubt and suspicion, but I had thrown all that overboard in my relations with you and had been totally honest and open with you, and something in the apparently cool tone with which you told me you would not be able to do 'Rose Tattoo' hurt me a great deal more than the professional set-back. Now you have dispelled that feeling and we can forget it."

Williams went on to unburden himself about where the story now stood:

> My main concern, now, is to know that you want to do it and to continue my work on it. I feel that the Rosario part is coming richly to life, and perhaps Cheryl has told you that I have a new (alternative) ending which *may* be better than the two women. I know what you'd dislike about the two women. It represents to you a retreat for Pepina. To me it was an advance on a realistic basis. But my objection to it is that it may be just a little bit cliché, a little expected or pat. Maybe that's only because of brooding too much about it. The other ending is really *wild* and it involves the children.—Of course Alvaro can't take the place of Rosario. Does anybody ever take the place of the first great love? What he accomplishes is her escape from the urn of ashes and her reconcilement with life! In the new ending I may go so far as to suggest, symbolically, that she will bear a child by him. I am sure that in playing, the feeling will be one of the affirmative statement, not decadent melancholy, because that is how I have conceived it. But the statement will have to have *pain* in it too.

Kazan, an expert philanderer, knew how to dissimulate and to seduce. He wouldn't commit to *The Rose Tattoo*, but he couldn't seem to let it go.

Even as he was assuring Williams of his allegiance, he was asking the novelist and playwright Irwin Shaw to give him a no-holds-barred second opinion about the play. Kazan was ambivalent; Shaw also had "mixed feelings." "It is not a continuation or an intensification, even," he wrote, comparing the play to Williams's other work. "It is new ore from the same vein, and not quite as rich in quality. The heroine is no Blanche du Bois, neither of the men is a Kowalski. They are single-faced, with the exception of Alvaro, who has overtones of the shnook (a la the character Karl Malden played in 'Streetcar') while representing some of the brutal and, to Tennessee, beautiful core of sex. I got a feeling while reading it that Tennessee had merely juggled a lot of his old characters, mixing parts of one up with parts of another, and leaving out, as was inevitable, the very best things." Shaw added, "It might be a good idea to burn this letter. And, of course, I won't tell anyone I've read the play. And I guess you won't either."

Williams continued to veer between hope and hopelessness. "Please keep after Gadg, and so will I," he wrote Crawford in late June. "I have a feeling that Kazan will like what I am doing in this last version of the play, as he originally said he thought Rosario was better as a memory." At around the same time, he was writing to Oliver Evans, "Kazan is still not entirely sold on the play and as yet I have no assurance that he will consent to do it. . . . Wonder if I should quit writing. But there is only one other thing I like doing very much, and you can't do that *all* the time. Or *can* you?"

By July, Kazan's continued silence was only part of the pall that hung over Williams's holiday, which seemed "infinitely *wrong*." The previous year's apartment had already been rented out; Williams and Merlo found themselves in a cramped, airless flat above a motorcycle garage, whose twelve-hour workdays sounded to Williams's ears "like the battle front in Korea" and made sleep impossible. "Key West seems like heaven in retrospect—the morning energy for work—the cool, sweet rooms—the night rides along the ocean highway," he wrote in his journal. "And Frank's friendliness. That's quite different here. I wonder if I have a single friend left?"

Williams was now not so much drifting as driven. "I have felt like a tired horse at the last high hurdle," Williams wrote to Wood and Crawford in mid-August. He was writing, he added, "by compulsion, not inspiration, and I am afraid that most of the progress I thought I was making was wishful thinking." Adding to the atmosphere of exhaustion was the vexed issue of the forty-two-year-old Anna Magnani, whom Williams always had in mind to play the widow. "The play is hung like a tent on the requirement for a magnificent performance in the part of Pepina. It demands the art of a Laurette Taylor or an Anna Magnani: the one is gone and the other may not speak English! . . . If the miracle of a Pepina comes to pass, I would like the male part to be offered to Marlon Brando," Williams wrote in the introductory note to the kitchen-sink version. Wood agreed. "If we don't get Magnani—where the hell we go from there I have not the remotest idea," she had written earlier in her letter of response to *The Rose Tattoo*.

Just trying to make contact with Magnani was an obstacle course. "Magnani told a friend of mine she was eager to meet me and read the play but she does not answer her phone," Williams wrote to Wood. "She has a new villa in the country and is at present incommunicado with a new lover." Finally, in the dog days of late July, Magnani consented to a tête-à-tête—at Doney, the most crowded of the Roman sidewalk cafés, at the most crowded hour of the day. She was forty-five minutes late, but it was worth the wait. "She has the warmth and vigor of a panther!" Williams gushed to Bigelow. To Crawford, he wrote a week later, "She was looking quite marvelous. She has taken off at least twenty pounds. Her figure is the very meaning of sex. Her eyes and her voice and *style* are indescribably compelling. She dominated the whole street. I was overwhelmed by her." Magnani demanded to read the script. When Williams explained that it was unfinished but offered to show her an early draft, she refused. "She would read only the final one," he explained to Crawford, adding, "At first she pretended not to speak English but after a while she began to speak it, with a clear accent and surprising fluency."

Nonetheless, Magnani was fearful of going onstage before the American public. "For an actor, one's language is like a flag," she told Williams. "In the movie studios, you can repeat a phrase, you can shoot a scene again, there are systems for correcting the sound. At night you know what you did during the day. In the theater, on Broadway, I would be alone in front of a demanding audience." Magnani's extravagant personality came with extravagant terms; she wanted "almost complete control over everything." To grant her this for a theatrical production would have been both impractical and unwise. From their brief encounter, Williams came away feeling that "it would be very easy to get her to do the *picture*," but not the play.

Whatever progress Williams felt he had made by befriending Magnani was stalled on August 12, when "the long dalliance with Gadg" came to an abrupt end. "Tell Tennessee how badly I feel about it, which I do," Kazan wrote to Wood, rejecting the play that his notes had been so crucial in salvaging. Williams gave up the idea of a fall opening. The script, he understood, still needed work. "If Gadg were available it might be worth risking," he wrote to Wood and Crawford, urging them to postpone scheduling the play. "He can do magic with fairly commonplace writing. Who else can? I feel as hurt as you must about his apparent dereliction—not resentful, but undeniably hurt!" As he sailed back to the United States, on September 1, Williams had no leading lady, no director, and, after eighteen months, no final script. "On the sea, returning. To what?" he wrote in his notebook.

"I STILL BELIEVE that the flat stretches in the play will ultimately come to life, that I *will* eventually have a period of real stimulation again when I can do warm, spontaneous work that will suddenly illuminate the script where it is now like dusty glass," he wrote that August. Between September and December of 1950, shuttling between New York, Los Angeles, and Key West, Williams rediscovered both his form and his equilibrium. Like Pepina, he made it through his impasse. James Laughlin, an honest broker when it came to the assessment of Williams's writing, declared himself "very impressed with it in certain ways." "The characters . . . move like veritable express trains through events more dramatic than those in plain and ordinary lives. . . . They are souped up, so to speak," he wrote to Williams, placing the play "in the romantic, not the classical tradition . . . where passion rules and not reason." He went on, "There are fewer of those beautiful poetic lines in this work. You probably know that. You probably intended it. More is done with motion and less with reverie. The wonderful dreaming quality of Menagerie is not here. But there is no reason that it should be. . . . You are breaking here into new ground."

The streamlined final draft of *The Rose Tattoo* had little in common with the kitchen-sink version. Gone were the symbolism, the moralizing, the indigestible Italian dialogue, the unfocused subsidiary characters, the scenic and verbal filigree of naturalism. The storytelling sparkled with a new impressionism, a theatrical shorthand in which Williams's familiar lyricism was not purely verbal but lay in his orchestration of the visual with the verbal. As Kazan had suggested, *The Rose Tattoo* became about the unlocking of the widow's frozen heart. Williams balanced the operatic passion of his widow (now named Serafina) with the tortured awareness of his stalled life, giving the widow a compelling new dimension. As a result, the play became a comic anatomy of Williams's own melancholy. Serafina, her cloistered daughter, and the idealized memory of her faithless husband were all drawn from the bewildering mad scenes of Williams's childhood: his mother's fainting fits, her terrified screams during sex, her Puritan strictures, her delusional grandiosity, his sister's knife-toting desperation and frustrated carnal longings, his father's womanizing, and his own incarceration in a grief-struck house were motifs rewoven into the final tale.

Serafina's second chance at life, with the uncouth Mangiacavallo, was also a slapstick simulacrum of Williams's relationship with Merlo. In the name of comedy, Williams steered the final version past heartache to an intimation of wholeness. "The heart should have a permanent harbor, but one that it sails out of now and again," he told Kazan at the time, adding, "Thank God Frank understands about that, and I can still do it sometimes." The play now incorporated both halves of Williams's romantic equation for happiness. Its debate was between Serafina, an ascetic hysteric who splits off from her erotic self and who sexualizes virtue, and Rosa, who fights free of her mother to pursue her carnal desire. "You wild, wild crazy thing, you—with the eyes of your—father," Serafina tells Rosa, when she arrives home from her graduation with her sailor-boyfriend, Jack Hunter, in tow. At the ceremony, in addition to her diploma, Rosa has been awarded "The Digest of Knowledge." For Williams, the royal road to knowledge *was* sexuality—an avenue that Serafina tries to block as much for her daughter as for herself.

Sex is inseparable from a sense of life and of loss. In her morbid isolation, Serafina tolerates neither. For three years, she has locked herself away with her husband's ashes and her daughter. (Rosa's clothes are temporarily stashed away so that she can't go out, and are surrendered only at the last minute so that she can go to her graduation.) Serafina is sexually and psychologically suspended. Her real erotic relationship, Williams makes clear, is with absence. "To me the big bed was beautiful like a religion," she tells the local priest. "Now I lie on it with dreams, with memories only!" She's "a female ostrich," one petulant customer observes in passing. Her abiding passion, it turns out, is a passion for ignorance. Instead of making love, Serafina makes scenes: her "slovenly deshabille," the stage directions read, "is both comic and shocking." She makes a spectacle of her own retreat from life by drawing attention to her grief and to her ghostliness. "Are you in there, Mama?" Rosa asks, calling into her mother's room from the parlor. "No, no, no I'm not," Serafina says from within. "I'm dead and buried!" At the beginning and end of the kitchen-sink version, Williams had imposed a "spectral rose": "Above the tin roof we see again the faint apparition of the rose between two curved hands." Now, instead of this external imposition of the ghostly, Serafina's hauntedness emerges directly from her own hysterical erotic imaginings.

Although Rosario never appears—his death and Serafina's subsequent miscarriage are offstage events—Serafina makes a permanent presence out of his memory. She idolizes Rosario's hair, his chest, his lovemaking; she counts the number of nights—four thousand three hundred and eighty—that they spent together in their twelve-year marriage. "Each time is the first time with him," she says. "Time doesn't pass." Her identification with Rosario takes her to the brink of mysticism. On the day of their second child's conception, she swears, Rosario's rose tattoo appeared on her own breast—with "a pain like a needle, quick little stitches." The tattoo plays as a sort of stigmata—a hysterical manifestation not of Jesus but of her husband, whom Serafina has turned into a kind of household god. When she first lays eyes on Mangiacavallo, she is suddenly seized by a similar kind of supernatural identification. "Serafina stares at the truck driver, her eyes like a somnambule's. All at once she utters a low cry and seems about to fall," the stage directions read. When Mangiacavallo

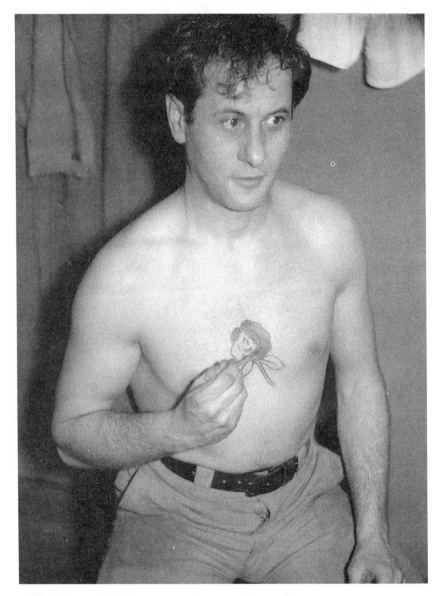

Eli Wallach sporting Alvaro Mangiacavallo's rose tattoo

walks into her life, he is crying over a fracas with a salesman. Serafina starts crying, too. "I always cry—when somebody else is crying," she says.

Mangiacavallo is another of Williams's primitives—a rambunctious handsome man with disarming appetites and a fierce immediacy. As the agent of lightness, and, therefore, of comedy, he is also vulnerable, down to earth, and honest. Unlike Rosario, with his vaunted patrician lineage, Mangiacavallo is spectacularly un-pedigreed ("the grandson of the village idiot," he says) and un-propertied ("Love and affection is what I got to offer"). He is at home in himself—and in Serafina's home. "You are simpatico, molto," he tells Serafina when they first meet. Psychologically speaking, Mangiacavallo is everything that Serafina is not. He flows, she is stuck; he is open, she is closed; she refuses loss, he accepts it as part of the comedy of life. "I like everything that a woman does with her heart," he tells Serafina. Inevitably, as the stage directions instruct, there is a "profound unconscious response" between them. As Mangiacavallo becomes increasingly Rosario's double—he even gets a rose tattooed on his chest—Serafina's atrophied heart is gradually resuscitated. Mangiacavallo's pragmatism punctures her grandiosity. He is present when she learns the name of Rosario's mistress, a blackjack dealer at a local casino, whom Serafina sets off to stab with a kitchen knife. Mangiacavallo literally and figuratively disarms her. Serafina smashes Rosario's funeral urn, then later that night sleeps with Mangiacavallo. But whom is Serafina really bedding? The still-virginal Rosa and Jack, coming home in the early hours from the graduation festivities, overhear Serafina in the bedroom:

SERAFINA: (*from inside the house*) "Aaaaaahhhhhhhh!"
JACK: (*springing up, startled*) What's that?
ROSA: (*resentfully*) Oh! That's Mama dreaming about my father.

The joke, which seems to be on the innocent Rosa, turns out to be on us. In a rubber-legged tableau of lust—"the scene should be played with the pantomimic lightness, almost fantasy, of an early Chaplin comedy," the stage directions say—the Spumanti-swigging Mangiacavallo emerges shirtless from Serafina's bedroom the next morning only to crouch over the sofa and ogle the sleeping figure of Rosa. "*Che* bel-la, *che* bel-*la*!" he whispers on his knees, staring at her "like a child peering into a candy shop window." His whispered words wake Rosa. Her screams at the sight of a stranger set in motion a whole series of farcical effects: Mangiacavallo falls on his back in shock; Serafina enters in her nightgown and lunges at him "like a great bird, tearing and clawing at his stupefied figure."

Despite his protestations of love, Mangiacavallo is driven out of the house. In the ensuing face-off with her daughter, Serafina lies to her ("I don't know how he got in"), which breaks the spell of maternal authority. Rosa understands what's going on; as in all fairytales, disenchantment sets her free. Rosa goes off to find Jack, who is on his way to New Orleans to join his ship, but not before a cruel argument. In the fracas, "abandoning all pretence," Serafina speaks an intimate truth to her daughter. "Oh cara, cara!" she says. "He was Sicilian; he had rose oil in his hair and the rose tattoo of your father. In the dark room I couldn't see his clown face. I closed my eyes and dreamed that he was your father." Although she can't meet her daughter's eyes as she leaves, they give each other their blessings. "How beautiful—is my daughter! Go to the boy!" Serafina tells her. Rosa, as she exits, tells Serafina that Mangiacavallo didn't touch her.

In his notes to Williams about the ending of the kitchen-sink version, Kazan had laid down to Williams what amounted to a theatrical gauntlet. "I was very surprised at the ending," he wrote. "Its main spirit up till then seemed to be in praise of life, and its sensual, undying base. Then comes the two women kneeling and gathering the ashes. That beat hell out of me." At the finale of the kitchen-sink version, Rosario's mistress, Estelle, stands nervously outside the door, returning to tell Pepina that Rosario had broken things off with her on the night he died. By having Pepina beckon Estelle inside the house to join in sweeping up Rosario's ashes—"The urn is broken. Help me gather his ashes, spilt on the floor!"—Williams demonstrated her acceptance of loss and forgiveness. Then, "quietly and gravely as two children gathering flowers, the women kneel together to collect the scattered ashes of Rosario and return them to the broken urn." Spelling out the play he'd like to see, Kazan continued, "It would be a comic Mass then between what man and woman are, and what they have made of themselves. And they sure as hell wouldn't be gathering ashes at the end." In the early version, the widow seems to accept loss, but she doesn't accept Mangiacavallo, who is shooed out the back door and never heard from again.

The play's emotional ambivalence mirrored Williams's own. Throughout much of the play's gestation, Williams was not certain whether he and Merlo had a future either. By the time Williams had finally understood his own story, Merlo was a fixture in his life. Mangiacavallo resuscitates Serafina in much the same humble way that Merlo bolstered Williams: he coaxed Williams reluctantly out of his isolation and into life. Williams's bravura final ending was a daydream of romantic transcendence—an eloquent image that was both an answer to Kazan's theatrical challenge and proof of Kazan's contention that Williams's plays "might be read as a massive autobiography . . . as naked as the best confessions."

For three years, in his "little cave of consciousness," Williams had labored to excavate comedy from his sense of collapse; for three years, struggling in a similar reverie of loss, Serafina buries herself in the shuttered gloom of her sewing room. Both are compelled to rendezvous with ghosts. Serafina's morbid lamentation is a way of keeping Rosario close to her; likewise, in his writing, Williams's habitual reconfiguration of his family and friends was a way of not losing his love objects, who were, as Vidal said, "forever his once they had been translated to the stage." In Serafina's story, Williams materialized the transfiguration he longed for in life. By the finale, she is no longer living in the past but in the moment. (The watch that Serafina meant to give Rosa for her graduation, which had stopped ticking, suddenly starts to work again.) The wind blows Rosario's spilled ashes away, and with it the sump of melancholy. "A man, when he burns, leaves only a handful of ashes," she says. "No woman can hold him."

The loss of Serafina's illusions is symbolized by a rose-colored silk shirt—a totem of Rosario's faithlessness—originally ordered by his mistress and sewn by Serafina with her own cuckolded hands. At the finale, reversing the negative trajectory of the end of *The Roman Spring of Mrs. Stone*, in which the widow invites destruction by throwing her keys *down*, Williams contrives to have the disputed shirt passed *up* to the temporarily banished Mangiacavallo, who is hiding out of sight on the embankment behind Serafina's house. Once an emblem of humiliation, the shirt is transformed into a semaphore of hope. "Holding the shirt above her head defiantly," Serafina throws it to the townsfolk, who rush it up the embankment "like a streak of flame shooting up a dry hill." "Vengo,

vengo, amore!" Serafina shouts, feeling a supernatural burning in her breast that signals to her that she is pregnant. As the curtain falls, she is heading up the embankment toward her new man—she is finally fecund and in motion.

In this last scene, Mangiacavallo is crucially not present; he is an immanence just beyond Serafina's horizon. This absence seems to inspire her passion. Desire, Williams once said, was "something that is made to occupy a larger space than that which is afforded by the individual being." *The Rose Tattoo*, which Williams called "my love-play to the world," was also a keepsake of a unique personal moment in his own life. Throughout the tale, Williams bore witness both to Merlo's liberating presence and to the shadow of autoeroticism in his romantic desire.

THE CASTING OF *The Rose Tattoo* coincided with the publication on September 27, 1950, of *The Roman Spring of Mrs. Stone*. Before the novella came out, Williams told Cheryl Crawford that he was "terribly afraid of critical reactions to the book!" "I am sure they will find it 'rotten,' 'decadent,' Etc. and will revive the charge that I can only deal with neurotic people," he wrote. He added, "My answer to that, of course, is when you penetrate into almost anybody you either find madness or dullness: the only way not to find them is to stay on the surface." After the publication, he was worried by the public indifference. "It comes at a point in my life when I have a need for some confirmation or reassurance about my work's value," he wrote to Laughlin, and sent the relevant portion of the letter to the *Herald Tribune*, one of the most egregious culprits. "The fact that the *Herald Tribune* has ignored it completely, both in the daily and Sunday book-review sections, is the worst sort of slap in the face, not only to this one book, but also, I feel, to all the work I have done, to my whole—*position* is *not* the word I want to use!"

But what was Williams's position? *Streetcar* had been closed on Broadway for nearly a year; the movie version wouldn't be released until the following year. The 1950 season had seen the debut of William Inge (*Come Back, Little Sheba*), the return to form of Clifford Odets (*The Country Girl*), and the premiere of *Guys and Dolls*, whose buoyancy and ambition defined the confidence of the new decade. Williams could be

forgiven for fearing that he had somewhat fallen out of the cultural discussion. "Critical reactions to the novel indicate a downward trend in my
favor with reviewers," he wrote to Wood. He felt himself "at a crucial
point when a failure might [be] final."

Wood had warned Williams that following *Streetcar* would be "a
gigantic task." So it was proving. Williams finally settled on the director
Danny Mann, who was responsible for staging *Come Back, Little Sheba*.
"He has your aliveness," Williams wrote to Kazan. "He is young and daring and says he is ready to rehearse the play as I wrote it and devil take
the hindmost! Why are most people so cautious when the whole scheme
of things is suspended by a single fine blond hair in the beard of God?"
One of Mann's other mots was "'Mood' is 'doom' spelt backwards," which
gave Williams pause. "Probably means that I shall have to put up a fight
for the plastic-poetic elements in the production," he wrote to Laughlin,
noting, however, that Mann was "no fool." Still, Williams had a new producer, a new director, a new leading man (Eli Wallach), and a play that
attempted a new theatrical form. All the more reason, the management
argued, for the box-office insurance of a star in the part of Serafina.

"Would Maureen Stapleton be all right?" Williams wrote to Crawford
in mid-August. "I have never seen her but have heard she is a somewhat
Magnani type." Stapleton was twenty-five, Irish American, and an
unknown who had appeared a couple of times on Broadway. She had
arrived in Manhattan from Troy, New York, at the age of seventeen, weigh-
ing a hundred and eighty pounds, determined to be an actress. By day she
worked as a billing clerk for twenty-nine dollars a week; at night, she studied theater with Herbert Berghof. At the Actors Studio and in a few character roles, she had, with her combination of volatility and vulnerability,
caught the attention of such Broadway nabobs as Guthrie McClintic and
Harold Clurman, whom she credited with planting the idea of her as the
middle-aged Serafina in the mind of Crawford. "Maureen must have been
a victim in her early life of some nameless wound," Clurman once wrote,
responding to the uncanny power of her playing. "To bear it she requires
the escape of acting and the solace of close embrace."

Williams's enthusiasm for Stapleton in her auditions overrode the collective anxiety about her age and her inexperience. According to Staple-

ton, that anxiety resulted in "a World Series of readings." Stapleton and Wallach auditioned together five times. "Finally, I assisted her in 'making up' for a reading," Williams recalled in *Memoirs*. "I had her dishevel her hair and wear a sloppy robe, and I think even streak her face to look like dirt stains. And that reading she gave made all agree that she was the one." "They seemed to want more assurance I could handle it," Stapleton said of her last audition. "I said: 'I can't promise anything. I might really be terrible.'" Williams stood up. "I don't care if she turns into a deaf mute on opening night!" he said. "That to me was extraordinary," Stapleton recalled.

Just before *The Rose Tattoo* company set off for Chicago, where the play opened on December 29 for a month of tryouts, prior to opening on Broadway on February 3, 1951, Williams wrote to his mother and grandfather. "The girl playing the lead is almost as good an actress as Laurette Taylor," he said. "In fact, she is like a young Laurette, which pleases me especially because nobody else wanted to cast her in the part, since they felt her youth and lack of experience would be too great a handicap." He continued, "She has tremendous power and honesty in her acting and I think she is going to put the show over. She is an Irish girl, not pretty in any conventional way and considerably too plump, but she has more talent than any of the leading ladies of twice her age, and half her size. The director is not as gifted as Kazan but he works twice as hard all day and half the night. It is his big chance."

For Williams, it was also a big roll of the dice. *The Rose Tattoo* was, he wrote in one elegant defensive preamble to the play, "the desire of an artist to work in new forms, however awkwardly at first, to break down barriers of what he has done before and what others have done better before and after and to crash, perhaps fatally, into some area that the bell-harness and rope would like to forbid him." In the weeks before the cast set off for Chicago, Williams took in some of the Broadway competition, including what he called "the Caesarean delivery" of John van Druten's *Bell, Book and Candle*, produced by Irene Selznick. Its success gave him pause and also fueled his malice. "It was the most miraculous opening I have yet seen on Broadway," he wrote to Kazan. "Although she had packed the house with her Broadway and Hollywood friends, there wasn't a genuine laugh in the house after the first act. I could amuse myself only

With Maureen Stapleton in rehearsal

by counting the number of times that Rex 'Sexy' Harrison planted his mouth on Lili Palmer's in a fashion so remarkably sexless that it seemed more like a pair of birds dividing a worm between them." He added, "The audience sat entombed in embarrassed silence. . . . The final curtain was jerked up and down like a man of eighty trying to jerk himself off, to the feeble patter of about ten pairs of hands, mine not included.—Then the great celebration at Irene's, climaxed by the reading aloud, the breathless incantation, of Brooks's 'Unqualified Rave!'"

At the opening-night party for *Bell, Book and Candle*, Williams received another rueful jolt. "For some time I have suspected that I am already washed up in the professional theatre," he told Kazan. "Rex Harrison put this feeling into words for me when he responded to my routine felicitations by saying, 'Yes, I think this play shows that the theatre has recovered its health after a recent period of sickness.'" Williams added, "Of course I am a little ashamed of my malevolence, of wishing [Selznick] bad luck . . . but I don't believe that she is at all ashamed of the letter she wrote from London about 'The Rose Tattoo' and I don't think she had any real concern for what it might do to me and what it did. (Spoiled my summer.) I think that my play is going to answer hers. I doubt that it will receive, even from Brooks, as good a notice as she got, but just the same it will contain the answer."

In Key West, less than a week before *The Rose Tattoo*'s Broadway opening, Williams, full of cold medicine and Seconal, sat up in the early hours listening to Merlo breathing beside him. "Four days now, and we will know," he scribbled in his notebook. "It seems like the whole future hangs on it. I mustn't ever again permit myself to care this much about any public success. It makes you little, and altogether too vulnerable. I wonder if I can try to concentrate on becoming a new, free person after this thing is over. It is mostly for Frank's sake that I care. Alone, I could run away from it. But with Frank I will have to face the possible failure more or less squarely. God be with us!" Williams added, "P.S. What do you think is going to happen?—*I don't know!!*"

CHAPTER 4

Fugitive Mind

Once Kazan and I were a perfect team.
— TENNESSEE WILLIAMS to Bill Barnes

"Now that the waiting is over, I can tell you that I was scared out of my wits," Williams wrote to Brooks Atkinson about *The Rose Tattoo* on February 5, 1951. "I knew that a sense of defeat at this point might have been altogether insurmountable." He added, "I feel invited to go on working for the theatre, and that is an invitation that I am only too eager to accept."

Although the *New York Post* condescended to Williams ("intermittently satisfactory"), the *New York Journal-American* brushed him off ("Play Isn't Worthy of the Fine Acting"), and the *Daily Mirror* more or less told him to pull up his socks ("We believe that the world today needs moral affirmation and not negation"), Atkinson, the most literate and fair-minded daily critic at America's most influential newspaper, the *New York Times*, was the person whose endorsement meant the most to the playwright and the producers. "His folk comedy about a Sicilian family living on the Gulf Coast is original, imaginative and tender," Atkinson wrote. "It is the loveliest idyll written for the stage in some time. . . . The respect for character and the quality of the writing are Mr. Williams at the top of his form." Later, in a more reflective follow-up piece, Atkinson observed, "Behind the fury and uproar of the characters are the eyes, ears and mind of a lyric dramatist who has brought into the theatre a new freedom of style."

The narrative advances of *The Rose Tattoo* were not the only news generated by the play; it also made stars of both Eli Wallach and Maureen Stapleton. (They, along with the play itself and the set design, won Tony Awards.) "If I keep working on it maybe I'll improve," Stapleton told

Brooks Atkinson, the influential drama critic of the *New York Times*

the *Times* in her first interview about the play. "Every time I open my mouth onstage, I seem to see people looking at each other and saying, 'This is no Magnani.'" Stapleton's combination of forthrightness, exuberance, and insecurity made her, over the years, a darling of the press, of the public, and of Williams, who called her "Maw" (she called him "Paw," a nod to the outlandish Mr. and Mrs. Kettles of screen comedy). At the outset, however, her freewheeling interpretation irked Williams, who tried, in his courtly way, to correct some of her "improvements" on the script. A day after her *Times* interview, just two weeks into the Broadway run, he wrote Stapleton a gossipy letter from Key West that praised her gift of gab ("You are good at public relations"), dishing Carol Channing ("She started giving me the needle. What is your name, how did you get it, how did you get that accent, my husband never heard of you. On that last remark, I got up and said, My wife never heard of you neither!"), and strategically slipping her his notes:

> I hope that you are "concentrating"—and making all the right "adjustments." The last time I saw you I only caught the last scene. You got some bad laughs on the stigmata bit. I think it was lack of "concentration" that did it. On the "ecco la comica" bit you seemed to be cross with the ladies. That is a wrong "adjustment." The right adjustment is one of *exultant* defiance—*exultant!* The way that the lone survivor of a fortress would brandish a flag in the teeth of too many assailants!— Wait for the tympani. Then get the stigmata with great *definition*, so that one really knows what and *when* it occurs!—You have great power to control your audience and you should never fail to exert it.

Although Williams claimed to Cheryl Crawford that putting on *The Rose Tattoo* had been his "happiest experience in the theatre so far," and that it was "the first time I have ever felt at home with a cast in the theatre," he kept a cold, clear eye on his show. And he continued to be distressed at Stapleton's attack on the role. "I am a little vexed by Maureen's attitude toward continued work on the staging," he wrote to Wood in March. "She knows we have to put up a fight for this play and she ought to be more than willing to make a real effort." He added, "Confidentially, I think if the show goes on the road we ought to give serious consideration to the idea of getting Judith Anderson, not only for box-office draw but for professional attitude toward work. *Talent is not enough, even in the young!*"

"This play *was* a radical departure," Williams wrote to Atkinson in his thank-you note for *The Rose Tattoo* review. To the Theatre Musicians Union, whose feather-bedding threatened to eliminate the use of music from the struggling production, Williams adamantly set out the nature of his theatrical innovation. "Modern creative theatre is a synthesis of all the arts, literary, plastic, musical, Etc.," he wrote. "'The Rose Tattoo' is a notable case in point since I think it has gone further than any recent legitimate American drama to demonstrate this fact." Privately, however, Williams feared that the Broadway production gave "only the barest glimpse" of what the play could have been, as he noted in an essay contemplating its adaptation as a film.

> Consequently many people missed altogether what was most original and distinguished in the play on paper. Many of the audience and critics had the mistaken idea that the community life, the Strega, the goat, and crowd scenes and the activities of the children were meant only to fill in and distract the eye. Very few seemed to realize that all of these were an integral part of the artistic conception of the play, that this was a play built of movement and color, almost as much as an abstract painting is made of them. This is arty talk. But what I am talking about is not "artiness" but something very rich and alive and universally appealing. . . . "The Rose Tattoo" should have been a riotous and radiant thing but the spatial limitations of the stage and the limits of time, etc., put it into a straight-jacket and only about two-thirds of its potential appeal came through.

Nonetheless, despite the mixed reception of the Broadway production, Williams could put his feet up on the railings of his Key West porch and relax with some satisfaction. "If it had been a smash hit like 'Streetcar' or a dismal failure like 'Summer and Smoke,' it would have been, either way, bad for me," he told Irene Selznick. "As it is, I think it provides what is always most essential, a bridge to the future."

The future, it turned out, was looming. In the eighteen months that it had taken Williams to bring his play to completion, the Soviet Union had acquired the atomic bomb, Mao Zedong had declared the formation of the People's Republic of China, and the Korean War had begun. "The big Chinese Red offensive in North Korea"—a rare political allusion—made its way into his story "Two on a Party," as a signal not of international threat but of sexual thrill. "Trade is always best when the atmosphere of a city is excited," Williams wrote, adding, "Anything that stirs up the whole population makes it better for cruising."

Williams could run from history, or trivialize it, but he could not avoid it. The world was "lit by lightning," which flashed across even Williams's backwater paradise. "Dakin, my brother's, number has come up again in the draft, although he did four years in Burma and India and lost most of his hair from malaria," Williams wrote to Stapleton, on returning, after the opening of *Rose Tattoo*, to Key West, where all his family were in temporary residence. "Mother is so upset that she fell down on the street. Grandfather was walking with her and came home alone and said, Your mother fell down. You had better go get her. She was still sitting at the side of the road when Frank picked her up with the car. She was not too seriously injured to eat a big 'Shore Dinner.'"

Cold War suspicion was the unmooring undertow beneath the placid surface of 1950s America. The new foreign war, the policy of containment abroad, and the purge of so-called subversive elements at home were the shadows that offset the glow of America's booming economy. Although it was true, as Kazan said, that politics was not Williams's "game," he had a clear perception of the toxic political landscape around him and its epidemic of fearmongering. "It is part of Nixon's job to show that if Americans want to rid themselves of Communism and *left-wingism* at home, they must throw the Democrats out," Williams, quoting a recent issue of *Time* magazine, wrote to Kazan. Nixon, he said, reminded him of the grade-school bully who "used to wait for me behind a broken fence and twist my ear to make me say obscene things." He continued, "Out in the open at last: the sneaking raid on all liberal thought and feeling under the transparent pretext of stamping out reds."

The growing national obsession with Communism was also a measure

With Edwina

of the country's insecurity about its new abundance, which had broug ht "the bright idea of property" within range of more citizens than ever before. Fueled by the single greatest rise of individual wealth in world history, the middle class grew to include 60 percent of Americans. In the same period, thirteen million new homes were bought; the number of two-car families doubled; and the nation, which was home to only 6 percent of the world's population, was consuming a third of the world's goods and services and producing two-thirds of its manufactures. The suburbs mushroomed; food and hotel chains spread. The increase in consumption led inevitably to a homogenization of taste; a pall of sameness settled over the land. In this, television had a seismic effect. Madison Avenue's total television billings were $12.3 million in 1948; by 1951, the figure had ballooned to $128 million. In 1949, Americans owned about one million television sets; by the end of the next decade, forty-eight million people did. They watched, on average, six hours a day. "Radio was abandoned like bones at a barbecue," the comedian Fred Allen quipped. In a real, as well as a symbolic way, society had become spellbound.

"It was a bad time to be very young, a bad time to enter the early chapters of your life, bad for curiosity or the impulse to explore," the journalist and film critic Nora Sayre wrote in her memoir *Previous Convictions*. "You heard a lot about fitting in; molds were awaiting you: professional molds, marital molds, ways of comporting yourself so that others would not think you were peculiar." This conformity did not go unnoticed by Williams. "Do you realize that there is scarcely a newspaper, magazine, radio or TV station or cinema in the whole country that doesn't represent practically the same old tired, blind, bitter and desiccated attitude toward life?" he wrote to Margo Jones in December 1950. "The Big Time Operators are all one guy and those are the qualities of him." The Broadway theater, which, more than any other art, survived by accurately reading the public mood, registered the new climate with an unmistakable tameness. "A lizardic dormancy seems to be upon us," Arthur Miller complained in the *New York Times*. "The creative mind seems to have lost its heat."

Williams, in his romantic rebellion, was always pitched against the restrictions of conformity: like that of the promiscuous characters in his story "Two on a Party," his existence was "a never-ending contest with the squares of the world, the squares who have such a virulent rage at everything not in their book." Williams, who had known rejection as a child, styled himself an outcast, a fox pursued by Philistine hounds, "calling the pack to follow / a prey that escaped them still." In his work and his life, he embraced the eccentric; tolerance was the flip side of his detachment. On his fortieth birthday, March 26, 1951, for instance, he attended a Broadway production of *Romeo and Juliet* in which the thirty-four-year-old movie star Olivia de Havilland played the thirteen-year-old Juliet. He was joined by the poet and professor Oliver Evans (on whom he based Billy, the lush in "Two on a Party"). At one point, late in the show, as de Havilland came downstage to deliver her soliloquy, the drunken Evans shouted up at the stage, "Nothing can kill the beauty of the lines!" then stalked out of the theater. Back in Key West, Williams wrote to Evans about his behavior. "One of the very few advantages of being my friend is that the point at which I become seriously offended, or even surprised, however moderately, is hard to reach," he said.

Gore Vidal, contemplating "a fermenting new world" of the fifties in his novel *The Golden Age*, cited *A Streetcar Named Desire* as one of its bellwethers: "When she was taken away at the end, barbarism—'the apes,' as Blanche had called the Stanleys of this world—had triumphed. Was this a warning or a prophesy?" he wrote. From where Williams sat, in Key West in the spring of 1951, that barbarism was already at his back door. "The town has changed much for the worse," he had written to Cheryl Crawford. "The campaign against 'Bohemianism' still virulent, a spirit of suspicion making you feel uncomfortable when you go out in the evenings, however innocently."

Strange things were happening in the rest of the country as well. In Indiana, wrestlers were required to sign loyalty oaths; in Ohio, Communists were declared ineligible for unemployment benefits; in Tennessee, anyone seeking to overthrow the state government faced a death penalty. The crusade for conformity extended to the gay world, with its perceived subversive and "degenerate" power. (The press dubbed what it saw as a cabal of powerful gay artists working to undermine the moral fiber of American life "the Homintern"—an invocation of the Soviet-sponsored Comintern.) In D.C., the police set up a special unit of the vice squad "to investigate links between homosexuality and Communism." "I would not say that every homosexual is a subversive," Nebraskan Senator Kenneth Wherry said in 1950. "And I would not say that every subversive is a homosexual. But a man of low morality is a menace in government, whatever he is, and they are all tied up together." Other senators were not so politic. "If you want to be against McCarthy, boys, you've got to be a Communist or a cocksucker," Senator Joseph McCarthy, the browbeating figurehead of the nation's reactionary delirium, told reporters. "The anti-fag battalions were everywhere on the march," Vidal explained. "From the high lands of *Partisan Review* to the middle ground of *Time* magazine, envenomed attacks on real or suspected fags never let up."

But it was in the swamps of the tabloid press that the bigotry festered. Walter Winchell, in his popular columns, for instance, regularly referred to "limp-wristers" and "whoopseys"; another Broadway pundit, Dorothy Kilgallen, declared it "time for TV to switch from switch-hitters." In 1951, *Washington Confidential* broadcast fears of America being "feminized";

the corruption, it gleefully reported, extended to the U.S. government, "more than 90 twisted twerps in trousers had been swished out of the State Department." (Even Alfred Kinsey, who wrote Williams after publishing his pioneering Kinsey Report, which lifted the lid off the hypocrisy of American sexual practices, couldn't bring himself to write the word "homosexual." According to David Halberstam, Kinsey "was prudish enough to keep the interviews that his staff did on homosexuality under a file that was known as the H-histories.") Homophobia extended even to such popular New York watering holes as the Plaza's Oak Room and P.J. Clarke's, which discouraged gay patronage by allowing at the bar only men who were escorting women.

This public mood so infected Key West that Williams contemplated selling his first, and only, home. "Fortunately property values are thought to be increasing," he told Crawford. "Although I paid too much for this house, I may be able to get rid of it without much loss—if the present atmosphere continues, which I suppose it is bound to do, or even increase—in the event of a war." Still, he clung to his identity as an outsider. Soon after returning from the opening of *The Rose Tattoo*, he packed off his mother and Dakin to St. Louis. He joked to a friend, "You can't run a Puritan and a Bohemian household under a single roof and expect the roof to stay on."

A few months later, after Atkinson had noted with pleasure, in his follow-up piece on *The Rose Tattoo*, the elimination of a controversial moment from the production in which Mangiacavallo accidentally drops a condom on the floor, Williams wrote to Atkinson about "the unmentionable article." "I would have removed it at once if it had not, somehow, failed to strike me as being at all vulgar, even though I knew it seemed that way to many people," he said, adding, "Bohemianism seems to take such a strong hold on someone from a background so intensely Puritanical as mine was, once it is broken away from. Then I am always wanting to say and do things in a play that are not ordinarily done, to make it closer to common experience, to prove, at least to myself, that there is nothing in experience that cannot be admitted to writing." In a subsequent letter to Atkinson, an exercise in special pleading written in April 1953, Williams returned to the theme of bohemianism, though now with a hint of hysteria brought on by the vicious and vituperative times he'd endured in the interim:

> I must tell you that I have lived in "the lower depths," which are a large strata of society, have fought my way only partially up out of them, and my work is a record of what I have seen, heard, felt and known on the way. I have known intimately a world haunted by frustrated and dreadful longings. ("Keen for him, all maimed creatures, deformed and mutilated! His homeless ghost is your own!") I have even spent nights in southern jails—wrist handcuffed to ankle and made to crawl—and seen negro women kicked and bludgeoned up and downstairs because the circumstances of their lives had turned them to prostitution, I have

With Paul Bigelow and the fleet

lived intimately with the outcast and derelict and the desperate and found in them the longing, passionate, and bravely enduring, and, most of all, the tender. I have tried to make a record of their lives because my own has fitted me to do so. And I feel that each artist is sort of bound by honor to be the voice of that part of the world that he knows.

Williams's letter to Atkinson, like his dramatic writing, was a calculated seduction, a way of using his heightened suffering to capture the imagination of the other. ("I have probably exhausted your patience now," he signed off. "But I hope I have not yet forfeited your friendship!?") For the hidebound section of the American community that feared contamination and clung to the bedtime stories being peddled in popular entertainment, the psychic romance of Williams's plays was viewed as a poisoned chalice.

WHILE WILLIAMS TRIED to cut down on both his drinking and his work routine in the Florida sun, the making of the film version of *A Streetcar Named Desire* brought into even bolder relief the battle that was being fought over America's cultural narrative. Hollywood had reinvented America as Superbia—a God-fearing, family-oriented land of blessing, where right and wrong were clear, progress was certain, and goodness prevailed. Williams's sense of moral order was not so doctrinaire. In his worldview, life couldn't always be repaired or people redeemed. He considered himself a romantic pessimist; optimism was not part of his narrative bargain. (When asked once about the secret of happiness, Williams answered, "Insensitivity, I guess.") With its complex view of human appetite and its pessimistic view of human nature, *Streetcar* challenged received opinion; inevitably, it forced out into the open the reactionary views of the power elite.

In 1934, in the name of civic responsibility, Hollywood created a Production Code Administration (PCA), headed by Joseph Ignatius Breen, through which the industry imposed its own unofficial form of censorship. Williams had his first skirmish with the PCA over the final cut of *The Glass Menagerie*. Breen's office suggested that Tom's last, elegiac lines— "Oh Laura, Laura, I tried to leave you behind me, but I am more faithful than I intended to be!"—implied incest and should be cut. In a rage, Williams wrote to the film's producers about "the foul-minded and utterly stupid tyranny" of the PCA. "The charge is insulting to me, to my family, and an effrontery to the motion-picture industry!" he railed. "I think you owe it to motion-pictures to defend yourselves against such prurience . . . by fighting it out with them." Williams added, "If I ever work in pictures, in America, I must know that my work is not at the mercy of the capricious whims that seem to operate in this office."

Now, the PCA rose again. As the epigram from Hart Crane announced, *Streetcar*'s ambition was "to trace the visionary company of love"; its truth was uncompromising and complex. The Breen office's self-proclaimed mission was to serve public taste, not truth, to ensure that "correct standards of life" were represented on the screen. "The stage got a shock from Tennessee Williams. We got twice the shock," Breen's assistant Geoffrey Shurlock said. From the outset, Kazan and Williams had thrown down the gauntlet. Kazan had been particularly combative. On April 27, 1950, he told the PCA operative Jack Vizzard, who thought the script "sordid and morbid," that "this story and this script are completely moral. . . . It ran two years and family after family came to see it." Unpersuaded and undaunted, the next day the PCA issued a report that outlined three problem areas: the "sex perversion" in regard to Allan Grey, whose discovery *in flagrante* and subsequent suicide haunt Blanche; Blanche's sexual avidity; and Stanley's rape of Blanche.

Williams spent a fortnight in Hollywood, at six thousand dollars a week, revising the screenplay, but the concessions he made were not enough. The primary sticking point was the rape scene. The PCA was prepared to let the implication of rape stand and to allow Blanche to sink into dementia afterward, but required that Stanley vigorously denounce the charge and prove his innocence. "The device by which he proves himself is yet to be invented," the PCA acknowledged. Jack Vizzard contacted both Williams and Kazan by phone to inform them of the PCA's conclusions. "The results were highly unsatisfactory," Vizzard reported. "Mr. Williams actually signed off in a great huff, declaiming that he did not need the money that much, and Mr. Kazan had to continue the second telephone call with a little more sobriety and temperateness than the writer."

In late May 1950, during a meeting at Warner Brothers with Joseph Breen in attendance, both Kazan and Williams threatened to quit if the rape scene was cut. "I only want to do this script if it can be done honestly and I don't want to do another story or a different story," Kazan said, according to notes taken at the meeting. "We think it has things which are pure and moral and are the very essence of the story and we have no intention of [making the cuts]. We will stop right here," he added, before storming out with Williams. The argument had not been resolved by the time the scene was scheduled to be shot in early October 1950. Kazan told the PCA that he would improvise a solution on the set. "If Mr. Kazan's solution was one of those fence-straddling devices which would let the scene be interpreted either way—either as a rape, or not—it probably would not be satisfactory," Vizzard told Breen, according to a written record of their conversation. "If protection shots were going to be taken, one should be made which would prove *affirmatively*, by any device they wished to invent, that a rape did *not* take place." As R. Barton Palmer and William Robert Bray wrote in *Hollywood's Tennessee: The Williams Films and Postwar America*, "In effect, Breen was asking Kazan and Williams not only to modify but to reject explicitly in the film version, the scene that, more than any other, had made the Broadway play a notorious, national sensation."

The brinksmanship continued throughout the shooting of the picture and into its editing. On October 29, 1950, Williams petitioned Breen directly by letter: "The rape of Blanche by Stanley is a pivotal, integral truth in the play, without which the play loses its meaning, which is the ravishment of the tender, the sensitive, the delicate by the savage and brutal forces in modern society. . . . 'A Streetcar Named Desire' is one of the truly great American films and one of the *very few* really *moral* films that have come out of Hollywood. To *mutilate* it, now, by forcing, or attempting to force, disastrous alterations in the *essential truth* of it would serve no good end that I can imagine." Williams went on, "When we have our backs against the wall—if we are forced into that position— *none* of us is going to throw in the towel!"

In the end, through the judicious use of close-ups, crosscut images of a shattered mirror, and a fire hose gushing water, the film conveyed the idea of rape without actually showing it. Kazan preserved Williams's

Marlon Brando and Vivien Leigh on the Hollywood set of *A Streetcar Named Desire*

poetry and his sensationalism; he saw this act of conversion as a commercial victory. "The thing that makes this piece great box office is that it has two things," he wrote to Jack Warner while completing the final edit in early 1951. "1) It is about the three F's. 2) It has class. No person who tries to keep in any kind of step can afford to miss it. Both are equally important. What made it a Pulitzer Prize winner—the poetry—must be kept in, untouched so that it will appeal to those who don't want to admit that they are interested in the moist seat department. (Everybody, of course, is!)" He concluded, "This is the only picture I ever made that I'm completely proud of."

The Breen office may have lost the battle; in an essential way, however, it won the war. In exchange for allowing the rape, Breen got agreement that "Stanley would be 'punished' and that punishment would be in terms of his loss of his wife's love. In other words, that there would be a strong indication that she would leave him." The bulk of Williams's story was preserved; the meaning of *Streetcar*'s ending was not. In the play, Stanley lies to Stella about the rape, and she decides to believe him. Blanche is sacrificed to the continuity of Stanley and Stella's sexual and family life. This preserving lie, and their collusion in it, is embodied in *Streetcar*'s final image, in which Stanley sits on the stairs beside Stella, who holds their child and sobs. "Now, honey. Now, love. Now, now, love," Stanley says, "voluptuously, soothingly" as his fingers unbutton her blouse. "The luxurious sobbing, the sensual murmur fade away under the swelling music of the 'blue piano' and the muted trumpet," the stage directions read. As the image of the Kowalskis' kingdom of self fades out, Stanley's poker-playing friends fade in. The play's last words—"This game is seven-card stud"—underscore its sexual ruthlessness. The game of life goes on at all cost; the driving force of passion includes a passion for denial. In the finale of the film, however, righteousness replaces selfishness, and the anarchy of desire is banished. "Don't you touch me," Stella says to Stanley, "shrinking from him," as she goes back to where her baby lies in his carriage. As Stanley yells her name, according to the screenplay, "Stella looks down at the infant. Crying, she whispers to the child these words of promise and reassurance:

STELLA: We're not going back in there. Not this time. We're never going back. Never, never back, never back again.
And then Stella turns and proceeds with strength and confidence up the stairs to Eunice's apartment.

Although this change ensured the PCA's rating of "acceptable," the Legion of Decency, a Catholic watchdog organization, whose self-proclaimed concern was "the primacy of moral order" but which had no statutory rights of censorship, objected to something much thornier and more fundamental in Williams's play: the erotic charge of the flesh. The sizzle of Stanley and Stella's coupling, not the brutality meted out to Blanche, was what threatened *Streetcar* with the Legion's C (Condemned) rating. "Joe, a very strange thing has happened," Vizzard wrote to Breen, after being tipped off about the Legion's complaints. "In concentration on our two leading characters, with whom most of the problems lay, we completely missed what this bastard Kazan was doing with Stella . . . the lustful and carnal scoring they introduced into the final print underscores and highlights what were mere subtleties and suggestions in a way I never thought possible." He continued, "The result is to throw into sharp relief in the finished film the purely lustful relationship between Stella and Stanley, that creates a totally different impression from the one we got when we saw it. . . . It makes it a story about sex—sex desire specifically— and this is the quintessence of the objection by the Legion."

Warner Brothers panicked. At the rumor of the Legion's disapproval, Radio City Music Hall canceled *Streetcar*'s grand opening. The studio imagined pickets, yearlong boycotts, and priests stationed in lobbies taking the names of parishioners who attended. "When you speak of the primacy of moral values, my only question is: WHOSE?" Kazan wrote to the Legion's spokesman, Martin Quigley, in August 1951, a month before the film's release. "My only objection is to a situation in which, regardless of motive, the effect is the imposition of the values of one group of our population upon the rest of us. This limits one of our fundamental American rights: freedom of expression." Kazan added, "This, to my way of thinking, is immoral." Quigley, who was an editor of a motion-picture trade paper and a Catholic with strong personal ties to Cardinal Francis Spellman, the Archbishop of New York, fired back, "You asked *whose* moral values I am talking about. I refer to the long-prevailing standards of morality of the Western World, based on the Ten Commandments— nothing, you see, that I can boast of inventing or dreaming up. . . . I have the same right to say that the moral consideration has a right of precedence over the artistic consideration as you have to deny it."

In an attempt to do an end run around the Legion of Decency, Kazan made a proposal to Jack Warner. Since the Legion had publicly argued that it was imposing its rating only for the protection of its flock, Kazan argued that the studio "should take them at their word." His idea was to open *Streetcar* in two different New York theaters: one showing the "condemned version" for the general public and the other showing an approved Legion of Decency version for Catholic audiences. "Think about it. Aside from everything else, I think it is great showmanship," Kazan wrote to his boss. "I even think some Catholics might sneak in to see the condemned version. I think it would gain you and your organization the respect of 98% of this country, *including most of the Catholics. . . .* I was brought up a Catholic in New Rochelle, New York, went to catechism school for two years, and am very intimately acquainted with nuns and priests. Believe me, *they like everybody else* despise no one so much as the people who knuckle under to them. In that respect they are only human."

Nothing came of Kazan's suggestion, however. Instead, a week before the film's opening, on September 18, 1951, without informing Kazan, Jack Warner dispatched a film editor to New York to carry out twelve cuts suggested by the Legion, which amounted to four minutes of film. "They range from a trivial cut of three words 'on the mouth' (following the words 'I would like to kiss you softly and sweetly') to a re-cutting of the wordless scene in which Stella, played by Kim Hunter, comes down a stairway to Stanley after a quarrel," Kazan wrote in an article on the subject in the *New York Times*. "This scene was carefully worked out in an alternation of close and medium shots, to show Stella's conflicting revulsion and attraction to her husband and Miss Hunter played it beautifully. The censored version protects the audience from the close shots and substitutes a long shot of her descent. It also, by explicit instruction, omits a wonderful piece of music. It was explained to me that both the close shots and the music made the girl's relation to her husband 'too carnal.'" Kazan continued, "Another cut comes directly before Stanley attacks Blanche. It takes out his line, 'You know, you might not be bad to interfere with.' Apart from forcing a rather jerky transition, this removes the clear implication that only here, for the first time, does Stanley have any idea of harming the girl. This obviously changes the interpretation of the character, but how it serves the cause of morality is obscure to me, though I have given it much thought."

In exchange for issuing a B rating, the Legion also insisted that the director's version not be shown at the Venice Film Festival. Outraged by this demand, and buoyed by the film's subsequent commercial and artistic success (it was nominated for Academy Awards in six categories, including Best Director), Kazan refused to let the issue drop. "My picture had been cut to fit the specifications of a code which is not my code, is not a recognized code of the picture industry, and is not the code of the great majority of the audience," Kazan wrote in the *Times* article, blowing the whistle on the studio's perfidy. Decades later, in his autobiography, Kazan recalled the incident and its implications. "The Legion of Decency had acted with a boldness and an openness that were unusual for them," he wrote. "What it meant—and I didn't immediately recognize this—was that the strength and confidence of the right in the entertainment world was growing stronger." The rising power of the Right, with its strategy of secrecy and intimidation, destabilized the cultural atmosphere. "Now an air of dissolution settled everywhere around me," Kazan noted. "From sources I didn't know, mysterious pressures were attacking the professional lives and, as a consequence, so it seemed, the personal relations of many of my friends. . . . Chaos was in the air."

O n May 18, 1951, Williams set sail for Rome. His retreat from America was a measure of his increasing sense of oppression at home. "It seems to me that the very things that make it uncomfortable for you here in the States are the things that make you write," Kazan wrote in a letter criticizing Williams's impulse to flee. "It seems to me that the things that make a man want to write in the first place are those elements in his environment, personal or social, that outrage him, hurt him, make him bleed. Any artist is a misfit. Why the hell would he go to all the trouble if he could make the 'adjustment' in a 'normal' way? In Rome, I'd say, you felt a kind of suspension of discomfort. . . . You are not really Tennessee Williams in Rome. . . . Blanche was a fragile white moth beating against the unbreakable sides of a 1000 watt bulb. But in Rome the 1000 watt bulb doesn't exist. The moth is more or less at home. . . . Whether you like it or not, and in a way, especially since you do not, you should stay here in the States. I think you'd soon have some new plays writing that NO ONE could turn you off."

It was a turbulent time. A month earlier, Julius and Ethel Rosenberg had been sentenced to death for allegedly passing a design for the atomic bomb to the Soviets, and in Korea, the Chinese and the United States were nearing a stalemate on either side of the thirty-eighth parallel. But Williams wasn't interested in making political statements; he worked from the inside out. Politics existed, like most of his relationships, somewhere on the periphery of his work, "a sort of penumbra outside the central mania." His plays wrestled with history only insofar as the contour of the times paralleled his internal drama. Abroad, during Williams's "summer of wanderings," a cold war of an altogether different kind loomed. "Yesterday was the first time in our lives together that I've known him to act like a bitch, and a rather usual one at that," Williams noted in his diary about Merlo's increasing truculence. "Of course there have been 'signs', now, for a number of months, but the resentment, the discontent—whatever it is—and he is still an enigma to me—are more and more exercised and displayed, now even publicly, adding humiliation to confusion, insecurity and sorrow. I can only wonder."

Like all factotums to the famous, Merlo was both needed and unacknowledged; he was trapped between empowerment and alienation. Throughout the rehearsals and the opening of *The Rose Tattoo*, he steadfastly supported the frantic Williams. But anything he did to help Williams only maximized the disparity between them. With the success of *The Rose Tattoo*, which was inspired by and about him, Merlo found it impossible to hide his ambivalence. Williams got the glory; Merlo got the grief. In Key West, before leaving for Europe, he dutifully oversaw the household affairs first for Williams's family, who had struggled with the flu during their stay, then for Rose and her caretaker, who visited. In order to relieve Merlo of some of his ever-increasing responsibilities, Williams hired the unflappable Leoncia McGee as cook and housekeeper, a position she held devotedly until Williams's death, in 1983. (Leoncia, Williams wrote, "makes the foulest coffee that ever made a man take to drink! It seems to be a distillation of volcanic ash. Tastes horrible but is so strong it blows your lid after the first dreadful swal-

With Merlo, *Vogue* session, 1949

low.") But Leoncia's presence in the eccentric ménage left Merlo even more restless; losing his daily chores, he also lost part of his identity. He now had no purpose. He was both the beneficiary of Williams's largesse and its captive. The glamour of their life—the famous friends, the exciting events, the travel—was to Merlo both a pleasure and a perpetual reminder of his own powerlessness. Inevitably, he kicked against his golden cage. Neither he nor Williams wanted to understand that his sudden disaffection (which he denied when Williams confronted him about it) was an envious attack on Williams and his writing. By making it hard for Williams to work, Merlo unconsciously was robbing him of some of his power and control.

For part of the summer, Merlo insisted that he and Williams go their separate ways. "He is not at all keen on seeing me at present," Williams noted in his diary on July 25. "It is unfortunate for me that this emotional dislocation had to come at a moment in my life when I most needed someone to give me the security that I used to feel in thinking myself cared for." Williams continued later the same day, "I called F. He made or suggested *no* appointment to meet. I feel as alone as a man must feel at the moment of his death. I know he will never really *say*—I will just have to try to guess what's happened, what I've done, what's wrong between us. I have no home but him. Can I find another? Can I live without one?"

In his letters Williams referred to this period as "the summer of the long knives." Wood had an appendectomy, Oliver Evans had an ear operation, Britneva an abortion, Paul Bigelow had surgery on his jaw, and Williams himself almost ended up on an operating table. In late July, heading from Rome to the Costa Brava, Williams drove his Jaguar into a tree at seventy miles an hour. "I had been quite witless for several days prior to the accident and should not have started out, but I felt that only a change could pull me together," he told Kazan. "So I filled a thermos with martinis and hit the highway." What happened next he recounted to Wood: "About one hundred miles out of Rome I became very nervous. I took a couple—or was it three?—stiff drinks from a thermos I had with me, and the first thing I knew there was a terrific crash! . . . It was amazing that I was not seriously injured. My portable typewriter flew out of the back seat and landed on my head. Only a small cut, no concussion, but the typewriter badly damaged!—Ever since, from the shock, I suppose, I have been very tense."

In Venice, recovering from the accident and "almost panicky with depression," Williams vowed to "be sweet to acquaintances and so to make friends." To get through the nerve-wracking string of evenings he had arranged with Peggy Guggenheim and Harold Clurman and his wife, the actress Stella Adler, Williams drank heavily. By day, he contemplated his loneliness, his self-loathing, and his boozing, adapting his "term in Purgatory" into a story called "Three against Grenada," a meditation on "Southern Drinkers," specifically a young Mississippian of "great vigor and promise," Brick Bishop, who succumbs to alcoholism. (The story, extensively rewritten and retitled "Three Players of a Summer Game," was published fifteen months later in *The New Yorker* and became the basis for *Cat on a Hot Tin Roof*.) Brick's hapless hanging-on mirrored Williams's bewildered mood. "No one noticed Mr. Brick Bishop and he noticed nothing; his eclipse was total," Williams wrote of Brick.

> He falls in love with his liquor with the same heroic abandon that he showed when he fell in love with and courted the girl he married. He loves it as if he had married it or given birth to it, it is his child now and his lover. Everything else disappears behind the comforting veil of his liquor or is seen through it with indifference and dimness, and then from that time on until the incredibly long time afterwards when it does eventually kill him, long after when it should have, in a crash on a highway . . . he seems to be throwing himself away like something disgusting he has found in his hands and has to get rid of as rapidly as he can.

Brick, who takes up residence in the bottom of a glass, embodied Williams's desire for retreat. "The crustacean world for a while!" Williams advised himself in the miserable dog days of July 1951. He was, he said, "drawing the sails of my heart back in, for the wind is against them." "Just taken: 2 phenobarbs, 1 seconal, 1 martini," he noted in his diary a month later. "Now already the magic begins to work. But I know it isn't right, it isn't well, this cycle of sedation." Williams, like Brick, "had not yet completely fallen beneath the axe blows of his liquor"; he was also "not long past his youth, in fact he was still in the further region of it." In the story, Brick is described emerging noisily from a car in order to kick down the "For Sale" sign on a property he has just bought, in defiance of his wife's power of attorney over their financial affairs. The scene inspires a recollection from the narrator's childhood—a childhood that exactly resembled Williams's own:

> I am telling you mostly what I saw out of a window one spring in my childhood when I was recuperating from a long childhood illness which had turned me an ordinary active boy of ten into a thin and dreamy little spectre of a boy who had to depend on girls for companionship. I was like a child in wet weather. I brooded about the house, inventing solitary games, and I spent a lot of time looking out of windows.

Brick's immobility certainly paralleled the creative and emotional still water in which Williams now found himself. Except for the story, Williams "couldn't get going on anything that seemed important" to him. He had been "working, working, working all summer," he confessed to Wood; for much of that time, he felt "like a man trying to run with a sprained ankle."

BY THE BEGINNING of August, Merlo and Williams were cohabiting again; the time apart, however, hadn't lifted Merlo's sour mood. To Williams, he appeared cagey, irritable, and sullen, exuding "all the warmth and charm of a porcupine." "I think the reason the Horse is so nervy and temperamental is that he has absolutely nothing, but NOTHING to do!" Williams wrote to Britneva. "I don't think I could stand another year without him being busy at something, and so I'm going to do everything in my power to get him to go to a secretarial school when we get back to the States. If not that, *both* of us to a good analyst!" Williams saw the problem; his solution, however, missed the point. He figured that the typing of his manuscripts would allow Merlo to share in the work. He didn't understand that Merlo's serving as an in-house secretary would only exacerbate the problem.

In the emotional standoff, Britneva's fierce allegiance—her *"amitié amoureuse,*" as she called it—became increasingly important to Williams, who longed to be kept in mind by someone. When he went to London without Merlo at the end of August, the high-spirited and affectionate welcome he got from Britneva was an answer to his prayers. "Thank God for Maria, if she still likes me," Williams noted in his diary. "I wonder if *anyone* does, and *why* if they do." But even the reunion with Britneva and her "good kind of mischief," as Williams called it, was dogged by fiasco.

On the way to watch a polo match, at the invitation of the playboy the Maharaja of Cooch Behar, Britneva and Williams were part of a caravan of Rolls-Royces that stopped to pick up the actress Hermione Baddeley and her twenty-two-year-old bisexual lover, the actor Laurence Harvey, from her small house in Chester Square. Among the matchgoers was the drama critic Kenneth Tynan, whose gift for limpid description—Britneva, he wrote, was "attractive in a wild sharp-toothed way, like a dashing stoat"—captured in his diary the world of brittle and bewildering folly into which Williams had wandered:

> We entered a small living-room, dark and shuttered despite the hot sun, full of bottles, glasses and party debris. Practical jokes were scattered everywhere, such as ashtrays in the shape of human hands and simulacra of lighted cigarettes lying on satin cushions. Laurence Harvey then staggered downstairs in a dressing gown, obviously hungover, to be introduced to us all and to pour drinks. He was followed by Hermione Baddeley, wearing an egg-splattered kimono. Hjalnar talked continuously; nobody else spoke except Tennessee, who muttered to me: "Do you know any of these people?" I shook my head. So did he. Hjalnar suggested we should leave: Miss Baddeley and Mr. Harvey got dressed; and as we were stumbling through the gloom to the door, Miss Baddeley said dramatically: "Larry—the beards!" "My God, yes," said Harvey and plunged back upstairs.
>
> He soon returned with an armful of long false beards made of crêpe hair and dyed extraordinary colours—green, yellow, purple, orange, puce. Solemnly he distributed them among the party: just as solemnly we hooked them over our ears. This was done without any

New York, 1948

Laurette Taylor, *The Glass Menagerie*, 1945

Laurette Taylor as Amanda, with jonquils

Backstage with set painters, *A Streetcar Named Desire*

Marlon Brando as Stanley and Kim Hunter as Stella, *A Streetcar Named Desire*

New York, 1948

Café Nicholson with (from left to right) Tanaquil Le Clercq, Donald Windham, Buffie Johnson, and Gore Vidal

Key West studio

suggestion of a prank but as if it were raining and he was handing out mackintoshes. "We turn up everywhere in our beards," said Miss Baddeley categorically. Flamboyantly hirsute, we piled back into the cars, and silently sped through the suburbs. As we stopped at traffic lights, people would stare curiously at the bizarre convoy, beards steadily wagging, myself in magenta quietly rabbiting with Tennessee in sky-blue.

At Cowdray Park we disembarked and the chauffeurs produced hock and cold pheasant from the boot. Some of us remained bearded, others did not. . . . All at once there was a scream: "Jesus Christ!" Mr. Harvey had been stung on the lip by a wasp. He danced around in a panic. "Christ, fuck it, I'm *filming* tomorrow and what happens to the fucking close-ups if my lip's swollen up like a fucking balloon?" Miss Baddeley soothed him, procured a bottle of brandy from a chauffeur and retired with him into one of the cars, closing doors and windows and pulling blinds behind them. Outside the car, conversation remained becalmed in the heat. . . . Tennessee became silently drunk. No one had any idea why they were there. My wife and I joined Baddeley and Harvey in the car for some brandy. Harvey was moaning, Baddeley philosophically drinking. Emptying the bottle, she peered through the window and said memorably: "I think I'll pop out for a mouthful of fresh wasp."

Harvey followed her, so noisily in need of medical attention that the kindly Cooch Behar decided we all had better return to London. . . . We climbed back into the cars. My wife and I travelled with Tennessee, Miss Baddeley and Miss [Susan] Shaw; our host went ahead with Hjalnar, Mr. Harvey and Miss Britneva who had already shown, in a number of flashing oeillades, that she had very little time for Mr. Harvey's tantrums.

As we were purring (I think that's the word) past the Albert Hall the leading Rolls drew up at the kerb and Miss Britneva flew out. She ran back to our car, weeping hysterically. Opening the door, she said: "Get me out of here, Tennessee. That shit Harvey has just spat in my face." It turned out that she had interrupted a monologue by Harvey on the subject of his film career to deliver herself of an incisive opinion on the effect of narcissism and megalomania on talent (if any). Whereupon Mr. H., who was facing her on a jump seat, had leant forward and let fly.

"The queen spat in Maria's face and called her the foulest names I've ever heard addressed to a woman by anyone but Pancho," Williams wrote to Merlo. "Of course Maria provoked the quarrel by some untactful remark, called him 'insufferably conceited' to his face." Williams's gossipy letter, which was meant to amuse, put a fine face on his aimlessness. "I've missed you an awful lot, both night and day, and Maria and I talk about you so much," Williams concluded, before adding a false note of ingratiation. "But I think we needed this period away from each other."

Over the next year, as Merlo's withdrawal of affection continued, Williams learned resignation. Like his character Brick, Williams adopted "the cool air of detachment that people have who have given up the struggle." "At times in life there is a big two-letter word that says 'No!' and you must learn how to read it," he admonished himself in his diary. "And if I don't read it and believe and accept it, at least for a while, I'm going to crack in so many pieces you couldn't find one of them!" Williams tried to achieve detachment. "I like being with Frank when he is friendly to me, which is only part of the time," he wrote in his journal on September 16, 1951, shortly after reuniting with Merlo. Two days later, the day that *Streetcar* was being praised by the American press as a contemporary film classic, Williams was being put down by Merlo in Rome. "The Horse is in bed, cross as two sticks—no, as five or six sticks!" Williams wrote to Britneva. "What are we going to do with him?!"

AS WILLIAMS STRUGGLED to distance his heart from Merlo, he began to invest it more in his work. In mid-September, buoyed by the response to *Streetcar*, Kazan contacted Williams about doing a theatrical evening of one-act plays from Williams's collection *27 Wagons Full of Cotton*, which he found "sexy, original and lively," plus *Ten Blocks on the Camino Real*, a recently published one-act play, two scenes of which Kazan had workshopped at the Actors Studio in 1949. With Kazan's rejection of *The Rose Tattoo* still not forgotten by either man, this suggestion of a new collaboration was a deep bow to Williams's talent. It elicited from Williams a deep curtsey in return. "The prospect of another Kazan production is a good enough reason for any living playwright to go on living and *even* return to America," Williams said. "Do you think he can be pinned down?" he wrote to Wood. "He would do a magnificent job and I think success, with him, would be fairly certain."

Of all the writers with whom Kazan worked—Arthur Miller, Thornton Wilder, John Steinbeck, and Archibald MacLeish among them—Williams was the one with whom Kazan, by his own admission, meshed best. The partnership was the most influential in twentieth-century American theater. "It was a mysterious harmony; by all visible signs we were as different as two humans could be," Kazan said. "Our union, immediate on first encounter, was close but unarticulated; it endured for the rest of his life." Kazan and Williams romanced each other. Kazan was "Gadg, baby" and "fratello mio"; Williams was "Tenn, honey." "I always had fun working with Kazan," Williams wrote in *Memoirs*. "Some day you will know how much I value the great things you did with my work, how you lifted it above its measure by your great gift," Williams wrote to Kazan after the first rehearsal of *Sweet Bird of Youth* in 1959. "I have been disloyal to nearly all lovers and friends but not to the one or two who brought my work to life. Believe me. I think I admire and value you more than any one I have known in this profession."

The intimacy of their collaboration owed a great deal to the similarity of their family histories. "Life in America made both of us quirky rebels," Kazan said. By reinventing themselves as artists—by rejecting the mediocrity of their brutal fathers—Kazan and Williams had each fashioned legends of daring. As a young writer, Williams had styled himself a pathfinder and adopted the name "Tennessee" in symbolic identification with his father's "fierce blood" and pioneer lineage. Likewise, Kazan credited his resourcefulness, his enterprise, his appetite for adventure to his Anatolian roots. "I come from a family of voyagers," he said. "My uncle and my father were transients, less from disposition than from necessity. They were slippery, had to be. Raised in a world of memories, they grew up distrustful of fate. 'Don't worry,' my uncle used to say. 'Everything will turn out bad.'"

Kazan's and Williams's suspicion of the world was a deep emotional bond between them. "We both felt vulnerable to the depredations of an unsympathetic world, distrustful of the success we'd had, suspicious of those in favor, anticipating put-downs, expecting insufficient apprecia- tion and reward," Kazan wrote. But the anxiety went further than that. Kazan shared with Williams an unstable metabolism; he too was a "dis- appearer." Although married with four children, he was always at work and on the move; his appetite for freedom was tinged with a sense of paranoia that made Williams's helter-skelter existence completely com- prehensible to him. "The one thing any ambitious outsider seeking recog- nition in an alien society cannot tolerate is to be trapped in an enclosure where the gate is locked and he doesn't have the key," Kazan, who kept bank accounts and complete sets of clothes in three different cities, said. "I've been obsessed all my life with the possibility that flight might sud- denly be necessary."

Kazan and Williams grew up in household atmospheres of danger. Distrust and insecurity were the legacy of their feared fathers, whom, in later years, they regretted not having gotten to know. The eldest of four boys, Kazan recalled himself as a teenager watching from the window while a taxi took his father, George (Yiorgos Kazanjoglou), a rug mer- chant, off to the train station. "The terror in the house lifted," he said. George Kazan, according to his son, "was a man full of violence that he dared release only at home. . . . The possibility that he might blow up at any time kept us all in terrible fear." Where Williams was mocked as "Miss Nancy" by CC, Kazan was humiliated as a "good for nothing" and a "hopeless case" by his father. George Kazan was an Old World patri- arch, oblivious to the needs of others except insofar as they served him. Kazan neither loved nor admired his father, though he shared a special bond with his mother, Athena, whose marriage to George had been arranged when she was eighteen. "We entered a secret life together, which Father never breached," Kazan wrote. "That is where the conspir- acy began."

Kazan's artistic destiny, like Williams's, was dreamed up by his mother, as a kind of joint rebellion against his father's overweening authority. Just as the teenage Williams had done in St. Louis, Kazan lived a kind of underground existence. "I learned to mask my desires, hide my truest feeling," he wrote. "I trained myself to live in deprivation, in silence, never complaining, never begging, in isolation, without expecting kindness or favors or even good luck." He added, "But I learned to keep coming back, to persist. I hardened. . . . I learned to live as an artist lives, empathically, observing, imagining, dreaming, all behind the mask." Convinced that his father "would be opposed to everything I wanted most," Kazan, with help from his mother and a supportive English teacher, applied to a liberal arts college rather than a commercial one. When he was accepted at the prestigious Williams College in Massachusetts, he couldn't bring himself to tell his father, so Athena did. "He hit her smack across the face, knocking her to the floor," Kazan recalled.

At college, where he was virtually friendless and isolated for four years, Kazan's otherness was forcibly impressed upon him. He joined no teams, attended no dances, rushed no fraternities. "I knew what I was. An outsider. An Anatolian, not an American," he said. Surrounded by wealthy Wasps, Kazan's sense of social and sexual inferiority festered. "I wanted what they had: their style, their looks, their clothes, their cars, their money, the jobs they had waiting for them, and the girls they had waiting for them," he recalled, adding, "Every time I saw privilege from then on, I wanted to tear it down or to possess it."

In the thirties, this corrosive longing for revenge led Kazan into an eighteen-month flirtation with the Communist Party; it also fueled his hunger for success. As an actor, he carried his chippie swagger onstage—"'Fuck you all, big and small!' I used to mutter during those years—to myself, of course, secretly," he recalled. Kazan's appetite for vindictive triumph—which drove his compulsive ambition and unrepentant womanizing—was partly rooted in one inescapable fact: Kazan was unhandsome. "Didn't you look in the mirror?" his father asked him when he first announced that he was going to Yale Drama School. His gnarly mug, with its large, jagged nose, telegraphed both his foreignness and his ferocity, and it made a Hollywood film career a nonstarter. Williams also felt blighted by his looks. "He didn't have the kind of physicality to lure," according to his friend, the actress Elizabeth Ashley. "He was one of those people who are more hungry than hungered for. . . . He was uncomfortable in his body. He was always fixing himself. He was always looking for something in the mirror that he knew he was never gonna find."

For Kazan, and for Williams, fame was the best defense against the humiliation of envy. Williams could write the anger out; in his acting, directing, and skirt-chasing, Kazan lived it out. "Women have always meant everything to me," he maintained. "I've never warmed to the so-called masculine virtues; I've lived apart from the male world and its concerns." Kazan related best to men like Williams who had "strong 'feminine' characteristics . . . sympathetic yielding qualities." "Baby, you know as well as I know, that, first of all, we've got to obey the first commands of our hearts," Williams wrote to Kazan about a business matter in late January 1952. "You know that or we wouldn't be so close to each other in spirit." Both men had educated themselves in desire; both saw sexuality as the pathway to knowledge. "Promiscuity for an artist is an education, a great source of confidence, and a spur to work," Kazan said. For Kazan, every woman was an adventure and an inspiration; for Williams, it was every man.

Kazan, like Williams, took a long time to grow into both his carnality and his talent. Directing allowed him to re-create the feeling of conspiracy he had shared with his mother, with whom he was, to use Freud's term, "the undisputed darling." "I wanted to be the source of everything," he said of directing. His rehearsals had, according to Arthur Miller, "the hushed air of conspiracy . . . not only against the existing theatre but society, capitalism—in fact everybody who was not part of the production. . . . People kept coming up to whisper in his ear." His approach to directing was a seduction: quiet, intuitive, penetrating. In his assessment of both the actor's and the character's psychology, Kazan was forensic. He paid his collaborators a kind of intense, strategic attention. In rehearsal, according to Miller, he "grinned a lot and said as little as possible," which had the effect of making his actors compete even harder for his affection. He worked by insinuation not command; stimulation and dissimulation were his twin gifts. "He would send one actor to listen to a particular piece of jazz, another to read a certain novel, another to see a psychiatrist, and another he would simply kiss," Miller recalled. He added, "Instinctively, when he had something important to tell an actor, he would huddle with him privately rather than instruct before the others, sensing that anything that really penetrates is always to some degree an embarrassment. . . . A mystery grew up around what he might be thinking, and this threw the actor back upon himself." Kazan's trick was to make his ideas seem like the actors' own discoveries. "He let the actors talk themselves into a performance," Miller said, which "they would carry back to him like children offering some found object back to a parent." And, like any good parent, when things were going in the right direction, Kazan knew how to stay out of the way.

To Williams, who refused any engagement with his actual father, Kazan was a kind of luminous, empowering father figure. "You are a man of action, Gadg," he wrote to him in 1949. "That is one of the beautiful things about you. You don't just talk and mess around. But translate yourself into dynamics! I wish I could do that." Kazan's straight talk challenged Williams; it set for him both tasks and boundaries. Kazan organized Williams and, figuratively speaking, forced him to clean up his mess. Like all sons of powerful fathers, Williams felt a certain ambivalence toward this authority. He needed Kazan's energy and inspiration; he also resented his intrusiveness. "I am very excited and a little dismayed and quite frightened over the rapid progress for the short plays," he wrote to Wood in October 1951. "He talks of 'work and work' (which sounds like an awful lot of it) but he doesn't say what it is to be, and I have never worked as badly in my life as I have these past few months." He added, "I do hope they don't include a desire to collaborate with me on the script! That is, to take part in the actual writing. On the other hand, Gadg has a very creative mind and he might stimulate me."

Around the time Williams returned to America, in late November 1951, the one-act idea had morphed into two projects. Williams was now expanding *Ten Blocks on the Camino Real* into a full-length play, which Kazan would direct when it was ready. Meanwhile, with the early studio excitement over *Streetcar* filling their sails, Williams and Kazan went full speed ahead on a screenplay based on *27 Wagons Full of Cotton*, tentatively titled *Hide and Seek*, which would become the basis for the movie *Baby Doll*. Feeling that "salvation lies only in new work," Williams wrote to Kazan pleading for literary assistance: "HELP! HELP! SEND ME A

WRITER!" He needed a collaborator who knew the Delta Country. In the end, opting for a bargain-basement solution to the problem, he invited his Maine-born, Cambridge-educated friend Paul Bigelow to join the ménage in Key West and help him with the script. Williams claimed "always to have had a slightly superstitious awe of Bigelow. I think he has magic powers, at least of divination."

Inevitably, Bigelow's stimulating presence and the obvious fun the two men had together—"We laugh our heads off while working," Williams said—disturbed Merlo, who continued to act out his disaffection at home as he had abroad. "F. and Bigelow joined us in bar and we saw a dull strip show," Williams wrote in a February entry in his 1952 journal. "F. took off by himself as usual. . . . I'm a dull boy, have been for a long time. Can't really blame F. for not desiring my company any more. . . . I'll find it hard to sleep tonight. The same old dull tedious resentment and hurt—why do relationships have to be turned into duels. I don't want to fight—I want to trust and love and feel loved. Or at least liked—not barely tolerated—Oh, shit—what's the way out?" He went on, "I do have love in my heart for Frank, which he seems to despise. Why? Because he feels confined by me—his dependence. And isn't reasonable enough to understand that the circumstance was and is his choice. . . . Nothing has changed much—but time goes on. I go on with it still."

Williams threw himself into work; Merlo threw himself into the local social merry-go-round. "Frank has found a crowd he enjoys," Williams wrote to Evans. "They do all the bars at night and he rolls in about daybreak. They're composed of the 'after the lost generation' guys and dolls who live on liquor and 'bennies' and the fringe of lunacy." He went on, "Frank dances wildly with the dolls. Possibly lays the guys. I wouldn't know. I've had a dry run as far as sex is concerned." In one moment of reprieve from that arid time, as Williams was undressing "a gorgeous . . . Adonis from Southern California" on the front-room sofa of the Key West house, Merlo pulled up in a taxi. "There was a real Gotterdamerung to pay!" Williams wrote to Evans, not disguising his pleasure at Merlo's surprising ardor. "Screams, protestations, fury and tears, winding up with Miss Merlo in her most becoming position on the living-room carpet and me wondering if Miss Southern California would be game for a second try under more discreet circumstances!—after being denounced as the whore of Babylon." Williams added, "I must say that Miss Merlo, when she is in a rage, pays very little attention to inequalities of size between her and the opponent."

To his friends, Williams struck a pose of defensive nonchalance. "Frankie is having himself a ball," he wrote to Crawford. "I'm just a bit cross about it, but he is like a kid at play and somebody ought to be having a good time in this sand-lot even if it can't be me." But in this fractious time his poems about Merlo were wistful, almost heartbroken. In "A Moment in a Room," for instance, he wrote:

> Coarse fabrics are the ones
> for common wear,
> the tender ones are those
> we fold away.
>
> And so I watch you quietly
> comb your hair.
> Intimate the silence,
> dim and warm.
>
> I could but do not break
> a thing so still,
> in which almost a whisper
> would be shrill. . . .
>
> For time's not cheated by
> a moment's quiet,
> the heart beats echo to
> eternal riot . . .
>
> But while it waits, I speak not
> false to you,
> something unspoken in
> the room is true,

And still it goes as though
it longed to stay,
this tender moment we
must fold away.

The year 1952 was a turning point for the country, as well as for Williams. On January 14, while Williams was at work on *Hide and Seek*, Kazan made the first of two appearances in front of the House Committee on Un-American Activities (HUAC). At this closed session, he refused to give names. "I decided to look the other way until forced," he recalled. In the meantime, he concentrated on *Hide and Seek* and the upcoming Academy Awards. *Streetcar* had been nominated in twelve categories: best picture, director, actress, actor, supporting actress, supporting actor, screenplay, art direction, cinematography, costume design, and music. "We made a clean sweep," Kazan wrote Williams on February 14. "I have a hunch, though, that 'A Place in the Sun' is going to get it because it's much more in the pattern of the way those people think. Why I don't know." Two days later, the Committee demanded that Congress punish espionage against the United States in peacetime as well as in war; it also took the film industry to task for not acting "with sufficient firmness to weed out Communists." Williams finished the screenplay for *Hide and Seek* on February 19; on March 7, he noted in his diary, "everyone seems pleased with the film script."

Prior to the Academy Awards, on March 20, Williams and Kazan met in Hollywood to pitch *Hide and Seek* to Warner Brothers and to do some politicking for *Streetcar*. Just as they arrived in Hollywood, however, news of Kazan's former affiliation with the Communist Party broke in the newspapers. Williams and Kazan, the two theatrical powerhouses of their time, could not make a deal. "Warner's stalled us with a lot of censorship objections and demands for revision without any signed contract," Williams told Crawford.

Hollywood lived and died by pleasing the public; the Red Scare petrified the industry. "Almost immediately that put him in the deep freeze out here," Williams confided to Britneva about Kazan, adding, "They are waiting to see what will happen next. There is even the possibility of a jail sentence if he persists in his determination not to reveal names of other party members when he was in it. This I think very admirable of him, and very brave, and all decent people ought to respect his sense of honor about it. But of course most of them don't." Williams continued, "Red hysteria has reached such a pitch that this disclosure may very well wreck his career as a motion-picture director."

Terror attacks thought. To avoid annihilating doubt, people rush to simplicities and make quick decisions. The 1952 Academy Awards was a small weather system that nonetheless reflected the larger national climate. *Streetcar* lost the best-picture award to the musical *An American in Paris*. Vivien Leigh, Karl Malden, and Kim Hunter won Oscars. "Gadg, Marlon and I were obviously screwed out of the Academy Awards," Williams said. He found the occasion "a hideous ordeal sitting there with your bare face hanging out and pretending not to care." Kazan claimed never to have seen anybody slumped so low in his chair as Williams. "I was afraid even to remove my flask from my pocket when Madame Clare Booth Luce got up on the platform and announced the writers awards," Williams confided to Crawford. "One part of me despises such prizes and the vulgar standards they represent, but another part of me wants to be 'The Winner' no matter what. When and how can we ever get over that, and have a dignified humility about us and a true sense of what matters?" The day after the awards, Kazan left Hollywood for New York. "I believed my days in that town and in that industry were over," he said.

While Kazan was contemplating his professional future, Williams was thinking about his personal one. Sometime between the Academy Awards and Kazan's second appearance before the HUAC—at a public session on April 10, 1952—Williams wrote to Kazan with a "desperate request." "He was asking me, in the greatest confidence, if I could arrange for a lady friend of his to be artificially inseminated," Kazan said. "He didn't say who the lady was, and perhaps, in this case, it didn't matter. The point was that Tennessee, still with Frank Merlo, very happy and likely to remain so, wanted offspring. He wasn't sure he could achieve the physical arousal necessary to penetrate a woman." Kazan added, "I told him I'd look around, but when I didn't hear any more about this from him, I forgot about it."

Unbeknownst to Kazan, of course, Williams was not happy. As implausible as it seemed, a child might have given Tennessee and Frank a shared enterprise beyond Williams's writing, as well as a focus for Merlo's restlessness. "He is going through some curious phase right now which I can't pretend to understand," Williams wrote to Britneva at the end of March. "I am not at all clever about people unless they're people of my own invention. I no longer complain about the Horse's behavior. He has a perfect right to behave as he chooses, and I can't say that he is ever deliberately done anything to hurt me, he has been very kind to Grandfather." Even Williams's ad hoc family setup now seemed precarious. "I say 'we' as if I felt quite certain the Horse were going with me," he wrote, alerting Britneva of his summer travel plans. "Actually I don't know."

With the situation with Merlo so unstable, Britneva found herself elevated in Williams's mind to his "five-o'clock angel." Presenting herself as a personification of allegiance and love, she offered Williams a kind of emotional home in exchange for his financial support. The only young and biddable female in Williams's close acquaintance, she was almost certainly the potential child-bearer he had in mind. At one point, earlier in the relationship, Merlo had offered to marry her to get her a green card, but the man she really loved was Williams. To a woman of Britneva's overweening social and artistic ambitions, an important marriage was crucial; from the start, she had eyes for Williams. "She was madly in love with Tenn," said the journalist Harriet Van Horne, who knew Britneva in her vagabond days, in the fifties in New York, when she was cooking dinner in a one-room apartment for, among others, William Faulkner and Marlon Brando. Although there is no evidence that Britneva and Williams ever had sex, Van Horne heard genuine passion in her talk about him: "Her description—'Tennessee is so tanned. His head is like a brown nut. I just love to run my fingers through his hair.' You don't say that unless you've got a physical attraction." Britneva wrote in her diary, "I do love Tennessee and don't think there is anyone alive who is more sweet and gentle, kind and generous and so full of talent. . . . His companionship and support are what I value now most in my life."

Maria consulted a psychotherapist about her relationship with Williams, and despite sensational evidence to the contrary, she tried to believe that he was a lapsed heterosexual. "To go around saying Tennessee wasn't a faggot is madness," Gore Vidal said. But at times she went around saying more than that. "She called me up and said, 'I've got to see you right away,'" Arthur Miller said. "'Tennessee and I want to get married'—not are *going* to get married. 'What do you think?' I was floored. I said, 'Are you sure you're both of the same mind?' I sensed a large element of fantasy in it. She was playing some kind of role, flying around the room and being extremely romantic and excited like a fourteen-year-old. All I could do was stall and think whether I'd heard right. I think she wanted me to talk to Tennessee and get him to marry her."

If Britneva's delusions amounted to nothing, the same could not be said for those of the House Committee on Un-American Activities. When Kazan appeared for the second time, he recanted his previous position and listed as Communist sympathizers eight members of the Group Theatre, whose names were likely already known to the Committee. "There was no way I could go along with their crap that the CP was nothing but another political party, like the Republicans and the Democrats," Kazan said, explaining his change of heart. "I knew very well what it was, a thoroughly organized, worldwide conspiracy. This conviction separated me from many of my old friends."

One of those friends was Arthur Miller, with whom Kazan had discussed his upcoming volte-face. Walking with Miller in the woods of his 113-acre Connecticut estate, Kazan explained that he couldn't see sacrificing his career for something he no longer believed in. "There was a certain gloomy logic in what he was saying," Miller recalled in his autobiography *Timebends*. "Unless he came clean he could never hope, at the height of his creative powers, to make another film in America, and he would probably not be given a passport to work abroad either. If the theatre remained open to him, it was not his primary interest anymore; he wanted to deepen his film life, that was where his heart lay, and he had been told in so many words by his old boss and friend Spyros Skouras, president of Twentieth Century Fox, that the company would not employ him unless he satisfied the Committee." Miller added,

"Who or what was now safer because this man in his human weakness had been forced to humiliate himself? What truth had been enhanced by all this anguish?"

Two days after his testimony, Kazan paid for a column-length ad in the *New York Times*—"A Statement by Elia Kazan"—which was written by his wife, Molly Day Thacher, but signed by him:

> . . . I joined the Communist Party late in the summer of 1934. I got out a year and a half later.
>
> I have no spy stories to tell, because I saw no spies. Nor did I understand, at that time, any opposition between American and Russian national interest. It was not even clear to me in 1936 that the American Communist Party was abjectly taking its orders from the Kremlin.
>
> What I learned was the minimum that anyone must learn who puts his head into the noose of party "discipline." The Communists automatically violated the daily practices of democracy to which I was accustomed. They attempted to control thought and to suppress personal opinion. They tried to dictate personal conduct. They habitually distrusted and disregarded and violated the truth. All this was crudely opposite to their claims of "democracy" and "the scientific approach." To be a member of the Communist Party is to have a taste of the police state. It is a diluted taste but it is bitter and unforgettable. It is diluted because you can walk out.
>
> I got out in the spring of 1936. . . .

"A very sad comment on our Times," Williams wrote to Wood.

Overnight, in left-wing circles, Kazan went from cultural prince to pariah. "I seemed to have crossed some fundamental and incontrovertible line of tolerance for human error and sin," he wrote. He was threatened, abused, and shunned. He changed his telephone number and hired a bodyguard for his wife and family. In Hollywood, the most popular director of his day was suddenly an undesirable. Even though he could continue to work, the crisis had made him a contractual cripple; he was relegated to the bottom of the studio heap. He had become, like Williams, a fugitive kind. (The ructions in Hollywood when he was chosen, four decades later, in 1999, to receive the Academy Honorary Award for lifetime achievement, demonstrated that Kazan had still not been forgiven his trespasses by a sector of the show-business community.) "He was, on the whole, the man who was least forgiven, because he had been the epitome of courage and strength," Irene Selznick, one of the many who stopped speaking to Kazan, wrote in *A Private View*. As Kazan put it, he was "on a great social griddle and frying."

Both Kazan and Thacher, whom Kazan described as "a passionate absolutist," put on stoic fighting faces. "Yes! You did a solid and brave thing," Thacher wrote to him. "Precisely because it did cut you off from all those people—outworn but familiar—knowing what they'd think—and still did what you found was right. Lonesome thing. And that's why it was brave. And I know that it was right; it's always felt right: like rock bottom, from which you can build up." She added, "I remember most sharply when you got out of the bathtub in 74th St. and handed me the subpoena. I said to myself, 'Nothing's ever going to be the same again.' I had a complete and final conviction of that. But it didn't occur to me then that things would be better."

Although most of the theater community rushed to judgment, Williams did not. "I take no attitude about it, one way or another, as I am not a political person and human venality is something I always expect and forgive," he told Britneva. For Kazan, "the most loyal and understanding friend I had through those black months was Tennessee Williams." Two days after the HUAC testimony, Williams sent Kazan an expanded version of *Camino Real*.

ON JANUARY 10, 1952, while he was writing the screenplay *Hide and Seek*, Williams reminded Kazan of *Ten Blocks on the Camino Real*, which seemed to have fallen out of their discussions. "Did some top-drawer work on 'Camino' lately. Do you remember 'Camino'?" he wrote. When Kazan and Williams discussed *Camino* the previous fall, it was still a one-act play, and the putative producer of the evening was William Liebling, who was ultimately unable to raise the money. Then Irene Selznick had poached Kazan to direct George Tabori's *Flight into Egypt*, for which Williams called her out as "treacherous." "There were tears and protestations and lavish gifts at Christmas!" he wrote to Britneva. "But she got Gadg and I got what the little boy shot at."

"Now to 'Camino'—ya gonna do it or not?" Eli Wallach wrote to Kazan in mid-February 1952. Wallach, who had played Kilroy—a bewildered former Golden Gloves champion and Williams's wandering hero and surrogate in the Actors Studio workshop—reminded Kazan that he was keeping up his body-building regime for the role. "Wish you luck? I wish you more. . . . I also wish you break your goddamn leg, if you don't do 'Camino.'" Kazan's HUAC appearance, and the news that Wallach would not be available until late 1952, led to yet another postponement. Kazan took another movie assignment (*Man on a Tightrope*). Williams took another Roman holiday. On June 10, the day before he sailed to Europe on the *Liberté*, he mailed Wood a copy of the full-length version of *Camino*. Williams saw the play, he said, as "an extension of the free and plastic turn I took with 'Tattoo.'"

In fact, *Camino* was a complete change of Williams's theatrical palette. He had written *Ten Blocks on the Camino Real* in 1946, just after the creative burst of *A Streetcar Named Desire*. At the time, he'd thought of combining it with another Spanish-themed play, with songs and dancing, and calling it "The Blue Guitar" or "The Guitar of Picasso." The titles themselves suggest a desire to change his style. "To me the appeal of this work is its unusual degree of freedom," he said. "When it began to get under way I felt a new sensation of release, as if I could 'ride out' like a tenor sax taking the breaks in a Dixieland combo." Williams claimed that *Camino* served him as a "spiritual purgation of that abyss of confusion and lost sense of reality" that he and others had "somehow wandered into." (The epigram to the play, taken from Dante's *Inferno*, set the stage for the spectacle of Williams's existential bewilderment: "In the middle of the journey of our life I came to myself in a dark wood where the straight way was lost.") In the exuberance of its dreamlike design and in the bold absence of psychology and of Williams's familiar lyric tropes, the play was an unfettered journey into his interior. "This play is possible because it deals precisely with my own situation," he told Kazan.

And what was Williams's situation? Like Kilroy, "the Eternal Punchinella," Williams found himself in an America "galloping into totalitarianism," which "struck terror in me." Driven, lost, and hounded by a neurotic sense that his theatrical time was running out, Williams, in his own mind, was a kind of former champion holding out the hope that "the old pure music will come to me again." "If you people . . . still take me seriously as a writer it is mainly because of what I did in the past," he wrote to Kazan, in the dog days of the summer of 1952. "I can't say what is the matter, why I accomplish so little. I work, God knows! But I'm not as 'charged' as I was, not as loaded. I have a sort of chronic fatigue to contend with. I used to have, say, two good days out of seven. Now I have about one good day out of fifteen to twenty. . . . I feed on delusion, beg for encouragement. In this situation the sensible thing to do would be to quit for a time, as so many writers have done, such as Rilke, and wait and pray for a new start, for a new vision, a regeneration of the tired nerve cells. But you see I committed myself completely to the life of an artist. I froze out almost everything else. I don't know how to live as anything else. . . . I have not made a success of life or of love. And if my work peters out, I am a bankrupt person."

Conceived as part protest play and part shadow play, *Camino Real* was both a phantasmagoria of Williams's turbulent interior life and a statement about "the all-but-complete suppression of any dissident voices" in American society, which "seems no longer inclined to hold itself open to very explicit criticism from within." Set in the imaginary plaza of a port town, whose central fountain has dried up—"The spring of humanity has gone dry in this place," Sancho Panza says—*Camino Real* weighed Williams's romantic idealism against the unforgiving reality of both his private life and the reactionary public sphere. In an arid, threatening, bizarre landscape, where dreamers and troublemakers are killed and swept away by street cleaners, where the word *hermano* ("brother") is forbidden, where the only birds are wild ones that have been tamed and are kept in cages, the denizens of the *Camino Real*—who are mostly romantic legends of literature—shuttle in perpetual jeopardy between a ritzy hotel and a flophouse. They live under constant financial threat, literally and symbolically in fear of being "discredited." From Kilroy to Gutman, the sinister hotelier who controls his guests' circumstances, to the trapped Romantics (Lord Byron, Proust's Baron de Charlus, Don Quixote, Dumas's Marguerite Gautier), the characters inhabit a freakish world, warped by desperation and pitched between desire and retreat. Their struggle for honor in dishonorable circumstances disfigures them. "It is they"—the Romantics—"who are being driven to the edge of the earth," Kazan noted of Williams's "v. personal" play. "It is they who have the problem of how to live and how to die, WITHOUT GIVING UP THEIR IDENTITY—even to realize their identity further through death."

"The people are nearly all archetypes of various human attitudes toward life," Williams wrote to Kazan.

> Marguerite Gautier is the romantic sensualist and her friend, Casanova, is an out and out rake but also with romantic yearnings that promiscuity did not satisfy. Baron de Charlus is the completely cynical voluptuary, and hedonist. They belong together because they have pursued a fairly similar course, so they all stay at the hotel which is the "haut monde," the prosperous side of the street. The Gypsy's establishment is the brutal enigma of existence. Her daughter is the eternal object of desire. Kilroy, like Don Quixote whom he eventually joins, is the simple, innocent adventurer into life, the knight-errant who has preserved his dignity, his sincerity and his honor, though greatly baffled and subjected to much indignity and grief. I am not sure how precisely all this adds up, but perhaps it doesn't have to, so long as the essential effect, of poetic mystery, is realized. I wrote it without figuring it out very logically in advance.

Kazan's identification with the perilous surreal nightmare of *Camino* was deep. "I was its unfortunate hero," he wrote. "I'd just been knocked down and was flat on the canvas. . . . I had to do what Kilroy—and Williams—did: get up off the mat and come back fighting. . . . Once when I asked him what the play was about, he answered, 'It's the story of everyone's life after he's gone through the razzle-dazzle of his youth . . . ' Then he went on, 'There is terror and mystery on one side, honor and tenderness on the other.'" The characters embody Williams's longing for a life beyond life, for an ecstasy not just of the flesh. This spiritual grasping for a way beyond, which appears, literally, in the topography of the set as the "Terra Incognita," a desert that lies between the walled town and the snow-capped mountains in the distance, is also embedded in the stylization of the writing. In its swift interplay of poetry and panic, beauty and barbarity, *Camino Real* serves up a kind of theatrical gallimaufry that resists traditional forms: an allegory and not; protest play and not; naturalism and not; poetry and not; drama and not. The play's rueful contortions express the surreal tragicomic mood of Williams's poem "Carrousel Tune," written in the same year:

> Turn again, turn again, turn once again;
> the freaks of the cosmic circus are men
> We are the gooks and the geeks of creation;
> Believe-It-Or-Not is the name of our star.

Camino Real—the punning pronunciation of the title itself broadcasts the paradoxical conflict of the spiritual and the political—was conceived in the giddy, alienated spirit of "Believe-It-Or-Not," that is, the spirit of the grotesque. The play's comedy was, according to Williams, "traceable to the spirit of the American comic strip, and the animated cartoons, where the most outrageous absurdities give the greatest delight . . . where the characters are blown sky-high one moment and are skipping gaily about the next, where various members of their bodies are destroyed and restored in the flicker of the projector." Kazan picked up on this need for incongruity. In his notes for the play, he wrote, "In the direction of this thing, keep it shimmering from violence and tragedy to broad wild humor, moving suddenly and always without transition." In its counterpoint of speech and symbol—"I say that symbols are nothing but the natural speech of drama," Williams contended—*Camino Real* embodies a kind of fugue state. "Conventions of dreams should be studied as a key to much of the play's staging and quality," Kazan wrote in his director's notes. "In dreams there is a continual flow and mutation: one identity melts into another identity without any interruption or surprise. . . . The play should set new limits of theatrical license and freedom." (*Camino Real*, Williams said, "literally got down on its knees and begged for imaginative participation.") For both the playwright and his characters, *Camino Real* was a leap into the unknown, which was part of its drama. "The essential stylistic problem is always to maintain the mood of mystery," Williams told Kazan, who wrote this definition in his script and added "+humor."

Nothing quite as poetic and visually playful had ever been tried on Broadway. "This play is moving to me because it describes what is happening in the world of 1952 to the people I love most in the world . . . all those blessed nonconformists," Kazan told Williams. (At a time when merely knowing a homosexual could justify an FBI investigation, Williams brazenly included the first unabashed portrait of a gay man on the Broadway stage, the promiscuous Baron de Charlus. "My suit is pale yellow. My nationality is French, and my normality has been often subject to question," he says.) Kazan continued, "I say, if the play IS about these people, let's speak out and say so clearly because they are being killed off and ironed out, they are being shamed out and trained out and silenced and shunted and shoved off the edge of the world. Let's speak out for them so everyone will hear and understand. If we don't no one else will."

"To the hard of hearing you shout," Flannery O'Connor observed about the use of the grotesque, "and for the almost-blind you draw large and startling figures." *Camino Real* did both. "Are you afraid of anything at all?" Williams's Gypsy asked the audience through a loudspeaker. "Afraid of your heartbeat? Or the eyes of strangers! Afraid of breathing? Afraid of not breathing? Do you wish that things could be straight and simple again as they were in your childhood? Would you like to go back to Kindy Garten?"

When Wood first read the play, she told Williams "to put [it] away and not show to anyone," he recalled, adding, "Her reaction had depressed me so that I thought the play must be really quite bad." But by June 1952, despite his morbid fears to the contrary, Williams was on a kind of artistic roll. The film of *Streetcar* was a hit; *Summer and Smoke* had been successfully revived Off-Broadway by José Quintero, who brought new luster to the play and to its star, Geraldine Page; and Williams had just been elected to the American Academy of Arts and Letters. These things and Kazan's enthusiasm for the full-length *Camino Real* renewed Williams's hope and his energy. "The script is only about 1/10 of the total quantity of writing done on it," he told Kazan, when he delivered it, adding, "The writing has a wild, breathless, stammering quality which reflects my own brink of hysteria, but nevertheless I feel tonight that it is the most original piece of writing I have done and is, in a way, as beautiful as 'Streetcar.' The texture of the writing is not as fine, of course, but the underlying spirit is finer. 'Streetcar' was fundamentally an encomium to the enduring gallantry of the human spirit. So that is how I feel about it tonight, and I am not drunk, though tanked up on coffee."

In mid-June 1952, Kazan and Williams met in Paris to discuss *Camino*. "I was prepared for anything, but to my happy surprise he seemed to be very favorably impressed," Williams reported to Wood, adding, "He says he wants to start rehearsals in late October. This suits me!" In late July, Kazan's suggestions for rewrites reached Williams. "I am *terribly stimulated* by these notes," Williams told him. But, privately, he worried that "The Terrible Turk" was a "slippery customer," liable to drop out of the project; strategically, he urged Wood to hurry the decisions about the show's producer and set designer. "The important thing is to keep Gadg occupied with it." Williams's own way of keeping Kazan occupied was to create a melodrama. *Camino*, he confided to Kazan, was "very likely my last [play]. I almost hope that it is." He added, "Except for some unexpected thing that will restore my old vigor, it would be better to put writing away, after this last job, and settle for whatever I could get out of just existing."

Kazan, who, like the characters in *Camino*, had his back against the wall and was making a daring fight for his integrity, responded in particularly pugnacious form. "We're fighting here for fun and for theatre and for self expression and not for money," he wrote to Williams about *Camino*, the day after he finished filming *Man on a Tightrope*. "So let's see to it that this once we do it really right, and not as a job. I don't want to do a job now. I'm not in the mood to overly respect that word." He went on, "Christ: let's have some fun! Let's have a costume parade that sends us home happy and relaxed and relieved. . . . I don't want to take the attitude towards this play that we're lucky to be able to GET IT ON at all. The hell with that. I'm in too mean a mood, and also too happy a mood, for that. . . . But I want the most difficult, the most experimental play to have the best help it can get. Who should 'experiment' except the best people."

But over the next few months it became apparent that the best people didn't know quite what to make of the experiment that Williams called "essentially a plastic poem on the romantic attitude toward life." The set designer Jo Mielziner, who had done three productions with Williams, "felt like an ungrateful dog" for his lukewarm response. Cheryl Crawford worried about cost, clarity, *succès d'estime*, and her preference for a "hot light" finale. "This play ends with a sort of 'misty radiance,' and I am not sure that will be, or can be, hot enough to suit her," Williams wrote to Kazan. "If you dissolve the shimmer of mystery over this thing, you lose its fascination."

Unsettled by the reactions of the other potential collaborators, Williams wrote to Kazan in late July: "I think it is remarkable that your own interest and faith in the play still survives. Mine is indestructible." But

With Elia Kazan and Cheryl Crawford

over the summer, after a couple of script-conference trips to Germany, where Kazan was filming, Williams began to discern "a retrenchment" of his director's enthusiasm. "Yesterday eve we read over the work I've done on 'Camino' under Gadg's direction," he noted in his diary on August 20. "He kept snorting and exclaiming, oh, this is wonderful! The way a doctor tells a dying man what perfect condition he's in. It seemed to me like one long agonized wail and I couldn't go out to eat with him. Said excuse me but I think I'll go cruising now."

"I hate writing that is a parade of images for the sake of images," Williams said. But *Camino* was in danger of becoming just that. The connections between his passages were not linear and naturalistic but imagistic and symbolic; the play was a delicate, elusive weave of ideas and metaphors, unified as much by the rhythms of the music as by the rhythms of speech. The problem with Williams's proliferating imagination was one of organization. Those poetic fragments had to be melded into a whole; a dramatic through-line had to be found in "a chowder of archetypes," as one wag called the play. "It's an almost super-human job," Williams said. It took Kazan more than a month to respond to Williams's September revisions. "I am very, very disturbed by the fact that you say that you have not read the script," Williams wrote to him.

As Williams suspected, a lot of Kazan's hesitation came from the reaction of his wife, Molly Day Thacher, who served as a kind of in-house critic for all her husband's work. Thacher was the playreader for the Group Theatre who had "discovered" Williams in 1939 and had been responsible for getting him to Audrey Wood. After the skirmishing over *Camino*, however, Williams came to see her as "the self-appointed scourge of Bohemia." At the end of September, still straddling the fence about *Camino Real*, Kazan wrote to Thacher, "About Tennessee: I called him yesterday, and he said he had finished the script and had sent one to Audrey, etc. As I told you, and then he said, he had the feeling I was going to run out on him again, he quoted from 'Glass Menagerie' and said: 'Don't fail me Tom! You are my right-hand bower!' Now, what can I possibly do but do his entire and utter bidding—at the same time of course making the script good which it is not yet." Kazan added, "I truly believe I can work with Tenn more, but he is the one guy that when I work with

him, the stuff doesn't turn out as I put it down in the outline. Not at all.
. . . I can certainly understand any queasy feeling about this venture, and
it is a staggering job, once embarked on. It seems to me life and death to
Williams, though."

Thacher, who hadn't read the play at that point, heard the doubt in
her husband's tone. "When you're sold, you just sell and don't take no for
an answer from anybody you want," she replied. "There's quite a difference. You said No to 'Tattoo' not too uncomfortably and with clarity.
Here, you're involved. And perhaps it wouldn't be fair to look at it as
though you'd never read it before and then decide. I sense a great hesitation or reluctance or something in what you write. I'm not talking about
what I think—I haven't read it—I'm talking about what you think, which
is important."

THACHER BROUGHT TO her passionate, articulate opinions an element
of the firebrand. (Three days before Kazan began shooting *On the Waterfront*, for instance, she went behind her husband's back to tell the producer, Sam Spiegel, that the script wasn't ready and the film would be a
disaster.) "Molly, to all extents and purposes, was smarter than Elia,"
their son, the screenwriter Nick Kazan, said. "They both knew it. He
desperately needed her critical input. It was one of the reasons he
respected her and one of the ways they kept their marriage together. But
once he felt that a play was going to work, he didn't want to hear everything that she had to say." He continued, "At some gut level, Elia worked
and lived out of his heart and groin; Molly lived in her head."

When Kazan first met Thacher, at the Yale Drama School (her
patrician pedigree included a former president of Yale), she had a more
academic and practical understanding of theater than he did. She had
studied drama, written one-act plays, and worked on productions with
Hallie Flanagan, who was soon to head the Federal Theatre Project.
She believed in Kazan's artistic potential and in his mind; for him, she
became a "talisman of success." "I came to rely on her judgment in
scripts. She made up for my lacks in taste and savvy," he wrote. Among
the writers who benefited at times from Thacher's forthright analytic
capacities were John Steinbeck, Irwin Shaw, Robert Anderson, and

Arthur Miller. For Williams, however, her finger-wagging over *Camino Real* went too far. In August 1952, having read the play, Thacher told Kazan, "I think you can help him, if he will help himself, for he clings to your strength. But what I began to feel out of the 'Camino' rewrite, was that—for this production—he was dragging you into his own swamp. And that's too high a price." To Williams, she said, "Never before with you and never with any writer have I seen so desperate and absolute an identification. It's dangerous." "She is my bete-noir!" Williams complained to Britneva, whose nickname for Thacher was "Catch-as-Catch-Can Kazan," adding in another letter, "Molly is a pain in [Gadg's] derriere but he has to make a public show of loyalty to her as the Mother of His Four Children, and so forth, while he puts on her more horns than cab-drivers blow in Paris!" In fact, Kazan made shrewd strategic use of his wife's well-argued notes to challenge his writers and to think against his own opinions.

In the meantime, Kazan had been offered Robert Anderson's *Tea and Sympathy*, a solid commercial bet, which he postponed in favor of *Camino Real*, which he saw as a way to refurbish his sullied public image in the eyes of the New York theater community. Thirteen of twenty-one actors in the *Camino* cast were from the Actors Studio. In hindsight, Kazan's commitment to the project, he said, came from a desire "to be accepted as their hero by the actors of that organization, to demonstrate my courage and my steadfast loyalty to them and to live up to an ideal to which I'd pledged support again and again and for which I'd demanded theirs. By demonstrating that I had the power to force things to happen our way, I would make the Actors Studio mine again. In plainer language, I wanted to be liked." Kazan forced *Camino Real* to happen; in December 1952, he was still trying to force Williams to impose a shape on the play.

Throughout the long process of rewrites, Williams both needed and resented Kazan's trenchant collaboration. "I have fallen off remarkably in the esteem of my co-workers when they start dictating my work to me," he noted in his diary. To friends like Paul Bigelow and Carson McCullers, Williams blamed this loss of creative control on the vagaries of the marketplace. "It's awful how quickly a theatrical reputation declines on the market," he told McCullers. "A few years ago and I could have anything I wanted in the theatre, now I have to go begging. Two plays that didn't make money and, brother, you're on the skids." But whether out of fatigue or fear, or both, Williams listened to Kazan. "This play moves me every time I read it," Kazan began in a long, excellent pep talk about revisions. "The author is saying a few thousand words in defence of a dying race, call them what you will: romantics, eccentrics, rebels, Bohemians, freaks, harum-scarum, bob-tail, Punchinellos, odd-ducks, the out-of-steps, the queers, double-gated, lechers, secret livers, dreamers, left-handed pitchers, defrocked bishops, Maria Britneva, the artists, the near artists, the would-be-artists, the wanderers, the would-be wanderers, the secret wanderers, the foggy minded, the asleep on the job, the loafers, the out and out hobos, the down and out, the grifters and drifters, the winos and boozers, the old maids who don't venture to the other side of their windows, the good for nothings, the unfenceables, the rebels inside, the rebels manifest, in fact all those blessed non-conformists of whom Kilroy is the present legendary hero and plain and simple representative." Kazan continued, "Incidentally wouldn't a list like this written by a man of talent be great somewhere in the play. Esmeralda speaking on the roof before she retires: 'Dear God, protect tonight, wherever they are, all the . . .' and then go into it. (It would also make abundantly clear whom the play is in praise of.)"

Williams took Kazan's idea and his rhythms and positioned the speech precisely where Kazan had instructed. The result was one of the play's bravura moments, and one of Williams's most brilliant soliloquies. Esmeralda's lyrical prayer became Williams's own romantic anthem:

God bless all con men and hustlers and pitchmen who hawk their hearts on the street, all two-time losers who're likely to lose once more, the courtesan who made the mistake of love, the greatest of lovers crowned with the longest horns, the poet who wandered far from his heart's green country and possibly will and possibly won't be able to find his way back, look down with a smile tonight on the last cavaliers, the ones with the rusty armor and soiled white plumes, and visit with understanding and something that's almost tender those fading legends that come and go in this plaza like songs not clearly remembered, oh, sometime and somewhere, let there be something to mean the word *honor* again!

Williams was less happy to take Kazan's cuts. For a backers' audition in the first week of December 1952, Williams wrote a preamble, "Invocation to Possible Angels," in which he explained that *Camino Real* asked, "Where are we, where do we come from and where are we going?" Two hours and forty minutes later—this was without the dance sequences— the bemused would-be backers had the same questions about the play. No one but Williams was in doubt about *Camino*'s vagueness or disarray. After the reading, Thacher had the temerity to tell him that forty-five minutes needed to be cut. "I screamed at her all the four-letter words that I could think of, and Gadg just sat there and smirked," Williams told Britneva later, adding, "She then sent out 'circulars' to everybody saying that I must cut 45 minutes of the play and that if 'we kept her with it we would have a play.'" As it turned out, Kazan held more or less the same view. "This play is at least twenty minutes too long by any standard and by any measure, including the only valid one: its own nature. It hasn't enough development of theme or plot to take on the jumbo length," he told Williams. Nonetheless, at a testy meeting in Crawford's office, Williams threw a tantrum. He balked at directorial interference; he claimed that neither Kazan nor Crawford had been frank with him. "Why stick to a conventional length?" he said.

The first person to call Williams on his intransigence was Thacher. In a letter written the next day, she accused him of using the legend of his own collapse to hold his collaborators to ransom. "You also exercise thru the intensity of your feeling a sort of psychological weapon against your friends and colleagues . . . a submission finally before your desperate and intransigent identification with the play," she wrote him, adding, "It's time for you to stop identifying with the play and, for a time, to identify with the audience. . . . The future of the play depends only on one thing: on you. . . . If this is treason—my husband is prepared to get on the *Titanic* with you anyway."

The Kazans were using different songs to deliver the same unhappy message: the play was not working. Kazan was the more collegial; his method was to pull no punches about either praise or problems. His forthrightness signaled equality and intimacy. "I'm not going to make any concrete suggestions to you. Or maybe I'll sneak in a few later. Probably. And incidentally I think you're quite right to do everything in your way ONLY," Kazan said, confessing himself "slightly singed" by Williams's post-audition outburst. Writing a five-page letter from the couchette of the railroad car that was taking him from New York to California, Kazan painted a comic picture of himself wading through the *Camino* rewrites "from A to infinity." "I sat down one morning and ripped the covers off and went through every page," he said. "By nightfall I was blind. (I recovered my sight just a few hours ago just to write this.) The floor of my compartment was a foot and a half deep with your crumpled efforts. . . . The point is that I got those goddamned versions out of my life. They're gone."

Kazan proceeded to lay down the law about reworking the first act. He commanded Williams to send Merlo out of the house for an hour, to put the telephone in a pail of lukewarm water, and to read act 1 through as if it were someone else's play. "Just do that," he said, adding, "Do you think the first act is ready to go into rehearsal? I don't. Probably there isn't an awful lot of work, mechanically speaking, pressing on typewriter keys and all that. I just think you've got to sit down and see that goddamn act thru. I mean see your way thru it, make some kind of one piece of it. It can be a bloody peculiar piece, but one piece it should be. It should have a sequence an audience can and will follow. And above all I think it should come to a climax—a real 'internal' one, a climax of a story and a climax of meaning, and one that calls for Act II." Kazan added, "A few 'ole's, a light change and a flurry of movement is not an act curtain. You can bring the rag down, but you still won't have an act curtain. You'll have a disaster."

For the final creative push before rehearsals at the end of January, Williams retreated to Key West and his quiet lemon-yellow studio. In this space, filled with the constant flickering of light and shadow, the rustling outside his windows of palm and pine trees "like ladies running barefooted in silk skirts downstairs," and the tinkling of glass pendants on the Japanese lantern above his head, Williams slogged away at his "perennial work-in-progress," which was "expanding in conception although it is now only ten or twelve days short of rehearsals." He was feeling, he said, "so beat!" "Kazan is still dissatisfied with the second-act curtain," he explained to Konrad Hopkins, his handsome new twenty-four-year-old Harvard-educated pen pal. "He is indispensable to this play so I must try to please him as well as myself. It's my most difficult undertaking so far and I regard it as a test of whether or not I can continue to write for Broadway."

The combination of good weather and the arrival of Mr. Moon, a four-month-old British bulldog, lent a distracting calm to the surface of Williams's life. "My dream-self betrays the true extent of anxiety," he noted to Hopkins. In one of the night sweats that Williams reported, he was in a house watching a parade. "All at once the paraders screamed and threw themselves flat against an embankment. The front wall of the house collapsed," he wrote. Williams saw a great black locomotive plunging directly toward him. Later the same night, "for some unfathomable reason—since no window was open more than two inches," a picture fell off the wall in his bedroom with a terrific crash. "I woke up screaming," he explained. "It was a picture of one of my play-sets. Baleful omens!"

The call for the first rehearsal of *Camino* was at 10:30 a.m. on January 29, 1953; by 10:00 a.m., the actors began drifting in. "All of us in the cast felt we were embarking on a trip to a world we had never encountered before," said Eli Wallach, for whom *Camino Real* would be "the greatest experience I had in the theater." At exactly 10:30, with the actors, the producers, the author's agents, and the nervous author himself assembled, Kazan strode onto the stage of the National Theatre. A hush came over the group, according to the production's stage manager, Seymour Milbert, who kept a journal of the rehearsals. "His air is one of unusual power, concentrated force," Milbert wrote. "Directness over everything: there is no latitude for anything but the most simple and meaningful communication." Kazan flung off his overcoat and moved to the small table that had been set up center stage for him, his assistant,

Anna Sokolow and Williams. He put his script on the table; inside it, highlighted in green, he had written:

Motto: No matter what you do, *what* tricks you pull, how "brilliant" you are, never forget the strength and truth of the play. We'll be lost unless the audience always feels the underlying reality . . . the pain & terror & emotion beneath the surface.

In black uppercase letters, just below the green words, he had added:

PAINFUL HUMOR, MOCKING HUMOR,
PLUS POETIC TRAGEDY

In his opening remarks to the cast, Kazan said, "This is a profound, emotionally charged play, with philosophically written lines, and poetry. Treat the philosophy and the poetry with reality, as simple meaning." He added, "When you come down to the apron and talk to the audience, find one person in it you can talk to. Above all, don't perform."

Later, after lunch, when he and the company were finally alone together, Kazan sketched out some thoughts on fantasy that he'd jotted in his script notes. "Fantastic events are played simply," he said. "Don't be sententious, or philosophic, or sorry for yourself. All these people in this play are engaged in a desperate struggle for existence. They have no time to feel sorry for themselves." He went on, "Death is too real for the people on this street. Have you ever been to Mexico and seen the disregard for the death of another human? It is fantastic for us Americans." Kazan divided the denizens of the Camino Real into Realists and Romantics. The Realists were "adjusted, make a living, have fun, are cruel, yet happy, behave sensibly, have all the good things, and can even afford to be generous! Remain calm, live by hurting and depriving, die." The Romantics, on the other hand, "behave absurdly, are anxious, don't fit, are 'guilty,' out of place, don't get ahead because they cannot live by hurting and depriving, are unhappy, always searching and always BROKE." Kazan's notes continued, "Marguerite, Jacques, Baron, Byron are all *legends*. If they give these legends up and live in an 'ordinary' way, they lose their identity and disappear. The legend of each is killing each, but they are fated to cling to it."

Of the autobiographical confusions that *Camino* explored—confusions about politics, sexuality, mortality, spirituality, and fame—the profoundest, of which Williams was then only dimly aware, was his confusion over the conflict between being great and being good. That moral quandary is represented in the play by the innocent, sweet-natured former champ, Kilroy, who is an essential link between the script and the audience. "Audience are his friends," Kazan wrote in his notes about Kilroy, who at one point is chased around the theater by police. "They are the witnesses to his final passion. . . . He goes and consults with them, protests to them and seeks refuge in their laps." (Kilroy was the first character in the legitimate theater to shuttle between the aisles and the stage.) Kilroy is a king who has lost his crown. He enters with the remnants of his glory—his golden gloves—around his neck. Kilroy has a golden heart the size of a baby's head. In order to woo the whore Esmeralda and to be her Chosen Hero, he foolishly sells his heart for cash, only to steal it back later. "He is the eternal spiritual wanderer," Kazan wrote. "He is romantic because he is looking, wandering in search of what does not exist—eternal love. He wants to fall in love with everybody. Meantime everyone is looking to take him. HIS ONLY WEAPON IS LOVE."

At the end of the first day's rehearsal, Kazan took Wallach aside to give him a keynote about Kilroy. "He is full of wonder. Jimmy Durante in wonderland." Kilroy is a totem of resilience, "utterly unaware of his own tragedy," Kazan wrote; like a slapstick burlesque clown, he bounces back from every blow. In the midst of an extravaganza of betrayal and death, Kilroy embodies Williams's faith in transcendence; at the finale, he and Quixote—both figures of absurd perseverance and hope—exit with a flourish through the Archway of the Camino Real and into "Terra Incognita." "The violets in the mountains have broken the rocks!" Quixote says in the play's penultimate tribute to romanticism.

On the second day—while the theater management struggled "like mad," Milbert noted, "to keep pace on the typewriter with the flood of rewriting that Tennessee is doing! Whole new scenes—passages torn out and new ones thrust in!"—Kazan worked privately, in the mezzanine,

Camino Real

with his principles. "During these sessions Kazan will tolerate no one about, neither an outside visitor, myself or any member of the company," Milbert wrote. He added, "When I have had to go up with a message which could not wait, or requests for immediate information, I could barely hear the voices at the table about fifteen feet away. The emphasis seems to be on quiet, meaningful communication, without projection."

Onstage, however, Kazan was a dynamo. "All day—Williams and Kazan finding moments—improvising lines—situations—moving people

—moving, moving!" Milbert noted. Kazan fed the actors word pictures and personal memories to give dimension to their characters. To Barbara Baxley, who played Esmeralda, for instance, he said, "Kilroy represents freedom to you, and the object of all your desires. Sure, he's a bum, a lousy American, but shut your eyes, and he's that man you want, that sexual experience, joy, happiness, that you want. You choose him and love him. All your life you have been raised to be a whore, but inside you're really imprisoned in the Gypsy's place. She's not your mother, she probably found you somewhere when you were a kid, and has raised you to make you go inside. So kick at the Nurse when you get excited, and he tries to make you go inside. Really fight him off, this is the one time you really want to break out." He went on, "I remember the kids I saw in Munich when I was there last summer, offering themselves to you for money. Were they whores? Not really: they're just kids, they want some fun, some joy, some escape from confinement."

To Wallach, Kazan laid out an emotional map for his romance with Esmeralda: "You, Kilroy, you're really jazzed now. You're caught up in the excitement of the chase, in Esmeralda's shouts of Champ. You're brought back to how it was, say, in 1934. You'd walk into a bar on 98th Avenue, and they'd want to buy you drinks, everybody wanted your autograph. All right, you love your wife, but Christ, twice a year or so, don't you want to break out and have yourself a real tear? This kid wants you, she's a real doll, so what the hell. In this Block, when you say 'I have only one ambition and that is to get out alive,' you really believe for the first time that you're going to live."

Sometimes Kazan worked by slyly generating conflict. He took Wallach aside at one rehearsal and said, "You're alone and you're scared, so go on and make friends." Meanwhile, according to Wallach, "he told the actors playing a motley crowd of peasants, 'Ignore this stranger; he's a gringo, and he has bad breath.'"

After the first run-through of acts 1 and 2, Williams noted in his diary, "Profoundly depressing. But Gadg remained strong—apparently confident and his spirit bolstered mine." Kazan's intention was to move Williams's poetic drama in the direction of dance; the choreography, he felt, would lift the everyday into the ritualistic. "I wanted a production that had the bizarre fantasy of the Mexican primitive artist [José] Posada," Kazan recalled in his autobiography. But he allowed his set designer, Lemuel Ayers—who had done the sets and costumes for *Oklahoma!*—to talk him out of his original impulse. Instead, Ayers provided a forbidding, realistic set, whose stone walls enclosed and muted Williams's gleeful game of the grotesque. "It made the fantasies that took place inside it seem silly," Kazan said later of the set. "I should have ordered a new setting, but I didn't."

On February 20, the day before *Camino Real*'s first out-of-town tryout, in New Haven, Williams allowed himself a moment of buoyancy. "The rehearsals are shaping up much better now," he noted in his diary. "I feel hopeful again. Very close to Gadg, and fond of him. I plan to inscribe the play to him." If the set ultimately failed the production, the wizardry of Kazan's showmanship did not. In Williams's judgment, at least, *Camino* was a much harder and more complex play to mount than either *Streetcar* or *Death of a Salesman*. Not only did it have an inadequate budget and inadequate rehearsal and tryout time, but, as he told James Laughlin, Kazan was working with players "at least half of which were dancers and had no previous speaking experience on the stage." He added, "Gadg is not as fond of verbal values as he should be, but of all the Broadway directors he has the most natural love of poetry."

Even in New Haven, the potential for controversy—the "pro-and-confusion," as Walter Winchell dubbed the out-of-town response to *Camino*— was apparent. "Some actually hiss it, others appear delighted," Williams wrote to Konrad Hopkins whom he was trying to coax up from Florida to the New York opening. "I think it will have the most divided reaction of any play I've done. Of course it's very hard on the nerves, and yet it gives life that feeling of intensity that most of the time I find lacking." In anticipation of the Broadway opening on March 19—a week before Williams turned forty-two—Kazan tried audaciously to preempt negative press by acknowledging *Camino*'s limitations in a Sunday *New York Times* essay. "I'm not sure 'Camino Real' is as much a play as a poem," he wrote. "It has faults, structural faults, as a play. These will be visible to the students in the drama group at Dalton School, of which my daughter is a member, as well as to the critics of the New York papers. But as a piece of direct lyric theater expression, it seems to me to stand rather by itself."

Nothing, however, prepared Kazan or Williams for what Williams called the "militant incomprehension" of the New York critics, which "seemed like an order to get out and stay out of the current theatre." The poetry, the politics, the play's path-finding structure were hardly noticed in the literal-minded first responses: "The worst play yet written by the best playwright of his generation" (Walter Kerr, the *New York Herald Tribune*); "an enigmatic bore" (Richard Watts Jr., the *New York Post*); "overall bushwah" (John Chapman, the *Daily News*); "Camino Unreal" (Eric Bentley, the *New Republic*); 'Camino Real' is a serious failure . . . not the failure of a theme, or even a vision, but the most self-indulgent misuse of a talent" (Louis Kronenberger, *The Best Plays of 1952–1953*, explaining why he excluded *Camino Real* from the list). The adamance of the naysayers reflected some of the reactionary hysteria of the American moment, society's refusal to reflect on its own dark side. Kerr actually counseled Williams to stop thinking: "You're heading toward the cerebral: don't do it."

Still, there were a few New York critics who got the aesthetic message in Williams's bottle. Robert Sylvester, writing in the *New York Daily News*, called *Camino Real* "the first real bop play." Brooks Atkinson noted, in the *New York Times*, "As theatre, *Camino Real* is as eloquent and rhythmic as a piece of music," though even he felt compelled to add, "Even the people who respect Mr. Williams's courage and recognize his talent are likely to be aghast at what he has to say."

Sitting in a box at the opening with his mother and brother, Williams told himself that although the play was flawed, "it surpassed its flaws." "I knew that I was doing new and different things and it excited me," he wrote in *Memoirs*. "I thought that they would work under Kazan. They did work, except the audience generally did not want them to work; the audience wasn't with it at the time." When it became clear that the critics weren't going to allow him the satisfaction of his achievement—"I was hardly conscious of anything about me except the one all-obliterating preoccupation and anxiety with the tragic little world of my play, whirling on its way to critical disaster," Williams said—he and Merlo, who was "a marvel of controlled cool empathy," fled the opening-night party and retreated to their Fifty-Eighth Street apartment. At around one that morning, Kazan and Thacher, accompanied by John Steinbeck and his wife, appeared. Kazan insisted on being positive about the experience. "I've come out of the production feeling healed. And reinstated," he wrote to Williams soon after the opening. "What we've done together has made me feel in the forefront again." But there was no consoling Williams. "How dare you bring these people here tonight!" Williams shouted at Kazan, before storming into his bedroom and bolting the door.

Steinbeck was one of several outraged fans of the play who over the next few weeks engaged in a public donnybrook with the critics. He wrote an open letter to Richard Watts Jr. of the *Post*. The British poet Dame Edith Sitwell wrote to the *Herald Tribune* ("I believe it to be a very great play, written by a man of genius and one of the most significant works of our time"). And after a second dismissive Sunday piece about the play, Williams himself wrote to Walter Kerr:

Molly Day Thacher, Elia Kazan, Elaine Steinbeck, and John Steinbeck, 1955

What I would like to know is, Don't you see that this play—as a concentrate, a distillation of the world and time we live in—surely you don't think it is better than a nightmare!?—is a clear and honest picture?

Two: don't you also recognize it as a very earnest plea for certain fundamental, simply Christian attributes of the human heart, through which we might still survive?

Three: have you no appreciation of the tremendous technical demands of such a work, its complexities and difficulties, and at least the technical skill with which all of us involved in the production have managed to meet them?—As far as I remember at this moment, you made no mention more than perfunctory of music or choreography or the great plastic richness contributed by the designer, Lem Ayers, and you certainly did not go a step out of your way to give due tribute to such brilliant performances as Wallach's and Barbara Baxley's. . . . And how about the work of Kazan? To undertake this play took a very notable courage, since no director ever tackled a play more difficult, and there were pieces of staging in it the like of which I know, and you know, that you'll wait many and many a season to see again.

Various theatricals lined up to offer praise for *Camino Real* in ads: Oscar Hammerstein, William Inge, Clifford Odets, Jean Arthur, Fredric March, Arthur Schwartz, Harold Rome, Gypsy Rose Lee, Valerie Bettis, and Libby Holman, among them. "A Statement in Behalf of a Poet" was published; its signatories included Willem de Kooning, Paul Bowles, Lotte Lenya, Gore Vidal, and John La Touche. "When a major work of dramatic art by some miracle of production manages to appear in the bleak climate of contemporary theatre, we believe this public ought to know about it," the statement read. "The reviews which appeared in the daily press gave no conception of the strength and perceptiveness of Mr. Williams's play. . . . Like *Alice in Wonderland* or *Ubu Roi*—it is a work of the imagination—romantic, intensely poetic and modern."

The brouhaha drew attention to the play. "The controversy over 'Camino Real' is paying off. Did better biz Holy Week than week before,"

Winchell noted in his column on April 6. The *Times*, under the headline "Concerning Camino Real," kept the argument going with a full page of contradictory opinions from such figures as Shirley Booth and Dame Edith Sitwell (again). The *Post's* "Sidewalks of New York" asked the Man in the Street, "What do you think of Tennessee Williams's controversial new play 'Camino Real'?" One of the five people questioned was the actress Geraldine Page. "I adore it, every minute of it," she replied. The producers, in their daily ad, tried to capitalize on the fun of the furor:

The Talk of the Town, Indeed!

"First bop show, sent me."

"A BURLESQUE for Ph.D.'s."

"Divided our town into roaring camps."

"Pure theatre poetry."

"Must see it for oneself."

"Felt less lonesome."

"Wanted to shriek."

"Felt dirty."

"Felt clean."

"Split my family asunder."

"Clear as sparkling crystal."

"I was confused."

"If you're alive, it's for you."

"The sexiest show in town."

"I've been three times."

"Should be 'Prize Play of the Year'—but won't."

"Sheer emotion."

"Sheer hogwash."

"You're conversationally sterile without it."

"See it before its First Revival."

A couple of days after the opening, just before he left for Key West by train, Edwina asked Williams to autograph her *Camino Real* program. "Bloody but unbowed. (Or more literally) Eggy but unbeaten," he scrawled across the cover. Still, Williams *was* beaten. On the train, he wrote a disconsolate letter to Atkinson, thanking him for his sympathetic notice, but adding, "I can't believe that you really think I have painted the world in blacker colors than it now wears, or that it is melancholia, psychopathic of me, to see it in those shades." (Atkinson's review had spoken of "psychopathic bitterness," "a dark mirror, full of black and appalling images," "a miasma of hopelessness, cruelty and decadence.") Williams's courtly words couldn't hide his bewilderment or his hurt:

> Has this play alienated your old regard for my work? Do you feel as others that it is a "mish-mash" of muddy symbols and meaningless theatricalism, were you pulling your punches? No matter what you say, I think it would help me in this dark moment if you would level with me.

Back in Key West, Williams received, he said, a "flood of correspondence . . . when so many people, more than were moved to write me about 'Street Car' and 'Menagerie' put together . . . tell me that it touched and moved them deeply, I can't keep on feeling that it was all in vain." But the most comforting of all the letters was from Atkinson. "You have no idea how much less lonely your letter made me feel," Williams replied, in a letter in which he cast himself as both a friend ("I hope I have not yet forfeited your friendship!?") and a fugitive ("I came out of the world that you belong to, Brooks, and descended to those under levels"). By mid-April, Williams's mood had lightened. "Of course soon as the notices came out Mother Crawford took us off royalties," he bitched to Britneva, adding that he had worked two years "mostly for nothing." "She is hoping, as usual, to scrape along by such economies as lighting the stage by fire-flies and a smokey old kerosene lamp, substituting a bit of percussion on an old washtub for a five-piece band, etc., but even so the prospects for an extended run are but dim."

On May 9, after sixty performances and a loss of $115,000, *Camino Real* closed. "The work was done for exactly what it has gained, a communion with people," Williams wrote to Atkinson. He had promised Atkinson a published copy, but now explained mournfully, "A published play is only the shadow of one and not even a clear shadow." He went on, "The colors, the music, the grace, the levitation, the quick inter-play of live beings suspended like fitful lightning in a cloud, those things are the play, not words, certainly not words on paper and certainly not any thoughts or ideas of an author, those shabby things snatched off basement counters at Gimbel's. The clearest thing ever said about a living work, for theatre or any medium, was said in a speech of Shaw's in 'The Doctor's Dilemma' but I don't remember a single line of it now, I only remember that when I heard it I thought, Yes, that's what it is, not words, not thoughts or ideas, but those abstract things such as form and light and color that living things are made of."

In the leafy calm of his Key West studio, contemplating the fifteen-year life expectancy of American literary talent, Williams did the math and found he had "long-exceeded" the mark. He was already living on creative borrowed time. He had a play by Donald Windham to direct in Houston, an around-the-world trip with Merlo planned for June, and the screenplay of *Hide and Seek* with Kazan to get back to. Although he felt that he should shift gears—he was diverting himself "with a little painting in oils"—he found his "daily existence almost unbearably tedious without beginning at the typewriter." There would inevitably be some kind of writing ahead of him. But what kind? Could he, like the poet in Esmeralda's prayer, find his way back to his heart's green country? He was now less sure than ever. He felt, he said, "shut out" from the theater world, and "the door barred against me." As summer approached, in the shifting landscape of his imagination only one thing seemed certain. "I have nothing more to expect from Broadway," he told James Laughlin.

CHAPTER 5

Thunder of Disintegration

I believe I said, "I am a furtive cat,
unowned/unknown, a scavenging sort of black alley cat
distinguished by a curve of white upturned
at each side of its mouth which makes it seem to grin,
denial in its eyes,
The negative: un-homed . . .

—TENNESSEE WILLIAMS,
"To Maria Britneva"

If only I could realize that I am not 2 persons I am only one.
There is no sense in this division. An enemy inside myself! How
absurd!   —TENNESSEE WILLIAMS,
Notebooks, 1936

In late December 1953, afflicted with "thrombosed hemorrhoids," which to his frightened eyes were "as large as a hen's egg," Williams found himself in a New Orleans hospital, where he was to undergo emergency surgery. "Don't think I ever spent such a night of pain not even at the time of the operation in 1946," he wrote in his diary.

Despite the lacerating pain—"this pain eclipses thought," he said—Williams had himself transferred from the prestigious but dry Ochsner Clinic to the "shabby" Touro Infirmary, where liquor was allowed. The failure of *Camino Real* and the devastations of the ensuing nine months—"a great storm has stripped me bare, like one of those stripped, broken palm trees after a hurricane passes"—had left Williams unabashedly dependent on his "pinkies" (Seconal) and his alcohol. The minor procedure had a major psychic impact; it seemed the culmination of his misery. "All hell is descended on me," he noted at the Touro Infirmary, "retribution for all my misdoings and the things undone."

Williams had written of "the catastrophe of success"; since the March premiere of *Camino* he had experienced its opposite: the catastrophe of indifference. It only fueled his paranoia. His journey two and a half months later on the SS *United States* began "not auspiciously," he noted, when a female friend of Merlo's collapsed in tears at their leave-taking and had to be supported off the ship. "A neurosis is worrying the ragged edges of my nerves," Williams wrote. "Bill Gray cried a little as he said goodbye to me but by no means so copiously as Ellen did over F. How could anyone manage to feel much concern over my coming and going I really don't know. Have thought of death a lot lately." The intensity of Ellen's feelings also fed anxieties about Merlo's loyalty. "These suspicions of mine are tiresome," Williams wrote. "I must at least cut them out of my list of torments this summer."

Back in Rome, however, his list of torments grew longer: at the top of the list was Merlo. "One gets tired of begging for crumbs under the table," Williams wrote in his diary on July 1. "Here is Kaput. But goot!" In a July showdown, Williams told Merlo that he was tired of being "treated like a stupid, unsatisfactory whore by a bad-tempered pimp." In a letter to Kazan, he expanded on the summer standoff. "Conversation had fallen to the level of grunts and barely varying inflections and simply coming into a room with him seemed to constitute an abuse of privilege," he wrote. "This went on for two weeks. Then I had it out with him ver-bally, and flew to Barcelona the next day. I don't think the poor bastard is even aware of what I protested about. He is sunk into such a pit of habit and inertia and basic contempt for himself or his position in life which I think he, consciously or unconsciously, holds me responsible for and almost if not quite hates me for. That old cocksucker Wilde uttered a true thing when he said, Each man kills the thing he loves. The killing is not voluntary but we sure in hell do it. And burn for it."

Neither travel nor writing worked their usual magic; Williams was mired in an enervating slough of defeat. "What a sorry companion I make for anyone young & alive," he wrote in mid-July. "'The Horse' and I never laugh together. Why? He has a sense of humor." Most of the summer was spent reanimating the "dreary" film script *Hide and Seek* and revising his 1940 play *Battle of Angels*, straightening out the story line and doing away with its "juvenile poetics" to shape a new version, which he called *Orpheus Descending*. By re-submerging himself in the world of *Battle of Angels*, in particular, Williams forced a comparison between his youthful romantic self and his ravaged middle-aged one, which only magnified his sense of impasse.

In his youth, back in 1940, his life had been spread out before him like a field to play on; he had been eager and energized. But success, which had expanded his literary horizons, had shrunk his personal ones. As early as 1946, in order to concentrate "on the one big thing, which was work," Williams had begun to draw a sort of psychic circle around himself. At age thirty-eight, he had characterized the pie chart of his existence as "work and worry over work, 89%: struggle against lunacy (partly absorbed in the first category) 10%, very true and tender love for lover and friends, 1%." Now, four years later, at forty-two, Williams complained of a "physical deterioration and a mental fatigue that makes me downright stupid"—Britneva nicknamed him "Forty Winks" for his new habit of nodding off over dinner—as well as a pervading sense of emptiness at the "nothingness of my world outside of work." His good writing days, "and they were not too good," totaled maybe three a month.

On September 7, 1953, Williams mailed a draft of *Orpheus Descending* off to Wood. By mid-October, he had her response. "Audrey wrote me a devastatingly negative reaction," he told Britneva. "I believe she thinks that I have 'flipped my lid' and will be waiting for me at the docks with a straight-jacket behind her back as she waves sweetly with the other hand." Williams, in his recent plays, had insisted on the promise of some kind of romantic transcendence: *Rose Tattoo* ended with Serafina finally in motion; *Camino* concluded with Don Quixote and Kilroy escaping the toxic plaza for the snow-capped mountains, with a grace note of romantic hope: "The violets in the mountains have broken the rocks!" But in the emotional sump into which Williams was now sinking, there was no flow to life or to the imagination. "Death has no sound or light in it, but this is still life," he wrote around this time.

In early October, finding himself in Madrid, Williams read through a new play he had been working on, whose tentative title—"A Place of Stone"—signaled his sense of petrified life. "Was so disheartened that I closed it and prepared to descend to the bar," he wrote. "What troubles me is not just the lifeless quality of the writing, its lack of distinction, but a real confusion that seems to exist, nothing carried through to completion but written over and over, as if a panicky hen running in circles." He added, "Some structural change in my brain? An inability to think clearly and consecutively. Or simply too much alcohol? . . . The prospect of returning to America with this defeat in my heart, which only drink can assuage, is a mighty dark one."

AT THE TOURO INFIRMARY nearly three months later, terrified, lonely, and in pain, Williams imagined himself on his deathbed. "If anything goes wrong, I want Frank to have the film play in addition to other items," he wrote in his diary. "I think he is loyal to me and possibly even loves me. Who else does? Audrey. Grandfather, Rose (as I was) and Mother in her way." Williams's connection of death to his love objects was not accidental. From childhood, he had associated loss with love, had felt an erotic attachment to pain, which he acknowledged in "Cortege," a poem about his thwarted family life:

> And on that morning—
> precociously—for always—
>
> you lost belief
> in everything but loss,
>
> gave credence only to doubt,
> and began even then,
>
> as though it were always intended,
> to form in your heart
>
> the cortege of future betrayals—

the loveless acts
of crude and familiar knowledge.

Even as he awaited the operation, which was called off at the last minute because the doctors thought better of it, Williams castigated himself for his fears ("I'm such a coward, oh, such a damned sniveling coward. It does disgust me so."); for his panicky hypersensitivity ("Anything strange upsets me"); and for his debasing loneliness ("Waiting for Frank like a dog for his bone and his master!"). Apocalyptic foreboding filled his diary: "If I am ever even relatively well again and free from pain I hope I will remember how this was." Williams clung to the memory of his few loved ones, listing them almost like talismans against his fear of cancer, a diagnosis that he "whispered" to himself. "Suppose someone said to me, Tennessee, you have cancer? How would I take it? Probably not well. And yet I suspect that I do." Nonetheless, when Oliver Evans visited him in the hospital on New Year's Day, and reported a conversation with Williams's doctor about the benign hemorrhoids, Williams took umbrage at even the mention of cancer. "He says you should have an operation as it could become malignant," Evans said. "I thought the remark at least unnecessary," Williams wrote in his diary, adding, "He has impulses of shocking cruelty sometimes."

More to the point was Williams's cruelty to himself. His New Year's resolution was to give up "that old breast-beating." About to leave the hospital, he resolved "to make no more incontinent demands on the exhausted artist. Let him rest. Even let him expire if his term is over. But since I want life, even without Creation, I must not whip myself for not doing what I've stopped being able to do. Whether the failure be only a while, or longer, or always."

"Oh, how I long to be loose again, entering the Key West studio for morning work, with the sky and the Australian pines through the sky light and clear morning light on all four sides and the warmth of coffee in me and the other world of creation," Williams wrote from the hospital on New Year's Day, 1954. By the third week of January, he *was* back in the sweet solitude of Key West with his grandfather, filled with a sense of both relief and release. "I am doing what I dreamed of doing again," he wrote. "Clear mornings, coffee, the studio—quiet, serene. But the Muse is not attracted. Not today."

A similarly potent constellation of warring internal forces—death and creativity, fear and freedom, doom and gladness—had occurred only once before in Williams's life. In 1947, after the trauma of his Taos hospital experience, Williams had sat down and projected, he said, "all the emotional content of the long crisis" into *A Streetcar Named Desire.* "Despite the fact that I thought I was dying, or maybe because of it, I had a great passion for work," he wrote in his *Memoirs.*

Now, seven years later, in the spring of 1954, Williams picked up "A Place of Stone," a short play that he hadn't been able to "get a grip on" when he started it the previous year and that had added to his "terrible state of depression last summer in Europe." In March, he wrote to Wood about it. "I'm . . . pulling together a short-long play based on the characters in 'Three Players'," he said. "Don't expect that till you see it, as I might not like it when I read it aloud." Nonetheless, within a week, although he judged the new play too brief and too wordy, Williams clearly saw that he had found a new imaginative seam. "I do think it has a terrible sort of truthfulness about it, and the tightest structure of anything I have done. And a terrifyingly strong final curtain." Back in Rome that summer, when Wood was visiting, Williams handed her a pile of pages he called his "work script," typed mostly on hotel stationery. By then the play was called *Cat on a Hot Tin Roof.* Wood stayed up reading until four in the morning. "I was terribly excited," she said. "In the morning I immediately told him this was certainly his best play since 'Streetcar', and it would be a great success. He may not remember this now, but he was then overwhelmed by my enthusiasm. It was obvious to me that he didn't yet know what he had done."

When Williams showed Wood the working script, he was, he said, "passing through, and still not out of, the worst nervous crisis of my nervous existence." During that parlous summer of 1954, he had arrived "at just about the pit." "I'm just holding on," he wrote in his notebook in June.

"Liquor and Seconal are my only refuge and they not unfailing." Williams's diaries also report a rueful hardening of his heart about love. "Am I worthy of it? Is anybody ever? We're all such pigs, I am one of the biggest"; "my soul, if I have one still, sighs. And shudders and sickens." In 1940, he had confessed to Margaret Webster, the director of *Battle of Angels*, that he had "begun to develop a sort of insulation about my feelings so I won't suffer too much." She replied, "That's a very dangerous thing for a writer." The observation had caught Williams's attention; he recounted it to Kenneth Tynan, fifteen years later. "Once the heart is thoroughly insulated, it's also dead," he said. "My problem is to live with it, and to keep it alive." At an emotional nadir, in his helplessness, he prayed for the intercession of a commanding presence, whose strength would resuscitate him. "Maybe Frank can help me. Maybe Maria will help me. Maybe God will help me," he wrote in his diary. In the end, Williams helped himself.

His feverish internal debate—between the dead heart and the outcrying heart—was built into the early structure of the script, which laid out the battle between the despondent, alcoholic Brick, son of Big Daddy Pollitt, "the Delta's biggest cotton-planter," and his beautiful, frustrated wife, Maggie, who wants both her husband's love and an heir to claim her dying father-in-law's wealth. "In this version, if you had a scene between Brick and Maggie, the first scene would be written from Brick's point of view," Wood recalled. "Then you'd turn a page and there would be the same scene from Maggie's point of view. Page after page it went on." Williams came to understand the play as "a synthesis of all my life." In Brick and Maggie's battle, Williams projected the war inside himself between self-destruction and creativity—his desire to reclaim his literary inheritance.

Brick, on crutches—he has broken an ankle in a drunken attempt to relive his glory days as a high-school athlete—is literally and metaphorically hobbled by his melancholy. He is, as his name indicates, inert. His life is the living death of resignation; he has thrown in the towel. Brick is not only blocked; he is a charming, laidback refusenik who stonewalls the world with drink, cutting himself off from fear, loathing, and life. "A man can be scared and calm at the same time," Williams had noted in the

New Orleans hospital. Brick personifies this infuriating passivity: he makes himself blank to his own desires. His deepest psychic relationship is with alcohol, which serves as a kind of mother, to nourish, calm, and contain him. "This click that I get in my head that makes me peaceful, I got to drink till I get it," he explains to his father, Big Daddy. "It's just a mechanical thing, something like a—like a—like a—switch clicking off in my head, turning the hot light off and the cool night on and—all of a sudden there's—peace!"

Brick is a monument to absence. He enacts onstage the same tactics that Williams did in life: he is compelling enough for other people to want to help him, but he never actually changes. His behavior inspires concern, but he feels concern for no one. His indifference is perverse. He externalizes the inner world of the hysteric—what Masud Khan calls "a cemetery of refusals"—in which the most sensational is his refusal to bed his beautiful wife. Maggie's goal throughout the play is to coax Brick back between the sheets, but, as far as he's concerned, Maggie the Cat can jump off that roof and take up with someone else who will satisfy her sexually.

Maggie, by contrast, is all combat: her hat, as she says, is in the ring, and she's determined to win. She wants Brick; she wants life; she wants, especially, to create a new life with Brick. "Born poor, raised poor, expect to die poor unless I manage to get us something out of what Big Daddy leaves when he dies of cancer," she confesses to Brick, who blames her for the death of Skipper, his beloved friend and former football team-mate. As Brick lashes out at Maggie, just missing her with swipes of his crutch, she forces him to face the truth: *"Skipper is dead! I'm alive!* Maggie the cat is—alive! I am alive, alive! I am alive!" She can still make a baby, she tells him; they can still claim their inheritance. "But how in hell on earth do you imagine—that you're going to have a child by a man that can't stand you?" Brick says. "That's a problem I will have to work out," Maggie replies.

"Did Brick love Maggie?" Williams wrote in a subsequent defense of

OPPOSITE PAGE: With British theater critic Kenneth Tynan at a festival in Valencia, Spain his characters. "He says with unmistakable conviction: 'One man has one great good true thing in his life, one great good thing which is true. I had friendship with Skipper, not love with you, Maggie, but friendship with Skipper . . .'—But can we doubt that he was warmed and charmed by this delightful girl, with her vivacity, her humor, her very admirable pluckiness and tenacity, which are almost the essence of life itself? Of course, now that he has really resigned from life, retired from competition, removed his hat from the ring, now that he wants only things that are cool, such as his 'click' and cool moonlight on the gallery and the deadening of recollection that liquor gives, her tormented face, her anxious voice, strident with the heat of combat, is unpleasantly, sometimes even odiously, disturbing to him. But Brick's overt sexual adjustment was, and must always remain, a heterosexual one. . . . He is her dependent."

Through Maggie, Williams gave a voice to his own imminent emotional atrophy. "I've gone through this—*hideous!—transformation, become—hard! Frantic!—cruel!!*" she tells Brick in the first minutes of the play. For Williams to keep his heart open, he had to lacerate it. "I never could keep my finger off a sore," Maggie says. Neither could Williams. Writing to Crawford in June 1954 (and, incidentally, asking her to recommend a stateside psychoanalyst for when he returned), Williams noted, "There is torment in this play, violence and horror—it is the under kingdom, all right!—that reflects what I was going through, or approaching, as I wrote it." He added, "Perhaps if I had not been so tormented myself it would have been less authentic. Because I could not work with the old vitality, I had to find new ways and may have found some."

Rather like an actor who stays in character offstage in order not to lose the reality of his performance, Williams had begun to intuit the utility of his masochism, to become a connoisseur of his own collapse. In *Cat on a Hot Tin Roof*, his friend Donald Windham correctly sussed a sea change in his writing; he called it a shift from self-dramatization to self-justification. "I'm not sure self-pity is the right term," Williams wrote to *Time* critic Ted Kalem, who had come to the same conclusion as Windham. "In the case of the 'highly personal' writer, I wonder if 'self-examination' isn't a more accurate way to put it. Does this make sense to you?" In fact, the shift in Williams was to self-cannibalization. He was prepared to destroy himself for meaning. He took himself right up to the precipice, so that he could stare into it.

While Williams was creating a drama around Brick's permanent state of inebriation, he, too, had formed an unrepentant appetite for what he jauntily called "a drinky-pie":

> When you're feelin sorry
> when you start to sigh,
> honey, what you're needin
> is a *little* drinky-pie.
> Yes, honey, what you're cravin
> is a little drinky-pie.
>
> Two or three ain't nothin,
> three or four won't make you high,
> but the fifth drink is the number
> that I call a drinky-pie!
>
> . . . You'll bust the sky wide open
> with a little drinky-pie.
> Drink a *little* drinky-pie, love,
> drink a little drinky-pie

Such anthems aside, Williams's drinking was no laughing matter. "It has gotten so bad," he admitted to Crawford, "I don't dare to turn down a street unless I can sight a bar not more than a block and a half down it." He added, "Sometimes I have to stop and lean against a wall and ask somebody with me to run ahead and bring me a glass of cognac from the bar." Williams was becoming simultaneously an actor and a voyeur, an exhibitionist and a spectator of his own suffering. He was scaring himself into new literary life.

"FOR THE NEW YEAR: may you write a play and may I direct it," Elia Kazan had written Williams on Christmas Day, 1953. Seven months later, Williams granted Kazan his wish. In July, Wood sent him *Orpheus*

Descending; by mid-August, Kazan declared his enthusiasm, dangling the possibility of a December production. "Of course I wrote it for you as I have all of my plays since 'Streetcar' but I had little hope that you would have the time or want to do it, probably as a result of Cheryl [Crawford]'s discouraging reaction," Williams replied, while reminding Kazan that another director, Joe Mankiewicz, was also in the hunt. He went on:

> Of course you know, as I've already told you, that I'd never give the play to Joe (assuming he still wants it) except in the unlikely event that there is an irreconcilable difference in your point of view and mine. I've never resisted any changes in work that you suggested for *any reason* except a *real inability* to make them, never because I didn't understand or approve of them. Sometimes you specify sweeping changes which would involve a sort of re-write that would occupy months of time, at my slower and slower pace of working. I'd hate to have to compute the amount of time I've already devoted to this re-write of "Battle": it would shock you!—and I just couldn't embark upon another very extensive revision of it, especially with two new plays in first draft which I think should now take precedence, although neither of them has, in my opinion, the potential stature of this one, but do have the advantage of complete newness. I believe Audrey feels the fact that this play is based on an old one would weigh against it critically. This may be true. But I feel that if it's powerful enough, as it surely would be in your hands, with the right cast, that disadvantage would be annihilated and even almost forgotten before it passed Philadelphia, because what they want is a *good* play, or a *strong* one, new or old.

In September, two weeks before his return from Europe, Williams wrote to Kazan again; in pencil, at the top of the letter, he scrawled, "Will return with 2 other plays besides 'Orpheus,' *no lie!*"

One of those plays was *Cat on a Hot Tin Roof*. When Williams had first shown the short version to Wood in Rome, he had floated the idea that it be part of a double bill. Wood was adamantly opposed. "I still wish it could be a full evening," she wrote to him in July, "and I'm still troubled by your desire to keep it in a length that will necessitate adding something alien to it." Wood felt the play was unfinished, but her idea challenged Williams's poetic conception of the play. He remained intransigent. "To me the story is complete in its present form, it says all that I had to say about these characters and their situation, it was conceived as a short full-length play: there are three acts in it. First, Brick and his wife. Second, Brick and Big Daddy. Third, The Family Conference," Williams wrote to Wood in September. "I thought at least structurally the play was just right, I liked there being no time lapse between the acts, one flowing directly into the others, and it all taking place in the exact time that it occupies in the theatre. I would hate to lose that tightness, that simplicity, by somehow forcing it into a more extended form simply to satisfy a convention of theatre."

Williams could straight-arm Wood with palaver about his artistic intentions; Kazan, however, was a cagier customer. At the prospect of getting his hands on a new Williams play, even before he'd seen it, Kazan passed on *Orpheus Descending*. "I'm quite exhausted. Out of gas. No gissum left," Kazan said, suggesting that Williams go with Mankiewicz and he would "wait for one of the new plays."

On September 30, accompanied on the *Andrea Doria* by Anna Magnani on her way to Hollywood to film *The Rose Tattoo*, Williams and Merlo docked in New York. Two weeks later, production plans for *Cat on a Hot Tin Roof* were already being formulated, with Wood and Kazan "both hot for it," according to Williams. "The only thing I want is Kazan," Williams wrote to Maria Britneva on October 17.

With two consecutive Broadway financial failures to his name, Williams needed a hit, and Kazan was a hit-maker. Before Kazan read *Cat on a Hot Tin Roof*, Williams wrote him a well-judged letter, and in it played both to his sense of friendship and to his artistic ambition. "You are on the threshold of your richest creative period. There were unmistakable signs of this in 'Waterfront' and in 'Tea and Sympathy,'" Williams wrote. "In both cases you triumphed over scripts which I personally don't care for and invested them with values without which they would have been red caviar: I mean salmon roe, not shad. All you need now is a thing that can rise when you rise, with the same sort of lift that you give it, and I am still hoping that something of mine will be it. I even dare to *believe* so!"

"I've occasionally lied to playwrights when they've offered me a play to direct that I've liked but with qualifications that were negative," Kazan wrote in his autobiography. After reading *Cat on a Hot Tin Roof*, however, he pulled no punches. He believed that Williams had written "a brilliant first draft," but he was convinced that there was more to do. "PLEASE PLEASE stop and don't rush into production," he said. "You're letting yourself in for a lot of grief if you do." In the push and pull of their collaboration, Kazan acted as a kind of clear-eyed father who had Williams's best interests at heart. "I'm scared to death to embark with you on this play before I think the script is ready," he insisted on October 18, in a three-page letter. "We did that on CAMINO and you had a sore blow. I don't think you should again." Kazan went on, "I told you way back then that I thought it was the wrong third act. About the wrong thing. You didn't really agree with that. But I still think so. I wish I JUST WISH to Christ you'd stop and think it thru. The script is 99% of the problem in the theatre. UNITY. Clarity. What the audience follows. What they are made to be interested in and what they want to follow." Kazan set out the problems as he saw them and challenged Williams to find solutions for himself. "I have no good suggestions," he told Williams in his notes. "You're out of my league. I don't think anyone else is going to help you, however. You're in a game where only you know the rules." Kazan's passion and prowess offered Williams a safety net, which emboldened the fearful playwright to write beyond himself.

The dying patriarch of Williams's tale, Big Daddy Pollitt, had risen from Delta plantation manager to become the owner of twenty-eight-thousand acres of "the richest land this side of the valley Nile." Into an early version of the play, Williams pasted a 1921 clipping from a local Mississippi newspaper about G. D. Perry—a friend of Reverend Dakin's—which had planted the seed that sprouted Big Daddy and his son and daughter-in-law Gooper and Mae's big family of "no-neck monsters":

From Manager to Owner of 7,400 Acres in Tunica

G.D. Perry and family of Hollywood, Miss. Mr. Perry has just closed a deal for one-half interest in the Duke Plantation which consists of 14,800 acres. This gives him 7,400 acres in Tunica County, Miss. He and his wife were reared in Tennessee. He is the son of Marshall Perry, formerly of Madison County, and grandson of Col. G.W. Day of Humboldt. His wife was Miss Sallie Jett Whitley of Mason, Tenn., at which place they were married in 1897. He went to the delta in 1900 as manager for B.F. Duke, better known as Tobe Duke, on this plantation which he has just closed the deal for. He managed for Duke 12 years. After Duke's death he leased this plantation and bought the plantation of W.M. Johnson and C.A. Barr——both of Memphis. Mr. and Mrs. Perry have nine children.

Big Daddy is a huge man, matched by a huge anger and a huge appetite for life. Williams seems to have borrowed the name and the look of the character from the father of his old Macon, Georgia, friend, Jordan Massie, a cousin of Carson McCullers, but for Big Daddy's bombast and bawdry Williams channeled his own bull-necked father. (The title of the play also came from CC. "My father had a great gift for phrases," Williams said. " 'Edwina,' he used to say. 'You're making me as nervous as a cat on a hot tin roof!' ") Big Daddy's voice—raffish, rough, rollicking—was mesmerizing and unique to the theater of its time, a twentieth-century manifestation of the folkloric American ring-tailed roarer. Big Daddy "strikes the keynote of the play. A terrible black anger and ferocity, a rock-bottom honesty," said Williams, who felt he had "reached beyond" himself to find a "crude eloquence" unmatched in any of his other characters.

In the play, Big Daddy, onstage or off, is the focus of the other characters' attention. It is his sixty-fifth birthday, and the household is celebrating his apparent clean bill of health after a struggle with cancer. He is the play's thematic catalyst, calling out the ambition in Maggie, the greed in Gooper and his wife Mae—"a monster of fertility"—who are intent on freezing Brick out of the family inheritance, and the self-delusion in Brick:

BIG DADDY: (*He snatches the glass from Brick's hand.*) What do you know about this mendacity thing? Hell! I could write a book on it! Don't you know that? I could write a book on it and still not cover the subject? Well, I could, I could write a goddamn book on it and still not cover the subject anywhere near enough!!—Think of all the lies I got to put up with!—Pretenses! Ain't that mendacity! Having to pretend stuff you don't think or feel or have any idea of? Having for instance to act like I care for Big Mama!—I haven't been able to stand the sight, sound or smell of that woman for forty years now!—even when I *laid* her!—regular as a piston. . . .

Pretend to love that son of a bitch Gooper and his wife Mae and those five same screechers out there like Parrotts in a jungle? Jesus! Can't stand to look at 'em!

Church!—it bores the Bejesus out of me but I go!—I go an' sit there and listen to the fool preacher!

Clubs!—Elks! Masons! Rotary!—*crap*! . . .

I've lived with mendacity!—Why can't *you* live with it? Hell, you *got* to live with it, there's nothing *else* to *live* with except mendacity, is there?

Despite the majestic energy of Big Daddy's personality and the brilliant extravagance of his talk, Williams, in his original conception of the play, did not bring him back in act 3. Instead, having learned from Brick that the family has kept his terminal prognosis from him, Big Daddy exits in act 2 and climbs up on the belvedere. For the rest of the play his offstage "long drawn cry of agony and rage" was the only thing that anyone in the Pollitt household heard of him. The banishment of Big Daddy from the last act was a narrative mistake. Wood remarked on it; Kazan jumped on it:

> This play is about what the second act is about.
>
> The first act needs work, yes. But it's not the crucial problem.
>
> I think the central problem is to find out what the second act is about and to resolve that in Act 3.
>
> The third act just plain loses me.
>
> I want to know what Big Daddy does, after he's been told. That isn't there. Simply and plainly, whom does he affirm? All right, I know you detest the word affirm. What does he do when he climbs up there?

I don't give a shit in hell how Big Mama takes the fucking news. We know.

It bores me to see Margaret and Mae squabble and bitch. It's beneath your play and we've had it. It's worth about a minute of action and not a second of act three. . . .

What is the hurry? A guy with talent the size of yours shouldn't put out something half-baked. You have a super superb second act. I know, I just know the third act is not right. I don't know what it should be. I think keeping the old man "alive" on the Belvedere is just a substitute.

Please don't satisfy me. Take time to satisfy yourself. Are YOU really satisfied with this play? You weren't at all when you gave it to me. . . . Tenn, this play is just not ready to have conferences about yet. That's the plain plain plain truth.

In another note, on October 20, Kazan added more fuel to the fire: "I am left at the end of Act II with an intense concern with Big Daddy's fate—and I want to see how he comes out, so to speak. I wouldn't even mind him just sitting on stage for a moment or two at the beginning of Act III. It would interest me more than what you have there now. . . . You can't get me all hot and bothered and then walk away and say let's look at the view." To the vinegar of his unfettered opinions—he delivered them in a back-to-back flurry of hastily typed notes over two days—Kazan added the honey of praise. "I think you've got the best play here potentially in years and years," he wrote. "Why throw that away because this wind of *let's get going* is pushing you? I'm not going anywhere. I want to do the play badly. I don't get but one play I really want to do every three years or so. I sure want to do this one."

On receiving Kazan's first set of notes, Williams couldn't sleep; nonetheless, at eight the next morning he was at the typewriter, determined, he told Kazan, "to get what you want without losing what I want." Williams added, "I dare to believe that I can work this out, but it would help me immeasurably if you and some producer would give me a vote of confidence by committing yourself to a date of production with the work still on the bench."

By October 29, as Williams reported to Britneva, Kazan "had committed himself (verbally) to do 'Cat on a Hot Tin Roof.'" The parenthetic word in Williams's sentence spoke volumes. Kazan was slippery. His power over a script's final shape was in direct proportion to the withholding of his complete commitment. Kazan knew his measure; even in production he was not above using his prestige as leverage to control Williams. At one rehearsal, Williams called up from the orchestra to Barbara Bel Geddes, who was the original Maggie: "More melody in your voice, Barbara. Southern girls have melody in their—" Kazan cut him off, then came up the aisle to sit beside Williams. "I whispered to him that if he did that again, I'd quit," Kazan recalled. Despite their loyalty, for both men, working together was a delicate dance.

In order not to lose Kazan, Williams had to find ways to answer his narrative demands, while keeping "the core of the play very hard, because I detest plays that are built around something mushy such as I feel under the surface of many sentimental successes in the theatre." Nobody has ever gone broke on Broadway purveying absolutes; as Williams saw it, however, he was dramatizing ambivalence. "This is a play about good bastards and good bitches," he told Kazan. "I mean it exposes the startling co-existence of good and evil, the shocking *duality* of the single heart." He went on, "I am as happy as you are that our discussions have led to a way of highlighting the good in Maggie, the indestructible spirit of Big Daddy, so that the final effect of the play is not negative, this is a forward step, a step toward a *larger* truth which will add immeasurably to the play's power of communication or scope of communication."

"Characters you can root for" was the mantra of Broadway's commercial swamis. In the case of *Cat on a Hot Tin Roof*, Williams heard the phrase from Wood, from Crawford, and from Kazan. "Vitality is the hero of the play!" Williams insisted. "The character you can 'root for' . . . is not a person but a quality in people that makes them survive." Nonetheless, as he told Kazan, he was rewriting act 1 in a tighter, straighter line, "and concentrating on the character of Margaret with emphasis on those things about her which make her human, understandable, and likeable. Someone who's always crouched at the feet of the rich and lucky with the smile of a beggar, and the claws of a cat. Expecting a kick, but begging for something better and willing to give for it plenty!—a normal, though desperate, person. A fighter."

Williams appropriated the nickname "Maggie the Cat" from Margaret Lewis Powell, a friend of Williams's friend Jordan Massie. But the prototype for Maggie's desperation, ruthlessness, outspokenness, and hyperbolic flair was someone who was closer to hand for the best part of the summer of 1954: Maria Britneva, to whom the play is dedicated. (An early version was dedicated to Wood.) "I think a lot of you has gone into the writing of it. Wit and gallantry etc.," Williams wrote to Britneva, while demurring on her characteristically brazen request to be elevated from bit player to star of *Cat* for its Broadway debut. The drawled iconic epithet in *Cat on a Hot Tin Roof*'s first line—"no-neck monsters"—was a piece of Britneva's comic vitriol: one of the many caustic mots that Williams enjoyed collecting and repeating. When Britneva read the final version of the script, she protested that she wouldn't talk like Maggie. "Honey! I'm writing about your spirit—your tenacity," Williams said. But he captured more than her tenacity; Britneva's flirtatiousness and her rapacity, her humiliated heart and her grandiose sense of entitlement were the elements from which Williams distilled much of Maggie's manic vitality. "You can be young without money but you can't be old without it," Maggie famously tells Brick. "You've got to be old *with* money because to be old without it is just too awful." Like Britneva, Maggie "always had to suck up to people I couldn't stand because they had money and I was poor as Job's turkey." She is a picturesque combination of sycophancy and ferocity—especially in the early versions of *Cat* where Maggie is even more extreme:

> The dress I married you in was my grandmother's wedding-gown and I had to pretend I wore it for sentimental reasons! Hell, I liked the moths better that ate it than that mean old witch that'd—*bequeathed* it to me, just about all that—
>   (*Jerks a drawer open*)
> —anyone *ever*—

(*Slams drawer shut*)

—left me, in *spite* of all my—

(*Dabs forehead*)

—bowing and scraping to them. . . .

(*Rises before the full-length mirror*)

So that's why I'm like a cat on a hot tin roof! . . . But I don't *look* like one, do I? Now? Or *do* I? Even *now*?

You're right. I must break myself of this habit of straining my throat muscles so they stick out!—like the neck of somebody rowning!—as if I was trying to keep my head above water. . . .

Well, I am!

In 1952, Britneva, "the furious Tartar," as Williams dubbed her, began a relationship with the talented, square-jawed James Laughlin, Williams's millionaire publisher. When Laughlin resumed an affair with an American cohort at his publishing company, New Directions, Britneva immediately glommed onto John Huston. "I introduced them on the set of 'Moulin Rouge,'" Williams wrote to Wood. "I had not been here a day when I received a wire from Maria. 'AT IT LIKE KNIVES. HUSTON A STEAMING HOT CUP OF TEA. WANT TO STAY IN PARIS CALL ME.'" Williams added, "I do hope she gets a job out of this, which was the original purpose of the meeting, and not just another one of her peculiar misadventures."

By the spring of 1954, however, Britneva was back together with Laughlin, and their engagement was precipitously announced in the *London Times*. The news, Williams wired them, "made me cry with happiness." Laughlin's patrician American mother, however, was not so happy. "Jamesie! A RUSSIAN! Can't you find a nice American girl who knows our ways," Laughlin recalled her saying. His mother's disapproval put Britneva immediately on her high horse. "Darling!" Williams counseled her, "Nobody loves honesty more than I, but honey! There are times, there are situations, there are circumstances in which the head must not rule the heart but at least act in collaboration with it. You seem to be doing and saying or thinking all the wrong things."

When Laughlin got cold feet and broke off the engagement several months later, it was ostensibly due to Britneva's avidity—she had gone out shopping in Florence to buy Laughlin a silk tie and returned with eight. "My God! What are you going to do with all *my* money?" Laughlin asked her. "I was genuinely surprised," Britneva recalled. "'Why, have you *got* any?—I'll spend it, of course!'" (Britneva knew perfectly well that Laughlin was wealthy. A press release she later composed, with the help of a New York PR man, refers to her having "broken her engagement to a multimillionaire steel heir.") It was Britneva's castrating willfulness that really terrified Laughlin. "I think you are one of the world's more attractive girls," he admitted to her in his Dear Maria letter. "But I'm also afraid of you—afraid of how you might wreck my life with all that mis-directed energy pouring out of you like a giant Russian dynamo." In a five-page handwritten letter to Williams, he spelled out his fears more directly: "She is so strong-willed and dominating and, to use her phrase, 'makes such rows' when I assert myself against her wishes. If anything, in the years I have known her, she has become *more* vital and active, more ready to get caught up in the interests and doings of people who do not really fit into the center of her picture." He added, "I doubt if she is really 'crushed,' as you say. I don't think you really understand what a vitality she has. *Nothing* could or would crush her."

For most of the summer of 1954, Britneva and Williams wandered around Europe. By September, she was still on Williams's meal ticket and "suggesting more trips," as he sourly admitted to Wood. "Poor little Maria!" he told Wood. "I said she must forget Jay and go back to her old life. She said, What life? I have none. I said, Well, you've got to make one. Nobody can be that Russian this long!"

By the end of the summer, Maria's freeloading, compounded with her high-handedness, had become a fractious issue in Williams's ménage. "All hell has broke loose here," Williams wrote to Wood. "Maria has denounced Frank as 'common, ill-bred, Etc.' and, at least for the past night, has removed herself from the premises." Williams went on, "The trouble is that she wants to be treated constantly as a guest although, since she has been with us all summer, we can only treat her as a member of the family without giving up our agreeable pattern of life. Another trouble is that she is without any personal funds to speak of, and is embarrassingly dependent on us. She will not be realistic about this but wants us to entertain her titled friends at expensive restaurants, Etc., and when she leaves in the mornings, there is usually a message on the table giving us instructions of what to do. I tolerate this because I am very fond of her and am keenly aware of her emotional upset over being jilted by Jay."

Throughout the summer of 1954, as he was finishing *Cat* and working on the revisions, Williams was enlisted in Britneva's real-life never-say-die battle to claim what she felt was her emotional and creative due. "Maria and I are writing letters beside the country club pool, she to Jay, I to you," Williams wrote to Wood. "I think I should let you know that M is probably flying to America this summer to have a showdown with Jay. She feels that it would strengthen, or dignify, her position if she had a job in the States and were not just pursuing him there. Can you think of anything for her? I have offered to pay her fare and allow her to occupy our NY apartment." Through the intercession of Williams, Kazan, and other theatrical grandees of her acquaintance, Britneva got a work permit, which allowed her, as "an artist of outstanding merit and ability," to perform in America. Her goal, however, was not to get work but to get Laughlin—and she was driving him half-crazy. "The help she needs is artistic and emotional, not material," Williams wrote Laughlin. "I am sorry if her presence in America complicated things for you or makes you uncomfortable."

"I don't think anyone has ever upset me so much," Laughlin told Williams. "She has wonderful qualities and if she would just get over her illusions—me, for one, and the idea that she has to be an actress for another—I think she would have a happy and useful life." Laughlin wanted to help Britneva financially, but his counselors argued for a clean break, because "as long as she thinks I am helping her she thinks that means in the end I will accept her and it just prolongs the illusion and her misery." Like Maggie, who refuses to lose, Britneva would not be denied. Once in America, she sought any means to inveigle her way back into Laughlin's life, including becoming a patient of the same psychotherapist. "The very fact that she went to such lengths to worm it out of the doctor where the help was coming from just proves that point," Laughlin wrote. "And her whole thought in going to him—as far as I can gather from talking to him—has been that by doing so she would alter her personality so that I would like her. In other words, she went to him not really to help herself, but just as a further means of getting at me."

If Britneva eventually had to relinquish her romantic dream, she clung staunchly to her artistic one. On March 3, 1955, three weeks before the Broadway debut of *Cat on a Hot Tin Roof*, she debuted as Blanche in a revival of *Streetcar* at the Originals Only Playhouse in Sheridan Square. In *Five O'Clock Angel*, Britneva refers to Brooks Atkinson's praise, in the *New York Times*, of her performance and her "exciting ideas about the doomed heroine." "She uses unexpected humor to reveal the gallant soul beneath the cracking veneer," Britneva quotes Atkinson. "The serenity of the final and complete escape from sanity, hitherto the weakest scene in the play, now comes as close to tragedy as anything by an American playwright since O'Neill." The review is more important for its retrospective revelations about Britneva than it is for her glory as an actress. Maggie, in her desperation, will do anything—even lie—to win the day; so would Britneva. Atkinson's favorable review, it turns out, was her own invention. In reality, what he wrote was, "There is no point in pretending that the acting conveys the intricate mysteries of the script. . . . Maria Brit-Neva, an English actress, is not able to express the inner tensions of that haunted gentlewoman."

Williams's compassionate interpolation of Britneva's character into *Cat on a Hot Tin Roof* actually prefigured her real-life marriage of inconvenience. On July 25, 1956, she married Peter Grenfell, Lord St. Just, the son of Edward Grenfell, the English banking partner of J. P. Morgan who had been made a baron in 1935. Peter, who had a love of country pursuits and ballet and opera, suffered from a manic depression that led to frequent bouts of uncontrollable shaking and crying. Britneva took him out of a sanatorium to marry him. While she was at Harvey Nichols buying gloves for the wedding, he bolted. They spent their wedding night at Claridge's, but after a furious row the next day, Lord Peter again ran off for a fortnight. "He was in kind of strange shape," Jean Stein, a friend of Britneva's whose father was the head of the media conglomerate MCA, recalled, adding, of Britneva's behavior, which was an eerie simulacrum of Maggie's scheming, "To be Lady St. Just and to have some money. Are you kidding?

She had nothing. Desperate. And to have that beautiful home in the country and to be legitimate!" "He thought she could help him," Bobby Henderson, a trustee of Peter St. Just's estate said. "She had an effect on him. She bemused him. Her amusingness distracted him. It was an escape. He certainly had strong feelings to be near her; and then he didn't."

Though the marriage produced two children, St. Just also fathered at least one and possibly two illegitimate children. And his mother treated Maria badly. Lord Peter and Lady Maria were put on a minimal allowance by his trustees. "Maria was living in a tiny, tiny flat with her two babies in London," Harriet Van Horne, an American newspaper columnist and friend who visited her there in the late 1950s, said. A house was eventually purchased for the couple but was put in the names of their children. "She lived there by grace and favor," Van Horne said.

By November 1954, Williams had turned in his revisions to Kazan. As part of his humanizing enterprise, he had given Maggie a different ending. "I am not at all sure that this new ending is what I want," he wrote to Wood. "Do you think it contains an echo of 'Tea and Sympathy'?" He went on, "Here is another case of a woman giving a man back his manhood, while in the original conception it was about a vital, strong woman dominating a weak man and achieving her will. Also: does Big Daddy's reappearance really and truly add anything that's important to the story besides making it softer or sweeter or easier to take?"

Williams's faith in his original play had recently been strengthened by Christopher Isherwood, to whom he had read his first typed draft. "He loved it, said he thought it in many ways my best play," Williams told Wood. He decided to fly to Los Angeles, where *The Rose Tattoo* was filming, to talk to Kazan. "Isherwood will be there and possibly the three of us could arrive at an agreement about the 'Cat' script that would satisfy both Gadg and me," he said. As late as November 23, Kazan had still not committed to direct the play. "I think Gadg must let us know right away if he is or isn't willing to make a definite commitment at a specific time."

Williams spent two lonely weeks in Los Angeles. ("Loathe every min-

Burl Ives as Big Daddy and Ben Gazzara as Brick in *Cat on a Hot Tin Roof*

ute of it," he wrote in his diary.) His talks with Kazan produced another five-page letter of director's notes about the outstanding problem: the dramatization of Brick, whose mystery, for Williams, was "the poem of the play, not its story but the poem of the story." "I do get his point but I'm afraid he doesn't quite get mine," Williams wrote in his diary. "Things are not always explained. Situations are not always resolved. Characters don't always 'progress.' But I shall, of course, try to arrive at an another compromise with him."

For Kazan, at least one crucial detail about the show was resolved: he would direct it. In a memorandum to Molly Day Thacher, he wrote:

I'm going to do the Williams play. I just admire that fellow. I really do. We've had some wonderful talks. We've got somewhere conceptually. He's terribly honest. Sometimes I fill with admiration for him. And I've never been able to talk to any author as I'm able to talk with him. Unreserved (Except Moss Hart on GA [*Gentleman's Agreement*] . . . The title of the play is CAT ON A HOT TIN ROOF. Isn't that just a hell of a title. Margaret now is "sympathetic" whatever the hell that means. Anyway I think the audience will end up with a tough grudging admiration for her. . . . And I've found something for Brick to do in Act Three AND I've influenced Big Daddy to totally reject Brick's explanation in Act Two. Or at least Brick's attack on his explanation.

From the beginning of their conversations about the play, Kazan had argued that Brick needed to be made theatrically dynamic, not just poetically impassive. "I 'buy' a lot of your letter but of course not all," Williams wrote to Kazan at 4:30 A.M. from his Beverly Hills hotel. "Possibly I 'buy' more than half, and after a couple of nights studying it out, I think I understand it." Williams went on, "To be brief: the part I buy is that there has to be a reason for Brick's impasse (his drinking is only an expression of it) that will 'hold water.'" Williams had come to the narrative conclusion that Brick did love Skipper, whom he identified with sports, "the romantic world of adolescence which he couldn't go past." Williams went on:

Further: to reverse my original (somewhat tentative) premise, I now believe that, in the deeper sense, not the literal sense, Brick *is* homosexual with a heterosexual adjustment: a thing I've suspected of several others, such as Brando, for instance. (He hasn't cracked up but I think he bears watching. He strikes me as being a compulsive eccentric.) I think these people are often undersexed, prefer pet raccoons or sports or something to sex with either gender. They have deep attachments, idealistic, romantic: sublimated loves! They are terrible Puritans. (Marlon dislikes me. Why? I'm "corrupt.") These people may have a glandular set-up which will keep them "banked," at low-pressure, enough to get by without the eventual crack-up. Take Brando again: he's smoldering with something and I don't think it's Josanne! Sorry to make him my guinea pig in this analysis (Please give this letter back to me!) but he's the nearest thing to Brick that we both know. Their innocence, their blindness, makes them very, very touching, very beautiful and sad. Often they make fine artists, having to sublimate so much of their love, and believe me, homosexual love is something that also requires more than a physical expression. But if a mask is ripped off, suddenly, roughly, that's quite enough to blast the whole Mechanism, the whole adjustment, knock the world out from under their feet, and leave them no alternative but—owning up to the truth or retreat into something like liquor.

Ripping away Brick's mask and then sustaining his story into act 3 was Williams's challenge. Less than a month before rehearsals, Kazan was still complaining. "Brick gives me a pain in the well-known part in Act III, the first seven-eighths of it. He seems to be exactly the same as he was at the beginning of Act I," he said, adding in a letter a week later, "Tenn, it's the job of the playwright to tell the truth. You aren't telling the final truth about Brick. You unveil a bit of him in Act I, another bit, a good-sized bit in Act II, and then back he goes hidden, hopeless, mannered, untouchable. And above all he acts as though Act II never happened." Kazan added, "Can't he be a lovable, bright, brilliant, funny drunk instead of a self-pitying, hopelessly immersed drunk?" At the climax of act 2, when Brick talks about Skipper's phone call—the call in which he issued the rejection that led to Skipper's suicide—Kazan urged Williams to "go a little further" and to exploit the situation "for everything it's worth" in order to hang "a heavier load of guilt on Brick" to explain his paralysis. Kazan dummied up some dialogue for his resistant author:

BIG DADDY: What did you say to him?
BRICK: Nothing.
BIG DADDY: Nothing?

BRICK: I hung up.
BIG DADDY: You said nothing? You hung up?
BRICK: I hung up. What could I say?
BIG DADDY: He was your friend. You had to say something to him.

In the rewritten scene, which upped the theatrical ante for both main characters, Williams transformed Kazan's suggestion into a sensational demonstration of Brick's habit of denial:

BIG DADDY: You musta said *somethin'* to him before he hung up.
BRICK: What could I say to him?
BIG DADDY: Anything. Something.
BRICK: Nothing.
BIG DADDY: Just hung up?
BRICK: Just hung up.
BIG DADDY: Uh-huh. Anyhow now!—we have tracked down the lie with which you're disgusted and which you are drinking to kill your disgust with, Brick. You been passing the buck. This disgust with mendacity is disgust with yourself. *You!*—dug the grave of your friend and kicked him in it!—before you'd face the truth with him!
BRICK: *His* truth, not *mine!*
BIG DADDY: His truth, okay! But you wouldn't face it with him!
BRICK: Who *can* face truth? Can *you?*

Kazan was "worried sick" about the third act, in which Brick kept singing and mooning about on the veranda but doing nothing. He kept wondering how to keep Brick center stage, how to keep his thinking and feeling, his experience continually before the audience. "God, Tenn, can't we bring that son of a bitch to life," he wrote. "Brick all thru! That's the job!" he wrote to Williams, before rehearsals started.

His case was strong. The arc of act 2 was entirely about Brick and the dilemma of bringing him back to life. "We see here, just as we did in Act I, that he is far, far, FAR from not giving a damn . . . that he is violent as a volcano underneath and is simply full of doubt and guilt," Kazan wrote to Williams. "Then something really revolutionary happens to him. Big

Daddy states that the mendacity that he is disgusted with is his own. That he has been blaming Maggie for a murder that *he* committed—that he is disgusted with himself for having betrayed his best friend." Kazan pressed on: "Now Brick has no answer to this. He, in fact, admits Big Daddy is right when he says: 'Can *you* stand the truth???' He admits, then, does he not, that what Big Daddy said was true." Kazan continued:

> The boy is aroused to murder at the end of Act I and around to practically killing his father in Act II. The playwright has done his job. He has put Brick into a situation that forces him out of his shell, that brings him out from under cover, and so on. And there is at the end of Act II this piece of SPIRITUAL RECOGNITION. The boy is brought face to face with his own lie.

> I should hope by this time in the play the audience will be FEELING (I'm not talking about thinking, or appreciating or enjoying—I'm talking about the basic theatre experience, the very basic one) I should hope by this time that the audience is sitting in the goddam theatre to see how two things turn out, sitting there very very partisan, as they should be. They should want Brick to face the lie he told himself and atone for the torture he perpetuated on Maggie. And DO something about it! They will want to see what he does. He's got to do something.

"It's only fair to put you on notice that I'll be striving—I can't do different—to keep Brick and his thinking, his development, smack in the audience's eye all thru Act III," Kazan told Williams as they approached rehearsals, adding, "I have to work to show that there *has* been a progression within him, no matter how deeply concealed." To that end, Kazan asked for Brick to sing; he got it. He asked for Brick to forgo the estate; he got it. Kazan wanted Brick to have more humanity and more agency. "Can we make him funny and truth-telling so IN THAT WAY reveal his pain and self-disgust? Can't we feel that above all he wants to make up to Maggie for the torture he gave her?" he asked Williams. Kazan got that too. As the family jostles for position in Big Daddy's will, the childless Maggie ups the ante by suddenly announcing in front of the patriarch that she's pregnant—a sort of Hail Mary pass that Brick witnesses with both shock and awe. "Truth is something desperate, an' she's got it," Brick says, coming to Maggie's defense when Gooper and Mae call it a lie. "Believe me, it's somethin' desperate, an' she's got it." Brick goes on, "An' now, if you will stop actin' as if Brick Pollitt was dead and buried, invisible, not heard, an' go on back to your peep-hole in the wall—I'm drunk, and sleepy—not as alive as Maggie, but still alive."

Williams's rewrites gave Kazan precisely what he had asked for. Kazan also had overridden Williams's initial disapproval of Jo Mielziner's abstract set ("a meaningless piece of chi-chi") and of the casting of Burl Ives as Big Daddy ("acted like a stuffed turkey") and Barbara Bel Geddes as Maggie ("inadequate"). Kazan had even coaxed Williams to soften his ending. On the first day of rehearsal, sensing a disaster, Williams wrote in his diary, "Already making plans for a far away flight (perhaps as far as Ceylon) the night the play opens in New York!" But, once the show was up and running in Philadelphia, it was hard to argue with its success. The reviews were rapturous; the box office, according to *Variety*, was "torrid." Kazan's structural demands had given the play its satisfying wallop, and Williams knew it. "I am being utterly sincere when I say that, on the whole, you have done one of your greatest jobs," Williams wrote to him after their last rehearsal before Philadelphia, signing himself, "Devotedly."

The thing that gave Williams the most pause was the show's revised ending, in which Brick was tempted back into the marital bed. All disclaimers to the contrary—"I didn't write, plan, or edit the 'commercial' third act," Kazan wrote in his autobiography, a statement that is belied by his notes to Williams—Kazan had winkled out of Williams this softer ending, which changed the play's thematic attack on the couple. At the finale, in the Kazan version, as she tries to coax him to create an heir, Maggie strikes a perverse bargain with Brick. "I told a lie to Big Daddy, but we can make that lie come true," she tells him. "And then I'll bring you liquor, and we'll get drunk together, here, tonight, in this place that death has come into! What do you say? What do you say, baby?"

Maggie has pitched all Brick's liquor bottles off the veranda, and he is unable to go and get more. He has lost his driver's license, and if he went to get booze himself, Maggie says, "I'd phone ahead and have you stopped

on the highway." He's checkmated. Now, however, she's prepared to collude in his self-destruction. Brick finds affirmative words. "I admire you,
Maggie," he says, sitting at the edge of the bed. Maggie kneels beside
him. "Oh, you weak, beautiful people who give up with such grace," she
says. "What you need is someone to take hold of you—gently, with love,
and hand your life back to you, like something gold you let go of—and I
can! I'm determined to do it—and nothing's more determined than a cat

Burl Ives in the dressing room during a production of *Cat on a Hot Tin Roof*

on a tin roof—is there? Is there, Baby?" For the first time, Brick allows himself to be touched by Maggie—"She touches his cheek, gently," the stage direction reads—a gesture that holds out the possibility of reunification. The curtain comes down on this moment of connection.

In the original ending, most of which Williams restored for the 1974 Broadway production and the play's subsequent republication, Brick refuses to surrender to Maggie and her blandishments. "What do you say?" she says. "I don't say anything. I guess there's nothing to say," he replies. His hatred for himself and for Maggie remains immutable; he submits to nothing but his own destructiveness. Nonetheless, Maggie whispers, "I *do* love you, Brick. I *do!*" Echoing Big Daddy's fierce words, in the play's curtain line, Brick says, "Wouldn't it be funny if that was true?" This ending, according to Williams, was appropriately hard for a play that said only one affirmative thing about man's fate: "that he has it still in his power not to squeal like a pig but to keep a tight mouth about it . . . and also that love is possible: not *proven* or *disproven*, but possible."

ON OPENING NIGHT, March 24, 1955, at the Morosco Theatre on Forty-Fifth Street, Williams took his seat beside Britneva, who was his date. During the first act, he was agitated, muttering to himself so loudly that people around him had to shush him. He and Britneva sat out most of the second half at a bar across from the theater; they returned to watch the crucial final scene between Maggie and Brick. "The New York opening of *Cat* was particularly dreadful," Williams recalled in *Memoirs*. The audience ovation and the backstage bravado only intensified his moroseness. By some miscue, Wood and Liebling did not go to celebrate with Williams at Kazan's house afterward; misreading their absence as a judgment on the evening, Williams took umbrage. When they met up later at the cast party, according to Wood, Williams "was in such a state of anger he would not speak to me. He behaved as if he were a deserted child who'd been abandoned in a snow-storm by untrustworthy relatives, or hurtful friends."

As diminutive and regal as she was, Wood was also the embodiment of Broadway commerce, a purveyor of quality goods: she had encouraged a full-length play, a third act, the return of Big Daddy, and a satisfying ending that gave Brick and Maggie at least some glimmer of hope. Williams, who judged the first night "a failure, a distortion of what I had intended," acted out his fury with the one person he trusted most in the world. He told Wood that she had ruined his play. Wood wanted to go home, but Liebling convinced Williams to go with them to get the first-night reviews.

"The wait for the morning notices to come out was one of the most unendurable intervals of my life," Williams said. They picked up the papers and went over to Forty-Third Street and Broadway to pore over them at Toffenetti's. "'Cat on a Hot Tin Roof' is Mr. Williams's finest drama," Brooks Atkinson wrote, adding, "Always a seeker after honesty in his writing, Mr. Williams has not only found a solid part of the truth but found the way to say it with complete honesty." "Mr. Williams is the man of our time who comes closest to hurling the actual blood and bone of life onto the stage," Walter Kerr said in the *Herald Tribune*. To Williams, each rave review—"the production has no flaw" (Walter Kerr), "enormous theatrical power" (Richard Watts Jr., *New York Post*)—was as much cause for laceration as celebration. He was convinced that, for commercial success, he had sold out the truth of his characters and his heart. In silence, at three o'clock in the morning, Williams, Wood, and Liebling sat together in a booth while Williams read his thick stack of opening-night telegrams one by one. "He studiously refused to permit us to see any of his messages. He continued to behave as if he were completely alone," the bemused Wood recalled. She and Liebling were witnessing in person what Williams had just dramatized in *Cat*: "the shocking *duality* of the single heart."

Williams's bread-and-butter note to Atkinson the next day—"Now that you've written your lovely notice I can tell you that I would have just died if you hadn't liked and praised 'Cat,'" he began—was full of self-loathing for his "fearful lack of security," his "abysmal self-doubt," his "invidious resentment of [William] Inge's great success," his "hideous competitiveness which I never had in me before!" In a postscript, Williams added:

Some time I would like you to read the original (first) version of Cat before I re-wrote Act III for production purposes. Both versions will be published, and, confidentially, I do mean confidentially, I still much prefer the original. It was harder and purer: a blacker play but one that cut closer to the bone of the truth I believe. I doubt that it would have had the chance of success that the present version has and since I had so desperate a need of success, and reassurance about my work, I think all in all Kazan was quite right in persuading me to shape Act III about the return of Big Daddy.

The published version of the play contained both the original and the Broadway versions. Williams perpetuated the legend of the play and its "commercial ending" in the accompanying essay "Note of Explanation," in which he portrayed himself as a hapless author victimized by the exigencies of commercial theater and the power of his director. "I wanted Kazan to direct the play, and though these suggestions were not made in the form of an ultimatum, I was fearful that I would lose his interest if I didn't re-examine the script from this point of view," he wrote. These weasel words, as Kazan later pointed out, "gave people generally the idea that I had forced you to rewrite 'Cat.' I can't force you to rewrite anything, first because you are strong, secondly because you are protected by your Guild." Kazan went on, "I've come to the conclusion that somehow you were willing to have me blamed for the faults in your plays, while you were praised for their virtues."

Williams owed Kazan more than he could admit to himself, or to the public. The thrust of the original version of *Cat* had certainly changed, but so had the play's clarity, depth, structure, and dynamism. It won every theatrical award for best play, including the Pulitzer Prize. By May 1955, the production had paid back its original investment of $102,000; it went on to play almost seven hundred performances. Williams owed Kazan, as he acknowledged in a letter, "a success when I had given up thought of anything but failure, and a sort of vague whimpering end to life."

In early July, Wood informed Williams that she was about to ask for half a million dollars from MGM, which wanted the play as a vehicle for Grace Kelly. "Figures stagger imagination approve get the loot," Williams wired back. Wood did as she was told. "You and I have come to know how difficult it is to get a hit play in New York City," she wrote to Williams afterward. "There are not too many 'Streetcars' and not too many 'Cats on Tin Roofs' in one man's lifetime for us to know no matter how well a man writes and how skilled he is as a playwright that it is improbable and very often impossible to continue writing good plays for any long amount of time. This is why I am more proud than usual to have been able to deliver the Metro-Goldwyn deal."

The cash and the kudos only intensified Williams's guilt and gripes. "I think he [Kazan] cheapened 'Cat,' still think so, despite the prizes," Williams wrote Wood. "That doesn't mean I doubt his good intentions, or don't like him, now, it's just that I don't want to work with him again on a basis in which he will tell me what to do and I will be so intimidated, and so anxious to please him, that I will be gutlessly willing to go against my own taste and convictions." Like Brick with Maggie, Williams projected onto Kazan his own moral failure and turned it into a kind of legend of betrayal. "I was terribly distressed by 'Cat on a Hot Tin Roof,' although I'm living on it and it's made me more money than anything else," he told Edward R. Murrow in a 1960 CBS TV interview. "People tell me it came off, but for me it didn't. It seemed almost like a prostitution or a corruption."

The corruption, however, was Williams's. Ten days before the New York opening, Kazan had offered to reinstate Williams's original, preferred third act. "You never stated that in your preface," Kazan wrote, in a letter that would end their professional relationship in 1960. "Nor did you note that I offered repeatedly to put your original third act into the road company. You made the decision not to. It's been four years now that this horseshit has been in the press. . . . YOU NEVER ONCE SAID A WORD!! . . . You should have come to my defense long ago. Ask yourself the reason why you didn't."

"ONE'S ENEMY IS always part of oneself," Williams wrote to Britneva in the slipstream of *Cat*'s success. Williams's need for triumph had trumped his sense of truth. "A failure reaches fewer people, and touches fewer, than does a play that succeeds," he wrote. Still, Williams needed to believe in the purity of his literary endeavor. A combination of vainglory and guilt compelled him to renounce the successful version. He couldn't quite admit his bad faith, or his dependence on Kazan, whose collaboration was essential not only to his success but also to his poetic expression. Williams felt shamed both by his calculated betrayal of the play and by his pleasure at its success. That shame had enormous reverberations; it consigned him, at the peak of his acclaim and his wealth, to the psychological penance of a half-life, "a sort of a lunar personality without the shine," as he described himself at the time. That summer he wandered aimlessly around Europe struggling to evade the truth of his artistic compromise. "I am running away from something, but don't know what I am running away from," he wrote to Wood from Barcelona in July 1955. "Each new place disappoints me, after a couple of days it seems like an awful mistake to have gone there. But when I return to Rome, that's no good either." Williams's real disappointment was with himself.

W illiams's losses that year were not just moral or aesthetic. His grandfather, Reverend Walter Dakin, his totem of luck and love, had died, at ninety-seven, just before the rehearsals of *Cat* began. In the middle of the summer, another true believer—Margo Jones—died, at the age of forty-three, apparently from accidental inhalation of a toxic carpet cleaner; she was buried with the brooch that Williams had given her at the Broadway opening of *Summer and Smoke*. In August, the set designer Lemuel Ayers—the only member of Williams's Iowa theater class to praise the quality of the dialogue and the atmosphere in the disastrous full-length play *Spring Storm*, thereby convincing Williams not to give up on theater—died at the age of forty. Each of these figures was a mainstay of Williams's art and his integrity. In his perfervid imagination, their deaths took on symbolic weight and added to his sense of his life as sullied and unmoored. "The reaper is not only grim but active and rapid this season," he wrote to Wood in late August.

According to the unedited manuscript of his memoirs, Williams that summer wrote only under the influence of stimulants. In his new one-act play "The Enemy: Time," he described this condition as "the drugged state of semi-oblivion which is what an artist has left when he abandons his art." Writing in the white heat of his internal crisis over *Cat*, the new

play was "an examination of what is really corrupt in life," an exploration
of the vying torments of his humiliation and his ambition. In *Camino
Real*, he had written about the difference between the will to be good
and the will to be great. The ructions around *Cat* made him agonizingly
aware of the gap between the two urges in his own character. "I believe
very strongly in the existence of good," Williams said. "I believe that honesty, understanding, sympathy, and even sexual passion are good." His
longing for goodness was broadcast in the last speech of the first draft of
"The Enemy: Time," a sort of prayer for blessing and purity: "Oh, Lady,
wrap me in your starry blue robe, make my heart a perpetual novena."
Williams was aware, however, that he had traded in his big heart for a
hard heart. "It is hard for me to like any playwright who is still writing
plays," he wrote to Wood at the end of his "vague summer." "Miller, yes!
Inge, sometimes . . . an ugly effect of the competitive system. They have
to stun me with splendor that drives vanity out! Or I wish they'd quit
writing as I have nearly this summer."

In April 1955, just after *Cat* opened, Williams entertained Carson
McCullers in Key West; although he had paid for his friend's ticket,
McCullers's presence made him feel emotionally bankrupt. "It's much
easier to give money than love," he wrote to Britneva, who had nicknamed McCullers "Choppers." "Choppers needs love, but I am not the
Baa-Baa-Black Sheep with three bags full for Choppers. I don't even have
any for the Master or the Dame or the Little Boy Down the Lane. I care
only, very much, about the studio mornings at the Olivetti." That summer, Williams was unable even to manufacture the energy to charm
Anna Magnani, who had just finished filming *The Rose Tattoo* and whom
he was now trying to corral for both a Broadway production and the film
of *Orpheus Descending*. "Magnani is outspokenly puzzled by my behavior, and I'm afraid we may lose her simply because I act like a Zombie
whenever I am with her," he told Wood.

Williams was still adamantly hiding from himself and from others the
bitter fact of his duplicity. "I am determined to express just me, not a
director or actors," he wrote later that year to Wood, refusing to beef up
the role of Val in *Orpheus Descending* in order to lure Marlon Brando.
He added, "Almost everybody of taste that I have talked to about 'Cat'

are disturbed and thrown off somewhat by a sense of falsity, in the ending, and I don't want this to ever happen again, even if it means giving up the top-rank names as co-workers." But even as Williams wrote these words, he was angling for Kazan to do the literary, heavy lifting on their two-year film collaboration, *Hide and Seek*. "Have to finish the film-script for Gadg and really don't know what more to do with the thing," he wrote to Britneva in June. "Catch-as-Catch-Can [Kazan] just says re-write, re-write, re-write, and I don't know what the hell for or about." Over the next few months, from Williams's various drafts and rewrites, often dispatched with the instructions "Insert Somewhere," Kazan assembled the script for the film, which was retitled *Baby Doll*—a work for which, at Wood's insistence, Williams took full screen credit and received an Academy Award nomination.

From November 1955 to January 1956, Kazan was in Benoit, Mississippi (population 341), filming *Baby Doll*. He took his family with him for the ten-week shoot; he had trouble, however, coaxing Williams away from Key West. "Those people chased me out of there. I left the South because of their attitude towards me. They don't approve of homosexuals, and I don't want to be insulted," he told Kazan. Nonetheless, he eventually turned up, only to excuse himself after a couple of restless days with the canard that he couldn't find a place to swim. "God damn it, I need an ending to this film," Kazan told him. Williams was distracted from the new play he had begun by the imminent opening of a production of *Streetcar*, starring Tallulah Bankhead and playing at the Coconut Grove Playhouse in Miami, that was billed as "under the supervision of Tennessee Williams," and by the glitzy New York premiere of the movie *The Rose Tattoo*, featuring the legendary Magnani's debut in American cinema. He seemed to want to be left more or less alone; so, really, did Kazan. "Now I was without an author, but I didn't mind," he recalled in *A Life*. "I was what I wanted to be, the source of everything."

On December 18, nearly a week after *The Rose Tattoo* premiere, Kazan sent Williams the scenes leading up to his proposed ending for

OPPOSITE PAGE: Anna Magnani as the seamstress Serafina in *The Rose Tattoo*

Elia Kazan setting up a shot with Carroll Baker and Karl Malden
on the Mississippi set of *Baby Doll*

Baby Doll. "There is one small element here following that you never
had in any of your bits, scraps, versions, rewrites or letters," he told him.
That "small element," it turned out, was a big narrative deal. Archie Lee
Meighan (Karl Malden) wins the hand in marriage of Baby Doll (Carroll Baker)—a nubile, manipulative nymphet of nineteen who still sleeps
in her nursery crib—by promising her father that he will not attempt
to consummate the union until she's twenty. It's a vow that drives the
loutish, sex-starved Archie Lee to distraction. In the meantime, as an
act of revenge, Baby Doll is pursued by Silva Vacarro (Eli Wallach, making his screen debut), a man whose cotton gin Archie Lee has burned
down. Although the film leaves open the question of whether he actually seduces Baby Doll, there's no question about the sexual heat generated between her and the Italian interloper. In Kazan's proposed ending,

Archie Lee, thinking he's been cuckolded, shoots up Vaccaro's place in a fit of fury, accidentally killing a black man before continuing his search for Vacarro—a finale that Kazan felt would be "both tragic and funny, El Greco and Hogarth, tiny and gigantic."

Kazan's idea was sensational, commercial, and bad; Williams was right back in the artistic tug of war he'd had over *Cat*. He showed no timidity, this time, in fighting his corner. "I simply can't believe that you have been shooting a film that demands a finish like this outline," Williams wrote, adding, "You say that whenever I am in trouble I go poetic. I say whenever you are in trouble, you start building up a '*SMASH!*' finish.—As if you didn't really trust the story that goes before. It is only this final burst of excess that mars your film-masterpieces such as 'East of Eden,' and it is in these final fireworks that you descend (only then) to something expected or banal which all the preceding artistry and sense of measure and poetry—yes, you are a poet, too! no matter how much you hate it!—leads one *not* to expect." Kazan's attention-grabbing finale was a piece of cinematic showboating, violent hokum that introduced a discordant note into Williams's *comédie humaine*. "Not false to the country. The hell with the Delta!" Williams said. "But false to the key and mood of the story." He went on, "Killing a negro is not a part of universal human behavior, witness all the universal Archie Lees in this world who never killed a negro and never *quite* would! They would commit arson, yes, they would lie and cheat and jerk off back of a peep-hole, but they wouldn't be likely to kill a negro and slam the car door on his dying body and go on shooting and shouting, now, would they?! . . . A killing is not so much a moral discrepancy as it is an artistic outrage of the film-play's natural limits." Williams suggested something more in keeping with the story's comic tone and scale—like Archie Lee blasting his shotgun at a car, then opening the car door to discover a black man inside, and saying, "Oh, it's you! Excuse me." Williams's version appears in the film; Kazan's does not.

When it came to promoting the movie, however, Kazan the showman— *Baby Doll* was the first picture produced by his newly formed Newtown Productions—won out. He had a billboard about the size of the Statue of Liberty (15,600 square feet, a third of an acre) built above the Victoria

Theatre on Broadway, where the movie debuted. It was the biggest painted sign in the world. "No one showboats anymore," he swaggered to Warner Brothers. "Trust my instinct."

Kazan thought he had made "a very cute movie." The Catholic Church, however, thought he'd made a very evil one. The Legion of Decency rated it C for "Condemned." Without ever having seen the film, Cardinal Spellman took to the pulpit of St. Patrick's Cathedral to denounce it. "I exhort Catholic people to refrain from patronizing this film under pain of sin," the Cardinal said. "The revolting theme of this picture, 'Baby Doll,' and the brazen advertising promoting it, constitute a contemptuous defiance of the natural law, the observance of which has been the source of strength in our national life." (Williams's brother, Dakin, then an officer in the Air Force and a recent Catholic convert, had to pay the church twenty-five dollars for a dispensation to see the film.) The tabloids spewed boldface headlines. "'BABY DOLL' IN NEW ROW," the *New York Post* shouted from its front page. En route to the premiere on December 18—"a harrowing experience"—Williams weighed in. "I cannot believe that an ancient and august branch of the Christian faith is not larger in heart and mind than those who set themselves up as censors of a medium of expression that reaches all sections and parts of our country and extends the world over." Kazan declared, "I am outraged by the charge that it is unpatriotic. In the court of public opinion, I'll take my chance."

What remained in public memory, over time, was not the film itself but the billboard. The behemoth image of Carroll Baker, sprawled the length of a city block in her short nightie, sucking her thumb, and reclining in a crib, became as iconic an erotic emblem of the era as Marilyn Monroe holding down her billowing white skirt in *The Seven Year Itch*. "This is the greatest idea since the days of Barnum," Kazan told Warner Brothers when he pitched the billboard; the sign, he assured the studio, would make *Baby Doll* "the talk not only of Broadway, but of the show world, of café society, of the literati, of the lowbrows, and of everybody else. I really don't see how anyone could avoid going to the picture if we put that sign up there." Kazan was right about the sign, wrong about the film. Generally speaking, the critical response to *Baby Doll* was muted. (Nowadays, Williams's half-heartedness is all too apparent in the strained, lackluster dark comedy.) Controversy, however, never hurt the box office. *Baby Doll* made news and money; it also made Williams a subject of scandal. The *New Republic* christened the film "The Crass Menagerie." "Just possibly the dirtiest American-made motion picture that has ever been legally exhibited," *Time* said. *Baby Doll* had no nudity, no simulated sex, no foul language, and little violence; by contemporary standards, it was Simon Pure. Nonetheless, in the popular mind, thanks as much to the sensational sign as to the story, the film became synonymous with louche sex. In the *New Republic*, Williams found himself dubbed "the high priest of *merde*." The attention only drove up his literary stock. MGM offered him another half-million dollars for his new play, still in its

The *Baby Doll* billboard in Times Square

unfinished first draft. Every ignominy, Williams was learning, fueled his fame; likewise, fame fueled his ignominy.

THE YEAR THAT ended in a public fracas over *Baby Doll* had begun, in January, with another one involving the fifty-four-year-old Tallulah Bankhead, who was playing Blanche in *Streetcar* at the Coconut Grove Playhouse. "She is the bitch of all time, but what a worker!" Williams wrote to Wood, after he was banned from rehearsals. From the outset, Williams had muddied the water between Bankhead and himself by bringing Britneva to Florida for the opening of a production for which she had unsuccessfully auditioned as Stella. "From the moment Miss Bankhead saw Maria, she would have none of her," Sandy Campbell wrote in *B*, a privately printed epistolary account to his partner Donald Windham about the production in which he had a small part. "Tenn is licking his lips with the prospect of an encounter."

On opening night—a performance that was overrun by Bankhead's rowdy camp followers—Williams came into her dressing room, got down on his knees, put his head in her lap, and said, "Tallulah this is the way I imagined the part when I wrote the play." At a party in honor of the cast that evening, however, according to Campbell, a juiced-up Williams, "in a voice all nearby (about a hundred or so people) could hear," told Jean Dalrymple that if B[ankhead] continued to give such an appalling performance he would not allow the play to open in New York. She was "playing it for vaudeville and ruining my play." Campbell added, "Maria, naturally . . . talking violently against B's performance." Inevitably, there was a showdown: Williams, who had hypocritically praised her, now told Bankhead she'd given a bad first-night performance. Campbell, who was present, recounted the scene:

> "And you had the nerve to say that after getting down on your knees to me in the dressing room," B said.
> "Are you calling me a hypocrite? . . ."
> "And bringing that bitch, Maria, to the party is shocking," B said.
> Tenn, standing up: "My dear, I do not have to stand for this anymore. Calling . . . my best friend a black bitch is more than I will take!" And he marched out.

Tallulah Bankhead as Blanche in *A Streetcar Named Desire*

When the show transferred to New York—"Batten the hatches! Hurricane Tallulah headed for Manhattan. Refugees pouring into Havana from Coconut Grove and Palm Beach!" Williams joked in a postcard to Paul Bigelow—he was forced to eat his words, backpedalling beyond hype into craven falsehood. In a *New York Times* tribute, Williams called Bankhead's performance "probably the most heroic accomplishment since Laurette Taylor returned in the Chicago winter of 1944–45 to stand all her doubters on their ears in 'The Glass Menagerie.'" Williams went on, "When the play opened at the City Center, this small, mighty woman had met and conquered the challenge." In her public reply to Williams's courtly *Times* flim-flam, Bankhead quipped, "Mr. Williams' talents as a playwright are considerable, but in his recent tribute he forever scuttled the ancient legend, *in vino veritas*." Privately she fumed, "If I am a small, mighty woman, he is a mighty small man."

Bankhead had Williams's number. She could tease him—"Tenn, you and I are the only consistently high Episcopalians I know"—and she could cut to the core of his insecurity. He was big in the world but not in himself. "Let's face it," Merlo, who had a ringside seat at their fight, said. "Tenn is vain and she wounds his vanity continually." The new play, the new movies, the new money, the new (and short-lived) Williams-Wood production company, intended to maximize his cash and his clout, were a testament to the momentum of Williams's career. (Even his Key West house was now "a regular stop for the sight-seeing buses.") The velocity of his life, however, had reached the point of disintegration. The latter part of 1956—"the worst I can remember," he told Britneva, who was now officially "Lady St. Just"—was spent "trying not to crack up." "I am far from sure that I have succeeded," he wrote. "I still keep up, as well as I can, a pretense of being a rational person. I have been absolutely alone during this ordeal. I have not been able to write a decent line since last spring and I believe my writing career is finished."

Throughout 1956, as if perched on some spiritual fault line, pulled apart by the opposing frictions of his accelerating career and his "lost decency," Williams felt himself approaching breaking point. "Living on Miltowns, seconals, and double shots of vodka with a splash of orange juice," he wrote to Christopher Isherwood and Don Bachardy in May 1956, after the Florida tryout of an early version of the new play "The Enemy: Time," now retitled *Sweet Bird of Youth*. "Frankie couldn't take it and has gone to New York: a purely geographic separation." On his own in St. Thomas, in the Virgin Islands, at the end of that enervating summer—"an almost unbroken decline in health and spirits"—Williams sat looking up at the stars. "I didn't feel the presence of God. I haven't felt it for a long time now," he wrote in his diary. "Something's awfully gone away from here, meaning me."

Merlo was another thing slipping out of Williams's reach. Although their relationship had begun to fray in private as early as 1951, Merlo's charm had still burned brightly in public. The gregarious Merlo was always a lubricant to conversation; he ran social interference for Williams in the world. To Françoise Sagan, the newly anointed nineteen-year-old *wunderkind* of French literature, who encountered them first with Carson McCullers in Key West in 1954, Merlo seemed "perhaps the most charming man in America and Europe put together"—"light-hearted, droll, good, full of imagination." A couple of years later, in Rome, Sagan joined Williams and Merlo at dinner with Anna Magnani, who spent the evening raging against men. After dinner, as they prowled Rome in Williams's car, which Merlo was driving, a streetwalker recognized him at the wheel. "She did not even laugh when a whore, a friend of Frank's called out to us gaily, or rather to him, pleadingly: *E quando Franco? Quando, quando, quando?*" Sagan added, "Tennessee, who was sitting in the back of the car, also smiled into his moustache, as if he were observing his rogue of a son chatting up a young girl. There was a great deal of tenderness between them, a very great deal."

But by the summer of 1955 that tenderness was in short supply; the distance between the two men was noticeably wider. For long periods, Williams found himself traveling solo. "The Horse gave me a very bad time in Rome; perhaps I gave him an even worse time," he wrote to Britneva. "He was always with that cynical street-boy Alvaro. . . . The Horse's character, each summer with Alvaro, is hardened and cheapened so that I can't stay with him but must keep flying around on these sad little trips." For a while, Merlo was laid up in Rome with a series of illnesses. "I don't think my company made him feel any better so it's just as well I went away," Williams wrote to Wood, adding a new regret to his litany of lamentations. "We never joke and laugh together, which is bad, as jokes and laughter do so much to relieve the human dilemma, but he touches me deeply, and while I doubt that I have ever deeply loved him, according to my extremely romantic conception of what love should be—as distinguished from the pleasures of the bed—still, he's given me an awful lot in a period when it was needed."

Williams longed for intimacy but shrank from its responsibilities. "He would be a trial to anyone who tried to take care of him. Frank Merlo, his man Friday, . . . has my sympathy," his mother wrote. "To know me is not to love me," Williams said. "At best, it is to tolerate me." Among the many things that Merlo had to put up with—the increase of Williams's work-load, his drinking, his depressions, his temperament—the greatest was the increase in his renown. Merlo's coolness to Williams was his way of con-tending with his own envy. "He is haunted continually by the feeling of insufficiency, that he is dependent on me, and yet doesn't seem to be able to bring himself to the point of taking any positive action to change this state," Williams confessed to Wood in 1955. Nonetheless, when the news of the half-million-dollar movie deal for *Cat* came through in the summer of 1955, Williams's first thought was of the security it would afford them as a couple. "We don't have to worry about 'the hard stuff' for another ten years, I guess," he wrote to Merlo from Barcelona. "We'll be old girls, by then, and can get our social security when it runs out, and by such little economies as saving old tea-bags and turning collars and cuffs, we can eke out a comfortable elderly existence in some quaint little cold-water walk-up in the West Nineties, with an occasional splurge at the YMHA when a surviving Sitwell gives a reading there. I'm afraid my eyesight will be get-ting rather dim, by that time, but my hearing may hold up."

But money—both Williams's earnings and the percentage that Merlo received from his plays—only dramatized the distance between them. Despite Williams's protestations to the contrary, Merlo was increasingly an extra in Williams's epic. As much as Williams wanted and demanded love, his first allegiance was to his writing; he could surrender himself completely to the page but never completely to a person. In the fall of 1955 and throughout the following year, he was engrossed in "The Enemy: Time," as it mutated into *Sweet Bird of Youth*. "This is the first time in years that I have been able to work with unflagging interest on a play script for six and eight hours a day," he said, adding, "It has the dynamics of what I think may very well turn out to be the strongest play I have written." The work got Williams's best self; his relationship got the rest. "'Attention must be paid to this man' before it's too late," Williams, contemplating sending Merlo to an analyst, wrote to Wood in 1955. The problem was that Williams *couldn't* pay attention.

A workshop production of the play was scheduled at the Studio M Playhouse in Coral Gables in April 1956. Merlo was present one night in Key West when Williams read a new scene to George Keathley, who was directing, lighting, and designing the work-in-progress. "They were having troubles," Keathley said. "Once, Tennessee turned to Frank after reading a new scene aloud and asked, 'Do you like it, Frankie?'—'No, I don't!'—'Why not?'—'I don't know, I just don't!'—"But why *not*? What's wrong with it?'— 'Don't ask me, I'm not your goddamned yes-man!' And with that Frank ran into another room, packed his bags and took off for a few days." Keathley added, "After this they separated more and more." Williams ended up moving to Miami to work in seclusion with Keathley while Merlo "held the fort during his absence, entertaining a wide circle of friends."

Four days after the workshop production of *Sweet Bird of Youth* opened, Williams, distressed about Merlo, wrote to Britneva. "For the

With George Keathley at the studio production of *Sweet Bird of Youth*

first time since I've known him, he's started drinking a lot, and is full of complaints about his health and generally depressed and distrait," he said. That summer, in Rome with Merlo, Williams tried to put into a poem, "How Can I Tell You?" the sense of wariness that had come between them:

> How can I tell you? With my lips and my hands?
> You might mistake their language.
> It isn't easily said.
>
> There's only moments when we can both believe it. . . .
>
> The trouble is that doubt is always half true,
> there is a hard kind of half accuracy in distrust which is hard, very hard,
> to let go of.
>
> Still: we stay with each other, we keep returning to places,
> the search continues.
> What are we looking for in the heart of each other?
> Will it ever be clearly
>
> the other and not the self that we so want to comfort?

By the summer of 1957, the crack in their relationship had become a chasm. "He has changed a great deal in the last month or two," Williams confided to St. Just. "DRINKING HEAVILY! A couple of double vodkas before dinner. At night, coming in LOADED!—but sometime you can't smell liquor on his breath. There is practically no real communication between us." Neither Merlo nor Williams could quite face up to his aggression toward the other. Both men felt aggrieved, sad, confused, unheard, unable to separate but unsure of how to continue. Williams's diary notes the constant flare-ups— "another big row with F." (August 1956); "bad, nearly disastrous, quarrel" (February 1957).

Williams's struggle to keep his relationship intact was played out, unconsciously, in his drama. His work of the mid-fifties acquired, according to Brooks Atkinson, a new "streak of savagery." In the plays of those years, the idea of the couple was continuously subverted, dramatized as a travesty (*Baby Doll*), a tragedy (*Orpheus Descending*), or an impossibility (*Cat on a Hot Tin Roof*). No connection was allowed to exist without being spoiled, falsified, mocked, obliterated, robbed of its goodness, or lost forever. Part of this violence was an expression of Williams's elemental rage, which the process of playwriting tapped into and released. "If something is wrong at the top, why not look at the bottom," he wrote in an early version of *Stairs to the Roof*. "Volcanic eruptions are not the result of disturbances in the upper part of the crater: something way, way down—basic and fundamental is at the seat of the trouble." Williams's ambivalence about love—his longing for it and his need to diminish it—had its origins in the primary couple in his life: his toxic, unreachable parents. He had grown up with the sense "that to desire a thing or to love a thing intensely is to place yourself in a vulnerable position. To be a possible, if not probable, loser of what you most want." While he was enduring the torture of increased separation from Merlo, and feeling both unloved and unlovable, his plays registered an ancient despair about the possibility of love.

I n 1939, Williams had described his play *Battle of Angels* as a tale about "a boy who hungered for something beyond reality and got death by torture at the hands of a mob." But in the intervening decade and a half, the valence of his life had dramatically shifted. Inevitably, so had his surrogate in the play. In *Battle of Angels*, Val was a hunted, primitive saint; in *Orpheus Descending*, he was a vagrant, jaded sensualist, "fighting his own descent into a hell of his own making," Williams explained to the *Miami Herald* in 1956. During the gestation of *Battle of Angels*, Williams himself had been a pilgrim soul, a newcomer to the "trapeze of the flesh," living from hand to mouth, with a literary reputation to gain and nothing to lose. By the time the play reached its final form in 1957, Williams was struggling with a sense that his heart had atrophied: "we persist, like the cactus," he wrote in his notebook. He had not so much transcended his wounded self as been trapped by his attempts to escape it. His life depended on his writing; his writing fed off his life, and his life had become attenuated by his wayward habit of being. "Unfortunately in 1940 I was a younger and stronger and—curiously!—more confident writer than I am in the Fall of 1953," he wrote to Wood after sending her the first draft of *Orpheus Descending*, which failed to impress. "Now I am a maturer and more knowledgeable craftsman of the theatre, my experience inside and outside the profession is vastly wider, but still the exchange appears to be to my loss."

In January 1957—two months before the Broadway opening of *Orpheus Descending*—Williams found himself in a hell from which even the big magic of writing could not seem to save him. "For the first time I think I may stay away from rehearsals," he wrote to Maria St. Just. "I am too destroyed at this time to be of any assistance." He continued, "Of course I have been through periods somewhat like this before, when the sky cracked and fell and brained me, but this time I seem less able to struggle out of the debris. I'm at a loss to explain it. I suppose it's partly Mother's nervous breakdown"—Edwina, suffering from paranoid delusions of being poisoned by her maid and murdered by her chauffeur, was briefly hospitalized in September 1956—"and the shock of Rose's sudden deterioration when I put her in the 'Institute for Living,' which I had hoped would do her so much good. But the unaccountable collapse of my power to work, since work has always been my escape and comfort, is more likely to be the root of trouble."

Williams longed, as he wrote to Kazan in March, to "recapture some of my earlier warmth and openness in relation to people, which began to go when I began to be famous." The guitar-toting Val of *Orpheus Descending* incarnated Williams's moral exhaustion. "He is still trapped in his corruption and engaged in his struggle to maintain his integrity and purity . . . a duality not reconciled," Williams said, speaking as much for himself as for Val. He spelled out his self-loathing most succinctly not in the play but in the opening minutes of his screenplay adaptation, *The Fugitive Kind* (1959). "I felt like my whole life was somethin' sick in my stomach and I just had to throw it up. So I threw it up," Val tells a judge who releases him from jail in the movie.

When the curtain rises on *Battle of Angels*, the dry-goods store is a reflective, even picturesque museum of the tragedy that the play recounts in flashback; in *Orpheus Descending*, we encounter an altogether more dynamic, foreboding, and oppressive landscape. Williams's stage directions suggest a crepuscular, deadly world: walls "streaked with moisture and cobwebbed," the "black skeleton" of a dressmaker's dummy, a "sinister-looking artificial palm," a "disturbing emptiness" outside the windows. Even the confectionery that is part of the store is "shadowy and poetic as some inner dimension of the play." The heart's calcification is central to the reconceptualization of *Orpheus*; it is the presenting symptom of both of the main characters when they first meet. When Val wanders into town, the sharp-tongued and volatile Lady Torrance, who runs the dry-goods store, pulls a gun on Val; "she's not a Dago for nothin'!" one character says. Lady has been "coarsened, even brutalized, by her 'marriage with death,'" Williams explained. Val also has been "brutalized by the places and circumstances of his wanderings."

Where the Val of *Battle of Angels* was full of rebellious romantic gas, the Val of *Orpheus Descending*, who wears a stolen Rolex from his hustling days, is full of moral atrophy. "Corruption—rots men's hearts and—rot is slow," he tells Vee, a mystic and painter who is married to the local sheriff and has seen lynchings, beatings, and convicts torn to pieces by dogs. Val understands Vee's paintings as an attempt to redeem the ugliness they've both witnessed, "from seats down front at the show," he says. He has paid a physical price for his life of indulgence. "Heavy drinking and smoking the weed and shacking with strangers is okay for kids in their twenties but this is my thirtieth birthday and I'm all through with that route," he says to the wild child Carol Cutrere, who recognizes him from her debauched past. Echoing his creator's frequent complaint, Val adds, "I'm not young any more. . . . You're not young at thirty if you've been on a Goddam party since you were fifteen."

In Williams's rewriting of the Orpheus myth, there are two hells into which Val descends: one is the degradation of his own desires, and the other is Lady's hell, a sort of trifecta of tragedy imposed on her by the brutish rural world in which she is trapped. Orphaned as a teenager, when her Italian immigrant father, "a Wop bootlegger," died fighting a blaze in his wine garden—which was set by racists because he sold wine to blacks—she was forced to have an abortion after her aristocratic lover, David Cutrere, jilted her for a society marriage. Of her sadistic and domineering husband, Jabe, one of the gossiping town biddies says, "He bought her, when she was a girl of eighteen! He bought her and bought her cheap because she'd been thrown over and her heart was broken by that." Lady's subservience is signaled by her bedridden husband's constant pounding with his cane on the floor above, which makes him a ghostly, terrifying, annihilating presence. ("He is death's self," one stage direction reads.) In his only appearance in act 1, Jabe, returning to his bed after a trip to the hospital, stops to notice a change Lady has made in the store. "How come the shoe department's back here now?" he asks. "Tomorrow I'll get me some niggers to help me move the shoe department back front." Jabe's voice is the voice of Williams's father, CC, the contemptuous, bullying Voice of No, canceling out Lady's imagination and innovation. "You do whatever you want to, it's your store," Lady says.

Dressed in black and always at Jabe's call, Lady is an embodiment of the living death of resignation. "I wanted death after that, but death don't come when you *want* it, it comes when you don't want it!" she confesses to David Cutrere, when they finally see each other again at the store. "I wanted death, then, but I took the next best thing. *You* sold *yourself.* I sold *my* self. *You* was bought. *I* was bought. You made whores of us both!" Loveless and full of loathing for her compromised life, Lady feels as corrupted in her own way as Val does. When she flirts with him as he applies for a job—"What else can you do? Tell me some more about your self-control!"—he swaggers, "Well, they say that a woman can burn a man down. But I can burn down a woman . . . any two-footed woman." Lady is disarmed; she throws her head back "in sudden friendly laughter as he grins at her." Burning is, of course, a symbol of both desire and purification, which is part of Val's powerful unconscious appeal to her.

Williams's spiritual problem was the same as Val's and Lady's: how to negotiate a path from corruption back to purity. While writing was his imagined redemption, guitar-playing was Val's. "I'm through with the life I've been leading," Val tells Lady. "I lived in corruption but I'm not corrupted. Here is why. (*Picks up his guitar.*) My life's companion! It washes me clean like water when anything unclean has touched me." When Val finally plays the guitar—which is autographed with the names of Lead Belly, Bessie Smith, and Blind Lemon Jefferson—he sings about a "heavenly itch," a will to believe in transcendence, which Williams, too, even in his darkest times, never surrendered:

> My feet took a walk in heavenly grass.
> All day while the sky shone clear as glass
> My feet took a walk in heavenly grass,
> All night while the lonesome stars rolled past.
> Then my feet come down to walk on earth,
> And my mother cried when she give me birth.
> Now my feet walk far and my feet walk fast,
> But they still got an itch for heavenly grass.

A self-proclaimed outsider, Val confesses to Lady that he's "disgusted" with the world he's known, a world composed, he says, of just two kinds of people: "the ones that are bought and the buyers." Val classifies himself in a third category—"bum"—a dreamer who tries not to be touched by life's craven hurly-burly. "You rise above it?" Lady asks. "I try to," Val says, at which point "off-stage guitar music fades in." Music—specifically the joyous and defiant music of the blues messengers who have signed his guitar—is the agent of Val's transcendence. The magic of creative freedom is the essence of the story that Val spins for Lady—in the play's most famous passage—about a bird that sleeps on the wind, never touching earth, except to die:

VAL: You know they's a kind of bird that don't have legs so it can't light on nothing but has to stay all its life on its wings in the sky? That's true. I seen one once, it had died and fallen to earth and it was light-blue colored and its body was tiny as your little finger, that's the truth, it had a body as tiny as your little finger and so light on the palm of your hand it didn't weigh more than a feather, but its wings spread out this wide but they was transparent, the color of the sky, and you could see through them. That's what they call protection coloring.

Camouflage, they call it. You can't tell those birds from the sky and
that's why the hawks don't catch them, don't see them up there in the
high blue sky near the sun! . . . So'd I like to be one of those birds;
they's lots of people would like to be one of those birds and never
be—corrupted!

LADY: . . . I don't think nothing living has ever been that free, not
even nearly. . . . I sure would give this mercantile store and every bit
of stock in it to be that tiny bird the color of the sky . . . for one night
to sleep on the wind and—float!—around under th'—stars. . . . *(Jabe
knocks on floor. Lady's eyes return to Val.)* Because I live with a son
of a bitch who bought me at a fire sale, and not in fifteen years have I
had a single good dream.

Val, of course, becomes Lady's good dream; desire is her escape route
from corruption. "Ask me how it felt to be coupled with death up there,
and I can tell you," Lady says, adding, "I endured it. I guess my heart
knew that somebody must be coming to take me out of this hell. You did.
You came. Now look at me! I'm alive, once more!" Having found him,
Lady is desperate to keep him. She latches onto Val like Ishmael to his
coffin. In her frenzy, she is ruthless. She threatens to frame Val; she holds
his guitar as ransom; she tries to bribe him by offering him the store
("Everything Death's scraped together down here!—but Death has got
to die before we can go").

This paradoxical spectacle of passion is played out around the opening
of a confectionery, which Lady is determined to reconstruct as a wine
garden and late-night club. The wine garden is a memorial to Lady's
father, a way of avenging his death that is a central part of Lady's story
and her psychology. "Electric moon, cut-out silver-paper stars and artificial vines? Why, it's her father's wine garden on Moon Lake she's turned
this room into," a character explains, just in case the audience missed the
visual clues. Lady's wine garden is a piece of theater, a production in
every sense of the word. Her strategy, like Williams's, is to restage her
oppressive history in order to defiantly triumph over it. "To—be *not
defeated!*" she swaggers, adding, "*You get me? Just to be not defeated.*
Ah, oh, I won't be defeated, not again, in my life!"

On the day of the confectionery's gala opening, in act 3, Jabe shuffles downstairs to inspect the room; he immediately understands what's
going on, and he matches Lady's aggression with his own. "Didn't I
marry a live one," he says, "with a muted ferocity" to his nurse. "Her
daddy 'The Wop' was just as much of a live one till he burned up. He
had a wine garden on the north shore of Moon Lake. The new confectionery sort of reminds me of it." Jabe adds, "But he made a mistake,
he made a bad mistake, one time, selling liquor to niggers. We burned
him out."

In *Battle of Angels*, Myra expresses her murderous feelings toward
Jabe from the outset. Lady, however, doesn't see her own rage until the
news of Jabe's complicity in her grievous loss calls it out into the
open. In act 3, pregnant with Val's baby and filled with triumphalist
hysteria—"Lady, you been a lunatic since this morning!" Val says—she
feels absolved of responsibility for anything that happens. "I was made to
commit a *murder* by him up there!—I want that man to see the wine
garden come open again when he's dying!" Lady says. She continues, "It's
necessary, no power on earth can stop it. Hell, I don't even want it, it's just
necessary, it's just something's got to be done to square things away."

Val knows that Jabe is dying upstairs; he also knows that Jabe sleeps
with a gun under his pillow. The event is too provocative. "You can't
open a night-place here this night," Val tells her, balking at changing
into his white waiter's jacket.

LADY: You bet your sweet life I'm *going* to!
VAL: Not *me*, not *my* sweet life!
LADY: I'm betting *my* life on it! Sweet or *not* sweet, I'm—
VAL: Yours is yours, mine is mine . . .

Although Val confesses in one breath that he feels "a true love" for
Lady, in the next breath he's telling her he'll wait for her somewhere out
of the county. Lady cuts him off. "Oh, don't talk about love, not to me.
Because I know what you are," she says. When Val learns, in the play's
penultimate beat, that she is pregnant, Lady finally releases him: "You've
given me life, you can go!" These are selfish, not star-crossed, lovers; Val

is caught in the slipstream of Lady's euphoric sense of liberation, which ends with her "in a sort of delirium" running to the upstairs landing, and "crying out," "I've won, Mr. Death, I'm going to bear!"

Lady's reckless words betray not only herself but also Val. She literally calls destruction down on both of them. "Oh, God, what did I do?" she says, almost instantly registering her mistake and retreating down the stairs as Jabe's clumping footsteps are heard. Jabe appears at the landing and fires all the bullets of his revolver into Lady, then tells the gathering crowd that Val has done it. Val bolts for the door only to be intercepted by locals, who pull him outside.

In the offstage commotion—the sound of voices, racing motors, baying chain-gang dogs—Val appears to break away from his captors, only to be cornered and torn apart. The revenge is not Lady's but Jabe's. In the end, Lady and Val don't evade their own corruption; they are claimed by it. Their new lives are defeated by the lethal forces of their old ones. With her dying breath, Lady repeats a line her father used to say: "The show is over. The Monkey is dead." It's a reference to a tale she has told Val about her father buying an organ grinder's monkey, who died in the middle of their busking act. But the strained, strange image resonates with other meanings. Williams himself was the performing monkey whose act was killing him. The garden of his own imagination was in danger of being overrun by destructive forces that he could name but not control.

ORPHEUS DESCENDING CIRCLED Broadway for two years before finally opening at the Martin Beck Theatre on March 21, 1957. Of the many impediments along the way—Williams's rewrites, settling on producing arrangements, the success of *Cat on a Hot Tin Roof*—the main one was wrangling Magnani, whom Williams dubbed "the Tigress of the Tiber." Although Lady's interior life, like Myra's in *Battle of Angels*, is modeled on Edwina Williams—"a woman who met with emotional disaster in her girlhood; verges on hysteria under strain"—her exterior displays Magnani's forthright toughness and sexual ripeness. "The only important thing in life is to be *authentic*," Magnani said. To Williams, she lived up to her credo. "She was beyond convention as no one I've ever known," he said. Although Williams was shy with Magnani at first—Merlo was "the intermediary between my reserve and her beautifully natural lack of it," he said—he soon fell under her darkly shimmering spell.

"Forget that bit about her being nervous," Williams wrote to Kazan in 1955, after Williams watched Magnani perform for her American film debut on *The Rose Tattoo* location next to his Key West house. "That dame is nervous in a way that's terrific! She takes over like Grant did at Richmond!" Even more admirable to Williams than Magnani's passion was her "incomparable sense of truth." To Williams, her face was "like a mackerel sky, altering from moment to moment and always the most precise gauge, accurate as a seismograph, of the varying quality of what she was listening to." He added, "She is almost a lie detector."

The size of Magnani's talent was matched by the size of her ego, which "surpasses mine but is more excusable," Williams wrote to Wood. Magnani was in the habit of rising at about three each afternoon. "Ciao, Tenn. What is the program," she'd say over the phone. Williams endured her habit of dining at eleven ("greater love (or is it endurance) hath no man"); the production she made of eating ("restaurateurs and waiters received her like a queen . . . she ordered wines, pastas, salads, entrees without consulting the menu"); and her midnight rambles, with the sack of restaurant leftovers she demanded, to feed the stray cats of Rome.

At the same time, there was continuing worry about her English, her schedule, her money, her weight, and her co-star. The news, in 1955, of Marlon Brando's interest in playing Val—"I know how to write for that boy," Williams said—got Williams back not only to rewriting the play but eventually to ghostwriting mash notes for Magnani to send to Brando. ("She has a genius for the wrong attachments," Williams wrote to Britneva, about Magnani's appetite for younger men. Sixteen years her junior, Brando fit her particular sexual sweet tooth.) The prospect of Brando was a spur to both Williams and Magnani. "This news gave me a great joy," she wrote to Wood. "Such a news gave me a courage of a lion and I'm ready to face this big struggle." But Brando, who thought Val's part was weaker than Lady's and demanded rewrites, wouldn't answer calls, not even from Williams.

By November 1955, exasperated by the silence, Magnani tried to get involved in the negotiation. "I know that Brando is very much interested in this play, and I also know that he asked Tennessee to alter the final part

of his character, and frankly for an actor of his calibre, it should be granted," she wrote to Wood. "Keeping in mind that with his talent and sensibility HE WILL NEVER ASK FOR SOMETHING THAT WOULD ALTER THE SPIRIT OF THE PLAY. Why not agree to that?" Magnani continued, "Do you realize the importance of giving to Broadway an important, if not the most important artistic event of the century by re-uniting the names of Tennessee Williams, Marlon Brando and Anna Magnani. . . . You must get Brando."

By September 1956, however, both Magnani and Brando had withdrawn from the Broadway production. Brando admired the play—"You wrote your funky ass off," he told Williams. Brando's problem was with Magnani. "When you play with her you either make sure that the parts are equally volatile or plan to carry a fair sized rock in your hand when you go on stage," he wrote.

> Magnani doesn't frighten me, how can any one so lonely and so choked with longing frighten anybody? I think that she is a woman of unusual force who has a very hard time because she can't find any one that would be willing to defeat her if they could. She yearns to be subjugated in a way that is natural to all women but she can't find anybody with enough fire to "burn her down." As well as strength she has aggression, and that makes her pitifully incongruous because it makes her domineering in her search to being dominated. The total effect of her force doesn't make her frightening it just makes her unattractive. When I refer to her wanting to be burned down, I don't mean just sexually, I mean she must find someone that will *utilize* her completely as a woman and love her too. As an actress she is a different rag on a different bush. I can't think of an actress I would rather play with providing the potential dynamics of the parts are equal.

It took three years and the first million-dollar contract in movie history to get Brando to play Val opposite Magnani in the film version, *The*

OPPOSITE PAGE: Anna Magnani and Marlon Brando in *The Fugitive Kind*

Fugitive Kind. "The money wasn't nearly as much a problem as the fact he wouldn't sleep with her," the director Sidney Lumet said. Brando and Magnani never shared off-camera the sweet sensuality of the romantic attachment between Val and Lady. "After we had some meetings in California, she tried several times to see me alone, and finally succeeded one afternoon at the Beverly Hills Hotel," Brando explained in his autobiography. "Without any encouragement from me, she started kissing me with

Sidney Lumet directs Marlon Brando in The *Fugitive Kind*

great passion." He went on, "To refuse her would have been a terrible insult. But once she got her arms around me, she wouldn't let go. If I started to pull away, she held on tight and bit my lip, which really hurt. With her teeth gnawing at my lower lip, the two of us locked in an embrace . . . we rocked back and forth as she tried to lead me to the bed. My eyes were wide open, and as I looked at her eyeball-to-eyeball I saw that she was in a frenzy, Attila the Hun in full attack. Finally the pain got so intense that I grabbed her nose and squeezed it as hard as I could, as if I were squeezing a lemon, to push her away. It startled her, and I made my escape."

Magnani posed problems for her director as well. "The essence of Anna?" Lumet said. "One day our call on set was 9:10, no Anna. 9:30, no Anna. 10:00, no Anna. I go, 'Fuck.' I went up to her dressing room. I come in. Marlon is there by the door, against the wall, shaking his head. She's seriously stain-faced, mascara running, the works. I said, 'Jesus, Anna, what's happened!' So help me God, she says, 'Even in Italy, even in Italy, he won't give me first billing!'"

Magnani commanded Lumet to shoot her only from the right side. "It completely ruined my staging," Lumet said. "It meant that everyone had to be in a certain position in relation to her. You never saw Marlon's right side, because he was always opposite her. I cannot tell you how destructive this kind of thing is to a movie." Lumet went on, "A very gentle cameraman will sometimes imply a tenderness to a scene. I used it on Marlon's big speech about the bird sleeping on the wind. I couldn't do those gentle movements right to left with her. I generally stayed above the eye level. It was fatal because of the lack of tenderness, the lack of knowledge." Despite Brando's opening five-minute monologue to the camera, which was done in one take and is among the finest, and least known, of his great film performances, and Magnani's magnificent fury, their chemistry never lived up to the shout line of the ads—"*Their fire! Their fever! Their desire!*" *The Fugitive Kind* "sputters more often than it sizzles," *Variety* said. The fact that the *New York Times*'s Bosley Crowther found his senses "throbbing and feeling staggered and spent at the end" hardly mattered. *The Fugitive Kind*, which Lumet knew was botched from "the first time I saw the rushes" because of Magnani's caveats, was a box-office disaster.

Williams had counted on Magnani to be a creative influence on Harold Clurman, the director of the Broadway production. As a co-founder of the Group Theatre in the thirties, Clurman had made his name directing the naturalistic work of Clifford Odets; by the late fifties, he had achieved a string of impressive Broadway hits, including *The Member of the Wedding*, *Bus Stop*, and *The Waltz of the Toreadors*. An early admirer of Williams, he had been a signatory of the "Special Award" from the Group Theatre that launched Williams's playwriting career in 1939. In 1940, he had offered to mount one of Williams's one-act plays at the Group just before it collapsed. Clurman had Williams's measure, if not his metabolism. "It is the 'peculiar people,' the unprotected, the innocently sincere, the injured, the estranged, the queer, the defenseless, the abandoned and the maimed whom Williams redeems with his compassion," he wrote.

Although Williams considered Clurman a "dear man and fine critic," as an artistic team the two were a forced fit. Clurman was a man of reason, not intuition; he had energy but not poetry. He was an explainer, an arguer, an inspirer, a man of vivacious intellect, but more boulevardier than bohemian. Penetrating in his analysis of plays and buoyant in his personality, he was romantic in his devotion to art but not in his relation to life. His mind was seductive, but his physical presence was not. Talk, for him, was the source of erotic connection. "Harold's rehearsals were like parties, at which he was the guest of honor," Kazan, who was Clurman's stage manager on *Awake and Sing*, said, adding, "He had trouble turning the psychology he had so brilliantly detailed into behavior on the same level of penetration and originality. There was often something inept about his staging; he had trouble getting people in and out of doors. He relied on the actors to work this out." "I know that Anna would break through his tendency to make a play a bit static or 'fixed,'" Williams told Wood.

Williams's verdict on Clurman's production, which finally starred Maureen Stapleton and Cliff Robertson, was that it was "under-directed." Prior to the opening, he leveled with the producer Cheryl Crawford: "For your own sake, honey, I am glad you are not doing 'Orpheus.' I think it is a beautiful and true play that says something very clearly but I don't think many people are going to like what it says." When he believed that his prediction had come true, Williams was devastated, "a truly shattering setback," he called it. In fact, the reviews were mixed but generally respectful. Atkinson damned *Orpheus Descending* with faint praise: "one of Mr. Williams's pleasantest plays . . . There are streaks of his special genius all through it." *Newsweek* concluded, "Something missing, but enough here." The *New York Post* called it "a drama of notable power, grim poetic insight, and disturbing fascination."

The most devastating of the notices came not from the daily critics but from the weekly *The New Yorker*. Under the headline "Well, Descending, Anyway," Wolcott Gibbs began, "The trouble with Tennessee Williams's new play is . . . , I should say, that the people in it aren't really terribly interesting." He continued, "In 'Orpheus Descending,' I could see nothing but purposeless ruin, and while the author writes a good many of his customarily vivid scenes, I don't believe that he has turned out a coherent play, or that he was quite sure of what was on his own mind." Williams claimed later that the critics of the play "put it down with a vengeance," but Gibbs's review seems to be the only one to live up to the legend of vitriol in Williams's memory. The trauma of the review was compounded by the news a few days before of his father's death on March 27, in Knoxville, Tennessee, at the age of seventy-seven. "There was an emotional shock, more than I would have thought," Williams wrote to Windham.

CC HAD BEEN out of touch with his famous son for more than a decade. "If he ever refers to my sister or me in any of his writing I will make him regret it as long as he lives," CC wrote to Wood in 1950, CC having been outraged by the publication of Williams's "devilish" short story "The Resemblance between a Violin Case and a Coffin." All of CC's obituaries contained his curt appraisal of his son as "a flop": "He didn't last long at anything until he started writing plays," CC had said. Nonetheless, by 1954, Williams had come to accept CC as "my desperate old father." "I've stopped hating my father and I do hope you won't put in any hurtful things about him," he told Kenneth Tynan in 1955, when he was writing an article on Williams. "He was not a man capable of examining his behavior toward his family, or not capable of changing it." Williams added, "My

Mother devoted herself to us three kids and developed an hostility toward him, which he took out on me, the first male to replace him."

CC was never so generous in the family home as he was when he was leaving it. Despite her newfound wealth from *The Glass Menagerie* royalties, CC gave Edwina their charming two-story Georgian house in St. Louis and a tranche of stock in the International Shoe Company, from which he had retired in 1945. "So a tragic situation works itself out, a little too late, but better than never at all," Williams wrote at the time. "As for the old man, he has probably suffered as much as anyone, possibly even more, and I am afraid it will be a lonely and bitter end to his blind and selfish life." CC decamped to his sister Isabel's home in Knoxville, then, when she couldn't handle him, to a hotel at a resort outside the city called Whittle Springs, where he lived out his days. "My father was really quite an embarrassment to me at this time," Dakin recalled. "He would be dead drunk in the hotel room. He would ask me to take him to Gulfport or Knoxville in my car. I would have to practically shovel him out of the hotel. He would gradually sober up on the trip."

After CC left St. Louis, Edwina never saw him again. Although both of her sons attended their father's funeral—"I was surprised that Tennessee came because of his feelings about my father," Dakin said—Edwina did not. In her memoir, she pictured him dying alone, drunk in a hotel room; in fact, CC, who had found a female companion in his last years, a widow from Toledo, Ohio, died at St. Mary's Hospital from complications from asthma. In Edwina's version of events, the children cast a cold eye on their father. "Dakin told me, 'Neither Tom nor I shed a tear,'" Edwina wrote. In truth, both Dakin and Tennessee cried over their father. "The Williams family was not one of the best families in Tennessee. It was *the* best family," Williams's Aunt Isabel used to say. But the gene of distinction had passed CC by. In his life, CC held no public office, wrote no poems, fought no battles except an ongoing humiliating war with his diminutive wife, who conquered him. He left his car to his autumn love; he left the modest remainder of his estate to his sister, his daughter, and Dakin. To Williams, he left nothing. "I wonder if he knew, and I suspect he did, that he had left me something far more important, which was his blood in my veins," Williams wrote in his autobiographical essay "The

Man in the Overstuffed Chair." "And, of course I wonder, too, if there wasn't more love than hate in his blood, however tortured it was."

CC was laid to rest in "Old Gray," as the Knoxville Cemetery was called. Williams remembered it as "an exceptionally beautiful service." Afterward, sitting on the Williams family tombstone, the disinherited son whom CC had called "Miss Nancy" signed autographs for his father's mourners.

ORPHEUS DESCENDING CLOSED after sixty-eight performances.

"Am I wrong in thinking that if you had directed 'Orpheus' it would have been one of our greatest successes?" Williams wrote to Kazan that April. "I don't think so. I think your appreciation of its basic truth would have inspired me to lift it above its theatricalism." Williams continued, "You could have staged the ending so it would play and score. You would have found the 'key' in which the play is written, not just intellectually but with an artist's and poet's vision, and gotten a stunning performance from Maureen all the way through."

"Tenn became a terrific hypochondriac that spring," Maureen Stapleton recalled. "He tried to act very bravely with us during the short run of 'Orpheus'—he was always trying to cheer us up, make us laugh when it was hard to laugh." Stapleton went on, "His paranoia could surface at the most unexpected times. More than once, we sat at a restaurant table and he would overhear someone nearby say something uncomplimentary— and invariably Tenn thought it was about him. And he'd be ready for a fistfight to defend an imaginary insult!" Williams had reached "a certain stop, or point of departure, in my professional life," he confided to Atkinson after the show opened. The loss of his father, to his surprise, made him even more convinced that he had come to some kind of turning point. "Since the failure of 'Orpheus' my stock has fallen enormously," Williams wrote to St. Just in June. His spirits had fallen just as precipitously. "What a season we've been having, Madam!" he told Wood. "A few more like it and we'll be ready for the glue factory or the soap works." Feeling that "I can't be the better part of myself anymore," Williams was finally ready for the psychiatrist's couch. "The moment has certainly come for psychiatric help, but will I take it?" he asked his diary.

CHAPTER 6

Beanstalk Country

Who am I?
A wounded man, badly bandaged,
a monster among angels or angel among monsters . . .

—TENNESSEE WILLIAMS,
"You and I"

On April Fool's Day in 1957, Williams found himself at the Starlite Lounge in Miami, nursing a third double-bourbon with the hard-drinking poet Gilbert Maxwell and Richard Leavitt, a new acquaintance who would become a friend and, in 1978, publish a biographical album about his life. Williams was having a good time. "I announced that I was retiring from the professional theatre and going to devote myself to friendship and a good, simple life in New Orleans, with analysis," he wrote in his diary. Then, he added, "Bull!—How on earth do I know what I'm going to do, except that it's fairly plain that I will go on drinking and drinking and *drinking*, and having a good time in bed whenever I can and hitting the keys on my new 'Olympia' typewriter—a good one."

By the end of May, however, Williams, carrying through on one part of his announcement, put himself into the care of the distinguished, sixty-one-year-old, New York–based psychiatrist Lawrence S. Kubie. Educated at Harvard, Johns Hopkins, and the London Institute of Psychoanalysis, Kubie was one of the leaders in a cluster of creative neurologists who saw early on the value and impact of psychoanalysis. A man of astringent and wide-ranging intellect—"He reminded me of Thomas Wolfe, who wanted to live every life, have every experience, be with every

Lawrence Kubie, psychiatrist

person," the psychoanalyst Eugene Brody wrote in *Symbol and Neurosis*, a collection of Kubie's papers published after his death in 1973—Kubie had been practicing his brand of Freudian psychology in New York since 1930. By the time Williams went to him, he had been president of the New York Psychoanalytic Society, he had taught at Columbia and Yale, and he was on the staff of Mt. Sinai Hospital. The author of three hundred psychoanalytic papers, reviews, and numerous books, among them a volume titled *Neurotic Distortion of the Creative Process*, Kubie was erudite, sophisticated, enthusiastic, and something of an intellectual maverick, whose often-repeated mantra was "The tree of psychoanalytic theory needs drastic pruning!"

Williams was a daunting analytic challenge: a borderline personality with tenacious addictive and depressive tendencies who was rich, famous, and a genius to boot. Many analysts would not have wanted to risk their reputations on such a quixotic, disturbed figure. But within the psychoanalytic and artistic communities, Kubie was the man—an expert at containing and commanding talented people lumbered with chronic personality disorders, especially those coping with homosexual issues. Many of the literary and theatrical stars of the day were Kubie's patients: William Inge, Leonard Bernstein, Charles Jackson (*The Lost Weekend*), Laura Z. Hobson (*Gentleman's Agreement*), Josh Logan, Vladimir Horowitz (who credited Kubie with "curing" him of homosexuality), Moss Hart, and Kurt Weill. (Kubie actually introduced Hart to Weill; the result was *Lady in the Dark*, a musical about psychiatry in which Kubie, with his "Harvard" accent and precise diction, was given fictional form.)

From the outset, Kubie's treatment of Williams was special. He judged his patient too disturbed to begin analysis immediately and insisted that he first dry out and undergo medical examinations for a few days at the expensive Harkness Pavilion. Pending the Harkness test results, Williams was to undergo a period of seclusion at the Austen Riggs Center in Stockbridge, Massachusetts, an open therapeutic community for severely troubled patients. (Kubie would publish a history of the place in 1960.) In those days, the Austen Riggs regimen involved a minimum stay of one year, during which the patient saw a psychiatrist three times a week and busied himself the rest of the time with such salubrious activities as painting, acting, walking, and writing, though the last item on the list was off limits in Kubie's program for Williams.

Kubie's approach for Williams involved cutting off all his addictions: drink, men, travel, and writing. This strategy of deprivation was a classical Freudian maneuver, predicated on the assumption that Williams's addictions were a form of acting out. "What is cut off will depend on which activity has been used persistently as a major escape from inner problems," Kubie wrote in *Practical and Theoretical Aspects of Psychoanalysis* (1950). Kubie's prescription of abstinence was mocked, by Vidal and other gay friends, as a clinical method of transforming Williams into "a good team-player." In fact, the deprivation was intended to force Williams's neurotic drives to find other routes of expression, specifically through interpretation during analysis—acting in, so to speak, instead of acting out. In his writing, Kubie preached the hard line he practiced on Williams:

> The psychoanalyst . . . will be tactful and judicious in his warnings, but in the end he must be merciless in forcing a patient to face his neurosis. Indeed, just as he must sometimes intervene actively to produce situations of deprivation, so he often has to tumble the patient into those very situations that arouse his fears, depression, and anger.

"I don't think I can stand much of it," Williams wrote, from his hospital bed at the Harkness Pavilion, of his "exquisite boredom." "Can do without the liquor and that's undoubtedly a wise move but—(interruption!?) Well—the boredom vanished when the two Docs entered and I felt suddenly *trapped*. Heart began doing flip-flops. I was nearly panicky." He went on, "I guess I've been hiding from this a long time, dodging, ~~cheating~~ kidding myself but maybe it's better, now, to have to collide with it, face to face, head on—Gosh, I'm downright incoherent."

Williams left the Harkness Pavilion on June 7, 1957, still uncertain whether surrendering himself to doctors and clinics would be his "salvation." Torn between facing his problems and fleeing them, he chose flight—a brief excursion to Havana, Cuba, "my favorite city in the Americas." En route, he "goofed" and fell off the wagon. "With the plane trip as an excuse (not a good one), I had at least 8 drinks during the day and had 3 Seconals, one before the flight and two later, combating an intense depression that had fallen over me," he wrote in his diary. Havana's sensuality worked its anodyne magic. In a letter to Kazan, Williams boasted that he'd cut down his drinking and "rarely take[s] more than one goofball a day." "The swimming and the fucking are wonderful here," he wrote. "It's cool summer weather, and the Cubans are socially compatible to me, they are bird-brains that sing like birds, especially for their supper, and don't seem to resent it. The revolution is very inconspicuous, and not at all scary to me. Sometimes I wish they would mistake me for an enemy and take an accurate pot-shot at me on the Prado. But most of the time I am happy enough to be at large." He added, "I am going on with my work, against the doctor's advice."

But during this Cuban interlude, Williams dropped his game face only for Merlo, to whom he had sent out an SOS. Kubie, he wrote, "had knocked me out so completely I couldn't put the pieces together again. For the first time, I've really been afraid that I was about to go out of my mind. I guess I am really going through a nervous breakdown. I couldn't ask you to help me because you're going through something similar, although, being much stronger, you have a lot more control." He added, "Perhaps the good Dr. Kubie can explain what's happened. I honestly can't guess!"

After this capriciousness, Williams set out on June 18 for Austen Riggs. For three nights prior to his departure, he had nightmares about it. To Maria St. Just, he referred to the institution as "a plush-lined loony-bin"; to Audrey Wood, however, he characterized it as "a Christian Retreat," "from which I hope to emerge a better Christian," he wrote, adding by hand, "less 'retreating'!!" Chauffeured by Merlo, Williams rolled up to Stockbridge from New York, ready to commit. But the collective doom of the other residents spooked him. "I stayed only five minutes in the Institute," he wrote to his mother the following week. "I took one look at the other patients and told Frank to carry my bags right back out to the car. I checked into the local hotel and stayed there over the weekend to make sure that this was not the place for me, then drove back to New York." He went on, "I think the psychiatrist, Dr. Kubie . . . is right in thinking I need some therapy of that kind to relieve the tensions that I have been living under, but I think it's unnecessary for me to live in a house full of characters that appeared to be more disturbed than myself."

Instead, Kubie cobbled together a new analytic plan for Williams that included five 50-minute sessions a week with him and a sort of forced separation from Merlo. "My analyst is very anxious for Frank to stay in

Key West till we have gotten over the hump of the analysis as during this period it is very difficult for me to share such a small apartment with another person as tense and temperamental as myself," Williams wrote to Paul Bowles. "We're like a couple of fighting cocks here lately, all but pecking each other's eyes out, and naturally that is not a healthy atmosphere in which I can go on with my work with Dr. Kubie." He added, "I give Dr. Kubie one year which expires in June. If, by that time, I am not on the way to something unmistakably better, I'll start travelling again." At the beginning of his treatment, Williams rented a second New York apartment, a sort of chic bolt-hole on the Upper West Side, with a fireplace and a calming vista of the Hudson and the George Washington Bridge. "Analysis is very upsetting at first," he explained to St. Just. "You are forced to look at and examine things in yourself that you would choose not to. So it's necessary to have a retreat, a peaceful place to retire. . . . At the same time, I feel very guilty about it because I know Frank interprets it as a threat to our relation."

Williams's West Side retreat was something of a sin bin, which might have reasonably been provocative to Merlo. On Saturday nights, Williams turned his eighteenth-floor apartment, he said, "into a swinging honky-tonk." "I had it all decorated like a chop-suey joint, I mean there were beaded string curtains, paper lanterns, kewpie dolls, every kind of outrageous tacky bit of decor I could pick up on Mulberry Street or Mott Street," he recalled to Oliver Evans. "Early Saturday morning I would get on the phone and call every swinger I knew and tell him to come to my West Side pad that night with any congenial friends he cared to bring. The number of guests usually ranged between twenty and thirty in number—if not also in age—and we had some high old times." He continued, "I laid in an abundant supply of liquor and Frank Krause—the steady occupant of the pad—would prepare a lot of dips and canapés and sometimes casserole dishes. . . . Sometimes we would take to the streets in the neighborhood to augment the guest list and it was on one such occasion that I first encountered Mishima"—Yukio Mishima, one of the most important Japanese authors of the twentieth century—"As a rule I only participated as host. Unless something very special was present."

Initially, Williams struck a cavalier pose about the analytic endeavor.

"I've been wanting to try it for a long time, and this seems a good time to do it, now that it seems advisable to stay at a safe distance from Broadway till the critics have a chance to forget my recent transgressions," he wrote to his mother. But he was serious about the process; he found it painful. "With Kubie I have worked mostly on negative points: my suspicions, fears, jealousies. I have deliberately painted a black picture of myself, a sort of 'mea culpa,'" he explained to Kazan. "If only we could turn up something nice," he complained to St. Just in October. "But so far nothing of that sort even worth mentioning, just envy, hate, anger, and so forth. Of course he is attacking my sex life and has succeeded in destroying my interest in all except the Horse, and perhaps the Horse will go next and I will start getting my kicks out of dirty pictures."

THE PROCESS OF analysis may not have been pleasant, but it did change at least one aspect of Williams's narrative: his story of his hated and hateful father. "Kubie would imitate my father and scream at me—to break the doors down, you know," Williams explained to *Playboy* in 1973. "What he gave me was not forgettable. I actually learned to respect my father, and now that he's dead, I love the old son of a bitch." Williams even took issue with a twelve-part *New York Post* profile in which Cornelius, who he now claimed "wasn't really that bad," was cast in a "terrible light." "My father was a totally honest man," Williams wrote in a protesting letter, which was published in full in the newspaper. "He was never known to tell a lie in his life or to take an unfair advantage of anybody in business." He continued:

> He had a strong character and a sense of honor. He lived on his own terms which were hard terms for his family but he should not be judged as long as he remains a mystery that he is to us who lived in his shadow. Maybe I hated him, once, but I certainly don't anymore. He gave me some valuable things: he gave me fighting blood, which I needed, and now he has given me, through the revelations of my psychoanalysis, a sense of the necessity to forgive your father in order to forgive the world that he brought you into: in my opinion, an important lesson which I hope I have really learned. Forgiving, of course, does not mean accepting and condoning, it does not even mean an end to the battle.

As for his being devoted to money, as my younger brother is quoted as having said of him, all American businessmen seem to have that devotion, more or less, mostly more, and I think it a sort of reverse sublimation. Disappointed in their longing for other things, such as tenderness, they turn to the pursuit of wealth because that is more easily obtainable in the world. My father got little of either.

Behind the tyranny of CC's anger, Williams came to see a punishing sense of resignation, a man exiled from those he ought to love and who ought to love him. In the poem "Iron Man," he imagined his father's "strangulated love":

I.

We cringed at his anger,
sudden as steel,
rapier-like,
but did not feel
his wounds that could not
utter their need
but bled in silence
as martyrs bleed!

II.

His rage over trifles,
his bitter smile
were the things that we noticed,
and yet all the while
a frustrated heart
was beating there
that wanted to love us
but did not dare!

In his essay "The Man in the Overstuffed Chair," Williams wrote, "A psychiatrist once said to me, You will begin to forgive the world when you've forgiven your father. I'm afraid it is true that my father taught me to hate, but I know that he didn't plan to, and, terrible as it is to know how to hate, and to hate, I have forgiven him for it and for a great deal else." He added, "Now I feel a very deep kinship to him." Through psychoanalysis, Williams achieved a less judgmental view of CC's boozing. "I think it was the constraint of working in an office after the free life on the road, and his unexpressed but deep feeling of guilt over his failure 'to be a good husband and father,'" he wrote in 1962 to Lucy Freeman, who helped Edwina to write her autobiography. "His nature was not to comply with accepted social modes and patterns without a restlessness that would have driven him mad without the release of liquor and poker and wild weekends." Williams recalled, "My mother would scream, 'I know where his liquor is. He's hidden it behind the bathtub.' If only she'd've sat down and had a sherry with him." In his son's eyes, CC had lived "a rather pathetically regular life." CC had played it safe; in the compromise, he lost everything. His sorry example inspired his son to take a more uncompromising approach to his own heart's desires, to gamble everything on his writing. "Oh, no, I can't make peace," he wrote in his diary. "I can't accept a little or nothing."

Williams's recognition through analysis of his underlying love for his long-absent, frustrated father was by itself a major accomplishment, but it was overlooked by friends in their posthumous accounts of Williams. "Happily, the Bird's anarchy triumphed over the analyst," Gore Vidal wrote, for instance. "After a troubling session on the couch, he would appear on television and tell Mike Wallace all about the problems of his analysis with one Dr. Kubie, who not long after took down his shingle and retired from shrinkage." This entirely misrepresented both Williams's hard-won emotional education and the analyst's role in it. Kubie did indeed retire, but to become director of training at the Sheppard and Enoch Pratt Hospital outside Baltimore; Williams did indeed talk to Mike Wallace, but with a new inward-looking tone, which demonstrated his serious attempt to reconsider his upbringing and to explore its effect on his character:

WALLACE: Richard Watts, whom I know you admire, has described your characteristic mood as "steeped in passion, hatred, frustration, bitterness and violence."

WILLIAMS: I'm having a big argument on this subject with my analyst, Mike. I tell him that I don't feel that way and he—he wants to find out if I do or I don't, and we're still exploring it. I think I feel more affection and love. He thinks that certain early conditions and experiences in my life made—created a lot of anger and resentment in me, which I am taking out now through my writing. He may be right. I can't say. . . . Have you ever heard of the term—he didn't want me to use these analytic terms, he doesn't approve of them, but I do a lot of reading and I use them to him, he doesn't use them to me—a term that I've come across lately is "infantile omnipotence."

WALLACE: "Infantile omnipotence"?

WILLIAMS: That is what we all have as babies. We scream in the cradle, the mother picks us up, she comforts us, she suckles us, she changes the diaper, whatever is giving us discomfort is tended to, and through this she rocks us to sleep and all that. And whatever gives us discomfort, we find, is—is relieved in response to an outraged cry. . . . This is the infant feeling omnipotent. All it has to do is cry out and it will be comforted, it will be attended to. All right. We grow up a little and we discover that the outcry doesn't meet this tender response always. After a while the mother realizes that it's no longer an infant, she gets impatient with its outcry or maybe the father gets impatient with it. Anyway, it meets the world which is less permissive, less tender and comforting, and it misses the maternal arms—the maternal comfort— and therefore, then, it becomes outraged, it becomes angry. And that's where most of our neuroses spring from, from the time when we— . . . We meet a more indifferent world, and then we become angry. That is the root of most anger.

The change in Williams's story about his father inevitably led to a recalibration of his story about his mother, and her legend as the put-upon family saint. Prior to analysis, Williams's narrative of his family was encapsulated in *The Glass Menagerie*, which (aside from its depiction of Amanda's inability to touch or comfort her children) essentially presented his mother's version of events. After analysis, Williams's attitude toward his parents (and himself) became more nuanced.

This new version of his story was incorporated into *Suddenly Last Summer*, which was a direct product of Williams's turmoil on the analyst's couch. "I was bored not working," Williams explained later. "I began to cheat. I'd get up at four, type a few hours, and then I felt fresh. The doctor finally surrendered." Kubie's diktats may not have broken Williams's writing habit—trying to was possibly even a strategic analytic mistake, too challenging for someone like Williams, whose self-worth was bound up entirely in his work—but they did allow him to come to terms with Edwina and her punishing passive-aggression, in which there was as much unacknowledged hate as love, as much selfishness as selflessness. When Edwina died, at the age of ninety-five, in 1980, Williams wryly acknowledged the lethal, castrating dimension of her "extraordinary power." "Only four feet eleven, she conquered my father who was six feet and drove him out of the house as soon as she received half of 'Menagerie.' Allowed the State hospital to perform one of the earliest lobotomies on Rose. Unconsciously managed to turn both her sons gay," he told Elia Kazan.

Suddenly Last Summer, which made a stylistic departure into the realm of the grotesque—a genre with "much of the beautiful, much of the wanton, much of the bizarre, something of the terrible, and not a little of that which might have excited disgust," as Edgar Allan Poe once described it—registered the roiling anger and the shock of disenchantment that his analysis had released. The play documents a furious struggle between Catharine Holly, a young woman who is driven mad by the gruesome death of her homosexual cousin, Sebastian Venable, and his mother, Mrs. Venable, who threatens to have her lobotomized for telling the truth about the circumstances of his demise. Set in a sort of festering and fantastical garden, "a well-groomed jungle," full of thrashing sounds, "as if it were inhabited by beasts, serpents and birds, all of a savage nature," *Suddenly Last Summer* was, according to its author, an allegory. The "prehistoric" jungle-garden was as much a simulacrum of Williams's unruly interior as it was a production of the decadent poet Sebastian Venable, who tended it. What has broken in Sebastian, in the play—"that string of pearls that old mothers hold their sons by like a—a sort of a—sort of—*umbilical cord, long—after . . .*"—was breaking in Williams too.

For the first time in his dramatic oeuvre, Williams allowed himself to face overtly the madness of his mother. Mrs. Venable, who idealizes her late poet-son, refuses to accept the shocking and contradictory account of his behavior delivered by the institutionalized Catharine, who claims that Sebastian used her as bait to attract young male lovers. "I was PRO-CURING for him," she tells her psychiatrist, Dr. Sugar. "*She* used to do it, *too,*" she says of Mrs. Venable. "*Not consciously!* She didn't *know* that she was procuring for him in the smart, the fashionable places they used to go to before that summer! Sebastian was shy with people. She wasn't. Neither was I." Mrs. Venable, who gasps "like a great hooked fish," clings to her delusions on the subject. "It wasn't *folie de grandeur.* It was gran-deur," she tells Dr. Sugar of the halcyon days she spent traveling the watering holes of Europe with Sebastian. In Mrs. Venable's mind, Cath-arine is a "vandal" bent on destroying the perfect image she has of her son and herself. "Really I was actually the only one in his life that satisfied the demands he made of people," Mrs. Venable tells the doctor, contend-ing that the forty-year-old Sebastian was "chaste," "not c-h-a-s-e-d." Mrs. Venable tries to use her wealth and her moral authority to bribe Catha-rine's family into having the incriminating details of Sebastian's sex life wiped out of her brain: the play is a negotiation for a lobotomy. "After the operation, who would *believe* her, Doctor?" Mrs. Venable says to Dr. Sugar, adding, from offstage, at the finale, "Cut this hideous story out of her brain!"

Suddenly Last Summer was a sort of autobiographical exorcism that worked through Williams's grief and guilt over his sister, Rose, as well as his anger at Edwina for deciding to allow a bilateral prefrontal lobotomy to be performed on her without informing him in advance about the procedure—an omission for which Williams never forgave his mother. ("*Do you want to bore a hole in my skull and turn a knife in my brain?*" Catharine challenges Dr. Sugar, adding, "You'd have to have my moth-er's permission for that.") "Now that it's over, I can tell you about Rose who has successfully come through a head operation," Edwina wrote to Williams on January 20, 1943. "What kind of operation was it and what

was it for?" he replied on January 25. "Please let me know exactly what was done with Rose."

In Miss Edwina's memoir, the date of the lobotomy was strategically fudged. By implying that the operation took place when Rose was first committed, in 1937, rather than nearly six years later, Edwina shifted the blame for the decision onto CC, who "had given up on Rose" and on himself, as his increasingly chronic boozing indicated. "The psychiatrists convinced Cornelius the only answer was a lobotomy," Edwina wrote, adding, "They tried to make me believe this was the only hope for Rose, that otherwise she would spend the rest of her days a raving maniac in a padded cell." In fact, what doctors had told CC was that the "only hope" was insulin treatments, which began to be administered at Farmington State Hospital, in Missouri, about seventy miles from St. Louis, on August 23, 1937. The insulin did not work, however. By August 1939, Rose's condition, if anything, had gotten worse: "Does no work. Manifests delusions of persecution. Smiles and laughs when telling of person plotting to kill her. . . . Admits auditory hallucinations. Quiet on the ward. Masturbates frequently. Also expresses various somatic delusions, all of which she explains on a sexual basis. Memory for remote past is nil."

Some part of Rose's unraveling *could* be blamed on CC, who, even the psychiatrist's report acknowledged, "has been eccentric most of his life." CC was always distant with Rose. "Any of the normal hugging or kissing between father and daughter would have embarrassed him, as it would have been discouraged by Edwina," Lyle Leverich writes in *Tom*. Rose never held a job, which only compounded CC's aloofness. In his mind, she was an economic burden who became an existential catastrophe. Over the years, his explosive scenes, his threats to leave the family, his drizzle of denigration unnerved and infuriated Rose, who began to show signs of erratic behavior at twenty-one. It was not uncommon for Rose, in front of guests, to accuse her parents of sexual immorality. She conceived the fantastical notion that Edwina was leading an immoral double life. "I remember her stalking into the front room one day, eyes

OPPOSITE PAGE: Elizabeth Taylor as Catharine Holly
in the film *Suddenly, Last Summer*, 1959

ablaze, and shouting at Mother: 'I know what you are doing and you are no better than a prostitute. You are keeping another apartment to have affairs with Dad's salesmen and you have a complete wardrobe there, you are practically a streetwalker and I am going to tell Dad!' " Williams told Oliver Evans in 1971. He added, "I think Rose was getting back at Mother for all those repressions which Mother forced upon Rose and which resulted in her breakdown."

Rose's scenes became increasingly sensational. On her way to a psychiatrist's office, she put a knife in her handbag; once, shortly before she was hospitalized, she wandered into Williams's room saying, "Let's all die together." In an attempt to stabilize her volatile and increasingly dissociated behavior, Rose's parents sent her to stay with CC's sisters in Knoxville over the Christmas holidays in 1936. The visit was not a particular success. Because of local flooding while she was traveling back to St. Louis a few weeks later, Rose was forced to sleep overnight at the Louisville train station "with refugees." She became agitated and began to rave as soon as she got home. Edwina wrote to her parents, "Cornelius . . . lost his temper, told her she was crazy and that he was going to put her in the State Asylum. He will do this too, if I don't do something else with her."

That March, Rose was committed to the psychiatric ward of Missouri Baptist Hospital and subsequently transferred on April 15 to St. Vincent's, a Catholic convalescent home. Dakin recalled, of her time there, "Rose was like a wild animal. Often I would hear her screaming long before the Catholic sisters would usher us into her presence. Our visits were almost always depressing disasters. Between screams and the most vile cursing, she would be chain-smoking and pacing up and down the corridor or visiting room. Finally the Mother Superior advised us there was no future for Rose at St. Vincent's, which was primarily equipped for 'custodial care.' " By the time Rose was admitted to Farmington, four months later, at the age of twenty-seven, her anger toward her parents, and CC in particular, was beginning to grow murderous. According to the Farmington report (Case No. 9014), she stated that "both of her parents had lost their minds." The report went on, "Frequently she appears mildly euphoric, but for the most part is bizarre, indifferent and shows no

normal concern about her family, usually condemning them." To mark
her tragic departure from home, Williams wrote the poem "Valediction":

> She went with morning on her lips
> down an inscrutable dark way
> and we who witnessed her eclipse
> have found no word to say.
>
> I think our speechlessness is not
> a thing she would approve,
> she who was always light of wit
> and quick to speak and move—
>
> I think that she would say goodbye
> can be no less a lyric word
> than any song, than any cry
> of greeting we have heard!

Edwina's consent to a lobotomy, in 1943, was brought on by Rose's
failure to improve during her hospitalization, and especially by her persistent graphic sexual outbursts—one of which Williams witnessed in
1939. "Horrible, Horrible!" he wrote in his diary. "Her talk was so
obscene—she laughed and spoke continual obscenities—Mother insisted
I go in, though I dreaded it and wanted to ~~go out~~ stay outside. We talked
to the Doctor afterwards—a cold, unsympathetic young man—he said
her condition was hopeless that we could only expect a progressive deterioration. It was a horrible ordeal. Especially since I fear that end for
myself." Still, Williams came to believe that the lobotomy had been "tragically mistaken." "I believe that without it Rose could have made a recovery and returned to what is called 'normal life,' which, despite its many
assaults upon the vulnerable nature, is still preferable to an institutional
existence," he said. Moreover, Williams thought that Edwina, who later
in life signed herself "Edwin" and thought a horse was living in her room,
"was essentially more psychotic than my sister Rose," he told the *Paris
Review* in 1981. He went on:

Mother chose to have Rose's lobotomy done. My father didn't want it. In fact, he cried. It's the only time I saw him cry. He was in a state of sorrow when he learned that the operation had been performed. . . . It didn't embitter me against Miss Edwina. No, I just thought she was an almost criminally foolish woman. Why was the operation performed? Well, Miss Rose expressed herself with great eloquence, but she said things that shocked Mother. I remember when I went to visit her at Farmington, where the state hospital was, Rose loved to shock Mother. She had great inner resentment towards her, because Mother had imposed this monolithic Puritanism on her during adolescence. Rose said, "Mother, you know we girls at All Saints College, we used to abuse ourselves with altar candles we stole from the chapel." And mother screamed like a peacock! She rushed to the head doctor, and she said, "Do anything, *anything* to shut her up!" Just like Mrs. Venable, you know, except Mother wasn't as cruel as Mrs. Venable, poor bitch.

Six months after the lobotomy, in a letter to "dearest brother," in a script no longer well formed, Rose wrote, "You made a bad appearance the last time you called on me. You looked murderous. I'm trying not to die, making every effort possible not to do so. . . . The memory of your gentle, sleepy sick body and face are such a comfort to me." She added, "I feel sure that you would love me if I murdered some one. You would know that I didn't mean to. . . . If I die you will know that I miss you 24 hours a day."

In addition to the lobotomy, in the nineteen years that she was in residence at Farmington, Rose underwent more than sixty-five electroconvulsive shock treatments. On December 31, 1956, Rose was discharged from Farmington. After a few botched attempts at residential care, Williams finally had her transferred to the deluxe Stony Lodge in Ossining, New York, high on a bluff overlooking the river. "Probably the best thing I've done with my life, besides a few bits of work," Williams said of this move.

During Williams's absences, his loyal coterie—the producer Charles Bowden and his actress wife, Paula Laurence, the actress Jane Lawrence Smith, and Maria St. Just—saw to it that Rose's rooms were well appointed (new flower arrangements arrived every week) and that she had frequent visitors. Her bedroom had a white canopy bed and white wicker furniture. In her wallpapered sitting room, a framed photograph of the actor Tristan Rogers, who played Robert Scorpio in *General Hospital*, her favorite program, sat atop the television set. Rose's walls were decorated with a framed poster of her famous brother, as well as with portraits of fictitious English nobles, who constituted part of the patrician family that Rose invented for herself.

Rose had her pleasures. She loved clothes. She loved churchgoing and the very loud and slow singing of hymns. She loved Christmas. Once, with some help from the Bowdens and Maureen Stapleton, Williams gave Rose a Christmas celebration in the middle of summer. "She and Tennessee sang carols and danced," Paula Laurence recalled. Rose also liked to be driven to the Highland Diner, in Ossining, where she would order a grilled-cheese sandwich and "a non-alcoholic" Coke. "She moved among her subjects" is how Bowden described Rose's air of noblesse oblige. "I do not desire it" was her ornate way of saying "no." She liked to go for drives, and over the years she acquired the habit of gesturing from the limousine, a semaphore that Williams dubbed "the Windsor Wave." He offered to take her to England to meet the Queen. "I am the Queen," Rose replied.

In 1988, five years after his death, Rose was moved again across town to the Bethel Methodist Home, a beautiful red-brick building with pillars and an American flag at the center of its circular driveway. There she lived out the rest of her long life (she died in 1996, at age eighty-six) in her own two-room suite—the only one at the home—at the cost of about $300,000 a year.

DURING THE AUTUMN of 1957, between undergoing analysis and writing *Suddenly Last Summer*, Williams visited Rose with unusual frequency, which even the Stony Lodge administrators remarked upon. "I've seen Rose four times since we went out together and you'll be happy to know that she is remarkably better," he wrote to his mother on November 19, 1957. He went on:

We have been going each Sunday to the lovely Tappan Hill Restaurant, near Sleepy Hollow famous for Ichabod Crane and the Headless Horseman. Rose is taking more interest in things and more pleasure, eating much better, putting on some becoming weight again, and has even started smoking. The last few Sundays she has asked for cigarettes, but she says she doesn't smoke except on these outings. She says that you wouldn't approve! She still complains that her parakeet [a gift from Williams] won't take a bath, but that's about her only complaint, and when I took her to the drugstore yesterday, she only bought candy and a toothbrush, not the usual ten or twelve bars of soap. For her birthday my old friend Jo Healy and I are taking her into New York for some shopping. She wants a winter coat so I think I'll give her one for

Rose Williams wearing her brother's Medal of Freedom, 1980

a birthday present, and take her afterwards to a good restaurant and maybe let her spend the night here with Jo, at a nice hotel.

In adulthood, Williams exhibited deep compassionate feelings for his sister. When, in passing conversation, Cheryl Crawford referred to Rose as "just a body," he took angry issue. "She isn't any more just a body than you and I are," he wrote to Crawford. "And if you looked at her, at her tortured face and observed her desperate effort to meet the terrible moment of facing the person she loved most as a girl, and to whom she was closest, and knew that she was a lunatic being visited by him in a bug-house, a plush-lined snake-pit, I don't see how you could call her just a body." He continued, "Madness doesn't mean the cease of personality, it simply means that the personality has lost touch with what we call reality, and I think, myself, that their mental and emotional world is much more vivid than ours is."

As a younger man, however, Williams had not been so attentive. *The Glass Menagerie* had appropriated Rose into his romantic myth, his legend of loss. "Oh, Laura, Laura, I tried to leave you behind me, but I am more faithful than I intended to be!" Tom says. But in October 1936, when she was in the process of losing her mind at home, to his abiding shame, Williams showed her no generosity and no compassion. "Rose in one of her neurotic sprees," he wrote in his diary on October 7. "Fancies herself an invalid—talks in a silly dying-off way—trails around the house in negligees. Disgusting." (Three years later, re-reading his journal, he wrote above this entry, "God forgive me for this!") The iconic scene of his never-to-be-forgiven callousness was a confrontation in the same year, after Rose had tattled to their parents about a boozy party he had thrown while they were on holiday in the Ozarks; Williams's newfound literary friends had been banned forthwith from the house. "We passed each other on the landing and I turned upon her like a wildcat," Williams wrote in *Memoirs*. "I hissed at her: 'I hate the sight of your ugly old face!' Wordless, stricken and crouching, she stood there motionless in a corner of the landing as I rushed on out of the house." He added, "This is the cruellest thing I have done in my life, I suspect, and one for which I can never properly atone."

By 1937, as Williams settled into life at the University of Iowa, the drama of his own survival prevented him from keeping Rose properly in mind. "I think of Rose and wonder and pity—but it is such a faraway feeling—how bound up we are in our own selves— our own miseries. Why can't we forget and think of others?" he noted. The day after her sexual outburst in 1939—"poor mad creature," he wrote in his diary— Williams was awarded a Rockefeller Fellowship, which would get him out of St. Louis and on his way. Rose was the dark cloud on his brightening horizon. "Rose, my dear little sister—I think of you, dear, and wish, oh, so much that I could help!" he wrote in July 1939. "Why should you be *there*, little Rose? And *me, here?* No reason—no reason—anywhere— why?—why?" Above these lines, two months later, he noted, "I seldom think of Rose anymore."

On the day of Rose's lobotomy—January 13, 1943—Williams was having "the most shocking experience I've ever had with another human being." "My trade turned 'dirt,'" he noted in his diary. "No physical vio-lence resulted, but I was insulted, threatened, bullied and robbed. . . . All my papers were rooted through and the pitiless, horrifying intimidation was carried on for about an hour. I felt powerless." Williams's 1943 diary is filled with news of his plays, his pickups, his pain; not until late March, however, is there mention of Rose, when she is included as part of "my lack of feeling, the numbness I have developed for my family. . . . The love seems all there, but the capacity to feel about them seems nearly gone." Two days later, he added a sort of haiku to his detachment: "Rose. Her head cut open. / A knife thrust in her brain. / Me. Here. Smoking."

In his work, Williams acted out his grief and his guilt over this youthful indifference. His plays were, in some sense, attempts at atone-ment, efforts to redeem Rose by elevating her to a literary motif, an invocation, an angelic immanence, an emblem of all the brave shadowy souls too delicate and too wounded to survive life's hurly-burly. In *Spring Storm*, which Williams wrote between 1937 and '38, the love-lorn Arthur makes a pass at Hertha Neilson—a librarian built along the same outlines as Rose: lean, with the same quick intelligence, the same need to "depend upon a feverish animation . . . to make her place among people." After a drunken kiss, Hertha blurts out her love for

Arthur. Appalled at the avowal, he pushes her away. "You—you *disgust* me. . . . !" he says. The words, which recall the rebuke that crushed Rose, send Hertha bolting from the library and ultimately to her death. (She throws herself in front of a train.) The moment is echoed in *Streetcar*, when Blanche attributes her husband's suicide to her comment on discovering him in a homosexual embrace ("It was because—on the dance floor—unable to stop myself—I'd suddenly said—'I saw! I know! You disgust me!'").

Catharine Holly, in *Suddenly Last Summer*, embodies both Rose's predicament and her defining characteristics: defiance, truthfulness, a love of smoking and of fashion, and a sense of mischief. Catharine's breakdown—a result of her having seen Sebastian eaten alive by "a band of frightfully thin and dark naked children that looked like a flock of plucked birds"—draws on a terrifying vision of devouring hordes that Rose confided to Williams during his first visit after the lobotomy. "The madness is still present—that is, certain of the delusions—but they have now become entirely consistent and coherent," Williams wrote to Paul Bigelow in April 1943. He went on:

> She is full of vitality and her perceptions and responses seemed almost more than normally acute. All of her old wit and mischief was in evidence and she was having great fun at the expense of the nurses and inmates. . . . She showed me about her building and I noticed the other girls regarded her very nervously. She said she had "publicly denounced them" that morning. She had the impression that I had been in the penitentiary and was sorry I wasn't, as she feels that an institution is "the only safe place to be nowadays, as hordes of hungry people are clamoring at the gates of the cities."

This image made a sharp impression on Williams, who repeated it in a 1943 letter that month to Donald Windham, as proof, if more were needed, of "what a dark and bewildering thing it is, this family group."

His writing hinted at even darker, more bewildering reasons for his guilt over Rose and his lifetime dedication to memorializing her. In his 1943 short story "Portrait of a Girl in Glass," Williams sketched out the characters and the central dramatic situation of *The Glass Menagerie*: Tom's desperate mother sees marriage as the only hope of salvation for his chronically shy and wayward sister, Laura, and pressures him to bring home an eligible man from the shoe warehouse where he works. Tom enlists the "best-liked," "warmly tolerant" Jim, whose "big square hands seemed to have a direct and very innocent hunger for touching his friends." Jim counts Tom, whom he nicknames "Slim," as a friend, and that endorsement has also greased the social tracks for Tom: "the others had now begun to smile when they saw me as people smile at an oddly fashioned dog who crosses their path at some distance."

The story contains the bare bones of the famous dinner scene and the postprandial flirtation of Jim and Laura: the mother's background babble, the lemonade, the record player, Laura's dissolving shyness, the dance, the rising hope, and then the devastating news that Jim has a steady girl-friend and is soon to marry. After Jim leaves, Tom's mother blurts out her bewilderment at her son's infuriating obtuseness:

> Laura was the first to speak.
> "Wasn't he nice?" she asked. "And all those freckles!"
> "Yes," said Mother. Then she turned to me.
> "You didn't mention that he was engaged to be married!"
> "Well, how did I know that he was engaged to be married?"
> "I thought you called him your best friend down at the warehouse?"
> "Yes, but I didn't know he was going to be married!"
> "How peculiar!" said Mother. "How very peculiar!"

At the beginning of the story, Tom speaks of Laura's habit of dissoci-ation—"I think the petals of her mind had simply closed through fear, and it's no telling how much they had closed upon in the way of secret wisdom." Jim's heartbreaking departure allows for an illustration of Lau-ra's secret wisdom, her ability to "pop out with something that took you by surprise":

> "No," said Laura gently, getting up from the sofa. "There's nothing peculiar about it."

She picked up one of the records and blew on its surface a little as
if it were dusty, then set it softly back down.

"People in love," she said, "take everything for granted."

What did she mean by that? I never knew.

She slipped quietly back into her room and closed the door.

Laura understands what Tom won't allow himself to know: he loves
Jim. His flustered response registers both his denial and his shock at
being, as Tony Kushner writes, "unceremoniously outed, by his mousey
sister, with his mother present." The awful implication of the innuendo,
which never made it into the play, is that Tom has used his fragile but
beautiful sister as bait to attract Jim to his home. In 1943, for an unknown
playwright who had not found his audience, such an idea was inadmissible
and un-stageable; by 1957, emboldened by craft, acclaim, and psychoanalysis, in *Suddenly Last Summer*, Williams was able to admit the idea of
using a woman as sugar to swat the fly of male attraction and to make it
the center of the scandal around Catharine Holly. Mrs. Venable wants the
idea cut out of Catharine Holly's brain just as Williams may well have cut
it out of his own consciousness through his legendary devotion to Rose.

At the beginning of his analysis, Williams worried that if he got rid
of his demons he'd also lose his angels. "I suppose this means the
end of my career in theatre," he told Paul Bowles in late December 1957.
On the contrary, when it opened Off-Broadway on January 7, 1958, *Suddenly Last Summer* received generally excited critical response. "Apparently, judging from some of the reviews I have read on my hillside, a
great light has broken through with 'Suddenly Last Summer,'" Katherine
Anne Porter noted in a letter to Williams. "An impressive and genuinely
shocking play," the usually un-biddable Wolcott Gibbs wrote in *The New
Yorker*. "An exercise in the necromancy of writing . . . A superb achievement," Brooks Atkinson called it in the *New York Times*. ("I don't think
I've ever been quite so grateful to you for a favorable notice," Williams
wrote to Atkinson.)

The analytic process seemed to have opened Williams up to the deeper reverberations of his unconscious. The most shocking element in the play—and the most central to the shift in Williams—was Sebastian's cannibalization. The gutted Sebastian, in Catharine's horrified description, looks as if "a big white-paper-wrapped bunch of red roses had been *torn, thrown, crushed!*—against that blazing white wall." The play is at pains to emphasize that the devouring was willed by the erstwhile poet. "*He!—accepted—all!*—as—how!—things!—are!—And thought nobody had any right to complain or interfere in any way whatsoever," Catharine explains to Dr. Sugar when he asks why Sebastian didn't resist it. She goes on, "Even though he knew that what was awful was awful, that what was wrong was wrong, and my Cousin Sebastian was certainly never sure that anything was wrong!—He thought it unfitting to ever take any action about anything whatsoever!—except to go on doing as something in him directed."

Dr. Kubie, who saw the play in the first week of its run, said that he was "emotionally stirred" by it. Williams had even worked Kubie into his macabre gothic fantasy. "Doctor—Cu?—Cu?" Mrs. Venable stammers, struggling with the name of the "glacially brilliant" psychiatrist who may operate on Catharine's brain. "Let's make it simple and call me Dr. Sugar," he replies. The line was a provocative wink at Dr. (Sugar) Kubie, who enjoyed the portrait. "Of all the many portrayals of the role of the psychiatrist that I have seen on stage and film, this rang truest," he wrote to Williams. "It had a quality of thoughtful, unpretentious, competence of responsibility and humanity. . . . And he did not have bed-side manner oozing out of every pore." Of all the reviews Williams got, Kubie's was perhaps the most probing. In the same letter, Kubie wrote at length about being "intrigued by the particular use you make of the fantasy of eating and being eaten":

> This is such an ancient component in human mythology: the "so sweet I can eat you up" routine with children; the lions of a child's nightmare; Prometheus; the Cocktail Party where the girl on the cross is eaten alive by ants; the carnivorous dreams of a young woman patient who is literally starving herself to death after an earlier period of compulsive

over-eating; etc. etc. You interweave this dream with a special meaning of the concept of God, which is pretty cloudy to me.

To Katherine Anne Porter, on the other hand, the idea of cannibalism didn't need any literary or psychoanalytic frame. "I am a realist in that sense that everything is real to me, nightmares, daydreams, the world visible and invisible," she wrote. "And that we eat and drink each other, as do all the other creatures, has been no news to me, any more than to you. . . . But Great God, as they say in Texas, what astounds me is that it is news to anybody at this late date." Williams told the press as much. "Life is cannibalistic," he said to Whitney Bolton in the *Philadelphia Inquirer*. "Truly. Egos eat egos, personalities eat personalities. Someone is always eating at someone else for position, gain, triumph, greed, whatever. The human individual is a cannibal in the worst way."

Williams himself was an unusual specimen in the annals of psychic cannibalism: he devoured himself. Although Sebastian's cannibalization plays as a generalized image of mankind's rapacious destructiveness, Williams's description of his body looking like "red roses" links the character to the iconography of his own public myth and gives the self-sacrificial game away. "I think we ought at least to consider the possibility that the girl's story could be true," Dr. Sugar says in the play's last line. The truth that Williams coaxed out of his unconscious was the imminence of his own decision to destroy himself for meaning.

During the first few months of his analysis, Williams reported unmistakable progress. For the first time in his life, he had become punctual; his panic attacks dramatically decreased; and his claustrophobia abated to the point where he could use the self-service elevator in the East Side gray-stone building where he shared an apartment with Merlo. One friend, who preferred to remain anonymous when interviewed by the *New York Post*, noticed a new relaxation in his demeanor. "I remember a couple of years ago if anyone even a dear friend, like say, Audrey Wood, kissed him on the cheek or put an arm around his shoulders, you could see him stiffen. Now if he likes somebody, it's more evident." Kazan saw a new centeredness in his nervy friend. "I'll tell you a new 'bit' I noticed about you," he wrote to Williams after the opening of

Suddenly Last Summer. "I don't think a couple of years ago you would have hung around the back of a lobby after one of your openings and gone up to a group of tough characters, Josh Logan and Molly Kazan, and sat down with them and asked 'How did you like it?' That's a new one and—oh, I forgot—Moss Hart—I really admired that, admired it because that much strength I don't think I have."

Kazan, who'd been sent two new scripts, including *The Loss of a Tear Drop Diamond*, noticed that Williams's point of view toward his characters kept shifting, as if to say, "'Just this second I'm fucking fed up with these goddamn types.'" "I think they as well as you are in a time of transition," Kazan wrote, adding, "I agree with Kubie. Don't rush. Please don't. You have the best record of anyone currently working in our Theatre. (Only except O'Niell [*sic*] and I can't even spell his fucking name. I don't know why I except [*sic*] his plays since I haven't read his plays since college). Anyway, don't hurry. No one is going to forget you. No one."

"Kubie has said for me, some way to quit work for a while and 'lie fallow,' as he puts it, till I have found myself; then go back to my work with a measure of inner composure," Williams told Kazan. "'A measure' of that is all that I can hope for. I'll never be as composed as Inge seems to be. I have one more job to do before the attempt to 'lie fallow.' I have to finish 'Sweet Bird.' At least a clean draft of it, and this I'll try to do in Key West and Havana during this two-week vacation." That exchange with Kazan was in January 1958. In late April, acutely depressed and in Kubie's words "passing through purgatory"—"I thought I had been going through that all my life," Williams wrote to St. Just—he wrote Kubie a long farewell letter. "But instead of posting it I delivered it by hand and of course he talked me into going on with it."

Williams's need for control meant that he was never going to submit easily to an analyst. The success of *Suddenly Last Summer* and the subsequent preproduction sale of *Sweet Bird* to MGM for $400,000, as well as the record-breaking release of the film of *Cat on a Hot Tin Roof*, virtually ensured that he wouldn't surrender to the analytic process. On June 27, 1958, Williams had his last session with Kubie. "It turned into a contest of wills," Williams told Kazan in his postmortem. "He got sore and wound up saying that I wrote nothing but violent melodramas that only succeeded because of the violence of the times that I live in."

Williams's account is not necessarily reliable. As Kubie noted, in a letter to Lucy Freeman in 1962:

> He is a strange and interesting phenomenon. Of course no matter what he says nor how he misquotes me I can never answer him in public print without violating his privacy. He has the right to indulge any public fantasies he pleases, but I do not have the right to correct him. His first reference to his treatment was in Newsweek (if I remember correctly). I vaguely remember that he had interrupted his analysis and was sorry and wished to go back but could not because his analyst was dead!! The more recent supposed quotation (put in quotation marks) bore not a remote resemblance to what I had actually said to him on that topic. However these are the hazards of the game and do not really worry me.

Writing was so successful a defense for Williams that he could not—would not—drop it even temporarily. "I had to defy my analyst to continue my work this past year," he wrote to Kazan, three weeks before calling it quits with Kubie, adding, somewhat disingenuously, "I wanted to accept this instruction but without my work, I was unbearably lonely, my life unbearably empty. And I didn't feel I could go on working with him while acting in total defiance of all his injunctions. So I quit for a while. I think maybe after this play I *could* do what he asks. Lie fallow. . . . The trouble, now, is that my personal life is all fucked up. Frank and I have drifted so wide apart and nobody else has come near enough to help me."

ON HOLIDAY IN Europe after concluding analysis, Williams used anger to separate from Kubie. "I resented him telling me that I must go through 'hell,'" Williams wrote to Wood that July. He also resented Merlo for putting him through it. At the beginning of the summer, in Barcelona, Williams was stung by a jellyfish, which, he noted in his diary, "seems to have set the keynote to practically all that has followed." He sank into a deep depression. As he saw it, he had success but no life. He couldn't live without Merlo, or with him. His work, which was his way of living, was also becoming his way of dying.

"Another day without coffee and work. Kubie would be pleased," he joked bitterly in his diary. Flying to Europe, he confided to Wood, had been a "grave error." "It was certainly not a good move. I became very paranoiac soon as I got here, fought with Frank," he wrote. During this lonely European sojourn, Williams was trying to bring more clarity both to *Sweet Bird of Youth*—"The truth of the play has not yet been quite reached. It's still a melodrama," he wrote to Wood in June—and to his bedeviling relationship. ("Frank and I never get along in Rome," he wrote to Jo Mielziner that summer. "Sometimes I wonder where we do get along, I'm not sure the place has yet been discovered on earth.") Sometime later, he addressed the temperamental and footloose Merlo with the state of their union.

I'm drunk enough to write you about you and me as I see us and the situation between us.

Something you said to me in the first few weeks that we lived together has stuck in my mind all these years. You said, "I hope you'll never be sick but if you were, then I could show you, prove to you, how kind I can be to you"—or something like that, that was the meaning of it.

I was already involved in a psychological and spiritual struggle that was slowly breaking me down despite the fiercest resistance. I needed exactly what you were offering to me and you were and are far too knowing not to have known it, but I don't think I'm being unfair when I say the promise was false.

You meant it, I'm sure you did, but you didn't carry it out. Your love never got out of bed, if you know what I mean, and you are far too knowing not to. I loved the bed but it wasn't what I needed, strictly speaking, I needed tenderness, sweetness, support and reassurance all the time, all the way, or a recognizable facsimile of it, and mighty damn little of it was forthcoming even in the beginning, and progressively less. It was you who "threw down the gauntlet" in the battle of wills, of egos, that our life together turned into over the years, progressively. You wanted it that way and I had to take it that way, and so the support, the spiritual sustenance, was not only withheld but in its place there was a continual duel, draining me emotionally, embittering me, turning me into an angry middle-aged man. Kubie was quick to see this, although I never told him anything more about you than the literal, day-to-day, blow-by-blow, account of our lives together in New York while we were there during my analysis. He came to the quick conclusion that the situation between us was "mutually destructive" and that's why he went out on a risky limb to try to put a stop to it. He knew I was at the point of a total crack-up and he saw that you not only did not care about it but gave a very suspicious appearance of pushing me toward it faster.

These are very harsh things to say and there may be some elements of injustice or misapprehension in them but this is the way it has been as far as I am able to see it, or Kubie could.

I know my faults and you know them so I don't have to tell you about them, you can tell me about them if you care to, and I will be glad to hear your full account of them. Intense irritability, raw nerves, chronic fatigue were the unavoidable concomitants of my endless struggle to carry on my vocation in years when energy was running low and lower, but it took far less than your native perception and wisdom to recognize the reasons and to understand and forgive them. If you did, you expressed it in strange ways, most of the time.—We still had the bed, and it was still good, but the love never got out of bed.

The bed-sweetness, the malignant dependency, the fear of running out of time, the hunger to hold onto fame's live wire, the longing for a pure love and the abuse of it, the issue of whether to stay with Merlo or to go, the artist's mortification at a "botched" work that turns into a big public success: all these intense personal issues in Williams's life found their way into the panorama of *Sweet Bird of Youth*. Analysis had given Williams a sort of detachment from his unfulfillable emotional demands, and that newly minted self-awareness lent a tragicomic flavor to the power play between *Sweet Bird*'s drugged, exhausted fading star Princess Kosmonopolis (aka Alexandra Del Lago) and Chance Wayne, her hapless, desperate, blackmailing gigolo and a would-be star who returns to his hometown in a doomed attempt to recover the love of his youth. Obsessed with her "outlived legend," the washed-up Princess is driven mad by the loss of her success; Chance is driven mad by his failure to achieve it. The drama that these two characters enact mirrored the conundrum of Williams's existence.

The Glass Menagerie had made a myth of Williams's escape through art from his "2 by 4 situation"; now, in *Sweet Birth of Youth*, he documented how his pursuit of art and fame had gotten him into an even tighter spot. Like the rat caught in a trap that Chance mentions in the play's penultimate moment—it "gnaws off its own foot . . . and then, with its foot gnawed off and the rat set free, couldn't run, couldn't go, bled and died"—Williams saw self-destruction as his only avenue of escape. Through both characters, he bore witness to his spiritual exhaustion. The Princess spoke for the abrasions of time and lost energy. "There's nowhere else to retire to when you retire from an art because, believe it or not, I really was once an artist. So I retired to the moon, but the atmosphere of the moon doesn't have any oxygen in it," she says, adding, "You can't retire with the out-crying heart of an artist still crying out, in your body, in your nerves, in your what? Heart? Oh, no that's gone." Chance spoke for Williams's moral exhaustion and the invidious pull of fame. "In a life like mine, you just can't stop, you know, can't take time out between steps, you've got to keep going right on up from one thing to the other, once you drop out, it leaves you and goes on without you and you're washed up." He added, "I'm talking about the parade. THE parade! The parade! the boys that go places."

Once, in 1955, while playing the truth game with Anna Magnani, en route to New York on the *Andrea Doria*, Williams had shocked her by calling her a "monster." "I told her that all good artists were monsters," he wrote. "In the sense of departing extravagantly from the norm, sometimes in a conspicuous fashion, sometimes in a fashion that almost escapes public detection, but I think they are always monsters if they have greatness. But try and try as I might, as I certainly did, to explain what I meant by 'monster,' she was still sorrowful over the term, and it lingered in her memory a long time. . . . For almost a year later, when I was back in Rome and she was driving me home from a late party her changeable face became dark and brooding and she lapsed into a long silence, and then she suddenly turned to me and said, 'Tennessee, you are also a monster.'"

By 1958, Williams had come to agree with her. The term "monster" was one that he regularly applied to himself, a defining descriptor in the idiom of his "out-crying heart." "I am a monster, but I don't hurt anybody by plan or intention," he wrote to Kazan as they were reworking *Sweet Bird of Youth*. "Am simply very self-centered without confidence in the center—Chance without looks, shall we say. And middle-aged and hate it." The play itself dissected the concept of monstrousness at length. "I wasn't always this monster," the Princess says. "Monsters don't die early; they hang on long, awfully long. Their vanity's infinite, almost as infinite as their disgust with themselves." (The eponymous reptile in *The Night of the Iguana*, which Williams would begin writing in 1959, while *Sweet Bird* was being mounted, embodied his next spiritual mutation: a monster at the end of its tether.) "Kubie said I can't believe anyone likes me because I despise myself," Williams told Wood, adding—in a phrase that foreshadowed Chance's struggle in *Sweet Bird*—"I want to become a decent person, as I used to be."

After a grueling decade of celebrity and literary striving, Williams had become all too aware of the shrunken circumference of his life, which brought with it the hardening of his carapace. Analysis had poisoned the pure well of his idealized self. "I came to discover a lot of very unpleasant things about my character," he wrote to Oliver Evans as 1958 drew to a close. "I doubt that I have improved as a result but at least I know they are there instead of considering myself as I used to, an unusually nice little man." To Kazan, he complained, "Kubie didn't seem to understand how much of my character is scar-tissue, an accumulation of traumatic experiences which have made me imitate the hermit crab, a crustacean way of living." Williams had become a stranger to himself. He could live successfully in his art but not in his life. By cultivating his literary persona, he had starved his private one. "A writer is always two beings, the part of him he works with and the part he lives with," he said. "Of course he lives with both, in a sense, but one is the more objective, the observer, and the other one, is the left-over one that he was born as." Williams went on, "This left-over one is constantly more left-over, more reduced, I'm afraid. It's an unfavorable contract between them, unfavorable to the original 'as born' being. It usually becomes unfavorable to both of them, after a certain point of difficult co-existence."

Sweet Bird was a kind of road map of this erosion. "It's the work of an older and more deeply troubled man than the author of 'Streetcar'—the simple and dreadful fact of the attritions of time can't be painted out of the picture," Williams admitted to Brooks Atkinson. "We know them and gauge them in advance—and we double the pressure on ourselves to make up for them,—but can we?"

In May 1958, when Kazan first read and responded to the script of *Sweet Bird of Youth*, he sensed in the play's intensity and in its eloquence that something had shifted in Williams. "I think the arias are wonderfully done and will be most effective and are an advance on CAT and can be staged more frankly even than those we did in CAT," he wrote to Williams. He added, "I think the psychoanalysis has done you good and you should go back." In a typed, five-page exegesis, Kazan told Williams that Chance Wayne had "the potential of being a character as memorable as any you have written . . . a sort of grotesque mid-twentieth century Hamlet." He added, "Chance smells of doom. It comes out of him like sweat, or like a radiation." To his set designer, Jo Mielziner, however, Kazan added another dimension to his interpretation. "I think this is the most truly autobiographical play Williams ever wrote," he confided. "Not in the way MENAGERIE was autobiographic—not a memory, softened and romanticized by time, of his youth, but Tennessee trying to describe his state of soul and state of being today and now." Kazan went on, "It is the frankest play he has written, dealing as it does with his own corruption and his wish to return to the purity he once had. . . . I believe it is Tennessee himself in disguise, right down to the thinning hair."

In Chance's existential quandary—he had broken his own heart—Kazan saw Williams's sense of shame and self-condemnation, an idea that Molly Day Thacher also raised in her perceptive five-page dissection of the play for her husband: "The play is an expression of a deepening theme of Tennessee's," she wrote. "What is coming clearer lately behind the fear is guilt and a sense of doom-that-is-punishment, a waiting for punishment that is like a seeking for it. This is one of the deep things that no one can or should try to touch or tamper with." In the play, Chance has come back to his hometown to try to reclaim Heavenly, the love of his youth, whose father, Boss Finley, drove him away after their affair. Chance, who doesn't know that he infected Heavenly with a sexually transmitted disease, is unprepared for the extent of Boss Finley's rage; twice faced with the threat of castration or murder, he refuses to leave town. Chance's stuckness—his reluctance to take action to save his own life—constitutes the suspense of Williams's story. As Thacher spelled it out:

> The PLOT of the play is that a man comes to his home town
> And is warned to get out of town
> And is warned again and we and he see that the threat is serious
> And more serious
> And he still doesn't go
> And the threat looms bigger
> And he's offered a chance to get out
> And the threat gets uglier and realer
> And he lets go his *last* chance to get out
> And we see that he wants to be destroyed
> And he wakes up to his destruction.

> *That's the play. You can't change that* without it turning into a half-play. . . . *What might be changed . . . is: the nature and the source of the threat.* . . . The threat could come from ONE person, be the twisted exaggerated vengeance of one person.

The greater the severity of Boss Finley's threat, the greater the paradox of Chance's refusal to save himself. "He is surrounded by murderous forces that want to do away with him or castrate him. . . . He is not strong enough to fight these murderous forces. And perhaps he doesn't even want to escape," Kazan told Mielziner, adding, "This is the strangely and unexpectedly puritanical side of Williams. He is obsessed with his own sin, and I suppose it is this sense of guilt that makes his vision universal."

For Mielziner's edification, Kazan recalled Williams's behavior on location in Greenville, Mississippi, during the filming of *Baby Doll*. "There, if ever I saw one, was a trapped man," Kazan said.

In one obsessive drunken moment he said he hoped he could get out of town alive, and he began to be panic stricken. . . . After three days he disappeared without warning. He had even felt, and I have felt this, trapped in his hotel room. That in case of an emergency or of sudden danger, there was no way out of the hotel room. And, after all, there was only one way out for him. Down through the lobby full of people that knew him and, as he saw it, hated him. You get the idea. It's all in the play. The scene in the cocktail lounge is exactly this. And, furthermore, I am only treating the matter superficially. He feels the whole world is against him as an artist and as a homosexual both. . . . Sometimes I wonder how the hell he lives! . . . How does Williams get out of this trap? Well, for one thing, which is like CHANCE, increasingly by drink. (His other forms of evasion, Kazan added, included "the act of loving" (although he "complains that as he gets older this is a decreasingly frequent escape for him") and, greatest of all, the "act of imagination.")

Kazan felt that the play called for a kind of "subjective scenery," which would dramatize both the trap that Chance is caught in and the imagination by which he escapes from it—scenery "from which Chance (Tennessee) can transport himself . . . by an act of art or by some extraordinary stimulus." He continued, "The PROCESS of the play is again and again how CHANCE passes from one world to the other. . . . CHANCE, and THE PRINCESS and even THE BOSS come forward under the author's direction, and recreate for themselves and for us their wish-dreams, their romanticized pasts, their lost glory. And as this happens, the author, now confident in the capabilities of the new stage says in his stage direction that 'Room changes.' 'Bar disappears.' 'They are alone in the Palm Garden.' 'He is alone with himself.' In other words, the TRAPPED ONE is transported on the wings of this spiritual experience—drink, dope, romance, sex, longing, imagination, memory, whatever—OUT OF THIS WORLD."

KAZAN WAS RIGHT to see a self-portrait in the character of Chance. But in the manipulative cohabitation of Chance and the Princess, Williams was also exploring the dynamics of his symbiotic connection to Merlo. The Princess, in her hysterical collapse, sees Chance, at first, as an agent of salvation. "Chance, you've got to help me stop being the monster that I was this morning, and you can do it, can help me," she tells him. Chance, in turn, latches on to the Princess as a means to the end of getting to Hollywood and redeeming his and Heavenly's blighted lives. But, in act 3, when Chance places a call to Sally Powers, a gossip columnist in Hollywood—hoping that the Princess will convince her to break the story of his and Heavenly's talent—the Princess launches into a megalo-maniacal aria. Her arpeggios of self-approbation begin to sever her con-nection to Chance, who, in the course of her speech, is transformed from savior to extra in her epic.

> PRINCESS: . . . I seem to be standing in light with everything else dimmed out. He's in the dimmed out background as if he'd never left the obscurity he was born in. I've taken the light again as a crown on my head to which I am suited by something in the cells of my blood and body from the time of my birth. It's mine, I was born to own it, as he was born to make this phone call for me to Sally Powers, dear faithful custodian of my outlived legend.

When the Princess learns from Powers that her latest movie is a hit—"Grown, did you say? My talent?"—Chance's needs are immediately erased from her mind. In its ruthlessness, the Princess's volte-face demonstrates the centrifugal force of fame, the destiny of "me," never of "we." Chance is no longer necessary to her. Aglow with a sense of her own importance, the Princess pushes him away with lacerating cruelty. "You've just been using me. Using me," she says, calling him "a beach-boy I picked up for pleasure, distraction from panic."

The parameters of the tale—the exhausted and demanding diva fear-ing the demise of her talent, and the beach boy/hustler trying to make meaning of his louche, wasted life—caught at least part of the struggle that bedeviled Williams's relationship with Merlo. The Princess and Chance need things in each other; they just don't need each other. "Frank . . . is so pitifully unable to think about anything but himself, especially at

Geraldine Page and Paul Newman in *Sweet Bird of Youth*

times when someone is making an emotional demand on him other than
the accustomed one of sex, which he answers with unfailing brilliance
always, and for which much is forgiven," Williams told Wood. "Each of us
is an island."

At the finale, the Princess is raring to return to Hollywood and to her
new celebrity. They sit together on the hotel bed in what the stage directions call "the huddling-together of the lost, but not with sentiment,
which is false, but whatever is truthful in the moments when people share
doom, face firing squads together." The Princess asks Chance to come

with her. "You're still young, Chance," she tells him. "Princess, the age of some people can only be calculated by the level of—level of—rot in them. And by that measure I'm ancient," he says. Chance balks at the offer of escape. "I'm not part of your luggage," he says. "What else can you be?" she asks. "Nothing," Chance replies, "but not part of your luggage."

Chance is resigned to staying in his hometown—"the home of my heart"—and to facing his destruction. "Something's got to mean some-thing, don't it, Princess?" Chance says in one of his last lines. Will he stay or will he go? Chance's decision, like Williams's, is to destroy himself for meaning. As Boss Finley's henchmen lurk on the periphery of the stage, Chance comes downstage at the finale and addresses the audience. "I don't ask for your pity," he says in the play's sensational last lines, "but just for your understanding—not even that—no. Just for your recognition of me in you, and the enemy, time, in us all." In these lines—too poetic and too eloquent for Chance—the character morphs into the playwright.

WITH *SWEET BIRD* completed and the prospect of another production on the horizon, throughout the spring and summer of 1958 Williams began to marshal his troops. In case Kazan turned the project down, he fired off to Wood a list of alternate directors, including José Quintero, Sidney Lumet, Bobby Lewis, and Josh Logan; he suggested the names of film production companies that might take a preproduction "big deal gamble." Once Kazan showed his hand—he was already fully committed for the fall of 1958, he told Williams, but "if you want to wait for me, I'll be your boy"—Williams began to worry, somewhat disingenuously, about the director's steam-rolling energy and his influence over "the most important thing, which is the play's truth." "Please help me not to be seduced or distracted by the great Mr. K!" he wrote to Wood, adding, "Hold on to Quintero till we know what Gadg wants, and are sure it's the truth of this play."

Kazan's instincts, as usual, were inspired. Williams had organized his original ending around Heavenly; Kazan insisted that "what happens to Chance" was the question that the audience would want answered and the proper end of the story. Williams began the second act without his main characters on the stage; Kazan found a way of keeping Chance at the center of the drama by having the blaring horns of the Princess's borrowed Cadillac call "attention to his presence in town and to his new affluence and power," as he drives around Boss Finley's home. Williams had planned to use the audience as stand-ins for the attendees at the political meeting hall where Boss Finley's rally takes place, a device that Kazan found gauche and old-fashioned; he suggested instead having the rally be conjured up by a huge upstage TV screen on which the characters were treated cinematically: "the camera cutting from enormous close-ups of the BOSS'S face to shots of the audience, to shots of the heckler, to shots of Heavenly," while "CHANCE is placed prominently on our stage watching what seems like a preview of his own fate."

The "stunt," as Kazan called this behemoth screen, was a piece of theatrical legerdemain that suggested the dimensions of both Boss Finley's power and the danger of his racist ideas to the community, while finessing the play's "obvious weakness": "The second act had very little relation to what had happened in the first and introduced a whole new set of characters who'd been barely mentioned before." Nearly all of Kazan's strategic suggestions—including the need to raise the stakes of Chance's guilt at the finale, in order to make him submit to a castration—were incorporated into Williams's final script and became part of his meaning.

Where Kazan was concerned, Williams never let his artistic vanity get in the way of commercial success. "I can't think of any other director who could touch Kazan, creatively," he told Wood, who was aghast at the price Kazan was asking for his services. "I am out," Kazan told Wood, when she balked at his terms. "I don't really make deals with agents," he explained to Williams. "The only one who can call a deal off between you and me would be you. You can call it off if you like, or I can call it off to you. But agent-talk is all . . . plumage display, flexing and unflexing of muscles and bullying, bullying bullying!" Their collaboration was golden, and Williams knew it. He told Wood, "I do think he's probably entitled to a better deal than he's gotten before in directing my work because, as we all know, this play has a kind of sensationalism which almost obscures its basic seriousness and truth. Blackmail, liquor, dope, an ovariectomy, a woman raping a boy, a crazy southern demagogue, the negro problem, a beating, Etc. Who but Kazan could hold these elements in control and still make dramatic use of them? And who could I work with as well as I can with this old pirate?" Williams added, "Meanwhile, please play it cool with the Greek." When it came to Kazan and *Sweet Birth of Youth*, Williams was willing to pay, and he got his money's worth. "I feel that this play needs him more than any other I've written," Williams wrote to Cheryl Crawford, the show's producer. By contrast, he balked at the exorbitant demands of the show's male star, Paul Newman. "He mustn't try to screw me: that I will only take from Kazan," Williams told Wood.

Kazan's other great contribution was to the play's casting. His prowess secured Newman's commitment to the production. For the bravura role of Princess Kosmonopolis, Kazan opted boldly "for the inner qualities" of Geraldine Page, an actress he "greatly admired" but who was no protection at the box office. As Alma Winemiller in José Quintero's 1952 Circle in the Square revival of *Summer and Smoke*, Page had turned in an uncanny performance that had made the name of the star, the director, and the play. "Miss Page is not the kind of actress who waits to give a performance on opening night," Quintero wrote in his memoir, *If You Don't Dance They Beat You*. "She plunges into her role at the very first reading. It's almost as if she wanted to forget herself as Miss Page and utilize everything that she owns to become the character that she is playing." Casting her was a brilliant decision, one that Williams had questioned. "I think it may demand more power and technique than a young actress like Geraldine could give it," he worried to Crawford, who agreed at first. "The Princess is a pretty cosmopolitan character and I would still be better satisfied with Page if I first heard Margaret Leighton, Vivien Leigh, Eileen Herlie and Edwige Feuillère and maybe even Siobhán McKenna," Williams wrote to Wood, adding, "It's a virtuoso part, demanding great stature, stage presence, power, vocal richness and variety, and so forth, but Gadg, we have to remember, has a genius for casting, second to no one's."

Kazan maintained that "consanguinity"—by which he meant being American—was a very important factor in casting the role. Still, Page struggled at first to locate the ravaged emotional geography of Princess Kosmonopolis's character. In preparation Kazan gave her a collection of photographs of silent-film stars and asked her to consider which one her

Princess might have been. Page discounted Greta Garbo as too remote, with a coolness that was not indigenous to the Princess's combustible nature. She discarded Mary Pickford, and her trajectory from sweetheart to diva, as a lazy choice. She was tempted by the steaminess of Theda Bara and the sassiness of Clara Bow. But in the end, she chose the complexity of Norma Talmadge, who seemed to have "an air of great vulnerability, as of someone who would greet everything and everyone with a spontaneous open-heartedness, and I was very touched by it," she explained. "I felt the shocks and hurts that would fall full force on a heart like that could turn someone into a complicated, volatile phenomenon like the Princess."

On the first day of rehearsal, at the Martin Beck Theatre, however, Page had two surprises for Williams. The first was that she would not sign her contract unless there was assurance in writing that she would play the lead in the film version. Wood was called to the theater, losing her fabled cool as soon as she marched through the lobby doors. "If Miss Page continues to insist on it," she told Page's agent, "we will have to find someone else to play the part." With the producer and the director standing within earshot, Wood prevailed. (Page, whose stage performance made her famous and earned her a Tony Award, starred in the 1962 film, for which she was nominated for an Academy Award.) Then, when the actors finally sat at the table to begin reading the play, Page's delivery was fearful and hesitant. Midway through, Williams bolted from his chair. "Stop it, stop it! It can't go on, it's too awful!" he said, and stormed out. Like the Princess in the play, who senses disaster and flees up the aisle at the premiere of her movie, Williams rushed home, refused to answer the phone, and knocked himself out with a cocktail of booze and pills. He craved a little of the *"temporary* obfuscation" he described in *Period of Adjustment*, a comedy he had premiered and directed at the Coconut Grove, in Florida, a few months before. Page's reading had convinced Williams that his first instincts were right and Kazan was wrong—that he was mistaken about the actress and, even worse, about the play.

Kazan spent the remainder of the afternoon dealing with Page, who had retreated to her dressing room in despair. "She was convinced that she couldn't do the part," he said. "I told her she could and would, that it was a stretch for her, true, but that she had to be courageous, and if she was, she would play the part precisely as I wished it played and no one else could or would play it as I wished." He added, "I knew I had to use some extreme measures—like making her 'camp' the part for a few rehearsals, to break down the inhibitions that the truth-seeking of the Method often causes in our actors. . . . It only needed me to hold her hand for a few days, then spur her on."

Sometime that evening, Williams roused himself to answer the insistent banging at his front door. Molly and Elia Kazan—"sweetly and genially smiling as if nothing has happened of an unusual nature"—were standing at the threshold. Williams had no choice but to invite them in. He was "now dreadfully ashamed of my conduct before the company but not yet swerved from my conviction that the play should not go on." The Kazans talked to him, he recalled, "as you do to a wounded animal or a sick child." Except for the time after the disastrous opening night of *Camino Real*, when Williams had locked himself in his bedroom, refusing even to receive the congratulations of John Steinbeck, who waited outside, Kazan had never seen Williams so distressed and timorous. "He doubted his own play; he wanted it withdrawn," Kazan said. "I believe that only the rather mystical faith he had in me persuaded him to go ahead." In a note to Kazan just prior to the beginning of rehearsals, Williams expressed that faith. "I think we have to go for broke," he wrote, adding, "I think we have got to draw out of Paul [Newman] an approximation of a kind of subtlety and sophistication and decadence that he doesn't have in him, and that is the 'rub.' I should have also put in the word ambivalence. If you can accomplish that, you'll have created a miracle almost. But I think you can."

Kazan once told Williams that he should never talk to actors; his combination of shyness and vagueness would make any suggestions more confounding than clarifying. "You get the impression, out of frustration really, 'Oh, I don't think he's read his plays even. He doesn't know anything about them,'" Geraldine Page recalled. "You want to shake him and knock him on his head and say, 'Open up and let me in to talk to you.' That 'you' that's way back in there, inside, that does the writing." She continued, "I imagine the number of people who have been able to really share that part of his work with him on a conversational level are very few."

Kazan, of course, was one of them. For *Sweet Bird of Youth*, Williams insisted that Kazan allow him "a close, undisturbed working relationship between you and me: no others." He felt an almost Oedipal connection to his director, which showed itself when he returned to the theater the day after his panicky scene. A young man—an Actors Studio "listener," unknown to Williams—was sitting beside Kazan, in the place usually reserved for the author. Convinced that the person had been "brought in to rewrite my work" and "jealous of his proximity to Gadg," Williams took a seat against the back wall. During the lunch break, he was introduced to the visitor, and his paranoid suspicions evaporated. For subsequent rehearsals Williams took his "rightful place next to our great white father."

As the play struggled to find its form in the Philadelphia tryout, the issue of whom Williams would collaborate with to solve its many structural and technical problems threatened to destroy the production and ruin his working relationship with Kazan. The problem was primarily Molly Day Thacher and her brusque opinions. "O.K. I'll play it cool and deal with MK's notes, but only on condition that from now on, in or out, there be no further exposure of my frayed nervous-system to notes, or discussions within my hearing, of this play . . . except between you and me," he wrote to Kazan. "I must not be demoralized at this point by the little group of well-wishers that close in for the kill when a play is in trouble. The moment that happens I'll close the play." The people to whom he would talk, he explained, were Kazan, Crawford, Mielziner, Wood, and "nobody else at all." Williams felt demoralized, exhausted, and under siege from other would-be advisors. "I will throw my typewriter at them if they come near me," he warned Kazan. "I will call on the Dramatists Guild for protection of my rights as an author to have exclusive control and authorship of this script. I have written a play about castration but refuse to enact the role of victim-protagonist in it."

When under attack, Williams could fight his corner with ferocious intelligence. In Philadelphia, sensing that Kazan was trying to "correct" his play in a "willfully, fatally wrong way"—he sparred even with his trusted director. "The sick fury that I felt last night at the demolition of the finest last scene that I've ever written, and I've almost always been best in my last scenes, has now died down and I am still alive, the fury is gone, just the sickness remains," Williams began a note to Kazan. Before launching into the most blistering, clear-eyed attack he'd ever leveled at Kazan, Williams praised his work with Newman ("You have given him, or drawn out of him, a really great performance") and his smooth handling of the play's flawed and faltering second act ("You have staged it as only you could. Nobody can equal you at obscuring the worst in a writer"). What threatened "to sever the Gordian knot of our friendship," however, was Williams's contention that Kazan was also "obscuring the *best* of my writing, in fact I might almost go so far as to say that you have obscured the play." At issue was Kazan's attitude toward the Princess:

> Your direction of her in the bar-scene, where the play is most elo-quently stated—the tragedy of people that need each other not reach-ing each other—seems, as I told you last night, as if you regarded that scene as a bit of lousy writing, a bunch of dummy lines, and that you wanted to throw it away by obscuring it with busy-busy direction which is not even interesting or good as direction alone.—I realize that you had built up a tension, a momentum, through your masterful staging of the crowd scene in the bar which a *quietly* passionate, lyrical scene between Chance and the Princess would appear to break. Actually, it's needed there!—I mean a break of pace, of momentum, of fury. It's set up that way in the script. They retreat to the gallery and the palm garden—everything is set up for an effective counter-point of some-thing tenderly human, meaningful and dramatic in a *quiet* way, with the influence of music and what you will have on the back-drop: sky and palm-garden. It's in this scene that you could score as a director who deeply understands and loves the true meaning and values of the material with which he is working, but you sacrifice it for what I sup-pose you regard as powerful staging, and I think you're so wrong!—but do you still care what I think?

In Kazan's strong hand, Williams sensed a certain hostility, which had as much to do with Kazan's growing frustration with his role as an interpretive artist as it did with Williams. (Kazan had recently finished his first original screenplay, for *Wild River*, and was in the process of translating William Inge's prose version of *Splendor in the Grass* into screenplay form.) "You know how suspicious, how paranoiac I can be and so often am, so you will not be surprised that I suddenly felt, last night, that your direction of Act III, your use of the Princess in it, was one of those unconscious acts of aggression that our analysts expose in us to our dismay—and that the aggression was really directed at the play's author, perhaps because you feel that I identify with the Princess and that I am a cheap, pretentious old bitch," he wrote in another furious note to Kazan. "Well, you're right in a way, but only in a way and to a degree. I am haunted all the time by 'the goddam end of my life,' by which I don't mean my physical death but my death as an artist: I am haunted by that terror, and that's why I drink as I do, and why I work compulsively as I do, shouting at life: 'IT AIN'T SO!'"

Williams was not wrong. "A sort of distortion was going on," Kazan admitted decades later in his autobiography. "I remember I felt an irritable impatience as I'd worked on those plays"—*Cat on a Hot Tin Roof* and *Sweet Bird of Youth*—"and, with it, a need to speak for myself at last. Here was born, I must suppose, the resolve to stop forcing myself into another person's skin but rather to look for my own subjects and find, however inferior it must be to Tennessee's, my own voice." In Philadelphia, incensed by laughter at the Princess in act 3—"the most truly powerful and moving scene in the play"—Williams called Kazan out about his competitiveness:

> A director of your skill and perception could not do such a thing without knowing what he was doing: consequently I must regard it as deliberate aggression, as an expression of disdain which you obviously now have toward me as a writer. You knew, you couldn't help knowing, that in the character of Ariadne del Lago I was expressing and tragically purging my own fearful dilemma, my own obsession, my terror, of losing my power as an artist and being obliged to live out the rest of my life with liquor and drugs and whores to stand the most unbearable loss

that anybody can suffer, and one that I wasn't suffering through any thing except terror of it. Don't regard this as mere Narcissism. I take a pretty objective view of myself, I see what I am in a clear mirror, which is merciless. This in its conception and writing is a scene of tragic stature, and pure dramatic theatre, the best I can do and have ever been able to do. The audience is meant to recognize the pathos of this woman . . . neither that nor her fiercely honest monologue while the phone-call is being put through, could be laughed at if it were played as conceived and written.—I don't mean it just incidentally when I add that it is also the sacrifice of a great talent in Gerry.

"I must know if you are now, finally, willing to regard me, and me alone, as your co-worker in the salvage operation that lies before us," Williams concluded, threatening otherwise to close the play, in which both men had large financial, as well as artistic, stakes. (Williams had invested $100,000 in the show; Kazan, $37,000.) Kazan took Williams's heat and agreed to return to their "original" version, which he felt "was more moving than the one we are playing now." In that version, Kazan said, "you watch the growing guilt, growing awareness of guilt which leads up to [Chance's] staying and submitting to (wanting the expiation of) castration." Because of cuts in the storyline, Kazan concluded, the bar scene in act 2, as it played in Philadelphia, was "shallow." "It seemed to be on the surface, concerned with external events. Occurrences in a bar! And instead of being INSIDE Chance, we are on the outside watching him bullshit and moan. . . . He seems like a callow and callous fool. The girl says they ripped my guts out. And he says I got it made. And carries on in the bar as if he still had a chance with her." The scene's construction was the problem, Kazan said, and he set Williams the task of rearranging the narrative elements so that Chance's crushing realization of his guilt mounts gradually. "If this is realized too early and he behaves semi-casually after it, then he stays for reasons that do not MOVE us," Kazan said. He added, "I think you and Audrey and I should have one fundamental talk. I'll ride up on the train with you or do or be anything and anywhere you want. But IT IS NOT TOO LATE to right ourselves."

SWEET BIRD DIDN'T get uniformly rave reviews—*Time* and *The New Yorker* adamantly dissented—but Williams got his Broadway block-buster. At the opening night, on March 10, 1959, he was called up onto the stage of the Martin Beck for a bow. "If this be blockbustering, we need more blockbusters. This is the noise of passion, of creative energy, of exploration, and adventure. Even in excess, it is enormously exciting," concluded the *Herald Tribune*. "One of his finest dramas," the *New York Times* said. "A play of overwhelming force" was the *Post*'s verdict. The combination of seven positive daily-newspaper reviews and the news of Geraldine Page's extraordinary performance—"a tigress with the voice of a trumpet," Walter Kerr called her—provided enough heat at the box office to propel *Sweet Bird of Youth* to a run of 383 performances.

Success immediately rewrote the public story of the play. "Kazan was marvelous: so patient and understanding during the whole ordeal," Williams wrote to Atkinson, thanking him for his *Times* review. "But I think these ordeals are WRONG! TERRIBLY, TERRIBLY WRONG! . . . I had never been through such a gruelling work-out in my—how many years on Broadway—19!—The whole trouble was in Act Two, as I see it. I just couldn't seem to write that damned act, I loved Act One and Act Three, but Act Two had to be forced out of me by all hands on deck. There must have been at least ten versions of it and I still don't know if we wound up with the right one: but at least we seemed to get by with it, with everybody but Tynan and Time, but 'getting by' with something is not, I know, the worthiest aim of an artist."

Williams had, in fact, written *Sweet Bird* with Atkinson's critical precepts in mind. In November 1958, he called Kazan's and Mielziner's attention to an essay on tragedy that Atkinson had published in the Sunday *Times*. "He thought the writing and the performance must rise to a level of eloquence and truth that will justify the point of view, however black it may be," Williams said. "I think this statement should serve as a warning for our production, since we need a good notice from Brooks. I don't want to suck up to any critic's artistic predilections unless I can sincerely buy them. In this case, I do. If he means what he says, I buy it. And so I am trying like hell to work into the last few minutes of this play some kind of summation comparable to Blanche's last line in Streetcar: 'Whoever you are, I've always depended on the kindness of strangers.' I think the audience, even the intelligent audience, and the good critic, will want something out of our main protagonist, Chance, besides his destruction. They'll want it to mean something to him. And to them. Otherwise it may seem like shooting cat-fish in a barrel. . . . I think that can only come out of a moment of dignity in him, which if I can find the words for it, he should express." In the last moment of Streetcar, Blanche threw herself into the arms of the doctor taking her to the asylum; with Chance's eloquent last lines in Sweet Bird, Williams threw himself into the arms of the audience.

In answer to the withering review in The New Yorker by his friend and early champion Kenneth Tynan, Williams opted for unbuttoned, rather than courtly, address. "Pride and dignity say SILENCE! ALOOFNESS!— All shit," he wrote to Tynan, adding, "What hurts and bewilders me is a note of ferocity in your notice. . . . I'm fighting the sort of game that you are peculiarly able to recognize with a real comprehension, and believe me, I have never surrendered knowingly to anything that I knew was false or cheap but in your piece about the play you imply that I have. WHY?" The virulence of Tynan's dismissal—"None of Mr. Williams' other plays has contained so much rot," he wrote—signaled an uncharacteristic refusal to think. In his vitriolic defensiveness, Tynan ignored the play's argument, which, as Williams's letter implied, struck a very particular, personal, and shared chord. "My complaint is that you didn't listen to Act One and Act Three which rank with the best work I've done," Williams told him.

Tynan, who was the most astute theater critic of his era, confessed to having been "dismayed and alarmed" by the play; he used wit to cover up Sweet Bird's central argument about the spiritual attrition of fame—a new theme in Williams's oeuvre and a subject that also went to the core of Tynan's own spiritual malaise. For Tynan, the play had hit a very raw nerve. Like Chance, who is ravaged by envy and guilt, Tynan relentlessly sought the public gaze and the legitimacy of the famous; and like the play's hero, he was full of self-loathing, compelled to pretend, as he put it, "to be somebody—anybody—else." "Something always blocks me," Chance says. By middle age, Tynan, a legendary enfant terrible, also found himself terribly blocked. "Still a non-smoker, but alas, a non-worker," he wrote to Louise Brooks. Williams's heroism lay in writing through his block; Tynan's tragedy was that he couldn't.

About the vexed issue of act 2, which dramatized the ruthless Boss Finley and his corrupt pursuit of power ("Big Daddy rewritten in the deep dyes of Victorian villainy"), Williams told Tynan, "You were obviously totally alienated by the dreadful but necessary Act Two. It is dreadful in *my* opinion. Maybe it really isn't dreadful at all but a very accomplished way of linking up the elements of a little play to those elements that make it a big one. That is Kazan's opinion, at least, anyhow, and I think Kazan has this time done a really wonderful job." To the columnist Max Lerner, Williams gave a more fanciful explanation of the play's luridness. "As an artist grows older he is almost always inclined to work in broader strokes," he wrote. "The delicate brush-work of his early canvasses no longer satisfies his demands of himself. He starts using the heavy brush, the scalpel and finally even his fingers, his thumbs, and even, finally, a spray-gun of primary colors. Act Two is written with that heavy brush, scalpel and spray-gun. Delicacy, allusiveness are thrown to the winds in writing, staging, performance. And I honestly think that was the only way to do it, and that if we hadn't done it that way the play would have failed to reach the mass audience that it seems to be reaching." He added, "Some day I am going to write a piece about the importance of sheer excitement in the theatre!—both seriousness and dramatic excitement!"

But of all Williams's postmortems of the play and himself, the most revealing was his letter to Kazan after Archibald MacLeish's *J.B.*, which Kazan also directed, won the Tony Award for Best Play. "You are tired but not half as tired as I am: I was BEAT!—and I don't mean 'Beatific,' just dead beat," he wrote. "I kept my critical faculties almost entirely intact, or so I believe, but I couldn't function on anything but the most hack sort of level and consequently a play that had the makings of greatness fell short of its mark. So the critics, rightly, gave their award to a play that set itself a much lower mark, and not only met it but passed it." The structure of *Sweet Bird* violated an essential rule. Williams, who streamlined the play after its first production, explained: "the rule of the straight line, the rule of poetic unity of singleness and wholeness, because when I first wrote it, crisis after crisis, of nervous and physical and mental nature, had castrated me nearly."

THE SUCCESS OF *Sweet Bird* propelled Williams, like the Princess, still farther "back alone up the beanstalk to the ogre's country where I live, now, alone." He was bigger than ever. By the end of 1959, the movie adaptations of *Suddenly Last Summer* and *Fugitive Kind* had been released; *The Roman Spring of Mrs. Stone* was about to go into production, with *Sweet Bird of Youth* soon to follow. "Are you driven and compelled as I am to keep *at it, at it, at it!*—because nothing else means enough," Williams asked Kazan three weeks after the opening of *Sweet Bird*. "I bet you feel like I do, that you have been through the meat-grinder. The consolation is that you turned our ground-up bits into successful chopped sirloin."

Kazan counseled his exhausted friend to stop work for a while. "You are giving me the same advice that Kubie gave me but with an important difference. You know me and care about me as a man and I don't think Kubie did except at moments," Williams responded. He continued, "There was a wonderful, beautiful speech, by far the best that Miller ever wrote, at the end of Death of a Salesman, something about him being 'Out there in the blue'—nothing solid beneath him to fall back on, to support him, except whatever natural, enduring power to rise or strength to stay up that he owned. That describes you and me. We are 'out there in the blue' with no net under. I'm SCARED! I think a lot more than you are. Out of my fright, as much as out of my love of creation, now, I am still working compulsively. The love of the work is greater than ever but the fear is too. The question is: If I go on this way, how long can I do so?"

In May, trying to negotiate some "freedom from pressure," Williams instructed Wood to "tell everybody who wants a quart of my blood that I am suffering from pernicious anemia." In July, as part of his campaign of rest and recuperation, he took a two-hour drive from New York to Pennsylvania to see Diana Barrymore, the daughter of the legendary actor John Barrymore, play Blanche in *Streetcar*. "She has the Barrymore madness and power and her last three scenes were remarkable," he told

St. Just, about the wafer-thin actress who shared his enthusiasm for "happy pills and sleepy pills" and whom he took to dinner afterward. "When we went backstage, the poor thing looked as if she had been drenched by a fire-hose." Williams went on, "What happens to actresses in my plays?! . . . I seem to push them over, I mean around that well-known corner, maybe because I'm around it too, and not pushing but calling?"

Williams was a performance without an intermission. By the fall, alternately polishing *Period of Adjustment* and working "like crazy on 'Night of the Iguana' and I do mean crazy," he found himself right up against his old malignant demons. To his friend Lilla Van Saher, Williams reported that several times on his travels he'd thrown awful, hysterical public scenes. "Something suddenly triggers my nerves and I flip! Really flip," he said, writing after a sleepless night, in such a state that he had "knelt beside the bathtub and prayed to God." "There is some volcano of violence in me and though I work every morning, as ever, it doesn't seem to release enough of the tension to get me peacefully and rationally through what is left of the day." As usual, Williams vowed to seek clinical help; as usual, the only interpretations to which he submitted were his own.

In December, Williams sent *Period of Adjustment* to Kazan. "Oh, God, Gadg, I don't know," Williams said, calling the play an "affirmation of sweetness in four troubled young people." "If it interests you, baby, please try not to think in terms of radical revision because I'm not up to it. . . . If you have some inspirations, aside from that, give them to me, but don't count on me being more than just *willing* to, for the Piper has arrived to collect his pay at my door and someone has let him in and told him that I am at home!"

To this rueful intimation, Williams added one last winded note. "I don't feel ready for the Sixties," he said.

CHAPTER 7

Kookhood

Perhaps my heart has died in me. If it is dead, I didn't mean to kill it.

—TENNESSEE WILLIAMS
to Hermione Baddeley, 1963

The sixties came in like a lion and stayed that way. On January 25, 1960, Diana Barrymore, one of the army of gallant lost souls whom Williams held dear, died at the age of thirty-eight from a heart attack apparently induced by an overdose of alcohol and drugs. The blanket of two thousand violets that draped her coffin at the Frank E. Campbell Funeral Chapel in New York was from Williams, who had flown from Key West to attend the funeral. "She had great honesty and a great capacity for love—and she died for lack of it," he told the press. Barrymore, who was given her first drink by her father at age thirteen, and was dubbed "Personality Deb No. 1" by the press at seventeen, had botched the early promise of her film career and lost many years to alcohol and drug addictions and three turbulent marriages. She chronicled her louche lonely life in her best-selling autobiography, *Too Much, Too Soon* (1957). In the book's final paragraph, she invoked Brooks Atkinson's review of her theatrical comeback, at the age of thirty-five, in 1956. ("Any time she wants to stop fooling around and learn the difference between acting and performing," Atkinson had written, "she can be an exciting actress. The stuff is there.") "I repeat my vow—and mean it," she wrote in the book's last lines. *"I promise. You'll see. You will indeed, Mr. Atkinson!* Perhaps I have begun to find my way."

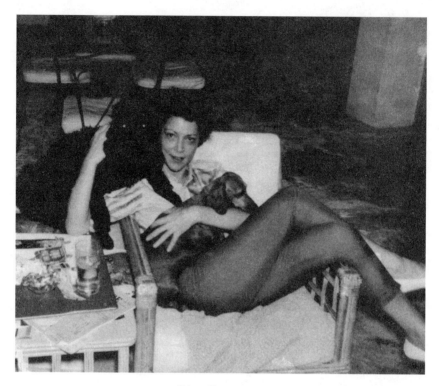

Diana Barrymore

For Barrymore, Williams was the pathfinder *and* the path. He was a kind of household god, an Orpheus who had led her back from her subterranean hell and into the light. "I don't mean this in a sacrilegious way, but *he is* my savior on earth," she wrote to Dakin Williams in April 1959. Barrymore was a wild but warm woman who often partied with Tennessee. Sometimes she dressed in male drag and pimped for him; sometimes, drunk and stoned, they would put Puccini's *Madame Butterfly* on the record player and act it out, with Williams playing Cio-Cio San to Barrymore's Pinkerton. She was also a frequent interpreter of his works. In 1958, she had taken on the role of Maggie in a touring production of *Cat on a Hot Tin Roof.* Good reviews had led to a successful engagement, the following year in Chicago, as Catharine Holly in *Suddenly Last Summer,* and finally as Blanche, in the summer-stock production of *Streetcar.*

"You can make a career of playing Tennessee Williams, and I almost have," Barrymore told the *Miami Herald.* "What shall I do when I finish him? I hope I never shall. Everything else seems weak and ineffectual." (At the time of her death, Williams was writing *The Poem of Two*, a play in which he planned to cast her opposite Maureen Stapleton.) Barrymore hoped that her performance as Blanche would be a springboard back to major critical acclaim as the actress playing Princess Kosmonopolis in the London production of *Sweet Bird of Youth*—a role that she was convinced would be her artistic redemption. "1960 is *our* year—I know it," she told the poet and actor Gilbert Maxwell. Barrymore's grand plan was confirmed by an astrologer she had consulted. "Not knowing anything of 'Bird,' she said, I would be going to England possibly in November—to do a play by the man who had changed my life (all this before she knew it was Tennessee)," Barrymore confided to Dakin. "The more I think about Tom (and that's most of my waking and *sleeping* time) I think it's going to come sooner."

Williams had given Barrymore a gold charm bracelet from which dangled an amulet the size of a quarter emblazoned with his familiar insignia: "10." "She flashed it everywhere and with it an implied story that Tennessee's promise to play the Princess had come with the bracelet. Although she said it many times, I doubt if it was true," George Keathley, who directed her in *Streetcar*, said. Williams encouraged Barrymore to try out for the role, and she did so twice, in front of Wood, Crawford, and Williams. Because the Princess reclines on a bed in the first scene of act 1, Barrymore performed for them while lying on her back. But for Williams, her performance "held no surprise." "I thought Diana was too much like the princess to play the princess well," he said. "She was a girl with talent but not enough talent and it haunted her and was destroying her." To Lucy Freeman, he wrote, "She read the part with a violence that defeated the part, which has to be held in the restraint, the controlled sense of measure, that Geraldine Page, under Kazan's direction, was able to give it."

Kazan refused to audition Barrymore for the New York production, which she considered "the most heart-breaking point in my whole life." "My hatred for Kazan burns black," she confided to Dakin. "If he had not wanted to play Svengali with Miss Page I would have done it—the woman is *me*—as I was—*Finished* at 36—I was! If I had been given a reading it would have been mine—Kazan could have started my life in November—now it will be a few months—it is hard to forgive a man who delays your *true* re-birth. But as in the Book of Job Love conquers all. My idolatry of Tom chases my black thoughts away. . . . So many nights I go to the theatre here [in Chicago] and I think of her in New York. She's in the dressing room making up for *my* part. I also comfort myself that Thank God I'm playing *Williams*—that is the one thing that makes this *waiting bearable.* I will pray for London."

Princess Kosmonopolis was not the only role that Barrymore wanted to play; she was also auditioning to be Mrs. Tennessee Williams. "The only strong men I had met were violent men," Barrymore wrote, at the end of *Too Much, Too Soon.* "What I needed, I thought, was a strong man who was gentle, who would be lover and father." Williams became her *idée fixe;* she campaigned for the author as well as the part. Barrymore charmed her way into the Williams family, by flying to St. Louis to take tea with Miss Edwina and cultivating a close friendship with Dakin (they referred to each other as "Sister" and "Brother"). "Just your brother matters to me—nothing else," she wrote to Dakin, as she was astonished to feel "for the first time in my life—my only concern was for someone else." She added, "This genius touched by God Himself is so helpless about everyday things. And like all true pure Geniuses he doesn't know how divine he is and how blessed."

After the run of *Suddenly Last Summer* she joined Williams and two other friends for a four-day holiday in Havana. "It was an idyll," she reported to Dakin. "In my whole life I've never been so happy—I'm not even used to spelling the word, I'm so unused to it!" She and Williams dined together at a restaurant where a band played and she sang; they took in the lavish floor show at the Tropicana Club; they joined Wood and Liebling, on their way back from a Caribbean holiday, for another congenial outing. "If you don't watch out, boy, I'm going to be flower girl at your wedding," Wood joked to Williams. In Barrymore's deluded imagination, the warmth of Williams's "sympathetic attachment" to her, as he called it, was blown up into the heat of romance. "Tom and I have talked of many things," she told Dakin. "He knows I love him now—it's going to take him time to realize how selflessly. Frankly, it appalled me to know at long last what it is just to love someone with your whole heart and soul."

Years later, Williams recalled Barrymore's glamour but not her avowals of love: "I remember her wearing a little red lady's riding jacket and black silk pants and one of those very crisply laundered white shirts with the black string tie," he said, of the Havana holiday. "She was so striking in it with her dark hair and flashing eyes. She was very lovely." To Lucy Freeman, he argued, "Diana loved me as a writer only. That's the truth and all of it. It couldn't have been otherwise. . . . I am peculiarly lacking in the qualities of a male-charmer and heart-breaker. I would say I am sort of the opposite, especially during these last five or six years when almost nothing but work meant anything to me. And I wasn't sure of the work." He added, "Diana's only great passion, perhaps her only true love, was her struggle to become a good artist."

Williams was "deeply disturbed" by Barrymore's death and concerned about his contribution to the professional and personal disappointments that pushed her over the edge. (The scenario echoed his guilt over the fate of his bright, fragile sister.) "I didn't think she would take it so badly. And, actually, 'Sweet Bird' has never been done in England. . . . If I had known how fully she identified with it and how deeply her heart was set on playing it, I might have tried to do something. But I didn't and I went south to Key West to work on something else and about a week later Diana Barrymore died," Williams wrote in *Memoirs*, a disingenuous account, as mistaken in its timeline as in its facts. Williams did know—had to know—about Barrymore's desire to play the Princess. She had proclaimed her entitlement to the heavens. She had spoken and written about it to Dakin; she had auditioned for Williams himself. At a Christmas party, a month before she died, she had even argued about the role with Williams, in front of Gilbert Maxwell. "The two of them were really at each other—Diana, on the floor by the sofa where he sat," Maxwell recalled. "I was *made* to play this part and I'm going to have it," she hectored Williams, shaking her finger at him, quoting the play. "*When monster meets monster*, remember." Maxwell observed, "It was half in jest, all of it, but there was a desperate seriousness in her intent. And at last, Tenn cried out, 'All *right*. I've told you I don't think it's for you, but if you want it this bad, I will do all I can.'" He didn't.

BARRYMORE'S COLLAPSE WASN'T the only one on Williams's mind. *Period of Adjustment,* the play that Williams was readying with Elia Kazan for a Broadway opening in November 1960, was a comedy in which a house—always a metaphor of the self in the Williams canon—is disappearing before its owner's eyes, "sinking into [a cavern] gradually, an inch or two inches a year." The cracks and lurchings of the play's Spanish-style suburban Memphis bungalow echo the internal disturbances of its lovelorn personalities: Ralph Bates, the homeowner, who has been abandoned on Christmas Eve by his wife and child, and George Haverstick, who is ready to call it quits after twenty-four hours of unconsummated marriage to a virginal bride. For both men, love has temporarily been lost, only later to be refound. "The human heart would never pass the drunk test," Ralph says. "If you took the human heart out of the human body and put a pair of legs on it and told it to walk a straight line, it couldn't do it."

Period of Adjustment—a play that, Williams said, "isn't my best by a long shot, but is nevertheless as honest a play as I've written"—meditates on changes of heart and the possibility of reconciliation. Written in a lighter, more benign tone than his usual, tormented one, and aspiring "to cast a kinder shadow, with more concentration on the quieter elements of existence," the play was Williams's demonstration that he was more than "the nightmare merchant of Broadway," as *Time* called him, and his answer to Dr. Kubie's accusation that he wrote "only violent melodramas" to appease his ambivalent, angry heart. "After my analysis I have reached a big decision about myself," Williams told the press that August. "I think perhaps I had too much hate in me. Hate can be constructive, but perhaps I hated more than I should. I am going to make a change." He had called it quits, he said, with "what have been called my 'black' plays. Maybe analysis has helped to get them out of my system. If it works, I owe it all to Dr. Kubie, a great and sympathetic analyst."

Subtitled *High Point over a Cavern: A Serious Comedy, A Period of Adjustment* expressed, Williams said, "more belief in the truth of people having tender need of each other, transcending their personal vanities and hurt feelings, than any of my other plays with the possible exception of 'The Rose Tattoo.'" The issues of frigidity, ambivalence, and bad faith that beset his mismatched couples are never seriously engaged, however, and a benevolent glow hangs over their fraught connections. "We all have to be smart and lucky," the virgin Isabel says to her new and temporarily impotent husband, "Or unlucky and silly."

Still, in the portrait of Ralph, one can see a stand-in for Williams in his relationship with Merlo: like Ralph, Williams wanted to renew the tenderness between him and his lover; like Ralph, he couldn't clearly see his own failures of compassion. For all of Ralph's vaunted capacity to feel—he is "one of those rare people that have the capacity of heart to truly care," a stage direction reads—he is habitually unfair toward his wife, Dorothea, whom he married for money and whom he describes as "a girl with no looks, a plain, homely girl that probably no one but me had ever felt anything but just—SORRY FOR." Williams shared with Ralph that capacity for unfairness and he knew it; he called himself "unintentionally unfair but sure as hell unfair. At least my analyst said so." So did Wood, who pointed out how he tended to "very often . . . misjudge Frank." Williams liked to portray himself as the victim of Merlo's emotional caprice, when his own temperament was equally infuriating, oblivious to its aggression. "It becomes difficult to distinguish between artistic temperament, simple temperament, and simply temper," Williams said. "In order to get along with me you have to be like my Frankie, and take a lot."

After having ministered to Williams during the ordeal of *Sweet Bird*—"he was an angel all during rehearsals and tryout," Williams said, declaring himself "more deeply in love with Frankie than ever before"— Merlo needed his own period of readjustment. "Frank made it clear that he didn't want me with him in Key West, that he wanted to be the 'Big Daddy' on that little plantation. Uncontested," Williams told Kazan in June 1959. "He feels he's done his bit for me and he's pushed me out of the nest, so I've got to fly alone again." But by the end of the year, Williams was contemplating pulling up his East Coast stakes and moving West with Merlo. "I think Frank would be reluctantly willing, and when he got out there he would be happy about it," he wrote to Christopher Isherwood. "Things are much better between us. There must be something. I don't know the mysteries of it, but there surely is something still very strong between us."

Williams and Merlo settled into a kind of negotiated truce, "in voices turned softer by love's exhaustion and hate's," as Williams wrote in "A Separate Poem" (1962), which memorialized the détente of their last months together. The poem, originally entitled "Lost Continent," was an anatomy of resignation and of love contaminated by disappointment:

> When we speak to each other
> we speak of things that mean nothing of what we meant to each other.
> Small things
> gather about us as if to shield our vision from a wide landscape
> untouched by the sun and yet blindingly lighted.
> We say small things to each other
> in quiet, tired voices, hoarsened as if by shouting across a great distance.
> We say small things to each other carefully, politely,
> such as:
> *Here's the newspaper, which part of it do you want?*
> *Oh, I don't care, any part but the funnies or ads . . .*
>
> But under the silence of what we say to each other,
> is the much more articulate silence of what we don't say to each other,
> a storm of things unspoken,
> coiled, reserved, appointed,
> ticking away like a clock attached to a time-bomb:
> crash, fire, demolition
> wound up in the quietly,
> almost tenderly,
> small, familiar things spoken.

The cocoon of medicated calm lasted into the summer of 1960. "The Horse is on pills and aged Cuban rum which he drinks out of ice-tea glasses filled to the brim, and is writing poetry, some of it remarkably good," Williams wrote to St. Just in August. "We don't quarrel anymore, it's all very sad, nice, and peaceful, with the Horse pushing forty and me pushing fifty. Where did the years go, so quickly? Even the dogs and the Parrott seem to wonder." Over the previous two years, Merlo had begun to drink harder than before; he was in the habit—Williams found it endearing—"of passing out stoned on the floor and me pouring a pitcher of ice-water over him in a useless attempt to revive him." A whiff of the autumnal had seeped into their life together and also into the poems that Merlo had begun to write, whose observations about the natural world contained a rueful intimation of endings:

> To beg a question
> Of the year's quartet:
> Winter, wolverine,
> Is present—
> Never past.
> Elusive summer, rare,
> Improvises—
> Thinks it is
> A tree,
> A blade of grass,
> A pollinating bee;
> While cold snakes
> Court
> July's warm air
> Under warmed rocks,
> And thrill,
> With coldly coursing blood,
> Thermal stone
> That happened to be there.
> Think hard
> On seasons flying fast.

If Williams's personal life was held in a precarious balance, his professional one had already begun to unravel. On April 21, 1960, Kazan, "looking rather shaky and gray in the face," according to Williams, met for a drink and told him that he was quitting as the director of *Period of Adjustment*—a seismic blow that ended the most important theatrical collaboration of twentieth-century American theater.

After the success of *Sweet Bird*, Kazan had told Williams that he would direct anything he wrote, "sight unseen and unread." The Broadway theater had been booked. The producing triumvirate of Kazan, Crawford, and Mielziner had been assembled. Kazan's surprise announcement pole-axed Williams. "I tried my best to make him change his mind, but he was adamant," Williams told the *New York Times*.

Williams's fury was compounded by the fact that Kazan was leaving the play in order to direct a film project by Williams's friend and theatrical rival William Inge (*Splendor in the Grass*), which Kazan said Williams took as a "signal that I preferred working with Inge." Williams was openly jealous, even sometimes bitchy about Inge, who'd had three hits in a row, including *Bus Stop* and *Picnic*. (Inge owed the launching of his career to Williams, who had befriended him in 1944 during the pre-opening run of *The Glass Menagerie* in Chicago, when Inge had interviewed him for the *St. Louis Star-Times*. Back then, Inge was trying and failing to write plays in the manner of Noël Coward. Contemplating the way that Williams converted the raw material of his life into drama, he saw a way forward. "Tennessee had shown me a dynamic example of the connection between art and life," Inge wrote in his diary. "I had never known where to look for material. . . . Now I knew where to look for a play—inside myself." The result was *Farther Off from Heaven*, a play based on his family; Williams liked the script and got it to Wood, who took Inge on as a client. The rest was Broadway history.) "I did promise to do your play," Kazan told Williams. "I did because I wanted to do it, and I wanted to do it because I think it's a beautiful play and a deep one. At that time I intended to get out of the Inge movie. . . . I couldn't . . . because I had initiated the project. I had made him write it. . . . How the hell can you pull out of a project that has cost a writer that much work and thought? . . . I couldn't. I didn't."

In the evening, after their drink, Williams called Kazan and, in a drunken paranoid outburst, berated him for his betrayal. "I'm furious at the way you spoke to me on the phone," Kazan wrote to him the next day.

OPPOSITE PAGE: With William Inge, friend and rival

"You haven't a right in the world to infer that I'm lying to you. I have never lied to you. And have I ever asked you to crawl? Has our relationship ever dealt in pity? We have a clean relationship and I did my share to keep it clean." He added, "I knew you were bound to think that I didn't really like your play. I expected that, but I didn't expect the insults."

Just a year before, Williams had described Kazan as "a very charged man. He is capable of error, and it has happened, but when he is right, he is blinding right." In this disagreement, the ugliest ever between them, Kazan was blindingly right. "Frankly, it appears to me that the loyalties in our relationship have run more from me to you than the other way," he said, and spelled it out:

> I stuck onto *Baby Doll* through the thick and thin of your indifferences and disappearing. . . . I stuck with *Sweet Bird* when you thought it was crap. I insisted on Gerry Page when you thought she was wrong. And I have taken for four years a whole campaign of vilification in the press to the effect that I was distorting your work. . . . I thought many times I should quit *P. of A*. But never seriously because I have always put you first. Then came Cassidy's piece, and I began to think. It isn't that I care what she thinks. I truly don't. . . . I only cared that YOU were silent. And I was forced to think that really and truly you felt the same way.

In her review of *Sweet Bird* in the *Chicago Tribune*, the theater critic Claudia Cassidy had tarred Kazan with a now familiar canard, that his vulgar influence marred Williams's poetic integrity: "The first and in part third are authentic Williams, while the inferior second act is shoddy compromise. Compromise with himself? With his director? Perhaps some of both." The play, she wrote, was "split down the middle by the same opposing forces that ripped 'Cat on a Hot Tin Roof'—the antithetical theatrical convictions of the playwright and of the dominant director, Elia Kazan. The valid pressure on Williams' characters comes from within. . . . Kazan's pressure often bears down from the outside, crushing the victim like a contracting cage. Compared with the inner violence of a Williams play the outer fringes of superimposed fury can be anti-climactic, even cheap."

Williams's past weasel words—referring to the Broadway third act of

Cat as "prostitution" and "Kazan's ending"—had fanned the flames of misconception and inevitably trivialized Kazan's subtle contributions to his work. In fact, Kazan's psychological and structural acumen provided Williams with a safety net that rallied him out of his writing blocks, challenged his melodramatic excesses, chivied him to work for greater depth, and allowed his imagination to soar. But Williams's artistic vanity would never allow him to acknowledge to the public or to himself just how much Kazan's prowess had affected his work. The art belonged to Williams; the inadequacies belonged to someone else. When it came to the critics' cavils about Kazan, Williams's silence was deafening. "I was surprised to find that they all had gotten under my skin," Kazan wrote of these accusations, adding that Cassidy's *Sweet Bird* notice was "the last bit of water that flushes the bowl." Now, in the face of Kazan's withdrawal, Williams told the *Times*, "The charge that Kazan has forced me to rewrite my plays is ridiculous. . . . Kazan simply tried to interpret, honestly, what I have to say." He went on, "The fact is, Kazan has been falsely blamed for my own desire for success." "He should have said that earlier," Kazan countered in the same article.

As it turned out, Williams's passion for success was the tipping point in Kazan's decision to say good-bye to him and to Broadway. (*Sweet Bird of Youth* was his last Broadway production.) He wrote to Williams:

> I thought, Why does he want me to direct his plays? The answer: Because of some superstition that I bring commercial success. Which you terrifyingly want. But that is part of the same distasteful picture. Just as I can't help but think you agree with Cassidy, I also think that you think of me as the person who can make your plays "go" and that you are willing to make some sacrifice in integrity and personal values to get the commercial success which I bring you. Well, Tennessee, fuck that! That is a hell of a humiliating position, and I don't want any goddamn part of it. . . . I'm not going to break my neck, slough off Inge's movie, do a half-ass job on *Period of Adjustment* only to be told in time, again, that I had misdirected your play into a hit. And then, to wait and wait for you to say something and wait for nothing. What the hell kind of position is that for a man? It's not for me. . . . Get a new boy and a new relationship.

For more than a decade Kazan had been the premiere American director of stage *and* screen; by 1960, however, he had grown weary of being handmaiden to other people's talent. "I wanted to be the unchallenged source," he wrote in his autobiography. His crack at the screenplay for *Wild River* had piqued his interest in his own self-expression; it was further buoyed by the script he had fashioned from Inge's prose treatment for *Splendor in the Grass*, which ultimately earned Inge the Academy Award for Best Screenplay. Walking away from Williams signaled a strategic volte-face in Kazan's psyche, as well as his career. He was walking away from commercial theater, from the studios, from his life as an interpretive artist. In time, he would become a best-selling novelist. "I no longer gave a damn about the themes of other men," he wrote in his autobiography. "How good it felt, despite the cold wind of Tennessee's disappointment, to be free." "Something has happened to me, no doubt," he told Williams after things had calmed down. "And is that bad? I don't think so. Something in me knows shock is necessary. Abrupt, jolting derailment. I'm sorry it all happened on your play."

Kazan "vowed not to look back." But how was Williams to look forward? To the *Times*, he insisted that for his future work there were other directors, in particular José Quintero, who was "just as brilliant as Kazan." Behind the scenes, after he'd cooled down, he returned, cap in hand, to Kazan. "I want you back if there is any way to get you back for this play," he wrote to him. "I'm confident that you are sincere about liking the play, and that this little play is one that you could give dignity and depth to, as well as a touching humor." He went on, "I said I wouldn't come creeping and crawling and I don't think I am. I am only telling you that I am still your mystified friend, and will remain so whatever your response to this appeal is. Yes, it is an appeal because I do want you and need you for the play and, without a sob, I don't think I am in any condition to have it without you. I'd rather put it away." Williams's pleading letter was signed "love," as Kazan's pugnacious one had been. "Please stay with me in spirit," he asked Kazan.

Kazan did. "I think our friendship will survive this and I think we will work together again. We're too close," Kazan told him in another letter, adding, "I can understand why you're sore at me. After all I said repeat-

edly I'd do it, and I was doing it, and then suddenly—. Well, I anticipated
how you'd feel. And I think, all considered, you behaved very well. . . . I
do think an awful lot of you, value you a lot, more than you know."

At the time of their split, neither Kazan nor Williams knew how long
their creative separation would last: it turned out to be forever. With the
frankness that characterized their collaboration, Williams finally
accepted the situation as blood under the bridge. "I don't know, and I will
never know, why you decided not to do the play," Williams wrote Kazan
some months after the break. "The message is that you made a big mistake and I suffered a big loss." Williams continued:

> Our association, personally and professionally, has always been a spe-
> cial one. Despite the fact that we had so much in common, but proba-
> bly it's the old story of conflicting egos of equally unsure people making
> a resentment and jealousy where there should have been faith and
> understanding and the brave use of peculiarly complementary talents
> for theatre, a mutual daring and a digging of each other's sense of life.
>
> We're both full of hate and love, but let's try not to hurt each other out
> of fear.
>
> Don't try to like me now. My psychic sickness and tensions, failure of
> analysis, self-facing and so forth, have made me at least temporarily
> impossible to like.
>
> You are in the same boat, I would say, right now, although you have
> the comfort of a home-life, your devoted children, etc., while I must
> make out with two dogs and a Parrott and someone I love who is in a
> relation with me that may make a truly reciprocal love a psychological
> impossibility.
>
> We are full of fear but also full of courage, and let's concentrate on the
> latter, and what does it finally matter whether we do more than under-
> stand each other's dilemma.

Williams remained true to Kazan in his fashion. When, in 1961, a year
after the walkout, during rehearsals for *The Night of the Iguana*, Wil-

liams's then director, Frank Corsaro, said in passing, "We young directors want to get away from Kazan," Williams chimed in, "Not too *far* away, baby, until you young directors are sure as hell that you're better."

Although the trajectories of their careers would take them in different directions, Williams and Kazan never lost their fraternal bond. They would continue to correspond, to seek each other's advice, to give notes on each other's scripts, and to support each other in moments of personal tragedy. At the beginning of rehearsals for *Period of Adjustment*, Kazan sent Williams a letter of good wishes and enclosed a turkey feather. "You monster," Williams joked in return, adding, "I wish I had an angel's feather to enclose in this letter to you but all my feathers are gray ones."

Period of Adjustment, directed by George Roy Hill, felt like a hit in Philadelphia; then, in New Haven, a frost settled "on more than the pumpkins," according to Williams. "I crept around like that man who'd slaughtered 5,000,000 Jews in Nazi Germany, I drank a quart of liquor a day; and then the bleeding started. . . . Only Thornton Wilder and his sweet old maid sister were nice to us there," he wrote to St. Just. Nonetheless, *Period of Adjustment* opened on Broadway on November 10, 1960. *The New Yorker* was the most virulent of the lukewarm press in its disapproval, referring to the play as "a turbid stew of immiscible ingredients." The rest of the reviews were sufficient for *Period of Adjustment* to eke out 132 performances and to secure a movie sale. "I figure that I have had my day in the Broadway theatre," Williams told St. Just. (Kazan "would have saved [it], if he'd staged it," he wrote to Wood, months later in a postmortem.) When the time came to stage his next play, *The Night of the Iguana*, Williams's name alone was, for the first time, no longer sufficient to guarantee a theater.

Back in 1959, Frank Corsaro had asked Williams to contribute a one-act play to be performed as part of a double bill with William Inge's *The Tiny Closet* at the Festival of Two Worlds in Spoleto, Italy. Williams sent Corsaro a twenty-one-page sketch based on "The Night of the Iguana," a short story he had written in 1946 inspired by his stint in

Mexico after his heartrending breakup with Kip Kiernan. The story focused almost entirely on Miss Edith Jelkes, a hysterical, reclusive thirty-year-old Southern spinster who is living at a lonely, envious distance from the two other guests—gay writers—at a ramshackle Mexican hotel. Drawn to the older writer, Miss Jelkes intrudes into the couple's solitary idyll:

> "Your friend—" she faltered. "Mike?" "Is he the—right person for you?"
>
> "Mike is helpless, and I am always attracted by helpless people."
>
> "But you," she said awkwardly. "How about you? Don't you need somebody's help?"
>
> "The help of God," said the writer. "Failing that, I have to depend on myself."

The older writer makes a clumsy pass at Miss Jelkes; she fights him off, but their brief botched sexual encounter severs "the strangling rope of her loneliness." Her predicament is mirrored by the plight of an iguana, who has been cruelly caught and tethered under the hotel veranda and is finally cut free from his torture.

Corsaro found the characters two-dimensional—the writer was "a bit of a louse," he recalled. He telephoned Williams to try to cajole him into giving them more depth. "As we're talking, something is coming to me," Williams replied. In Williams's recalibration of the story into "an expression of my present, immediate psychological hassle," as he described it to Corsaro, the tale became more about spiritual exhaustion than sexual frustration. Almost nothing of the original story ended up in the script, which Williams considered "more of a dramatic poem than a play."

The Night of the Iguana deposits a defrocked-priest-turned-tour-guide, Reverend T. Lawrence Shannon, on a hilltop in a tropical Mexican paradise, positioned strategically between the awe of creation and the awe of disintegration—news of world war is reported from the radios of some jocund German guests (who did not appear in the short story), the world is at a spiritual tipping point, and so is the feverish Shannon. As he climbs the hill to the Costa Verde Hotel, he is on the verge of a second nervous breakdown. Down below him, a busload of unhappy ladies from a Texas women's college—"a football squad of old maids"—complain loudly about the tour, of "the underworlds of all places" that he has taken them on. Shannon is a kind of pilgrim, a "man of God, on vacation" who has lost his way, trying vainly to wrestle under control his lust for young girls and alcohol. Scrambling uphill for the solace of male company—the hotel's owner, Fred Faulk—he is almost immediately walloped with more calamity: Fred has died, and Shannon comes face to face with Maxine, Fred's predatory widow who has, in her newfound freedom, been entertaining herself with local youths.

In this revised drama, whose theme, according to Williams, is "how to live beyond despair and still live," Shannon is the hysteric, and Miss Jelkes is transformed, for the purposes of dramatic debate, into the calm, saintly, androgynous Hannah Jelkes, a guest at Maxine's hotel. "Ethereal, almost ghostly. She suggests a Gothic cathedral image of a medieval saint, but animated," the stage directions say. Unlike the story's Edith Jelkes, "a dainty teapot," Hannah Jelkes is an intrepid Nantucket artist and traveling companion to the wheelchair-bound, ninety-eight-year-old Nonno, "the oldest living and practicing poet on earth" who is struggling to finish his last poem. Nonno, which means "grandfather" in Italian, was Merlo's nickname for Reverend Dakin.

The portrait was Williams's tender homage to his proud, histrionic grandfather: Nonno is a home to Hannah, just as Reverend Dakin's presence in Key West gave Williams "a sense of really having a home." "When he died, something in me died, too, and it's hard to revive it," Williams wrote to Katharine Hepburn, when pitching her to play Hannah Jelkes on Broadway. "He didn't like my plays, although he would never admit it to me directly, but he always would say to others 'Tom is a poet, he will be remembered as a poet'—In his middle nineties he could recite Poe's 'The Raven' and 'Annabel Lee' by heart, and quote long speeches from Shakespeare. . . . He wanted his Manhattan with two cherries before dinner every evening, could charm lady birds out off bushes, loved eau-de-cologne, even perfume." Williams explained to Corsaro, "When the old keep serenity and dignity and sweetness in them as long as he did, life turns to poetry and, without that, to cold prose. Their memorial is almost a religious recognition of them." (Williams's subtitle for the original play was "Three Acts of Grace"; in its post-Spoleto 1960 version, it was subtitled *Southern Cross* and "dedicated to the memory of Reverend Walter Dakin.")

In the short story, which was written in the full flush of Williams's romantic rebirth in Mexico, Edith Jelkes glimpses salvation in the carnal. In the play, however, Shannon, who is set upon by both a nubile teenage tourist he has seduced and her outraged guardian, has been betrayed by his carnal impulses, driven out of his church for fornication and heresy, and he strains beyond them for transcendence. "See? The iguana? At the end of its rope? Trying to go on past the end of its goddam rope? Like *you*! Like *me*! Like Grampa with his last poem!" he says.

The play was a sort of summa of Williams's warring urges, of his humiliated Puritan soul, fighting a pitched, and likely losing, battle against self-destruction. "It's horrible how you got to bluff and keep bluffing even when hollering 'Help!' is all you're up to," Shannon says. His "reaching-out hands"—"as if he were reaching for something outside and beyond himself"—perform the emblematic gesture, at once a plea and a prayer, with which Williams ends the second act.

"My life has cracked up on me," says Shannon, trapped, like Williams, by his past, his appetites, his lost goodness, his isolation, his winded hankering for grace. "I am a little bit in the condition of the Reverend Shannon right now," Williams told Corsaro in 1960, in the early stages of their collaboration, "as a result of corresponding tensions, I mean correspondingly great, which have gone on longer than anyone but a tough old bird like me would be able to survive, even physically."

As Williams's relationship with Merlo continued to unravel, Shannon's tormented voice became a kind of fever chart of his isolation and self-loathing. "We—live on two levels, Miss Jelkes, the realistic level and the fantastic level, and which is the real one, really," Shannon confides to Hannah. "But when you live on the fantastic level as I have lately but have got to operate on the realistic level, that's when you're spooked, that's the spook." Devoured by fear and feeding off it for inspiration, Williams faced the same predicament. "Don't ask me why I've fallen into this state," he wrote to Wood from Egypt in late October 1959. "Because I couldn't tell you except to say that something 'spooked' me somewhere, sometime, somehow, and I can't shake the spook. The lucky thing is that I'm writing about just exactly that thing."

Hannah Jelkes, by contrast, is a model of containment and compassion; she is a new type of Williams heroine, one who speaks for his embattled moral side, holding out the hope of an escape from the self. (She was also his first non-Southern lady.) "Hannah is not a loser," he explained to Corsaro, his "other Sicilian Frankie." "She is profoundly understanding and compassionate but still a fighter and winner. She doesn't bow to the terms as Alma, or crack under them completely as Blanche who could only accept a doctor's arm at the end. She rises to a sort of necessary pride and austerity like the Oriental concept of living with a 'cool' God." Williams went on:

> She is unseduced by any worn-out and weakly sentimental concept of Christian-Hebraic philosophy of human behavior, but—and yet—she, out of her austerity, her coolness, can escape from herself, her personal dilemma and crisis, to concern for a captive lizard: she forms a workable synthesis between the Western and Eastern concepts of morality. And feeling. ~~An affirmation of the human spirit undefeated.~~

Hannah's stoic composure puts into bold relief Shannon's hysteria and his compulsion to use his woundedness—his "Passion Play performance," as Hannah calls it—as a lure, as well as a lament. Through his connection to her, Shannon achieves what Williams couldn't manage in life: "understanding and kindness, between two people at the end of their ropes."

"As we were working, pages kept coming in from Williams until I had ninety pages of script," Corsaro said of the Spoleto version of *The Night of the Iguana*, which had a completely new, almost symphonic, tone. He added, "I knew I had something very special." So did Williams. "I'm tired, the energy's low from the long, hard screaming I've done for help, for light and forgiveness," he wrote to Atkinson in the summer of 1959. "But I've just now finished a scene about forgiveness, and help, and maybe there is some light in it to make up for the fatigue. I think the hate of the world has worn itself out, for a while—There never was hate of people—

and if 'the hazards' of this long trip are lucky I will come back with a play or two for you that you may be able to like as well as admire technically." In May 1959, Williams wrote to Wood, "I think the play for Spoleto can be made very good." "Tenn dear, you're right to say that in this latest work of yours there is all your heart. ONE FEELS IT!" Anna Magnani wrote after reading *Iguana*. "Once I said to a journalist . . . 'the characters of Tennessee Williams are always looking at the sky/heaven.' And it's true! They are always seeking salvation, in the purest and most noble sense."

IN THE THIRTY months or so that it took to complete *The Night of the Iguana*, Williams's world, like Shannon's, came down around him. He lost his longtime director, Kazan, and then his most consistent and insightful public champion, Brooks Atkinson, who retired from the *New York Times* in the spring of 1960. The rumble of paranoia began to shake even Williams's bedrock faith in Audrey Wood. "In all the letters and phone-calls and talks between us about the 'Iguana' there was a great area of ambiguity, which unnerved me and made it harder for me to complete the work with any confidence in it," he wrote, forgetting his own initial doubts about the play's viability. "You never said *clearly*, I am deeply interested in this work and think it is valuable. So I had to represent myself and make my own decisions about its production some of which may have been faulty."

Finally, Williams lost his longtime lover. In the battle of attrition with Merlo, Williams officially waved the white flag on January 2, 1961. "Dear Horse: or Saint Francis," he wrote:

I guess you win, like Mizzou in the Orange Bowl Game. Thirteen years, the longest war on record, but that's not a nice way to put it. Anyhow I am going back to Key West since I feel like I have a ton of lead in my legs and island-hopping doesn't seem possible for me.

Please be a good winner. A good winner respects a good loser, which I hope I will be. He enjoys his victory over him, but he treats his surrendered opponent with courtesy and consideration, not rubbing his nose in the ground.

I hope to behave as my father did when he lost but I hope that unlike him, I won't be locked out of the house. I have no Knoxville to go back to, and no widow from Toledo. If it should not turn out to be an honorable capitulation, I suppose I could still employ a traveling companion who would take me away to Europe but then victory, yours, would lose its glory and even its just reward, and I do mean just because I think to have passed thirteen years with me, the gloomy Hun of all time, must merit a crown in heaven.

Blanche was a bit of a Hun, too, but I think she was quite sincere when she said, "Thank you for being so kind, I need kindness now."

Kindness in one makes kindness in the other. Love, T

Williams's courtly request put a shellac of civility on his own cruelty. Prior to the tryout of *The Night of the Iguana* at the Coconut Grove in Miami in August 1960, Merlo had gone up to New York for medical tests to explain a mysterious loss of weight and energy, which Williams attributed to drugs. In Merlo's absence, Williams took up with a painter. Alerted by a Key West friend who had walked in on Williams's frolics, Merlo flew home unannounced. (Merlo was no stranger to Williams's provocations; earlier in the year, by his own admission, Williams had spent an afternoon in a drunken orgy with three queens in a South Beach hotel, after which he returned home for a home-cooked dinner with Merlo. "I set myself down at our patio table like a king, waiting to be served. The kitchen door banged open and past me sailed a meat loaf, missing my head by inches," Williams recalled. Before bolting in their car, Merlo managed to throw the succotash, the salad, and the Silex of coffee at him as well. "When people I care for turn violent," Williams told Gore Vidal solemnly, "I have no choice but to withdraw from the field. I abhor violence of any kind." "There was no use in saying that Frank had a good case for throwing a lot more than a leg of lamb at the maddening Bird," Vidal wrote in his memoir *Palimpsest.*) Having come home to Williams and the painter, Merlo "declined to eat and he hardly spoke . . . his great eyes fastened upon the painter and me," Williams wrote in *Memoirs.* "Then the scene exploded. Like a jungle cat, Frankie sprang across the room and seized the painter by the throat and it appeared to me that the painter was being strangled to death—that is one evening when I am pretty sure Frankie was deep under drugs." Williams called the police; Merlo slept at a friend's house. The next day, as Williams prepared to decamp to a Miami motel with his painter and his papers, Merlo ran down from the porch. "Are you going to leave me without shaking hands, after fourteen years together?" Merlo said.

The incident marked the beginning of their end. For the next year, they lived separately in their Duncan Street house. Merlo found a new friend and a new life. "I'm not any longer his 'Embraceable You,' at best, a tolerated guest in my Key West refuge, my place where I fight for survival, my wild beast's cave, as it were," Williams wrote to Wood in March 1961, alternately outraged and avuncular. Even as he pushed his loved

With Marion Vaccaro and others on holiday adventure

ones away, Williams was compelled to hold onto them. "I have never stopped loving anyone that I ever loved, and I have loved everyone who was considerate of me and my trouble," he told Wood. "In one of my plays, I don't remember which one, somebody says: 'He liked me and so I loved him.' Oh, yes, in 'Suddenly Last Summer'—Catharine speaking to the doctor about her feeling for Sebastian. I was speaking for myself, too. I love anyone who likes me, even if I know it may be illusion."

In April 1961, Williams set off alone for Europe in the company of Marion Vaccaro and her gigolo. "Perhaps I will meet with someone who can stand me—somewhere," he said. About once a week during his time away from Key West, even after swallowing three Miltowns at night, Williams couldn't sleep. He reported being overcome by "terrific waves of loneliness [which] sweep into my single room." When he counted up "the dreadful facts of my life," Merlo was high on his list. "I gave my love, so much of it that there was hardly enough feeling left for friendship, to someone who seems to hate me," he said. Nonetheless, he couldn't resist trying to call Merlo. The overseas operator got through, but, as Williams explained to Wood, "the answering party said that he didn't know me. I said, never mind let me speak to this person. I waited a while and the operator called back, and said, The person doesn't want to speak to you and I can't force him.—Then he said to me: Why don't you get off that streetcar named desire?—I said: I know what you mean, get off it and lie on the tracks."

"I suppose he is so revolted by my sickness, my state of mind which I think is close to lunacy, that he will take no more of it, and I mustn't ask for it," Williams wrote melodramatically to Bob MacGregor, his editor at New Directions, adding of the upcoming production of *Iguana*, "I doubt that Frank will be with me, he doesn't answer my letters or even the phone."

In May, from Rome, Williams tried phoning Merlo again, only to be stung once again by his ex-lover's tormenting refusal to speak to him. Sometimes Williams tried to joke about the telephonic stonewalling and Merlo's refusal to recognize his name ("Sic Transit Gloria Swanson"); inevitably, bitterness percolated through the posture of nonchalance. "I've always tried to respect his pride but now I think he is confusing it with cruelty of a frightening nature, and that he wants to break all pride in me, which I mustn't permit, for then I would turn to a worm, which is worse than having turned to a bit of a monster," Williams confessed to Wood. He went on, "Why do I still care about him? He gave me an escape from loneliness, which I think is the worst affliction in life, and he gave me a sense of life all these years when I've been so inclined to think too much about death." "Magnani says, 'Fuck it,'" Williams reported in a joint letter to Bowden and Corsaro in mid-May. "But I still hold the torch for 'The Horse.' And I long for the peace of my little house there, to help me get through one more Broadway production."

Merlo's silence cast a long shadow over Williams's travels, and also over the rewriting of *Iguana*. In their life together, Williams had been the engine and Merlo the caboose. Now, for both parties, the ride was over. So it was for Shannon. The argument with Merlo became the argument of the play.

Dispossessed of his keys, his tour bus, his job, and his confidence, Shannon is hounded into frantic retreat. Facing off against Miss Fellowes, the infuriated leader of his tour group's insurrection, Shannon repeats almost verbatim Williams's words to Wood about Merlo: "Don't! Break! *Human! Pride!*" he says. At the end of the play, Hannah faces the prospect of continuing on alone without her beloved Nonno. "I think of a home as being a thing that two people have between them in which each can . . . well, nest—rest—live in, emotionally speaking," she says. "How will it seem to be traveling alone after so many years of traveling with . . . ," Shannon asks Hannah, who replies, "I will know how it feels when I feel it." "I wonder . . . if we couldn't *travel* together, I mean just *travel* together," Shannon suggests. Hannah demurs. "Don't kid yourself that you ever travel with someone," she says. "You have always traveled alone except for your spook, as you call it. He's your traveling companion. Nothing, nobody else has traveled with you."

Like an amalgam of his characters, Williams felt at once incensed and unmoored. "The Horse has done just about all in his power to shatter me and humiliate me, so I must find the courage to forget and put away a sick thing," he wrote to St. Just in the summer of 1961. "To be fair, it isn't easy to live thirteen years with a character walking a tight rope, and a thin one, over lunacy. But the time has come to 'cool it' and I trust I can."

ON JANUARY 8, 1961, six days after Williams officially called it quits with Merlo, he also cut loose his producer, Cheryl Crawford, who had mounted four of his plays and had told him, after seeing an Actors Studio workshop of *Iguana* in May 1960, "In Iguana you can have your finest play to date and a play, stealing movie slogans, I would be proud to present." Williams had asked Crawford for notes; she gave them. "During the intermission I want an audience to be saying 'What's going to happen next?' '*What* is he (or she) going to do?' They weren't," she wrote, adding, "The audience simply does not know who or what to follow by the end of Act Two. Consequently, they were not identifying and not caring."

Although Crawford had correctly identified a problem—which Williams would elegantly solve in his final version—she didn't hear from him for six months. His letter of January 8 informed her that Charles Bowden would be his producer. "This play is a dramatic poem of the most intensely personal nature and Bowden, for some unknown reason, seemed to want it like that," Williams wrote. Once again, in a sensational bit of backpedaling, Williams imposed on his own bad faith the posture of reasonableness. "I never thought that you really wanted 'Iguana'; I thought that, being a truly kind person, you wanted to encourage me by seeming to want it, just that, and when I got your notes, I realized I couldn't please you with it and still please myself," he explained, adding defensively, "I think you need this play like a hole in the head. Surely you know that, don't you?" Having declared *Iguana* his "probably last play," in the next paragraph Williams wrote, "I hope and trust and pray that one of the [plays] I am holding in reserve will be a right one for you." His careless kiss-off was signed, "My heart's true love to you, darling!" Their collaboration was over.

The Night of the Iguana would make its way to Broadway with Williams now cast as the seasoned captain of a new team. "I want to be around for the staging of this one," Williams told Bowden. "Corsaro would need me and want me, since the play is such a highly personal play, dealing with emotional things that only a man of my history (and age) has experienced enough to understand them, totally." To Williams, the Harvard-educated Bowden, an actor-turned-stage-manager-and-producer, was "a terrifically dynamic man"; to Corsaro, however, Bowden was "silly putty—a silly person who had a coterie of people around him right out of a Tennessee Williams waxworks" and who "almost wrecked the play." While teaching them how to cope with his own wayward style of living and writing, the befogged playwright struggled to hold these incompatible elements of himself together.

In order to free himself from inhibition and test out dramatic possibilities, when he worked on a play Williams would often forget the logic of his plot and fill in scenes without necessarily picking up where he'd left off the day before. "My scripts at this stage are a shambles of inconsistencies, repeats, contradictions, because of my methodless method of work, my not reading over yesterday's work, just going on, on, like a madman, spooked chased by a spook," he explained to Chuck Bowden. From this crazy quilt of reimagined strands, the play was finally assembled: an act of collage as much as construction. "The revisions extended certain areas and, in some ways, they overwhelmed others," Corsaro recalled of the daunting task of pulling together Williams's eloquent mess. He remembered Williams handing him three versions of a scene in the third act in which Shannon tells Hannah about him and his tour group spotting some natives consuming "undigested" scraps from a dung hill. "I said, 'What do I do with them?' 'I want you to see what you think is right, or whether any of them are right.' I said, 'You're giving me a big responsibility, Mr. Williams,'" Corsaro recalled.

In the old days, Williams had relied on Kazan to bushwhack through his tangle of scenes, to winkle out his strongest themes, and to take the lead in their dramatic rearrangement. Now, to his rookie collaborator, Williams had to be both coach and cheerleader. "Despite your talent, your sensibility, your understanding, you seem to be distrustful of your ability to solve dramaturgic problems which are surely not as challenging as the ones you bravely confronted in such fearfully challenging works as 'Oh, Dad' and 'Short Happy Life,'" Williams wrote to Corsaro. "Let us stick, in our personal relations as a company of artists, to a thing which the play has to say, that it is possible and surely most desirable for desperate living creatures to make up for the deficiencies in the world's creation: to play a compassionate and understanding deity as if we were under-studies or stand-bys for our mysterious creator who behaves as if he had flown to another part of the universe and had forgotten ours." Williams added, "(Rah-Rah, yeah, Team, Etc.)"

For the show to move from the Coconut Grove to Broadway, it needed to have a star. Williams set his cap at Katharine Hepburn, whose "aristocracy of spirit"—her combination of backbone and cool—made her a perfect fit for Hannah Jelkes. "I wrote the part of Hannah for Hepburn and I still can't see anyone else playing it with that odd combination of astringency and lyrical feeling that Katie could give it, not even Page, unless she were staged by Kazan," he said. "For Katie, I might even find a way to eliminate the dung-hill speech at the end, although I think it makes the strongest statement in the play about what Shannon is showing his ladies:—'the horrors of God's world' as it exists without His intervention."

When Williams called Hepburn that January, her immediate response was "absolutely impossible." "You say 'absolutely impossible,' and I know you mean it right now but, being an incurable romanticist, I think that nothing is absolutely impossible when it is right as you and Hannah Jelkes, since I have never written a part so perfectly right for an actress as Hannah is for Kate Hepburn, at least not deliberately," Williams wrote to her the next day. He added, "Someday, somehow, it *will* happen."

"You're a hustler, aren't you, you're a fantastic cool hustler," Shannon says to Jelkes, who answers, "Yes, like *you*, Mr. Shannon." In the confidence game, Williams himself was no slouch. In the unctuous last paragraph of what he called his "pitch" to Hepburn, he played his wild card. Their discussion the previous evening had included talk about the film version of *Suddenly Last Summer*, in which Hepburn played Mrs. Venable and which Williams considered "an abortion." Now he reminded Hepburn of how, on the last day of shooting, after her final take, she spat on the sound stage to show her contempt for the director, Joseph Mankiewicz. "I don't mean to put down [Montgomery] Clift and Liz [Taylor] or anybody connected, really, but you, only you, resisted the misconception," Williams wrote. "How awful it must have been for you to play that last bit! If it isn't too late, I would like to make it up to you." In the end, Bowden's shuttle diplomacy, Williams's flim-flam ("Yes, I know, I'm coming on like a huckster, like a cool hustler"), and the script itself captured Hepburn's imagination. "Bit by bit, we are going to go on submitting bits of this play written for you till the voice of Hannah says, 'Yes, you win, I'll do it,'" Williams wrote in his emboldened next letter.

Hepburn saw that she was right for the part and that she could be great in it; she had already begun to imagine her way into Hannah. She agreed to talk contract. "You must understand something! I love this work! I'm ninety-five per cent of the way home with Hannah in the dressing room!" she told Bowden, as they drove through the Hollywood Hills trying to finalize a deal. Bowden insisted that he needed more than a six-month contract. "Not a moment more!" Hepburn said. For Bowden, this was a deal-breaker. "She won't give us more time because [Spencer] Tracy is in a bad way again, and she feels she is the only one who can save him," he explained to Williams. So Hepburn gave up the role of Hannah onstage to play it offstage, and Margaret Leighton, the ethereal thirty-nine-year-old British actress, was signed for the part—for which she would win the 1962 Tony Award for Best Actress.

The blockbuster name that finally gave the Broadway production commercial viability was "that wonderful old bitch" Bette Davis, who signed on to play the blowsy, sluttish widow Maxine Faulk. Davis, who in 1949 was the highest-paid woman in America, earning $10,285 a week, was by 1961 financially strapped and looking for a movie comeback. She last appeared on the legitimate Broadway stage in 1929. Williams was dubious. "Granted she is a name, one of the biggest, and has had the scarcely credible humility to offer to play the second female part," he told Wood. But he had concerns: "Is she physically right for the part, and still more important, does she have the right style for it? If she played it like almost any of her film roles, since 'Human Bondage,' the effect might be very funny in a very wrong way, and I say this as a great fan of Bette Davis."

To Williams, Maxine was the "living definition of nature: lusty, rapacious, guileless, unsentimental"; Davis, by contrast, was the living definition of artifice—the Hollywood star system. The fifty-three-year-old actress may have been nearly a decade older than Maxine's suggested age; she may have had a potbelly, a sagging chest, and a coarseness that had evolved over a decade of hard drinking and brawling with the actor Gary Merrill, her recently divorced fourth husband; nevertheless, she was a box-office beauty. With an unknown—Patrick O'Neal—playing the male lead, the producers had eyes only for her drawing power. According to Corsaro, who was against the ploy, Bowden told Davis that "the play wasn't completely finished," and she signed with the understanding "that her part was going to be developed." Corsaro warned the team that "when she discovers that the play is not really about Maxine Faulk, we're going to have a great storm on our hands." For his part, with all his theatrical ducks now in a row, Williams was sanguine. "I love the play and I love the players, and the rest is prayer," he wrote to Bowden five days before the *Iguana* campaign began, which Williams would later call his "longest and most appalling tour I've had with a play."

The first read-through was held in the Stratford Suite of the Algonquin Hotel on October 9, 1961. Davis arrived seven minutes late in a black pancake hat, with her hair loose to her shoulders and her mouth "over made-up like a mailbox," as the stage manager, John Maxtone-Graham, observed in his tart diary account of the eleven-week pre-Broadway tryout. When they began rehearsals at the Belasco the next day, the division between Davis and the rest of the cast was made physical. Bowden had arranged for bleachers to be set up in front of the playing area for the company to sit on; for Davis, he created a special space apart. "No one was to go near," Corsaro said. "It was a horrendous atmosphere." Davis's first words to Margaret Leighton only reinforced the sense of her separation from the rest of the production. "We don't have to be friends, do we, to work together?" Davis said. By the third day of rehearsals—in "a piece of superb one-upsmanship," as Maxtone-Graham noted—Leighton had learned all her lines while Davis, who hadn't acted onstage in twenty-five years, was still struggling with the book, knowing nothing. "She was frightened to death, you could tell: the hands were cold when they grabbed you," Corsaro said.

Davis objected to the unpredictable mannerisms of her introverted leading man; she objected to the size of her part; she objected to the internal practices of the Method. At one point, when Corsaro was trying to explain the sexual subtext between Maxine and Shannon, he recalled, "she came up behind me and put her tits against my back, grabbed me, and rubbed. 'That's what is needed here. Right out,' she said." When

Davis wasn't running her scenes, she either paced and smoked inside her exclusive area—"doing Bette Davis," as Corsaro put it—or sat smirking and glowering at the actors. In the first week, according to Corsaro, Leighton played Hannah "unfortunately as a very conventional spinster; she was not showing herself." Corsaro took her aside and suggested an attitude adjustment. "When you come in, you own this place, you already know everything about it. You're not begging—you are the mistress of the inn," he told her. The advice gave Leighton's Hannah a new, quiet, but startling authority. "She was marvelous," Corsaro said. "Davis was looking at her in horror, because suddenly this woman was transformed. From that moment on Davis became a demon."

Before the show even began its tryouts, Davis quit twice. Her first blowup came at the beginning of the second week, when she dressed down her leading man in front of the company. "I'm sick of this Actors Studio *shit*," she screamed at O'Neal, who bolted out of the theater. "When she is on a rampage . . . she projects rather like the man who calls the states at national conventions," Maxtone-Graham noted. At one point, Corsaro knocked on her door; getting no response, he opened it. "This was the sight: Bowden and Tennessee Williams on their knees in front of her," he said. Davis stayed away from rehearsals for two and a half days. Rumors circulated, correctly as it happens, that Jo Van Fleet had been sent a script.

At noon on October 27, a few days before the play was to open in Rochester—a booking made at Davis's request, at the theater where she'd made her professional stage debut, thirty-three years earlier— Davis reappeared. Her return had been announced the previous day in a statement read to the cast, which said "that she had an *artistic* difference . . . and no mention of the incident was ever to be made to her." On her return, Davis looked "a little red-rimmed around the eyes, slightly over-weight and seemed as though she had been on some kind of toot," Maxtone-Graham noted. "Needless to say, the producer, director, author, stage-manager, actors—everybody—had a large mouthful of humble pie, and every time Miss Davis made the most pathetic joke, there was roar upon roar of laughter. Giggles and chuckles at her slightest whim. Rather like a very badly or, rather, well-paid canned-laugh audience."

The opening night of *Iguana* in Rochester was like "a wild comedy," according to Corsaro. "Tennessee and I looked at each other. It was as if the people were not used to seeing live theater." After opening night, Davis claimed to have sprained her ankle; she was forced to wait out the next day's performance in a wheelchair ("suffering from a wrenched knee, as well as a secondary part," as one local paper reported). "She was only good on opening night because she was nervous. Then out came the cigarettes and the strut," Corsaro said. "She was really very disruptive at this point. She never allowed the play to take on any momentum."

To Williams, behind her back, she was "La Davis"; to the cast she was "Jessica Dragonet" and "Lydea Leadflipper," and to Corsaro she was "La Bête." "She was asking for rewrites, rewrites all the time. There were no rewrites. Tennessee gave her dribbles," said Corsaro, who within a fortnight held a secret cast meeting to discuss replacing her. "I'm sorry to have to agree with that," Leighton said at the meeting. "But I don't think she's doing any service to the play." However, the one service that Davis provided—advance ticket sales—made it almost impossible to confront her, let alone fire her. She was the star—an economic fact of life that Davis would periodically underline to the company by refusing to perform a matinee while one of her assistants stood inside the box office to tally the number of people asking for their money back.

The tour quickly became a battlefield, "perfidy galore," as Corsaro called it. Even the stage manager got into the rancorous spirit of things. "I can't help feeling that Chuck Bowden and Frank Corsaro, all these people, as they listen to Tennessee, perhaps feel at the back of their minds that here is a rather drunken old reprobate telling them what to do with his play," Maxtone-Graham remarked. As the troupe rolled into Detroit, where Davis was photographed on crutches while getting out of the limousine that had carried her all the way from Rochester—"IGUANA LIMPS INTO DETROIT," read one newspaper headline—chaos ruled. Davis was fighting with O'Neal, Leighton, and the management; Corsaro was fighting Bowden's increasingly intrusive suggestions; and Williams was fighting with Merlo, whom he had managed to cajole into accompanying him on the road. In addition to the personal wars being waged, an artistic Rubicon remained to be crossed: the length of the play had to be dealt with; the curtain was coming down at 11:30. "Overlong, dreadfully overlong," Maxtone-Graham said. "I think they must cut twenty-five minutes." But Williams wouldn't, or couldn't, cut. The obvious place for cuts was in Davis's part; if he tampered with her role, she would walk out.

W hile trying to box clever with Davis, Williams was already dazed by harrowing bouts with Merlo, which made it almost impossible for him to concentrate on the professional task at hand. "Frank is not a bad boy," Williams had written Wood. "In certain ways, his devotion to our pets, his devotion to the outcasts of society, the whores of Rome, the beatniks of New York, the cracked or cracking up 'lost ones' in Key West, even the chronic jail-birds and the heroin-addicts, is a bit like Saint Francis of Assisi who embraced the leper in the woods who cried 'Unclean!'" Merlo, who couldn't resist the desperate and the wounded, couldn't say no to Williams.

But Merlo, too, was ailing. He "really didn't feel well," Paula Laurence, who was understudying Davis, recalled. "He used to walk the streets at night because he felt so poorly and didn't want to upset Tennessee." Williams, however, misconstrued Merlo's late-night absences as rejection; "It's over between us!" he bleated repeatedly to Corsaro in Detroit. Feeling the need for devoted attention, Williams had their black Belgian shepherd, Satan, acquired in Rome at Anna Magnani's urging, shipped up from Key West. "He is a handy thing to have around when you are entertaining strangers whose kindness you aren't quite sure of," Williams wrote to Oliver Evans, with an admission that he was "a little scared of him myself." (The previous summer, Satan had put a bite that required seven stitches in Marion Vaccaro's hand.) Satan was good company at first. "He used to sit in front of me at the Book-Cadillac Hotel in Detroit, staring into my eyes with those lovely yellow eyes of his, and occasionally sticking out his tongue to give my hand a lick," Williams recalled.

But one morning, after his stint at the typewriter, Williams went into

the bedroom and stepped over Satan, who lay "like a guardian by the twin bed of Frankie." As Williams slid into Merlo's bed, Satan growled his displeasure. That night, the dog savaged Williams in his own bed and bit both his ankles to the bone. "He was starting for my throat when Frankie rushed out and pulled him off me," he said. Merlo had the dog put down the next day. A week later, after his ankles, he claimed, "had swollen up almost to the size of an elephant's," Williams was hospitalized. He was under heavy sedation, but there was no way to calm his rampaging paranoia: Merlo had set Satan on him; Merlo wanted him dead; Merlo wanted his money.

After his release from the hospital and the transfer of the show to Chicago, Williams continued to fear for his life. Bowden and Laurence successfully arranged for him to attend a private mass at six in the morning, to pray for the troubled production and himself—they chose the early hour in order to evade the *Time* photographers, who, Williams imagined, had staked out the hotel for the cover story they were writing on him. Out of gratitude, Williams insisted on taking the Bowdens out to a Chinese meal. That evening, he was sitting with them in his suite. "I'll have a drink and then we'll have that banquet," he said, adding to Bowden, "Open a new bottle." "So I opened a new bottle of vodka," Bowden recalled. "By that time, Frankie had gone out. I said, 'Tennessee, what is this about opening a new bottle? There's a new bottle over there, just one drink is out.' He said, 'Frankie's putting ground glass in the bottles. He's trying to poison me.'"

Williams's delusional outbursts were too much for Merlo, who decamped to Key West, leaving the playwright to his own demented devices. "Frankie had dealt so well with [Tennessee's] paranoia," Maureen Stapleton said. "The craziness began with those awful crazy pills he was getting." (A microbiologist, writing about Williams's gargantuan intake of drugs, called it "a pharmacology of the lost.") The pills, in this case, included barbiturates and "fire-shots"—injections that could include amphetamines, pain-killers, vitamins, and human placenta—

OPPOSITE PAGE: Bette Davis and Patrick O'Neal in *The Night of the Iguana* doled out by Dr. Max Jacobson, a purveyor of speed to the rich and famous whose nickname was "Dr. Feelgood." "I hope to get through this final Broadway production, Iguana, and I think I will need someone like Max Jacobson to help me make it," Williams had written to his editor at New Directions six months earlier. Williams joined a long list of high-rolling recipients of Jacobson's shots: Marlene Dietrich, Alan Jay Lerner, Truman Capote, Nelson Rockefeller, and John F. Kennedy, among them. "I don't care if it's horse piss—it works," President Kennedy said. It also caused symptoms that resembled those of paranoid schizophrenia: wild mood swings, hyperactivity, impaired judgment, and, in the case of the amphetamine-poisoned presidential photographer Mark Shaw, death—a result that contributed to the revocation of Jacobson's medical license in 1975.

Williams became quite an aficionado of Jacobson's "miracle tissue regenerator," which the doctor insisted should not, under any circumstances, be mixed with alcohol—a caveat that Williams overlooked to his cost. Eventually, he learned to inject himself, using the needles and ampules that Jacobson mailed to him around the world; he followed the intramuscular injections with a 500-milligram chaser of Mellaril, an antipsychotic whose side effects included irregular heart rates, tremors, severe confusion, and unusual body movements. Williams referred to this high-low drug combination as "the Goforth Syndrome." "I felt as if a concrete sarcophagus about me had sprung open and I was released as a bird on the wing," he said of his first Jacobson injection. (For one of his early injections, Williams had taken Corsaro with him to Jacobson's office on East Eighty-Seventh Street in New York. "Would you like to try it?" Williams asked. "Holy shit, no, I'll just sit here," Corsaro said, who found the German-born doctor "right out of 'The Cabinet of Dr. Caligari.'")

After the Chicago reviews, Williams certainly needed something to boost his spirits and to keep him at work. The *Tribune*'s Claudia Cassidy— the critic whose review of *The Glass Menagerie* had launched Williams's career—now seemed to want to revoke his artistic license. "EVEN FOR A MAN OF LESS TALENT THIS WOULD BE A BANKRUPT PLAY," the headline of her column read. Cassidy had thrilled at Tom Wingfield's romantic pursuit of his destiny; fifteen years on, she was appalled at

Shannon, whose collapse was a kind of betrayal of that renegade imagination. "I would almost have paid a psychiatrist to save me from having
to listen," she wrote.

"What is rather pathetic is the shock which the bad reviews were to
Charles Bowden and Tennessee Williams," Maxtone-Graham observed.
As the show got closer to New York and the author and the cast were, in
Leighton's words, "punch-drunk with new pages," Williams grew even
harder to wrangle. "Flushed with whisky and battered with failure, I
think the Chicago reviews have hurt him more than he admits,"
Maxtone-Graham reported. A dictum about contacting the playwright
was sent out to the stage management. "[Williams] is to be notified in
writing the day before he is needed," Maxtone-Graham reported. "He is
then telephoned at half-hour intervals during the morning to assure that
he will be there. This morning's visit required constant attention by a
secretary. Four different calls, practical administration of Bromo-Seltzer
to get to the theatre."

In Chicago, *Iguana* found itself in the paradoxical position of being a
critical catastrophe and a box-office success; nonetheless, Cassidy's vitriolic response was a kind of wake-up call. Williams and Corsaro had no
choice but to cut half an hour out of the play. The situation was so drastic
that Corsaro had Wood, who also believed the play needed a severe hair-
cut, fly in from New York to convince Williams. Corsaro recalled Williams yelling, of Davis, "I can't. I'd be taking her part." "But, Tennessee,
your play will be ruined," Wood insisted.

After reviewing the cuts, Davis called a meeting onstage with the
management. With three weeks to go before the Broadway opening, she
demanded that Patrick O'Neal be fired. "It was insane," Corsaro said.
"Patrick O'Neal had been with this show from the very beginning, and he
had been just brilliant. But his performance was suffering because of her.
He couldn't stand everything that was going on, and he started to act like
Shannon offstage, drinking and holing himself up in his hotel room. He
didn't tell anyone his phone number; you couldn't reach him. He was
completely incommunicado, hiding out from Bette Davis." In her demand
to the management, according to Maxtone-Graham, Davis struck the
bullying tone that the company had come to dread—"that rather hyster-

ical, over-definite pronouncement of hers, usually abysmally ignorant. That led to an impasse of the kind: I'll have my way, or you'll have no way at all." Davis claimed that O'Neal's constant improvisation was a deliberate attempt to undermine her performance, an idea of which Williams had tried throughout the run to disabuse her. "I can't agree with you that he means to be that way, that he is doing it deliberately," Williams wrote to Davis, who remained adamant on the issue even after the show had opened. He continued:

> I think he is just trying very hard to correct the flaws in his performance, just as I have always kept making little revisions in a script. Actually, Bette, you are fully able, in my opinion, to cope with these little variations of Pat's, that is, so long as he doesn't give you a wrong cue. You have more virtuosity as an actress than you know. Remember that he is playing the part of a very disturbed man, about to have another crack-up. If you keep that in mind, I believe you will find that you are able to "use" those bits of variation that seem to be so much a part of his style. I remember how Eddie Dowling used to try little changes with Laurette Taylor in "Menagerie." She didn't like them, but she "used" them, sometimes just by some little variation of her own, sometimes just by giving him a "good look," a good hard look that took his measure, and invariably this little variation of her own would be entirely in the frame and key of the play and would actually work better for her than Eddie's variation would work for him.—Please don't be mad at Pat! I know this sounds like easy advice. But try to remember that Pat is struggling with a feeling of disappointment in himself.

News of Davis's demand somehow got back to O'Neal in his dressing room. He slipped into the theater. Davis saw him coming up the aisle. "Where have you been?" she said. O'Neal charged up the stairs onto the stage. He lunged at Davis, knocking her to the ground and grabbing her by the throat. "Patrick almost killed her," Corsaro recalled. "We had to run up and pull him off her. The thing that was amazing was, as he was doing it, she was smiling." O'Neal ranted at her—"You filthy *cunt!*"— threw a table across the stage and stormed out of the theater.

O'Neal wasn't fired; but the next day, at Davis's command, Corsaro was. "I can feel vibrations between he and I," she said, quoting a line from the play. Williams didn't defend him. "He was a frazzled man," Corsaro said. "You couldn't depend on him. He didn't want to get involved. Bowden, who was a wriggly guy, saw his chance to take over the production. Tennessee just sort of fell in with him." Corsaro fought for two days to keep control of his production, "hiding down in the back of the theater until the curtain went up and then taking notes." He was discovered by one of Davis's factotums and banished to New York. "We now have no director and our producer has just today gone into hospital for a three-day check up," Maxtone-Graham said in the last entry of his backstage chronicle. "I asked him before he left who was in charge, he said gaily, 'Oh, Mr. Williams.' And if that sodden relic who sits in the back row of the orchestra every night is in charge, I think it's time that I packed up my tapes. Good night, and to all a merry Christmas."

In the end, Corsaro's work was saved by the surprise intervention of Elia Kazan, who came to see the Chicago production at Williams's request. "He told Williams and Bowden. 'The play is very well-directed. Davis is gonna do exactly what she's gonna do and there's nothing you can do about it but don't change the staging,'" Corsaro recalled. Nonetheless, Williams maintained his focus on Davis's performance, trying to chip away by degrees at her tense, mannered, self-conscious characterization, which even her biographer called an "unabashed disregard of the playwright's specifications."

In an effort to spackle over the emotional cracks in her portrayal, Davis imposed on Maxine a lurid vividness—a lacquered, ketchup-colored wig, brassy makeup, a brazen blue shirt unbuttoned to the waist, a push-up brassiere. "I think this creation of Maxine will be enormously helped when all these 'externals' have been set right," Williams wrote to Davis in Chicago. "One of these 'externals' that isn't right, yet, is the wig. I like the color of it but it is too perfectly arranged, too carefully 'coiffed.' It ought to look like she had gone swimming without a cap and rubbed her hair dry with a coarse towel and not bothered to brush or comb it. When she says, 'I never dress in September,' I think she means just that. Her clothes shouldn't look as if they'd just come from the laundry: there's nothing 'starchy' about her. . . . She moves with the ease of clouds and tides, her attitudes are free and relaxed. There's a touch of primitive poetry in her."

Even though the show had been "frozen" in Chicago, as it shifted to New York, Williams was still at work trying to give Maxine more dramatic impact at the finale; he had figured out a way to bring her pagan presence into the center of the play's argument about body and soul. He pitched his new ending to Davis as "giving color and visual poetry." Maxine has Shannon tied up in a hammock to suffer through his breakdown, and then leaves. "It is made apparent that, Shannon being roped up, she has reverted to the Mexican kids for companionship. (I don't mean sex.)" Eventually she returns; "she's ready for a night swim so she checks on Shannon. She discovers that he's out of the hammock. It doesn't particularly surprise her but she's happy to see that he's hitting the booze since this is what makes Shannon acceptable, mostly." Williams added, "In her silk robe and her vivid-striped towel there is something a little suggestive of some ancient female (Egyptian or Oriental) deity . . . and, without stressing it too stylistically, the two kids are like a pair of pagan acolytes attending her, till she dismisses them."

The Night of the Iguana opened at the Royale Theatre on Broadway on December 28, 1961. "I thought Maggie Leighton's final bit with the grandfather one of the most beautiful moments I have ever seen," Kazan wrote to Williams, adding, "It's so far ahead of any other play this season that I have seen, in my feelings, that I can't really compare it with anything." He continued, "All that pain and so on the road was worth it. Incidentally, I thought Frank Corsaro did an excellent job and don't let anybody ever tell you different."

In the twenty-two years of life that remained to Williams, he would have seven more Broadway openings, but *Iguana* would be his last hit. The play's arrival in New York was preceded, in late November, by a front-page article by Brooks Atkinson in the *New York Times Book Review* on two biographies of Williams. ("Mr. Williams is the most gifted theatre writer in America," Atkinson said.) The play's opening was followed, in March, by Williams's appearance on the cover of *Time*, a portrait of tweedy, cigarette-smoking composure. *Time*, which had been

Williams's homophobic nemesis in the fifties, had changed its theater critic and its allegiances; the magazine became his champion, declaring him "in his best dramatic form since 'Streetcar'": "*Iguana* served to bracket the whole range of Williams's achievement, a body of work so substantial that it now casts a larger shadow than the man who made it."

On opening night, as she entered to a barrage of cheers, Bette Davis broke out of character, walked downstage, jutted out her chin to the audience, who stood for her, then lifted her hands above her head like a prize fighter who had just knocked out an opponent. "I fell down," Corsaro, who had been "allowed" to come to the opening, said. Davis's grandstanding meant that when Patrick O'Neal made his entrance, he was, he said, "greeted by a flat, dead house. It was difficult."

A couple of weeks later, after reading the glowing reviews of Margaret Leighton's performance and her own tepid press (Walter Kerr spoke of her "tattered and forlorn splendor"), Davis considered stopping the show another way. "The day I left New York I was informed that you might be about to quit," Williams wrote to Davis in early January. "Of course you know that this [will] automatically close it, and if you're sincere in your stated love of the play and your part in it, and I am pretty sure that you are, I know that you don't want this to happen anymore than I do, which is not at all. We've had a wonderful bit of luck with the critical reception, the play is regarded as a hit, at least enough of one, and if we play our cards right, to carry it to the end of the season, possibly even further." He added, "For both of us this is desperately important, it would be very bad for us both if . . . the play should expire prematurely."

Williams, who seemed incapable of saving himself, would do anything to save his play. At some personal cost to his notion of truth and honor, he managed to persuade Davis to stay until the theater parties were finished. "I want to tell you that, believe it or not, I love you," his begging letter began. "And, more important than that, I admire and respect you. You are a good, hard fighter, you have terrific courage and stamina." He added, "It thrilled me the way the public responded to you on opening night, I don't think I've ever witnessed an ovation for an actress quite like that."

After 128 performances, Davis left the show in April. (Shelley Winters replaced her and stayed with the show until it closed, after 316 performances. "It is hard to say which was worse but at least La Davis drew cash and La Winters seems only to sell the upper gallery," Williams wrote to St. Just.) After her final performance, Davis called the cast out onto the stage of the Royale to bid them farewell. "I'm *so* happy that everyone thinks Maggie is so *charming* and Patrick is *so* brilliant! I'm sorry I had to irritate you for so long with my professionalism. You obviously like doing it your way much better. *Well!* Now you can," she said. Five months later, Davis took out ads in the "Situation Wanted" section of *Variety*, which famously read, "Thirty years experience as an actress in motion pictures. Mobile still and more affable than rumor would have it. Wants steady employment in Hollywood. (Has had Broadway.)"

After the play became a hit, Williams welcomed Corsaro back into his circle. Corsaro, who hired Winters to replace Davis, oversaw the production for the remainder of its run. He had delivered to Williams the prize of commercial and critical success—Williams won the New York Drama Critics' Circle Award and a Tony nomination for best play. It was the kind of victory that ordinarily would lead to a creative partnership, but Corsaro never worked with Williams again. For a while, during the run, they'd meet at the Isle of Capri, an Italian watering hole on Sixty-First Street and Third Avenue, which had become their hangout during the many months of planning and revisions. "We would sit there and he would just mumble his way through a meeting. You almost felt there was nobody there, in a way," Corsaro said. "I lost a certain kind of compassion for his view of himself and the world, his desire, literally, to extinguish himself." He added, "He was not a very good person, really. He became very much the monster of the theatre, the man who was at the top." One night late in the run, after dropping in on the actors before curtain, Corsaro went over to the Isle of Capri for dinner. Through the restaurant's glass front door, he saw Williams at a table nursing a drink. "I turned around and went to another place. I just didn't want to go near him," Corsaro said. He never saw Williams again.

IN *THE NIGHT OF THE IGUANA*, Nonno, "a minor league poet with a major league spirit," struggles throughout the play to finish his last poem. When he finally speaks it at the finale, the poem tells the story of a piece of nature's perfection—a golden orange—as it plummets to the ground, only to lose its radiance to "the earth's obscene, corrupting love." The orange dies, the poem says, "Without a cry, without a prayer / With no betrayal of despair." The poet, one of the "beings of a golden kind," asks for a similar grace. The completion of the poem is the answer to Nonno's prayer. The ability to express himself manufactures courage and calm; it reverses the natural order of things. Where death turns everything into nothing, art makes everything into something. Speaking "in a loud exalted voice," Nonno achieves eloquence, then almost immediately dies, with a grateful, not a "frightened heart." "Yes, thanks and praise" are Nonno's last words as he drifts poignantly out of consciousness.

For Williams, *The Night of the Iguana* was also, in effect, an act of grace. Exercising colossal will, and fearing, like Shannon, that "my . . . brain's going out now, like a failing—power," Williams had drawn out of himself a well-formed, eloquent expression of his internal world. Onto the absurd, problematic nature of his existence—his losses, his longings, his self-loathing, his unexplained and unexplainable emptiness—he had imposed a meaning. Some critics complained of the aimlessness of the plot. ("The play may seem meaningless, shapeless, a little unreal," Harold Clurman said in the *Nation*, while conceding that it was "the best American play of the season.") The fact was that *Iguana* lacked the melodramatic fireworks of Williams's earlier work; its main event was not an external battle but an internal one: the spectacle of one man's losing struggle to save his soul.

The positive reviews of *Iguana* called attention to the unusual depth of its lyricism: Williams was "writing at the top of his form" (the *Times*), "at his poetic, moving best" (the *Daily News*); it was "perhaps the wisest play he has written" (*Time*), "one of [his] saddest, darkest and most contemplative plays" (the *New York Post*). The intensity of its language was in direct proportion to the precision of its metaphor. Williams himself was at the very psychological crossroads that his characters dramatized: like Nonno, he felt his brain and his talent dying out; like Shannon, he was pulled toward the amnesia of self-destructive indulgence; like Hannah, he was exhausted by a lifetime of solitary struggle.

At the finale, Shannon retreats to the beach for a swim with the bawdy

Maxine. "I can make it down the hill, but not back up," he tells her. "I'll get you back up the hill," she says, "half leading half supporting him," according to the stage directions. Maxine, with her siren song, lures Shannon back onto the rocks of his own deracinating addictions; she offers to make him her companion in waywardness—he can help manage the Costa Verde and continue his habit of fornication, pleasuring the women guests to his heart's content. It's an ambivalent ending, which plays, on the surface, as a cheerful one: Shannon "chuckles happily" as he heads down through the rainforest. (John Huston's outstanding film adaptation, with Richard Burton, Deborah Kerr, and Ava Gardner, makes this ironic penultimate scene into an upbeat final one.) The play may be "a dream of immobility from which the dreamers never awake," as Walter Kerr claimed in his follow-up *Herald Tribune* review, but by the end, Shannon is finally in motion, and the vector of his momentum is decidedly downward. "Shannon has given up and is being sentenced to Hell" was how Patrick O'Neal interpreted it.

Williams gives Hannah the last words in the play and the last image. "Oh, God, can't we stop now? Finally? Please let us. It's so quiet here, now," she says. Only then does she realize that Nonno has slumped in his chair, dead. "She looks right and left for someone to call to," the stage directions read. "There's no one." Hannah is alone with her grief and her terror; like Williams, she must soldier on under new circumstances, with only the memory of love and loyalty to guide her.

"I'M SORRY YOU'RE not feeling well," Kazan wrote to his frazzled friend at the beginning of 1962. "Put part of it down to after-opening slump." He continued, "One thing you should try to cultivate just a little bit is the ability to enjoy success, even if you consider it partial, still it is there, and very real, you really do *accomplish* you know." But in the punishing struggle to bring *The Night of the Iguana* to life, Williams had sniffed the winds of theatrical change, and his accomplishments were no solace. Despite *Iguana*'s acclaim, Williams did not win the Tony Award; he was snubbed in favor of Robert Bolt's middle-brow British historical play *A Man for All Seasons*. More significantly, *Iguana* did not get a national tour. "I think my kind of literary or pseudo-literary style of writing for the theatre is on its way out," Williams said. If Williams had been Broadway royalty, he was beginning to feel deposed.

As early as 1960, Williams and his thematic tropes had become sufficiently common currency to be parodied from the Broadway stage by the most sophisticated comedy team of the era, Mike Nichols and Elaine May. In their sensational show *An Evening with Nichols and May*, Nichols, playing the playwright "Alabama Glass," took a very long gulp from the tumbler beside him, and then drawled, "I want to tell you tonight about my new play, 'Pork Makes Me Sick in the Summer.'" He went on:

> It is a simple story of degradation. The scene is a basement apartment in the Mexican quarter of Detroit. Before the action begins the husband of the heroine, Nanette, has committed suicide on being accused of *not* being a homosexual. Distraught, she has an affair with a young basketball team, after which she turns to drink, prostitution and putting on airs. During the course of the three acts she gradually begins to go downhill and, finally, she disintegrates and has to be put away.

Williams saw the show; according to Mike Nichols, however, he didn't go backstage. "I didn't and don't blame him," Nichols said. "The piece was nastier than necessary, especially if you add my voice and character when doing it. It was less Williams than Capote, whom I truly disliked. I always felt bad about this since I admired Williams inordinately and still do."

By 1962, a new wave of American and European playwrights was bringing to their storytelling an allusive minimalism, which challenged both Williams's florid narrative style and his hegemony. Williams was beginning to feel not just old but old-fashioned. "I'm so tired, so terribly, terribly tired. And now anything that I do is going to be compared to the savagely truthful work of the best New Wave playwrights," he complained to the director Herbert Machiz in the fall of 1962, after seeing a preview of Edward Albee's *Who's Afraid of Virginia Woolf?*, which he judged to be "one of those works that extend the frontiers of the stage." The spareness of Samuel Beckett—whose *Waiting for Godot* Williams helped to produce in its debut American production—and the "astringency" of Harold Pinter drove him "crazy with jealousy." Speaking of Pinter's *The*

Caretaker, which was competing with *Iguana* on Broadway, Williams was almost in awe. "While I'm in the theatre, I'm enthralled by it and I say, 'Oh, God, if I could write like that.' If only I were twenty-five and just starting out, what these boys could have given me." During the course of the year, he'd written two "long-short or short-long plays" under the collective title *Slapstick Tragedy* that were perhaps, he told Jay Laughlin, "my answer to the school of Ionesco." "They're not just funny, they're also supposed to be sad: I mean 'touching,'" Williams explained. "Who is touched and by what is the big question these days, which are the days of the untouchables, the emotional astronauts. In which I'm beginning to feel like Louisa May Alcott or the early Fannie Hurst."

If Williams couldn't die, he could imagine his death. So, too, could Flora Goforth, the indefatigable "dying monster" of *The Milk Train Doesn't Stop Here Anymore*, the play that Williams was working on for the 1962 Spoleto Festival—"a poem of death," he called it—about the last two days of an imperious wealthy woman's existence on her mountaintop estate in Italy, where she has gone to finish writing her memoirs. "Ahhhhhhhh, meeeeeeeeeee! . . . Another day, Oh, Christ, Oh, Mother of Christ!"—the first lines that Mrs. Goforth delivers, from offstage— sounded the unmistakable note of Beckett's tragicomic ennui.

Throughout his life Williams's work had always been a kind of mother to him, nourishing and containing him. The title *The Milk Train Doesn't Stop Here Anymore*—its reference to the drying up of a life-giving supply evoked the breast, even if it didn't name it—signaled both a pining for his fecund youth and a profound sense of abandonment. (Subsequent play titles, such as *Small Craft Warnings* and *The Mutilated*, about a woman and her humiliation at losing a breast, also hinted at his fear of losing his power.) Walter Kerr, in his review of *Milk Train*, unwittingly hit upon the psychological issue at the center of the play, which was not just the drying up of the milk of human kindness but the drying up of Williams's trust in his unconscious. "Which brings us to Mr. Williams' own predicament," Kerr wrote. "He has not yet heard from his muse, from his mind, from his typewriter, what needs to be said." "Courageous title, by the way," the twenty-six-year-old director John Hancock said to Williams during his subsequent production of *Milk Train* for the San Francisco Actor's Workshop. "He looked at me carefully and replied, 'That's right, baby. Glad you appreciate that.' Of course he knew what he was writing about. The content of the exchange was clear. He'd always been a house on fire, but he couldn't read the smoke signals anymore." As Williams kidded on the square to Hancock, he was "'the daid Mistuh William.'"

Williams claimed that *Milk Train* was the most difficult of his plays to write. Woven from the tattered strands of his imploding life, the play is a kind of fairy tale of his own decline: The name "Goforth" was an echo of Williams's mantra of endurance, "En avant!" (The title itself was an acknowledgment of his fear of creative paralysis, of the extinction of his "go forth" spirit.) The insignia on a flag that marks the first and last moments of Mrs. Goforth's residency in her mountaintop aerie—"a golden griffin. A mythological monster, half lion, and half eagle"—is a simulacrum of Williams's own family coat of arms: a fighting lion above a peacock. Even the epigram, from William Butler Yeats's "Sailing to Byzantium," proclaimed Williams's lostness: "Consume my heart away; sick with desire / And fastened to a dying animal / It knows not what it is."

In a letter to John Hancock, Williams claimed that *Milk Train* was "a portrait. An allegorical portrait." The allegory was in Mrs. Goforth, the pill-popping Georgia "swamp-bitch" who is trying to complete her "demented memoirs" and whose willful perversion and mysterious empowerment were a simulacrum of the destructive and creative sides of Williams, vying for domination of his overworked, balky imagination. A kind of broken, exiled, clownish monarch, Mrs. Goforth was a compendium of Williams's deliriums—his stagnation, his fierce battle to defeat the enemy Time through literary endeavor. ("We're working against time, Blackie," she tells her beleaguered secretary, who tries to make sense of the diva's scattershot ramblings about her six husbands and her famous life as an international beauty.) Mrs. Goforth acted out Williams's own refusal to accept the inevitability of decline. As Blackie says, she "apparently never thought that her—legendary—existence—could go on less than forever!" "A legend in my own lifetime, yes, I reckon I am," Mrs. Goforth says at one point, adding, "I'm a little run down, like a race horse that's been entered in just one race too many, even for me." To Hermione Baddeley, the first actress to play her, Williams wrote:

I beg you to play the broken queen of a corrupted material domain who knows she's broken and the domain is corrupted, and offers her abdication, not her surrender, her strength, not her dissolution. She is a Napoleon wearing a sort of badge of honor on her regal garment. . . . She was a queen of the world as it is, and we know what it is. She's exiled to Elba, yes, but exiled monarchs have pride, and speak out proudly. Their voices don't lose the proud and imperious tone, no matter how they're reduced, circumstantially. . . . Suddenly facing the false premise of their position, on a mountain, they remember how hard they had to climb up there, what it cost them in their hearts, now dying, and no matter how exiled and lonely they are on Elba, they know they fought as best they could however completely they lost. It's only at the end, as everything dims out, that they appeal for the comfort of a death angel, and even then, without shame in the appeal. Their pride stays with the appeal.

Mrs. Goforth is at the watershed between life and death when her castle keep is breeched by Christopher Flanders, a sweet-talking, insistent "death angel," the author of a slim volume of poetry and a maker of mobiles who takes his name from the First World War killing fields of Belgium. Chris is, from the outset, associated with art and the higher mysteries of creation. Williams characterized him as "a guest desperately wanted but not invited." He's an interloper who trespasses on Mrs. Goforth's hilltop compound, intent on bringing her some kind of salvation that will assuage her desire and ease her out of life. "Sometimes, once in a while, I've given [people] what they needed even if they didn't know what it was," he tells Mrs. Goforth of his ministrations. "I can't explain Chris," Williams said. "I can only reveal Mrs. Goforth." Unlike Mrs. Goforth, who was modeled on divas well known to Williams— Tallulah Bankhead, Anna Magnani, himself—Chris was impossible for Williams to explain precisely because he was not a person but a phenomenon: an emissary of the intuitive, the imaginative, the mystical: those unconscious realms over which Williams felt he was losing his grip. At its most literal dramatic level, Chris embodies the question that Williams was asking about his own imagination: Can it be trusted? Will it deliver? Can you lose it by abusing it?

Mildred Dunnock and Hermione Baddeley in
The Milk Train Doesn't Stop Here Anymore

Inevitably, the protean Chris is both a seer and a seducer, a saintly
angel and a predatory hustler, courtly and unbiddable. "There's the element of the con man in him, but there's also an element of the mystic,"
Williams said. ("Everything about him was like that, a contradiction," one
of Mrs. Goforth's acquaintances tells her.) Chris is at pains to explain to
Mrs. Goforth that he is a representative of another reality—a reality that
could be misconstrued as insanity. "We don't all live in the same world,
you know, Mrs. Goforth," he says. "Oh, we all see the same things—sea,
sun, sky, human faces and inhuman faces, but—they're different in *here!*"
(He touches his forehead.) "And one person's sense of reality can be
another person's sense of—well, of madness!—chaos!" Chris is a messen-
ger of the unknown and a votary of it. He carries in his backpack a book
titled "Meanings Known and Unknown." "It sounds like something reli-

gious," Mrs. Goforth says. She can't attract Chris, who refuses her imperious sexual command. "You have the distinction, the dubious distinction, of being the first man that wouldn't come into my bedroom when invited to enter," she tells him. The pleasure with which he tantalizes her is spiritual. "You need somebody or something to mean God to you," he tells her.

Writing was the ruthless something that meant God to Williams, a manifestation of the miraculous that had, several times, engineered his own resurrection. Through the blessings of his imagination Williams had been comforted and reborn. The drama onstage is not whether Chris will have sex with Mrs. Goforth; it is whether Chris will be the catalyst that allows her imagination to re-engage, her calcified heart to reopen. Flora Goforth—isolated by geography, money, celebrity, and competitive ruthlessness—is the *reductio ad absurdum* of the spiritual trap that Williams had spelled out to Kenneth Tynan almost a decade earlier: "Once the heart is thoroughly insulated, it's also dead. At least for my kind of writer." (Mrs. Goforth, whose motto is "Grab, fight, or go hungry," admits to having built "a shell of bone round my heart with their goddamn loot.")

Mrs. Goforth's indifference to others ensures her isolation; she exudes an epic ennui comparable to Williams's. At the same time, the dying diva longs for and fears Chris's life-giving touch. The play's contest takes place between competing internal forces: it's a drama of withholding and surrender, in which one frustrated half of Williams is shown struggling to communicate with the other half. Chris, looking out over the Mediterranean from Mrs. Goforth's balcony, for instance, turns the vista into a poetic vision. "Here's where the whole show started, it's the oldest sea in the Western world, Mrs. Goforth, this sea called the Mediterranean Sea, which means the middle of the earth, was the cradle of life, not the grave, but the cradle of pagan and Christian—civilizations, this sea, and its connecting river, that old water snake, the Nile." Mrs. Goforth short-circuits his meaning. "I've been on the Nile," she replies. "No message." Mrs. Goforth has no symbolic imagination. She is comically literal. When she complains that her work is "burning me up like a house on fire," Chris turns her platitude into something visionary: "Yes, we—all live in a house on fire, no fire department to call; no way out, just the upstairs window to look out of while the fire burns the house down with us trapped, locked in it." "What do you mean by—what windows?" she counters.

Williams's addictions, he knew, were shrinking his creativity even as they were meant to sustain it. "In my own writing, I look back wistfully on the years, many of them, when I only needed two cups of strong coffee," he said. "Now I wouldn't dream of attempting to reach my unconscious mind without some other device in the nature of two or three martinis." Williams couldn't properly nourish himself, and neither could Mrs. Goforth, for whom feeding is a crucial issue. Living mostly off pills and coffee—"Anything solid takes the edge off my energy," she says—she can't receive much nourishment or give it. At the same time, she is suspicious of Chris's desire to nurture her. "One long-ago meeting between us, and you expect me to believe you care more about my spirit and body than your own, Mr. Flanders," she tells Chris, who admits to being "panicky when I have no one to care for." Mrs. Goforth also perversely refuses to feed Chris. He hasn't eaten in five days; he is "famished." But at the beginning of the play, before they've met, she has her servants remove a tray of food that's been brought to him; when they meet the next day on her sumptuous patio, she orders the breakfast tray removed because she "can't stand the smell of food." By the time Blackie manages to sneak a bottle of milk into Chris's rucksack, the play is nearly over. As the very particular stage directions indicate, milk is meant to suggest food for the soul, not just for the body: *Chris opens the milk bottle and sips the milk as if it were sacramental wine. . . . He catches some drops of milk that have run down his chin, licks them almost reverently off the palm of his hand.*

The drugged Mrs. Goforth is a mess; like Williams, she can no longer find herself to know herself. Just as Williams took up residence in the virtual world of his characters, Chris proposes to take up residence on Mrs. Goforth's estate. The collaboration he suggests is an antidote to existential abandonment:

> We're all of us living in a house we're not used to . . . a house full of—voices, noises, objects, strange shadows, light that's even stranger—We can't understand. We bark and jump around and try to—be—*pleasingly playful* in this big mysterious house but—in our

hearts we're all still very frightened of it. Don't you think so? Then
it gets to be dark. We're left alone with each other and give those
gentle little nudges with our paws and our muzzles before we can slip
into—sleep and—rest for the next day's—playtime . . . and the next
day's mysteries.

Chris is one of those mysteries. His first and last word is "Boom!"—a
mysterious sound that mimics the waves crashing on the Divina Costiera
below and carries the paradox of the waves' resounding power: explosion
and erosion, creation and destruction. "Boom" is the title of a mobile that
Chris wants to construct. "That's what it means. No translation, no explanation, just 'Boom,'" Chris says in the play's last lines.

To Williams, "Boom" was "the sound of shock felt by people each
moment of still being alive." Even in these metaphoric terms, the word
contains the pulse of paradox—the sound of both heartbeat and heart
attack. (In 1962, after the Cuban Missile Crisis, the word echoed Williams's fear not only of his own demise but also of the demise of the
Western world. The sound was so central to *Milk Train* that Williams
titled his screenplay for Joseph Losey's 1968 film adaptation *Boom!* In
the film, which Williams considered "much better written than the play,"
Chris doesn't clamber up the mountain onto Mrs. Goforth's property;
instead, significantly, he emerges from the sea—the mother ocean—an
emissary of the unconscious who may, or may not, help Mrs. Goforth.
"*Don't leave me alone till—*," she whispers to Chris at the finale. "Be
here, when I wake up," she says with her last breath. "You always wonder
where it's gone, so far, so quickly. You feel it must be still around somewhere, in the air. But there's no sign of it," Chris says of the end of Mrs.
Goforth's "fierce life." Between existence and extinction, there is only
one infinite, unfathomable explosion.

Milk Train is a murky play, but it accurately describes the confounding creative and emotional knife-edge on which Williams was perched; a
vision of Williams's creative demise and a prayer for his own imaginative
salvation. It is also a portrait of Frank Merlo, who is the emotional and
physical impasto with which Williams painted the characters around
Mrs. Goforth. In Mrs. Goforth's description of her thrilling first nights

with Husband No. 3, and how he looked as he closed the curtains ("clothed in a god's perfection, his naked body!—he went from window to window, all the way round the bedroom, drawing the curtains together"), Williams was specifically reworking his image of Merlo in "A Separate Poem": "You put on the clothes of a god which was your naked body / and moved from window to window in a room made of windows, drawing, closing the curtain . . . then came to rest, fleshed / in a god's perfection beside me." Even Christopher, the hustler with artistic ambitions, contains a wash of Merlo and his charm. But most obviously, as the pun on his name indicates, Merlo was written into Blackie, the forthright, compassionate, put-upon factotum who is abused by her imperious employer. ("Blackie, the boss is sorry she took her nerves out on you," Mrs. Goforth says.) Like Merlo, Blackie is at once feisty—she threatens to quit—and unable to leave, trapped in her boss's psychic net.

IN LATE JUNE 1962, "just barely marching . . . stopping is not appealing," Williams took his new play and his new "Angel," as he called him— the poet Frederick Nicklaus—to Tangiers, where he had rented a house for four months: "He's a desperate young man and I'm a desperate old one—a basis for some degree of communication, perhaps," Williams wrote. A graduate of Ohio State University with a degree in art history, Nicklaus had migrated to New York from Columbus, Ohio, to pursue a poet's calling. He was a handsome, tow-haired, gentle man—a cousin of the golfer Jack Nicklaus—to whom Williams had been introduced in September 1957 by Gilbert Maxwell at Brentano's bookstore on Fifth Avenue, where both men were working to support their writing habit. "I was stacking books. And Gilbert came over and said, 'Oh, Freddy, I want you to meet Tennessee Williams,'" Nicklaus recalled. "He was wearing a gray suit and dark glasses. He was tan. And he was smiling—a strange, ambiguous smile. You couldn't tell if he was happy or if he was just disguising something." Nicklaus added, "I blushed."

"I have engaged a very gentle, kind young man to watch out for me," Williams wrote to Lilla Van Saher in August. But before he agreed to accompany Williams on his travels that summer, Nicklaus did a great deal of "soul-searching." "I didn't want to be a home breaker," he said,

With Frederick Nicklaus

adding, "I asked Tenn emphatically, 'What is Frank going to think about this?' And he said very harshly—you know Tennessee had a hard side to him—'It doesn't matter what he thinks.'"

But it did. The previous months had been tempestuous ones for Williams and Merlo. That March, Robert Hines, a New Orleans realtor who managed Williams's recently purchased property at 1014 Dumaine Street, and his friend Robert Lee (aka "The Dixie Doxie") had stayed with Williams and Merlo at their Duncan Street "villa," as Merlo called it. "The 'fireworks' started immediately upon my arrival," Hines recalled. "Tenn was standing on the front porch naked from the waist up screaming, 'the Sicilian Bitch has locked me out of my own house!' So Dee Dee and I started to burgle a window when Frankie drove up and easily opened the patio glass door which evidently was left permanently unlocked—just slightly difficult to shove open, and Tenn obviously knew this." Hines continued, "I quickly realized that Tenn had all along been grooming me as an ally versus Frankie . . . (i.e. 'Frankie takes the afternoon off for drug runs,' when actually Frank came home after running errands for laundry, dog care, groceries, plus planning to cook). Tenn then discovered Frank and I spent hours drinking and talking about our shipboard lives as sailors (we both did medical work for years at sea). This excluded Tenn, naturally. Frankie and I were also avid opera buffs and sat up late, playing grand opera from Frank's great collection, which enraged Tenn, as he would shout down the stairs, 'I can't sleep in my own house!' Frank would yell back, 'Shut up, you don't sleep anyway, you're like a vampire roaming the place!'"

To Hines, the outbursts seemed to come more from Williams than from Merlo. After one scene—which was caused by Williams having it off with Dee Dee under Merlo's nose—Williams stormed out of the house. "Robert, Sir, do me the honor of driving me to the nearest motel, away from this pack of lies and [this] poisoned roof," Hines recalled him saying. Hines agreed to chauffeur Williams and Dee Dee away. "Frankie was hurt and stunned, helpless. Dee Dee stuttered, 'T-T-Tenn, what about clothes?' Tenn shot back, '*What* clothes? Buy clothes, the only thing important are my manuscripts,' which he put in the trunk of my car!" Hines went on, "Off we went and travelled about four blocks when Tenn suggested I pull over to a liquor store and purchase a pint of Old Grandad—'One should never be caught without *stash!*'" After a few hours at the local public beach with a bottle of Old Grandad, the theatrical trio returned to the compound. "All quiet," Hines noted.

But the recriminations between Williams and Merlo spilled out into public scenes. At an Italian restaurant, according to Hines, "Tenn took to baiting Frankie, I tried to make peace, . . . Frank called Tenn a 'phony Southern Gentleman,' whereupon, Tenn stood up and stomped his foot. Frankie told him he was playing 'Mrs. Stone.' Tables fell over, waiters came running, the tourists gaped and whispered. Tenn hailed a taxi while I sat there paying the bill before the owner arrived. Disaster." Hines went on, "In retrospect, I felt Tenn treated Frank pretty bad."

In the winter of 1962, as Williams began *Closing Time*, a reworked one-act play that he dedicated to Merlo, "who understands life so well that, over the course of our fifteen years together, he nearly succeeded in making me understand it, too," Williams noticed a certain change in

Merlo's behavior. In February, for instance, on an impulse Merlo had headed off to New York City to take part in a "Strike for Peace Demonstration," a silent picketing of the Japanese embassy with white chrysanthemums and white daisies. "It has, or seems to have, given Frank something to be seriously involved in for the first time since I've known him, which is almost fifteen years now," Williams told Andreas Brown, his bibliographer. A month later, in a letter to Kazan, Williams worried about Merlo, who "has lost so much weight and has the shakes and vomits when he gets up in the morning. He's spending today at the local hospital getting all kinds of tests and x-rays. I suspect that his chief problem is the old one of having nothing to do that gives him enough sense of doing." Williams added, "Since I have noticed he seems to get better when I am away for awhile, I am planning to keep away several months."

That April, to ease the friction between them, Williams offered to buy Merlo a house in Key West. "I feel that if we didn't have to share the same roof we might become friends again," he wrote to St. Just. "He says flatly no. I think he wants me to get out of the house, it is the only home I have known." Williams continued, "Perhaps if I can drum up the energy for a summer abroad, things will right themselves in both our minds. I am fond [of him], there is still some kind of attachment. But it would be nice to know if it was a good or a bad one. I can't tell anymore." In his first letter to Nicklaus, on May 6, 1962, Williams wrote of his New York pied-à-terre: "I may not be in the apartment as Frank is now occupying it. That's why I suggest your leaving your new address (if any) with Audrey instead of my answering service. I have a long story to tell you, a long, sad story to tell you." Williams signed off, "I love you."

The story Williams had to tell was of his meeting with Merlo to finalize their separation. "I was as frightened to see him as I was of seeing [Pancho Rodriguez] after the violences of 1947," Williams recalled in *Memoirs*. The negotiation took place at their apartment on East Sixty-Fifth Street. "Frankie was on his best behavior: dignified, calm, and expressing hurt and bewilderment over our estrangement. Miss Wood was her coolly diplomatic self," Williams wrote. After agreeing to continue to give Merlo his salary, Williams insisted that Merlo leave with Wood; ten minutes later, Merlo was on the phone saying that it was impossible to talk privately in Wood's presence. He wanted to return to continue the conversation. Williams would meet him only at a local bar. "I remained curiously resolute," Williams wrote. "I remember saying to him, 'Frank, I want to get my goodness back.' He looked at me silently and with understanding."

Williams found Nicklaus to be a congenial, tolerant traveling companion. He had to be. Williams's fear of drying up manifested itself physically; during the trip, he was afflicted by a bedeviling inability to speak. "My young companion, 'The Poet.' / Fair as Adonis but rational as ten hatters at Alice's tea-party. / Seems to be succumbing to my iron of silence / which is so desperately unwillful. / Can he still, at times, like me?" he wrote in "Tangiers: The Speechless Summer." In "Tangier 1," a poem dedicated to "T.W.," Nicklaus told his own story of Williams's fears:

> . . . You woke in the night,
> following some white spook of noon;
> the cat, hissing,
> was gone through the high grill.
>
> The night at least seemed a little safe:
> doors barred from the inside,
> black tile on white.
>
> Asleep, I dreamed us safe and near,
> till a thing that stole so quietly in,
> hissing, leapt through an open grill,
> and left you trembling by a chair.

If Nicklaus lacked Merlo's combustible, outgoing nature, he also lacked his efficiency. He was, as Williams wrote to Andreas Brown, "inept at anything of a practical nature so our travels are one continual fantasy of confusions. He doesn't know how to open a door with a key, find a light-switch, count change, and this morning he didn't even know how to flush the toilet. So I am having to acquire a lot of mechanical aptitudes which other persons provided in the past. But we have some good laughs together and he writes some rather beautiful poems." (Nicklaus's first volume, *The Man Who Bit the Sun*, was published by New Directions in 1964 after a nudge from Williams.)

Despite the solace of Nicklaus's company, Williams was restless and unwell for most of the summer, hopping around Europe "like a flea." "The beauty of my companion made us desirable as guests," he recalled in *Memoirs*, adding, "Even with the young poet I could barely communicate except in bed." By August, Williams, who had gloomily submerged himself in rewriting the tale of Mrs. Goforth's death, was reporting a litany of suffering that included "internal bleeding and terrible weakness and fatigue." "I am still able to do my morning's work but after that I am barely able to move," he noted. "Although it is only a three-minute walk to the beach from this house in Tangiers, I am sometimes unable to make it and just lie in bed all afternoon, dragging myself out for a bite to eat and eating only a bit of it as my appetite has gone with my strength." After Tangiers, Williams checked in to a London hospital for a few days, before returning Stateside, where "the Merlo situation" was still "a difficult and painful thing to work out."

Williams wasn't sure that he could return to Key West; he contemplated pulling up stakes and settling in New Orleans or somewhere along the Gulf Coast. "I'm still desperately looking for '*the* place' and '*the* friend,'" he wrote to Andreas Brown in September 1962. "Perhaps I've found the latter in the young poet now living with me, but the place is elusive as ever. Key West is great except that it was Merlo, not Williams, who claimed it. I understand that and I hope I don't resent it, but it does make me feel like a man who has lost his island even when he is still living on it."

The ordeals of the summer, however, were nothing compared to those of bringing Williams's *Milk Train* to the stage that fall. "Get on your knees and pray, baby! We are coming in on a wing and a prayer, God help us," he told the director Herbert Machiz. Writing to Hermione Baddeley the following year, trying to interest her in a London production, Williams looked back on the first staging ruefully: "There was just too much double-talk and socializing instead of enough hard work at understanding. And the play wasn't ready. . . . Machiz has talent but somehow he fucks himself up repeatedly by not concentrating his vitality where it serves the play best. 'Tis true, 'Tis pity, and pity 'tis true." From Philadelphia, the beleaguered author wrote to Wood, "Unless a miracle happens in Philly, I think the play should close there, since I am totally exhausted and couldn't help Herbert even if he would accept it. . . . I have lost my moral strength as a writer. Also I've lost my respect for myself as a person, and when you lose self-respect, you lose respect for others and you turn into a monster."

The play opened at the Morosco Theatre on Broadway on January 16, 1963, and closed after sixty-nine performances, the victim of a 114-day newspaper strike and poor reviews. In their acerbity, the critics bristled with a new and unmistakable tinge of condescension. Richard Gilman, one of the brainier members of the critical corps, for instance, titled his rebarbative review in *Commonweal* "Mistuh Williams, He Dead." ("Why, rather than be banal and hysterical and absurd, doesn't he keep quiet? Why doesn't he simply stop writing, stay absolutely unproductive for a long time in Key West, or the South of Spain, or the corner of any bar, and just think?" Gilman wrote.) The words haunted Williams. "The truth I guess. Only a bitch would say it, but he is and I am one, too," Williams said. That March, his face "swollen up like a pumpkin," his nerves "dancing like monkeys," his throat wracked by a hacking cough, Williams told Robert MacGregor, confiding the morning's conversation with himself, "Face it, baby, you're dying. Can you do it decently or will you make a mess of it like most things in your life?" He added, "Suspect following circumstances: lung cancer."

Williams's dire self-diagnosis was yet another example of his porous genius, the hysteric's uncanny ability to identify with others. He was not dying of lung cancer; but, as he'd recently learned, Merlo was.

CHAPTER 8

Waving *and* Drowning

Nobody heard him, the dead man,
But still he lay moaning:
I was much further out than you thought
And not waving but drowning.

—STEVIE SMITH,
"Not Waving but Drowning"

On September 9, 1963, eleven days before Frank Merlo died, at the age of forty, Williams wrote to Elia Kazan from Abingdon, Virginia, where he was "waiting shakily" for a new version of *Milk Train* to be performed at the Barter Theatre. "Do you know about Frankie?" he asked. "He has been in and out of Memorial Hospital since a lung cancer operation last winter. Right now he's in the New York apartment and I know he'd love a call from you as he's mentioned the fact that he hasn't seen or heard from you, and he's always liked and admired you. He is down to 114 pounds but his spirit's unbroken and his mind is sharp and clear. Wish I could say the same for myself." Williams continued, "I don't see many old friends, in fact scarcely any, because I don't want to 'spook' them with my crazy, bearded appearance. I grew the beard to disguise, if possible, a persistent swelling of the lymph nodes on either side of my face. It goes up and down and back up again like a false pregnancy. Some people think it's a psychosomatic reaction to being eclipsed by Albee."

At first, Key West doctors had attributed Merlo's exhaustion, his hacking cough, and his "shakes," which had become so bad that Leoncia, the housekeeper, had to hold his morning coffee for him, to a range of possible illnesses, including bronchial pneumonia, mononucleosis, anemia, and tuberculosis. In Williams's diagnosis, Merlo's nervous state and his weight loss were more likely due to drug use and to "the cumulative effect of passing 14 years of his life in my company." But soon after Williams and Nicklaus got back from their summer travels in 1962, Vaccaro called from Florida to say that Merlo had boarded a plane to New York, to undergo an operation at Memorial Hospital for suspected lung cancer. Some weeks before, over lunch with friends at a Key West café, Merlo had coughed up spumes of blood; he went immediately to his Key West doctor, whose X-rays revealed a dark area on his lung. "I was stricken with remorse," Williams recalled.

Williams visited Merlo the day before his operation. "He was quite matter-of-fact about this thing of which I would have been crazed with apprehension," Williams said. He was with Merlo in the recovery room when he came to, and saw him every day that he was in the hospital. When Williams spoke to Merlo's doctors, however, they explained that the cancer was situated alongside Merlo's heart and was too advanced to be operated on: the surgeons had sewn him back up and told him nothing. When Williams asked how long Merlo had to live, the answer was six months. "I hung up and burst into tears," he said.

Merlo returned alone to Key West. Along with their dog, Gigi, and Creature, a nervous, bad-tempered monkey, he moved into a frame cottage on Bakers Lane about ten blocks from Duncan Street, where Williams and Nicklaus were cohabiting. Williams had rented it for him from the writer James Leo Herlihy. "Frankie was quite unaware that effective surgery had not been performed and during the first month or two he gave every evidence of thinking himself quite recovered," Williams wrote in *Memoirs*. "I remember him doing one of his wild 'Lindy hops' in a local Key West night spot, but also remember that at its conclusion he seemed about to collapse." Writing to Edwina in February 1963 about "the sudden and shocking illness of Frank," Williams noted, "I see him daily and we are pretending that he is recuperating. Nothing else to be done." Three days after this stoic pronouncement, on the back of an airmail envelope addressed to the actress Claire Luce, Williams scribbled the poem "Morgenlied," an augury of the emptiness to come, which both masked and admitted the guilt he felt over Merlo:

I saw a white dove in a tree.
The tree was white, the leaves were three.

These leaves, I noticed as I passed,
were shaped as bells of crimson glass

And azure glass and emerald glass:
I felt them tremble as I passed.

The dove stood in the tree alone
and in her beak she clutched a bone.

This was my love, I heard her cry,
I drank his blood and watched him die.

I drank his blood, the dove confessed,
because I loved him to excess.

Then as I passed my body thinned,
it lifted on a gust of wind,

And I was high above the hill,
the universe was white and still

And there was neither tree nor bird
and no bell struck and no leaf stirred.

In April, Williams reported brightly to St. Just from Key West that Merlo was in his nearby pad, while "waiting to take over the house when Charlie Nightingale [Nicklaus] and I go back abroad, later this month or early next. It isn't a perfect arrangement but nothing in life is." Williams added, "He is full of energy and spirit and when I saw him at dinner last night, a fabulous pasta which he cooked with his culinary genius, he coughed only once and was jumping and charging about with all his old vitality." Nicklaus's memory of the time was grimmer. "Tennessee got Frank a television set, and we went over to see him one night," he recalled. "We pulled up to the house, and it was dark, but the television screen was flickering. We talked briefly, and then we left. Tennessee was very upset. 'His legs are so thin,' he said. 'He used to have such strong legs. He just looks so gaunt. I just can't stand the idea of him sitting there by himself like that.' He asked me, 'Do you think maybe it would work if Frank came back and we stayed together in Duncan Street?' I said, 'Sure.'"

When Merlo moved back, he stayed upstairs in the master bedroom while Williams and Nicklaus slept downstairs. The new living arrangement created some inevitable confusion: Williams found himself emotionally re-involved with Merlo; Nicklaus found himself marginalized. "I think Tennessee's and my relationship would have lasted much longer without these awful pressures being brought upon it," he said. "I became less and less real and Frank became more and more real. I could sense that I was receding in this entire picture. For all practical purposes, Frank and Tennessee were lovers again. I would wonder at times, Why am I here?" As Williams wrote in *Memoirs*, Frank "seemed annoyed that I remained so long in Key West that spring. . . . This was not because he resented Nicklaus—the poet was wonderful to him; but he treated Nicklaus almost as if he didn't exist, which was close to the truth, by this time: I mean in my heart." Williams went on, "Frankie didn't want a witness to his decline, not such a close one as I. So in the middle of May, Nicklaus and I flew North." In fact, Williams and Nicklaus flew to Europe.

Though Williams and Nicklaus's first year together had gone "swimmingly," according to Nicklaus, the second year brought "some pretty bad arguments." The worst flare-up occurred in Key West just before they left. After a night of drinking and bickering, Nicklaus lay down on the living-room couch. "Tennessee was ready to go to bed. He didn't stay up late in Key West. He liked to get up in the morning and work," Nicklaus recalled. "Time went by, and Tennessee shouted through the bedroom door, 'Well, are you coming in?' I said, 'I think I'll sleep here on the couch.'" Nicklaus continued, "Tennessee came and poured some Scotch in my ear. I happen to be very sensitive about my ears. I was infuriated. It came to blows." The row—"the worst crisis in our relationship," according to Nicklaus—was forgiven but not forgotten.

After bouncing around Rome, Barcelona, and Tangiers, by mid-June, Williams and Nicklaus were in England, enjoying the hospitality of Lady St. Just, who threw a few star-studded parties in Williams's honor. Despite the fun, Williams was still preoccupied with thoughts of Merlo. On a trip to Brighton—"the air is as stimulating as the new green pills," he wrote to Vaccaro—Williams and St. Just called Merlo in Key West. "Although he made no reference to it, I sensed that he was not as well as before I left," Williams wrote to Vaccaro. "Anyway I have him on my mind too continually to enjoy being on the other side of the sea." Writing to Paul Bowles from London on June 13, he said of Nicklaus, "He has seen me through an intolerable period in my life but now I think my place is alone with Frank till things work out whichever way they are going to. He's one of the few I've loved deeply."

Williams decided to return to Key West. "All this, the cutting short of the holiday and the return alone to Frank, is a bit hard on Frederick," he told Vaccaro, "but home is where you've hung the most years with someone, and Frederick will stay on the pay-roll and perhaps he'll like being alone for a while, or with other companions." Finding the climate too hot, however, Williams convinced Merlo to join Nicklaus and him in Nantucket—a trip that Merlo, it turned out, was too debilitated to enjoy. He didn't like the rented cottage. He wouldn't go out. He picked at his food. The ménage stuck it out together for only a week. "I'd rather bear the heat of New York or Key West," Williams wrote to Wood. "Socially and emotionally, there's only Frank right now, and I think we'll stand by each other. There's that much to cling to beside my work." Williams dispatched Nicklaus to Florida and holed up in New York while Merlo underwent cobalt therapy at Memorial Hospital, treatments that burned his chest black. Merlo would never see Key West again.

"We do very little," Williams wrote to St. Just on August 5. "Read and watch television." Merlo slept in the bedroom; Williams took the long couch in the study. "Each night—this is what is particularly painful to remember—I would hear him turn the bolt on the bedroom door," Williams recalled. By the time Merlo returned to the hospital later that month, he weighed less than a hundred pounds. The Horse, who had looked like "a little Hercules," now called to mind a skeletal sparrow. He had to be wheeled to his bed, which was on a ward for brain-cancer patients. "It was a nightmare to look at them," Williams recalled. "I begged him not to stay in that ward but to take a private room. He said sharply, 'It doesn't matter at all to me now, I think I like being with them.'"

The opening of the newest version of *Milk Train*, in Abingdon, Virginia, called Williams away from Merlo's bedside for a week and a half. "I remember seeing Frank in the hospital during his final days," Williams's lawyer, Alan U. Schwartz, who also represented Truman Capote, Tom Stoppard, and Aleksandr Solzhenitsyn, said. "Tennessee had not communicated with him and he was anxious to hear about Tennessee and to send messages to him through others. I think he felt isolated, deserted, and bruised and abused. Despite the fact that Frank was always sort of a rough-and-ready guy, at this stage he was anything but rough and ready." In *Memoirs*, Williams defended his absence by claiming that Merlo "had been in and out of Memorial so often, I did not recognize this time as the final one." Maureen Stapleton, who called Merlo "my dear buddy" and who was with him at the hospital almost every day, chivied Williams to get back to his bedside. So did Williams's cousin, the Reverend Sidney Lanier. The day after *Milk Train* opened in Virginia—September 16—Williams got a call from Al Sloane, a Key West friend of Merlo's who'd been in attendance during his hospitalization; Merlo had taken a turn for the worse. "I said, 'He'll die this Thursday. I'll fly back at once,'" Williams wrote in *Memoirs*, adding in a chilling, defensive sentence. "And I flew back before the reviews of the Barter Theatre production came out."

On the day of Merlo's death—Friday, September 20, 1963—Williams was with him. Merlo was moved to a private room. In the shift from the ward, however, his oxygen cylinder was left behind; it took about half an hour to catch up with him. Merlo was restless and gasping "like a hooked fish," Williams said. Every few minutes he'd get up from his bed to sit in a chair, then, unable to get comfortable, stagger back to bed a few minutes later. (One punishing fact excluded from Williams's

account both in his memoir and in his 1981 play *Something Cloudy,
Something Clear* was acknowledged in his unpublished poem "The Final
Day of Your Life": "You sat up in the chair next to mine. / We didn't look
at each other, and all I was able to say / is that you seemed to be stronger.") The last exchanges of the "dreadful vigil" would replay in Williams's mind for the rest of his life:

> "Frankie, try to lie still."
> "I feel too restless today. The visitors tired me out."
> "Frankie, do you want me to leave you now?"
> "No, I'm used to you."

Merlo then turned onto his side, facing away from Williams, and "pretended to sleep," Williams said. "The statement of habituation was hard
to interpret as an admission of love, but love was never a thing that
Frankie had been able to declare to me except over a long-distance
phone," he recalled. At the beginning of their relationship, Williams had
written poignantly in a poem, "My name for him is Little Horse / I wish
he had a name for me." At the end of their fifteen years together, he still
hadn't won any terms of endearment from Merlo.

Williams sat silently beside Merlo for a while; then, around four
o'clock that afternoon, he left. He went straight to the office of his psychiatrist, Dr. William G. Von Stein. After Williams "told him rather hysterically what a nightmare Frankie's last days at Memorial had turned into,"
Stein gave him a sedative shot. Then, Williams said, "my hysteria took a
different turn." "Tennessee just couldn't stand it anymore," his friend
Richard Leavitt recalled. "He suggested we go out. He just wanted to be
around people, in bars full of bodies, people living." With Leavitt, Nicklaus, and Gilbert Maxwell—"friends that were mine not yours," as he
wrote in "The Final Day of Your Life"—Williams hit a series of gay bars,
ending up "quite drunk." Around 11:30 P.M., he was back in his apartment on Sixty-Fifth Street when a phone call came from Merlo's friend,
the Key West architect Dan Stirrup. At 11:05 Merlo had died while sitting up in bed to take his medicine. "I usually answered the phone and
took messages," Nicklaus recalled. "But Tennessee answered it. I thought

New York, 1952

With Anna Magnani on the set of *The Fugitive Kind*

With Maureen Stapleton, *Orpheus Descending*, 1957

With Anna Magnani on the set of *The Rose Tattoo*

Geraldine Page and Paul Newman, *Sweet Bird of Youth*

With Maria St. Just, Key West, 1974

Key West

Malibu, 1978

to myself, 'Oh my goodness, this is probably it.' Tennessee hung up and said, 'Well, Frank's gone.'"

"I AM JUST beginning, now, to feel the desolation of losing my dear little Horse," Williams wrote to St. Just, three days after Merlo's death. "I saw him yesterday, lying in state at the family wake, and he looked like a saint, and like himself, too." Merlo had two funerals. The first, arranged by his family, was a requiem mass held at St. Ignatius Loyola on Park Avenue and Eighty-Fourth Street in New York; the second was at Frank E. Campbell's Funeral Chapel, a few blocks away, on Madison Avenue, where Williams had Merlo's corpse transferred to a less garish casket. Williams organized the second service and the star-studded guest list, which included Marlon Brando, who arrived on his motorcycle. Although Williams wrote Merlo's eulogy, he wasn't able to read it at the service. Instead, in front of a packed room, the Reverend Sidney Lanier read "a recollection written by someone who knew and loved him":

> He was a man of honor.
>
> He had a clearly defined code of behavior which nothing in life or death could make him alter. . . . The way would not change. It could not be changed. And when you had learned it, you knew that it was right.
>
> In some persons such an inalterable character might be irritating. In the case of Frank it was, on the contrary, a source of unfailing reassurance as a beacon light in a harbor.
>
> He had no onstage part in the theater: he didn't act for it or write for it. But for more than fifteen years he was a vital part of it. He loved people in the theater and he knew their names, first and last names, and a star meant no more to him than a player who had just a walk-on. He knew the first and last names of the men on the light board, the stage manager, the propmen, the stage doorman.
>
> He had a unique capacity for knowing and liking people, and all he demanded of them for his understanding and liking was a decent honesty in them, and he had a unique gift for drawing out of them the best that they had to give.

Frank Merlo at age forty, the year of his death, 1963

Being above all honest, he had a phenomenal instinct for that quality in others. And he had a personal warmth and sweetness that could evoke those sometimes timid qualities in all whom he knew and accepted. . . .

He was a giving person, always giving of himself and whatever he owned. The generosity of his heart, and its gift for understanding, made him superior to us in a way he probably never knew.

He had the kind of pride which is nobility and it was never broken once by the illness that has ended his living, visible presence. . . .

One time on a two-motor plane flying over high mountains, one of the plane's engines suddenly failed. His companion, as the plane lost altitude steadily over the mountain range on its way back to its point of departure, found it necessary to wash down two pills with the contents of a pocket flask of whiskey in order to endure the apparently imminent prospect of crashing in flame. But Frank sat quietly reading his book, after saying casually, "Oh, I've flown back over the South Pacific, after a bombing mission, on a four-motor bomber with only one or two motors working a lot of times, and made it home safe. Drink? No, I don't want a drink. There's nothing to worry about."

And it was the proudly unafraid face of his companion that kept Frank's friend from giving in to his panic, not the medications and the liquor but that seemingly casual reassurance and that seemingly calm concentration on the book that he held before his beautifully, strongly cut face.

As an epigraph to the poem of Frank's life and death, his plane companion, over mountains and oceans, can think of none more suitable than Stephen Spender's line: "I think continually of those who were truly great."

After the funeral, Williams did not follow the cortege to the cemetery; he couldn't bear to see Merlo lowered into the ground. Instead, he returned to the apartment with Elia and Molly Kazan. A few days later, the Kazans, with the Steinbecks in tow, dropped by Williams's apartment to console him. "He was pacing the floor, saying, 'How am I ever gonna live without Frank?'" Elaine Steinbeck said. "When Frankie was dying, there was a new form of grief, and maybe a new form of guilt, for Tennessee to deal with, and I think it broke him," Cheryl Crawford shrewdly observed.

When Alan U. Schwartz came to the New York apartment one day to discuss some professional matters, Williams discouraged even the mention of Merlo, which "made the talk somewhat dull on his part," Schwartz said. The two men drank martinis and tried to make conversation. Off to the side of the large room in a golden cage, Creature, the monkey that Merlo had cared for in Key West (and cried over when he thought it had escaped—"I don't know why this creature appealed so strongly to Frankie," Williams wrote), was making chirping noises. After a while, Schwartz looked over at the cage and noticed that the monkey seemed to be in some difficulty; he was not chirping as much and his movements were disjointed. "Tenn, your monkey seems to be sick," Schwartz said. "Tennessee raised his lidded eyes and glanced over at the cage and gave me one of his knowing smiles. 'No, Alan, he is just fine,' he said." The conversation meandered on until Schwartz realized that the room had gone quiet. "When I looked over at the cage, the monkey was lying motionless at the bottom. He didn't seem to be breathing. . . . 'Tenn, I think your monkey is dead!' I said. Tennessee slowly moved his gaze from me to the cage, studied it for a moment, then looked back at me and in his slightly drunken Southern drawl said, 'Why so he is. So he is.'"

A week after Merlo was buried, Williams left with Nicklaus for the Mexican resort town of Puerto Vallarta, where John Huston was filming *The Night of the Iguana*, with Deborah Kerr, Richard Burton, and Ava Gardner. "My heart is heavy, but I couldn't have chosen a better place, not to forget, but to remember as peacefully as I can," Williams wrote to Vaccaro, trying to coax her to join him. "The sea is just warm enough and the streets are full of creatures. Burros, horses descended directly from that horse of Don Quixote, wandering hogs." He added, "Yesterday I made myself popular by re-writing a scene for Burton and Sue Lyon, which everyone liked. Today I'm re-writing the ending which had been sentimentalized. I'm trying to replace the sentimentality with some honest emotion and the producer, Ray Stark is adding several feet to the speed-boat or fishing boat that he's offered to pay me with."

But neither the glamour of the surroundings nor the company worked its distracting magic. "I have been very depressed over the loss of Frank," Williams wrote to his mother and brother. "It was so awful to watch a young person so full of vitality before slipping so steadily away and trying so desperately not to face it." "Things were never the same after Frank died," Nicklaus said. Key West, to which Williams returned with Nicklaus in October, was no longer emollient. "The house, in fact the whole island, is haunted by Frank and our happy years together," Williams wrote to Wood.

Bound up in his grief over Merlo's death was a projection of his own demise. (Williams, who was almost always photographed with a cigarette in hand, immediately stopped smoking.) In his mind, *Milk Train*, which he was revising for a second opening on Broadway within a season after the play's previous failure—an unprecedented opportunity that he considered "almost a miracle"—became a kind of swan song. He hoped for a stellar, uncompromised production "to conclude my Broadway career." "I have no more illusions about the Broadway establishment," he had written to Wood in July 1963. "A writer is valued only as long as he is in current fashion, and I have had my day. I was always psychologically prepared for this eventuality and I think I am able to face it, now that it's come, having acquainted myself with the fate of other writers like Fitzgerald."

THE FLAMBOYANT BROADWAY producer David Merrick (nicknamed the "Abominable Showman"), seeing an opportunity to corner Williams's future output and turn himself into a producer of serious drama, had proposed the restaging of *Milk Train* to Williams in May 1963. He began his charm offensive by praising the play as "one of your best" and declaring Williams "the greatest playwright, now or ever." Merrick "liked writers in the way that snakes like live rabbits," John Osborne, whose plays *Look Back in Anger* and *Luther* had been produced by Merrick on Broadway, once observed. Nonetheless, Williams was easily seduced by his flattery. And, like all producers, Merrick paid to play. He hired the British director Tony Richardson, whose film adaptation of Henry Fielding's *Tom Jones* was one of the year's cinematic sensations. ("Tony is a man of genius—only a man of genius could have directed that film so fabulously," Williams said after seeing it.) Merrick's other big move was to lure back to Broadway the legendary Tallulah Bankhead.

Given her precarious health, her notorious louche life, her addiction to pills, and her scabrous manner, Bankhead seemed like she was typecast for the role of Mrs. Goforth. In 1962, without Williams's consent, she had been sent a copy of *Milk Train*, perhaps because she was—as she recognized—cruelly caricatured in it. "Every good female part you've ever written you've written for *me!*" she brayed to the author. She was "more than slightly right," according to Williams. Of the four roles that Williams acknowledged having based in part on Bankhead—Myra Torrance, Blanche DuBois, Princess Kosmonopolis, and Flora Goforth—she had played only one. The evening she finished reading *Milk Train*, Bankhead told the actress Eugenia Rawls and her husband, the producer Donald Seawell, who were with her, "Tennessee has written a play that's absolutely right for me—in fact, he has written it for me and I am going to call him right now and tell him I want to play it." She placed a call to Key West. "It was an occasion when I might have lied if I had time to think of a lie," Williams recalled, adding, "So I said: 'Tallulah, I wrote it for you but it wasn't ready for you, so I tried it out in Spoleto with an English actress, Hermione Baddeley, and she was so terrific that I staggered into her dressing room after the Spoleto opening, and said, 'Hermione, this play will be yours if you want it next season on Broadway.'" The Seawells couldn't hear Williams's words, only Bankhead's reply to them: "Well, dahling, that's all right, and I *do* understand if you've promised it to someone else, but you *did* write it for me, and I just want you to know that if anything happens, I want to play it, and I *will* someday."

Richardson knew next to nothing about Bankhead. Before engaging her for the role, he went to meet her. "I saw exactly what Tennessee meant," he said. "In appearance and personality, Tallulah was the thing itself: the heavy-lidded, drooping ruins of a proud and striking beauty, with a growl of a voice, worn low by alcohol and cigarettes chain-smoked until she had burnt the flesh of her fingers down from the scarlet-lacquered nails to, quite literally, the bone." In her prime, Bankhead had memorably created Regina in Lillian Hellman's *The Little Foxes* and Sabina in Thornton Wilder's *The Skin of Our Teeth*, but Richardson wasn't sure she was still up to Flora Goforth. Williams was; he saw Bankhead, after her long, sodden hibernation, being revived by *Milk Train*, the way Laurette Taylor had been by *The Glass Menagerie*. After trying and failing to get Katharine Hepburn for the role, Richardson capitulated. "It was either Tallulah or not do it," he said.

The price that Richardson extracted for his compromise was the casting of Tab Hunter—the buff, blond, B-movie heart throb, whose cover of "Young Love" had gone to No. 1 on the record charts in 1957—as Chris Flanders, the hustler and "Angel of Death." "I have spent a sleepless night, the second in a row, examining my conscience about this Tab Hunter business, and now that I have examined my conscience and despaired of getting to sleep, I have risen, more like Lazarus than Jesus, to say that my conscience has said, No, no, no, no, NO!" Williams told Wood. He added, "It's really a question of whether or not I am a serious

With Tallulah Bankhead

writer. If I am a serious writer I can't give such an intensely seriously created part as that of Flanders to one of those young men who have come into the theatre, *if* they have come into it, really not by the grace of God but that of Henry Willson. It would be a catastrophic injustice not only to the play, but to Tallulah and Tony and Merrick, to be a party to such a folly." Even after Hunter was signed, as late as October 31, Williams was badgering Wood to use "your beneficent witch-craft to spare us all the embarrassment of starting rehearsals with Tab Hunter." "Everyone who mentions the production to me says the same thing," he wrote. "'Bankhead and Richardson, sounds wonderful, but why Tab Hunter?' Some even imply that I must have some non-professional attachment to the boy."

Williams even sought his brother's legal advice on ways to break Hunter's contract. But, as it turned out, the problem with the second Broadway production of *Milk Train* was not Hunter, who gave a creditable performance—"YOUR PERFORMANCE IS ONE OF THE MOST DELIGHTFUL SURPRISES OF MY LIFE SINCE I HAD SEEN YOU ONLY IN FILM PARTS THAT GAVE LITTLE INDICATION OF YOUR RANGE AS AN ARTIST," Williams wired Hunter on December 18, 1963—but Bankhead, who did not.

Even before they got into the rehearsal room, Bankhead and Richardson were at loggerheads. At a pre-rehearsal cast dinner, thrown by Bankhead at her Fifty-Seventh Street apartment and served by her maid, whom Bankhead referred to as "Cunty," Richardson found himself blurting, "Fuck you!" to his rebarbative leading lady. The relationship between director and actress was toxic. "Tallulah was the most unpleasant person I've ever worked with," Richardson said. He found the rehearsals—"though they really couldn't be called that"—"torture." "On the way to rehearsal I'd have a frantic inner dialogue: 'I've got to find a way to like her, to like something—even to feel sorry for her, feel pity, feel compassion.'" Richardson couldn't relate to Bankhead, or she to him. "Loud or soft—how do you want it?" she'd say when he would try to give her a note. "There wasn't any choice," Richardson said. "Tallulah was simply past it. She couldn't remember, she couldn't perform."

Each morning, Bankhead would hobble into the theater, sit down at a table center stage, and apply makeup to the wreckage of her face, a messy ritual that included smearing her gums with grease, which, she claimed, helped with speech. "Then, like a hideous old vulture on a carrion heap, she'd look around for which of the understudies or assistants had the cleanest newest shirt or sweater, beckon, 'Come here, darling,' and wipe her hands on their fresh clothes," Richardson recalled. She frequently chose for this duty the black actor Bobby Hooks—later the co-founder of the Negro Ensemble Company—who played one of the two Stage Assistants, who move props, comment on the action, and add an Oriental artifice to Williams's opaque storytelling. At one point, anticipating the segregation problem that awaited them at hotels in Baltimore, where the show was to begin tryouts, Bankhead said to Hooks, "Don't worry, darling—I'll say you're my chauffeur."

Bankhead proved to be an equal-opportunity abuser. Marian Seldes, who played Blackie, was frequently dragged to the ladies' room by Bankhead to run lines with her while she sat on the toilet. From almost the first day, Bankhead took against Hunter, who had the temerity to call her out for her incessant interruptions during rehearsals. "Why the *fuck* don't you shut up!" he screamed. As revenge for his insubordination, when asked by a reporter about Hunter's sexual taste, according to Hunter, Bankhead said, "Tab *must* be gay—he hasn't gone down on me."

On November 22, 1963, when news of President Kennedy's assassination drifted into rehearsals, national tragedy trumped theatrical calamity. At first, only the soft, unexplained offstage crying of Ruth Ford, who played the Witch of Capri, was audible. Then the stage manager brought the news to Richardson, who made the announcement to his players. "So that's what the bitch has been wailing about," Bankhead screamed. "My daddy was a senaatorrr!" She rushed toward the edge of the stage, threw herself onto her knees, and began to sob. Ford came in from the wings and joined the downstage caterwauling. As Richardson recalled, "In the middle of this, Tennessee arrived, pulling at his little silver pocket-flask of vodka, half in tears, half hysterically giggling, and murmured to me, 'There, Tony, I told you—Tallulah should have had a frontal lobotomy.'"

"The second Milk Train just about killed me," Williams wrote to Herbert Machiz, the play's first director. "I was treated like a dead author, with cuts and transpositions made without any consultation, and Bankhead—well, you must have observed. She didn't have a chance." As early as the Baltimore tryouts, the debacle was apparent. "There was no way 'Milk Train' should have opened in Baltimore, or anywhere else," Richardson, who had become "La Richardson" in Williams's deflated estimation of him, said. "He showed a strange indifference to its disintegration on the road," Williams wrote. Richardson couldn't save the production, and he didn't want Williams's help. In a flop sweat, he imposed a cool Kabuki-like style on the play, which lent a strange Brechtian detachment to Williams's impassioned words. After Williams vociferously objected to some piece of direction, he recalled, Richardson told him, "I don't think you're insane but you are a chronic (or natural) hysteric." In Baltimore, where Merrick joined Richardson and Williams for a crisis meeting, Richardson pleaded with Merrick to close the blighted show. "I think it would kill Tallulah if we closed it," Williams said.

So the play staggered onward to Broadway. In the last week of New York previews, Richardson jumped the sinking ship to meet his family in Europe for the holidays. Although this had been contractually agreed upon, his departure was seen as "desertion" by Williams; and, in a way, it was. Richardson didn't return to New York for the show's opening on January 1, 1964. *Milk Train* closed three nights later, after five performances. ("Half the seats in the Brooks Atkinson [Theatre] were empty," Hunter recalled.) No Williams play had ever received such a crushing rejection. The critics' gloves were off. "For the kind of playgoer who has hailed Williams the King of Broadway for a dozen years, it was undoubtedly an ordeal of tedium and a sad signal that he may indeed mean to quit," *Newsweek* wrote. To *The New Yorker*, "Miss Bankhead was hoarse and unhappy," and Hunter was "about as stimulating as the greasy-kid-stuff addict in that television commercial." Bankhead's was "not a performance" but an "appearance," according to the *Herald Tribune*; as for Hunter, "what vigor he brings with him is born of the gymnasium."

Williams's desolation was so great that he fled immediately back to Key West, leaving his mother and brother, who had flown in from St. Louis for the opening, to fend for themselves in New York. "I felt very badly about leaving New York before Mother left," Williams wrote to Dakin. "But I was simply unable to endure another day in that place, after the fate of 'Milk Train II.'" He added, "Everything has gone so wrong this year that the time to come could hardly be anything but better. I try to keep in mind that Chinese philosophy 'Mei you Guanchi,' 'no sweat,' but it's been really tough going."

Williams subsequently claimed that Merlo's death was the catastrophe that precipitated his seven-year depression—his "Stoned Age," as he called it. He likened his collapse to the slow-motion destruction of a building by dynamite. "It occurred in protracted stages, but the protraction gave it no comfort," he said. The loss of Merlo certainly shook him;

the real unmooring catastrophe, however, was the loss of his literary power, that sure connection to the green world of his imagination. "The colored lights" that had sustained him since childhood were starting to flicker. "I work but I have no faith left in what I am doing," he wrote to Lanier in January 1964, three weeks after *Milk Train's* second humiliating collapse. He added, "I work too much under liquor that kills the critical sense for a couple of hours and gives the illusion of doing what you're not really doing."

"I am floundering in the boon-docks of my life and at the present time, I see no way out," a grim Williams wrote to Nicklaus in April, who was now more or less living a separate life. "Must try to believe there is one, besides the last one." He added, "Gloom is heavy and tiresome. I must discard it somehow or no one will be able to bear me." Entombed in grief, unable to write or to reach out to friends, Williams hid himself away in Key West. Marion Vaccaro was enlisted to keep him company; in May, she camped out at Duncan Street, a stay that seemed to her like "an extended visit to Grant's Tomb." "I came for a weekend and have been here over 2 weeks," she wrote to the producer Chuck Bowden, another of Williams's stone-walled but stalwart friends. "Every time I plan to go back to Miami, he says, 'Wait till tomorrow.' . . . Every night we plan to go out to dinner, he backs out and says, 'Let's have a sandwich here.' . . . Between us, we fix lunch, listen to the news on TV, and those fascinating 'Search for Tomorrow' soap operas, and commercials with the sound turned off. We have been out to dinner three times—and once in a while for a late swim—only wish I knew what to do—hate to leave him here but can't stay indefinitely—since apparently I am no solution. . . . Tom looks fine—outside—it's something else—and I am not the answer, even if he does hold on to me."

Williams may have been uncommunicative with his friends, but they communicated their worries to one another. "I have been hoping each day that there would be some word from Tenn that would open the door to him so I could be of some help," Bowden wrote to Vaccaro in mid-June. "If I call him outright I am afraid he will react against us—more importantly you—feeling that we are ganging up against him. . . . I am afraid to make bad matters worse if I force much harder at the moment."

Even the novelty of summer travel couldn't shake Williams's depression. With Vaccaro in tow, he spent three weeks in Barcelona and a month in Tangiers. "He was in such a depressed condition that I hesitated to leave him," Vaccaro wrote to Henry Field, a Miami psychotherapist whom Williams knew. "Apparently there was no one he could put up with, and he was frightened of being alone. I stayed near, but there were days when we scarcely spoke, beyond 'good morning,' 'What shall we have for supper.'" She added, "I wonder if I was any help at all. . . . He had been talking so much of doing away with himself that I simply couldn't just go away and leave him in his black world."

On his return to New York, Williams learned that in his absence the Sixty-Fifth Street apartment, which he'd shared with Merlo, had been looted twice; he moved into a duplex next to City Center on Fifty-Fifth Street. Williams took the seventeenth floor; his roommate on the sixteenth floor was his young Tennessee cousin, Jim Adams, who was studying ballet and the dramatic arts. Adams, whom Williams said had been "bitten by the culture bug on both cheeks of the ass," suggested Williams see his analyst Ralph Harris. In the first few months of treatment, even though he was living a celibate life, visiting Harris at eight every morning Monday through Friday, and going to bed by 10:30 every night, Williams exhibited signs of breakdown. The symptoms—insomnia, loss of curiosity, loss of sex drive—were sufficiently serious for Harris to monitor him over the weekends. "He calls me up on Saturday and Sunday to check on my mental and physical state, too," Williams wrote to Paul Bowles that September. "He is very anxious for me to resume some kind of sex-life but I have no interest in it, it seems like something I'd never heard of."

When he felt he needed to lift his spirits, Williams popped Elavil, an antidepressant. "To believe in pills you have to believe in magic, but maybe they do help a bit and I have always clung to some belief in magic," he told Bowles. "Tom came here to dinner, alone, on Monday," Bowden's wife, the actress Paula Laurence, reported to Vaccaro in mid-September. "I think he looks better—slimmer—and I think he *is* better. Not happier, but more open and inclined to talk about how he feels. He goes to the doctor every day and swims and did some excellent work on the plays"— *The Gnadiges Fraulein* and *The Mutilated*. (Williams had returned to rewriting two one-act plays he'd written in 1962, under the collective title *Slapstick Tragedy.*) Bowden, Laurence explained, was planning to produce them, for a February opening. By late January, Williams was writing to St. Just about the double-bill. "I am going into rehearsal in a couple of weeks with a couple of very odd plays," he wrote. "I don't suppose the critics or public will know what to make of them, and I can't say that I do either. But it is better to be occupied with something rather than with nothing." By the end of the month, however, Bowden postponed the show. He was unable to raise enough money for a Williams production, even with major theatrical talent—Alan Schneider, Margaret Leighton, Kate Reid, and Zoe Caldwell—attached. Williams now had to face a harrowing new prospect: not only had he lost his inspiration, he seemed to have lost his audience.

W illiams first found his audience as the Second World War was ending. In 1945, *The Glass Menagerie*'s elegiac tone of promise and regret caught the wave of history and rode it to glory. Almost twenty years to the month later, *Slapstick Tragedy* caught the undertow. America was back at war, fighting an undeclared battle both abroad and at home, and wartime was no time for Williams's particular brand of talent, as he himself had shrewdly concluded as early as 1940. War terrified and isolated the country, making it increasingly suspicious of ambiguity and resistant to thought. "We are not soft people and the war is making us even harder," Williams had written to Mary Hunter in 1943. "There is a great deal of pity and tenderness in all of us, but when a certain balance is broken by things that create exhaustion, I think the underground devils come out—which makes for naked and savage kinds of creation."

Like the citizens invoked in the prologue of *The Glass Menagerie*— "matriculating in a school for the blind . . . having their fingers pressed forcibly down on the fiery Braille alphabet of a dissolving economy"— Americans of the floundering, bewildered sixties had their fingers forcibly pressed down on a social fabric that was unraveling under the pressure of racial unrest, radical political protest, and social, cultural, and aes-

thetic upheaval. "We are on the verge of Armageddon and await an apocalypse," the usually even-handed Harold Clurman, dean of American
theater critics and co-founder of the Group Theatre, noted in the *Nation*
in 1967. The theatrical paroxysm—whether the grimace of laughter that
refused suffering (Joe Orton, Charles Ludlam's Theater of the Ridiculous), violent physical transformation (Jerzy Grotowski), startling enact-
ments of rebirth (Sam Shepard, the Living Theatre, the Open Theatre),
or the absurdist context of no context (Beckett, Ionesco, Pinter, and so
on)—held up a mirror to the desperation of the times. To more overtly
political playwrights, such as Arthur Miller, this agitation signaled a
"thrilling alienation." "Once again we were looking almost completely
outside ourselves for salvation from ourselves," he wrote in *Timebends*.
"In the absolutely right and necessary rebellion was only a speck of room
for worrying about personal ethics and our own egoism."

In this roiling atmosphere, however, Williams's confessional style
didn't play well; his solipsistic Southern voice sounded both familiar and
trivial. As one critic, writing in *Life*, put it, "The new theatre is lunging
into uncharted waters; Williams is caught looking in the rearview mirror.
Other playwrights have progressed; Williams has suffered an infantile
regression." The mission to which Williams's great plays of the forties and
fifties had been dedicated—the emancipation of desire and the celebration of the wild at heart—no longer held the same subversive romantic
novelty. The underground, in all its political and psychosexual extremes,
was now out in the open and making a public spectacle of itself. "The
permission that Williams helped create sort of robbed him of a platform,"
the playwright Tony Kushner said. "He found himself a revolutionary in
a post-revolutionary era. By the time the sixties rolled around, the things
that Williams had liberated were everywhere irrelevant."

A similar mutation had taken place across the Atlantic, in the late
fifties, when the lords of British West End theater—Terence Rattigan
and Noël Coward—had found themselves deposed almost overnight by a
new wave of playwrights. For nearly two decades, Rattigan had been the
West End's most successful playwright; at one time, in the forties, he'd
had three plays running in adjacent theaters on Shaftesbury Avenue.
Unable to fathom how deeply the welfare state's working-class ethos had

altered the British imagination, he protested to Kenneth Tynan. "Why pick on me?" he had asked the critic who had led the bloodthirsty charge for the new guard. It was not just the plays but the pukka upper-middle-class personas of Rattigan and Coward that the public and the critics were rejecting. A few years later, caught in the slipstream of different but equally ferocious social crosscurrents, Williams found himself similarly dismissed *and* despised. But where Rattigan had retreated to Hollywood and Coward had taken himself on the road as a cabaret turn, Williams, defiant and heartbroken, pressed on.

The widening division within American society between young and old, progressive and reactionary, antiestablishment and establishment was mirrored in New York's theatrical landscape. The time was confrontational; the mood, polemical; the aesthetic, presentational. The adventurous "avant-garde" fare moved downtown to small Off-Broadway venues; by the mid-sixties, Fourteenth Street had become a kind of Maginot Line, dividing intellectual theater from escapist theater. At the birth of Off-Broadway, in the late fifties and early sixties, Williams had been part of the experimental repertoire at Caffe Cino and La MaMa; for reasons of commerce and kingship, however, he insisted that his major work be staged on Broadway. Writing in the *New Republic* in 1966, Robert Brustein, one of the swamis of postwar dramatic criticism who that year founded the Yale Repertory Theatre company, observed that "the Broadway audience has changed its character radically over the past fifteen years." He went on, "To playwrights of previous generations, the customer was always a known quantity, but few dramatists today have any clear idea about who this middle-aged behemoth is or how to feed it."

Faced with the growing public and critical resistance to his work, Williams was confounded; he groped for ways to reconnect with his perplexed and wayward public. As early as 1964, he began to experiment with a freer, more surreal form of storytelling that, he said, "fits people and societies going a bit mad." The second part of *Slapstick Tragedy*, *The Gnadiges Fraulein*, a clown play first published in *Esquire* in 1965, was, for Williams, an act of theatrical and personal artificial respiration. "It's harder as you get older," he said in 1965, a year before *Slapstick Tragedy* was finally mounted on Broadway. "You have to work much harder and much longer on everything you do. The human animal is subject to attrition, he gets tired. And he has to go to wonderful doctors like Doctor Max." The manic *Gnadiges Fraulein* was written while Williams was on Dr. Feelgood's amphetamines. Set in "Cocaloony Key," the play is a funhouse reflection of Key West. A group of zany characters, dodging the buzz-bombing, scavenging Cocaloony birds at the end of the municipal pier, live, like their author, under a state of perpetual siege, but with this difference: they are detached from pain.

Williams's rambunctious one-act was a preemptive strike against his critics; it was also an identification with them. ("I decided they were right," he said later, of the deluge of bad press he received in the sixties.) With its slapstick high jinx, *The Gnadiges Fraulein* sends up the themes and the lyricism that the critics had dismissed as hysterical and passé, mocks Williams's self-pity, and subverts his gloom. The first beats of the play lampoon Williams's own florid Southern idiom. "Everything's southernmost here because of a geographical accident making this island, this little bit of heaven dropped from the sky one day, the southernmost bit of terra firma," Polly, the gossip columnist of the *Cocaloony Gazette*, drawls. She goes on, "I did the southernmost write-up on the southernmost gang-bang and called it Multiple Nuptials, which is the southernmost gilding of the southernmost lily that any cock-eyed sob-sister and society editor, even if not southernmost, ever dreamed of. . . . Yais, everything's southernmost here, like southern fried chicken, is southern-*most* fried chicken."

Molly, who is hustling up publicity for the guesthouse she runs, where the eponymous Fraulein—a Viennese *chanteuse* who can no longer properly render a song—is in precarious residence, pokes fun at another of Williams's theatrical tropes: Southern gentility. "You'd go a long way out of your way to find a richer gold mine of material in the class category than I got here in The Big Dormitory, under the roof-tree of God," she says. "I've got REAL PERSONAGES here." When Joe, a half-naked, blond Indian "with Caribbean blue eyes," makes a brief monosyllabic appearance, Williams even parodies his erotic ideal—the hunky primitive male object of desire.

POLLY: HOW.
INDIAN JOE: POW.
MOLLY: WOW.

The most underrated of Williams's sixties plays, *The Gnadiges Frau-lein* is a surrealist romp, which plunders the freewheeling presentational style of the newly fashionable theater of the absurd. Intended as a vaude-ville on the edge of a cliff, the garish cartoon makes symbolic and linguis-tic nods to Ionesco and Beckett. The set, as prescribed by Williams's stage directions, is a sort of Cubist parody of Southern Gothic. It features a stylized Key West frame cottage skewed as if "Picasso designed it," with a zinc roof that sits "at the angle of Charlie Chaplin's derby on the house." In this off-kilter world, Williams's sense of persecution is reimagined as comic pandemonium; his public collapse is turned into the symbolic tri-umph of the pratfall. To maintain the farcical momentum of the play, even his distinctive lyric idiom is translated into the "gunfire dialogue" of comic cross talk.

The Fraulein—with an orange fright wig, a bloody eye patch over a recently pecked-out eye (Williams at the time was blind in one eye), and an eccentric costume that "would not be out of place at the Moulin Rouge in the time of Toulouse-Lautrec"—is a fantastical battered figure, pre-served in the aspic of her former glory. "Her scroll has been charged with a good deal of punishment lately," Molly explains to Polly. "Don't mock her," she adds. "In spite of her present condition she's still a personage." "Having passed and long passed the zenith of her career in show-biz," the Fraulein has hit rock bottom; like her creator, she has lost her status, her concentration, and her audience. When she was a star, her scene-stealing gambit was to snare in her mouth the fish tossed by a trainer to his per-forming seal. Now she is doomed to repeat the trick, without the applause: she must perform for her two sadistic spectators—Polly and Molly, a sort of Vladimir and Estragon to the Fraulein's brutalized Lucky.

As the Fraulein dashes back and forth from the pier, the wacky biddies sit in rocking chairs on the guesthouse porch, smoking grass and keeping up a cruel running commentary. To earn her place at the guesthouse table and civil treatment from the society there, she must produce fish for dinner. "Three fish a day to keep eviction away and one fish more to keep the wolf from the door," Molly explains. At the sound of an approaching fishing boat's third whistle, the Fraulein hightails it to the docks, hoping to beat the vicious birds to the boat's discarded catch. The question—for both the Fraulein and her creator—is whether she'll be able to beat what Polly calls "the competish." At the finale, the Fraulein "assumes the starting position of a competitive runner and waits for the third whistle"; as the stage dims, she starts a "wild, blind dash" for the docks.

The Gnadiges Fraulein was a daring departure, intended to take on "the competish" and to win back the public's flagging interest. The gigantic Cocaloony bird—part pelican, part raptor, all cartoon—makes a brief, strutting nightmarish appearance, preying on the Fraulein with the same dopey malevolence with which Williams felt the critics went after him. The play's giddy despair plays as a metaphor both of Williams's crumbling competitive consciousness and of the social havoc of the nation's habitual pursuit of victory. ("The Disunited Mistakes" is how Williams jokingly refers to his country in the opening speech; he underlined the point with a reference in the Broadway program to the Vietnam War's "incomprehensible evil.")

The double bill of *The Mutilated* and *The Gnadiges Fraulein*—a smorgasbord of Williams's old and new theatrical styles—opened at the Longacre Theatre on Broadway on February 22, 1966. According to the actress Zoe Caldwell, who won a Tony Award for her performance as Polly, the director, Alan Schneider, "didn't have a clue to what the play was about." In fact, according to the producer, Chuck Bowden, Schneider confessed as much two weeks before the opening. Schneider imposed on Williams's gaiety a heavy, elaborate set, by Ming Cho Lee, as well as his own heavy directorial hand. The result: *The Gnadiges Fraulein* was a clown play directed with no authentic antic touch. As Margaret Leighton, who played the embattled Fraulein, observed, in Schneider Williams had an earnest director "who followed the printed script too literally." While Kate Reid, who played Molly, was having trouble remembering her lines, Leighton, the night before the show opened, cracked her shoulder blade and lost her voice. "I had my arm in a sling, actually, and no voice. So I had to find another voice, which was a kind of man's voice, somewhere," Leighton recalled. Sensing disaster, Caldwell, who had threatened to quit the show, battled her preopening sense of doom by writing doggerel:

I doubt the audience will see
This second play by Tennessee,
A play that's fraught with homely birds,
If only Kate could learn the words.
They'll not hear our Huff, huff, wheee,
We are so sorry, Tennessee.

Cocaloony Bird, Zoe Caldwell, and Kate Reid in *The Gnadiges Fraulein*

William Inge, who second-acted *Slapstick Tragedy* on opening night, found the play "marvelous" and Williams's writing "more and more personal." "'The Gnadiges Fraulein' was just a beautiful conception and the humor in it, the personal humor that no one saw, no one—no critic really dealt with what the play was about," he said. After its opening, *Slapstick Tragedy* lasted seven performances. "The press hit me with all the ammo in their considerable and rather ruthless possession," Williams wrote. "A brilliant talent is sleeping. . . . Mr. Williams has neither grown nor changed," Stanley Kauffmann sniffed in the *Times*. Walter Kerr slapped down *Gnadiges Fraulein*: "savage slapstick is not the playwright's happiest vein," he said. ("Walter Kerr dismissed 'Gnadiges Fraulein' in one line. He said, 'Mr. Williams should not attempt black comedy.' I'd never *heard* of black comedy, though I'd been writing it all my life," Williams told *Playboy* in 1973.) The most seasoned of the critics, Harold Clurman, however, writing in the *Nation*, acknowledged the injustice of the play's critical reception, as well as the folly of producing one-acts on Broadway when, Off-Broadway, "they might have gained considerable esteem." "However we interpret this nightmare it is written in an odd but effective mixture of gallows humor and Rabelaisian zest," Clurman wrote. "On opening night the audience laughed uproariously at the broad-stroked slapdash language, but though I was able to appreciate the style I could not bring myself to smile. I was too conscious that its author was in pain."

IN THE NEXT two years, Williams, rather like the frantic Fraulein, brought three offerings to the public table, all of which were rejected more or less out of hand: *The Two-Character Play* failed in its London debut (1967); the film *Boom!* (1968) received derisory reviews; and *Kingdom of Earth*, retitled *The Seven Descents of Myrtle* (1968), lasted only a month on Broadway. On December 12, 1967, returning drunk to his London hotel suite after the opening night of *The Two-Character Play* at the Hampstead Theatre Club, Williams told Wood and St. Just, "I want to die. I want to die." "Nothing but this, over and over," Wood recalled. "He was totally submerged in his own misery."

Although Williams later put a high-camp spin on his collapse in the late sixties—"I would fall down often, yes, but was put down only by reviewers"—at the time he retreated from the world as perversely as the world, so it seemed, was retreating from him. "I was abandoned by friends to a large extent. People ceased to think of me as an existing person. I was, you know, a sort of apparition. I was only interested in work and I had just *three* sexual experiences in four years," he said.

A self-proclaimed "zombie," Williams gave himself a kind of social lobotomy, joining his sister as one of the living dead. (The deaths of two close friends—Carson McCullers and Lilla Van Saher—during this period only compounded his sense of morbidity.) In a work meeting with the director John Hancock, Williams staggered to the bar to get a drink and fell down. "I did not pick him up," Hancock recalled. "I figured if you want to stagger over and get yourself another drink while you're discussing something that's important to the work of your life, and you fall doing that, you can pick yourself up, right?" For six months, Hancock didn't hear from Williams; then he called to arrange a dinner at Elaine's. "He confessed that he'd been furious at me for not picking him up when he fell," Hancock recalled. "He said, 'Now I've been thinking about it, and I realize you were trying to tell me that I could pick myself up. You know, my mother used to fall. I always thought maybe it was to seduce my father. Maybe I was trying to seduce you.'" Hancock continued, "The past was always in Tennessee's present. He was stuck in his childhood. In that sense, he was ghostly."

Williams haunted everyone with his sensational absence. "WRITER TENNESSEE WILLIAMS DROPS FROM SIGHT HERE" was a June 24, 1968, headline in the *New York Post*. Shortly before, Dakin Williams, fearing that his brother was "in quite imminent danger," alerted the police. He had received a letter from Williams scribbled on stationery from New York's L'Escargot restaurant, which said, in part, "If anything of a violent nature happens to me, ending my life abruptly, it will not be a case of suicide, as it would be made to appear." When police found Williams four days later, he was holed up at the Hotel St. Moritz. But his sequestered, unsettling regression continued. "Please check up on my son, Tom, and let me know how he is," Edwina wrote to Marion Vaccaro in December 1968. "He has so bravely met all the 'arrows of outrageous (mis)fortune.'"

Williams could no longer pull himself together for "the life bit," as he called it. He had taken up desperate residence in his imagination. *The*

Two-Character Play was rewritten over the next three years, before its American debut in Chicago in July 1971, under the title *Out Cry*, both as a road map and as an allegory of his disintegration. "I wrote it when I was approaching a mental breakdown and rewrote it after my alleged recovery," he said. "I was thoroughly freaked out." "To play with fear is to play with fire.—No, worse, much worse, than playing with fire. Fire has limits": the play's opening lines launch Williams's depiction of the claustrophobic, deracinated tumult that engulfed him. Set backstage, amid a clutter of unassembled scenery and props indicating an "incomplete interior," the play suggests both the broken world of the theater and the disorder of Williams's own hermetic mind. The play was a sketch of the kind of autistic enclave Williams had organized for himself.

Clare and Felice, like Williams, were the playwrights, performers, and audience of their own self-destruction. Here, Felice and Clare, his hysterical sister, have been deserted by their touring company, which announced its departure with a telegram calling them "insane." To fill their awful isolation, the pair reprise a familiar two-hander about two parentless children, also called Felice and Clare, whose father has killed their mother in a murder-suicide, and who survive by lying to the outside world. (Brother and sister improvise and twist their memories of the text; in this hall of mirrors—"a play within a play within a play," Williams called it—the playwright also clearly inserted memories of his own parents.) "So it's a prison, this last theatre of ours?" Clare says. They are trapped in a perpetual performance, their lives and their stage roles so confused that they cannot find their way out of the crepuscular gloom and back to the guilt-ridden reality of themselves. Illumination and order lie only in play. "If we can imagine summer, we can imagine more light," Felice says. "If we're lost in the play?" Clare asks. "Yes, completely—in 'The Two-Character Play,'" her brother replies. Their elaborate and confounding game is a sort of three-card monte with reality whose obfuscation was a simulacrum of the perverse psychological magic of Williams's drugged existence: if you don't know where you are, you can't be lost.

The issue of suicide is raised in the play's final beats. Clare finds a revolver hidden behind a sofa cushion and aims it at Felice. "*Do it while you still can!*" Felice says "harshly." Clare cries out, "I can't," and drops the revolver; Felice picks it up and tries to execute Clare, but he can't either. As the lights start to fade, "in both their faces is a tender admission of defeat." But the ending is ambivalent. "They reach out their hands to one another, and the light lingers a moment on their hands lifting toward each other." The embrace, when it comes, is in "total dark." Have they reconnected in life? Or in death?

Around this time, at a Chinese restaurant in New York, Williams had a stoned lunch with Yukio Mishima, also a New Directions author, whom he'd first met and befriended while traveling in 1956. "Mishima told me then . . . that I was 'killing myself' and I said something like 'why not?'" Williams recalled. His latest play, *The Seven Descents of Myrtle*, was about to open on Broadway; a sense of doom hung heavily over him. He felt, he said, as if he'd "been ravaged, without Vaseline, by a troop of elephants." To a recent acquaintance, his Canadian pen pal David Lobdell, he wrote, "I am in a state of panic and confusion. Although I may like the play—it is hard not to like something on which you've worked a long time—I feel that the critics will put it down. I feel that I am out of fashion as a writer." In April, after the predicted critical bashing, Williams's psychological situation grew worse. "I don't believe God is dead but I think he is inclined to pointless brutalities," he said. The reviews of *Myrtle*, however, were tame compared to the hoots of disapproval that awaited him in late May, when Joseph Losey's film version of *Boom!* was released. The almost gleeful critical contempt for the movie had him reeling. Williams fled to England; but he could find no succor even in the emollient presence of St. Just, who reported his awful state in a distressed letter to Audrey Wood.

Things had not improved by mid-July 1968, when Williams was back in New York. "He still is not taking care of himself," Wood wrote to St. Just. Nonetheless, Williams forced himself to the typewriter. "Everyday I work slowly but carefully as possible on a middle-length play called 'Two Scenes in the Bar of a Tokyo Hotel,'" he told Laughlin. "I drink much less, but sometimes I fall out of my chair in a restaurant. Do I have brain cancer?"

The new play, according to Williams, was about "an artist's one-ness with his work, and growing estrangement from the world outside it." But

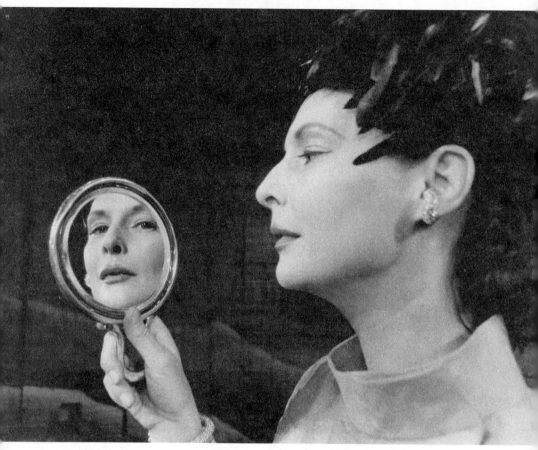

Anne Meacham as Miriam, *In The Bar of a Tokyo Hotel*

within that familiar theme, Williams called out of himself something new and startling. Through the character of Miriam, the disenchanted wife of a befogged world-famous painter named Mark, Williams introduced the unsparing, objectifying voice of his own self-loathing.

Miriam, who hates color and flowers, personifies the pure negative. Onstage, she spells out in physical terms something that Williams tried to define in poetic form: "The Negative: unhomed, unowned, by preference alone. / And that is all: why do you stay? Is it not time to go?" When the curtain comes up, Miriam is unhomed and in the process of leaving her husband. For fourteen years, she has lived in a fierce, fraught symbiotic relationship with Mark—each "the constant unbearable" of the other.

Now, seated in the bar of a Tokyo hotel, alternately trying to pick up the barman and to compose an SOS to Mark's agent, Leonard, summoning him to Japan to clean up after Mark's "total collapse of the nervous system," Miriam is calling it quits with the marriage. "He is mad," she says. "I am married to madness! I need some space between myself and.—A man raging in the dark!" Miriam has lost faith in Mark's new paintings, which are an "adventure" to him and a "crock" to her. "He's gone through drip, fling, sopped, stained, saturated, scraped ripped, cut, skeins of, mounds of heroically enduring color, but now he's arrived at a departure that's a real departure that I doubt he'll return from. Oh, I'm no fool about the. His sacred studio, talking to his. And his black and white period before he," Miriam tells Leonard, when he arrives a few days later.

Williams, like Mark, was in the throes of fashioning a new style—a literary attack that was as free and conspicuous as Mark's vivid painterly gestures. To demonstrate the psychic static between Miriam and Mark, he came up with a new theatrical idiom, a sort of linguistic stammer, in which the characters anticipate and finish each other's sentences.

> MIRIAM:—Are we two people, Mark, or are we—
> MARK: (*with a force of dread*) Stop there!
> (*She lifts her hands to her face, but the words continue through it.*)
> MIRIAM: Two sides of!
> MARK: Stop!
> MIRIAM: One! An artist inhabiting the body of a compulsive—
> MARK: Bitch!
> MIRIAM: Call me that, but remember that you're denouncing a side of yourself, denied by you!

Struggling to explain the discoveries he is making upstairs in the hotel room, where he works obsessively with a spray gun to translate his incoherence, Mark stammers.

> MARK: For the first time, primary colors and no. No technique that sep, sep!
> MIRIAM: Are you trying to say separates?

MARK: Yes, separates, holds at some dis!
MIRIAM: . . . holds at some distance, is that it?
MARK: You understand what I'm trying to say.

"I don't complete many sentences these days," Williams told a reporter in 1969. The ravaged and rumpled Mark is a doppelgänger for the derelict Williams at the time of writing, a personification of the "peculiarly humiliating doom of the artist," as Williams said. When Mark makes his entrance in the middle of the first scene, he attempts to pull a chair up to Miriam's table "but stumbles to his knees: staggers up with an apologetic laugh." "Too soon after work," he explains, his hand so tremulous that he needs help lifting the cocktail the barman puts in front of him. "Sometimes the interruption of work, especially in a new style, causes a, causes a—loss of momentum that's never recovered!" he tells Miriam, when she literally holds up a mirror to his "shaking, unbathed, unshaved," demented self.

Miriam sees only his breakdown; Mark sees only his art. He is compelled to return to his canvases, which are "demanding what I can't give them yet." It's exactly because he can't function that he can't achieve his artistic aim.

MIRIAM: You'll return to the States and you will consult a.
MARK: He would only tell me what I already know. You know there isn't much further.
MIRIAM: Your least attractive quality is self-pity.
MARK: I was being objective.

Mark feels his inspiration—a word synonymous with breathing— waning. He is winded. "I'll tell you something about what's called—the breath of life in us. No, I don't have the breath to tell you," Mark jokes. In the second scene, he staggers up from Miriam's table, promising to "be back in ten minutes, exactly," and then falls to the floor. For both the characters and the audience, the shock is that Mark's much-vaunted forward movement is a race toward death after all.

The question that haunts the play, as it did Williams, is why does

Mark, a man of great attainment who has found his creative bliss, destroy it. Williams wrote a kind of explanation, in a letter to Herbert Machiz, the play's original director, which he asked to have read to the company. (In his references to the "wife or lover," Williams was clearly referring to his relationship with Merlo, which had split along similar fault lines.)

As Mark truthfully says, the intensity of the work, the unremitting challenges and demands that it makes to him and of him (in most cases daily) leaves so little of him after the working hours that simple, comfortable *being* is impossible for him. . . . For a few years this wife or lover will accept, or appear to accept, his primary commitment to his work. Then the wife or lover will reasonably resent being so constantly in second place, and will pay him back by promiscuities, sometimes as ravenous as Miriam's. His youth passes. The health of his body fails him. Then the work increases its demand from most of him to practically all of him. . . . As death approaches, he hasn't the comfort of feeling with any conviction that any of his work has had any essential value. The wife or lover is repelled by his shattered condition and is willing to be with him as little a time as possible. Somewhere in her or him there remains, unconsciously, a love for him that can only be expressed in her or his feeling when the artist is dead.

By associating love with *posthumous* feelings, Williams pointed to the murderous impulse of envy that is at the core of Miriam and Mark's toxic relationship:

MIRIAM: I have clipped flowers outside your studio and heard you talk to your work as if you were talking to another person in the studio with you.
MARK: No. To myself.
MIRIAM: And I was clipping flowers. It's natural that I.
MARK: Felt?
MIRIAM: Sometimes a little excluded, but I never spoke of it, did I?
MARK: The work of a painter is lonely.

MIRIAM: So is clipping flowers. . . .

MARK: When I heard you clipping flowers outside my studio, it would sometimes occur to me that you wished the flowers you were clipping were my.

MIRIAM: What's become of the man that?

MARK: What's become of the woman that?

Miriam has played midwife to the artist whose achievement is both her validation and her alienation. She is in the paradoxical position of needing Mark to succeed and wanting to undermine his success. Her promiscuity is dramatized as both an attack on and revenge for Mark's creativity. And her unconscious wish to steal his power is dramatized by her conscious choice to rip off his work in order to finance a future without him. "I have, under my own name, in Morgan Manhattan Storage, about, no less than two hundred of his best paintings before he discovered color with spray guns, and I also have a hell of a lot of his drawings," she tells Leonard. When Leonard feels Mark's pulse and pronounces him dead, "Miriam appears to see and feel nothing," the stage directions read. Eventually, she says, "Released! . . . I am released."

In the Bar of a Tokyo Hotel acts out Miriam's envy of Mark; it is also an unusually raw and baldly autobiographical meditation on the problem of self-envy, of the artist whose best work may be behind him. Mark speaks for Williams's romantic, heroic side; Miriam, for his perverse, capricious side. Mark seeks illumination through struggle; Miriam seeks escape through distraction: "Animation. Liveliness. People at a smart restaurant talking gaily together." The creative life she has shared with Mark is literally and symbolically behind her. In the play's final moment, Leonard asks Miriam, "What are your actual plans?" She replies, "I have no plans. I have nowhere to go." She is at a loss; she can't move. "With abrupt violence, she wrenches the bracelets from her arms and flings them to her feet," as the lights fade to black. For the first and only time in his canon, Williams ends on a harrowing image of impasse.

The last words spoken over the dead artist in Tokyo Hotel are, "He thought that he could create his own circle of light." By the end of 1968, Williams, in his drugged-out paranoid blur, was living entirely in darkness.

In early January 1969, Dakin flew down to Key West. "At this moment, and not for the first time, he looked as though the death bed might not be far away," Dakin recalled of his gaunt, withdrawn brother. In the 1962 *Time* cover story, the piece mentioned Dakin's "broad hints in person and in print" about how his beleaguered brother could "achieve peace of soul" through religion. "If it would make him happy, I would have a deathbed conversion. It might help to distract me too," Williams had joked. Now, when Dakin raised the issue of conversion again, Williams was in forlorn agreement. Dakin arranged a meeting and a baptism with a Jesuit priest, Father Joseph LeRoy of St. Mary Star of the Sea Catholic Church.

On January 10, flanked by Dakin, Bill Glavin (Williams's secretary and companion since 1965), Leoncia McGee (his housekeeper), and Margaret Foresman (a longtime friend and the editor of the *Key West Citizen*), a haggard Williams, "weakened by the flu" and "wobbly when he went to the altar," was baptized into the church. "I also received the last rites, assuring my ascension to heaven after a relatively short stay in purgatory," Williams wrote later to Robert MacGregor, adding, "I have always been a Catholic in my work, in the broadest sense of it. Don't be disturbed. I question the canons of all faiths. I love the chanted Mass, and the rich ceremony. At best, I will be a very eclectic Catholic." "Salty Author Williams Takes Catholic Vows" was a headline in the *Miami Herald*. Father LeRoy gave Williams a copy of Thomas Merton's *No Man Is an Island*; Williams gave Father LeRoy a book of his plays, which he inscribed, "Dear Father Joe, Faith is in our hearts, or else we are dead." According to Father LeRoy, Williams, in his profession of faith, accepted everything except the idea of immortality. "He didn't understand much about that," he said. When asked later by the press why he had converted, Williams said to "get my goodness back." As Dakin said, "Tenn thinks his conversion will cause him to write better and clearer. He expects that his best plays are ahead."

Although Williams believed that "the eventual, unavoidable doom of an artist is a thing that's appallingly simple," the staging of it was not. After a few weeks of rehearsal for *In the Bar of a Tokyo Hotel* at the East-side Playhouse in New York, Williams himself replaced Machiz as the director. "He seemed to be interested only in stage movement, no comprehension of anything else," Williams told Laughlin. *In the Bar of a Tokyo Hotel* may not have been one of Williams's great plays, but it was a good one, a fascinating dissection of the perversity of his psyche. The play had obvious structural limitations—no satisfying arc, no empathetic characters—and a flawed central performance ("Anne Meacham as Mark's wife *italicizes* every word she utters," Harold Clurman observed). Nonetheless, it had more intellectual sinew, moral complexity, and psychological nuance than the critics acknowledged. With the exception of Jack Kroll, the sophisticated culture editor of *Newsweek*—"In the age of the heartless avant-garde it is good to see that Williams still has the touch," he wrote—the press was deaf to the new tones in Williams's outcry. *In the Bar of a Tokyo Hotel*, critics judged, was "almost too personal, and as a result too painful" (the *New York Times*), "more deserving of a coroner's report than a review" (*Time*). "Tennessee Williams appears to be a White Dwarf"—a star at the end of its life cycle—*Life* magazine reported. "We are still receiving his messages, but it is now obvious that they come from a cinder." Of all the reviews, however, the most annihilating came from Williams's mother, who attended the opening night on May 11, 1969, with Dakin. "Tom, it's time for you to find another occupation now," Edwina said. That afternoon, Williams had delegated Wood to accompany Edwina to Bergdorf Goodman to be fitted for a fur coat. "Whatever the exact price was, I do not remember, but it was in four figures," Wood recalled. "Mrs. Williams was delighted." After Edwina's comment, Williams canceled the purchase.

In the Bar of a Tokyo Hotel lasted for twenty-five performances. In May, Williams was awarded the Gold Medal for Drama by the American Academy of Arts and Letters; in June, a full-page ad for *Life* magazine appeared in the *New York Times*. In it, a picture of Williams's mustached profile was captioned, "Played out? 'Tennessee Williams has suffered an infantile regression from which there seems no exit. . . . Almost free of incident or drama . . . nothing about *In the Bar of a Tokyo Hotel* deserves its production.' That's the kind of play it is, and that's the kind of play it gets in this week's *Life*." "I really began to crack," Williams said.

In desperation, Williams, accompanied by Anne Meacham and his bulldog, Gigi, fled to Japan, ostensibly to see rehearsals of *Streetcar* at the renowned Bungakuza Theatre Company in Tokyo, but quarantine issues with the dog sent him into an even deeper tailspin. "I had an evening with very sad Tennessee Williams and Anne Meacham," Yukio Mishima

With Bill Glavin

wrote to Robert MacGregor. "I did not understand his talking at all because he was drunken being so shocked by Japanese custom officers' bureaucratic treatment to separate him and his sweetheart Gigi (a dog). It was a very very sad but very impressive evening. I took care of him with Anne beside of his bed in order to give him a good sleep and sweet dream. He was just a big baby with beards drinking alcohol instead of milk." "My condition had so deteriorated that I do not even recall my seeing Yukie," Williams confided later to Oliver Evans. After the fiasco of Japan, where Williams proved impossible for Meacham to wrangle—he ended up accusing her of stealing his drugs—he reunited with Bill Glavin in San Francisco, for a dismal three-week stay at the elegant Fairmont Hotel.

Glavin was a charming New Jersey–born lost soul, with azure eyes, half-moon teeth, rotted away, and nice cheekbones, who had a "rollicking nature" and "an almost suspect glamor," according to Williams. He was tall, cast against type for Williams. "Tennessee always preferred someone of his own height as a companion," Bill Gray, a professor of English who befriended Williams in the late forties, said. "He did not like a person of ideas. He did not like an intellectual. God knows Glavin filled *that* bill." Many people who saw Williams and Glavin at close quarters felt that Glavin treated Williams shabbily. "He didn't look after him. He didn't do the job. Glavin was never there," the realtor Robert Hines said. According to Jack Fricks, Hines's partner, Glavin "would get Tennessee knocked out and have him back home by ten or eleven in the evening, and then Glavin would take off and go out and stay out till four in the morning." Even a laissez-faire freeloader like Glavin had his work cut out trying to take care of Williams. "There's a limit to what anybody could do with Tennessee in that period," Dakin Williams said. "Glavin couldn't handle Tennessee because of his temperament—an explosive type Irish temperament."

Nonetheless, for five years until 1970, Glavin ushered Williams through his Stoned Age, that twilight zone in which Williams "elected to be a zombie except for my mornings at work . . . [and] didn't know if I wanted to live or not." Glavin accompanied Williams on his daily Manhattan walkabout—to his analyst's office, to see Dr. Feelgood, to swim at the Y, to lunch at L'Escargot, to the previews of *Gnadiges Fraulein* at the

Longacre, where they sat in a box and laughed uproariously, and where the producer, Charles Bowden, caught them in the men's room "shooting up with Dr. Feelgood's amphetamines." Glavin was bisexual and "very attractive to ladies," according to Williams. He also had a ruthlessness that made him "perhaps . . . closest to representing Chance Wayne in 'Sweet Bird of Youth' in my life." But Williams's attachment was more to Glavin's managerial skills than his erotic expertise. "During our nearly five years together he offered himself to me only three or four times, and, as best as I can remember, I had no carnal knowledge of anyone but him during his time with me."

"Tennessee made impossible demands on Glavin," Dakin Williams recalled. "They would go to Europe, and Tennessee would have forgotten his syringes that he'd gotten from Dr. Feelgood. He would accuse Glavin of having stolen them. He would make Glavin pack up and go back to New York with him. Tennessee would find them in his room." In Williams's fragile, drugged, paranoid state, Glavin frequently became the object of his boss's furious projections. Once at lunch at L'Escargot, they got into a shouting match over Williams's accusations of disloyalty and theft. Glavin walked out, which is when Williams penned his paranoid SOS about being murdered.

In the early days of their relationship, when they were living in separate bedrooms in the thirty-third-floor penthouse at 15 West Seventy-Second adjacent to The Dakota, a pill-popping guest took Williams aside and said, "Tennessee, how do you dare live on the thirty-third floor of a building with a man with eyes like that and with a balcony he could throw you off of." The next day—"being a madman"—Williams had his furniture put into storage and moved alone into a nearby hotel for a few days, until Glavin discovered his whereabouts and joined him. "[Glavin] probably started, then, to hate me," Williams wrote in *Memoirs*. Toward the end of their relationship, Williams gave Glavin a copy of August Strindberg's *Dance of Death*, one of his "three favorite modern plays." In an appended note, he wrote, "It isn't so much my life that I value but what I live for—my work. In destroying *me*, you are destroying *that*, and are you *sure* you're *worth* it? Think hard! And fast! So will I!"

When Glavin rejoined Williams in San Francisco after the Japan debacle, Williams's paranoid scenes grew so bad that they were turned out of the Fairmont. Williams moved on to New York to oversee the duplication of his scripts and to score a hundred tablets of Doriden, and then to New Orleans for a rendezvous with Pancho Rodriguez. Williams was in free fall, a king dethroned by his critics and divested by his own caprice of imaginative command, sent to wander alone in the wilderness. The gauge of Williams's melancholy was his rage at the loss. In the poem "Old Men Go Mad at Night" (1973), he looked back at this ugly period of paranoid turmoil and gave brilliant poetic shape to his sense of depleted inspiration:

> Old men go mad at night
> but are not Lears
>
> There is no kingly howling of their rage,
> their grief, their fears, dementedly,
> from sea-cliff into storm. [. . .]
>
> No title of dignity, now,
> no height of old estate
>
> Gives stature to the drama . . .
>
> Ungrateful heirs, indeed!
> Their treacherous seed
>
> Turns them away from more than tall
> gold-hammered doors:
>
> Exiles them into such enormous night
> skies have no room for it
>
> And old men have no Fools except themselves.

On September 7, 1969, not having spent more than a month in one place for more than a year, Williams straggled back to Key West, with

Glavin, whom he promptly sent away for a week. Confused and alone, without even the feckless Glavin on hand for company, Williams sank like a stone. "He never knew where he was most of the time," his friend the novelist David Loomis recalled. "He staggered. His hands shook. He was incoherent. He'd get paranoiac and scream and shout and cry." Williams was living under a demented state of siege. He placed a frantic call to his Key West friend Margaret Foresman. "He insisted someone was going to break in the house and kill him," Foresman said, adding, "He'd call me to come over and check around the house—he was convinced there were prowlers and murderers. He wouldn't call the police himself, he had me do it—he was used to having people do things like this—and when the deputy sheriff arrived, Williams insisted that someone guard the house all night. All that week he became worse and worse."

Foresman contacted Wood, who had also been called by Vaccaro; she in turn called Dakin. Having experienced Williams's capricious rage-outs when he was in this kind of paranoid condition, Vaccaro was chary to intervene. The following week, Williams picked up a Silex containing boiling coffee from a stove that had been set up on the patio while his new kitchen was being installed, then slipped on tiles and scalded his naked shoulder. "The rest is not a blur but is too fragmented and chaotic to be sorted out so far," he wrote later. The burn was not bad but was sufficient proof to Williams that someone was trying to kill him. "Dakin, an attempt will be made on my life tonight," he told his brother in a distressed call at ten o'clock that night. "Well, Tom, I can't do anything about it tonight," Dakin recalled replying. "Is it all right if I come tomorrow morning?"

The burn may have been superficial, but Williams's collapse was profound. Dakin saw his opportunity. Using the burn as an excuse, he asked Williams to come to St. Louis, to Barnes Hospital, where a cousin, Dr. Carl Harford, was in residence, a guarantee of proper attention. On the plane, when the flight attendant refused to give Williams more than the two-drink limit in first class, he made a scene. Dakin was forced to leave the plane during a stopover in Chattanooga, to hunt for booze. It was a Sunday; he came back empty-handed. Williams threw a fit. When they arrived in St. Louis, Dakin rushed Williams to their mother's house, where there was liquor, and Williams was finally pacified.

The plan was for Williams to go to Barnes Hospital by ambulance the next morning, but when the time came, Williams balked. Around noon, with Dakin's intervention and accompanied by Edwina, Williams admitted himself as "Thomas L. Williams" and underwent tests while ensconced in "Queeny Towers"—the deluxe top-floor wing of Barnes. His room, not far from the swimming pool, had blue satin curtains and a large television on which he watched Shirley Booth in *Hazel*. ("I thought Shirley was making veiled innuendoes about me," Williams said.) He was allowed to keep his blue kit bag full of pills, speed, and syringes by his bedside table. Propped up on pillows, with a little stocking cap on his head, as Dakin recalled, Williams "thought he was in full control of everything."

That evening, Dakin arrived with a bouquet of flowers and get-well notes to Williams from his nieces; his mother also reappeared, looking like "a little Prussian officer in drag," Williams recalled in *Memoirs*:

> There was now, quite clearly, something impending of a fearful nature. I sensed this and scrambled with remarkable agility out of bed and said, "I'm going home right now," and I ran into the closet to get into my clothes.
>
> "Oh no, Son."
>
> "You all will drive me right home or I'll walk."
>
> I got myself dressed with amazing alacrity, all the while shouting abuse at Dakin.
>
> "God damn you and your two adopted children. How dare you give them our family name."
>
> Dakin: "I don't have to sit here and listen to this abuse."
>
> Now fully dressed and totally out of my mind, I charged into the corridor and down to the elevators. I started to enter one, was blocked in this escape effort by a huge young man in hospital uniform. He was blond, I remember, with a beefy, sneering face. I somehow slipped past him into the elevator but he wouldn't let the doors close.

OPPOSITE PAGE: Photograph by Richard Avedon, 1969

Raging and storming invectives, I rushed back past him to the room where Mother was asking a nurse for smelling salts. Jesus!

Then I lit into her with a vengeance.

"Why do women bring children into the world and then destroy them?"

(I still consider this a rather good question.)

Said Miss Edwina—sincerely?—"I just don't know if we're doing the right thing."

The "thing" to which she was referring was committing Williams to the hospital's psychiatric ward, the Renard Division. Alarmed by Williams's state, Dakin had asked his cousin at the hospital for advice on how to handle the emergency. "He told me that I could sign a letter at the hospital admitting him for ten days. After that Tennessee could get out any time he wanted to," Dakin said. He went on, "Of course, I never told Tennessee that. He had no legal advice. If he'd had legal advice, he could've gotten out in ten days which, of course, would have killed him. Ten days would have done him no good at all."

In Williams's account of his futile dash for freedom, he was intercepted "by a wheel-chair with straps and by a goon squad of interns. . . . Clutching the flight bag that contained my booze, my pills, my vial of speed . . . I was strapped into the chair and rocketed out of Queen's Division to Friggins Violent Ward"—Williams's mocking epithet for the Renard Division. "There the flight bag was snatched from me, and at this point I blacked out." Williams's story omits Edwina's "fainting as Tennessee was being wheeled to the elevator," according to Dakin. Dakin, who was then running for the U.S. Senate, had come with Bob Arteaga, a photographer friend, who attempted to calm Williams by placing his arm around him. "Who are you?" Williams asked Arteaga. "I'm a friend of Dakin's." "I wouldn't brag about that," Williams said. As he was wheeled into the elevator, an intern "got behind him and injected him with something in his arm that put him to sleep," Dakin said.

Technically, according to Williams, he was considered a voluntary admission. "It wasn't voluntary at all. It was forced. I was given a paper to sign and told that if I didn't sign it I would be legally committed," he explained. "I thought it better to sign it, as, technically again, you are in a position to sign yourself out. But how can you do that without your doctors' and relatives' permission? I mean approval?" Dakin's decision, which would cost him his inheritance, kept Williams in the hospital for three months. It also saved his life. The tests revealed that Williams was dying of acute drug poisoning. To get him off the drugs would require a prolonged stay. For Williams, whose life had been ruled by a rebellion against any proposition of control, the idea of such a confinement was repellent and terrifying, "a 2 by 4 situation."

When he woke up, according to Dakin, Williams's first words were, "Where am I? At the Plaza?" In the Renard Division, a lock-down ward where he was kept for the best part of a month, his cell was checked "every half hour by an intern—the door would open noisily and a flashlight would be turned on you." Williams dubbed the place "Spooksville" and "nightmare alley." He claimed to have been driven crazy by days of sleeplessness. In addition to the intrusive interns, he had been given a whitewashed room (No. 512) beside the incinerator, whose rumblings were another barrier to his getting any sleep on his steel cot. The demented haunted the hallways. For nearly two months of his stay, Williams was not allowed to write letters, to make phone calls, or to receive unopened mail. When a package of books from Elia Kazan was inspected by an orderly before it was handed over—"Hospital policy," the orderly said—Williams flew into a rage. "Upset the card table and started screaming at the orderly and screaming at me. I didn't do anything except walk out," Dakin said, adding, "I was the only one allowed to see him besides the doctors."

"I am a completely disenfranchised citizen," Williams wrote to Glavin, when he could. He later claimed to have had three "convulsive seizures" during his withdrawal from Doriden and Mellaril. Over time and retellings, those seizures escalated to "heart attacks." Williams's medical files have been destroyed, so the facts of his condition cannot be corroborated, but the emotional thrust of his account, however melodramatically embellished, never varied. "The circumstances under which I was treated were totally unsuitable and demoralizing and would most certainly have destroyed me had I not been so fiercely resolved to complete my life, what was left of it after those convulsions and heart attacks—which Dr. von Stein has told me were altogether unnecessary—in a state of freedom, not behind the bars of a violent ward in a snake pit, in filthy clothes because neither the hospital nor my brother were willing to have my clothes laundered till toward the very end when it became apparent that something in me would prevail," Williams later wrote to MacGregor. When he was finally allowed to write letters, he titled one of his first, to Wood, "De Profundis 200,000," drawing an invidious comparison between his own confinement and Oscar Wilde's ruinous imprisonment. In Williams's mind, the hospital was a jail, a kind of sadistic internment camp, from which there was no escape and where his literary fame and his celebrated eloquence had no purchase.

In Williams's accounts of the hospital's abusive treatment, there is no mention of the cruel abuse that he dished out—the overturned tables, thrown cups, scurrilous graffiti, snarling insults. Nor, in any written account, is there an acknowledgment of the indisputable, not incidental fact that the medical team he vilified gave him back his life and another decade of writing.

Instead, Williams adopted the posture of shanghaied victim, dragooned into a hell of his brother's making. "I'm afraid I bear him malice, permanently, after those months in the St. Louis snake pit he put me into," Williams wrote to Paul Bowles after his release in late December 1969. "I suspect he'd love to do it again. Given the slightest excuse. I think the sight of him would freeze my blood." Two years earlier, Williams had spoken lovingly of Dakin as "sort of a Quixote—my favorite character in life and fiction. . . . Honesty and humor are a rare combo, but Dakin has both." Now, Dakin was "Brother Cain." Williams's hospitalization, he concluded, was "legalized fratricide." Where Williams saw betrayal, Dakin saw love. He insisted he'd saved his big brother's life. Many of Williams's closest acquaintances—Laughlin, Wood, Vaccaro, Stapleton, and Brown, among them—agreed. "I know that you never intended (consciously) to do wrong," Williams wrote to Dakin in 1970. "And yet how can I forget the day you picked up a post-card photo of Edwin Booth in my Cell at Renard and said, 'This man's brother shot Lincoln. I guess he felt his brother had up-staged him.'" Williams continued, "It is hardly accurate to say that you 'saved me' by putting me in the violent ward of a psychiatric hospital where I had three convulsions in a single morning because of cold-turkey withdrawal under the care of a sadist resident-physician and three pompous neurologists, two of which were indifferent at best, and one of them unmistakably hostile."

While on the psychiatric ward, Williams had a dream so vivid and extraordinary that years later he included it in his memoir. He saw himself moving slowly down a corridor with a drag queen's mincing, exaggerated gait and chanting a poem. The recurrent line of each verse was "Redemption, Redemption." "Redemption from what?" he wondered. Was it about his brother, his homosexuality, his waste of life and talent? "How terribly I've abused myself and my talent in the years since . . . I suppose since Frankie's death," Williams wrote to his New Directions editors from the hospital. But to pour scorn on his brother and the doctors was easier than to face the losses he'd brought about himself. In his excoriating (and hilarious) prose-poem account of his hospitalization, "What's Next on the Agenda, Mr. Williams?" (1970), Williams loudly proclaimed his innocence—a riff that demonstrated, among many things, that anger was a great antidepressant. (The two neurologists attending Williams, Dr. Berg and Dr. Levy, were rechristened here "Ice Berg" and "Leviathan.")

> "You say you do not sleep well." . . .
>
> "No, I do not sleep well," I said to this mammoth neurologist, the one of the three that came on with an air of tired but benign intentions, unlike Dr. Ice Berg whose questions I rarely answered. . . . "No, Dr. Leviathan," I said to this doctor whom I could talk to, "your sleeping medications give me palpitations like the hoof-beats on a fast-track at the derby, and also, every half hour during the night, an orderly bangs my cell door open and flashes his goddamn flash-light directly into my eyes, for what reason I no more know than why they're giving electric shock therapy to that sweet old lady, seventy-five years old, worn thin as a finger by life but not the least bit senile, who nearly shakes to pieces with terror when she is informed, which is every night, that she'll be subjected to shock again the next morning.

"She's not one of our patients," the doctor said blandly, "so let's stick to you, Mr. Williams. Now couldn't it be that you don't fall asleep because you associate falling asleep with dying?"

"No, Sir, I don't think so."

"Perhaps, you don't think so but you unconsciously feel so."

"No, I still know what I unconsciously feel which makes it a conscious feeling, if not at night, at least by this hour the next day."

"What patients think they feel isn't always reliable here. You know, I think that your brother told you, that you have suffered what's called a silent coronary which showed up on the electro-cardiogram taken of you before you were admitted to Friggins Division."

"Oh, yes, he did give me that bit of false information with quite an interesting smile the first time he called on me here; yes, false it was as his smile was shockingly true. Now, doctor, I know and you know, we both know, that I did not have a coronary, not a silent nor a loud one, before I had three convulsions in one morning while under the skilled, conscientious care of the resident physician here at Friggins; but during and since those three cold-turkey convulsions, I have had and survived two of them, I mean coronaries, the first one during those spasms of my brain-waves, the stabbing pain of it is all that I remember about that first coronary, and I know that I suffered another, a second one, since, when I was pursued by a bitch of a night-nurse into this cubicle where I'm afraid you must be very uncomfortably seated." . . .

And while I said this to myself, confronting the fact that I was being a son of a bitch, he thanked me for being concerned concerning his comfort.

"Thank *you*," I said, "for caring how I don't sleep."

Still, Dr. Levy, who "was fully aware of who Tennessee was," according to Dakin, gradually broke down Williams's bumptiousness. "He was very clever at motivating him," Dakin recalled. "He said, 'Tennessee, if you co-operate with us, you'll write better when you come out than you did before.' It was then that he began to cooperate a little bit." As Williams dried out and slowly returned to his senses, by degrees his privileges were reinstated. In late October, the writing ban was lifted; he was allowed envelopes and a rental typewriter, which had to rest on his bed because the table was too high for it. "The worst may be over," Williams wrote to Glavin, who was housesitting in Key West. "It was the withdrawal from Doriden. It was a cold-turkey withdrawal." The letter contained the first signs of Williams's chastened recovery:

> I'm having dinner with Dake tonight—I now have the privilege of dining in a very attractive top-floor restaurant in another (non-psychiatric) part of the hospital, on the condition that I don't order a drink. It's hardly credible but I've not had a drink for over a month—I believe that's about how long I've been confined. Some nights I can't sleep at all and I sure miss the presence of a Scotch on the bed-side table. However it's just as well that I don't attempt to go into the matter of things that I miss. Well, perhaps I might mention you and Gigi and the little house and—nope, I'd better not remind myself of other remembrances.
>
> . . . The present circumstances are relatively agreeable. Most of the patients appear to be reasonably normal, at least by my standards which are not the strictest. A certain number are taking electric shock treatments. You can tell which ones they are by their dazed expressions. I've not been given that kind of shock, probably because my electro-cardiogram shows that I've had a serious heart attack, "some time in the last few years."
>
> I registered here as Tom Williams but Dakin gave a press-release so it's now widely known that Tennessee is here, too.
>
> I walk quite steadily now and I notice nothing particularly eccentric about my behavior—but when the doctors will release me is something I've yet to learn. "We don't expect to keep you here forever" is the closet approximation I can get out of them. They say they can't yet trust me to stay off Doriden and liquor, the combination of which was responsible for my general disequilibrium. You know, I really didn't drink so very much. I rarely finished a Scotch and only had two or three a day. Of course there were the martinis and wine at meals. But

the doctors have an exaggerated idea of my drinking habit and seem very skeptical when I tell them I was a minor-league drinker. . . .

I'll seem quite well when you see me and I'll be careful thereafter. . . . Take care. I've learned it's necessary.

Around the same time, in the last days of October, Williams made contact with Wood. The gloom seemed to be lifting. He was full of ideas for rewrites of a new short play, *Will Mr. Merriweather Return from Memphis?*, and a reworking of *Tokyo Hotel* ("I was obviously quite ill when I wrote that play but stripped to its essence, it could have an original quality and a degree of poetic power"). Williams was coming back to life.

Today, for the first time, the neurologist, Dr. Levy, spoke of my going home (Key West) as something not months away. Perhaps in three weeks I'll be ready. Just imagine, for a month and a half now, I have existed without a drop of liquor!—I am given countless un-named pills, mostly anti-depressants. Levy says that I have been living in a "fog" of depression for "several years" but that I am lucid now.—The agony has been the sleepless nights. Two or three in a row without sleeping a moment. Withdrawal from Doriden is harder, he says, than withdrawal from heroin. . . . Did you know that Dakin is running for nomination to the Senate? That he has five television sets in his house, two of them in color? What an eccentric family Rose belongs to!

On November 7, almost two months after his committal, Williams stepped out of the hospital and into the light of a lovely Indian summer morning for a sanctioned excursion. He had lost weight in the hospital; his clothes no longer fit. Dakin drove him to a men's store in the suburbs of St. Louis to replenish his wardrobe. Williams wrote to Lobdell:

I'd planned to get a couple of suits but I felt too nervous, too tense, to spend that much time in the store. So I settled for two pairs of slacks and a red sweater-shirt. Dakin disappeared. I got panicky and shouted for him. He was trying on a suit. I insisted that we leave at once. How selfish sickness makes you! He really needed a suit. He is running on a peace and Civil Rights platform, I'm happy to say. He is on the side of the young. Our country seems to be divided between young and old. It's a tremendously dramatic confrontation. . . . I hope that some entirely new idea of government will evolve, perhaps it could happen within the framework of democracy that is *really* democracy. But I must leave polemics to my brother, I am not running for anything but my personal liberation and the night sky in Key West and the morning light in my studio where I can sit under the long slanting window in the ceiling and say to myself: "I have come through, I am home!"—it doesn't even matter too much if I find myself unequal to the challenge of the typewriter under the skylight. Perhaps it won't be a challenge, only an invitation, and perhaps I'll find myself able to accept it. Gears have been shifted, values have been re-assessed. The question is: is there time?

On November 20, Williams was "sprung" from Barnes Hospital a week early. "The prospect of early release makes me feel stronger," he wrote to Andrew Lyndon, a hard-at-heels Southern writer and former lover of Christopher Isherwood's who had volunteered to fly with him to Key West after a couple of days' recuperation at his mother's house. He added in another letter, "My mind is quite clear, now, I have acquired the poor man's courage, which is stoicism. I have an awful suspicion that I pity myself, but perhaps that is only human. . . . I'll have to retire to the little compound and live very quietly. That's all I hope and pray for. It would seem a miracle to me to achieve that much."

Settled back in Key West, Williams limited himself to a drink at dinner and only the occasional hour at his typewriter. "Perhaps that's for the best," he told Paul Bowles in mid-December. "I had written myself very thin and become dependent on hypnotic drugs to reach my unconscious in order to work at all." He was also resolute about changing his living arrangements and resolved "to ship Glavin off, preferably to Siberia." Within a few months of his return, Williams was paying Glavin three hundred dollars a week to stay away from Key West. "With his facile Irish charm, Glavin has this town sewed-up," he complained to Wood in February 1970. "It is apparent to me that his intention is to drive me out of this house which is the only place where I have known any true happiness since my childhood. (No sobs. Just a statement.)" During Williams's three-month hospitalization, "without my knowledge or authorization," according to Williams, Glavin had spent more than twenty thousand dollars redoing Williams's kitchen and expanding his patio. Williams came to see Glavin more as a symbol of his madness than as a savior from it, "at best, he's pitiable; at worst—*sinister*!" "Nobody knows the true desolation, the absolute moon-surface emptiness of my life with that humanoid creature who blandly escorted me down and down and down till delivered by my brother to a snake-pit. Would you like me to suggest you set up house-keeping with Dracula?" he wrote to Jo Mielziner, who'd had the temerity to suggest that Williams and Glavin might reunite.

Glavin's real crime, in Williams's mind, at least, was the effect he had on Williams's work. "Tennessee wanted out, he said, because he couldn't write around Glavin," Dotson Rader, who lived with Williams and wrote a book about him titled *Tennessee: Cry of the Heart*, recalled. "He blamed him for fucking up his mind. Tenn was big in giving blame to others." Williams had returned to his senses; the question he couldn't yet answer when he entered his writing room for that daily rendezvous with his harried unconscious was whether his muse had returned to him. In a letter to Wood from the hospital, he had confessed that "most of the stuff" he'd finished over the last few years read as if he had been tired when he wrote it. "Dear, dear Tenn," Wood replied. "You weren't tired my love— you were way out on a light beam in a world that didn't exist except in your own confused mind." Wood preferred not to dwell on the past but to celebrate Williams's return to sanity. "On to the future—and all the plays you are going to write—and see—and hear—and watch over with both eyes open and a mind going clickety-clack as of yore," she wrote. "Much love, darling, I *am so looking forward to the future.*"

CHAPTER 9

The Long Farewell

Time betrays us and we betray each other.

—TENNESSEE WILLIAMS,
Camino Real

On July 7, 1971, the night before the opening of *Out Cry*—a rewritten and renamed version of *The Two-Character Play*—at the Ivanhoe Theater in Chicago, Williams, Audrey Wood, Maria St. Just, the director George Keathley, and the actors Eileen Herlie and Donald Madden, who played Clare and Felice, assembled in Madden's dressing room for notes. Madden had wallpapered and painted the place himself; as a finishing touch, he'd draped a few strands of Christmas lights around the room to give it a festive feeling. The night's performance, however, put a damper on the stage-managed atmosphere of cheer. Although the response to the first preview had been heartening—some audience members had stood to applaud—the cool reaction of the second-preview crowd had unsettled everyone. The play, according to Keathley, who was holding pages of notes, "was choppy as hell." "Tennessee had been obstreperous all during the performance, braying loudly at the slightest joke," Keathley said. "Everyone knew—instantly—that he was very high."

Out Cry was Williams's first new production in more than two years. He felt, he said, "sort of like Sister Elizabeth planning to kidnap Kissinger and bomb the Pentagon." Prior to setting off for Chicago, he had confessed to Oliver Evans that he was "petrified." "I can't do a thing now but cut it and people who know her tell me that Eileen Herlie comes on like a bellowing ox in a slaughter-pen, which is hardly a desirable approach to

With Audrey Wood

the part of Clare," he said, adding, "I think I am a bit sick of this whole writing bit now, perhaps I'm just too old for it."

From the moment he hit town, first in the company of his new best friend, the writer and antiwar activist Dotson Rader, and then with St. Just, whom he flew in from London for the opening—"It's a cold world without you," he said when issuing the invitation—Williams was managing his panic with liberal cocktails of Ritalin and Nembutal, a downer that counteracted Ritalin's amphetamine-like rush. "The results were awful to see," Keathley recalled. "He would come in giggling in a high-pitched voice, his eyes bulging and looking off to the side while he opened his mouth as wide as he could—as if to stretch the skin. There was incredible tension in every movement. He truly looked like a spastic. It bordered on the grotesque." Keathley added, "It was uncomfortable. He had moved into a place where he no longer cared. He screamed at everybody."

Because the theater couldn't afford to pay for newspaper ads to spread the word about its premiere, Keathley took it upon himself to accompany Williams to the all-important media interviews. "He could not respond with any degree of sensibility," he said. "And still he drank. And still he drugged. And still he sank deeper and deeper into a terrible despair."

For all of 1970, Williams had hounded Wood about the urgency of producing *Out Cry*. Wood was emphatic that wherever the play was finally mounted, it was crucial that Williams be present. "We should not again make the mistake of having this play done without the author, as we did in England. If ever a play needed the watching over, every hour of rehearsal, it is this one. I urge you to be here when this work goes into rehearsal," she wrote to him in November. But by the time the Chicago production began rehearsals, eight months later, Williams had so over-shot the runway that he was of little use. "In one of our arguments about the text, Tennessee let it slip that Dotson Rader had said such and such," Keathley recalled. "So there it was. Tenn was being pumped from the outside by Rader and would listen to no one else. . . . It was not a happy-making situation." Inevitably during the fraught rehearsals, alliances were formed: Madden sided with Williams, Keathley with Herlie. At several points, Keathley became so frustrated that he broke down in tears in front of the cast.

IN MADDEN'S DRESSING ROOM the night before the opening, the mood was somber. There had been a jubilant dinner after the first pre-view, but Wood had seemed oddly withdrawn. "Did you notice how Audrey was?" Williams remarked to Lady St. Just. Wood had, as Williams wrote, "an uncanny sense of not only what is good but what will go." Her reticence now in Madden's dressing room spoke volumes.

The conversation turned to the play's excessive running time and to cuts. "Tennessee, I have a thought," Keathley said.

"What?" Williams snapped.

"Why don't we cut the references late in the play about . . ."

"Do you think I would introduce something in the first act and not make reference to it in the second act?" was Williams's curt retort.

"Now, now, Tennessee," Wood said.

Her maternal tone—her "will to manage, to control her sometimes recalcitrant son," as Williams described it—always got his goat and fed an ambivalence that he freely admitted to, even when publicly praising Wood. Williams was now of an age as an artist where he felt humiliated by "too much domination, too many decisions for him not made by himself," and where "he would rather make wrong decisions than accept right ones from someone else." "Now Williams whirled on her and spat the words out with a terrible anger," Keathley recalled. "You must have been pleased by the audience reaction tonight. You've wanted me dead for ten years. But I'm not going to die," he yelled. In that shocked and shocking moment, Williams made probably the worst decision of the rest of his life. "I became a sort of madman," he wrote in *Memoirs*, omitting any mention of the drug-addled state that had fueled his paranoid rage. Although he insisted that he spoke to Wood with "quiet ferocity," to the ears of everyone around him, he was screaming hysterically. As a parting shot, according to Keathley, Williams snarled, "And you, you bitch, you've been against me from the beginning. I'm through with you. You're fired!" Williams yanked open the dressing-room door and stormed out.

"No one knew what to say or what to do," Keathley said. "Although he thought he was making a grand exit, Tennessee had, in fact, gone to the bathroom, and soon everyone realized where he was. We were still silent, each of us, wondering just exactly what Tennessee was going to do. After what seemed like hours, he suddenly threw open the door and, without a word to anyone, left."

For Wood, and on some level for Williams, the moment was indigestible. "For the first time in all our years together . . . I wanted only to slap him hard on the face," Wood wrote later. Still, during the outburst, she maintained a dignified silence, refusing her client the pleasure of an extended scene. Once he was gone, her impulse was "to get the hell out of there, one, two, three!" Nodding to the embarrassed group, she managed a quick exit. In her retelling of the story, Williams was still within earshot as she hurried away; she heard him say, "That bitch! I'm glad I'm through with her!" "After such a trauma, one needs to find a chair and a stiff drink," Wood recalled. She found both at the Ambassador East, where she and Williams were staying. Soon after she had gotten settled, Williams rushed into the bar with St. Just in tow. "When he saw I had arrived before him, he went charging out in a further rage," she said. That night, Wood told herself, "I have been through similar Williams scenes through the years. I am strong. I have humor. The play will open. I can get by for a few days more. I will see him as little as possible. . . . I won't talk." Unable to bear the heartbreak and the humiliation, however, the next morning Wood rented a car and driver to speed her away from Williams and Chicago to Milwaukee, where she visited the graves of her parents.

THE NEWS OF Wood's firing traveled fast. Alan U. Schwartz, Williams's lawyer, was at LaGuardia Airport about to board a plane to Chicago for the opening night of *Out Cry* when he got the word. "'Don't come, or come if you want, but you're gonna be very unhappy,'" Schwartz remembered Wood telling him. "I didn't go. I was in shock. She came back to New York, and *she* was in shock." Schwartz continued, "She blamed a lot of it on Maria."

As early as 1963, Wood had called St. Just out on her subversive double-dealing. "Dear, dear Maria," she began,

> The world we live in is indeed small. An old friend returning from London the other day apparently saw you during one of your social evenings in London either in May or June. With eyes popping with friendly interest I was told how gleefully you were announcing in London that I no longer represented Tennessee Williams.
>
> As a very old friend I know you will be pleased to know that Tennessee has signed agency contracts with Ashley-Steiner, and I am continuing to work with him and for him as in the past. Knowing how many people you know in London I felt I must write this information to you so you could bring your party conversation up-to-date.

When Wood confronted Williams with the rumor that he had left her agency, he dismissed it. He wired back:

> DEAREST AUDREY PLEASE DON'T WORRY ABOUT ME HAVE GONE A LONG WAY TOGETHER AND HOPE HAVE LONG WAY TO GO. LOVE TOM.

Now others reinforced her suspicions about St. Just. Incredulous at the news of "Tenn's defection," James Laughlin, who had almost walked down the aisle with St. Just, wrote to Wood, "I wonder what part M. plays in all this. I understand that she has been very much in the picture again, and that Tennessee may be with her now. She has many fine qualities, but the intensity of purpose is a little frightening." Rader also saw her as the culprit. "I don't believe he would have broken with Audrey if he had not been under the stress of a new production or if that stress had not been exacerbated by drink and drugs, and if his suspicions had not been reinforced by insinuations against Audrey made by close friends, notably, Maria, Lady St. Just," he wrote.

A telltale clue to St. Just's culpability in the Wood-Williams breakup is her silence about it. St. Just was in the room at the time of the firing and by Williams's side immediately afterward. She also lived on the same floor with him at the hotel, so "she could share the use of my suite which includes parlor, kitchen and a nice little dining room so that I can 'eat in.' . . . I have developed a taste for cooking and Maria is good at it, too." However, at this pivotal event in Williams's career, in *Five O'Clock Angel*—her self-aggrandizing collection of Williams's correspondence, in which in an astonishing act of ventriloquism she is both the subject of the narrative and the omniscient narrator—St. Just puts herself in the room but nowhere near the scene.

For the first three months of 1970, Williams had been full of gratitude for his sobriety and for Wood. "I find myself thinking of you often and with the deepest respect and with an affection I have reserved in my life for fewer persons than I could count on the fingers of one hand," he wrote to her in March, adding, "Time draws short. . . . We must be careful with my last long play!" Together, they agreed on a strategy for *Out Cry*: to pursue Rip Torn and Geraldine Page in America, and Paul Scofield and Margaret Leighton in Britain. On both sides of the Atlantic, however, the actors proved hard to corral, and the play's progress seemed to stall. It was then that the perfervid and proactive St. Just returned to the scene.

The friendship had been on the back burner during Williams's Stoned Age in the late sixties. "I had stupidly feared you'd dismissed me from mind and heart," Williams wrote to her, in March 1970, after receiving a letter she'd written while he was at Barnes. (It had gone undelivered because Wood had refused to give St. Just his hospital address.) Now the relationship was quickly rekindled. Whereas Wood sometimes seemed underinvolved and unavailable to Williams, St. Just was ardent and on call. Williams, who admitted to Wood that he had "little faith left in my own judgment" about *Out Cry*, also started to doubt Wood's faith in him. "My agent Audrey Wood never sends me anything good about me," he complained to Rex Reed. St. Just's unalloyed enthusiasm for the work was in dramatic contrast to Wood's measured admiration. "You have written a poem of extreme, staggering sensitivity and elegance and strength," St. Just told Williams. Among his circle of intimates, St. Just also had the emotional advantage of being untainted by the plot, as Williams saw it, to have him committed. He had cut himself off completely from Dakin (who went so far as to protest outside Williams's Key West house with a placard reading, "TENNESSEE WILLIAMS UNFAIR TO HIS BROTHER"). "I'll never understand why my frantic male sibling, that intrepid actor and statesman, was permitted to put me into the sadistic hands of that threesome," Williams wrote to Wood. The implicit reproach to Wood, whom Williams suspected had been "in on the conspiracy," was clear.

By May 1970, Williams had become sufficiently agitated over the fate of *Out Cry* to face Wood with his fears. "I have a suspicion that you don't really want it produced during my lifetime," he wrote to her, "and don't start thinking I am paranoiac because I entertain such a suspicion . . . since ordinarily by this time, a production would have been set up and scheduled in the foreseeable future, if for no other reason, at least for the psychological comfort of the author. So do please speak up on the subject, I simply don't have any time left anymore for the long, cool, silent treatment."

"Once she got the inkling that Tenn was beginning to get suspicious of someone, she would pee in their ear," Rader said of St. Just's habit of playing on Williams's paranoia. "Obviously Audrey has a pair of wire clippers connected to the New York telephone exchange from her office to the Plaza," St. Just wrote to her "dearly beloved Tenn." "Because the second you said, 'Well, now for Audrey,' there was a crackling sound of burning flesh and a hissing sound. I got a short, sharp electric shock, and I imagine the operator is a small pile of ashes." Part of their "*amitié amour-*

euse," as St. Just dubbed their friendship, was the delicious intimacy of collusion. In July 1970, in a playful poem, Williams appealed for Wood's affection: "Remember me as one of your clients / not the greatest of these, not the least / but in some small way distinguished from all of the others"; by August, he was gleefully betraying it. "I knocked Audrey's little hat off her head this p.m. by informing her that I wanted you to receive 15% of my royalties on this play (if any) and for that tricky lawyer of mine (Alan Schwartz) to get cracking on the 'agreement,'" he swaggered to St. Just. "I feel that you have done far more to advance the production of this play than the Lady Mandarin."

That summer, behind Wood's back, Williams had begun to cut deals for himself. He wired a producer in August:

DO NOT BE CONCERNED IF YOU RECEIVED COMMUNICATION FROM MY AGENT SINCE I INTEND TO ACT QUITE INDEPENDENTLY WITH YOU ON OUR DEALS ON THE WEST COAST. HAVE LATELY DISCOVERED THAT REPRESENTATION SOMETIME OBSTRUCTION

While he complained to Wood that he felt like "a forsaken creature," Williams was quite prepared to do the forsaking himself. In late September 1970, without telling Wood, he deputized St. Just to be his European agent. "It appears for all practical purposes, and some of an entirely spiritual nature, you are now representing me, not Audrey Wood. She will continue to collect her ten percent and I don't begrudge it, but you are now my functioning representative and from now on whatever you place for me, for publication or production, I want you to receive fifteen percent." ("Naturally, I never took the fifteen percent," St. Just said. "I'm not an agent, nor have ever considered myself capable of being one.") What St. Just was looking for wasn't a promotion to agent but a pole position to Williams's heart. For a while, she reigned as his saving angel, albeit of the five o'clock variety. Inevitably, the news put Wood into "one of her Old Testament furies," according to Williams, who now surmised, "No support can be expected from that quarter."

On December 29, 1969, William Liebling, Wood's business partner and husband of thirty-one years, died; she was in mourning. Although

Williams wrote her an eloquent condolence letter, her loss won her a new nickname in his cruel conspiracy with St. Just: "Somehow we must circumvent the machinations of the Widow Wood—never up to no good! . . . oh, I do wish you were here to deal with this situation!—as only you could," Williams wrote to St. Just at the beginning of 1971. In July 1970, Williams had vowed "by hook or crook—any means, however devious" to see *Out Cry* mounted. He was now fully in devious mode. Despite Wood's having written "for the 94th time" to clarify Scofield's position on joining the British cast, Williams had St. Just working on the sly to chase the actor down, and he brazenly went behind Wood's back to petition Schwartz to make overtures to the director John Hancock. "I would like *you* to act as 'liaison' between me and Hancock, not *Audrey*," he wrote.

In his complaints to Schwartz about Wood's dilatory responses, Williams made no reference to the fact that Wood was still grieving. "Audrey informed me on the phone a couple of days ago, in her most elegiac tone, that the scripts had arrived and that she would be reading one at some unspecified date and would let me know her opinion," he wrote to Schwartz. "I said, 'Please don't.'" Williams continued:

> For the past ten years—and the fault may be principally mine—my relations, professional and personal, with this extraordinary woman have undergone a steady deterioration and it has now come to a point where I feel quite convinced that if I am to retain my license to practice as a writer—and if I am not a practicing writer I feel that I am just about nothing—I must somehow by-pass "Miss Wood's office." . . . Although Audrey would probably never admit this even to herself, it is quite apparent to me that she does not want this last long play of mine to be done while I am living. . . . If you wish evidence to support this conviction of mine, I can provide you with it by the boat-load!

Williams could point to a few galling recent confusions in his dealings with Wood. Although, for instance, he had made two trips to New York to rescind Dakin's power of attorney over his corporations—"He is an ethical idiot," Williams said—he was shocked to discover that this hadn't been done. "Why didn't anyone tell me?" he wrote to Wood in late 1970, adding, "After all, I have not accumulated too much money for these years of terrific effort as a writer and it must be protected for my sister and me: neither of us is likely to succeed in a future career." He also claimed to have almost signed a contract with ABC Television, which would have meant that after his death the network could cannibalize his oeuvre to make series about his characters. Because she was in on the deal, Williams claimed, Wood had not brought this fine point to his attention. After his death, he said, she was also planning to develop a Tennessee Williams theme park. "Tennessee was adamant in his belief that such were the evil designs Audrey had on his work, a conspiracy he had discovered and exposed in the nick of time," Rader said. (There is no archival evidence to support Williams's notions.)

One week after their blowup in Chicago, Williams wrote to Wood:

> To quote a line now deleted from the script, "The punctuation marks in life include periods which includes one that is final." It is not a good line in a play but it is a true statement. I feel we have both felt for nearly ten years that a long and mutually beneficial professional relationship was wearing itself thin and has now at last worn itself out. . . .
>
> Of course there are many, many specifics that it would be only hurtful to go into regarding this break in our professional relations. I have been through quite enough of an upsetting nature to feel justified in sparing myself a further account of why the change must be made.
>
> I hope you will be as willing as I am to remember only the many good things about our relationship and forget what is unpleasant and could only hurt us both.
>
> I hope you will still regard me as a friend.

Over the next couple of months, Williams and Wood made stabs at civility; a few cordial letters were exchanged. Wood now worked for International Creative Management (ICM), one of the most powerful agencies in the entertainment industry; Bill Barnes, a new recruit to ICM, was suggested as a suitable replacement for Wood. He was handsome, Southern, and gay; formerly he had been an assistant to Otto Preminger. According to Rader, Milton Goldman, the head of ICM's theater department, saw this as "a temporary holding action until things with Audrey could be patched up."

Many months later, while Wood was having Sunday brunch at the Algonquin with the novelist Sidney Sheldon, she heard a voice say, "Hello, Audrey," and saw a hand extended in her direction. Instinctively, Wood reached out to take it. She looked up; Williams was standing in front of her. "Then something happened over which I had no control. My hand involuntarily withdrew," Wood said. Williams stalked away angrily; Wood excused herself from the table and stepped into the hotel lobby to calm herself with deep breaths and tranquilizers. The encounter brought into focus the depth of her wound. The friendship, which had sustained them both for more than three decades, was no longer possible. "There was no way she could take him back," Arthur Kopit, another of Wood's stable of star playwrights, who visited with Wood in her Westport cottage soon after she'd been fired, said. "Maybe if Liebling had still been alive she could have. She was a very proud woman, and he had done something terrible to her. She could not allow it to happen again."

No playwright-agent relationship in American theater history had had a longer or more glorious story than Williams's partnership with Wood. "She was way more than an agent to him, and she knew it," Kopit said. "She had no children of her own. Her clients were her children, and Williams was No. 1 son." Wood had been a kind of taproot, a connection to the idealism and the adventurousness of Williams's literary journey. Without her keen critical eye, her deep knowledge of the theater, and her understanding of his complex personality, he was adrift, with no one to guide him. In the course of a year, the bulwarks of Williams's emotional and professional support—Wood, Marion Vaccaro, Oliver Evans, and Dakin Williams—had either died or become dead to him, and Williams was left more alone than ever, making him easy prey to the mindless Key West brotherhood he gathered around himself. Of that "weird tribe," David Lobdell, Williams's poet pen pal who became his house sitter, wrote, "It has the makings of a good horror movie." Like the characters in *Out Cry*, Williams was now lost in his own theater.

Although Williams had many explanations for his rash act, there was an irrational one that he couldn't directly acknowledge. Wood, with her criticism and her austere presence—"There is much about her that reminds me of eighteenth-century women of note," he said—was a reminder not only of the past but of what *he* had been and knew he could no longer be. She saw—or he thought she saw—that his writing was less powerful than it had been in their salad days. Wood's devotion had been a kind of inspiration; now it was a kind of humiliation. In firing her, Williams was also releasing himself from any obligation to his past, including the obligation to be great. He projected the shame of his own behavior onto Wood. "She found it quite easy to manipulate me when I was too ill and drugged and disintegrated to resist manipulation," he explained defensively in September 1971 to Floria Lasky, his new lawyer. "There has been an outrageous betrayal of trust and that is something which I cannot accept, especially since I gave the betrayer more confidence and license than would any other of her clients, for many years."

To the upbeat Bill Barnes, whom he dubbed "the Dixie Buzz Bomb," Williams wrote, "I feel that since we've met everything has gone for the best, you and I, because there is a wonderful balance between our psychic vibes." Not all of Williams's friends held Barnes in the same esteem. "He is a thoroughly dangerous and faggoty intriguer of the first order," Chuck Bowden wrote in 1972 to St. Just, with whom he had joined forces to produce *Out Cry* in London. "He has Tenn completely mesmerized and under his thumbs, what with pot, whores, personal appearances, spies and his pretensions to being A SOUTHERN GENTLEMAN."

Under his peppy regime, Barnes churned the water while Williams rode the waves. "I need the fact or the illusion of continuing activity in the theatre which is—any theatre—the only real home I have had in so many years," Williams told him. He was, he told Lasky, "boiling with something, and I don't know what it could be if it isn't an absolutely imperative call of action. Audrey keeps insisting that I am crazy. I am. Like a back-house rat! I know exactly where I am at, now, and I am going to *go on!*" The undefined but passionate "something" that Williams described was more profound than the hubbub of his career: he longed for a rebirth. "I am making a number of changes, and pray that God will give me the strength to be a bit of a Phoenix after all," he said.

On Christmas Eve in 1971, Williams sent off the final draft of a new play, *Small Craft Warnings*, to its director, William Hunt. The play, which had begun as the one-act *Confessional*, had been written out of a despair "just this side of final," Williams said. It marked his transition to sobriety and his reconnection with the world. A necessarily cautious work that Williams considered "minor," *Small Craft Warnings* is a collage of mostly static character sketches: a collection of derelict lost souls who gather in a California seaside bar to drink, carouse, look for love, and flounder eloquently in the avant-garde of suffering. It has no plot structure, no real dynamic besides that of language sometimes beautifully used. "I have no intention—and no power—to change it much from that state of being," Williams told Hunt. To the *Times*, he said, "The thing you mustn't lose in life is the quality of surprise. I lost it at the time I was writing this play."

When Harold Clurman came to review *Small Craft Warnings* in the *Nation*, he observed that the play almost felt like a revival—"it repeats the mood and mode of much earlier work." In a way, it did. But after nearly a three-year theatrical absence from New York, Williams had reemerged with a somewhat different song, one that engaged new tropes for newly tempestuous times. The Stonewall riots of June 1969 and his own coy coming-out on *The David Frost Show* in 1970 ("I don't want to be involved in some sort of a scandal, but I've covered the waterfront") had emboldened Williams to portray homosexuality directly for the first time, rather than simply implying it. Because of his complicated, at once unabashed and guilty feelings about his sexuality, Williams was no poster boy for the strident absolutes of the emerging gay liberationists; and despite his increasing interest in progressive politics, he was also avowedly "not a person dedicated primarily to bettering social conditions." He was too oblique and allusive a writer for polemical drama.

Nonetheless, the student demonstrations, the riots at the 1968 Democratic National Convention in Chicago, and the furor of anti-Vietnam protests abroad and political chicanery at home compelled him to embrace the romantic idealism of the youth culture that was rising up around him. "Young people were the world. It was all suddenly visible to me," he said. His primary incentive for mounting *Small Craft Warnings*, he told Hunt, was to explore "the only thing at this point in my life worth my personal belief and conviction": "this possibly ingenuous but truly and deeply felt commitment to what I've observed and experienced in a new generation." He went on, "I have struck an elegiac tone over and over during those awful years when I really had no other note to strike. Now, strangely, you might say incongruously, I do have this new non-elegiac but affirmative thing to say to an audience. And it just might make the difference between rejection and acceptance of the work."

Into his own struggle for psychic regeneration—"I am too ornery a mother to let go," he said—the sixty-year-old Williams had absorbed the youth culture's hankering for radical transformation. Dotson Rader, a baby-faced twenty-nine-year-old writer for the *New Republic* and other magazines, with a left-wing pedigree that included four arrests for protests against the war, was Williams's Chingachgook, a raffish guide to this wild political territory. After a teenage breakdown, the Minnesota-born Rader had rebelled against the strictures of his preacher-father's Puritan fundamentalism and his military-school education and cut out to New York. By the time Williams had met him, he was a contributing editor to the *Evergreen Review*, America's foremost avant-garde magazine and part of Grove Press, which published works by many of the firebrands who were fueling the protest movement: Frantz Fanon, Malcolm X, Abbie Hoffman, Amiri Baraka. Rader was soon to publish a provocative, successful first novel, *Gov't Inspected Meat and Other Fun Summer Things*.

Tall, adventurous, and wayward, Rader knew the counterculture's high-rollers and lower-riders. Dressed in black leathers, Frye cowboy boots, and a black Rancher hat, which he donned for his nighttime crawls with Williams, he even looked the part of pathfinder. Rader's curious mixture of fun and ferment made him a controversial figure among some of Williams's older, stuffier friends, including Vidal, St. Just, and Ruth Ford, but that only added to his renegade appeal for Williams, who enjoyed setting the cat among the pigeons. Rader was, Williams said, "indispensable" to his project of staying contemporary. "You gave me charm and lightness and I love you for it," Williams told him later.

Rader was in his full outlaw regalia the first time he met Williams, at a SoHo party, where he was introduced by his friend Candy Darling, the drag queen and Andy Warhol "Superstar," who was Williams's date (and who would be cast as a replacement for the hapless and homeless Violet, in the original production of *Small Craft Warnings*). "We both seemed much older than we were," Rader said, recounting Williams's flirtatious opening conversation in his memoir:

> "How much do you get a night?"
> "One hundred bucks," I replied, playing along.
> He paused, rolling his blue eyes at Candy, his heavy black-rimmed glasses slipping down his nose. "Well, baby, what do you charge to escort an older gentleman to dinner?"
> "Fifty bucks."
> Feigning shock, he felt in his pockets for money, pulled out a few bills. . . . "Do you suppose we could settle for *lunch*?"

"I want to meet your underground friends," Williams wrote to Rader in August 1971. "Would they take me seriously or just say, 'Oh, that old fart!' And put me on? It will not be easy for you to make your friends believe in me as, for so many years, I have passed as an establishment writer because they preferred to see me that way, never bothered to get the message at all."

With Rader, Williams went places and met people far outside his usual ambit—young people who didn't know him or want anything from him. "How liberating that was!" Rader said. "It must have been like when he was young and still unknown and penniless. When people liked him for himself. The affection was disinterested." The pair spent a lot of time in subterranean New York haunts. "In a night, we'd go to dinner, two-three parties, two-three bars, and pick up people as we went, ending up back at whatever hotel or apartment he was at. The laughter went on until late," Rader said. "Being places where respectable people thought it unsuitable to be seen, he formed a kind of cockeyed solidarity with those who shared with him a hatred of the rich . . . the cake-eaters who despoil the poor, who eat the earth." Williams told Rader, "For you . . . being part of the movement has become a bit too familiar . . . but for me it is quite fresh and exhilarating as mountain air."

With Dotson Rader, 1972

Among the things that attracted Williams to the antiwar movement, according to Rader, "was the fact that young people, most especially those committed to media-centered action, made him feel alive, in contact with history, in a way that books and theatre did not." Through them, he was able to rejoin life and the cultural conversation. "My bringing Tennessee to anti-war and other left events—demonstrations, protests, meetings—didn't make him radical," Rader said. "It simply brought him home politically to the place where his heart already was. He detested authority in general, and felt like an outsider with no loyalty to the undemocratic dominant class, which is why he didn't vote anymore."

Williams, who was by his own admission "drifting almost willfully out of contact with the world," may not have gone in search of the bold-faced names of the counterculture, but he found them. Rader introduced him to leading feminists (Kate Millett, Jill Johnston, Betty Friedan), underground figures (Robert Mapplethorpe, Christopher Makos, Parker Tyler, Charles Ludlam, Gregory Corso, Cal Culver), and uptown grandees (Peter Glenville, Pat Kennedy Lawford, George Plimpton, Ruth Carter Stapleton, Anthony Perkins). Williams also kept company with some of the movers and shakers of the Movement (Dave Dellinger, Tom Seligson, Abbie and Anita Hoffman, Jerry Rubin, Carl Oglesby, Gus Hall, William Kunstler). Over time, Dellinger, the radical pacifist, became an admired friend to whom Williams later lent his Key West house. Williams also befriended Eric Mann, of Students for a Democratic Society, and Mark Kluz, who had been imprisoned for his antiwar activities. (Williams thought of these men as "pure revolutionaries," but in his own political enthusiasms he was no purist. Offered a choice between going dancing with gay friends on Fire Island and meeting Daniel Berrigan, the Catholic priest and activist who was on the FBI's Ten Most Wanted List, Williams chose Fire Island.)

When New York's Governor Nelson Rockefeller let the National Guard and state troopers loose on rioting Attica prisoners in 1971, a decision that resulted in forty-three deaths, Williams and Rader joined the outraged public protest. "It is impossible to overstate how morally repugnant the system was in his eyes," Rader said. Of the Left's challenge to authority, Williams wrote to Rader:

> It becomes very easy, thinking of it, to abandon hope: but that hope is all that we've got: to give meaning to our lives. . . . The bright side is the strength of our moral leadership: the blacks ("We're willing to do the dying"). The unwavering resolution of Dave Dellinger and the brilliance of his mind, tempered by humanity. That quality in Abbie Hoffman that made me feel in the presence of a holy man. And all our true caring for each other. It really is, for me, a religious conversion, my first one that is ~~socially~~ humanly meaningful. We must be constantly on guard against finks and ego-trippers and opportunists. There are questions we mustn't even ask, information we must not have, such as: do we have an arsenal? Are we armed at all, in case it comes to fighting for our lives. . . . I am not yet ready to know Weathermen or share their

secrets, not because I can't be trusted but because it is mortal danger to trust almost anybody—the blacks are right about that.

Inevitably, to raise both money and visibility for the Movement, Williams was drawn into political action by Rader, who was helping put together a massive benefit on December 6, 1971, at the Cathedral of St. John the Divine. The Peoples Coalition for Peace and Justice, which was organizing the event, had gathered a panoply of celebrity supporters in order to break the press blackout on their activities and "to subvert the media image of protesters as a bunch of wild-eyed, drug-crazed violent hippies trying to overthrow the government," according to Rader. Unbeknownst to Williams, Rader had included Williams's name on the letterhead of the "Remember the War" Benefit Committee—in a list that included, among other distinguished and outspoken progressives, Rennie Davis, Jules Feiffer, Susan Sontag, Paul Goodman, and Martin Duberman. Williams, however, was balky about being used as bait for the mass media. "I must be rehabilitated as a playwright before I can offer much power to the movement," he told Rader. "Baby, I am wise as a shit house rat and know what I'm doing. You will hear and see. I got politics in my blood, and you know that I can use it to both our advantage if I do it my way."

Williams's way was to write a poem entitled "Ripping off the Mother" for *Evergreen Review,* and a polemic, "We Are Dissenters Now," for *Harper's Bazaar*—and to donate both fees to the People's Coalition. In the *Harper's Bazaar* piece, Williams railed against "pig-dom." Invoking the pioneer heritage of his distinguished family tree, he recounted how one of his female ancestors had been scalped by Indians but survived. "Some of her [blood] is still running on through my arteries this morning shouting to you 'Right on.'" Williams continued, "We're all dissenters now. . . . You don't have to spell America with a 'k' to know the condition it is in. . . . More than one side can cry 'Charge!' and surely the side with love for and faith in humanity will finally prevail over those whose faith is only in death and whose love is a lust for blood."

Still, Rader pressed Williams for more active participation. He wanted him to speak at the event: the playwright's first public statement against the Vietnam War would obviously be newsworthy. But Williams proved hard to snare. In mid-November, in desperation, Rader wired him:

> IF WE DO NOT ACT TO END WAR AND RACISM THEN HOW WILL IT EVER END. THE FROST SHOW ON THE 24TH AND THE CAVETT SHOW ON THE 26TH ARE ESSENTIAL. WE CANNOT GET AIR TIME WITHOUT YOU. WE ARE COUNTING ON YOU

"I am certainly in favor of those great abstractions but the prospect of talking politics is alarming," Williams wrote to his director, William Hunt. "Being a human centipede I will probably manage to get all 100 feet in my mouth at once."

In the end, he capitulated to Rader and came north to do his bit for the People's Coalition. On the day of the event, wearing a sort of Confederate uniform in a misguided attempt to look young and cool, Williams, accompanied by Bill Barnes and a camera crew from the Canadian Broadcasting Company, who were filming him, arrived to take part in the exercise in radical chic. Williams sat in the fourth row with Rader and the British director Peter Glenville, while Charles Mingus, the Chambers Brothers, Phil Ochs, and Edgar Winter and White Trash performed for the nearly five thousand people who had paid up to fifty dollars a ticket to show their solidarity. A parade of speakers followed: the Episcopal bishop of New York Paul Moore Jr., Gloria Steinem, Ossie Davis, David Dellinger, and Williams. "I am too old to march anymore," Williams said in his peroration. "No, no!" the audience yelled back. Williams held up his hand for silence. "But I will march on paper!"

Williams sat down to an ovation. He was followed by Norman Mailer's forty-five-minute protest play *Why Are We in Vietnam?*—a work whose profanity on the cathedral's high altar so offended Williams that he stalked out in protest. "Suddenly 'The Movement' was unmasked for me by the Cathedral's desecration and by the display of shallow exhibitionism," he wrote later. "By the drugs, the decadence, the spitefulness and finally by the hideous blasphemies of the play." He remembered the benefit as "probably the most shocking and disillusioning experience of my life, which has contained a great deal of shock and disillusionment." The event, an organizational fiasco that ended up losing nearly ten thousand dollars, put a crimp in his relationship with Rader and brought a full stop to Williams's political activism. "I avoided all affiliations of a political nature all of my life till I met you," he wrote to Rader. "And I'm going to avoid them totally from now on."

Still, the rhetoric of the protest movement stayed with him—and was built into his Last Will and Testament, which was written on June 21, 1972, and witnessed by Rader. In it, Williams requested a burial at sea, in the Caribbean, north of Havana, near the spot where Hart Crane took his life. The document instructed that his obsequies were "to be conducted by my revolutionary comrades . . . those desiring freedom from an imperialistic and militaristic regime." Williams's jejune quest had led to some enduring and defining emotional knowledge. In himself and in the embattled political world around him—"this ambience of continual dreadfulness"—he registered a growing barbarity. "I was thinking last night . . . that there has been a terrible erosion of the capacity for sympathy and for pity among us all," he wrote to Rader that July. "So much horror . . . the heart wears out the breast and we stop feeling as we did for each other."

THAT PSYCHIC NUMBING found its way into the rewrites of *Small Craft Warnings*, in a soliloquy delivered by Quentin—a washed-up homosexual screenwriter, in blazer and ascot, who has "a quality of sexlessness, not effeminacy"—that Williams considered "the finest writing I've done since the early plays"; it was also the finest he would do in the last decade of his theatrical life:

QUENTIN: . . . There's a coarseness, a deadening coarseness, in the experience of most homosexuals. The experiences are quick, and hard, and brutal, and the pattern of them is practically unchanging. Their act of love is like the jabbing of a hypodermic needle to which they're addicted but which is more and more empty of real interest and surprise. This lack of variation and surprise in their . . . "love life" . . . (*He smiles harshly.*) . . . spreads into other areas of . . . "sensibility"? (*He smiles again.*) . . . Yes, once, quite a long time ago, I was often startled by the sense of being alive, of being *myself, living!* Present on earth, in

the flesh, yes, for some completely mysterious reason, a single, separate, intensely conscious being, *myself: living*! . . . Whenever I would
feel this . . . *feeling*, this . . . shock of . . . what? . . . self-realization? . . .
I would be stunned, I would be thunderstruck by it. And by the existence of everything that exists, I'd be lightning-struck with astonishment . . . it would do more than astound me, it would give me a feeling
of panic, the sudden sense of . . . I suppose it was like an epileptic
seizure, except that I didn't fall to the ground in convulsions; no, I'd be
more apt to try to lose myself in a crowd on a street until the seizure
was finished. . . . They were dangerous seizures. One time I drove into
the mountains and smashed the car in a tree, and I'm not sure if I
meant to do that, or . . . In a forest you'll sometimes see a giant tree,
several hundred years old, that's scarred, that's blazed by lightning,
and the wound is almost obscured by the obstinately still living and
growing bark. I wonder if such a tree has learned the same lesson that
I have, not to feel astonishment anymore but just to go on, continue for
two or three hundred years more? . . . This boy I picked up tonight, the
kid from the tall corn country, still has the capacity for being surprised
by what he sees, hears and feels in this kingdom of earth. All the way
up the canyon to my place, he kept saying, *I can't believe it, I'm here,
I've come to the Pacific, the world's greatest ocean!* . . . as if nobody,
Magellan or Balboa or even the Indians had ever seen it before him;
yes, like he'd discovered this ocean, the largest on earth, and so now,
because he'd found it himself, it existed, now, for the first time, never
before. . . . And this excitement of his reminded me of my having lost
the ability to say: "My God!" instead of just: "Oh, well."

Williams went into rehearsals feeling, as he wrote to Bill Barnes, that
the play "can do no harm, even if it fails to do good."

Still, the rehearsals were fraught. Hunt was dismissed; for a time,
until Richard Altman was hired to finish the job, Williams himself served
as director. "I certainly had no desire to take over direction, but I felt
obliged to since all the stage movements seemed arbitrary," Williams
said. "Someone has just told me that when I took over the direction the
leading lady said, 'Why should I take direction from this old derelict?'"

On Easter Sunday, April 2, 1972, *Small Craft Warnings* opened at the Truck and Warehouse Theater, near the Bowery, a venue that Williams thought a "metaphor for posterity," signaling a change in fortune if not in style. The Easter opening worried Williams, for it might give the critics a stick with which to beat him. "They'll say the Resurrection didn't come off," he joked. If *Small Craft Warnings* wasn't exactly a resurrection and wasn't exactly a hit, it was still a comeback of sorts. The reviews were mixed. "The critics in New York are no longer inclined to make allowances for my advanced age nor for the dues I've paid," Williams complained to St. Just after the opening. "They keep saying, 'This is not up to Williams' best, such as *Streetcar* and *Cat*'—Well, for Chrissake, how could it be? If it were a major play such as 'Out Cry,' it would not have opened at the Truck and Warehouse in the Bowery, would it?"

In fact, the reviews of *Small Craft Warnings* were sufficiently positive to give Williams hope that the narrative about his work might be changing. *Show*, a posh short-lived theater magazine, ran a long article subtitled "The Revitalization of a Great Dramatist," and Clive Barnes's review in the *New York Times* concluded that *Small Craft Warnings* "may survive better than some of the much-touted products of his salad years." In *Time*, Ted Kalem welcomed the play as "a five-finger exercise from the man who is the greatest living playwright in the Western world." "Surely you meant 'playboy of the Western World'—but never mind," Williams quipped, when thanking Kalem for his "incredibly beautiful notice."

Small Craft Warnings turned out to be Williams's most successful new theatrical outing in nearly a decade; it played two hundred performances, in a run of nearly six months. That June, when ticket sales dipped, and the actor playing Doc—a doctor who has lost his license to drink but practices clandestinely—left for a four-day film gig just as the play was transferring to the New Theatre uptown, Williams stepped in. "Goddam it, no, I will play it myself!" he told the producers, who took him up on the offer. "A star is born," Williams wrote to St. Just. "We have played to packed houses. And no cabbages thrown. I guess I have to admit that I am a ham and that I loved it." Although Williams's performances gave the show a commercial kiss of life, onstage he was something of a loose cannon, prone to ad lib. "He never shut up," the actress Peg Murray, a veteran of three of Williams's late plays, said. The other actors never knew when their cue was coming. "Just watch his lips," William Hickey, who played Steve, a short-order cook, said. "When they stop moving, you come in." When nobody was depending on him for a cue, however, as Murray recalled, "he was wonderful in the part."

That September, *Small Craft Warnings* was forced to close, to make way for *Oh, Coward!*, a Noël Coward musical revue ("a pair of jerks imitating Gertie Lawrence and Nelly Coward in a nostalgic tribute to their— whatever they did," Williams called it). In the last few days of the run, Williams's behavior, by his own admission, became alarming. In a rage over the impending closure, he ranted at the theater management in his opening monologue ("A synonym for a manager in the theatre is a con-man—and all playwrights are shits with their back to the wall") and threw a glass at the audience. In another performance, in a scene in which Doc returns from losing a mother and her baby in a botched deliv-

Playing "Doc" in the Off-Broadway production of his *Small Craft Warnings*, 1972

ery and is asked how things went, Williams replied loudly, "Not as bad as they'll go at the New Theatre tomorrow if they close us for Nelly Coward." At one performance, when a heavy-set drunk in the audience shouted abuse at the stage, Williams leapt off the proscenium. "We were all terrified," Murray recalled. "This little round man in his white suit went up to this big guy. 'You will not insult the artists!' Tennessee said. It was overwhelming."

Earlier in the run, the management had complained about Williams's failure to project his voice, but toward the end he said, "I was belting out every line like Ethel Merman through an amplifier. . . . I guess I am just getting a bit bored with so-called 'rational behavior' now in these 'vintage years.'"

For a decade, drama critics had been reminding Williams that he was a thing of the past; now, some zealous members of the gay liberation movement were also calling him a relic of reactionary times gone by. "Tennessee, look, an army of lovers is beginning to arise. It is being born from among the victims, the queers, the women you were among the first to love," Mike Silverstein wrote in an open letter on the pages of *Gay Sunshine* in 1971. "We were queer like you, victims like you. But now we are gay, no longer accepting our victimization, and proudly proclaiming our humanity." Silverstein, a fan, addressed Williams demanding a new narrative; other activists were less polite, characterizing Williams as a fogy, whose writing had no purchase on homosexual reality.

In a 1972 *New York Times* article, "Why Do Homosexual Playwrights Hide Their Homosexuality?," for instance, "Lee Barton"—a pseudonymous writer who had also written "Nightride," an Off-Broadway drama about a black-white gay marriage—wrote from the perspective of a man looking forward to "the 'freed' generation": "One work of art dealing truthfully with homosexual life is worth a hundred breast-beating personal confessions," he said, throwing down the gauntlet. "Who really gives a damn that Tennessee Williams has finally admitted his sexual preferences in print. He has yet to contribute any work of understanding to gay theater, and with his enormous talent one of his works would indeed be worth any amount of personal data." Williams responded a month later in the *Village Voice*: "I feel sorry for the author. He makes the mistake of thinking I've concealed something in my life because he writes under a pseudonym. I've nothing to conceal. Homosexuality isn't the theme of my plays. They're about all human relationships. I've never faked it."

Years later, in a reply to an annihilating *Gay Sunshine* review of Williams's *Memoirs*, which called his plays "lies" and "complicated misrepresentations of reality," Williams took issue at length with the "shocking misapprehension of my work" and with the review's rhetorical incivility, inadvertently underscoring the distance between Williams's view of himself as the "founding father of the uncloseted gay world" and that of the bumptious new generation:

> Now, surely, Mr. Dvosin, you don't believe that the precise sexual orientation of a character in a play is what gives validity to the play. Is there such a thing as precise sexual identity in life? I've never encountered it in sixty-five years of living and getting about widely. Nearly every person I've known has either two or three sexual natures, that of the male, the female, and that of the androgynic, which is far from being a derogatory classification to my way of feeling and thinking. Now, a confession: I contain all three. The reason that I have no difficulty at all in creating female characters is because, in my psyche, there is a little congregation of panicky ladies and/or tramps. Why panicky? Because they are confined there. . . . I have always had something to say in my plays, which was more important to the play, to me, to the audiences than the non-existent thing, a precise sexual identity of a character. Have you read my plays, have you seen them performed in the theatre as well as in the usually distorted film-versions? I doubt it, somehow. . . . Finally, can you really think of a reason why a person like myself—one of divided (psychic) gender—should find it difficult or at all disagreeable to write about love, sexual or spiritual between a woman and a man? I tell you honestly, it was always to me as natural as a duck taking to water or a bird to the air. I could say what I needed to

say as easily through love-scenes between a man and woman as I could between two Gays: that I swear.

So where's the lie?

I feel it would be more profitable for you to look for rigidities and repressions in your attitude as a reviewer, in this instance.

Over the years, Williams had been the target of repeated homophobic abuse, both from the press and from the Key West locals. "There are a great many people in this town who don't like Tenn, who feel that he is a disgrace to the town and who take it upon themselves to 'punish' him," David Lobdell wrote. Junk was frequently thrown over the fence, plants urinated on, eggs and gunshot blasts aimed at the house, obscene calls received late at night, and obscenities shouted from passing cars. "Certain people on the streets look at me as if to say, 'I know who you are,'" Lobdell added.

The threat was real. In the late seventies, while sauntering down Duval Street singing Southern hymns, Williams and Rader encountered a group of five young men seated on a concrete planter on the sidewalk. As they sang, the men accosted them and announced that they knew who Williams was. One of them had a knife. Rader wanted to run and grabbed Williams's sleeve; Williams shook him off. "My name is Tennessee Williams! And I am not in the habit of retreat!" he said to the punks. Rader was punched in the mouth; Williams was pushed on top of him. Williams and Rader both took a kicking, but Williams had stood his ground. To face down the bullying gay libs—"to whom my heart is committed, categorically, in a bruised-ass way"—Williams adopted the same kind of gallant staunchness. But he was shaken, nonetheless.

On the first day of 1972, he confided to Bill Barnes that the "relentless thing called time" was taking its toll. "I feel like it's running out on me," he said. "I feel so OLD," he told one reporter after *Small Craft Warnings* opened. "You know people want you to be rejuvenated at sixty-one. One can't be rejuvenated at sixty-one. One must consider one's vascular system." To the *Saturday Review*, a couple of weeks later, he said, "At sixty-one you do not expect your powers to increase, you know, unless you're crazy. . . . The power of a writer is very closely related to sexuality,

sexual power. Not that I have lost my sexual power. No, that is very persistent. But there is a decline in sexual security, of mental assurance."

Williams's insecurity was compounded by the decline of his body,
which gravity seemed to be pulling inexorably toward the earth: his eyes,
his cheeks, his neck, his stomach were sagging. ("Time had interred his
looks," Truman Capote wrote, in a thinly disguised, malicious portrait of
Williams—whom he described as a "chunky, paunchy, booze-puffed
runt"—in "Answered Prayers," which was published in installments in
Esquire between 1975 and 1976.) When Williams looked in the mirror,
he saw a person he characterized as "fat," "ugly," "unattractive," no longer
"presentable with my clothes off." "Perhaps I'll have a face-lift—a bit of
counterfeit youth, well, at least middle-age, could improve my chances,"
he wrote in a late diary. (He eventually got an "eye-lift.")

In an effort to recover and feed off the memory of his youth, Williams
began to write his autobiography, which crosscut between his current life
and his past—"an aging man's almost continual scuttling back and forth
between his recollections and his present state," he said. He also submerged himself in a new work titled *Vieux Carré*, a reimagining of his life
at 722 Toulouse Street, the New Orleans boardinghouse where his literary adventure and his sexual coming-of-age had begun. This surge of
creative energy coincided with a surge in romantic agitation. "My best
work was always done when I was deeply in love," he told the *Saturday
Review* in April 1972. Sometime near the beginning of his adventure
with the New York staging of *Small Craft Warnings*, Williams met a
handsome, pony-tailed, twenty-five-year-old veteran who had survived
three years of military service in Southeast Asia, and who was writing a
novel mostly about Vietnam and "the charm of the Orientals," Williams
said. His name was Robert Carroll. "I was comforted greatly during this
time of durance vile by [his] nightly presence . . . and even more so by his
daily presence," Williams wrote to a Washington friend.

"Little Robert," as Williams called him, was the son of a coal miner
from West Virginia, the youngest of nine children who had lost touch with
his family. At least that was the story that Williams told and seemed to
believe. "Robert was very, very, very quiet about his life pre-Tennessee,"
Rader said. Williams was smitten. "He drives well, cooks very well,

With Robert Carroll

and is sexually permissive to my occasional wishes," Williams said.
But there was nothing femme about Carroll; he was streetwise, independent, impetuous, and Southern. He looked out at the world over his
wire-rimmed glasses with a skeptic's impudent, practiced indifference.
He had disabused himself of all certainties; he was no sycophant. At
once un-biddable and untameable, unknowable and unreachable, Carroll
appeared to be unimpressed by Williams's fame, his theatrical milieu,
and even, sometimes, Williams himself. A temperamental maverick—"he
alternates in moods like mistral and sirocco," Williams said—Carroll
didn't want to be made over in a relationship; he wanted to be left alone.
In fact, when Rader was first introduced to Carroll at a New York party,

he noticed that "Tennessee would touch him, and Robert would pull way. Robert sort of kept his distance from Tennessee." "There was something about him like a coiled cat," Rader recalled. "You never knew when he was gonna spring. He could turn on Tennessee just as quickly as he could turn on someone who was a danger to Tennessee, which is what Frank [Merlo] was known for. He kind of acted as a bodyguard."

"My young writer friend, the Enfant Terrible, has been mysteriously difficult," Williams told St. Just, who thought it "a disastrous and destructive liaison." But in Carroll's prickly, paradoxical personality—defiant and depressed, ambitious and impoverished—Williams recognized some part of himself, "a nature I know to be as difficult and torturous as my own." Years later he would salute Carroll as "Traveller, stranger, son—my friend"; even in the early stages of their relationship, his bond to Carroll was almost filial. In October 1972, he reported "a beautiful dream" in which "I had a new brother, a few months old but already on the streets, hard to keep up with. I loved him very dearly and I remarked to Maria, who was with me, searching for him, 'He is the only one of us that has the eyes of my grandmother and he's just a few months old but is already brighter than Dakin.'"

Unlike many of Williams's crew of haphazard companions who were his intellectual inferiors, Carroll had the brains, the backbone, and the vocabulary both to fight and to delight Williams, who compared his imagistic stream-of-consciousness writing to the work of Carson McCullers. For the first time since 1946, when he and McCullers had written at opposite ends of a Nantucket kitchen table, Williams was able to create in the same room as someone else. In New York, Carroll worked on a rental typewriter at the coffee table and Williams at his desk. In Key West, writing in different shifts, they shared Williams's studio. (Williams also installed Carroll in the Key West "master bedroom," clearing away the madonna, the vigil candle, the Hindu god, the photo of Rose, and the scarlet silk cloth from the little tabernacle where he'd prayed after his conversion to Catholicism, to make room for the person who seemed to be the answer to his prayers.)

When Williams and Merlo first got together, Williams had lamented, "My name for him is Little Horse. / I wish he had a name for me"; early in the relationship with Carroll, Carroll gave Williams a nickname, one with a typically sardonic kick: "Hound Dog" (for his "cryin' all the time"). Often Williams's baying was over the absence of the feckless Carroll, who had a habit of wandering off the compound for days at a time. To Williams, for whom absence was always the route to desire, Carroll's mercurial nature—intimate and elusive, sweet and abusive, seductive and hard—made him a tantalizing figure. In the unpublished poem "Robert," Williams wrote:

> Where is Robert?
> Gone away.
>
> Willingly?
> Who can say . . .
>
> Ever lesser
> to be known
>
> Living flower
> or flower of stone.

In October 1972, while waiting in the early hours for Carroll to return home from a date, Williams wrote a mutual friend, "He got himself a ravishingly becoming pair of black and white striped double-knit slacks, a black t-shirt that sets off his bewitching tan as well as the slacks did his almost incomparable little ass, and after delivering me to the little compound here on Duncan Street, he sashayed off again in our rental car and has yet to return at 6:15 a.m.—I have a dreadful feeling that all of those vigil lights in the cathedral have blown out tonight."

At once thrilled and pained by Carroll's comings and goings, Williams sometimes colluded in his companion's disappearing acts. "He has a young (twenty-year-old) admirer in town," Williams reported to Harry Rasky, who was making a documentary on Williams that October. "I did not complain when he stayed out all night the first time with the youth: and last night the youth returned at my invitation and I stayed at the opposite end of the pool while the intimacies occurred, not even looking at them, and went to bed while they remained in progress." Williams went on, *"Mais le coeur a ses raisonne que la raison ne connait pas.* And when I woke up long past midnight and discovered that they had retired to my studio, I really blew it. I mean it. It blew my mind, and I shouted to Robert, 'If you don't get that bitch on his two wheels'—he came on a bike—'I am going to do it much less pleasantly than you would!'"

THE TUG OF WAR between Williams and Carroll was a drama that played out for years, lending eventfulness to what Williams saw as his flat-lining career. In June 1972, in a spirit of capricious desperation, Williams had double-crossed St. Just and Bowden, who for nearly a year, at his instigation, had been hard at work setting up a production of *Out Cry* in London with Paul Scofield. Instead, with Barnes's encouragement, Williams jumped at a Broadway production starring Michael York and directed by the British director Peter Glenville. For a while, St. Just stopped speaking to him, and she made a show of returning the copyright of the play to Williams. "All rights, moral, or in writing, have no meaning," she said. The Broadway staging of *Out Cry*, which Williams later referred to as "Glenville's abortion," was a disaster: devastating reviews closed the show on March 10, 1973, nine days after its opening. "You don't recover from a failure like 'Out Cry,'" Williams said, adding, "I feel like my writing career is washed up. I go on writing but it means nothing to me."

Williams's relationship with Carroll was equally bewildering. Carroll's moods, Williams reported to St. Just, continued to alternate between "great sweetness to me" and "down-right beastliness of behavior which makes it all but impossible for me to go out with him in public." Carroll's unsuitable dress, his surly silences, his habit of introducing himself as a "hired companion" disconcerted Williams and his friends. Despite his feigned indifference to Williams's fame, Carroll's impulse to rob Williams of his power, even in a social context, broadcast his envy. In Positano, Italy, for instance, at a lunch party given by Franco Zeffirelli, Carroll ignored the guests and, according to Williams, "just lay there chain-smoking. Franco whispered to me, *'Maria a ragione'*"—Maria is right. (St. Just had dubbed Carroll "the Twerp" and had, according to Williams, an "implacable Tartar hatred for him.") Williams suspected Carroll's moods were drug-induced. "That 'grass' he smokes is making him 'un peu dérangé,'" Williams told St. Just. "A little period of separation seems to be in order since I must not be bugged while 'Out Cry' is going on." Carroll was a kind of psychic shadow of Williams—at his best, a lifeline, and, at his worst, an embodiment of Williams's own rage at himself. Like Felice and Clare in *Out Cry*, the two tussled in an unbreakable, confounding embrace.

Williams's increasing difficulty with Carroll as a travel companion added to his depression. In Bangkok, Carroll not only insisted on having his own room; he wanted it to be in a different hotel. "I said: 'You find me intolerable.' He said: 'I find you repulsive.'—And I said, going into my Blanche bit, 'Not as repulsive as you'll be a year from now.'" By the time they arrived in Positano at the end of May 1973, the skirmishing had escalated into something like outright war. One night, over dinner, Carroll "was talking persistently about a wish to kill himself," Williams wrote to St. Just. "I finally got fed up and said, 'Oh, you mustn't do that, it would please too many people!'"

A few days later, Williams sent up warning flares to Bill Barnes. "The co-habitation with Carroll is approaching its pre-destined finish," he said. "He is an insupportable drain on my nerves this summer which I must devote to things that restore me such as work, swimming and gentle society. Oh, how home-sick I get for gentle voices and people—I've had my share of the opposite." Williams added, "This sick person continually hassles me about money, pretends not to receive weekly pay-checks insults people quite gratuitously and could isolate me from all agreeable society. I know I'm up-tight about it but I have endured it too long. The bed-sweetness, I'm afraid, is a professional trick. And I can do without it." By the end of his Positano stay, Williams was living alone. "It turned out that 'enigmatic' does not completely describe him," he wrote to Oliver Evans. "Just before his departure he threatened to kill me."

The breakup was a temporary one, however. Back in Key West, that October, Williams wrote to St. Just about Carroll's latest scene: "The West Virginia Kid suddenly decided yesterday to smash up all his possessions including a camera that cost him $260 in Vietnam and is worth $800 in the States: then practically all his clothes.—I have locked his mss. in my studio to save them from destruction, too." He added, "Of course you won't believe this, but his revised book, *Old Children*, is a terrifyingly beautiful accomplishment: yet he wants to destroy it." Two years later, when Williams and Carroll arrived in England to spend Christmas with St. Just, she insisted that Carroll be dispatched to Morocco for the holiday. At first Carroll agreed, then "abruptly decided he wouldn't leave till I did," Williams said. "The best I could do was to move him to a different hotel—a rather nice one on Half Moon Street. . . . Then one night he went berserk. Got hold of barbiturates, took enough to go into a coma and towards evening they transferred him by ambulance to a public hospital where he broke a window, a door, struck a 'Sister' and landed in a straight-jacket in a padded cell." He added, "For hours I could get very little information about him. Then at last I got him released after paying a large sum in 'damages' and he is now back at the Fleming—still sleeping off injections they gave him."

In Williams's descriptions of Carroll's scenes—at once awful and thrilling—there is a kind of startled innocence. Williams was perpetually grieving for the genuine self who had been sacrificed to his fame. Carroll's sensational recklessness had the whiff of the authentic; it made a spectacle of all that Williams had lost. "When Tenn was with Robert, stoned or sober, he had to be on his toes, alive, alert," Rader said. "It didn't thrill Tennessee, but it brought him into life. It slapped him awake." Over the years of fights, separations, reunions, and expulsions, the relationship had intensity in place of intimacy. "You see, you had laid a heavy number on the head of the old hound dog," he wrote to Carroll in the late seventies. "But the dog is faithful of heart and would doubtless tag your heels to the end of the earth if permitted. We are roving creatures, being born of woman, we are full of sorrow and not inclined to long stays. Yet I've always wished it could be together, a restless caravan for two."

In 1978, on a flight to San Juan, the caravan came a cropper. "Robert seemed to be going through a terrible mental crisis, probably drug-induced, possibly systemic," Williams wrote.

He never flies with grass, being afraid of narcs, but crazes himself with booze. On the flight over to San Juan he had six double rums and went berserk. Shouted "This plane is full of Jews!"—which happened to be a true observation but nearly provoked a riot. Then when the handsome young steward refused to serve him more drinks he denounced him as a faggot. Finally, he started hammering on the door to the pilot's cabin which might have got him shot as a suspected hijacker. It is now clear to me that he can't leave Key West anymore, unless it is to be for a stay at the Veteran's Hospital for withdrawal from these angel-dusted joints.

Back in New Orleans that November, Pancho Rodriguez, the violent man of Williams's youth, bore witness to the violent man of Williams's old age. "My beloved Genius is in town for a few days," Rodriguez reported. "Seems he and Robert arrived in New Orleans ten days ago and as they were checking into the apartment Robert started attacking him, refusing to take Tennessee's bags upstairs. Before you knew it, Robert was on top of him, Tennessee was yelling for help, and the tenants came out to the rescue. The police came, Robert was incarcerated, but bailed himself out. Ten flew out next morning for California and came back Sunday with the companionship of a very intelligent young man by the name of David Peterson who will remain with him indefinitely. Tennessee claims Robert had been acting up for some time and he had to be put away. I always found him silent and evasive. Of course, there are two sides to every story. It takes two to tango." Rodriguez went on, "I see the Great One again tonight. . . . Out of all this will emerge another tempestuous, violent masterpiece."

Until Carroll was evicted for keeps in the late seventies—"I hope to see you some day when you have proven the strength that I think is latent in you—but not until then. . . . I must avoid further calls upon my exhausted resources," Williams wrote to him—he lived apart from Williams in a small guesthouse next to the studio by the pool. But the years of ruction and anxiety took their imaginative toll on Williams. "Robert was far more confident of his hold over Tennessee than Tenn was sure of

OPPOSITE PAGE: "Torito" and Pancho

his control over Robert," Rader said. "And control was what it was all about. . . . Whether intentionally or not, this endless battle for control between Tenn and Robert rendered Tenn incapable of focussed, sustained writing." Why did Williams endure this emotional storm for so long? To those who lived around him, including Rader, the answer had to do with guilt over his treatment of Merlo. "The banishment of Frank was, along with his silent complicity in Miss Rose's lobotomy, the most regretted act of his life. He could not forgive himself. He did not want to make the same irredeemable mistake again with Robert," Rader said.

Long after the breakup, Williams kept Carroll in mind. He transferred to him the deed to a farm in West Virginia that had been left to him by his painting teacher, Henry Faulkner; in 1980, he took the liberty of correcting the punctuation and syntax of Carroll's latest novel ("There are not many readers in publishing houses . . . who will see through weak syntax and punctuation and focus on the important thing—a highly original and impressive talent"); and in his will, he left Carroll a yearly sum of $7,500, the only person, besides Rose, to whom he bequeathed money. To the end of his days, Williams dished out avuncular advice to Carroll. "Take care and spit in the face of depression," he said.

After Williams's first split with Carroll in Italy in 1973, Bill Barnes found the playwright a stand-in for the last segment of his trip. Indifference, however, proved to be the galling drama of Williams's later years. He took personal rejection with more humor than the public variety. "It is true that my charms continue to elude him," Williams wrote of his new escort, "that expensive hotel doors remain locked between our adjoining rooms. It is true that he took the midnight air with the proprietor of the hotel at Ravello. It is true that he neglected to provide me with my thermos for coffee at four a.m. as well as my little toddy essential to the flow of creative juices, all of these misdemeanors are true as charged, but still he is a highly presentable public companion, he practices a pleasant air-steward's politeness. . . . When I asked him if he would love me or hate me when we parted, he reflected only a few seconds and then replied: 'I will remember you.'—What more could I ask? Après tout."

To be sensational, that is, to give others a *sensation* of his internal world, is part of the hysteric's performance, which Williams had turned into his own art form. But now that he had lost his currency, it was becoming increasingly difficult for him to find an audience. "I have a conviction that I have been professionally assassinated stateside," Williams wrote to his agent in the spring of 1973, adding, "Maybe I ought to consider myself irrevocably eighty-sixed out of the States and emigrate to another English-speaking theatre such as Australia—and then England. I'm serious." Barnes, however, encouraged his new client to take himself and his story on the road. To raise his visibility and his asking price, Barnes proposed that Williams sing the song of himself on numerous national TV talk shows, in a *Playboy* interview, a memoir, and an autobiographical novel (eventually titled *Moise and the World of Reason*) in which Williams and many of his famous friends would be incorporated. The novel was "a kind of autobiographical peep show," Michael Korda, the editor of *Moise*, wrote. But the autobiography turned out to be the real striptease. Williams had pulled his punches when it came to discussing his sexual identity on television with David Frost. *Memoirs* would bring him spectacularly out of the closet and answer his critics within the gay community, if not the heterosexual one. "If he hasn't exactly opened his heart, he has opened his fly," one droll critic put it.

Williams was well aware of the spectacle he was going to make of himself. "I am knocking it out at an average of sixteen pages a day and—although I may have to emigrate permanently from the States when it is published—I feel there's a cool million in it!" he wrote of his memoir to St. Just. To Kate Medina, his editor at Doubleday, he wrote, "I don't plan to turn out a discreet piece of work in my lifetime. I think that all good literature is an indiscretion." Williams's loosey-goosey discursive style and his sexual outspokenness quickly proved a challenge for Medina, whose robust editorial suggestions earned her a charming but firm "dear Kate" letter. "I feel that the project could not interest you unless you were involved in the actual writing or shaping of it," Williams wrote. "The book can only be successful if it is a work of total and personally unsparing honesty about myself and by myself. . . . The book when finished will not be 'sensational' in a bad way but in a good one."

Tom Congdon, another Doubleday editor, took over the general supervision of Williams and his manuscript. "You impressed me by your patience and understanding," Williams wrote to him. "I know, now, that, much as I continue to like Kate Medina, it was best that we all decided that you supervise and advise my work on the memoirs." Although Williams told the press that his autobiography was the first thing he'd ever written for money, by the time *Memoirs* was published, in 1975, he was complaining about his fifty-thousand-dollar advance. "I feel I've been had for a button," he said. "I laid my whole life on the line. My WHOLE life." The memoir received mixed notices, but it was on the *New York Times* bestseller list for nine weeks. If nothing else, Williams had proved a point: he couldn't—and wouldn't—be ignored.

The great revelation about Williams's life, however, came two years later, with the publication of *Tennessee Williams' Letters to Donald Windham: 1940–1965*, an extraordinary volume of correspondence written before Williams became famous, which expressed the full power of his romantic connection to his life and his talent. Williams considered the letters "amusing and well-written"; they were far more than that. Full of wonder, humor, struggle, and vivid description, the book made a claim for Williams as one of the best letter writers of his time, and certainly the most eloquent among American playwrights. Williams had, twice, given permission to Windham and his partner, Sandy Campbell, for a small private publication, without realizing that he was signing over all rights. When, to Williams's surprise, the book was commercially published— Windham got a twenty-five-thousand-dollar advance—he was drawn into a public feud with his old friend.

Williams had cause to feel aggrieved. Windham had promised him galley proofs of the letters before their publication; these were never sent, and for good reason. The extensive (and mischievous) footnotes were full of Windham's sour critical comment, which Williams rightly found "insulting and damaging." "What makes a Windham?" he asked in his diary. "Inherent cruelty, I would guess, and that invidious rage that comes from writing well without much financial reward. Does he truly believe that the sketch for 'Camino Real' is superior to its final form, and that between the sketch and the final form, I abandoned, or lost, my power and purity as a writer?" Williams went on, "His footnotes and his appen-

dix to my collected letters to him are remarkably venomous to his disad-
vantage, not mine." In a mean-spirited review in the Sunday *New York
Times*, Robert Brustein, then dean of the Yale School of Drama and the
go-to critic for high-tone put-downs of Williams, gave the letters a
homophobic thumping. "The love that previously dared not speak its
name has now grown hoarse from screaming it," he wrote. Although
Brustein's blatant misreading caused much consternation and vociferous
squabbling on the *Times* Letters page, the short-term effect was to mute
the reception and the luster of what was probably the major Williams
artifact of the seventies.

The glaring difference between the vivacity of Williams's early letters and his garrulous memoirs demonstrated an internal sea
change: at the start of his career, Williams had survived to write; now, he
wrote to survive. *"I can't live in a professional vacuum, I must have new
productions to make my life seem worth continuing a while longer—and
the big one seems to be still a bit in the distance.* Lemme know, lemme
know, lemme know!" he wrote to the producer Hillard Elkins in 1974
about *The Red Devil Battery Sign*, a political allegory begun in the radical upheaval of 1972 and optioned in its first draft in 1973 by David Merrick, who had produced Williams's three previous Broadway flops.

With all its dark, conspiratorial political overtones, the play, which
is set in Dallas after the Kennedy assassination, allowed Williams to
explore his sense of being, like his characters, a dead man walking. ("Did
I die by my own hand or was I destroyed slowly and brutally by a conspiratorial group?" Williams wrote in his late "Mes Cahiers Noirs." "Perhaps
I was never meant to exist at all.") His heroine, named only "Woman
Downtown"—the rich, wayward wife of a nefarious industrial kingpin
involved in political chicanery who keeps her under surveillance—recalls
the corrupt bonhomie of the lavish parties she once hosted as "one big
hell-hollering *death grin.*" "Oh, they trusted me to take their attaché
cases with the payola and the secrets in code, and w*hy not? Wasn't I
perfectly NOT human, too?!*" she tells King, a bar pickup whose sexual

David Merrick, "the abominable showman"

connection to her brings her back to life. "Human!" she shouts, throwing her head back. King, who is struggling to recover from a brain tumor, was formerly the charismatic star turn of a mariachi band called the King's Men, which featured Nina, his flamenco-dancing daughter. He dreams of singing again and of reclaiming his old glory. "Tonight? I got up on the bandstand with the men and I—*sang!*" he tells his wife, who has to support him now. "And there was applause almost like there was before. Soon I will send for La Niña and we will hit the road again. Remember her voice and mine together."

In this daydream of corruption and redemption—a hallucinatory vision in which "grief and disease receive little pity, where men live in chronic dread and howl in city canyons like coyotes at the moon," as Herbert Kretzmer wrote in London's *Daily Express* when the play was performed there in 1977—the living dead are briefly shocked into new life. As King dies of a brain seizure, he manages to tell Woman Downtown, "Dreams necessary." King loses his kingdom on earth; Downtown Woman, wild by nature and truthful in spirit, gains the kingdom of revolutionary immortality. At the finale, the play shifts from impressionistic reality to poetic prophesy. Woman Downtown is still a ghost of sorts, but one who haunts the audience with righteous outrage, joined hand in hand with the spectral protesting young—"outlaws in appearance . . . streaks of dirt on their faces, bloodied bandages, scant and makeshift garments." The stage directions tell us, "They seem to explode from a dream—and the scene with them . . . eyes wide, looking out at us who have failed or betrayed them. . . . The Woman Downtown advances furthest to where King's body has fallen. She throws back her head and utters the lost but defiant outcry of the she-wolf."

Merrick and Williams struggled to find a director for this challenging, opaque melodrama, which Williams subtitled in its early drafts "A Work for the Presentational Theatre." Williams wanted Milton Katselas or Elia Kazan; Merrick was pressing for Michael Bennett, a choreographer-turned-director who was best known at that time for his work on Neil Simon's *Promises, Promises*. "He's just 32—and at that age, how can he dig the depth of life and death which are inseparable from this play? I still love Gadg Kazan," Williams wrote to Merrick. To Barnes, he said, "In the old days I usually had a director before I had a producer. . . . The director is invariably more objective than the author, especially an author like me who is full of anxiety and uncertainty, who even doubts the sun will come up tomorrow. None of these . . . incontestable facts have occurred to David."

Throughout the play's gestation, Merrick treated Williams like a dead

man. For critics to call Williams a ghost of his former self, or even, rhe-
torically, to declare him "dead," was par for the course by the late seventies. But for Williams to be treated as invisible by a collaborator was an
insult of an altogether different order. Merrick often refused to communicate directly with Williams or to answer his letters. "If the play has not
your confidence and I have not your friendship, then maybe I should just
concentrate on the approach of the Christmas season and go back to New
Orleans and continue work on the play," Williams wrote to him in November 1973, adding, "I thought we had arrived at the point where you could
call me but I still hear nothing from you. . . . This is not the way an
important play is prepared."

Emotionally and artistically, Merrick and Williams had reached an
impasse. That December, with no production scheduled and no director
assigned, the momentum of the play seemed to have evaporated. Williams wrote to Kazan for help: "I sensed that you were seriously interested
in the play. Of course it would add to my feeling of security—and I am
sure of Merrick's, too—if you would make some sort of commitment, no,
I don't mean commitment but printed statement of 'involvement'—such
as 'Tennessee is going to Mexico to pull an exciting long play together,
and if he is not raped or slaughtered by lascivious and blood-thirsty ban-
dits, I might resume my directorial activity, that is, if Tennessee and I
are both convinced that he has pulled the opus together.'—Well, you
don't have to phrase it that eloquently, but some sort of little item in
Variety or the *Times* would vastly increase my momentum and also the
public interest."

But Kazan didn't take the bait, and Merrick continued to drag his
feet. "What's the matter, David? Don't you have the money?" St. Just
brazenly asked the producer, who, according to his biographer, "seemed
to choke on her words." On August 18, 1974, after Merrick's option lapsed,
Barnes saw the opportunity to jump ship to the team that had just given
Williams a spectacular success with a London revival of *A Streetcar
Named Desire*, starring Claire Bloom and directed by Ed Sherin. Hillard
Elkins, the revival's producer, who was then Bloom's husband, began
negotiations for *Red Devil*, a move that so outraged Merrick that he
threatened to sue for breach of contract, until Williams agreed to extend

his option. "None of us wanted to be involved in litigation with such a moneyed and powerful man," he said. In the end, for a while, Merrick and Elkins joined forces. By then, Williams's director of choice was Sherin, who considered *Red Devil* "one of the most important works of the decade, with a clear warning about the destructive forces rampant in our society," but who was unwilling to commit if Merrick was the sole producer. "I felt that David Merrick hadn't the patience, understanding or compassion to produce this particular work," Sherin said, who pushed Elkins to do the play alone. Elkins insisted that he could work with Merrick and that Sherin's feelings "were paranoid."

Red Devil was scheduled to begin tryouts in Boston in mid-June 1975, then travel to Washington, and open on Broadway in August, with a star-studded cast that included Anthony Quinn, Katy Jurado, and Claire Bloom. Setting off for rehearsals in New York, Williams wrote to St. Just, "I fancy this will be a summer of drama, mostly offstage." And so it proved. Merrick, who was also acting as the company manager, demanded that the set be redone by a new set designer; the union would not allow the hiring of Mexican mariachis, and the New York variety turned out not to read music; Katy Jurado found it difficult to pronounce or to understand Williams's words; and Bloom, whose acting style didn't mix well with Quinn's, was having trouble finding her character. One afternoon during rehearsals, Quinn took Sherin aside and suggested that "another actress be found or he would leave," Sherin said, adding, "Four days before we travelled to Boston, the play was unrealized, the acting was uneven, the mariachis were nowhere, but we were going to perform for the public the following Saturday." At one of these unhappy rehearsals, Merrick put in a rare appearance. "As I live and breathe, it's Mr. Broadway," Williams drawled. Merrick shot him a look. "I thought you said you'd be dead before we went into rehearsals," he said. Williams replied, "Never listen to a duck in a thunderstorm."

Red Devil didn't make it to Broadway or even to Washington. Its first Boston preview, on June 14, 1976, was four hours long, and even the director judged it "amateurish, ponderous, inaccurate and incomplete." When it opened on June 18, critical opinion was mixed, with reactions varying from "a mess" (the *Boston Globe*) to "cause for rejoicing . . . a haunting

Claire Bloom, Anthony Quinn, and Ed Sherin rehearse *The Red Devil Battery Sign*

theatre piece" (*Christian Science Monitor*). Nonetheless, the audiences were lively and at near capacity. Then, just as the play was "beginning to emerge," according to Sherin, Merrick announced that the entire $360,000 investment had been spent and that there might not be enough left over to cover the cost of closing. (According to Sherin, his co-producer subsequently claimed that "only $260,000 or less had been spent.")

Ostensibly to save the production, Merrick presented a plan that would require the creative team to make drastic cuts to royalties and the actors' salaries. When Merrick's numbers were challenged, he refused to show his books and countered with the threat that if his plan was not immediately adopted, he would remove the equipment he personally owned (all the lights and the winches used in set changes). In a late-night meeting that weekend, peace between the management and the cast seemed to be negotiated; but on Merrick's orders at 7:00 P.M. on Monday, at the beginning of the run's second week, a closing notice was posted. "I stood in disbelief, before moving on to all the dressing rooms to assure the company that there had been some mistake," Sherin wrote. "Claire Bloom, who only drinks wine occasionally, was downing a shot of vodka from a freshly opened bottle on her dressing-room table. Anthony Quinn was seething with anger and talked bitterly of a double-cross. The notice must have been all the more bitter for Quinn, when at the final curtain that night, he received a standing ovation for his performance as King."

That Tuesday, Sherin called Williams to tell him the bad news. "He gave me this shocking report of a statement by Merrick. He declared before witnesses that he had always hated me and the play and that he had only produced it to destroy it. Mr. Sherin is not a man to invent such a story," Williams wrote in a memo to himself. "If Merrick does indeed think that he has destroyed the play, I think he is totally unaware of my dedication to my work, the tenacity of my resolve to resist its destruction. I have many enemies; but I feel these enemies are greatly out-numbered by those who understand and admire the work which [is?] the heart or truth of my being." Williams added, "Bill Barnes invited me over last night to inform me of the posted notice. We sat upon his terrace as dusk fell. . . . It was a curiously emotionless occasion." Other members of the production were not so laid back. Quinn told a reporter, "Tennessee Williams, one of the great talents of all time, has been treated like an assembly-line butcher." Sherin saw Merrick's draconian actions as indicative of the ominous undertow of a corrupt culture, "the very forces in our society about which Tennessee Williams is writing in 'The Red Devil Battery Sign,'" he said. "If these forces are already so powerful that they can silence the warnings of our greatest artists, then it may already be too late."

Red Devil ended its Boston run on June 28, 1975, the first Williams play to close out of town since *Battle of Angels*, thirty-five years earlier. "It's not closing for good," Merrick told a reporter from the *New York Times*. "It's closing for bad." When the play was staged in a tighter, angrier, more political version by the English Theatre in Vienna in 1975—"Burn, burn, burn," the cast chanted at the finale—it was praised as "one of the most thrilling tragedies of love and hate in Williams's work" (*Frankfurter Allgemeine*) and "a blazing torch illuminating the very core of life" (*Die Presse*). But in the society at which Williams's howling vision was aimed, *Red Devil* went unheard and unnoticed.

IN THE YEARS after *Red Devil* closed—a "coup-de-disgrace," Williams called it—the playwright felt as if he were vanishing in plain sight. Despite his self-deprecating laughter and his gallant public shows of endurance—"I am like some old opera star who keeps making farewell appearances," he said—he was fading like a photograph. "Aside from you, the New York *Times* appears to ignore my continuing efforts and sometimes accomplishments in the theatre," Williams wrote to Walter Kerr. "I wonder if you might encourage them to give me a sense of continuance. . . . I'm sure you understand my longing for these little reminders . . . that I am still living." When Roger Stevens, the chairman of the Kennedy Center, called Williams in 1979 to tell him that he was to be celebrated in the second annual Kennedy Center Honors, Williams replied, "Why, Roger, you must think I'm dead."

Writing in the *New York Times* in May 1977, Williams noted, "I am widely regarded as the ghost of a writer, a ghost still visible." The declaration, which was meant to both disabuse and defy his critics, was a brazen maneuver that went well beyond the usual game of show-and-tell that he played with the public. Although his near-death experiences were a frequent part of his public palaver—he was "imminently posthumous," as he confessed to Dick Cavett in 1979—Williams had never before declared himself dead. For him to admit to his ghostliness in print was a signal of his desperation, as well as his self-loathing.

He did, on occasion, however, play dead. At a boring Key West production of *Twelfth Night*, Williams extricated himself from his fourth-row center seat before the intermission by gasping loudly, "Help! Get me some medicine! Help!" "I phoned Tennessee to see if he was alright," William Prosser, the director who was near him, said. "He replied in full health, 'Oh, you know baby, I never did much like *Twelfth Night.*'" In 1975, dismayed at the early rehearsals of the Vienna version of *The Red Devil Battery Sign*, Williams had a large oxygen tank brought up to his hotel suite, sent for the leading lady and the director, who were the husband-and-wife owner-managers of the small theater, and pretended to be stricken, "so they might hear the dying playwright's last words on how the production was killing him," St. Just, who was present at his performance, said. In his diaries, on December 16, 1976, Peter Hall, then the artistic director of Britain's Royal National Theatre, reported Williams's glee at another "death." "The lady who produced my new play on Broadway organised a seminar," Williams told Hall. "As I went into the seminar I saw that the notice for closing the play was up on the stage-door notice board. I thought this odd as I was doing the seminar to boost business." Williams continued, "After the seminar I asked the lady producer why the notice was up. She said she had no more money. I told her this was a shock to me as I had a cardiac condition. I threw myself down on the floor. She screamed and called for a doctor. I rose from the floor roaring with laughter."

Implicit in the dramaturgy of these scenes was Williams's almost compulsive desire to compel emotional surrender. "Tenn used death to control the play," said Rader, who sometimes "played second lead in Tennessee's death act when we were trying to get drugs from a doctor." "I saw him use it most in places where he was trying to pick up a reluctant boy who had never heard of him and hoped that an appeal to their common humanity might do the trick. It usually did. It didn't in the case of Hiram Walker, an actor I knew who told me about it. Tennessee staggered over to the bed and, facing him, rolled his eyes and fell backward on the mattress. 'Hold me, baby, I'm dying,' Tenn said. Hiram sat beside him and held Tennessee's hand, which annoyed him. Hiram asked if he should call the doctor. 'Doctor? It's too late for the doctor,' Tennessee said. 'Leave! I prefer to die alone.'"

For Williams, who claimed to be "inordinately possessed of the past," playwriting had always been a negotiation with the dead; by calling ghosts out of himself and onto the stage, he allowed them to reenter the realm of time. Now, in his later years, he was haunted not only by the ghosts of others but by the ghost of himself. His plays teemed with apparitions. The resurgence of the spectral in his drama began with two excellent pieces: the poignant teleplay *Stopped Rocking* (which was never filmed) and *Vieux Carré*, a memory play about his journeyman days in

New Orleans, both of which Williams completed in 1974 as "alternate projects" during the long wait for *Red Devil* to be mounted.

Stopped Rocking, originally titled "A Second Epiphany for My Friend Maureen," was written for and dedicated to Maureen Stapleton. The story maps the trajectory into ghostliness of the fragile Janet Svenson, whose husband, Olaf, is having her transferred from the Catholic sanatorium, where she has spent the past five years, to the state mental facility. Since Janet's hospitalization, Olaf has built a new life and plans to move out of state with his new partner. Guilt-ridden and gauche, he treats Janet as a kind of disembodied figure, at once trapped in time and outside of it. In order to break the news gently to Janet, who still pines for him, Olaf takes her on a tragicomic trailer "holiday" in the Ozarks. On their trip, Olaf and Janet pass through a "spectral country" that is symbolic of the internal retreat that Olaf predicts for her:

> No, not alone, with fantasies, apparitions, perfect companions for you. Creatures you invent make no demands on you. You'll dream your own world, Maw, with complete possession of it. . .
>
> Reality gives no rest, it gives no peace. For you: stopping, resting.

Janet, however, envisions a different form of oblivion. "No more Sunday visits, now, ever, not longer between but never, never ever—those—long words, never ever," she says in a heartbreaking line that doesn't move the stolid Olaf. Doomed to a living death, Janet throws herself into a river, only to be saved and stuffed with antidepressants by Olaf, who returns her to the sanatorium and, as the play's title indicates, to oblivion. In her last close-up, Janet is shown as a kind of disembodied lost soul, "utterly peaceful and 'resigned from life.'" By the end of the play, although he is still moving among the living, Olaf, too, has "stopped rocking." Olaf, who is nicknamed "Stone Man," has become one: "stone outside and in, all the way through, in other words, plain heartless."

Stopped Rocking was proposed as a Hallmark movie of the week. Williams requested John Hancock as the director and met with him in Los Angeles to discuss the script. In the years since Williams had last seen Hancock, he had transitioned from theater to film, directing *Sticky My Fingers, Fleet My Feet* (1970), a live-action short that was nominated for an Academy Award, and *Bang the Drum Slowly* (1973), a feature about baseball that gave Robert De Niro his first major role. During his first meeting with Hancock, Williams complained about his physical transformation. According to Hancock, "he told me ruefully how difficult he was finding it to get laid because his body 'well, isn't as nice as it once was,' he said."

But Hancock came to see that the changes in Williams were more than physical. One night, they ended up at an Italian restaurant on Melrose and Robertson, on the border between Beverly Hills and West Hollywood, because Williams wanted to eat "calamari fritti." "He was drunk but not out of control," Hancock recalled. "He was having balance problems as he often did—the synergy, I guess, of downers and booze—and he took my arm to cross the street from the limo to the restaurant. As we approached the far side, there was an opening in the gutter that leads down into those big storm drains that underlie the north-south streets in that area, and, seeing that, he whirled on me with crazed eyes and drew away from me in fear. Later, he confessed that he thought I was going to push him down into the storm drain. I hadn't realized he was that crazy. It was all chuckled over as if it were some kind of joke, but I remember thinking, Is he still talented enough to be this crazy? I decided he was, but he had greatly changed from the man I'd known earlier."

In Hancock's opinion, Williams, in *Stopped Rocking*, "had written another of his great hysteric females and . . . the madness of the middle-of-the-night camping disasters could provide an opportunity for her to have some spectacular arias." Hoping to make him see how "skimpy" the middle of the script was and to get him excited about expanding it, Hancock collected a distinguished crew of actors—Richard Jordan, Blair Brown, and Harry Hamlin—to read through a few scenes in Williams's presence at his Malibu house. "I knew we were in trouble when I saw Tennessee get out of the car and stagger toward the front door," Hancock said. "Here was a ghost. Bill Barnes was with him. They came in, Tennessee stumbling slightly as he came down the three stairs to our sunken living room, and met everybody."

The actors were arranged in a circle; Williams sat in a chair, with a well-thumbed copy of the screenplay in his lap. He began to read, slurring wildly. "The actors were stunned, embarrassed. We looked at each other. I didn't know what to do," Hancock said. "After a page or so I gathered my courage and said, 'Excuse me, Tennessee, but I don't think I was clear—we have all these wonderful actors and we want to read the play to you, not you to us.'" Williams closed his script, took off his glasses, sat back, and the actors began to read. After a few pages, Hancock looked over at Williams; he was asleep. "Tennessee stirred. Maybe he wasn't asleep? The actors plowed grimly on. But he was fast asleep," Hancock recalled. When it was over, Williams mumbled his thank-yous and staggered out to the car. "I never heard from him again," Hancock said. "Nor, I think, did I see Tennessee ever again, but in a way, he was vanishing even before he had gone."

VIEUX CARRÉ, A crepuscular spectacle of dead souls, includes among its spectral figures the jejune Writer himself. First conceived as an evening of two one-act plays (*The Angel in the Alcove* and *I Never Get Dressed until after Dark on Sundays*), it picks up Williams's story from the end of *The Glass Menagerie* and fills in the journeyman years, when he was a nearly destitute twenty-eight-year-old living in a New Orleans boarding house, afflicted by loneliness and by "a passionate will to create." Beneath its lyric veneer *The Glass Menagerie* was a battlefield of fierce contending forces: a son trying to break free of a controlling and toxic mother, and a put-upon mother trying to keep her son in place. *Vieux Carré*, a memory play, has no such urgency or argument. "Once this house was alive, it was occupied once. In my recollection, it still is, but by shadowy occupants like ghosts. Now they enter the lighter areas of my memory," the Writer/Narrator says in the play's opening lines.

By the play's end, the Writer has been buffeted as much by a vision of his future as by his past. The last words of *Vieux Carré* resonate two ways: as an augury and as an epitaph. Setting out on the literary adventure of a lifetime, the Writer opens the door to the boardinghouse:

(*As he first draws the door open, he is forced back a few steps by a cacophony of sound: the waiting storm of his future—mechanical racking cries of pain and pleasure, snatches of song. It fades out. Again there is the urgent call of the clarinet. He crosses to the open door.)*

WRITER: . . . They're disappearing behind me. Going. People you've known in places do that: they go when you go. The earth seems to swallow them up, the walls absorb them like moisture, remain with you only as ghosts: their voices are echoes, fading but remembered. *(The clarinet calls again. He turns for a moment at the door.)*
This house is empty now.

In early drafts of *Vieux Carré*, there is a scene in which, in the excitement of collaboration, a playwright accidentally tips backward into the orchestra pit. He clambers out. "Old cats know how to fall," he says. By the time *Vieux Carré* got to Broadway, Williams wasn't so sure he could bounce back. Shuttling between Bermuda, Atlantic City, and Key West, he avoided most of the previews. "None of us saw Tennessee for a long time until we had major problems with several scenes," Sylvia Sidney, who played Mrs. Wire, the witchy, intrusive landlady, said. "When he finally arrived, his excuse was, 'I need to see it on its feet!' By then it was almost too late." Williams was hiding from the critics even more than from the production. "I am as frightened as ever of the critics," he wrote to his director, Arthur Allan Seidelman, in early May 1977, contemplating the prospect of bad reviews. "If we get a 'Stop' sign from them, I think we should do something quite spectacularly unusual like publicly challenging them to a debate." Williams went on, "I am personally quite ready to have a final showdown with them before flying to England and emigrating to Australia because of an unremitting barrage of excrement from those or those who employ them."

As it happened, *Vieux Carré* lasted only five hapless performances, defeated by poor direction, poor design, and poor producers. "It developed that the backers lacked cash," Williams wrote in his postmortem, adding, "Behind my back the director went ga-ga and removed the climactic scene of Part One. The narrator (his boy-friend) was an amateurish performer in a part that demanded high professional skill." Although the production was given a drubbing, Williams's writing was not. "Tennessee Williams's voice is the most distinctively poetic, the most idiosyncratically moving, and at the same time the most firmly dramatic to have come the American theatre's way—ever," Walter Kerr wrote in the *New York Times*. "No point in calling the man our best living playwright. He is our best playwright, and let qualifications go hang." A few American critics, Kerr among them, indicated an interest in seeing future productions. In August 1978, a revised London production of *Vieux Carré*, directed by Keith Hack, was a hit, and it restored honor to the play, which went on to be one of Williams's most popular late works.

IN *VIEUX CARRÉ*, Williams wrote himself from the outside; in his next major play, *Clothes for a Summer Hotel: A Ghost Play*, Williams wrote himself from the inside. He took as his subject the tormented, romantic saga of F. Scott and Zelda Fitzgerald, a move that Brendan Gill of *The New Yorker* likened to "body snatching." The play is set in Highland Hospital, the asylum near Asheville, North Carolina, that burned down with Zelda in it, seven years after Scott had died, in 1940. The literary couple, now ghosts, argue and mingle in flashback with apparitions from their reckless heyday in the twenties: Ernest and Hadley Hemingway, Gerald and Sara Murphy. Walter Kerr spoke for the largely bemused general public when he declared in his negative review in the *Times*, "We are simply being told what we already know. We *don't* know why we are bothering to retrace the terrain now."

What was Williams really trying to tell the public? He was far too clever and too committed a playmaker simply to rehash the famous dead for profit. By making the Fitzgeralds ghosts, Williams abstracted them from history and from their social façade; they existed for him as pure idea. "In a sense all plays are ghost plays, since players are not actually whom they play," he said in an author's note. "Our reason for taking extraordinary license with time and place is that in an asylum and on its grounds liberties of this kind are quite prevalent: and also these liberties allow us to explore in more depth what we believe is truth of character." Williams was haunted not so much by the truth of the Fitzgeralds' story, which was well known, as by the spiritual truth of his own story, which was not.

"Zelda is the type of character I can deal with very easily, having a sister who suffered from mental illness and myself having perhaps moments of it," Williams said, when the play went into rehearsal on New Year's Day in 1980, adding, "Yes, I guess I also felt a kind of kinship with Scott. He was a prodigy when his first book came out, but he was afflicted by alcohol, and during the last years of his life, his books were virtually out of print. I also have gone through a period of eclipse in public favor." On the surface of the Fitzgeralds' tale—the waste of talent, the mental illness, the tempestuous lives lived on the edge—it was easy for Williams to draw lines of emotional connection. But their story also spoke to something deeper in Williams's own creative survival, something he both knew and didn't know, what he called "the brutality of the unconscious": his cannibalization of himself and others for his art.

On the day that *Clothes for a Summer Hotel* went into rehearsal, the director, José Quintero, told the press, "In Tennessee's work, it is always the question of survival. Imagine this man to whom people have said, 'You're dried up, you can't write any more,' still writing, still coming to rehearsals in his raccoon coat. That's what it's all about—surviving in the theatre, surviving in the profession." *Clothes for a Summer Hotel* was about the price of that survival.

"Scott used Zelda's life in his books, and that theme echoes Tennessee's use of his own experience and his sister's experience in his work," Geraldine Page, who played Zelda, said. That appropriation is at the core of the argument between Scott and Zelda. "Is that really you, Scott? Are you my lawful husband, the celebrated F. Scott Fitzgerald, author of my life?" Zelda asks, in her first line to Scott, who is waiting for her on a bench outside the "unrealistically tall" black iron gates of the asylum. Later, in the same scene, she charges Scott with being a kind of psychic imperialist who has eaten her alive: "*What was important to you was to absorb and devour!*" she says. The real Zelda's claim—as laid out in her own novel, *Save Me the Waltz*, and in Nancy Milford's 1970 biography, *Zelda*—was that her husband not only had used her as a model for the heroines in his fiction, and published her stories under his name, but also had borrowed freely from her letters and diaries for his fiction. ("Mr. Fitzgerald . . . seems to believe that plagiarism begins at home," the real

Zelda wrote in a review of *The Beautiful and Damned* in 1922.) Her artistic ambitions thwarted, Zelda went slowly mad, obsessed in her later years with the idea of becoming a ballerina. "The will to cry out remains," she says in the play.

At the opening of the play, Scott offers Zelda a duplicate of the wedding ring she's thrown away. "Call it a ring of, of—a covenant with the past that's always still present, dearest," he says. Scott will not accept responsibility for his part in her destruction. Toward the end, in a memorable final aria, Zelda calls Scott out on his image of himself as a good man—a gentleman and an artist—which has prevented him from seeing the damage he has inflicted:

> ZELDA:—I'm approaching him now, no son of God but a gentleman shadow of him. It's incredible how, against appalling odds, dear Scott achieved a Christly parallel through his honoring of long commitments, even now to me, a savage ghost in a bedraggled tutu, yes it's a true and incredible thing.
> SCOTT: (*softly, as he falls back onto the bench*) Incredible?—Yes.
> (*She pauses briefly before him; then touches his shoulder and crosses to downstage center.*)
> ZELDA: . . . The incredible things are the only true things, Scott. Why do you have to go mad to make a discovery as simple as that? Who is fooling whom with this pretence that to exist is a credible thing? The mad are not so gullible. We're not taken in by such a transparent falsity, oh, no, what we know that you don't know—(*She is now facing the audience.*) Or don't dare admit that you know is that to exist is the original and greatest of incredible things. Between the first wail of an infant and the last gasp of the dying—it's all an arranged pattern of—submission to what's been prescribed for us unless we escape into madness or into acts of creation. . . . The latter option was denied me, Scott, by someone not a thousand miles from here. (*She faces Scott.*) Look at what was left me!

But Scott cannot, will not, take in what she's saying. He changes the subject. Zelda sits down beside him and continues her speech—a speech whose litany of loss recalls Williams's own retreat from real and imagined defeats:

> —As I grew older, Goofo, the losses accumulated in my heart, the disenchantments steadily increased. That's usual, yes? Simply the process of aging.—Adjustments had to be made to faiths that had faded as candles into daybreak. In their place, what? Sharp light cast on things that appalled me, that blew my mind out, Goofo. Then—The wisdom, the sorrowful wisdom of acceptance. Wouldn't accept it. Romantics won't, you know. Liquor, madness, more or less the same thing. We're abandoned or we're put away, and if put away, why, then, fantasy runs riot, hallucinations bring back times lost. . . . —Yes, I went back to the world of vision which was my only true home.

At the finale, as Zelda moves for the last time through the gates and back into the asylum, Scott tries to follow her. "The gates are iron, they won't admit you or ever release me again," she says, as the gates close behind her. "I'm not your book! Anymore! *I can't be your book anymore! Write yourself a new book!*" Scott thrusts the ring through the bars. "The ring, please take it, the covenant with the past—[*she disappears*]—still always present, Zelda!" he says, in the play's final line. *"His haunted eyes ask a silent question which he must know cannot be answered,"* the last stage direction reads.

On its surface—the level on which the first-night critics dealt with it—*Clothes for a Summer Hotel* was the somewhat aimless tale of a celebrated embattled couple airing their differences. However, it was, on a deeper psychological level, an argument within Williams's famously divided self. Both victimizer and victim, Williams had devoured himself for the sake of his work. This idea is spelled out in the play by the ghost of Hemingway, who talks about his whole-cloth appropriation of Fitzgerald's life for his own short stories. "You see, I can betray even my oldest close friend, the one most helpful in the beginning," he tells Scott. "That may have been at least partly the reason for which I executed myself not long after, first by attempting to walk into the propeller of a plane—then having failed, by blasting my exhausted brains out with an elephant gun."

Hemingway continues, "I may have pronounced on myself this violent death sentence to expiate the betrayals I've strewn behind me."

Williams, similarly consumed with guilt over his exploitation of himself and of Rose for his greater glory, chose a slower suicide than Hemingway, but it was self-destruction nonetheless. When Zelda screams at Scott to "write yourself a new book," her words play both as an indictment of Fitzgerald and as an injunction from Williams to himself—to stop feeding solipsistically off his own demise. From the mid-fifties, in Williams's mind, creation and betrayal were psychologically conjoined. To give life to his characters Williams preyed on himself—drawing on drugs and promiscuity to engineer the extravagant conversion of despair into art. In seeking his liberation, he became his own oppressor. The beseeching hand, pushing a ring through the asylum bars in *Clothes for a Summer Hotel*, is a punishing image of this tormented, tormenting stalemate. Like Fitzgerald, Williams remained devoted to a covenant that he'd long since betrayed: the purity of romantic transcendence through art.

The play opened at the Cort Theatre on March 26, 1980, Williams's sixty-ninth birthday. At the curtain call, the audience stood to applaud Williams; he took a bow. The next day—"Tennessee Williams Day" by mayoral proclamation—Williams took brickbats. At the opening-night cast party, Williams had sat downcast in a shadowy corner of a Third Avenue restaurant, with St. Just by his side, as news of the first reviews filtered in. "He said he wanted to fly away on angels' wings," Rader, who had brought Pat Kennedy Lawford with him to the party, recalled. "Maria snapped, 'You'll get those soon enough.' She was pissed at the clear failure of the play and, as usual, responded by patronizing him. 'We did our best, didn't we, dear?' 'We mustn't be too hard on ourselves.'" Williams had, he said, "hung on for ten years to have a success

OPPOSITE PAGE: Kenneth Haigh and Geraldine Page as Scott and Zelda Fitzgerald in *Clothes for a Summer Hotel*

in the American theater; *Clothes*, with its celebrated cast and its popular subject matter, was his best roll of the dice, but he had crapped out. Pat sat down beside him and held his hand. "She thought he was dangerously despondent," Rader said. "To cheer him up she offered to give him a party that weekend." Williams "beamed," according to Rader, and said he'd be delighted to come.

When Williams arrived at the party, with St. Just in tow, most of the twenty or so guests, who included Anne Jackson and Eli Wallach, Philip Kingsley, Vass Voglis, Jan Cushing, and Rader, were having drinks in the flower-filled drawing room of Kennedy's elegant eighth-floor Sutton Place South duplex, overlooking gardens and the East River. The foyer of the lobby had been decorated with a five-foot-high balloon that read "HUR-RAY FOR TENNESSEE," but Williams brought little of that good cheer with him across the apartment's threshold. "He seemed nervous, depressed, and unsure of himself," Rader said. Williams had been there for about ten minutes when he bolted across the drawing room, pulled open the French doors, ran out onto the balcony, and clambered over the railings to throw himself off. "Eli was the first to grab him," Rader said. "It was very alarming. Resisting, he was pulled back into the room, then sort of threw his shoulders back and gave a sickly smile and shrugged. It was a close call."

Later that evening, Wallach read Williams's comic poem about post-coital palaver, "Life Story," then pointed out a ring he was wearing, on which the face of tragedy morphed into the face of comedy. "I have had it all my life," Wallach said, "and there is nothing that I cherish and value more than this ring. It has brought me luck. And there is no one I would give it to, no man I love more, than you." He took off the ring and handed it to Williams, who accepted it tearfully. Wallach then raised his glass and toasted "the greatest living playwright." The others stood for Williams and raised their glasses. "Eli, thank you, baby," Williams said. "I don't know how true what you say is, or whether it matters if it is. It's nice to hear it from a friend."

Williams certainly didn't hear it from the critics. As the reviews rolled in, so did the vitriol, which could be measured by the headlines alone: "Slender Is the Night" (*Newsweek*), " 'Clothes' Needs Some Tailoring" (*New York Post*). "There is nothing necessary about this ghost play, nothing that needed saying in *this* world," John Simon wrote in *New York*. "The action is set in the 1940s, the design comes out of the 1950s, the ideology belongs the 1960s. Leaving the theatre, I felt in my 80s," Robert Brustein remarked in the *New Republic*, adding that Williams should perhaps book "a flight to Three Mile Island on a one-way ticket." "This is an evening at the morgue," Rex Reed declared in the *New York Daily News.*

For all its narrative problems, *Clothes for a Summer Hotel* is a much better written and more evocative play than the version those first-nighters saw. As Williams wrote to Kazan, "'Clothes' was a victim of a bad first act, miscasting of Scott"—who was played by the British actor Kenneth Haigh—"a stingy producer, and Gerry Page's problem with projecting her voice, so bad that all the theatres we played had to be miked. Much as I love Quintero, he vacillated too much over crucial problems, in my opinion." Nonetheless, in a desperate gesture, so that word of mouth would have time to build, Williams stumped up twenty thousand dollars to help cover the costs for a second week. "Couldn't the son of a bitch at least let us get out quick?" Page said on hearing the news. The actors got out quick enough. The play closed on Easter Sunday, having played seven previews and fifteen performances in New York, twenty-three shows in Chicago, and thirty-nine shows in Washington, and losing the best part of half a million dollars. Williams told Earl Wilson, the *New York Post*'s gossip columnist, that he'd been a victim of "critical homicide." He vowed never to return to Broadway, which was just as well because his illustrious career on the Rialto was over.

In 1976, at his induction to the American Academy of Arts and Letters, Williams had heard the words of Robert Penn Warren: "No dramatist writing in English has created a more strongly characteristic and memorable world." At the Kennedy Center Honors, in 1979, he heard Kazan call him "a playwright in the way that a lion is a lion. Nothing but." Accepting the 1980 Presidential Medal of Freedom, Williams heard President Jimmy Carter say that he'd "shaped the history of modern American theater." But for the remainder of his life, Williams never heard a major American critic praise a new play of his.

"I WILL NEVER recover from what they did to me with 'Clothes,'" Williams wrote to Mitch Douglas, his new representative at ICM. (Barnes had left the agency.) "But I will not stop working till they drop me in the sea. . . . I think I know better than anyone how little time there's left for me. I'll use it well. I trust you to help me with it." Douglas had been a Williams fan before he became a Williams functionary; he had read every published work. He was firm, feisty, and fun. He began at ICM as a temp typist between acting jobs; in 1974, he became a full-time agent, and by 1978 Williams was his client. "Tennessee was difficult because Tennessee was crazy. There's no diplomatic way to say that," Douglas said. "He ate Bill Barnes alive. One of the reasons Billy was out at ICM was because Tennessee was taking all his time. I was told, 'Don't let him take up all your time the way it was with Billy Barnes.'" Williams's literary life—the calls, the productions, the correspondence, the personal appearances, the travel—was a three-ring circus, of which Douglas became the harassed ringmaster.

On his first trip to Key West, to discuss *Stopped Rocking*, Douglas called Williams from his hotel and asked to come over. "Well, that would be difficult," Williams said. "Robert got wasted last night and wrecked the car. Now he's sitting on the front porch with a gun in his lap threatening to blow the brains out of anyone who approaches. I would say we're under siege." Douglas quickly learned that to handle his new client, strict boundaries would have to be maintained. When St. Just called him to complain about Williams's New York apartment—"Mitch, the windows are filthy and the floors are even worse"—Douglas told her, "I don't do windows. You want a maid, call a maid service. You need some help with business, I'll be happy to help." Inevitably, though, even the no-nonsense Douglas sometimes had to deal with Williams's transgressive antics. At the Kennedy Center Honors luncheon, for instance, Williams and Maureen Stapleton got drunk. After lunch, as they waited for their limousine, a Marine band was playing beside the driveway. Stapleton went up to the conductor. "You guys play so fucking good. Do you know 'Moon River'?" she said. The band struck up the song. Stapleton and Williams began dancing; they waltzed themselves into a forbidden area of the White House. "I went to the Sergeant of Arms, and I said, 'Will you help me get them out of here?'" Douglas recalled. "Two Marines got under Tennessee and two under Maureen's arm. They walked them to the limo."

Feeling that "time runs short," and determined to live in the slip-stream of his fame, Williams proved increasingly difficult for Douglas to wrangle. In July 1981, a few months before the Off-Broadway premiere of *Something Cloudy, Something Clear*—a memory play in which the adult Williams revisited and commented on his first experience of love, with Kip Kiernan, in 1940—Williams wrote to Douglas suggesting that they "level with each other." "Let's do," Douglas replied; in a piquant, four-page, single-spaced letter he made clear a lot of what was cloudy in Williams's behavior:

> You've been quoted in the press saying that you did not approve the STREETCAR remake deal and the negotiations went forward without your knowledge. Also you've stated that you never approved of Sylvester Stallone as Stanley. Obviously you've forgotten that we discussed the possibility of selling these rights for a year before the Martin Poll negotiation began. When I told you I could get a lot of money—$750,000 or a million—for these rights, but Stallone would be included as Stanley, you indicated that you didn't care if Stanley were played by a banana. You indicated that you needed the money and might as well have it while you were around—"I'm not interested in anything posthumous." And I do agree with you. You've worked long, hard and well and should enjoy the rewards—and *now*. When the Jerry Parker *Newsday* article appeared quoting you as saying you didn't know about the deal and that Stallone was a "terrible actor," you called me denying the story, asking to get a denial and attributing the comment to one of the several people in the room with you when Parker was interviewing you. I got a denial through Liz Smith, and within a day you went to North Carolina and made the same comments to a different set of reporters. Stallone has walked out of the project. Martin Poll wants to honor the deal and put it together with a cast of your approval in spite of the fact that none of the major studios

think that STREETCAR is now a hot property, and in fact the highest previous offer I could get was $250,000. Do you want this $750,000 deal . . . or not? A simple yes or no will do.

You also commented in North Carolina, "Not only do I work very hard but I have to represent myself as well. My representative is only interested in using me for profit." I resent this type of abusive statement. I work very hard for you and always with a two-fold purpose: to do the best for you artistically and financially. When I book you at the Jean Cocteau Repertory Theatre [*Something Cloudy, Something Clear*] or allow you to sign for a small film such as THE STRANGEST KIND OF ROMANCE, it isn't for the money—it's for the artistic merit and for the possibilities of getting a work done that otherwise might not be done, with the hope of future financial rewards. I'm sorry, but your plays since IGUANA haven't done well financially and you aren't an easy sale commercially. I try to offset the not-for-profit situations, since you often cry, "I'm not a wealthy man," with sales like that of STREETCAR to the movies. . . .

Yes, Tennessee, let's level with each other. You wrote recently of Audrey Wood saying theatre people are often impossible people and that you were never an easy client for Audrey even from the beginning. Well let me confirm something I think you already know—You aren't an easy client now. You're inconsistent, unreliable, you make commitments you don't honor and your attitude and approach are often less than gentlemanly. . . .

. . . You attack me in Chicago because ICM didn't send you a birthday telegram. I reply, "But Tennessee, I *came.*" "Well, baby we all come sometime if we're lucky!" Or in Orlando, "I want my wine in an opaque glass. Mitch, do you know how to spell opaque?" I have a duty to you, but it doesn't include being abused by you. . . .

Also in your recent comments about Audrey you said that Audrey understood. I think I understand too, Tennessee. We come from the same area, have the same background (good lord, we even have the same birthday), and like you I've worked hard to attain my position as a skilled professional. . . . You *are* our greatest American playwright, living or dead, and it's a honor for me to be associated with you. . . . But

I must also tell you, dear Tennessee, that I don't intend to have my first heart attack because of you.

Williams dismissed "Bitch Douglas" gently but immediately. "I wish you luck and I do believe that you wish me the same," he wrote, adding, in a reference to the last ICM agent he'd fired, "I know that you'd never draw back your hand and make a hissing sound if I pass your table at the Algonquin." To Milton Goldman, the head of the agency's theater division, Williams wrote, "Can you place me in the hands of some agent at ICM who is not and never was one of 'Miss Wood's' people!?" From then on, Goldman, who represented actors, fronted as Williams's agent while Douglas did the work. "I will not again open an envelope with his name on it," Williams wrote to Goldman, adding, "What most concerns me is that if Mitch does not do the graceful and dignified thing (for me and ICM) he will still have his hand in my affairs when I split the scene which I think is not long away."

IN HIS REVIEW of *Clothes for a Summer Hotel*, Harold Clurman argued that Williams's creative practice had become disconnected from his inner self. On the contrary, the apparitions, the shadowy reality, the double exposures of past speaking to present and present to past that dominate Williams's thin late plays dramatize precisely the retreat of his attenuated self—a self that had been desiccated by his adamantine will to write. The activity that had given him life also gave him death. "There are periods in life when I think that I want death, despite my long struggle against it all these years," Williams wrote to Oliver Evans at the beginning of 1981. Edwina Williams died in June 1980. (Gore Vidal referred to her as "666" in his condolence note; "that stands for 'The Beast of the Apocalypse,'" Williams explained to Kazan.) Audrey Wood, who had been a kind of surrogate mother for thirty-one years, had a stroke in 1981 and never regained consciousness. Williams sent one of his paintings—*Christ on a Cross*—to Wood's nursing home, where it hung over her bed for the four years she clung to life. Williams saw "a long, long stretch of desolation about me, now at the end." Even his handwriting signaled a shift; the bold flow of his signature was suddenly

Williams's painting of the Crucifixion

feathery, no longer an assertion of energy and confidence. "When I am very ill, as I am now—diseased pancreas and liver—I am unable to carry out even the most important things that I should do," he told Evans at the beginning of 1981, adding, "It is only good to think back on the times when life was lovely—at least comparatively."

Williams's memory plays were written in this wistful vein; blending elegance and anxiety, they failed to make his turbulent hauntedness dynamic. "There's an explosive center to 'Something Cloudy, Something Clear'—if only Mr. Williams would light the fuse," Frank Rich wrote in the *New York Times*. In his final full-length play, *A House Not Meant to Stand: A Gothic Comedy*, a "spook sonata" that was almost giddy with bleakness, however, Williams lit the fuse and turned his sense of being a "still living remnant" into something savage and sensational.

"Never, never, never stop laughing!" Williams counseled Truman

Capote, during his "period of disequilibrium." Williams practiced what he preached. Developed in three versions at the Goodman Theatre in Chicago between 1980 and 1982—it began as the one-act *Some Problems for the Moose Lodge*—*A House Not Meant to Stand* was a complete stylistic departure. In its embrace of the comic grotesque, it announced Williams's refusal to suffer. The play's aspiration—to combine stage mayhem with moral outrage—also broadcast the influence of the British playwright Joe Orton, to whom Williams dedicated *The Everlasting Ticket*, a play he worked on during the eighteen-month gestation of *A House Not Meant to Stand*. "I don't compete with Joe Orton. I love him too much," Williams said at the time. Nonetheless, he adapted Orton's game of dereliction, delirium, and denial into his own allegory of decay.

At curtain rise, the decrepit Cornelius and Bella McCorkle are returning, at midnight, to their dilapidated, rain-swept Mississippi house, which has a perpetually leaky roof and a threadbare interior, whose "panicky disarray" is intended "to produce a shock of disbelief." The first sound of the play is "a large mantel clock," which "ticks rather loudly for about half a minute before there is the sound of persons about to enter the house." The relentlessness of time is the issue. The imminent threat of structural collapse is meant as "a metaphor for the state of society," Williams says in the play's first stage direction. (The epigram, by Yeats, is equally explicit: "Things fall apart; the center cannot hold.") In its loquacious Southern way, the play aspires to a kind of farce momentum: at a certain speed all things disintegrate. But as Williams's alternative titles for the play indicate—"A House Not Meant to Last Longer Than the Owner," "The Disposition of the Remains," "Terrible Details," "Putting Them Away"— he was also prefiguring his own ending. The play talks about the specter of "sinister times"—nuclear war, inflation, overpopulation—but the haunting it demonstrates is Williams's.

A House Not Meant to Stand is a funhouse of mirrors in which comic images of Williams's humiliated past distort his fury and reflect back his pain as pleasure. Williams's ornery, bombastic father, CC, returns, under his own name, as the comic menace, Cornelius. Although he has acquired new illnesses (osteoarthritis, pancreatitis) and new pills (Cotazym, Donnatal) from his author, his overstuffed chair and his brutish detachment

from his family are very much his own. "I don't respect tears in a man, and over-attachment to Mom, Mom, Mom," Cornelius tells his feckless, second son, Charlie. In the play, as in Williams's life, Cornelius's hectoring has already driven two children out of the house: Chips, the gay and now dead first son, and Joanie, the daughter, the unseen resident of a lunatic asylum. CC referred to the young Williams as "Miss Nancy." Cornelius similarly taunts Chips's effeminacy—"I remember when he was voted the prettiest girl at Pascagoula High." At the opening, returning from Chips's funeral, Cornelius and Bella try to understand their son's tragic early death; Cornelius puts Chips's homosexuality down to Bella's cosseting:

CORNELIUS: You encouraged it, Bella. Encouraged him to design girls' dresses. He put a yellow wig on and modelled 'em himself. Something—*drag* they call it. Misunderstood correctly—by the neighbors.
BELLA: He could of grown outa that.

CC threatened to kick Edwina and her children out of the family home; in *A House Not Meant to Stand*, Cornelius threatens to commit Bella to a mental home in order to get his hands on her "moonshine money," the cash he thinks his wife has inherited from her bootlegging grandfather and stashed away. (She has.) In a plot point that Williams adapted from his own brother's folly, Cornelius decides to make a run for Congress and wants the money from Bella to pay for his campaign—the very skulduggery that Williams feared Dakin had become involved in when newspapers reported that Edwina had made a fifty-thousand-dollar contribution to his ill-fated Illinois senatorial bid. ("No one whom I have discussed the question with has any doubt that he will be defeated in this race," Williams wrote to his mother in 1972. "Please assure me that you have not thrown so much money away on such a hopeless cause.") Williams wickedly transforms the incident into the driving force of his com-

OPPOSITE PAGE: In rehearsal for his last full-length play,
A House Not Meant to Stand, 1981

Helping brother Dakin Williams run for governor of Illinois, 1978

edy: Will Cornelius get his hands on the "Dancie money"? Will the confused Bella manage to hang on to it?

But the real autobiographical revelation of the play is the psychic atmosphere beneath it. Bella's confounding maternal non-communication is a re-creation of the emotional absenteeism in Edwina that triggered her son's compulsion to be seen, to turn his inner life into unforgettable event. Cornelius tells Charlie that "lunacy runs rampant" in his wife's family, the neurasthenic "Dancies" (a variation on "the Dakins")—just as CC used to berate Edwina's ancestral line, which was filled with "alarming incidences of mental and nervous breakdowns." Moving heavily around the house, confused and demented by grief at the loss of her eldest child, Bella is a sort of saintly sleepwalker, whose mind is always elsewhere:

CHARLIE: Mom?

BELLA:—Chips?

CHARLIE: No, no, Mom, I'm Charlie.

"Bella should be presented as a grotesque but heart-breaking Pieta," Williams wrote in his notes. "She all but senselessly broods over the play as an abstraction of human love and compassion—and tragedy." Retreating into herself, projected backward into the past and never alive to her present, she is haunted, and haunting. "My eyes keep clouding over with—time," she says at one point. When she pokes around the kitchen, Charlie asks her what she's looking for. "Life, all the life we had here!" she says. Bella pines for her children as they once were; she can't think of them as adults. Bella is shown as a dutiful wife and mother. Unbidden she serves up an omelette to her son; she insists on doing the shopping; she responds without complaint to her husband's imperious commands:

CORNELIUS: (*half-rising and freezing in position*) TYLENOL THREE. TYLENOL THREE!

(*Automatically Bella crosses to him and removes the medication from his jacket pocket.*)

CORNELIUS: Beer to wash it down with.

BELLA: Beer . . .

(*She shuffles ponderously off by the dining room.*)

Her actions appear nurturing; her aggression—her refusal to take in her children—is harder to see. At one point, Bella admits to her neighbor, Jessie, that "Little Joanie" is in the state lunatic asylum. "How did this happen to Joanie?" Jessie asks. "I don't know," Bella says. Joanie has sent a letter. Bella's first instinct is not to face it, to have Jessie read it for her. In the end, Bella reads it aloud, an exercise that demonstrates to the audience, if not to Bella, that hearing is not understanding: "All I had was a little nervous break down after that sonovabitch I lived with in Jefferson Parish quit me and went back to his fucking wife." Bella stops to apologize, and offers her only insight: "She seems to have picked up some very bad langwidge somehow." A hilarious, subtle piece of invention, the letter is a testament to the family's climate of denial. Bella can't fathom the landscape of impoverishment that Joanie's language betrays. She has loved her children but has not connected to them. She frets about them, but she has never known them or understood her own contribution to their haplessness.

As Bella approaches her end, in a reversal of the trope of *The Glass Menagerie*, where, in an exhibition of his literary aplomb, Tom at the finale silences the ghosts of his past ("Blow out your candles, Laura—and so good-bye"), Bella now summons up her own specters. According to the stage directions, "Ghostly outcries of children fade in—in Bella's memory—projected over house speakers with music under. She moves with slow, stately dignity." The children's voices bring with them the "enchanting lost lyricism of childhood":

VOICE OF YOUNG CHIPS:—*Dark*!
VOICE OF YOUNG CHARLIE: *Mommy*!
VOICE OF YOUNG JOANIE: We're *Hungry*!

At the moment that Bella delivers the Dancie money into safe hands, the ghosts of her children gather around the kitchen table. "Chips—will you say—Grace," she says. The line echoes Amanda's first words in *The Glass Menagerie*: "We can't say grace until you come to the table!" Amanda's prayer for grace is answered, at the finale, by Tom's empowered survival. In Williams's final full-length play, thirty-seven years later, however, grace is only a memory. "Ceremonially the ghost children rise from the table and slip soundlessly into the dark," the stage directions say. At the last beat, each ghost turns at the kitchen door "to glance back at their mother. A phrase of music is heard." The ghosts' departure brings the curtain down on Bella's struggle; it also hints at Williams's sense of an ending: a farewell to lyricism and to the spectral absences that have tormented and inspired him since childhood. With their stately exit, Williams seemed to imply, consciously or not, that he had said all he had to say.

"WHEN I HEAR [the critics] say that I have not written an artistically successful work for the theatre since 'Night of the Iguana' in 1961 they are being openly, absurdly mistaken," Williams wrote in 1981. *A House Not Meant to Stand* was proof that Williams was right. The play, which ran for only a month at the Goodman, received generally positive local press, but the *New York Times* didn't bother to send a critic to review it. When it played for a week at the New World Festival of the Arts, *Time* mentioned it as "the best thing Williams has written since 'Small Craft Warnings.'" In terms of narrative scope and theatrical daring, it was far better. Nonetheless, although he didn't stop writing, for all intents and purposes Williams's legend as a playwright ended in Chicago, where it had begun.

Still, if the world was uninterested in Williams's new work, it continued to honor the old. Williams turned seventy in 1981, on the heels of receiving the Common Wealth Award of Distinguished Service in Dramatic Arts, a twenty-two-thousand-dollar prize that he split with Harold Pinter. In June 1982, Harvard University, to which he had willed a large cache of his papers, after much badgering from St. Just, gave him an honorary degree. Open-collared and in a sports jacket amid the sea of crimson-gowned academics, Williams was ushered into Massachusetts Hall before the procession, where he mingled uncomfortably with the scholastic scrum and signed the guest book with the other honorands. Looking around the room, he noticed two nuns sitting on a sofa saying their rosaries, ignored by the milling crowd. "My God, that's Mother Teresa," he whispered to Robert Kiely, then master of Adams House, who was his escort. "In the strangest introduction I have ever made, I said respectfully to the tiny wrinkled nun, 'Mother Teresa, this is Tennessee Williams,'" Kiely recalled, adding, "She looked up kindly, obviously having no idea who Tennessee Williams was." Williams fell to his knees and put his head in her lap. Mother Teresa patted his head and blessed him.

While the parade of honors rolled on, there were signs that Williams was readying himself to leave it. That September, back in Florida, sitting alone in a bus-stop café, he struck up a conversation with a young novelist, Steven Kunes, and his wife. Charmed by their enthusiasm, he invited them back to his house. Williams asked Kunes about his novel-in-progress; after a while, he got up from the table, where they were having coffee, and returned with a large black case. He asked Kunes to look inside. "It was an Underwood typewriter from the nineteen-forties," Kunes said. " 'I write very rarely on this anymore,' he said. 'But I used it for "Summer and Smoke" and "Cat on a Hot Tin Roof." It needs a new ribbon, and perhaps some oil. I didn't know I'd be finding a place for it so soon. Write a play, Steven. Just write a play.' " In November, in his last public appearance, at the Ninety-Second Street Y in New York, Williams told the audience that he'd almost forgotten to show up. "He looked old," John Uecker, a theater director and Williams's caretaker at the time, recalled. "I knew that mortality had entered the picture." Williams read for half an hour, then abruptly stood up. "That's the end of the performance," he said.

"I don't understand my life, past or present, nor do I understand life itself," he had written to his Key West friend Kate Moldawer that May. "Death seems more comprehensible to me." On Christmas Eve, worried that their persistent telephone calls to Williams had gone unanswered, Moldawer and Gary Tucker, the director who had mounted the early versions of *A House Not Meant to Stand*, went to Williams's house. He had locked himself inside three days earlier. The door had to be broken down. They found Williams on the floor, wrapped in a sheet, with pill vials and wine bottles around him. He was dehydrated, frail, and incoherent. He was rushed to a hospital, where, under a false name, he spent several days recovering. His Key West doctor told him that he could not continue much longer without prolonged hospitalization. "He just wouldn't have it," Uecker said. "You couldn't tell him anything. He would only do what *he* wanted to do."

Since the spring, Williams had toyed with the idea of renting out his Key West property. After his collapse, he finally decided to sell it. Sometime in the last days of December, Leoncia McGee, his housekeeper, overheard Williams calling for a taxi. When she inquired about the car, he told her that he was going to New York. She asked when he'd be coming back. "I won't ever be coming home again," he said. He handed her a check for her weekly salary and explained that she'd be receiving her future checks from New York. "Before Mr. Tom went away from the

In academic procession to receive an honorary degree from Harvard University, 1982

house alone, he came back into the kitchen and handed me another check, one for a thousand dollars," McGee said. "'What's this for?' I asked Mr. Tom. 'For Christmas,' he said. I walked with him to the front door, and before he left he kissed me on the cheek, a thing he never done before. That's when I knew he wasn't coming back. He kissed me, and he was travelling alone, and he never done them things before."

In January 1983, Williams sat down to write an encomium to James Laughlin, to be read at an awards dinner at the National Arts Club in New York. New Directions, which Laughlin founded and whose backlist forms a canon of modernism, had published forty-eight of Williams's books—which have, collectively, sold five million copies, helping to sustain the independence of the house and making Williams its best-selling author. After celebrating his friend—"It was James Laughlin in the beginning and it remains James Laughlin now"—Williams invoked the work that Laughlin had published enthusiastically over the decades. "I know that it is the poetry that distinguishes the writing when it is distinguished, that of the plays and of the stories, yes, that is what I had primarily to offer," Williams wrote. He crossed out a tentative modifying clause; by hand, he added, "And now as a time for reckoning seems near . . ."

In February, unhappy and unwell, Williams took himself off alone on a panicky junket to London, Rome, and Taormina, in Italy. Within a week, he was back in New York. At the time, a small not-for-profit theater on Forty-Second Street was reviving *Vieux Carré*; the production didn't get reviewed. When Rader asked Williams about it, he said, "I've gone from good reviews, to bad reviews, to no reviews."

On the day in 1939 when Williams first met Audrey Wood and his professional career officially began, he joined Wood and her husband in their suite at the Royalton Hotel. Wood served sherry and proposed a toast. "To us," she said. "Let's be honest and each of us drink to himself," Williams replied, saluting his newly minted public identity as "Tennessee Williams." In the more than thirty plays and seventy one-acts, written over six decades, Williams built a kingdom of the self, at once glorious and onerous. "*I, I, I!*—a burden to be surrendered," he noted in his sixty-ninth year. In 1983, sometime between the moment when he was last seen, at 7:30 P.M. on February 24, and 10:30 A.M. the following day, when he was found in the Sunset Suite on the thirteenth floor of the Hotel Elysée in New York—the "Easy Lay," as he called it—Williams surrendered the self that he had liberated, lacerated, pleasured, mythologized, and destroyed.

CHAPTER 10

The Sudden Subway

Tennessee called death the sudden subway and now he has
taken that train.

—JAMES LAUGHLIN,
"Tennessee"

He wrote his own life; he wanted to write his own death.

—JOHN UECKER

There was a "Do Not Disturb" sign on the door when the police
arrived at Williams's room at the Hotel Elysée at 12:40 P.M. on February 25, 1983. For three days, Williams had been holed up inside, refusing entry to the cleaners and to almost everyone, except his new agent,
Luis Sanjurjo, and occasionally John Uecker, who kept an eye on him
from the sitting room of the suite and his adjacent bedroom. (Williams
declined at least five long-distance telephone calls from Lady St. Just.)

In his poem "Cried the Fox," Williams had likened the panicky perpetual motion of his life to that of a fox pursued by hounds:

> I run, cried the fox, in circles,
> narrower, narrower still,
> across the desperate hollow,
> skirting the frantic hill

Now, without the energy to make another run for it, he seemed cornered. Outside his room, Uecker waited, ready to order up the breakfasts

that Williams picked at, to watch television with him, or to read to him from the satchel of books he'd brought along for that purpose. "I knew he was dealing with his whole life—where he was gonna go next. He had nobody; he had no home; he didn't have me, either—I was temporary," Uecker said.

In *The One Exception*, a prescient one-act play—and his last piece of writing—completed in January 1983, Williams predicted his own parlous situation. His heroine, Kyra, soon to be hospitalized and "deathly afraid of institutions," has "retreated to her room." "She dreads any encounter," her caretaker, May, tells Viola, a former roommate from happier times who has come to visit. "Don't be offended. It's the same with everyone except me, now, and even sometimes with me." May and Viola huddle outside Kyra's room to discuss the best way of negotiating a meeting between the old friends. "She used to have periods of depression but pulled out of them," Viola says. "She had her work and us, her friends, to offer our moral support, in those days."

When Kyra does finally appear, her first halting words are "I—can't talk much. The past is—passed." Brusque and tense, Viola pours out a cascade of gossip before trying to buttonhole Kyra for an urgent loan. Kyra, however, is in a different realm of urgency. "Yes. Alone," she says, mishearing, "except for . . . Noth-nothing. Just—" Viola tries to touch her. Kyra trembles, calls out, apologizes, and, with the help of May, is ushered back to her room, where she locks herself in. Worried that her friend is suicidal, Viola says to May, "I wonder if it wouldn't be better to put her in right away or there could be a repetition of the attempt to—" When May calls the doctor and pleads with Kyra to eat and to prepare herself to go to the hospital, Kyra "nods with a senseless look." She is petrified; in the last words Williams ever wrote, his character closes down the world and herself:

> Kyra takes a few hesitant steps in one direction, then another. Frightened by the sound of her slippers on the floor, she removes them: then crosses to each door and bolts it stealthily. That done, she is again undecided of what to do next: at last, she seats herself rigidly in a chair stage center and closes her eyes.

"Tennessee begged me not to call the hospital, not to put him in hospital," Uecker said. At one point, after watching a television news report about a man who'd pulled the plug on his mother-in-law, Williams asked Uecker if he'd do that for him. "I most certainly will not," Uecker said. "This man's up on charges of manslaughter. I can't do that." Williams looked at him. "Well, the only one that I could talk to is Lady Maria. She's strong and rich," he said. Then he fell silent. After a while, he said, "But only if there's little, or no, hope."

"Every time I'd go in the room I had to get myself centered," Uecker said. "He was watching me, worried if I was going to turn him in or not, if I was going to betray him. He didn't want a public death." A loyal, if nervy, companion, Uecker had Williams's measure as an artist and a man. In the previous few months of being Williams's "right-hand bower," Uecker had shepherded his boss through a series of punishing abdications. "It was like watching a titan come down," Uecker said. "You watched his vital forces leave." He continued, "He was interested in nothing. Not in meeting or being with young people. Not once did I see him look at anyone. He was not looking at beauty at all, whether male or female beauty. He was removed from everything."

Williams had thrown away his paints; stopped swimming; sold the Key West house. On the Monday before he died, over a half-eaten sandwich at the Drake Hotel, he told Uecker, "I can't write. And if I can't write. I don't want to live. I'm gonna get some Seconals. I know you don't approve, but you understand?" On Tuesday night, at dinner with his good friend, the actress Jane Smith, who had flown to Key West after his collapse and brought him back to recover at her New York apartment for the first two weeks of January, he confided, "I have faced the fact."

On Thursday, Uecker, worried about Williams's exhaustion and the Seconals he had stashed in the safe in his room, called Williams's doctor: "I said, 'What if he should take the whole bottle?' He thought I was hysterical and said, 'If there's no liquor there, just don't worry about it. His system is accustomed to the medication. He can't do damage without alcohol.' I said, 'But he hasn't eaten enough to sustain himself.' He said not to worry." Unable to calm his fears, Uecker enlisted Vass Voglis, another of Williams's friends, to help hospitalize him. They planned to do it the next day—Friday.

On Thursday evening, Uecker awakened Williams at seven to tell him that Jane Smith was in the sitting room, eager to see him. Williams came out to see her; he was embarrassed to be in his bathrobe. "He just seemed to be in dreamland," Uecker recalled. "He half blushed that he had slept so long. He said, 'Oh, Jane, I just can't go out.' He talked to her a few minutes and went back into his room. 'You and John go out to eat.'" They went downstairs to the hotel's La Veranda Restaurant.

When Uecker returned to the suite later that evening, he put his ear to the door and heard Williams's snoring; the next morning, he listened again and heard nothing. At 10:30 A.M., Uecker opened the door. The curtains were drawn; the place was a sour, pill-strewn mess. "It was bad. If you just took a photograph, oh my God," Uecker said. Williams was not in his bed. "I didn't feel his presence at all. I thought, Oh, God, he's gonna be in the bathroom and in terrible shape. I was just totally prepared for this whole trail of blood, or something like that. I looked in the bathroom, and he wasn't there," Uecker recalled. "My next thought was that he got his coat on in the middle of the night and started walking around the streets. Then I saw that the hotel key was still there. When I saw the key, I knew he was on the other side of the bed. I just had to face it, you know, with my eyes."

Williams was in his Jockey shorts, curled in a half-fetal position on the green carpet. He had slipped between the bed and the night table. He was on his right side; his glasses were still on. His right arm was extended backward, his forearm, bent at the elbow, rested against the mattress. Under the glass-covered night table was an empty vial of Seconal and a couple of corks from bottles of Corvo Salaparuta dry red wine, a half-full glass of which was on the night table. A photocopy of "Some of These Days," a short story by Williams's friend James Purdy, about a boy who dies of a broken heart, was also on the table. At the top of the page, as a sort of epigram, Purdy had written out some lines by Thomas Chatterton: "Water witches crowned with reeds / Bear me to your lethal tide."

When the police arrived on the scene, they sealed off the bedroom.

On the dresser they counted thirteen bottles of prescription drugs, including Aldomet, Zyloprim, Reglan, Cotazym, and HydroDiuril. Under Williams's right hand, they found one Seconal capsule; when they turned his body over, another one was uncovered. Once the bedclothes and sheets were removed, the total came to five.

The suite, which had been a cave of solitude all week, was suddenly overrun. Police, a couple of photographers, and the city's chief medical examiner, Dr. Elliot M. Gross, filled the room. Williams's close friends and business associates—Luis Sanjurjo, Milton Goldman, Vass Voglis, and Jane Smith—also joined the scrum. "There were so many people it was unbelievable," Uecker, who by his own admission started "to freak out" at the hubbub, recalled. "It all became so totally inhuman. The police came in with their Philistine ideas. *Oh, look at all these drugs—ha, ha, ha.* Their rolling eyes, giggling, smirking. *A rich decadent dies.* The whole bring-down of someone who has a great gift that people don't understand and don't have themselves. I just wasn't braced for that," he said. "I saw them making conclusions. I heard people say the press were outside." Uecker tried to speak to Gross. "I said, 'Look, it's not what it looks like. I know what it looks like—that's not what was happening. I swear to you.'" Gross walked away.

Williams was put in a body bag and placed on a stretcher. The ambulance crew wheeled him out of the bedroom; before they could get to the front door of the suite—reporters were crowded just outside it—Smith, who was watching with Uecker from his bedroom, said, "I've got to see him!" She bolted toward the stretcher, forcing her way through the phalanx of ambulance men to Williams's body. "It was like watching some incredible opera," Uecker said. "The whole room seemed to stop." Smith got down on her hands and knees and held Williams in the black rubber bag. "She just cried, and cried, and cried, and kissed him," Uecker said.

Fame, which was problematic for Williams in life, also proved a difficulty in death. On February 26, Gross announced to the press that he did not suspect foul play. "The cause of death is asphyxia due to obstruction of the glottis," he said, "by a plastic over-cap." According to Michael Baden, a forensic pathologist and a former chief medical examiner of New York, however, the bottle cap "was not wide enough to stop up

Williams's airway. In fact, it was not even *in* his airway. It was in his mouth." Nonetheless, the tale of Williams choking on a long thin rubber medical-bottle stopper was the news headline, and the official public story about his death; it is included in St. Just's *Five O'Clock Angel* and on the final page of Williams's own edited voluminous *Notebooks*. Gross also told the press that "an autopsy was performed this morning on the body of Thomas L. Williams. . . . Further studies, including chemical tests, will be performed." Gross had indeed sent samples to the lab for analysis, but he had sent them under another name, that of a drug-addicted youth who had jumped off a roof. Later Gross claimed that it was fear of foul play, along with the need to prevent press leaks about the famous, that had led him to do this. In 1985, Gross's controversial practices—and his behavior at the time of Williams's death, in particular—were featured in a *New York Times* exposé. "Gross told me it was a very important case and that he did not want anybody to know that they were working with this material," Dr. Milton L. Bastos, the former toxicology director for the Chief Medical Examiner's Office, told the *Times*. "This was not regular or proper. But I did it. These were orders." About five months after Williams's death, digging his heels in about asphyxia as the cause of death, Gross issued a statement amending his initial findings but going only so far as to admit that "apparently the overcap was being used to take the barbiturates." Weasel words aside, it was clear from the toxicology report, which had been completed two months before Gross's statement to the press, that whether by accident or by choice Williams had ingested a toxic level of Seconal. The report showed that Williams's brain, blood, stomach, liver, and kidney were saturated with secobarbital.

WHEN NEWS OF Williams's death first hit the front pages, he was prayed over, wept over, recited, and lauded. At a crowded memorial at the Shubert Theatre, in a letter read by Hume Cronyn, Elia Kazan called on the theater community to stop making "sad group noises" over Williams's death. "The man lived a very good life, full of the most profound pleasures and he lived it precisely as he chose," Kazan said. "That is allowed to few of us." The actress Elizabeth Ashley, who had been Williams's definitive "Maggie the Cat," said, "In order to negotiate life most people sort of chart an emotional course to avoid the rocks and shoals. . . . But Tennessee wrote about all of those shoals and the monsters in the sea that come up and eat the boat. He went into the taboos of the heart and let us know that we don't have to carve out of our souls, the innocence and the madness—the things society wants to amputate. He saw life whole—not just the skin on the hand, but the bones and the blood in the veins underneath." Arthur Miller, who, like Williams, had endured a critical fall from grace, cut to the nitty-gritty of Williams's career and courage: "For a while the theater loved him, and then it went back to searching in its pockets for its soul. He chose a hard life that requires the skin of an alligator and the heart of a poet. To his everlasting honor, he persevered and bore all of us toward glory."

The day after Williams's death, the lights of twenty Broadway marquees were dimmed. At Frank E. Campbell's funeral parlor, on the Upper East Side, Williams's body lay in state for three days in a simple wooden coffin without handles—"the Orthodox Jewish coffin," as Dakin Williams and St. Just called it. A Russian Orthodox priest had been imported by St. Just for the occasion, and a Russian icon was placed in Williams's folded hands. Williams's cousin the Reverend Sidney Lanier led the service. "It is a time of reconciliation for all who knew and shared life with him. He might laugh at our mood—we all remember his unique laugh, don't we?" Lanier began. When a second memorial service was held at the end of the week in St. Louis, darker laughs were in store.

Williams had wanted to be buried at sea. His wish was spelled out in a notarized letter; he had spoken about it to friends and even to the camera. "I'm to be borne out to sea in an inexpensive little vessel, perhaps a shrimping boat. I suggest it put out from my island home at Key West, and when this small craft has arrived at the point most nearly determined as the point at which Hart Crane gave himself to the sea, there, at that nearest point that can be determined by any existing records, I wish to be given back to the sea, from which life is said to have come," he said in the documentary *Tennessee Williams' South*.

The decision to bury Williams, instead, at the Calvary Cemetery in St. Louis was made by his brother, Dakin, whose "intimate biography" was to be published that April. The previous December, Dakin had flown to Key West to show Williams the galleys and to get his blessing; Williams had sent him away without seeing him. "If he had to die, and everyone has to die, he couldn't have done so at a more opportune moment," said Dakin, who envisioned a literary windfall—and a huge print run—after his brother's death. "Suddenly out of obscurity, to headlines across the nation. I think my life is beginning to take shape," he told the *Washington Post*. Being in Williams's shadow, Dakin said, "has forced me to run for public office, do everything but jump off the Empire State Building." He went on, "I didn't have a lot of pleasant times with him. When he was well, he didn't want to have anything to do with me. And when he was sick, he was very disagreeable to be around. I got him mostly when he was sick. I guess you could say I got in on all of the funerals and none of the picnics."

For Dakin, who made no bones about his sibling rivalry, Williams's funeral was a picnic of sorts. At the two-day St. Louis wake, where Williams lay in an open coffin with an Orthodox cross around his neck, Dakin sashayed around the airless funeral-home room in his "Parisian outfit," a pea-green leather jumpsuit that zipped up the front. Copies of *Vieux Carré* and Dakin's own *Bar Bizarre*, a privately published account of his legal career, with an introduction by his brother, were prominently displayed on a coffee table. Dakin had briefly entertained the idea of burying Williams beside his beloved grandparents in Waynesville, Ohio, but he'd judged it impractical. "The milk train doesn't stop in Waynesville anymore," he said. Of his decision to make St. Louis Williams's final stop, Dakin said, "I'm sure he'd disapprove of being buried here. But I'm his only survivor and this is where I think he should rest. Where else should I put him?" He added, "This way he'll be in a centrally located spot for people to pay their respects to the world's greatest talent since Shakespeare." If Dakin's hyperbole had the ring of P. T. Barnum, it was perhaps because he had plans to turn the grave site into a tourist attraction. "Dakin planned a concession stand peddling refreshments, trinkets, souvenir key chains, and Dakin's books," Dotson Rader said. "Good old Dakin always trying to cash in. There'd be admission charged to visit the grave site, like Graceland." By this time, Dakin knew that he had been mocked in his brother's will: of an estimated five-million-dollar estate, Dakin was willed a derisory twenty-five thousand dollars but only after Rose died. He had the last laugh, however. If he couldn't make Williams pay attention to him in life, Dakin could make him pay in death.

On March 5, more than twelve hundred mourners gathered for a ninety-minute requiem mass at the Byzantine-style St. Louis Cathedral. Afterward, a cortege of mourners, stretching for more than a mile, wound its way past 4633 Westminster Place, where the transplanted Williams family had first settled in St. Louis, in 1918, when Tom Williams was seven, to Calvary Cemetery. A tent had been set up on the greensward in front of the plot, with chairs for the mourners and a trestle for the pallbearers to rest the coffin on. With a light rain falling and the forsythia beginning to bloom, Williams was lowered into his grave. And so it came to pass that Tennessee Williams was buried in the city he called "St. Pollution"; an Episcopalian by birth and a Roman Catholic by conversion, he went to his resting place in a Jewish coffin marked by a gravestone emblazoned with an Orthodox cross. The man who had wanted to be absorbed back into the Mother Ocean ended up spending eternity next to his mother, the woman he'd fled and kept at a distance for a lifetime.

The dispute over Williams's physical remains was over; the quarrel over his literary remains was not. Williams's Last Will and Testament set off as sensational a display of mendacity and manipulation as any he wrote in life. In the penultimate paragraph of *Five O'Clock Angel*, St. Just wrote, "Tennessee's two great loves had been his work and his sister Rose. In his Will, he entrusted the care of both to Maria." How well St. Just succeeded in purveying this myth for the rest of her life can be seen in her own obituaries. "THE ARISTOCRATIC HELLCAT WHO LOVED TENNESSEE WILLIAMS" was the *London Evening Standard* headline. The *Guardian* spelled out her story in calmer detail: "She was Williams's closest woman friend, and her almost familial devotion was acknowledged upon his death, when she was named as his literary executor. His artistic heritage could not have been entrusted to a more vigilant administrator."

Despite all pronouncements to the contrary, Williams did not actually name St. Just as his literary executor. His will is explicit in its intention to separate the trustees of his estate—St. Just and John Eastman, who had fiduciary power and responsibility for Rose—from the people evaluating his literary legacy: in a codicil to the will—drawn up on September 11, 1980—Williams designated Harvard University as the sole arbiter of such judgment. In revising this history, St. Just was revising her place in Williams's story, which had been a bone of contention between them since the publication of his *Memoirs*, in 1975. As St. Just frequently told the press, she had thrown *Memoirs* into the wastebasket. She had been offended, she said, by its louche tales. She was even more offended by Williams's having made only eleven mentions of her in the book, referring to her as "an occasional actress," and promising the reader, "I will write more about Maria later." The most memorable remark about her in the book is "The lady is afflicted with *folie de grandeur*." St. Just put the screws on Williams, and his apology was a few typewritten pages about their relationship, which he promised would be published in the British edition. In the end, they were published in St. Just's book *Five O'Clock Angel*. Williams wrote, "In the American edition of my memoirs, this richly sustaining attachment was, for some reason, reduced by the editors to the point where it seemed to be little more than an acquaintance, practically unexplained."

But had the St. Just–Williams *amitié amoureuse* been blue-penciled out by others? "The answer is no," Kate Medina, the original editor of the book, said. Williams himself had virtually left St. Just out of the official story of his life. She had absorbed him, but had Williams, as she claimed in *Five O'Clock Angel*, absorbed her? "I suppose in a way he had," Gore Vidal said. "Although he was a *very* solitary cat. He appreciated, to a degree, what she did for him, which was just kind of looking after him. But I don't think he ever had any affection for anybody." At the finale of Williams's 1976 play *This Is (An Entertainment)*—which was about St. Just and dedicated to her—the General offers an affectionate envoi to St. Just's stand-in, the Countess: "My last request is a last command. Give the lady safe passage through the mountains! Will you? For old times' sake?" In a sense, Williams had offered St. Just a safe passage through life. But in the fifteen years between the writing of that play and Williams's death, their relationship had declined. Williams's last, garbled story, "The Negative," written in November 1982, tells of a has-been poet who can't finish the poem he's writing and is about to be sent to a nursing home. He gets a phone call from the mysterious Lady Mona, who seems to know all his difficulties and wants to be his muse. They meet in a dark café. The poet, horrified by the woman's rapacious eyes, throws himself in the Thames.

Of St. Just, Bruce Smith—whose memoir *Costly Performances: Tennessee Williams: The Last Stage* recounted his friendship and PR work with Williams on his late plays—said, "He knew that she had exaggerated and exploited the level of their friendship beyond all recognition." At the end of his life, Smith added, Williams was "weaning himself away from her. There were unopened letters from her even when I was around there and she was back in London. He was emotionally through with her. He said to me, 'I don't know why she bothers to come over here for these openings because she isn't needed and she really isn't wanted.'" Mitch Douglas recalled the rehearsals of Williams's last Broadway play, *Clothes for a Summer Hotel*. "Maria was very much a presence," he said. "There were lots of notes, and, if I may respectfully say so, she was getting in the way. Tennessee would smile and be very nice to her and then turn around to the people at hand and say, 'Well, you know, she really doesn't understand this kind of theater.'" According to Charles Carroll— the personal representative of the Southeast Banks of Florida, which was the sole executor of Williams's estate until his will was probated in June 1988—Williams, before his death, considered striking St. Just's appointment as a co-trustee from his will, but "he was a procrastinator, and he never got it done."

Inevitably, Williams's will was the focus of much powerful and ambivalent feeling between him and St. Just. "She was always whining about money," Dotson Rader said. "About her future. She was getting old. He'd say, 'Oh, baby, don't worry. You're in the will.'" Rader added, "Tennessee was always telling people they were in his will." St. Just argued with

Williams—and even fell out with him for a number of years, friends said—over her potential inheritance. This estrangement accounts for the meager twenty letters from Williams to St. Just between 1959 and 1967 that appear in *Five O'Clock Angel*. "Ultimately, money was the root of her evil," Paula Laurence said. "She loved money. Money was all tied up with security, with love, with emotions." With a large estate to manage, two daughters in private school, and an erratic husband, financial security was always an issue for St. Just. She wanted Williams to leave her a percentage of the royalties to one of his major plays—a gesture he'd made to other important caretakers. But the only royalties Williams left to St. Just were the proceeds of his rarely performed *Two-Character Play*—which, in fiscal terms, was as impudent a joke as Shakespeare's leaving his wife the "second best bed." Williams also made St. Just's co-trusteeship of the Rose Williams Trust—and the substantial stipend that eventually came with the job—dependent on Rose's life span. According to the will, when Rose's life ended, so would the salaries and benefits of the co-trustees. This was a guarantee, above and beyond St. Just's avowed devotion to Rose, that proper care would be taken of her.

When St. Just was devotedly nursing her sick husband, Peter St. Just, near the end of his life, the New York columnist Harriet Van Horne asked her, "Suppose both Peter and Tenn were terminally ill? At whose bedside would you sit?" According to Van Horne, St. Just replied, "Well, Tennessee's, darling, of course." As it happened, Williams died a year and a half before Peter St. Just. In the remaining years of her life, St. Just frequently asked Paula Laurence, "What do you think? If Tennessee had lived, how would this have ended?" Laurence explained, "She wanted us to reassure her that he would be with her somehow. Maybe not in a legal marriage, but together. You felt so sad about that. 'Get real, girl!' Jesus!"

St. Just's frustrations and her fantasy of being Williams's widow coalesced in her role as co-trustee of the Rose Williams Trust, which held the majority of Williams's estate, about five million dollars. In her care of Rose, St. Just was imaginative, warm, and dutiful; in her involvement in Williams's literary affairs, however, she was fanatical. St. Just had played a large part in getting Williams to sign the codicil to his will, withdrawing the bequest of his papers to the University of the South—the alma mater of his beloved grandfather, in whose name a literary fund was to be established—and giving them to Harvard University instead. (This legal hornet's nest was resolved behind closed doors when the University of the South agreed to receive the assets of the trust—including the earnings of the published works—while Harvard got clear title to the manuscripts.) The producer Lyle Leverich had been in New Orleans with Williams when St. Just called him about the codicil. "'Tell her I'm asleep,'" he recalled Williams saying to his companion. "Then he turned to me and said, 'They want me to change my will.' Those were exactly his words. He mumbled something about not wanting to do it. He shook his head." But under continuing pressure, Williams did sign the codicil, and Jeanne Newlin, then the curator of the Harvard Theatre Collection, became the person in charge of the papers after his death. Daunted at the prospect of managing the estate with John Eastman—who had drawn up Williams's will but didn't know him well, and was busy with many other celebrity clients, including Paul McCartney (who was married to his sister), Andrew Lloyd Webber, David Bowie, and Billy Joel—Newlin pressed St. Just to get involved. "I knew that *she* was the one who knew Tennessee, and I was beginning to be worried about the material," Newlin said, adding, "And I'll tell you something: it was necessary. A Tennessee Williams person was necessary, who was familiar with the work."

Because the trust owned the copyrights to the plays, St. Just found herself increasingly in a position to give or to deny permission to produce them. She attacked the job with the vindictive enthusiasm she'd brought to her overhaul of Wilbury, her husband's family estate, once her mother-in-law was dead. ("BANG, BANG, BANG, and out like stout go the following," she'd written gleefully to Williams about firing the cook, the butler, the pantry boy, and the chambermaid.) Like Mrs. Goforth in *The Milk Train Doesn't Stop Here Anymore*, St. Just consigned anyone who wouldn't do her bidding to "the oubliette." She held sway with such ferocity that even her own solicitor, the legendary fixer Lord Arnold Goodman, told her she was out of line. In his 1993 memoir, *Tell Them I'm on My Way*, Goodman wrote, "She was engaged in vigorous battles to maintain the integrity of various productions, despite my constant remonstrances that it is no part of her duty as a trustee to engage in casting the play. However, remonstrances to Maria are about as futile as persuading a charging bull of the error of its ways." "Maria was the greatest cheerleader Tennessee Williams will ever have," Eastman said. "Sometimes cheerleaders aren't so pretty once you get them off the field." To those who worked with the estate, however, Eastman seemed only too glad to have St. Just oversee the literary side of Williams's affairs. "Eastman is perfectly willing to get out of any aspect which is not going to bring in money, which means the literary aspect of it," Vidal said.

In the most literal sense, St. Just and Eastman fulfilled their mandate as trustees, which was to increase the economic value of the estate. Between 1984, when St. Just and Eastman began to assist the Southeast Banks of Florida in administering the estate, and 1989, Williams's earnings jumped from $349,000 to $545,000 a year; by 1993, they were up to $809,000 a year. But St. Just had no academic training and no understanding of how a literary reputation is made or sustained. She understood that Williams's work was a financial asset, but for more than a decade, because of her draconian desire to retain control over literary matters, she managed to freeze almost all critical discourse about it. Williams's royalties went up, but the discussion of his work went down. Scholars were refused the right to quote from Williams's unpublished writings, or even to Xerox material from his early papers, which occupy a hundred boxes at the Harry Ransom Center at the University of Texas at Austin. "These are the people who keep Williams's reputation alive by writing about him and by teaching him in their classes," Cathy Henderson, then the librarian who oversaw the collection, wrote to St. Just in 1992. "Denying this group of users the option of doing at least a portion of their research from photocopies discourages critical attention and sets the stage for there being less of an audience for his works." "Maria wasn't really interested in the scholarship or the longevity of Williams for the future," said Elizabeth McCann, the American co-producer of Sir Peter Hall's 1989 revival of *Orpheus Descending*. "She was only interested in what was in it for her. Now. This moment."

In the first nine months after Williams's death, St. Just tried to stop many of the productions that the Southeast Banks of Florida had approved, including a cable-TV production of *Streetcar* with Ann-

Margret—a project that had been initiated in Williams's lifetime. Two months after Williams's death, Ed Sherin—who held both a letter of support from Williams for a mooted second 1983–84 production of *The Red Devil Battery Sign* and the agreement of Shirley Knight to play Woman Downtown—wrote to St. Just for permission to mount the play at the Hartman Theatre in Stamford, Connecticut, where he was the artistic director. St. Just said no. If he was shocked that she'd made other plans for the play, St. Just wrote, pissing on him from a great height, she was shocked that he hadn't expressed any sympathy for the tragic loss of her beloved Tennessee.

Rocco Landesman, then head of New York's Jujamcyn Theaters, approached St. Just about using Williams's name for a Broadway theater. "I wanted to name what is now the Walter Kerr Theatre after Tennessee," Landesman said. "I called Maria St. Just. She talked quite a lot and listened not at all. The gist of the conversation was that if we'd produce 'Orpheus Descending' on Broadway, she'd arrange this. Which was too bad, because Tennessee would have had the most beautiful theater in New York named after him. But I wouldn't submit to blackmail."

Because of St. Just's bow-wow caprice, *Something Cloudy, Something Clear*, a play she disliked because it was "homosexual," wasn't published until 1995. *A House Not Meant to Stand* wasn't published until 2008. Gregory Mosher, who had moved from being the artistic director of the Goodman Theatre in Chicago to running the Vivian Beaumont Theater at Lincoln Center, offered the estate a major New York production of *A House*, which St. Just declined. "She said, 'The play is not doable,'" Mosher recalled. "I said, 'You didn't even see it. How do you know if it's doable or not?'" St. Just was charming and biddable when seasoned British directors, such as Peter Hall or Richard Eyre, came calling, but younger directors who lacked Hall's and Eyre's cachet and charm were in for heavy weather. Simon Curtis, then the head of BBC television drama, tried to persuade St. Just to let him produce *Stopped Rocking*. "She pretended an awful lot," Curtis recalled. "'Who's going to write the screenplay?' she said to me. 'It *is* a screenplay,' I said."

Since St. Just's public persona was an elaborate house of cards, any scrutiny was a threat, and she was determined to have a say in the choice of Williams's biographer. "His personal image has been appallingly tarnished," she said, of the spate of inadequately researched memoirs about Williams—including his own—that emphasized drink, drugs, and homosexual promiscuity. "I explained to her, 'All you care about is how you come out of the story,'" Gore Vidal said. "'Any biographer will give you the right to censor anything about yourself, since the biography is not of Maria but of Tennessee.'" Many biographers were called, and one was chosen. Margot Peters, the author of biographies of Charlotte Brontë and the Barrymore family, worked on a Williams biography from 1989 to 1991. The process did not go smoothly. "She definitely wanted to vet the manuscript," Peters said of St. Just. "I just kept telling her, 'Maria, this is my own biography. You're giving me the rights, but it's mine. I can't work if you're going to vet the manuscript.' There were some things that she wouldn't even let me examine. First I could use quotes, then perhaps I couldn't." The project was off; then it was on again. Finally, the two women parted ways in a bitter transatlantic phone call. "I would never trust you with him," St. Just told Peters. Peters screamed at St. Just, "You have ruined Tennessee Williams! You're ruining him! You're ruining his reputation! You're ruining scholarship for him! I wouldn't work on him or with you for anything in this world!" And she slammed the phone down.

St. Just, an admirer of Margaret Thatcher, adopted the former prime minister's tactic when faced with opposition: she took no prisoners. Obliteration, not negotiation, was her style. She never mentioned—not even to the "authorized" Peters—that for five years prior to his death, Williams had cooperated with Lyle Leverich, who was planning a two-part biography and who possessed two letters from Williams naming him the authorized biographer and allowing him "full access to my private correspondence and journals." Williams had first met Leverich in 1976, when Leverich was managing a small San Francisco theater called The Showcase, which successfully produced *The Two-Character Play*. The following year, Leverich wrote a long letter to the *New York Times* in response to Robert Brustein's review of *Tennessee Williams' Letters to Donald Windham: 1940-1965*, and Williams wrote to thank him for his support. The next year, over dinner, Leverich suggested that Williams's own *Memoirs* had done him a disservice, and proposed that a book be written about Williams's work in the theater, whereupon Williams said, "Baby, you write it!" In January 1979, Williams instructed Bill Barnes to represent Leverich. Subsequently, he decided that Leverich should be his biographer—a task that Leverich, who had never written a book, accepted. In 1984, shortly after Williams died, Charles Carroll confirmed Leverich as Williams's official biographer.

Leverich worked on his first volume—*Tom: The Unknown Tennessee Williams*—in ten years of relative tranquility. The book was scheduled to be published by Grove Weidenfeld in the fall of 1991. By mid-1988, however, Williams's will had come out of probate, and St. Just had ascended to her self-appointed role as Williams's literary guardian. She set out to retroactively deny Leverich permission to publish, on the grounds that Williams's two letters of authorization did not specifically say that Leverich could quote from correspondence and journals. Leverich contended that he had indeed obtained the required approval from the Southeast Banks of Florida, and had proceeded in good faith since then, but St. Just dismissed Leverich's work as just another "pirate book." She took up the matter with Andreas Brown, the owner of the Gotham Book Mart and an appraiser of literary archives who had been hired by Audrey Wood in the sixties to catalogue and appraise Williams's papers and had resumed the task after Williams's death. In a letter, St. Just upbraided Brown for helping Leverich and assured him that Leverich would never be the authorized biographer. Brown wrote back to say that he had helped Leverich on Williams's instructions. Nonetheless, even though Leverich's publishers thought he had a good case, they were not willing to take on a potentially expensive crusade against the quixotic Lady St. Just. Plans to publish were dropped, and the book was kicked into the long grass.

In another letter to Brown, St. Just laid the responsibility for the estate's hard line on James Laughlin, to whom Leverich had submitted an early draft of his manuscript for comment. Laughlin returned the manuscript in the spring of 1989, claiming that he was unable to read it because he was coping with fire damage to his Connecticut home. He added, however, that he didn't think it would "fit into Maria's plans," because "she wants something far shorter and with a different slant." Subsequently, Laughlin wrote to the estate's lawyer about the biography: "I admired the depth of its research but did not feel that the book had the literary qualities requisite for designation as an authorized biography of Tennessee Williams."

What had happened? Brown, who knew both Leverich and Laughlin well, wanted to know. "As I recall," he wrote to Laughlin on June 27, 1990, "Lyle submitted his early unedited draft to you for general comment, not as a screening process for Maria and the estate to accept or reject Lyle's work as 'authorized.' Further, I do not recall your saying at any time during those occasions when the two of us discussed Lyle and his manuscript that you had concluded that his biography did not 'warrant' authorization." Brown got his explanation from Laughlin on a handwritten postcard, postmarked July 5: "The answer is spelled blackmail. Sorry!" St. Just had played her ace. As the holder of the copyrights, she could choose to move any future Williams books to another publishing house or to block Laughlin's plan to publish a volume of Williams's letters to him. In May 1992, Laughlin wrote to Leverich, "I must remain friends with the estate because we have business to do with them, but I don't like the censorship bit at all."

Others, including Vidal, lobbied St. Just on behalf of Leverich and academic freedom. "I've denounced her," Vidal said. "I've bawled her out. She knew (a) that he was very thorough and (b) that he was onto the abortion thing. And I said, 'Everybody has abortions, for chrissake. What's the big deal? It's not as though you're in line to be Queen of England, and this might be bad P.R. You're just an actress—actresses go in for that sort of thing.'" Taking matters into her own hands, St. Just went to the Williams archive at the Harry Ransom Center, in Austin, and demanded, as his literary executor, that she be allowed to read his letters alone in a private room. With a razor, she cut out any incriminating words in Williams's letters. (She didn't realize, however, that the library kept microfiche copies of every document and could access the excised content.) Leverich wrote to St. Just and offered to "submit for your review and comment" any sensitive material he had uncovered. She never replied. "Maria wreaked havoc on this man's life," Brown said. "It's a real moral crime."

In 1994, the year of St. Just's death, and at the end of a three-month *New Yorker* magazine inquiry into the Williams Estate's fiduciary and literary high jinx, John Eastman finally allowed Leverich's biography to proceed to publication. Thirteen years after Williams was buried, the conversation between America's greatest playwright and the world he'd once bustled in could properly begin. The results of this reinvigorated discussion could be seen at the box office. In 2000, there were 246 productions of Williams's plays, which earned a total of $1.15 million; by 2011, the number of worldwide productions had risen to 309, and the receipts to $1.4 million.

IN HIS STRUGGLE to unlearn repression, to claim his freedom, and to forge glory out of grief, Williams turned his own delirium into one of the twentieth century's great chronicles of the brilliance and the barbarity of individualism. In order to name our pain, he devoured himself:

> . . . this much will be clear as any of his lost mornings,
> that he did own one essential part of a hero,
> the idea of life as a nothing-withholding submission of self to flame.

Out of the sad little wish to be loved, Williams made characters so large that they became part of American folklore. Blanche, Stanley, Big Daddy, Brick, Amanda, and Laura transcend their stories—sensational ghosts who haunt us through the ages with their fierce, flawed lives. Williams allowed words to live like anthems in the national imagination: "I have always depended on the kindness of strangers"; "Sometimes—there's God—so quickly"; "Nowadays the world is lit by lightning"; "*Make voyages!—Attempt them!*—there's nothing else."

Grabbing both the brass ring of success and the trapeze of the flesh, Williams swung high and low. His passage through time was sensational. He contended doggedly with his own roiling divided self. In him, until his last breath, the forces of life and death were pitched in clamorous battle. Art was his habit, his "fatal need," and his salvation. Foraying into those ineffable realms of sensation where language has little purchase, he uncovered our sorrow, our desire, our hauntedness. At the same time, he

changed the shape and the ambition of the American commercial theater, which ultimately couldn't support the paradoxical truth, "the tragic
division of the human spirit," that his stories tried to trap.

In his single-minded pursuit of greatness, Williams exhausted himself
and lost his way. "I want to get my goodness back," he frequently said. If
he didn't find the light, his outcrying heart certainly cast it. "What implements have we but words, images, colors, scratches upon the caves of our
solitude?" he asked. In the game of hide-and-seek that he and his theater
played with the world, Williams left a trail of beauty so that we could try
to find him.

Acknowledgments

I'M AWARE THAT many Williams fans have been waiting a long time for me to cough up this book. A biography takes time; I wouldn't have been able to rush it even if I'd wanted to. Nonetheless, twelve years from start to finish is pushing the envelope. I'm grateful to have lived long enough to complete this particularly challenging narrative trek. The climb would not have been possible without the generous and loyal support of many others along the way.

I salute: David Aaronovitch, Ginny Agnew, David Allentuck, Katherine Allentuck, Hilton Als, Jesse Angelo, Herman Arrow,° Elizabeth Ashley, Mary Babcock (copy editor), Jonathan Baker, Emilio Banda, Milly S. Barringer, Gregg Barrios, Megan Beatie, Joseph P. Benincasa, Megan Bernard, Georges and Anne Borchardt, Robert Bray, Andreas Brown, Ann Caserta, Mark Cave, Frank Corsaro, Meg Courtney, Jere Couture,° Paul Davis, Josephine DePetris, Mitch Douglas, Julia Druskin, Richard Eyre, Arcadia Falcone, David Finkle, Roy Flukinger, Horton Foote,° Patrice Fox, Peggy L. Fox, Leslie Garis, Lynn Goldberg, Ann Goldstein, Robert Gottlieb, Julie Grob, Harold Guskin, Allean Hale, John Hancock, Cathy Henderson, Kenneth Holdich, Trudie Homan, Anne Jackson, Frances Kazan, Nick Kazan, Thomas Keith (Chronology), Arthur Kopit, Shelagh Kufpfe, Tony Kushner, Jane Lahr, Stanley Ledbetter, Jennifer B. Lee, Margo Lion, Felicia Londre, Zoulema Loup, Sidney Lumet,° James Malcolm, Kendra Malinowski, Lynne Maphies, John Maxtone-Graham, Peter Mears, Mike Medavoy, JoAnne Metsch, Richard Mikel, Seymour Milbert,° Arthur Miller,° Judy Morris, Gregory Mosher, Peg Murray, Linda Briscoe

° Deceased

Myers, Mike Nichols, Sean Noel, Richard Oram, Harold Paisner, Jay Parini, Kent Paul, Michael Polonsky, Daniel Rabinowitz, Dotson Rader, Leo Rangell,° Rachel Routh, Michael Ryan, Alan U. Schwartz, Ann Schneider (photo editor), Daniel H. Sheehan III, Ed Sherin, Katie Smither, Declan Spring, Thomas F. Staley, Elaine F. Tankard (research), Margaret Tufts Tenney, John Uecker, Jeff Umbro, Eli Wallach,° Rick Watson, George C. White, David Wilk, Dakin Williams,° Richard Workman.

A tip of the cloth cap also to friends in London's psychoanalytic community whose conversation and insights over the years have helped to broaden my understanding of Williams: Gregorio Kohon and his paper "Kafka at the Borders," Donald Campbell, Stephen Grosz, Priscilla Roth. A special shout-out to Christopher Bollas, whose books (*Hysteria, Shadow of the Object, Being a Character*) and high-spirited gab fests have been a constant source of provocation and revelation.

The New Yorker has been the joy of my writing life. It has also brought many literary angels to my table: Ty Baldwin, my steadfast right-hand man; Jennifer Stahl, the supremo of fact-checkers; and Deborah Treisman, my inspired editor for the last thirteen years whose finesse has been a great gift. The manuscript bears the marks of these experts. At Norton, it was my good fortune to have found a splendid, caring collaborator in John Glusman, the editor in chief of the publishing house and my editor, who has overseen this complex project with elan. The enthusiasm and generalship of Bill Swainson at Bloomsbury, my English publisher, has also been the biography's good fortune.

As I draw the final curtain on this endeavor, I would like to clasp hands with Lyle Leverich, who started me off, and with my wife, Connie Booth, whose faith in me and the project has kept me going through the book's long gestation. From the outset of our courtship nearly twenty-five years ago, Tennessee Williams has been a constant part of our conversation. In her earlier career as a professional actress, Connie played Laura in the 1977 London production of *The Glass Menagerie*, a performance that was admired by Williams, who came backstage to tell her so. Her intuitive understanding of the man and his family unhappiness informs these pages.

JL
London
October 9, 2013

Chronology

1907   Edwina Estelle Dakin (1884–1980) and Cornelius Coffin Williams (1879–1957) marry in Columbus, Mississippi, on June 3 and then move to Gulfport, Mississippi.

1909   The couple moves to Columbus, Mississippi, to live in the Episcopal rectory where Edwina's father, the Reverend Walter E. Dakin (1857–1954), and her mother, Rosina Isabel Otte Dakin (1863–1944), lived. A traveling salesman, Cornelius is on the road for long periods of time.

   Rose Isabel Williams is born on November 19.

1911   Thomas Lanier Williams III is born on March 26. In the family, he is known as "Tom."

1913   The family moves to Nashville, Tennessee, where the Reverend Dakin becomes pastor at the Church of the Advent.

1914   Cornelius takes a job as a traveling salesman for the International Shoe Company of St. Louis.

1916   The Reverend Dakin returns to Mississippi in January to become rector of Grace Church in Canton, and St. Mary's in Lexington, as well as serving as the minister in Durant. During this time, the Williams family lives in Canton.

   Tom contracts diphtheria, almost dies, and is bedridden for at least a year.

1917   In February the Reverend Dakin becomes rector of St. George's Church in Clarksdale, Mississippi. The Williams family joins him there later that year, and Tom is enrolled in the first grade for the 1917–18 school year.

1918   Cornelius accepts a managerial position in the St. Louis, Missouri, office of the International Shoe Company. Edwina and Tom arrive in St. Louis in July. When Rose joins them in September, the children attend Eugene Field Elementary School.

1919 Tom's brother Walter Dakin Williams, called Dakin, is born on February 21.

1920 Tom stays with his grandparents in Clarksdale, Mississippi, for the 1920–21 school year.

1921 For the next decade, Tom will spend the majority of his summers either in Clarksdale or in the other Southern towns where his grandparents are residing.

1922 Tom attends Stix School, where he meets his future girlfriend, Hazel Kramer.

1924 Edwina buys him a secondhand typewriter for ten dollars.

Tom's first published story, "Isolated," appears in Blewett Junior High School's newspaper, *The Junior Life*, in November.

1925 His first published poem, "Nature's Thanksgiving," appears in *The Junior Life* in November.

Rose is sent to All Saints College in Vicksburg, Mississippi.

1926 Tom enrolls in Soldan High School in January and transfers to University City High School in June.

1927 His essay "Can a Good Wife Be a Good Sport?" wins the third prize of five dollars in a *Smart Set* magazine contest and is published in May.

1928 While attending University City High School, his short story, "The Vengeance of Nitocris," is published in an August issue of the pulp magazine *Weird Tales*.

Tom's maternal grandfather Dakin takes him to New York City, where they see the original Broadway production of *Show Boat*, then board the RMS *Homeric* for an eleven-week tour of Europe, from July 6 to September 12, with visits to London, Paris, Monte Carlo, Naples, Rome, Milan, and Cologne, among other locations.

1929 Tom graduates from high school and enrolls at the University of Missouri, Columbia, in September, where he joins the Alpha Tau Omega fraternity.

1930 His first one-act play, *Beauty Is the Word*, wins sixth place in a Dramatic Arts Club contest at the university—it is unusual for a piece by a freshman to make it to the finals.

1931 Tom enrolls at the University of Missouri School of Journalism in September.

In October he is inspired by Russian actress Alla Nazimova in the Theatre Guild's touring production of Eugene O'Neill's *Mourning Becomes Electra* and decides that he will write for the theater.

1932   He fails ROTC during the spring term and is taken out of college by his
       father and put to work as a clerk at the International Shoe Company.

       Three hundred miles north of Havana, Hart Crane jumps to his death from
       the ocean liner *Orizaba*.

       That November Tom casts a vote for president for the first and last time,
       pulling the lever for Socialist candidate Norman Thomas.

1934   Tom continues writing daily in the family attic and while on the job at the
       shoe company.

1935   He collapses from exhaustion in January, is relieved from his job at the
       International Shoe Company warehouse, and is sent to Memphis to spend
       the summer with his grandparents.

       A "one-act melodrama" by Dorothy Shapiro and Tom Williams, *Cairo!*
       Shanghai! Bombay! is performed by local children in July in the Shapiro's
       Memphis backyard.

       In the fall Tom audits classes at Washington University in St. Louis, where
       he meets aspiring poets William Jay Smith and Clark Mills McBurney.
       Mills introduces Williams and Smith to the poetry of Hart Crane, Rim-
       baud, Rilke, and others.

1936   Tom is admitted to Washington University in January.

       In October his one-act *The Magic Tower* is produced by the Theatre Guild
       of Webster Groves, an amateur group just outside of St. Louis.

       Attending a touring company of Ibsen's *Ghosts*, he sees another inspiring
       performance by Alla Nazimova.

1937   In March, the Mummers of St. Louis produce his first full-length play,
       Candles to the Sun.

       Rose is committed to a psychiatric ward in St. Louis, then diagnosed with
       schizophrenia at a Catholic convalescent home. In the summer she is
       moved to a state hospital in Farmington, Missouri, where she is given shock
       treatments.

       Tom transfers to the University of Iowa in September to study playwriting.

       In November the Mummers produce *Fugitive Kind*.

       He completes a draft of *Spring Storm*.

1938   Williams receives a bachelor's degree from the University of Iowa in
       August.

       He begins work on *Not about Nightingales*.

       He submits his full-length plays and a group of one-acts under the name

"Tennessee Williams," and mails them from Memphis on his way to New Orleans, where he arrives for the first time on December 28.

1939   He lives in the French Quarter at 722 Toulouse Street until February 20, when he and Jim Parrott leave on a trip to California.

In August, three one-acts from the series he then calls *American Blues* wins him "a special prize" of $100 from the Group Theatre. Attention from the prize brings him in contact with Audrey Wood (1905–1985), who becomes his agent.

His name "Tennessee Williams" appears for the first time in print with the publication of "The Field of Blue Children" in the September–October issue of *Story* magazine.

He receives a $1,000 grant from the Rockefeller Foundation in December.

1940   Williams moves to New York, where he studies playwriting with John Gassner and Erwin Piscator at the New School.

That summer in Provincetown, Massachusetts, he falls in love with a Canadian dancer, Kip Kiernan (1918–1944); their affair lasts only a few weeks.

Williams travels to Mexico in August and September.

The Theatre Guild produces *Battle of Angels*, which opens out of town in Boston on December 30.

1941   *Battle of Angels* closes in Boston after two weeks. The Broadway run is canceled.

His first published one-act play, *Moony's Kid Don't Cry*, appears in *The Best One-Act Plays of 1940*, edited by Margaret Mayorga (published by Dodd, Mead of New York).

1942   Throughout most of 1941 and 1942, Williams keeps traveling, primarily between New York, St. Louis, New Orleans, Macon, Mexico, Jacksonville, and Provincetown.

At a New York cocktail party in December, he meets lifelong friend and publisher James Laughlin (1914–1997), founder of New Directions Publishing.

1943   On January 13 a bilateral prefrontal lobotomy is performed on Rose.

From mid-May to mid-August, Williams works in Hollywood at $250 a week for MGM, where he is assigned to write scripts for Lana Turner and Margaret O'Brien.

He adapts his draft play "The Gentleman Caller," based on his short story "Portrait of a Girl in Glass," for the screen, which MGM rejects.

You Touched Me!, co-authored with Donald Windham, opens at the Cleveland Playhouse on October 13.

1944   Williams's beloved grandmother Rosina—known as "Grand"—dies on January 6.

Kip Kiernan dies from a brain tumor on May 21.

Williams receives $1,000 from the American Academy of Arts and Letters.

New Directions publishes twenty-six of his poems in *Five Young American Poets, 1944* and the text to *Battle of Angels* in a literary journal. (Future trade editions of all plays and other writings are published by New Directions unless otherwise indicated.)

The Glass Menagerie opens to favorable reviews in Chicago on December 26.

1945   *Stairs to the Roof* premieres at the Pasadena Playhouse in California on March 25.

The Glass Menagerie opens on Broadway on March 31 and goes on to win the New York Drama Critics' Circle Award for best play of the year.

You Touched Me! opens on Broadway on September 25 and is later published in an acting edition by Samuel French.

27 Wagons Full of Cotton: And Other One-Act Plays is published.

The Glass Menagerie is published by Random House.

1946   Williams lives in the French Quarter of New Orleans with Pancho Rodriguez y Gonzales (1921–1995); they live together for the next two years.

1947   Williams meets Frank Merlo (1922–1963) in Provincetown that summer. Beginning in 1948 they become lovers and companions and remain together for nearly fourteen years.

On December 3, *A Streetcar Named Desire*, directed by Elia Kazan and starring Jessica Tandy, Marlon Brando, Kim Hunter, and Karl Malden, opens on Broadway to rave reviews and wins the Pulitzer Prize and the New York Drama Critics' Circle Award.

1948   *Summer and Smoke* opens on Broadway on October 6 and closes in just over three months.

A collection of five one-act plays, *American Blues*, is published by the Dramatists Play Service.

Williams returns to Europe for the first time in a decade and meets Truman Capote and Gore Vidal in Rome.

One Arm and Other Stories is published in a limited edition.

1949   Williams takes his grandfather and Merlo to Key West, where Williams
        buys the house at 1431 Duncan Street.

1950   His novel *The Roman Spring of Mrs. Stone* is published.

        He transfers his sister, Rose, to the Stony Lodge clinic near Ossining, New
        York.

        The Warner Brothers film version of *The Glass Menagerie* is released.

1951   *The Rose Tattoo*, starring Maureen Stapleton and Eli Wallach, opens on
        Broadway on February 3 and wins the Tony Award for Best Play.

        The film version of *A Streetcar Named Desire*, starring Vivien Leigh as
        Blanche and Marlon Brando as Stanley, is released.

1952   A revival of *Summer and Smoke*, directed by José Quintero and starring
        Geraldine Page, opens Off-Broadway at the Circle in the Square on April
        24 and is a critical success.

        The American Academy of Arts and Letters inducts Williams as a member.

1953   *Camino Real*, directed by Elia Kazan, opens on Broadway on March 19 and
        closes within two months after a harsh critical reception.

1954   *Hard Candy and Other Stories*, Williams's second book of stories, is pub-
        lished.

1955   At the age of ninety-seven, his grandfather the Reverend Dakin dies on
        February 14.

        On March 24, *Cat on a Hot Tin Roof*, directed by Elia Kazan and starring
        Barbara Bel Geddes, Ben Gazzara, and Burl Ives, opens on Broadway. *Cat*
        wins both the Pulitzer Prize and the New York Drama Critics' Circle
        Award.

        The film version of *The Rose Tattoo*, for which Anna Magnani later wins an
        Academy Award, is released.

1956   The film *Baby Doll*, directed by Elia Kazan with a screenplay by Williams,
        is released amid some controversy and is blacklisted by Cardinal Francis
        Spellman.

        In the Winter of Cities, Williams's first book of poetry, is published.

1957   *Orpheus Descending*, a revised version of *Battle of Angels*, directed by Har-
        old Clurman, opens on Broadway on March 21 and closes after two months.

        Williams's father dies on March 27.

        Williams begins psychoanalysis with Dr. Lawrence S. Kubie in June and
        continues for a year.

1958   On February 7 *Suddenly Last Summer* and *Something Unspoken* open Off-Broadway under the collective title *Garden District*.

       The film version of *Cat on a Hot Tin Roof*, directed by Richard Brooks, is released.

1959   His final collaboration with director Elia Kazan, *Sweet Bird of Youth*, opens on Broadway on March 10 and runs for three months.

       The film version of *Suddenly Last Summer*, with a screenplay by Gore Vidal, is released.

1960   The comedy *Period of Adjustment* opens on Broadway on November 10 and runs for over four months.

       The film version of *Orpheus Descending* is released under the title *The Fugitive Kind*.

1961   On December 28 *The Night of the Iguana* opens on Broadway, where it runs for nine months and wins the New York Drama Critics' Circle Award.

       The film versions of *Summer and Smoke* and *The Roman Spring of Mrs. Stone* are released.

       Williams becomes a patient of Dr. Max Jacobson, known as "Dr. Feelgood," who provides him with injectable forms of barbiturates and amphetamines.

1962   The film versions of *Sweet Bird of Youth* and *Period of Adjustment* are released.

       Williams buys a townhouse at 1014 Dumaine Street in New Orleans's French Quarter.

1963   *The Milk Train Doesn't Stop Here Anymore* opens on Broadway on January 16 and closes after two months due to a blizzard and a newspaper strike.

       Estranged from Williams for nearly two years, Frank Merlo dies of lung cancer on September 20.

1964   On January 1, *The Milk Train Doesn't Stop Here Anymore* is revived in a Broadway production starring Tallulah Bankhead and Tab Hunter; it closes within a week.

       John Huston's film version of *The Night of the Iguana* is released.

1965   *The Eccentricities of a Nightingale*, his revised version of *Summer and Smoke*, is published.

1966   Two one-act plays, *The Mutilated* and *The Gnadiges Fraulein*, open on Broadway on February 22 under the collective title *Slapstick Tragedy* and run for seven performances.

       A novella and stories are published under the title *The Knightly Quest*.

1967   His initial version of *The Two-Character Play* plays at the Hampstead The-
        atre Club in London and is published in a limited edition.

1968   On March 27 *Kingdom of Earth* opens on Broadway under the title *The
        Seven Descents of Myrtle*.

        A film version of *The Milk Train Doesn't Stop Here Anymore*, directed by
        Joseph Losey, is released under the title *Boom!*

1969   Tennessee's brother, Dakin, arranges for him to convert to Roman Cathol-
        icism in a ceremony on January 10.

        In the Bar of a Tokyo Hotel opens Off-Broadway on May 11 and runs for
        three weeks.

        Williams is awarded a doctorate of humanities by the University of Mis-
        souri and the Gold Medal for Drama by the American Academy of Arts and
        Letters in May.

        Dakin commits Tennessee to the Renard Psychiatric Division of Barnes
        Hospital in St. Louis, where he stays for three months.

1970   The film version of *Kingdom of Earth*, with a screenplay by Gore Vidal, is
        released under the title *Last of the Mobile Hot Shots*.

        In an interview on David Frost's television show, Williams discusses his
        homosexuality.

        A book of plays, *Dragon Country*, is published.

1971   Williams breaks with his agent Audrey Wood. Bill Barnes assumes his rep-
        resentation; then Mitch Douglas, in 1978; and Luis Sanjurjo, in 1981.

        In a December rally organized by Norman Mailer at the Cathedral of St.
        John the Divine in New York, Williams speaks out against the war in Viet-
        nam.

1972   Williams is awarded honorary degrees by the University of Hartford and
        Purdue University.

        Small Craft Warnings opens Off-Broadway on April 2 and runs for a total
        of six months, first at the Truck and Warehouse Theater and later at the
        New Theatre, where Williams plays the role of Doc to boost ticket sales.

1973   *Out Cry*, a revised version of *The Two-Character Play*, opens on Broadway
        on March 1 and runs for just over a week.

1974   *Eight Mortal Ladies Possessed*, a book of short stories, is published.

1975   Williams is presented with the Medal of Honor for Literature from the
        National Arts Club.

The novel *Moise and the World of Reason* is published by Simon and Schuster and *Memoirs* is published by Doubleday.

1976 *This Is (An Entertainment)* opens at the American Conservatory Theater in San Francisco on January 20.

The final version of *The Two-Character Play (Out Cry)* is published.

The Red Devil Battery Sign closes during its out-of-town Boston tryout in June.

The Eccentricities of a Nightingale premieres on Broadway on November 23 and runs for two weeks.

Williams serves as Jury President at the Cannes Film Festival.

He is elected to the American Academy of Arts and Letters.

1977 *Vieux Carré* opens on Broadway on May 11 and closes within five days.

His second volume of poetry, *Androgyne, Mon Amour*, is published.

1978 *Tiger Tail* premieres at the Alliance Theater in Atlanta, Georgia, and a revised version premieres the following year at the Hippodrome Theater in Gainesville, Florida.

A selection of his essays, *Where I Live*, is published.

1979 *A Lovely Sunday for Creve Coeur* opens Off-Broadway on January 10 at the Hudson Guild Theatre, where it runs for a month.

Kirche, Küche, Kinder runs as a workshop production Off-Broadway at the Jean Cocteau Repertory Theatre.

He is presented with a Kennedy Centers Honors medal by President Jimmy Carter at the John F. Kennedy Center for the Performing Arts in Washington, D.C.

1980 *Will Mr. Merriwether Return from Memphis?* premieres on January 25 for a limited run at the Tennessee Williams Performing Arts Center in Key West, Florida.

On March 26 his last Broadway production, *Clothes for a Summer Hotel*, opens and then closes after fifteen performances.

On June 1 Williams's mother, Edwina, dies at the age of ninety-five.

He is awarded the Presidential Medal of Freedom by Jimmy Carter.

1981 *Something Cloudy, Something Clear* premieres Off-Broadway on August 24 at the Jean Cocteau Repertory Theatre, where it runs in repertory into the next year.

The Notebook of Trigorin, his free adaptation of Chekov's *The Seagull*, premieres November 12 at the Playhouse Theatre in Vancouver.

1982 The second of two versions of *A House Not Meant to Stand* opens for a limited run at the Goodman Theatre in Chicago on May 8.

A workshop production of *Gideon's Point* is produced in August at the Williamstown Theater Festival.

Williams receives an honorary degree from Harvard University.

1983 Williams is found dead in his room at the Hotel Elysée in New York City on February 25. He is later buried in St. Louis.

Clothes for a Summer Hotel is published.

1984 *Stopped Rocking and Other Screenplays* is published.

1985 His *Collected Stories*, with an introduction by Gore Vidal, is published.

1988 *The Red Devil Battery Sign* is published.

1995 Lyle Leverich's biography, *Tom: The Unknown Tennessee Williams*, which chronicles Williams's early life, is published by Crown Publishers.

Something Cloudy, Something Clear is published.

1996 On September 5, Rose Williams dies at the age of eighty-six in Tarrytown, New York.

The rights to all writings by Williams transfer to the University of the South, Sewanee, Tennessee, and his papers are a bequest to Harvard University.

The Notebook of Trigorin, in a version revised by Williams, opens at the Cincinnati Playhouse in the Park on September 5 and is published in 1997.

1998 *Not about Nightingales*, directed by Trevor Nunn, premieres at the Royal National Theatre in London on March 5 and later moves to the Alley Theater in Houston, Texas.

1999 *Spring Storm* premiers at the Actors Repertory of Texas, Austin, on November 6 and is published the same year.

On November 25, *Not about Nightingales* opens on Broadway.

2000 Volume 1 of *The Selected Letters of Tennessee Williams* is published.

Stairs to the Roof is published.

2001 *Fugitive Kind* is published.

2002 *Collected Poems* is published.

2004 *Candles to the Sun* is published.

Volume 2 of *The Selected Letters of Tennessee Williams* is published.

2005   *Mister Paradise and Other One-Act Plays* is published.

2006   Williams's personal journals are published by Yale University Press under the title *Notebooks*.

2008   *A House Not Meant to Stand* and *The Traveling Companion and Other Plays* are published.

Dakin Williams dies at the age of eighty-nine in Belleville, Illinois.

2009   *New Selected Essays: Where I Live* is published.

2011   *The Magic Tower and Other One-Act Plays* is published.

Celebrations and productions around the world are dedicated to Williams during his centennial year.

The Comédie-Française in Paris produces *Un tramway nommé Désir*, staged by American director Lee Breuer, the first play by a non-European playwright in the company's 331-year history.

Notes

ABBREVIATIONS USED

BDC—Betty Davis Collection, Howard Gotlieb Archival Research Center, Boston University.

BRTC—Billy Rose Theatre Collection, New York Public Library for the Performing Arts.

Columbia—Tennessee Williams Papers, Rare Book and Manuscript Library, Columbia University.

CP—The Collected Poems of Tennessee Williams, by Tennessee Williams. Edited by David Roessel and Nicholas Moschovakis. New York: New Directions, 2002.

CS—Collected Stories, by Tennessee Williams. New York: New Directions, 1985.

CUCOHC—Columbia University Center for Oral History Collection, Columbia University.

CWTW—Conversations with Tennessee Williams, edited by Albert J. Devlin. Jackson: University Press of Mississippi, 1986.

Delaware—Tennessee Williams Collection, Special Collections, University of Delaware Library.

DPYD—Don't Put Your Daughter on the Stage, by Margaret Webster. New York: Alfred A. Knopf, 1972.

Duke—Carson McCullers Papers, David M. Rubenstein Rare Book and Manuscript Library, Duke University.

ESC—Ed Sherin Collection, Howard Gotlieb Archival Research Center, Boston University.

FOA—Five O'Clock Angel: Letters of Tennessee Williams to Maria St. Just, 1948–1982, by Tennessee Williams. With commentary by Maria St. Just. New York: Alfred A. Knopf, 1990.

Harvard—Tennessee Williams Papers, Harvard Theatre Collection, Houghton Library, Harvard University.

Houston—Cheryl Crawford Collection, Courtesy of Special Collections, University of Houston Libraries.

HRC—Tennessee Williams Collection, Harry Ransom Center, University of Texas at Austin.

Huntington—Manuscripts Department, Huntington Library.

ISC—Irene Mayer Selznick Collection, Howard Gotlieb Archival Research Center, Boston University.

JLC—John Lahr Collection, Howard Gotlieb Archival Research Center, Boston University.

JLI—John Lahr Interview. John Lahr Collection, Howard Gotlieb Archival Research Center, Boston University.

KAL—A Life, by Elia Kazan. New York: Alfred A. Knopf, 1988.

KOD—Kazan on Directing, by Elia Kazan. New York: Alfred A. Knopf, 2009.

L1—The Selected Letters of Tennessee Williams, vol. 1: *1920–1945*, by Tennessee Williams. Edited by Albert J. Devlin and Nancy M. Tischler. New York: New Directions, 2000.

L2—The Selected Letters of Tennessee Williams, vol. 2: *1945–1957*, by Tennessee Williams. Edited by Albert J. Devlin, co-edited by Nancy M. Tischler. New York: New Directions, 2004.

LIB—Laurette: The Intimate Biography of Laurette Taylor, by Marguerite Courtney. New York: Limelight Editions, 1984.

LLC—Lyle Leverich Collection, attached to the John Lahr Collection, Howard Gotlieb Archival Research Center, Boston University.

LLI—Lyle Leverich Interview. Lyle Leverich Collection, attached to the John Lahr Collection, Howard Gotlieb Archival Research Center, Boston University.

LOA1—Tennessee Williams: Plays 1937–1955, by Tennessee Williams. New York: Library of America, 2000.

LOA2—Tennessee Williams: Plays 1957–1980, by Tennessee Williams. New York: Library of America, 2000.

M—Memoirs, by Tennessee Williams. New York: Doubleday, 1975.

Maryland—Katherine Anne Porter Collection, University of Maryland Libraries.

Morgan—Carter Burden Collection of American Literature, Morgan Library and Museum.

Ms.—manuscript.

Ms. "Memoirs"—"Memoirs" (unpublished manuscript), by Tennessee Williams. Lyle Leverich Collection, attached to the John Lahr Collection, Howard Gotlieb Archival Research Center, Boston University.

N—Notebooks: Tennessee Williams, by Tennessee Williams. Edited by Margaret Bradham Thornton. New Haven, Conn.: Yale University Press, 2006.

NSE—New Selected Essays: Where I Live, by Tennessee Williams. Edited by John S. Bak. New York: New Directions, 2009.

RBAW—Represented by Audrey Wood, by Audrey Wood, with Max Wilk. Garden City, N.Y.: Doubleday, 1981.

RMTT—Remember Me to Tom, by Edwina Dakin Williams, as told to Lucy Freeman. New York: G. P. Putnam's Sons, 1963.

RS—The Roman Spring of Mrs. Stone, by Tennessee Williams. London: Vintage Classics, 1999.

Sewanee—Archives of the University of the South, Sewanee, Tennessee.

THNOC—Fred W. Todd Tennessee Williams Collection, Williams Research Center, The Historic New Orleans Collection.

TWIB—Tennessee Williams: An Intimate Biography, by Dakin Williams and Shepherd Mead. New York: Arbor House, 1983.

TWLDW—Tennessee Williams' Letters to Donald Windham, 1940–1965, by Tennessee Williams. Edited and with comments by Donald Windham. New York: Holt, Rinehart & Winston, 1977.

Wisconsin—Wisconsin Center for Film and Theater Research, Wisconsin Historical
   Society.
WUCA—Elia Kazan Collection, Cinema Archives, Wesleyan University.

EPIGRAPH

 ix "Art to me": Mark Rothko, *Writings on Art* (Dexter, Md.: Thomas Shore, 2006),
     p. 45.

PREFACE

 xiii "The one duty": Oscar Wilde, *Oscar Wilde: The Major Works*, ed. Isobel Murray
      (Oxford, U.K.: Oxford University Press, 2000), p. 256.
 xiv "a picture of my own heart": *N*, Apr. 9, 1939, p. 147.
 xiv "to be simple direct": Ibid.
 xiv "The real fact": Robert Van Gelder, *New York Times*, sec. 2.1, Apr. 22, 1945.
  xv "to report his cause aright": Lyle Leverich, *Tom: The Unknown Tennessee Wil-
      liams* (New York: W. W. Norton, 1995), dedication page.

CHAPTER 1: BLOOD-HOT AND PERSONAL

  1 "Into this scene comes": Clifford Odets, *The Time Is Ripe: The 1940 Journal of
     Clifford Odets* (New York: Grove Press, 1988), pp. 217–18.
  1 8:50 P.M.: In an earlier era, Broadway show time was 8:40 P.M.—a fact memorial-
     ized in one of the most famous revues of the thirties, *Life Begins at 8:40*.
  1 "like a farm boy": *TWIB*, p. 125.
  1 "You're only as good": *RBAW*, p. 143.
  2 "It seems to me": Audrey Wood to Tennessee Williams, Apr. 1, 1939, *L1*, p. 164.
  2 "not a finished dramatist": Audrey Wood to Tennessee Williams, Apr. 28, 1939,
     ibid., p. 172. Wood was "deeply impressed" by Williams's theatrical sketches,
     American Blues, but thought his dramatic problem was "going to be how to sus-
     tain a dramatic idea in a full length play." On May 4, 1939, Williams wrote to his
     mother, "The Group Theatre and my new agent, Audrey Wood, both urge me to
     devote all my time to writing one long, careful play as they feel I have been work-
     ing too rapidly and without sufficient concentration on one thing." (Williams to
     Edwina Williams, May 4, 1939, ibid., p. 168.)
  2 "You are playing a very long shot": Williams to Audrey Wood, June 25, 1939, ibid.,
     p. 178.
  2 "I'd reached the very, very bottom": *CWTW*, p. 330.
  2 "Yes, I have tricks": LOA1, p. 400.
  3 aftermath of an Actors' Equity suspension: Lyle Leverich, *Tom: The Unknown
     Tennessee Williams* (New York: W. W. Norton, 1995), p. 547.
  3 "on the longest wake in history": *LIB*, p. 415.
  4 "She'd closed many a show": Reminiscences of Eddie Dowling, Nov. 21, 1964,
     Columbia University Center for Oral History Collection (hereafter CUCOHC),
     p. 815.
  4 "the alcoholic of alcoholics": Ibid.
  4 "Nothing like this": Ibid., p. 819.
  4 "It's Amanda": Ibid., p. 165.
  4 "This was just about the time": Ibid., p. 820. Dowling's account of the first lines

doesn't correspond with the printed text. But, as Williams knew to his cost, Dowling and Taylor were chronic ad-libbers.

4 "Audrey I love the play": Dowling, Nov. 6, CUCOHC, p. 165. Wood at first refused. "Eddie, this is the wrong way. This boy has all these failures," Dowling recalled her saying. (Ibid., p. 166.)

4 "a sick, tormented boy": Ibid., pp. 165–67.

5 "Success is like a shy mouse": Williams to Donald Windham, Apr. 1943, *TWLDW*, p. 58.

5 "a nauseous thing": *N*, p. 413.

5 "I gave up a sure $25,000": Dowling, Nov. 6, 1963, CUCOHC, p. 171.

5 "I said, 'Make up your mind.'": Ibid., pp. 170–71.

7 "she'd been hibernating": Ibid., pp. 171–73.

7 "jam about money": Laurette Taylor to Dwight Taylor, undated, HRC.

7 "Between two and three in the morning": Effie Allen, "You Can't Whip the Charm of Laurette Taylor," *Chicago Tribune*, Feb. 1945. Taylor is quoted as saying, "Tell them there is no escape from grief. They had to stand and face it. I know because I tried to escape. . . . I know now that you can't outrun sorrow. You just have to learn to bear it."

7 "I could look back": Helen Ormsbee, "Laurette Taylor Knew Amanda Was Her Absolutely Right Part," *New York Herald Tribune*, 1945.

7 "tobacco-spitting mammas": Allen, "You Can't Whip the Charm."

7 "She'd spruced up a little bit": Dowling, Nov. 6, 1963, CUCOHC, pp. 173–74.

8 "Oh, Mr. Dowling": Ibid., p. 817. Williams wrote to Donald Windham that even in Chicago, Taylor still sounded like "the Aunt Jemima Pancake Hour." (Dec. 18, 1944, *TWLDW*, p. 155.) Taylor, however, claimed Williams as the model for her Southern accent. "All during rehearsals I'd say to him, 'Just talk to me, Tennessee. Don't explain how to pronounce the words; just keep talking to me.' We had quite a lot of talks. Amanda's drawl is the result." (*LIB*, p. 397.)

9 "Wouldn't it be great, George": Dowling, Nov. 6, 1963, CUCOHC, p. 177.

9 "As Tiny Tim said": Ibid., Nov. 21, 1964, pp. 177–78.

9 "Ilka Chase": Ilka Chase (1900–1978), a well-born, droll actress of stage and screen, was in the original Broadway productions of Claire Booth Luce's *The Women* (1938) and Neil Simon's *Barefoot in the Park* (1963). For a few years in the forties she hosted a radio show, *Luncheon at the Waldorf*. Her epitaph reads, "I've finally gotten to the bottom of things."

9 "Laurence Stallings": Laurence Stallings (1894–1968) was a playwright, screenwriter, and novelist. On stage, he collaborated with Maxwell Anderson in *What Price Glory?*; on the screen, his credits included John Ford's *She Wore a Yellow Ribbon* and King Vidor's *Northwest Passage*. He was a member of the Algonquin Round Table.

9 "He doesn't mean to hurt you": Dowling, Nov. 6, 1963, CUCOHC, pp. 179–80.

9 "It's just in the lap of the gods": Williams to James Laughlin, Dec. 15, 1944, *L1*, p. 539.

11 "Well, it looks bad, baby": *N*, Dec. 9, 1944, p. 431.

11 "My God, what corn!": Williams to Donald Windham, Dec. 18, 1944, *TWLDW*, p. 155.

11 "What was she working toward": Tennessee Williams, "On Laurette Taylor," undated, HRC.

12 "Mr. Dowling": Laurette Taylor to Dwight Taylor, Chicago, undated, HRC.

12 "I can't find the tranquility": Ibid.

12 "Tennessee, don't change that ending": Murray Schumach, "A Texas Tornado Hits Broadway," *New York Times Magazine*, Oct. 17, 1948.

12 "It was a strange night": Dowling, Nov. 21, 1964, CUCOHC, p. 796.

12 "the greatest play in fifty years": Advertisement in clipping file, LLC.

12 "was respectful but hardly ecstatic": *RBAW*, p. 142.

13 "For eight weeks, we starved": Dowling, Nov. 6, 1963, CUCOHC, p. 183.

13 writing was on the fourth wall: "Finally when we announced we're going to leave in two weeks, they tore the doors down. We had to give two extra matinees, and it was the consensus of opinion that we could have stayed there for a couple of years. But we had to come in because Singer had come on and made a contract for the Playhouse Theatre on 48th Street." (Ibid.)

13 "When Miss Taylor plays": Laurette Taylor correspondence, Chicago, undated, HRC.

13 "the distortions that have taken place": Williams to the Editor, Feb. 25, 1945, *L1*, p. 546.

13 "Pandemonium back-stage!": Williams to James Laughlin, Mar. 11, 1945, ibid., p. 553.

13 "We arrived in New York": Dowling, Nov. 21, 1964, CUCOHC, pp. 813–14. "Taylor has been drinking, but so far no sign of drunkenness," Williams wrote to Windham a week before the Chicago opening. (Dec. 18, 1944, *TWLDW*, p. 155.) By February, there were plenty of signs. "Worried about Laurette," Williams wrote to Audrey Wood. "She got terribly drunk at a party night before last. Literally passed out cold and fell on the sidewalk—first time this has happened." (Williams to Audrey Wood, Feb. 5, 1945, *L1*, p. 545.)

14 "a quick run-through": Dowling, Nov. 21, 1964, CUCOHC, p. 815.

14 "It seemed incredible to us": *LIB*, p. 412.

14 "All the company were on me": Dowling, Nov. 21, 1964, CUCOHC, p. 815.

14 "artistically my big brother": John Lahr, "Lucky Man: Horton Foote's Three Acts," *The New Yorker*, Oct. 26, 2009, p. 90.

14 "a torrential downpour": Dowling, Nov. 21, 1964, CUCOHC, p. 816.

14 "The most beautiful rainbow": Ibid.

15 "thanking all of the gods": Ibid., p. 818.

15 "soaking, wringing wet": Ibid.

15 "Hel-lo, Ray": Ibid.

15 "We could hear the buzzing": Ibid.

15 "Eddie, can you get him a seat": Horton Foote, *Beginnings: A Memoir* (New York: Scribner, 2001), p. 258.

15 "a pineapple ice cream soda": Lahr, "Lucky Man," p. 90.

15 kept Foote in Williams's mind as possible casting: Williams to Horton Foote, Apr. 24, 1943, *L1*, p. 443. "I have been working with tigerish fury on 'The Gentleman Caller,'" he wrote Foote in 1943, adding in the next sentence, "It has at least one part in it for you and maybe two, if you can imagine such a thing."

15 "Tennessee, tell them in front": Foote, *Beginnings*, p. 258.

16 "Oh, my God, our fate": Dowling, Nov. 21, 1964, CUCOHC, p. 817.

16 "Now is the time for unexpected things": LOA1, p. 187.

16 "a huge advance over its predecessors": Williams to Theatre Guild, Sept. 20, 1940, *L1*, p. 279.

16 "to fuse lyricism and realism": *N*, Dec. 11, 1939, p. 173. " One must learn . . . to fuse lyricism and realism into a congruous unit—I guess my chief trouble is that I don't. I make the most frightful faux pas. . . . I feared today that I may have

taken a distinctly wrong turn in turning to drama—But, oh, I do feel drama so intensely sometimes."

16 "Onto it I projected the violent symbols": Leverich, *Tom*, p. 383.

18 "one of my biggest troubles": LOA1, p. 212.

18 "When people read it": Ibid., p. 243.

18 "Says he's exploring the world": Ibid., p. 199.

18 "always feel that I bore people": *N*, June 14, 1939, p. 187.

18 "I, too, am beginning to feel": *DPYD*, p. 74.

18 "Decent is something that's scared": LOA1, p. 235.

18 "Passion is something to be proud of": Ibid., p. 258.

19 "We of the artistic world": Williams to Donald Windham, Sept. 1940, *TWLDW*, p. 14.

19 "shiny black satin": LOA1, p. 207.

19 "an enemy of light": Ibid., p. 270.

19 "You heard me cussing": Ibid., p. 211.

19 "new patterns": Williams to Joseph Hazan, Sept. 3, 1940, *L1*, pp. 274–75.

19 "I have spent so many years": Williams to Donald Windham, June 19, 1945, *TWLDW*, p. 174.

19 "a shameless, flaunting symbol": LOA1, p. 273.

20 Conjure Man: "The Conjure Man, if you are looking for a symbol, represents the dark, inscrutable face of things as they are, the essential mystery of life—'the one who knows but is not telling'—omniscience, fate, or what have you, of which death, life and everything else are so many curious tokens sewn about his dark garments." (Williams to Lawrence Langner, July 3, 1941, *L1*, p. 320.)

20 "seems to make a slight obeisance": LOA1, p. 274.

20 "BETTER RETURN AT ONCE": Tennessee Williams, "Better Return at Once" (unpublished), HRC.

20 "I am becoming more and more": Williams to Donald Windham, May 1, 1941, *TWLDW*, p. 22.

20 "twenty-six years of living": He was actually twenty-nine. Tennessee Williams, undated Ms., HRC.

20 "I remembered particularly": Williams, "Better Return at Once," HRC.

21 "Old," Williams said: Ibid.

22 sent Odets into semipermanent theatrical retirement: Between 1935 and 1940, Odets wrote seven plays; from 1940 until his death in 1963, at the age of fifty-seven, he wrote only three more.

22 "What can we produce": Williams to Paul Bigelow, Oct. 23, 1941, *L1*, p. 352.

22 "We were deceived by the maturity": *DPYD*, p. 69.

22 "Probably no man has ever written": LOA1, p. 275.

22 no experience with casting: Lawrence Langner and Theresa Helburn, the Guild's co-directors, were described by Margaret Webster as "masters of miscasting." (*DPYD*, p. 68.)

22 "before I knew": LOA1, p. 275.

22 "low and common": Leverich, *Tom*, p. 363.

22 "It's impossible, darling": Ibid., p. 364.

23 "a deep collective death wish": *RBAW*, p. 136.

23 "a bunch of prissy old maids": Williams to Joseph Hazan, *L1*, Jan. 2, 1941, p. 297.

23 "raised the roof": Williams to the Williams Family, Nov. 18, 1940, ibid., p. 293.

23 "seem much interested": *DPYD*, p. 69.

23 "I am old, I am tired": Williams to the Williams Family, Nov. 18, 1940, *L1*, p. 293.

23 "For heaven's sake, do something": LOA1, p. 283.

24 "a not very satisfactory cast": *DPYD*, p. 71.

25 "Up and down the aisles": LOA1, p. 285.

25 "To an already antagonistic audience": Ibid., p. 285.

25 "The bright angels": Williams to Joseph Hazan, Jan. 2, 1941, *L1*, p. 297.

25 "He appeared so suicidal": William Jay Smith, *My Friend Tom: The Poet-Playwright Tennessee Williams* (Jackson: University of Mississippi Press, 2012), p. 54.

26 "The play gives the audience the sensation": Leverich, *Tom*, p. 393.

26 "which seemed to us the roar of a cannon": *RBAW*, p. 136.

26 "I will crawl on my belly": Ibid., p. 137.

26 Lawrence Langner: In subsequent correspondence with Audrey Wood, Williams referred to Langner as "Lawrence Stanislavsky Langner, the one who operates that famous Art Theatre on E. 56th St." (Williams to Audrey Wood, June 20, 1945, *L1*, p. 565.)

26 "At that moment": Audrey Wood to Williams, undated, HRC.

26 "putrid": Gilbert Maxwell, *Tennessee Williams and Friends: An Informal Biography* (Cleveland: World Publishing, 1965), p. 51.

26 "improper and indecent": Ibid.

26 "too many of the lines": Leverich, *Tom*, p. 394.

27 "DIRT": *L1*, p. 298.

27 "Tennessee was completely taken by surprise": *DPYD*, p. 72.

27 "censors sat out front": LOA1, p. 286.

27 "an insult to the fine young man": Leverich, *Tom*, p. 394.

27 "MIRIAM HOPKINS SAYS": *DPYD*, p. 72.

27 "You don't seem to see": Maxwell, *Tennessee Williams and Friends*, p. 50.

27 "You must not wear your heart": Leverich, *Tom*, p. 395.

27 "I don't think I had an answer": Ibid.

27 "for recasting, re-writing, re-everything": Williams to Joseph Hazan, Jan. 2, 1941, *L1*, p. 297.

27 "What a failure!": Williams to James Laughlin, Apr. 2, 1944, ibid., p. 521.

27 "Nothing whatever in this whole experience": *DPYD*, p. 72.

27 "the play was more a disappointment": Leverich, *Tom*, p. 395.

27 "I am right smack behind the eight-ball": Williams to Lawrence Langner, Feb. 26, 1941, *L1*, pp. 305–6. When the rewrite was rejected by the Theatre Guild, Williams wrote to Audrey Wood, "Spit in Langner's face for me." (Williams to Audrey Wood, Sept. 2, 1941, ibid., p. 318.) On June 27, 1941, Williams's revised script of *Battle of Angels* was rejected by the Theatre Guild. He was philosophical about it. "It is apparent that no definitive script has yet emerged, though . . . one eventually will—and 'Battle of Angels' can afford to wait, perhaps more than such plays as 'Watch on the Rhine,' 'There Shall Be No Night,' Etc.," he told Langner, adding, "I have made this play out of such enduring stuff as passion, death, and the spiritual quest for the infinite, which are elements that time can only improve." (Williams to Lawrence Langer, July 3, 1941, ibid., p. 317.)

29 "O lonely man": "Speech from the Stairs," CUCOHC, p. 819.

29 "That is the one ineluctable gift": Williams to Joseph Hazan, Sept. 3, 1940, *L1*, p. 275.

29 "the days AB—After Boston": *N*, Feb. 16, 1941, p. 221.

29 "This is a one-way street": Williams to Audrey Wood, Feb. 27, 1941, *L1*, p. 308.

30 "I have diverted myself": *N*, June 27, 1941, p. 227.

30 "a rich and exciting period sexually": Ibid.

30 "a celluloid brassiere": Williams to James Laughlin, May 29, 1943, *L1*, p. 455.

30 "Dear Child of God": Williams to Audrey Wood, June 20, 1945, ibid., p. 564.

30 "I want an *audience*": Williams to Audrey Wood, Sept. 1, 1942, ibid., p. 402.

30 "I cannot see ahead nor can anyone": *N*, July 9, 1942, pp. 301–3.

30 "The things that I have to sell": Williams to Joseph Hazan, Sept. 24, 1940, *L1*, p. 285. The undertow of war also seemed to drown the highfalutin poetic drama of Maxwell Anderson as well as the work of George Kelly, Robert Sherwood, Paul Green, and Philip Barry, who had dominated Broadway theater in the thirties.

31 "I must be able to be a post-war artist": *N*, Feb. 25, 1942, p. 281.

31 "a new form, non-realistic": Williams, undated, HRC.

31 "I think there is going to be": Williams to William Saroyan, Nov. 29, 1941, *L1*, p. 359.

31 "We must remember that a new theatre": Williams to Horton Foote, Apr. 24, 1943, ibid., p. 443.

31 "It is appalling": *N*, Oct. 26, 1943, p. 401.

31 "no overwhelming interest": Williams to Donald Windham, July 28, 1943, *TWLDW*, p. 94.

31 "I have been horribly worried": Williams to Margo Jones, Aug. 27, 1943, HRC.

32 "Have finished 'The Caller,'": Williams to Donald Windham, Aug. 1944, *TWLDW*, p. 148.

32 "I said, 'Ma, c'mon, now,'": Dowling, Nov. 21, 1964, CUCOHC, p. 819.

32 "The few minutes she had": *LIB*, p. 412.

32 "She played almost through a fog": Dowling, Nov. 21, 1964, CUCOHC, p. 820.

32 "There was nothing left inside of her": *LIB*, p. 412.

32 "supernatural quality on stage": Williams, "On Laurette Taylor," HRC.

32 "Laurette's basic tragedy": Ibid.

32 "There is an inexplicable rightness": Stark Young, *New Republic*, Apr. 16, 1945.

33 "Stop all this hand clasping": *RBAW*, p. 143.

33 "haunted household": Williams to Donald Windham, Apr. 1943, *TWLDW*, p. 57.

33 "We can't say grace": LOA1, p. 401.

33 "I begin with a character": *LIB*, p. 412.

33 "in exact ratio to the degree": Williams to Kenneth Tynan, July 26, 1955, *TWLDW*, p. 306.

33 "There are only two times": Williams to Donald Windham, July 28, 1943, ibid., p. 91.

33 "that thing that makes me write": Williams to Brooks Atkinson, Sept. 2, 1959, BRTC.

34 "I have a vast traumatic eye": *CP*, ["I Have a Vast Traumatic Eye"], p. 173.

34 "sixteen cylinders inside a jalopy": Williams to Lawrence Langner, Aug. 22, 1940, *L1*, p. 267.

34 "the climate of my interior world": Greil Marcus and Werner Sollers, eds., *A New Literary History of America* (Cambridge, Mass.: Harvard University Press, 2009).

34 "The turbulent business of my nerves": LOA1, p. 276.

34 "It seemed to me that even the giants": Ibid.

34 "a frustrating lack of vitality": Ibid., p. 275.

34 "had not seen more than two or three": Ibid.

34 "In five years' time": *CS*, "Portrait of a Girl in Glass," p. 119.

35 "irreconcilably divided": Williams to Jessica Tandy, as quoted in Mike Steen, *A Look at Tennessee Williams* (New York: Hawthorn Books, 1969), p. 181.

35 "his basic repertory company": Gore Vidal, "Tennessee Williams: Someone to Laugh at the Squares With," in Gore Vidal, *Armageddon? Essays 1983–1987* (London: Andre Deutsch, 1987), p. 53.

35 "so absorbed": JLI with Gore Vidal, 2000, JLC.

35 "Nowhere was ease": *CP*, "Cortege," p. 30.

35 "was completely unshadowed by fear": *RMTT*, p. 19.

36 "had fallen in love with long distances": LOA1, p. 401.

36 hung onto his mother's skirts: Williams observes, "My mother's overtly solicitous attention planted in me the makings of a sissy." (*M*, pp. 11–12.)

36 "His winter breath": *CP*, "Cortege," p. 30.

36 "the blue devils": Williams to Donald Windham, July 28, 1943, *TWLDW*, p. 91. "It's like having wild cats under my skin."

36 "When my family first moved": Tennessee Williams, "Why the Title" (unpublished), HRC.

38 "was no tenement": *RMTT*, p. 28.

38 "We could not afford": Ibid., p. 32.

38 "The Williamses had fought the Indians": *NSE*, p. 59.

39 "In the beginning there was high adventure": "The Wingfields of America" (unpublished), HRC.

40 "the saddest man I ever knew": *N*, "Mes Cahiers Noirs," 1979, p. 751.

40 "the emollient influence of a mother": *M*, p. 12.

40 "fierce blood": Williams to Donald Windham, *TWLDW*, p. 298.

41 "continual excitement": Leverich, *Tom*, p. 519.

41 "I have an instinct for self-destruction": LOA2, p. 221.

41 "the least demonstrative person": *RMTT*, p. 162.

41 "not the most masculine of men": *Time*, Mar. 9, 1962.

41 "Grecian vice": JLI with Gore Vidal, 2000, JLC.

41 "he is humble and affectionate": *CS*, "Grand," p. 379.

41 handed over most of his wife's savings: Leverich, *Tom*, p. 152. See *CS*, "Grand."

41 "She said 'Why, Walter?'": *CS*, "Grand," p. 384.

42 "The Bird told me": Vidal, "Tennessee Williams," p. 52.

42 "I want to go to Key West": Dennis Brown, "Miss Edwina under Glass," *St. Louisian*, Mar. 1977, p. 62.

42 "You'd think": Ibid.

42 "like a ghost": Williams to Donald Windham, Nov. 23, 1943, *TWLDW*, p. 121. As Williams grew increasingly a stranger to himself, the notion of being a ghost increased. To his pen pal–turned–house sitter, the poet David Lobdell, Williams signed off in one letter, "I offer you a ghostly hand, David, on your hand, your face, your hair." (Williams to David Lobdell, Sept. 14, 1968, LLC.)

42 "ineluctably smiling": LOA1, p. 400.

43 "gross lack of sensitivity": *N*, Nov. 20, 1941, p. 257.

43 when he met Edwina: "My mother's marriage ceremony in Columbus, Miss. came as a complete surprise to nearly all her friends in the town," Williams wrote to Audrey Wood. "It was performed in the church but privately and was a shocking surprise to the congregation as my father was considered 'too fast' for a minister's daughter." (Williams to Audrey Wood, Nov. 26, 1946, HRC.)

43 "One thing your father had plenty of": LOA1, p. 410.

43 "Before we arrived in St. Louis": *RMTT*, p. 34.

43 "I never could understand": Leverich, *Tom*, p. 70.

43 "Edwina can't sew": *RMTT*, p. 186.

43 "Baucis and Philemon": *CWTW*, p. 87.

44 "the house as though he were entering it": *CS*, "The Man in the Overstuffed Chair," p. vii.

44 "It was as though a thunderclap": Leverich, *Tom*, p. 34.

44 "We don't think much of that new baby": Ibid., p. 36.

44 "Then it isn't mine": Ibid., p. 48.

44 "was eager to get as much as he could": Dakin Williams interview with Robert Bray, *Mississippi Quarterly*, vol. 48 (Fall 1995), p. 777.

44 "great but confused vitality": LOA1, p. 394.

44 "turbulence": Leverich, *Tom*, p. 520.

45 "Most of the time, life with him": *RMTT*, p. 39.

45 "Come out of there": Ibid., p. 63.

45 "You wanted to shrink": Ibid., p. 26.

46 "I made the mistake of protesting": Leverich, *Tom*, p. 138.

46 "And I—I had to endure him!": LOA1, p. 266.

46 "two breathing things": *RMTT*, p. 35.

46 "Just like a moo-cow": Ibid., p. 56.

46 "designed for insanity": Harold Bloom, ed., *Tennessee Williams* (Broomall, Penn.: Chelsea House, 2003), p. 24.

46 "a whole lot more than he was worth": Durant Da Ponte, "Tennessee's Tennessee Williams," Tennessee Studies in Literature, University of Tennessee Studies in the Humanities, 1956, p. 14.

46 "Dad resented any money": Dakin Williams to Lyle Leverich, Aug. 16, 1984, LLC.

48 "Off and on he would make abortive efforts": Williams to Kenneth Tynan, July 26, 1955, *TWLDW*, p. 302.

48 "I think he loved me": *CWTW*, p. 258.

48 "[Tom] did not defy his father": *RMTT*, p. 62.

48 "I had begun to regard Dad's edicts": Ibid., p. 69.

48 "It was like walking on eggs": Ibid., p. 35.

48 "Cold, cold, cold": *CP*, "Cortege," p. 30.

48 "The old man has just now": Williams to Donald Windham, Apr. 1943, *TWLDW*, p. 58.

48 Another sign of his internal alliance: LLI with Dakin Williams, 1985, LLC.

48 "My father—how to meet him again": *N*, Aug. 23, 1942, p. 323.

48 "We made talk alone": Williams to Donald Windham, Apr. 1943, *TWLDW*, p. 56.

49 "What a dark and bewildering thing": Ibid., p. 57.

49 "Does nothing but stay home and drink": Williams to Audrey Wood, Jan. 15, 1946, HRC.

49 "Any excuse just to get away": Williams to James Laughlin, Mar. 11, 1945, *L1*, p. 554.

49 "He could recite poetry by the yard": *RMTT*, p. 167.

49 "Pitch now your tents toward Heaven": Papers of the Rev. Walter Dakin, Sewanee.

51 "Is my mother a lung lady?": *RMTT*, p. 15.

51 "She was always talking": JLI with Dakin Williams, 2001, JLC.

51 "she was trying to gain the stage": JLI with Dakin Williams, 2004, JLC.

51 "Miss Edwina will still be talking": Tennessee Williams, "Let It All Hang Out," *NSE*, p. 174.

51 "rarely if ever bested": *RMTT*, p. 202.

51 "It wasn't enough for a girl": LOA1, p. 403.

51 "I always like to forget": *RMTT*, p. 14.

51 "I often pretended to feel gay": Ibid., pp. 254–55.

52 "TOM: I know what's coming!": LOA1, p. 403.

52 "You couldn't sit with Edwina": JLI with Gore Vidal, 2000, JLC.

52 "was exceptionally observant as a child": *RMTT*, p. 15.

52 reenacted by Amanda: "Dakin said that the characterization was so accurate, Edwina could have sued Tom. 'Her fainting act and her "suffering Jesus" facial expressions were the most lethal (and unendurable) bits of her repertoire.'" (Leverich, *Tom*, p. 567.)

52 "looked like a horse eating briars": Leverich, *Tom*, p. 560.

53 "Well, Mrs. Williams": Ibid.

53 "a moderately controlled hysteric": *M*, p. 116.

53 trouble with her body: In 1920, Edwina miscarried; in 1922, her persistent illness was diagnosed as incipient tuberculosis; in 1926 she had a hysterectomy from which she nearly died.

53 "She used to scream every time": *CWTW*, p. 327.

53 "president of the anti-sex league": Leverich, *Tom*, p. 61.

53 "She didn't believe in sex": JLI with Dakin Williams, 2001, JLC.

53 "She just didn't touch you": JLI with Dakin Williams, 2004, JLC. Edwina claimed that her own mother, Williams's beloved "Grand," was "never very demonstrative, the least demonstrative person I've known, but she felt things deeply." (*RMTT*, p. 162.)

53 "Don't quote instinct to me!": LOA1, p. 421.

53 "an almost criminally foolish woman": *CWTW*, pp. 326–27.

53 "monolithic Puritanism": *M*, p. 119.

53 "all the errors and mistakes": Williams to Audrey Wood, Jan. 15, 1946, HRC.

53 "Achievement, of whatever kind": The typing exercise is filed in the Rose Williams folder at HRC.

54 martyred look: Leverich, *Tom*, p. 567.

54 "She fixes on him her look": *CS*, "Man in the Overstuffed Chair," p. x.

54 "maniacal fury": Ibid.

54 "imposed": *N*, p. 751.

54 Dakin remained sexually inexperienced: "I knew next to nothing about sex and was a 'virgin' when I married Joyce in 1955 at the age of thirty-seven." (Dakin Williams to Lyle Leverich, July 15, 1987, LLC.)

54 "reaction to delusions": "Psychiatric Summary": Farmington State Hospital, Dr. CC Ault, Dec. 16, 1937, LLC.

54 "and then not with my hands": *N*, pp. 751–53.

54 "highly sexed": *M*, p. 119.

54 "She made no positive motion": *CS*, "Portrait of a Girl in Glass," p. 110.

54 "to associate the sensual": Leverich, *Tom*, p. 63.

54 "almost entirely impossible": *M*, p. 23.

54 "Almost without remission": Ibid., p. 17.

55 "What taunts me worst": *N*, Sept. 23, 1942, p. 325.

55 "the only psychiatrist in whom I believe": *RMTT*, p. 244.

55 "essentially more psychotic": *CWTW*, p. 327. Edwina herself was committed for

a time; at the end of her life, she dropped the "a" from her name and signed herself "Edwin Williams."

55   "Like a force of nature": Williams to Elia Kazan, July 5, 1980, Harvard.

55   "You're my right-hand bower!": LOA1, p. 419.

55   "Resume your seat, little sister": Ibid., p. 402.

55   "Nonsense! Laura": Ibid., p. 410.

55   "AMANDA: It's almost time": Ibid., p. 404.

56   "My mother was extremely": LLI with Dakin Williams, Apr. 15, 1985, LLC.

56   "Her husband had deserted her": Tennessee Williams, "Stairs to the Roof" (unpublished story), HRC.

56   "mah writin' son": Leverich, Tom, p. 65.

56   "Within a few months": Williams to Elia Kazan, undated, WUCA.

56   "thought writers were complete zeroes": Dakin Williams to Lyle Leverich, Aug. 16, 1984, LLC.

56   "I feel uncomfortable": N, Oct. 7, 1938, p. 125.

56   "doubled her support": Leverich, Tom, p. 65.

56   storytelling became a kind of collusion: M, p. 15.

57   "I was a sweet child": N, Oct. 10, 1943, p. 395.

57   "the same precarious balance of nerves": Williams to Audrey Wood, Sept. 4, 1942, HRC.

58   "all of the family were mentally deranged": Leverich, Tom, p. 247.

58   "like a somnambulist"": M, p. 119.

58   "Rose is liable to go down": RMTT, p. 85.

58   "Tragedy. I write that word": N, Jan. 25, 1937, p. 73.

58   "Insight was entirely absent": "Psychiatric Summary."

58   "Mother chose to have Rose's lobotomy done": CWTW, p. 327.

58   "now lived in a world": RMTT, p. 14.

58   "outer oblivion and inner violence": NSE, p. 76.

59   "reclaiming dead bodies": Leverich, Tom, p. 65.

59   "somatic delusions": "Psychiatric Summary."

59   That ghostliness: To Williams, playwriting was a sort of haunting. "A play just seems to materialize, like an apparition it gets clearer and clearer and clearer," he said. (CWTW, p. 330.) He would later write to Elia Kazan about "the detached eye of art" and its ability to see human character in all its contradictoriness, "as if a ghost sat over the affairs of men and made a true recording of them." (Williams to Elia Kazan Apr. 19, 1947, WUCA.)

59   CC's abandonment: On seeing The Glass Menagerie for the first time, CC's only comment was, "Well, I never deserted the family."

59   "interior storms": Williams to Donald Windham, July 28, 1943, TWLDW, p. 91.

59   "You know it don't take much": LOA1, p. 417.

59   "I traveled around a great deal": Ibid., p. 465.

60   "almost dancelike": Ibid., p. 425.

60   "my doomed family": Williams to Donald Windham, Apr. 1943, TWLDW, p. 56.

60   "interior pantomime": LOA1, p. 465.

60   "Never before in my experience": Dowling, Nov. 21, 1964, CUCOHC, p. 820.

60   "holding out the ruffles": LIB, p. 413.

60   "All the people backstage": JLI with Betsy Blair, 2002, JLC.

60   "Author, Author!": Life, Apr. 30, 1945.

61   blushing: Irving Hoffman, Hollywood Report.

61 "Eddie, I can't remember anything": Dowling, Nov. 21, 1964, CUCOHC, p. 820.

61 "It was like after a World Series game": Ibid., pp. 821–22.

61 "the real and first talent of them all": Stark Young, as quoted in *LIB*, p. 408.

62 "pretty run-of-the-mill": *CWTW*, p. 239.

62 "Her talent was luminous": Williams, "On Laurette Taylor," HRC.

62 "I don't remember feeling": Leverich, *Tom*, p. 585.

62 "providential": *CWTW*, p. 330.

62 "a planetary tie-up": Scrapbook, HRC. The chart goes on: "Around this chart are most of the significant contacts-by-conjunction made to the players and author's planets by the planets on that exciting opening night. (And note first that the only planet uncontacted is Saturn, the planet generally debited with obstruction and failure, nothing of that kind about this opening—and Saturn has no contact, on the negative side of analysis)."

62 "a revolution": Arthur Miller, "Tennessee Williams' Legacy: An Eloquence and Amplitude of Feeling," in Arthur Miller, *Echoes down the Corridor: Collected Essays: 1944–2000* (New York: Penguin Books, 2000), p. 204.

62 "It seems to me that your glass menagerie": Carson McCullers to Williams, Feb. 10, 1949, Duke.

63 "I was happy to have my freedom": *RMTT*, p. 200.

63 "The postman can ring twice": As quoted in the *Knoxville News-Sentinel*, Apr. 22, 1945.

63 "there was a feeling of release": *New York Times*, Apr. 1, 1945.

63 "REVIEWS ALL RAVE": *TWIB*, p. 126.

64 "snatches of talk about the war": Lewis Nichols, "The Glass Menagerie," *New York Times*, Apr. 2, 1945.

64 "Such a response and attitude": Stark Young, *New Republic*, Apr. 15, 1945.

64 "in playing Amanda": *LIB*, p. 415.

64 "The whole week has been fantastic": Laurette Taylor to Dwight Taylor, Apr. 8, 1945, HRC.

64 "the greatest moment of collective inebriation": Philip Roth, *American Pastoral* (New York: Vintage Books, 1997), p. 40.

64 American per-capita income would triple: Harold Evans, *The American Century* (New York: Alfred A. Knopf, 2000), p. 435.

64 "Everything was up for grabs": JLI with Arthur Miller, 2004, JLC.

65 *The Inside of His Head*: John Lahr, *Show and Tell: New Yorker Profiles* (Woodstock, N.Y.: Overlook Press, 2000), p. 94.

65 "There is no dynamic in life or art": Odets, *Time Is Ripe*, p. 344.

65 "Overcome selfishness!": LOA1, p. 422.

65 "the destiny of me": Walt Whitman, "Out of the Endless Rocking."

65 "I build a tottering pillar of my blood": *CP*, "The Siege," p. 9.

65 "that long upward haul": *CS*, "Grand," p. 383.

65 "I am thy frail ghost-brother": *N*, Aug. 23, 1942, p. 325.

65 "Breathe into me a little of thy life!": Ibid., Sept. 17, 1941, p. 239.

65 "I will burn one for you": Williams to Paul Bigelow, Oct. 10, 1941, *L1*, p. 348.

66 "Homo Emancipatus—the Completely Free Man": Williams, "Stairs to the Roof," HRC. "Freedom for him wore the bright face of danger and he was willing to contemplate it only from a safe distance," Williams wrote in an early short-story version of the expressionistic *Stairs to the Roof*, subtitled *A Prayer for the Wild at Heart That Are Kept in Cages*. The play made its unremarkable debut a week

before the opening of *The Glass Menagerie* at the little Pasadena Playbox. In Williams's mind, freedom had a spiritual dimension. In his stage directions to *Stairs to the Roof*, he left no doubt as to what the roof represented: "Below this region the world may be grooved repetition, but here it is the transcendental—light, light, light! The last high reach of the spirit, matter's rejection, the abstract core of religion which is purity, wonder and love." ("Stairs to the Roof," HRC, p. 90.) Before he disappears in a cloud of smoke into a new orbit, the hero, Ben Murphy, tells the girl who goes with him, "The roof is only the jumping-off place to a man with my ambitions." His last words, shouted "from a long way off" to the hordes of workers who scream his name and "cast their ledgers, their papers, and pencils away with joyful cries for freedom" are "Hello—goodbye." (Ibid., p. 98.)

66   "The poet, the dreamer": The endpapers of Williams's copy of the *Collected Poems of Hart Crane*, which he carried with him. Columbia.

66   "When will the cool white time": *N*, Aug. 14, 1942, p. 321.

66   "Am I still looking": Ibid., June 27, 1941, p. 229.

66   "We can't say grace": LOA1, p. 401.

66   "the time when I would first catch": *NSE*, pp. 77–78.

66   "We come to each other": Ibid., p. 78.

67   "I guess I'm getting spoiled": *New York Times*, Apr. 4, 1945.

67   "This is the twilight of an era": Williams to Paul Bigelow, Apr. 10, 1943, *L1*, p. 438.

CHAPTER 2: THE HEART CAN'T WAIT

68   "What do I want?": *N*, Apr. 29, 1938, p. 229.

68   "May God be merciful to me": Ibid., Sept. 17, 1939, p. 165.

68   "a last, desperate throw of the literary dice": Williams to Erwin Piscator, Aug. 13, 1942, *L1*, p. 393.

68   "drizzle puss self": *N*, Oct. 6, 1943, p. 3.

68   "spiritual dislocation": *NSE*, p. 33.

68   "Once I ordered a sirloin steak": Ibid.

69   "I nearly went crazy": Williams to Guthrie McClintic, May 23, 1945, *L1*, p. 560.

69   "I have met the following here": Williams to Audrey Wood, June 20, 1945, *L2*, p. 7.

69   "Tennessee Williams, Writer": Lyle Leverich, *Tom: The Unknown Tennessee Williams* (New York: W. W. Norton, 1995), p. 280.

69   "About an hour after my arrival": Williams to Audrey Wood, Dec. 14, 1945, HRC.

69   "no telephone": Ibid.

69   "I am switching back and forth": Williams to Audrey Wood, Jan. 15, 1946, *L2*, p. 36.

69   most fecund of his writing life: Between 1945 and 1947, after the success of *The Glass Menagerie*, Williams wrote *Summer and Smoke*, *A Streetcar Named Desire*, the first draft of *Camino Real*, two of his major short stories, "One Arm" and "Desire and the Black Masseur," as well as *The Night of the Iguana* in story form.

69   road company of *The Glass Menagerie*: *You Touched Me!* closed after 109 performances; *The Glass Menagerie* closed on August 3, 1946, after 563 performances; the road company—according to Williams in a letter to Audrey Wood written in late March 1947, was "really a travesty of the play, mainly because of the glaring, stupefying incompetence of one member of the cast, Eddie Andrews." (Williams to Audrey Wood, Mar. 1947, *L2*, p. 88.)

70   "I was not a young man": *M*, p. 52.

70 "I never put on a shirt": Williams to Audrey Wood, Jan. 3, 1946, *L2*, pp. 31–32.

70 "I am going through quite an experience": Williams to James Laughlin, Jan. 25, 1946, ibid., pp. 39–40: "I am so shy with this girl Sylvia that I suffer acutely when alone in a room with her. Have you ever felt that way with anyone? I have told her I feel that way—she makes it worse by enquiring every few minutes, 'Am I making you uncomfortable?' 'Do you want me to go out now?' 'Is it all right if I sit here?' 'Don't talk to me unless you want to? Etc.' Then she sits there with her brilliant eyes taking in every embarrassed change of expression as if she were conducting some marvelous experiment in a lab so that I don't know where to look, let alone what to say. Exactly like Lillian Gish or at best Harold Lloyd in an old silent film. What are women made of?!"

70 command performance of *The Glass Menagerie*: Williams failed to attend the performance; he fell asleep and also missed the White House reception.

70 "She is one of these people": Williams to James Laughlin, Jan. 25, 1946, *L2*, pp. 39–40.

70 "particular milieu": Williams to Audrey Wood, Jan. 3, 1946, ibid., p. 31.

70 "more restful": Williams to Audrey Wood, Dec. 14, 1945, HRC.

70 "If you can imagine how a cat": Williams to Audrey Wood, Jan. 3, 1946, *L2*, p. 31.

70 "my dear Daughter": Williams to Oliver Evans, Jan. 1946, ibid., p. 37.

71 "my sainted Mother": Oliver Evans to Williams, undated, LLC.

71 "I am purring with gratitude": Williams to James Laughlin, Jan. 4, 1946, LLC.

71 "across the street from a Negro Convent": Williams to "Rod" (letter signed by "John"), Oct. 19, 1945, HRC.

71 Amado "Pancho" Rodriguez y Gonzalez: LLI with Pancho Rodriguez, 1983, LLC. Both Donald Spoto, in *The Kindness of Strangers*, and the Library of America volumes on Tennessee Williams maintain incorrectly that Williams met Rodriguez in Mexico, who then followed Williams to New Orleans. "I met him here in New Orleans in the winter of '45," Rodriguez said. "He was coming back from Mexico. I didn't realize who he was because I wasn't too keen on theatre then."

71 "dark of skin, dark of hair": *CS*, "Rubio y Morena," p. 261.

71 "I wish I had a lovely little clown": *N*, Oct. 23, 1943, p. 401.

71 "rambunctious": *KAL*, p. 334.

71 "Companionship was not a familiar": *CS*, "Rubio y Morena," pp. 259–61.

72 "took to be a man": Ibid., p. 258.

72 "I have been having quite a hectic time": Williams to Paul Bigelow, Feb. 27, 1946, *L2*, pp. 43–44.

72 "his bedroom with the bottle": Williams to Audrey Wood, Jan. 15, 1946, ibid., p. 35.

72 "Conditions at home must be worse": Williams to Audrey Wood, Jan. 3, 1946, HRC.

72 "In spite of basic damnation": Williams to Donald Windham, Sept. 8, 1943, *TWLDW*, pp. 103–4.

73 "I am waking up": LOA1, p. 440.

73 "It takes five or six years": *Time*, Mar. 9, 1962, p. 55.

73 "a picture of my own heart": *N*, Apr. 9, 1939, p. 147. On Easter Sunday, 1939, after the Group Theatre had acknowledged his work with a $100 prize, Williams rededicated himself to his vision of playwriting: "a picture of my own heart—there will be no artifice in it—I will speak truth as I see it—distort as I

see distortion—be wild as I am wild—tender as I am tender—mad as I am mad—passionate as I am passionate—It will be myself without concealment."

73 "ideal conditions": Williams to Audrey Wood, Jan. 3, 1946, HRC.

73 "He had no idea": *CS*, "Desire and the Black Masseur," pp. 205–6.

73 "His desires": Ibid., p. 206.

73 "Miss Alma grew up": *CWTW*, p. 228.

74 "Please be sure that no single copy": Williams to Audrey Wood, Sept. 24, 1941, *L1*, p. 341.

74 "By the flesh is meant": Papers of the Rev. Walter Dakin, Sewanee.

74 *The Ascent of the Soul*: Amory H. Bradford, *The Ascent of the Soul*. Williams's volume is in the Washington University Library in St. Louis. The inscription reads, "For T. Lanier Williams from his Grandfather Walter Edwin Dakin, Christmas 1933. May he 'read, mark, learn, and inwardly digest' the thoughts of this book."

74 "Character is the man": 4–5 Eastertide, Acts 24:14–16, Papers of the Rev. Walter Dakin, Sewanee.

74 "I had begun to associate": *CS*, "The Resemblance between a Violin Case and a Coffin," p. 277.

75 "the proud proprietress of a virgin mind": Tennessee Williams and Donald Windham, *You Touched Me!* (New York: Samuel French, 2010), p. 115.

75 "a youth of twenty-one": Ibid., p. 4.

75 "the fears and reticences": Ibid., p. 116.

75 "not predatory maternity": Ibid., p. 5.

75 "like being under water": Ibid., p. 18.

75 "The Victorian actually prevailed": Williams to Audrey Wood, Sept. 4, 1942, HRC.

75 "Virginity is mostly the consequence": Williams and Windham, *You Touched Me!*, p. 84.

75 "Without intervention": Williams to Audrey Wood, Sept. 4, 1942, HRC.

75 "who found it too much": Ibid.

76 "I doubt that anything": Williams to Elia Kazan, Nov. 18, 1950, WUCA.

77 "catches her fingers": Williams and Windham, *You Touched Me!*, p. 115.

77 "Where are you going?": Ibid., pp. 113–14.

77 "the little puritan": *CWTW*, pp. 228–31.

77 "HADRIAN: . . . I grew up": Williams and Windham, *You Touched Me!*, pp. 50–51.

77 "Don't hang back with the beasts": LOA1, p. 511.

77 "To me—well": Ibid., p. 612.

78 "Don't quote instinct to me!": Ibid., p. 421.

78 "body electric": Williams to Donald Windham, Jan. 3, 1944, *TWLDW*, p. 126.

78 Hazel Kramer: Williams met the redheaded, spirited Hazel Kramer (1912–1951) when he was eleven and she was nine. "Some young hoods were . . . throwing rocks at a plump little girl. I went to her defense . . . and thus began my closest childhood friendship which ripened into a romantic attachment," Williams wrote in *Memoirs* (pp. 14–15). Around puberty, Williams recalled, "I had a sexual desire for Hazel and it was in The West End Lyric, a movie house on Demar Blvd. Sitting beside her before the movie began, I suddenly conscious of her bare shoulders and I wanted to touch them, and I felt a genital stirring." (Leverich, *Tom*, p. 73.) CC, who didn't think she was "good enough for Tom," according to Edwina, opposed them attending the same university. She attended the University of Wisconsin.

78 "She was frigid": *M*, p. 29.

78 "deeply in love with my roommate": *CWTW*, pp. 230–31.

78 "Faults—I am egocentric": *N*, Oct. 9, 1937, p. 109.

79 "stunted": Ibid., Sept. 14, 1941, p. 235.

79 "Why do women ignore me": Ibid., May 30, 1938, p. 119.

79 "genuine nympho": *M*, p. 43. Regarding his vomiting: "All of a sudden I felt nauseated from the liquor consumed and from nervous strain and embarrassment. I rushed into the bathroom and puked, came out with a towel around me, hangdog with shame over my failed test of virility."

79 "I was . . . terribly impressed": Ibid.

79 "'I fucked a girl tonight'": Ibid. The affair lasted a few months before Williams was "thrown over by the beloved bitch—but the experience was valuable." (*N*, Apr. 29, 1938, p. 115.)

79 "finally fully persuaded": *M*, p. 49.

79 "This part down here is the sex": LOA1, p. 624.

79 "I must get my mind": *N*, Nov. 23, 1937, p. 69.

79 "to the artistic and Bohemian life": Ibid., Jan. 1, 1939, p. 133. The phrase "mad pilgrimage of the flesh" was first mentioned in ibid., Jan. 14, 1939, p. 133: "Am I all animal, all willful, blind stupid *beast*? Is there another part that is *not* an accomplice in this mad pilgrimage of the flesh?" In the short story "The Malediction" (1945), the phrase appears for the first time in print.

80 "discovered a certain flexibility": Leverich, *Tom*, p. 278.

80 "Rather horrible night": *N*, June 11, 1939, p. 153.

80 "I had the experience Sat. night": Ibid., June 14, 1939, p. 153.

80 "I seem to be my *normal* self again": Ibid., June 25, 1939, p. 153.

80 "It is good for me to have somebody": Ibid., May 25, 1939, p. 149.

80 "I felt like I was going to cry": Ibid., Mar. 7, 1939, p. 141.

80 "appalling loneliness": Ibid., Mar. 8, 1939, p. 143.

80 "If only tomorrow": Ibid.

80 "a delightful personality": Ibid., July 6, 1939, p. 155.

81 "I want something straight": Ibid.

81 "I demand so much": *N*, July 30, 1939, p. 161.

81 "enduring for the sake of endurance": LOA1, p. 587.

81 "Now I must make a positive religion": *N*, July 30, 1939, p. 161.

81 "an expert at graceful retreat": Ibid., Aug. 11, 1936, p. 49.

81 complaints that signaled his quiet desperation: Ibid., Oct. 16, 1938, p. 125. "The fear is so much worse than the thing feared—the heart defect, however actual, would cause me little discomfort, no actual pain—if I were not afraid of it—it is the fear that makes all the concomitant distresses, the dreadful tension, the agora and claustro-phobia, the nervous indigestion, the hot gassy stomach."

81 "a strange trance-like existence": Ibid., July 30, 1939, p. 161.

81 "The dreadful heavy slipping": Ibid.

82 "was caging in something": *CWTW*, p. 83.

82 "I need somebody to envelop me": *N*, Oct. 3, 1939, p. 166.

82 "What taunts me most": Ibid., Aug. 23, 1942, p. 325.

82 "I am so used to being": Ibid., May 27, 1937, p. 87.

82 "I've never had any feeling": *CWTW*, pp. 229–30.

82 "It is so easy to ignore": *N*, Oct. 6, 1943, p. 391.

82 "to know me is not to love me": *M*, p. 131.

82 "I am a problem": *N*, July 1, 1942, p. 297.

83 "I am as pure as I ever was": Ibid., Jan. 28, 1940, p. 185.

83 "Thank god I've gotten bitch-proof": *N*, Dec. 15, 1939, p. 179.

83 "My first real encounter": *CWTW*, p. 231.

83 "Ashes hauled": *N*, Jan. 12, 1940, p. 183.

83 "Oh, Lord, I don't know": Ibid., Jan. 26, 1940, p. 183.

83 "the restless beast in the jungle": Williams to Joseph Hazan, Sept. 1940, *L1*, p. 276.

83 "I ache with desires": *N*, Feb. 7, 1940, p. 187.

83 "The big emotional business": Ibid., Mar. 11, 1940, p. 191.

83 "this awful searching-business": Williams to Joseph Hazan, Aug. 18, 1940, *L1*, p. 262.

83 "My emotional life has been a series": *N*, May 26, 1940, p. 195.

84 "His practice in a room": Donald Windham, *As If: A Personal View of Tennessee Williams* (Verona, N.Y.: Privately published, 1985), pp. 17–18.

84 "He would dispatch me": *M*, p. 53.

85 "quotidian goal": Windham, *As If*, p. 17.

85 from prude to lewd: Anna Freud, *The Writings of Anna Freud*, vol. 2: *Ego and the Mechanisms of Defense* (Madison, Conn.: International Universities Press, 1936), pp. 153–54: "Young people who pass through the kind of ascetic phase which I have in mind seem to fear the quantity rather than the quality of their instincts. They mistrust enjoyment in general and so their safest policy appears to be simply to counter more urgent desires with more stringent prohibitions. Every time the instinct says 'I will', the ego retorts, 'Thou shall not' much after the manner of strict parents in the early training of little children. . . . But in the repudiation of instinct characteristic of adolescence no loophole is left such substitute gratification . . . turning against the self we find a swing-over from asceticism to instinctual excess, the adolescent suddenly indulging in everything which he had previously held to be prohibited and disregarding any sort of external restrictions."

85 "I was just terribly over sexed": *CWTW*, p. 231.

85 "I'm getting horny as a jack-rabbit": Williams to Donald Windham, Oct. 11, 1940, *TWLDW*, p. 17.

85 "the most uncompromising of southern Puritans": Williams to Theresa Helburn, Oct. 11, 1940, *L1*, p. 290.

85 "So line up some": Williams to Donald Windham, Oct. 11, 1940, *TWLDW*, p. 17.

85 "deviant Satyriasis": *M*, p. 53.

85 "Sexuality is an emanation": Ibid.

85 "I went out cruising last night": Williams to Paul Bigelow, Sept. 27, 1941, *L1*, p. 333.

85 "I am always alarming bed partners": *N*, Jan. 15, 1943, p. 409.

85 "As the world grows worse": Williams to Donald Windham, May 1, 1941, *TWLDW*, p. 22.

86 "I'd like to live a simple life": *N*, July 12, 1942, p. 303.

86 "I think for a good summer fuck": Williams to Donald Windham, July 23, 1942, *TWLDW*, p. 37.

86 "I cruised with 3 flaming belles": *N*, Oct. 4, 1941, p. 243.

86 "Tonight ran into some 'dirt'": Ibid., Oct. 29, 1941, p. 255.

86 "unspent tenderness": Williams and Windham, *You Touched Me!*, p. 65.

86 "When I now appear in public": Williams to Paul Bigelow, July 25, 1941, *L1*, pp. 325–26.
87 "Sometimes I feel the island": *CP*, "The Siege," p. 910.
87 "I always want my member": *CWTW*, p. 229.
87 "In his room, amid the disordered contents": Windham, *As If*, pp. 16–17. See also "Portrait of a Girl in Glass" (*CS*, p. 119, originally published 1943): "In five years' time I had nearly forgotten home. I had to forget it, I couldn't carry it with me."
87 "I think I have gone": *N*, Oct. 28, 1946, p. 447.
87 feeling like a ghost: "I felt like a ghost." Williams to Donald Windham, Nov. 23, 1943, *TWLDW*, p. 121.
88 "Evening is the normal adult's time": *N*, Feb. 25, 1942, p. 281.
88 "to find in motion": LOA1, p. 465.
88 "spiritual champagne": *N*, Mar. 29, 1940, p. 191.
88 "the asking look in his eyes": *CS*, "The Malediction," p. 147.
88 "*You* coming toward me": *N*, May 26, 1940, p. 195.
88 "rebellious hell": *M*, p. 53.
88 "I know myself to be a dog": *N*, May 30, 1940, p. 195.
88 "I wonder, sometimes, how much": *M*, p. 53.
88 "at the nadir of my resources": Williams to Luise Sillcox, July 8, 1940, *L1*, p. 257.
88 "mad pilgrimage of the flesh": Williams to Joseph Hazan, Aug. 18, 1940, ibid., p. 262.
88 "beautiful and serene": Williams to Donald Windham, Aug. 1940, *TWLDW*, p. 11.
89 pictures he would carry in his wallet: LLI with Joseph Hazan, 1985, LLC.
89 "Neither of us had any talent": LLI with Joseph Hazan, 1985, LLC.
89 "My good eye was hooked like a fish": *M*, p. 54.
89 cataract in one eye: Ibid.
89 "I will never forget the first look": Ibid.
89 "slightly slanted lettuce-green eyes": Ibid.
89 "When he turned from the stove": Ibid.
89 "with Narcissan pride": *M*, p. 54.
89 "He had Southern charms": LLI with Joseph Hazan, LLC.
90 "crazed eloquence": *M*, p. 54.
90 "Tom, let's go up to my bedroom": Ibid., p. 55.
90 unique account of his ravished surrender: Hazan insists that between Kip and Williams there was only one sexual encounter and that Williams embellished his sexual life with Kip. (See *N*, p. 202.) In *Memoirs* (p. 55), Williams implies that their affair was more than one night. "After that, we slept together each night on the double bed up there, and so incontinent was my desire for the boy that I would wake him repeatedly during the night for more love-making . . . ," Williams wrote. In any case, the entire relationship lasted no more than six weeks.
90 "We wake up two or three times": Williams to Donald Windham, July 29–30, 1940, *TWLDW*, pp. 9–10.
90 "little boy's face": Ibid.
91 "Last night you made me know": *M*, p. 55.
92 "I know Kip loved me": Ms. "Memoirs," p. 237; in the published book, he adds: "after his bewildered fashion" (*M*, p. 55). The last two sentences were cut from the published version.

92   "ecstasy one moment": Williams to Donald Windham, July 1940, *TWLDW*, p. 8.

92   "Kip turned oddly moody": *M*, p. 55.

92   "Moves me to find someone afflicted": *N*, July 29, 1940, p. 201.

92   "Will it be all gone": Ibid., July 19, 1940, p. 199.

92   "I am being courted by a musician": Williams to Donald Windham, July 1940, *TWLDW*, p. 8.

92   "a girl": Ms. "Memoirs," p. 56. In an edited passage, "The girl was the sister of Kenneth Tynan's wife, Elaine."

93   "Tenn, I have to talk to you": *M*, p. 56.

93   "made a horrible ass of myself": *N*, Aug. 15, 1940, p. 205.

93   "*C'est fini*": Ibid.

93   "I can't save myself": Ibid., Aug. 12, 1940, p. 203.

93   "You whoever you are": Ibid., Aug. 15, 1940, p. 205.

93   "Oh, K.—if only": Ibid., Aug. 19, 1940, p. 207.

93   "I hereby formally bequeath you": Williams to Kip Kiernan, Aug. 22, 1940, *L1*, p. 269.

93   "Do you think I am making too much": Ms. "Memoirs," p. 240.

93   "K., if you ever come back": *N*, Aug. 19, 1940, p. 207.

93   died of a brain tumor: Williams visited Kip as he lay dying in a hospital bed at the Polyclinic Hospital near Times Square. By then, Kip had married; from his bed he had been asking for "Tenny." Williams, who was afraid to visit him alone, brought Windham. "As I entered Kip's room he was being spoon-fed by a nurse; a dessert of sugary apricots. He had never looked more beautiful," Williams said in a 1981 *Paris Review* interview. "We spoke a while. Then I rose and reached for his hand and he couldn't find mine, I had to find his." Afterward, he sent Kip a cream-colored Shantung robe. He commemorated the encounter in "Death Is High": "Return, you called while you slept. / And desperately back I crept / . . . my longing was great / to be comforted and warmed / once more by your sleeping form, / to be, for a while, no higher / than where you are, / little room, warm love, humble star!" Williams to Paul Bowles, Feb. 23, 1950, HRC. This early draft was later published in a much-revised version as "Death Is High," without the dedication to Merlo.

94   "Tennessee could not possess his own life": Gore Vidal, "Tennessee Williams: Someone to Laugh at the Squares With," in Gore Vidal, *Armageddon? Essays 1983–1987* (London: Andre Deutsch, 1987), p. 59.

94   "For love I make characters": *CS*, "Preface," p. xv.

94   *Something Cloudy, Something Clear*: This title refers to Williams's eyes at the time he met Kip, and represented to Williams "the two sides of my nature. The side that was obsessively homosexual, compulsively interested in sexuality. And the side that in those days was gentle and understanding and contemplative." (*CWTW*, p. 346.)

94   "has a fresh and primitive quality": LOA1, p. 199.

94   "fresh and shining look": Ibid., p. 575.

94   "is one of those Mediterranean types": Ibid., p. 701.

94   "still slim and firm as a boy": LOA1, p. 884.

94   "the body electric": Williams to Donald Windham, Jan. 3, 1944, *TWLDW*, p. 126.

94   "I love you": Williams to Kip Kiernan, Aug. 22, 1940, *L1*, p. 269.

94   "I screamed like a banshee": *CWTW*, p. 229.

95   "I have just had an orgy": Williams to Donald Windham, Sept. 20, 1943, *TWLDW*, p. 105.

95 "Why do they strike us?": *N*, Jan. 5, 1943, p. 339.

95 "Not that I like being struck": Ibid., Jan. 7, 1943, p. 339.

95 "What do you expect to get": Tennessee Williams, "The Primary Colors" (unpublished), HRC.

95 Sexuality: In an early version of *Streetcar*, Blanche says to "George" (Mitch), "What people do with their bodies is not really what makes good or bad people of them!" Ibid.

95 "The truth of the matter": *N*, Aug. 25, 1942, p. 327.

95 "tricks in my pocket": LOA1, p. 400.

95 "charged with plenty": Williams, "Primary Colors," HRC.

95 "She tries to explain her life": Williams to Audrey Wood, Mar. 23, 1945, *L1*, p. 557.

96 "We ought to be exterminated": *N*, Sept. 14, 1941, pp. 232–33. Evans was also the model for Billy in Williams's short story "Two on a Party."

96 "sad but poignant": Ibid., Sept. 14, 1941, p. 235.

96 "What are we doing": Williams to Erwin Piscator, Aug. 13, 1942, *L1*, p. 393.

96 "Mr. Williams, you have written": Williams to Audrey Wood, July 29, 1942, ibid., p. 387.

96 "underground devils": Williams to Mary Hunter, mid-April 1943, ibid., p. 438.

96 "naked and savage kinds of creation": Ibid.

96 "vast hunger for life": Williams to William Saroyan, Nov. 29, 1941, *L1*, p. 359.

96 "long fingers": Williams to Donald Windham, July 18, 1943, *TWLDW*, p. 88: "We must have long fingers and catch at whatever we can while it is passing near us."

96 "too selfish for love": LOA1, p. 265.

97 "Who, if I were to cry out": Ibid., p. 565.

97 "Probably the greatest difference": Williams to Donald Windham, Sept. 20, 1943, *TWLDW*, p. 106.

97 little devil of the prologue: John: "They told me I was a devil. . . . I'd rather *be* a devil." The script even has Buchanan driving like "a demon." LOA1, p. 610.

97 "unmarked by the dissipations": Ibid., p. 575.

97 "a Promethean figure": Ibid.

97 "worn-out magic": Ibid., p. 622.

97 "It's yet to be proven": Ibid., p. 611.

97 "the everlasting struggle and aspiration": Ibid., p. 612.

97 "I should have been *castrated*": Ibid., p. 624.

97 "I'm more afraid of your soul": Ibid.

97 "I came here to tell you": Ibid., p. 638.

99 "narcotized tranquility": Ibid., p. 504.

99 "I cannot create": *N*, June 27, 1941, p. 229.

99 "I pray for the strength": Williams to Joseph Hazan, Aug. 20, 1940, *L1*, p. 265.

99 "the cage of Puritanism": *CWTW*, p. 83.

99 "The prescription number is 96814": LOA1, p. 642.

99 "And still our blood is sacred": *CP*, "Iron Is the Winter," pp. 60–61.

99 "I need a soft climate": *N*, Nov. 28, 1945, p. 437.

100 "N.Y. holds me only by the balls": Williams to Donald Windham, Dec. 18, 1945, *TWLDW*, pp. 178–79.

100 "Our friendship was more spiritual": LLI with Pancho Rodriguez, 1983, LLC.

100 "the rare and beautiful stranger": *N*, Aug. 18, 1940, p. 206.

100 "I don't think he was disappointed": LLI with Pancho Rodriguez, 1983, LLC.

100 "Right in the thick of it": Williams to Margo Jones, Oct. 17, 1946, *L2*, p. 75.

100 "It was not until I met him": LLI with Pancho Rodriguez, 1983, LLC.

100 "the bright side of myself": Williams to Joseph Hazan, Aug. 22, 1940, *L1*, p. 270.

101 "Tennessee: This is Vanilla Williams": Tennessee Williams/Pancho Rodriguez record, BRTC.

101 "Well bred people find it difficult": *Miami Herald*, Mar. 30, 1958.

101 "comes from deep underground": LOA1, p. 640.

101 "was willing": Williams to Studs Terkel, radio interview (Blackstone Hotel), Dec. 1961, LLC.

101 man-child of twenty-five: Pancho Rodriguez was born Dec. 1, 1920.

102 primitive: "He was a primitive," the New Orleans artist Fritz Bultman said, as quoted in Donald Spoto, *The Kindness of Strangers: The Life of Tennessee Williams* (Boston: Little, Brown, 1985), p. 122.

102 "All of my nights with Pancho": Ms. "Memoirs," p. 24.

102 "sort of an off-beat saint": *M*, p. 106.

102 "At first I entertained him": Ms. "Memoirs," p. 24.

103 "My deportment wasn't too exemplary": LLI with Pancho Rodriguez, 1983, LLC.

103 "The scenes he created": Ms. "Memoirs," p. 24.

103 "He could not explain this thing": *CS*, "Rubio y Morena," p. 259.

103 "had never been able to believe": Ibid., p. 257.

103 "restored his male dominance": Ibid., p. 261.

103 "some loud tacky thing": Ibid., p. 595.

103 "where anything goes": Ibid., p. 610.

103 "gay, very gay": Ibid., p. 642.

103 "Did anyone ever slide downhill": Ibid., p. 618.

103 "widened the latitude": *CS*, "Rubio y Morena," p. 265.

103 "sentenced to solitary confinement": LOA2, p. 875.

103 "Of all the people I have known": Williams to Pancho Rodriguez, Nov. 1947, *L2*, p. 130.

103 "had grown to love": *CS*, "Rubio y Morena," p. 260.

104 "to breathe the fine air": Ms. "Memoirs," p. 28.

104 "I have learned how to use": Williams to Audrey Wood, Apr. 21, 1946, *L2*, p. 46.

104 "When I got home": Williams to Donald Windham, Apr. 1946, *TWLDW*, p. 188.

104 "I'm sorry I couldn't talk": Williams to Pancho Rodriguez, Apr. 1946, *L2*, pp. 48–49.

105 "Jack in Black": Ms. "Memoirs," p. 29.

105 "The altitude affected my heart": Williams to Audrey Wood, May 27, 1946, HRC.

105 "Pancho sat in the hospital with me": Ms. "Memoirs," p. 32.

105 "He always had moments of great style": *M*, p. 103.

105 "a sensation of death": Ibid., p. 104.

105 "Claustrophobia, feeling of suffocation": Williams to Kenneth Tynan, July 26, 1955, *TWLDW*, p. 304.

105 "I'm dying! I'm dying!": Ms. "Memoirs," p. 32.

105 "I don't know why I said it in Spanish": Williams to Audrey Wood, May 27, 1946, HRC.

105 "a rare intestinal problem": Ibid.

105 "Well, you're all right now": Williams to Kenneth Tynan, July 26, 1955, p. 304.

106 "One of the good sisters of the Holy Cross": Williams to James Laughlin, July 1947, *L2*, p. 57.

106 "I don't know what you got": Williams to Kenneth Tynan, July 26, 1955, *TWLDW*, pp. 305–6.

106 "Since then, and despite": Williams to James Laughlin, July 1946, *L2*, p. 57.

106 "I am sitting up here smoking": Williams to Donald Windham, May 1946, *TWLDW*, p. 191.

106 "This was when the desperate time started": Williams to Kenneth Tynan, July 26, 1955, Ibid., p. 306.

106 "a dying man": Ms. "Memoirs," p. 42.

106 "As everyone remarked": Williams to Margo Jones, Sept. 5, 1946, HRC.

106 "She was a crashing bore": JLI with Gore Vidal, 2000, JLC.

106 "The minute I met her": Williams to James Laughlin, July 1946, *L2*, p. 58.

107 "Those who find it a little harder to live": From "Love and the Rind of Time," the lines continues: "As struggling gene in oceanic plant / Predestine voluntary cells that give / The evolutionary turn to fish, then beast . . . " Carson McCullers, *The Mortgaged Heart: Selected Writings*, ed. Margarita G. Smith (London: Penguin, 1975), pp. 290–91.

107 "I feel that once": Carson McCullers to Williams, May 11, 1948, Columbia.

107 "the last good year": *CWTW*, p. 199.

107 his first sighting of McCullers: Ibid.

107 "Are you Tennessee or Pancho?": Virginia Spencer Carr, *The Lonely Hunter: A Biography of Carson McCullers* (New York: Doubleday, 1975), p. 272.

107 "For some reason Pancho": *M*, p. 107.

107 "by no means convinced of this": Ibid.

107 "spuds Carson": Ibid., p. 275.

108 "Carson is the only person": *CWTW*, p. 200.

108 "I feel you are a true collaborator": Carson McCullers to Williams, May 11, 1948, Columbia.

109 "Pancho was subdued for a while": Ms. "Memoirs," p. 37.

109 "My friend Pancho has been cooking": Williams to Audrey Wood, Sept. 29, 1946, HRC.

109 "As you ought to know": Williams to Pancho Rodriguez, July 1946, *L2*, p. 61.

110 "When Tennessee would mention": LLI with Pancho Rodriguez, 1983, LLC.

110 "a violent dislike": Paul Bigelow to Jordan Massie, Oct. 16, 1946, LLC.

110 "the Mexican problem": Williams to Margo Jones, Oct. 1947, *L2*, p. 129. "The Mexican problem returned to Manhattan a couple of days ago, quite unexpectedly, and is now sharing the one-room apartment with me. *Manana* he will look for a job. (Always Manana)."

110 "Don't, for God's sake": Carson McCullers to Williams, undated, Columbia.

110 "Carson says that Ten's Mexican": Paul Bigelow to Jordan Massie, Oct. 16, 1946, LLC.

110 "I had peeled down": *TWIB*, p. 142.

110 "Dakin stayed up all night": LLI with Pancho Rodriguez, 1983, LLC.

110 "an asset to you socially": Dakin Williams to Williams, Mar. 8, 1947, HRC.

110 "How can you do this to me": *TWIB*, p. 142.

111 "had the predictable effect": Ibid.

111 "No amount of reassurance": Paul Bigelow to Jordan Massie, Sept. 20, 1946, LLC. "I refused to go, of course, and gave Liebling some stern instructions about not ever mentioning any of this, even obliquely, to Tenn. Since to do so would mean that Audrey would no longer be Tenn's agent—Pancho would see to that, even if Tenn did not get sufficiently offended—and that is unfair to Audrey's long and unselfish interest in Tenn's work."

111 "She resented me": LLI with Pancho Rodriguez, 1983, LLC.

111 outraged her: Paul Bigelow to Jordan Massie, Oct. 30, 1946, LLC. "I don't blame Audrey for having felt deeply offended when Tenn brought Pancho to all meetings with her, turned to him for opinion and consultation on points that concerned only Audrey as his representative, and particularly by the extremely patronizing tone Pancho assumed toward her, including a reference to the delay in bringing the elaborate moving picture arrangements to a conclusion."

111 "Audrey, what happened to the money": LLI with Pancho Rodriguez, 1983, LLC.

111 "Audrey wanted to ask my advice": Paul Bigelow to Jordan Massie, Sept. 29, 1946, LLC.

111 "A deal has been completed": Tennessee Williams/Pancho Rodriguez record, BRTC.

112 "It was an error": Paul Bigelow to Jordan Massie, Oct. 30, 1946, LLC. In the same letter, Bigelow writes, "I am horrified that such tales are circulating about in the circles where his career must be, for the theatre has always been curiously prudish and like many a slut is more cautious of scandal than the respectable. And as for Hollywood, there is no more certain end to a career. I simply don't believe there have been attacks upon Tenn's life."

112 "I was jealous of all of them": LLI with Pancho Rodriguez, 1983, LLC.

112 detail of passion in *A Streetcar Named Desire*: Stella: "No, it isn't all right for anybody to make such a terrible row, but—people do sometimes. Stanley's always smashed things. Why, on our wedding night—soon as we came in here—he snatched off one of my slippers and rushed about the place smashing the light bulbs with it. . . . He smashed all the light-bulbs with the heel of my shoe. . . . I was–sort of—thrilled by it." (LOA1, p. 504.)

112 "You take your friends out": LLI with Pancho Rodriguez, 1983, LLC.

113 "We're the sugar daddies!": Windham, *As If*, p. 81.

113 "Tenn . . . disappeared": Ibid.

113 "You ought to see your room": Ibid.

113 "A portable typewriter": Williams to Donald Windham, June 6, 1947, *TWLDW*, p. 200.

113 "on the other side of a center": *CS*, "Rubio y Morena," p. 263.

114 quiet days to write: In the manuscript of "Memoirs" (p. 42), Williams wrote, "I would work from early morning to early afternoon, and then, spent from the rigors of creation, I would go around the corner to a bar called Victor's and revive myself with a marvelous drink called a brandy Alexander which was a specialty of the bar. I would always play the Ink Spots rendition of 'If I Didn't Care' on the juke box. Then I'd eat a sandwich and then I'd go to the Athletic Club on North Rampart Street."

114 "the always turbulent return of Pancho": Ms. "Memoirs," p. 42.

114 "Situation of my psyche": *N*, Nov. 15, 1946, p. 447.

114 "The nightingales can't sing anymore": Ibid., Dec. 16, 1946, p. 451.

114 "Nausea persists": Ibid., Dec. 19, 1946, p. 453.

114 "Undoubtedly a lot of my symptoms": Williams to Audrey Wood, Dec. 3, 1946, HRC.

114 "STILL DISSATISFIED": Audrey Wood to Williams, Nov. 18, 1948, HRC.

114 "I agree with Guthrie": Ibid.

115 "Still here, still working": *N*, Dec. 1, 1946, p. 449.

115 "He kept yawning as I read": Ms. "Memoirs," p. 41.

115 "Maurice's negative reaction": *N*, Dec. 16, 1946, p. 451.

115 Jones liked: Ms. "Memoirs," p. 43. "Margo Jones and her friend Joanna Albus arrived from Dallas and I read the first draft of *Streetcar* aloud to them. I think they were shocked by it. So was I. Blanche seemed too far out. You might say out of sight." (*M*, p. 111.)

115 "Quarreled with Pancho": *N*, Dec. 19, 1946, p. 453.

115 "feeling pretty desolate": Ibid.

115 "with newspaper and Crane and Hemingway": Ibid.

115 "Somehow or other": Williams to Audrey Wood, Jan. 9, 1947, *L2*, p. 83.

115 "I haven't caught sight": *N*, Dec. 16, 1946, p. 451. The "pipe dream" is a reference to *The Iceman Cometh*.

116 "Pancho is home with me": *N*, Dec. 24, 1946, p. 455.

116 "I . . . find it surprisingly close": Ibid.

116 "rather harsh, violent": Williams to Audrey Wood, Jan. 9, 1947, *L2*, p. 83.

116 "desultorily": *N*, Jan. 2, 1947, p. 457.

116 "She is probably disgusted": Ibid.

116 "this huge, dreadful game": Victor Campbell Collection, Oct. 2, 1946, THNOC.

116 "Thinking of driving down": *N*, Jan. 2, 1947, p. 457.

116 "Grandfather was a wonderful": *M*, p. 111.

116 "over a clean sweep of the sea": Williams to Donald Windham, Jan. 28, 1947, *TWLDW*, p. 193.

116 "You cannot imagine": Williams to Pancho Rodriguez, ca. Jan. 31, 1947, *L2*, p. 85.

117 "By the calendar": Williams to Rev. Walter Dakin, Oct. 10, 1946, ibid., pp. 71–72.

117 "You are one of the youngest people": Ibid. The other is "Grand," Dakin's wife; see Williams's story "Grand."

118 "Just being with him": *M*, p. 111.

118 "I think the change was good": Williams to Pancho Rodriguez, ca. Jan. 31, 1947, *L2*, p. 85.

118 "It went like a house on fire": *M*, p. 111.

118 first-draft scenes of "The Poker Night": Under the title page, Williams wrote, "With careful editing, I think a reasonably complete play script could be made out of these rough scenes: that is, if I am unable to do this myself." Tennessee Williams, "The Poker Night" (unpublished), HRC.

118 "loved me with everything": Ibid.

118 "an awful city wilderness": Ibid.

118 "a different species": Ibid.

118 changed to "Stanley": In the original manuscript, Williams wrote at the top of the script, "Typist—change name 'Ralph' to 'Stanley' when you find it in script." Williams, "Poker Night," HRC.

119 "the soft people": LOA1, p. 515.

119 "Be comfortable is my motto": Ibid., p. 482.

119 "slowly and emphatically": Ibid., p. 506.

119 "Nobody sees anybody *truly*": Williams to Elia Kazan, Apr. 19, 1947, *L2*, p. 95.

119 "Damsel in Distress": Kazan notebook, WUCA.

120 "I kept puzzling over the play": *KAL*, p. 349.

120 "threatened to leave": Williams to Donald Windham, Mar. 26, 1947, *TWLDW*, p. 197.

120 "Somehow in my life": *N*, Mar. 30, 1947, p. 461.

121 "a desperate driven creature": Williams to Elia Kazan, Apr. 19, 1947, *L2*, p. 95.

121 "To breathe quietly": *N*, Mar. 29, 1947, p. 459.

121 "a cleft in the rock": LOA1, p. 546.

121 "It was because": Ibid., p. 528.

121 "the searchlight": Ibid., p. 538.

122 "Sometimes—there's God": Ibid., p. 529.

122 "mortuary equipment and appliances": Tennessee Williams, "The Primary Colors" (unpublished early version), HRC.

122 "The first time I laid eyes on him": Ibid.

122 "He's *common!*": LOA1, p. 510.

122 "This Stanley never forgets": Production script of *A Streetcar Named Desire*, WUCA. Elsewhere in his notes, Kazan writes of Stanley, "The one thing that Stanley can't bear is someone who thinks that he or she is better than him. His only way of explaining himself—he thinks he stinks—is that everyone else stinks. This is symbolic. True of our National State of Cynicism. No values. There is nothing to command his loyalty. Stanley rapes Blanche because has tried and tried to keep her down to his level."

122 "red-stained": LOA1, p. 470.

122 "We've had this date": Ibid., p. 565.

122 "I'll put it to you plainly": Jeff Young, *Kazan: The Master Director Discusses His Films* (New York: Newmarket Press, 1999), p. 83.

122 "She simply seemed to exist": *M*, p. 109.

122 "He is a man of thirty-two": Williams, "Primary Colors," HRC.

123 "Sometimes my violence": LLI with Pancho Rodriguez, 1983, LLC.

123 "I felt that he was exploiting me": Ibid.

123 "I had a great fondness": *M*, p. 133.

123 handsome, well-built young man: Frank Merlo, who would later become Williams's companion for fifteen years.

124 "I have never regarded sand": *M*, p. 133.

124 "Pancho gave her a clout in the eye": Ms. "Memoirs," p. 56.

124 "With that protective instinct of mine": Ibid., p. 58.

124 "Pancho drove the car into the field": Ibid.

124 "It looks like P and I": *N*, Mar. 16, 1947, p. 457.

124 "A relative success": Ibid.

124 "It makes me shiver and shake": *NSE*, p. 132.

124 "She said something like this": Ibid.

125 "Tennessee's script was as close": *RBAW*, p. 152.

125 "Don't think about this": Audrey Wood to Williams, Mar. 22, 1947, HRC.

125 smacked of a Western action novel: *RBAW*, p. 151.

125 "Do you think anything will be done": Williams to Audrey Wood, Mar. 1947, *L2*, p. 89.

125 "safe": Williams to James Laughlin, Apr. 9, 1947, ibid., p. 92.

125 "MY TRAIN LEAVES 5:30": Williams to Audrey Wood, Apr. 8, 1947, ibid., p. 91.

125 "Audrey repeated twice on the phone": Williams to Donald Windham, Apr. 10, 1947, *TWLDW*, p. 198.

125 "the Princess": Ibid.

126 highest-paid man in the United States: From 1937 to 1946, Mayer earned one million dollars a year, the equivalent in today's money of over twenty million a year.

126 "I did not know that Mrs. Selznick": Williams to Donald Windham, Apr. 10, 1947, *TWLDW*, p. 198.

126 "I have always proceeded on the theory": *RBAW*, p. 141.

126 "Lawrence Stanislavsky Langner": Williams to Audrey Wood, June 20, 1945, *L1*, p. 565.

126 "wanted any part of Singer": Williams to Audrey Wood, Mar. 1947, *L2*, p. 88.

126 "deeply indignant": Ibid. "It is really a travesty of the play, mainly because of the glaring, stupefying incompetence of one member of the cast, Eddie Andrews [the Gentleman Caller]. I think if they had really respected the play, even just as a commodity, they would not have allowed it to drag about the country in this disgraceful condition when all they had to do was fire or buy out one intolerable actor to make a creditable company of it. Of course I realize that Singer probably does not know a bad actor from a good actor but Dowling certainly does and he should have paid some attention."

126 *Heartsong*: Arthur Laurents's second play was later reworked into his hit, *The Time of the Cuckoo*.

126 "My heart was with the playwright": Irene Selznick, *A Private View* (New York: Alfred A. Knopf, 1983), p. 291.

126 "I wanted to find someone with money": *RBAW*, p. 152.

126 "Third and last call, my girl": Selznick, *Private View*, p. 294.

127 "Why me?": Ibid., p. 295.

127 "Find me someone else": Ibid.

127 "The play was bigger than I wanted": Ibid.

127 "I have a distinct feeling": Audrey Wood to Irene Selznick, June 1, 1947, ISC.

127 "Feeling like a marriage broker": *RBAW*, p. 153.

127 "I walked looking straight ahead": Selznick, *Private View*, pp. 296–97.

127 "The only time he seemed impressed": Ibid., p. 297.

127 "Enough": Ibid.

128 "Let's get this over with": Ibid.

128 contract: Williams received a $2,000 advance; he agreed to extend the production date from November 15, 1947, to January 15, 1948, if the production team could show that they had "signed a director meeting with the approval of the author; and signed a leading player for the part of 'Blanche' or 'Stella' meeting with the approval of the author." (Apr. 19, 1947, ISC.) The author also had approval of scenic designer and incidental music. He was guaranteed four and a half weeks on the road prior to opening, and four house seats in the first six rows.

128 "a Female Moneybags from Hollywood": Williams to James Laughlin, Apr. 9, 1947, *L2*, p. 92.

128 "I was prepared for anything but this": Selznick, *Private View*, p. 297.

128 "BLANCHE HAS COME TO LIVE": Ibid.

128 "shocked": *KAL*, p. 327.

128 "seething": Cheryl Crawford, *One Naked Individual: My Fifty Years in the Theatre* (Indianapolis: Bobbs-Merrill, 1977), pp. 184–85.

128 "There was a hysteria of snobbery": *KAL*, p. 327.

128 "none of his clients": Ibid., p. 328.

128 "Irene is nice": Williams to Pancho Rodriguez, Apr. 15, 1947, *L2*, p. 94.

129 "strong but fastidious director": Williams to James Laughlin, Apr. 9, 1947, ibid., p. 93.

129 "peculiar vitality": Williams to Audrey Wood, undated, LLC.

129 "The cloudy dreamy type": *KAL*, p. 328.

129 "Gadg likes a thesis": Ibid., p. 327.

129 "reservations": Ibid.

129 "I wasn't sure Williams and I were the same": Ibid., p. 328.

130 "What our stage does": Elia Kazan, *Elia Kazan: Interviews*, ed. William Baer (Jackson: University Press of Mississippi, 2000), p. 67.

130 rabble-rousing theatrical mantra of the decade: *KAL*, p. 116. "It was the most overwhelming reception I've ever heard in the theatre. The audience of *Death of a Salesman* may have been more deeply stirred; I believe they were. And *Streetcar Named Desire* may have stayed in the audience's memories more enduringly—it did. But *Lefty* 'killed' them." (Ibid., p. 115.)

130 "Proletarian Thunderbolt": Ibid., p. 116.

130 "I was intense": Ibid.

130 "The best actors' director": Marlon Brando with Robert Lindsey, *Brando: Songs My Mother Taught Me* (New York: Random House, 1994), p. 170.

130 "emotionalism": Kazan, *Elia Kazan*, p. 16.

130 "All his characters are felt for": Ibid.

130 "His modestly took me by surprise": *KAL*, p. 328.

130 "We were both freaks": Ibid., p. 335.

130 "My curiosity was satisfied": Ibid., p. 336.

130 "a perfect team": Williams to Bill Barnes, Dec. 28, 1973, private collection.

130 "Our union, immediate": *KAL*, pp. 334–35.

131 "I read the play again last night": Ibid., p. 329.

131 "I believed that those same powers": Ibid., p. 338.

131 "pretty stiff": Williams to Irene Selznick, May 1947, *L2*, p. 102.

131 "Considering that I felt our producer": *KAL*, p. 331.

131 "an alternative": Williams to Irene Selznick, May 1947, *L2*, p. 102.

131 "In writing a play": Ibid.

132 "I was not going to knuckle under": Selznick, *Private View*, p. 300.

132 "In time she would": *KAL*, p. 338.

132 "I was rude": Ibid., p. 339.

133 "Tennessee went off his noodle": Irene Selznick to Irving Schneider, July 2, 1947, ISC. "Jo's designs for *Streetcar* are almost the best I've ever seen," Williams wrote to Margo Jones. "The back wall of the interior is translucent with a stylized panorama showing through it of the railroad yards and the city (when lighted behind). It will add immensely to the poetic quality." (Williams to Margo Jones, July 1947, *L2*, p. 109.)

133 "We all went to the show": *KAL*, p. 340.

133 "It has been a pretty fabulous time": Williams to Donald Windham, July 29, 1947, *TWLDW*, p. 202.

133 drawn up on July 19, 1947: Contract on file in ISC.

133 "about the biggest headache": Williams to Audrey Wood, Aug. 25, 1947, *L2*, p. 115.

133 "much pressure from Greek headquarters": Irene Selznick memo to Irving Schneider, July 28, 1947, ISC.

133 "Kazan tried to persuade me": Irene Selznick to Irving Schneider, July 2, 1947, ISC.

134 "I therefore had a final luncheon": Ibid.

134 "I entered the agreement with Selznick": Williams to Audrey Wood, Aug. 25, 1947, *L2*, p. 115.

134 "To lose him now": Irving Schneider telegram to Irene Selznick, Sept. 15, 1947, ISC.

135 "low as a snake": Irene Selznick to Irving Schneider, Aug. 18, 1947, ISC.

135 "I HAVE GARFIELD-ITIS": Irene Selznick telegram to Irving Schneider, Aug. 19, 1947, ISC.

135 "a minute on the stage": Margorie Loggia and Glenn Young, eds., *The Collected Works of Harold Clurman: Six Decades of Commentary on Theatre, Dance, Music, Film, Arts, and Letters* (New York: Applause Books, 1994), p. 977.

135 "I don't think he ever did anything better": Ibid.

135 "That boy's having a convulsion!": Patricia Bosworth, *Marlon Brando* (New York: Viking, 2001), p. 31.

135 "There was nothing you could do": Young, *Kazan*, p. 81.

136 "He even listened experientially": Ibid., p. 83. "His performance was full of surprises and exceeded what Williams and I had expected," Kazan wrote.

136 "There are no 'good' or 'bad' people": Williams to Elia Kazan, Apr. 19, 1947, *L2*, p. 95.

136 "epochal": *New York Times*, July 2, 2004.

136 "Gadg and Irene both said": Brando with Lindsey, *Brando*, p. 118.

136 "a size too large": Sam Staggs, *When Blanche Met Brando: The Scandalous Story of "A Streetcar Named Desire"* (New York: St. Martin's Press, 2005), p. 31.

136 "The line was busy": Ibid.

136 "a shot in the dark": *KAL*, p. 342.

136 "That's all I said": Ibid., p. 341.

137 "domestic cataclysm": Williams to Audrey Wood, Aug. 29, 1947, *L2*, p. 119.

137 blackout during the Wingfields' supper: Ibid.

137 "into everlasting darkness": Ibid.

137 "It was all too much for Pancho": Ibid.

137 "He was just about the best-looking": *M*, p. 131.

137 "You'd think he had spent": *CWTW*, p. 204.

137 "just as he played it": Ibid.

137 "I was the antithesis of Stanley Kowalski": Brando with Lindsey, *Brando*, pp. 121–22.

137 "Get Kazan on the phone!": *M*, p. 131.

137 "A new value came out": Williams to Audrey Wood, Aug. 29, 1947, *L2*, pp. 118–19. Brando was signed within four days; on September 3, 1947, his photo and the news of his signing ran for the first time in the *New York Times*.

137 "smiled a little": *M*, p. 131.

137 "Things were so badly arranged": Williams to Audrey Wood, Aug. 29, 1947, *L2*, p. 118.

138 "God-sent": Ibid.

138 "When an actor has as good a play": Brando with Lindsey, *Brando*, p. 122.

138 peculiar shyness: *M*, p. 132. "Brando was always shy with me for some reason," Williams wrote.

138 "And so we did—in silence": Ibid.

138 "I am hoping he will go home": Williams to Audrey Wood, Aug. 29, 1947, *L2*, p. 119.

138 "It took some doing": *M*, p. 134.

138 "quite gratefully so": Ibid.

138 over a hundred line changes: Brenda Murphy, *Tennessee Williams and Elia Kazan: A Collaboration in the Theatre* (Cambridge, U.K.: Cambridge University Press, 1992), p. 22.

138 "There is still something too cut-and-dried": Williams to Irene Selznick, Sept. 8, 1947, *L2*, p. 123.

139 "dim white against the fading dusk": Williams, "Poker Night," HRC.

139 "Now, now, love": LOA1, p. 564.

139 "fidelity": Williams to Elia Kazan, Apr. 19, 1947, L2, p. 96.

139 "After this experience": KAL, p. 353.

139 "Probably I would want him back": Williams to Donald Windham, Mar. 26, 1947, TWLDW, p. 197.

139 "He needed me as much as I needed him": LLI with Pancho Rodriguez, 1983, LLC.

139 "I cannot find words": Williams to Margo Jones, Oct. 1947, L2, p. 128.

139 "Today I am particularly aware": N, Oct. 20, 1947, p. 463.

139 "I wish I could write you": Williams to Pancho Rodriguez, Oct. 1947, L2, p. 126.

140 "Reisito, Torito": Ms. "Memoirs," p. 61.

140 "Unable to break down the door": M, p. 135.

140 "I am terribly troubled": Williams to Margo Jones, Oct. 1947, L2, p. 129.

140 "He was like a father": LLI with Pancho Rodriguez, 1983, LLC.

140 "to take a man's place in the world": Williams to Pancho Rodriguez, Nov. 1947, L2, p. 131.

140 "This play is hardly your dish": Williams to Edwina Williams, Nov. 1947, ibid., p. 133.

140 "I shall not listen to any moral homilies": Ibid.

140 "Life is hard": Williams to Pancho Rodriguez, Nov. 1947, L2, p. 130.

141 "had been persuaded": M, p. 135.

141 Pancho moved back in with him: Williams to Margo Jones, Oct. 1947, L2, p. 129.

141 last scene mounted for the first time: "Gadg's method is to stage one new scene each day and to go over all the preceding scenes in sequence," Williams wrote Jones. "Tomorrow, Monday, he will stage the final, eleventh scene, which I think is the crucial one." (Williams to Margo Jones, Oct. 1947, L2, p. 128.)

141 "My feeling for P. has more or less": N, Oct. 27, 1947, pp. 465–67.

141 "I thought, privately, this character": M, p. 136.

141 "But people are complex, Thorn": As quoted by Kim Hunter, in Myrna Katz Frommer and Harvey Frommer, eds., It Happened on Broadway: An Oral History of the Great White Way (New York: Harcourt Brace, 1998), p. 7.

141 "a performance miracle in the making": KAL, p. 343.

142 "Because it was out of balance": Brando with Lindsey, Brando, p. 124.

143 "I looked to my authority": KAL, p. 344.

143 "If Tennessee was Blanche": Ibid., pp. 347, 350.

143 "is attracted to a murderer": Young, Kazan, pp. 83–84.

143 "fearsome commotion": KAL, pp. 346–47.

143 "I left New York two or three weeks": LLI with Pancho Rodriguez, 1983, LLC.

143 "I used to try and hurt him": Ibid.

144 ". . . I have never said": Williams to Pancho Rodriguez, Nov. 1947, L2, p. 132.

144 "I knew that he loved me": LLI with Pancho Rodriguez, 1983, LLC.

144 "as if a ghost sat over the affairs": Williams to Elia Kazan, Apr. 19, 1947, L2, p. 96.

144 "When you see that someone needs peace": Williams to Pancho Rodriguez, Nov. 1947, L2, pp. 130–31. "Right after Frank Merlo's death, Tennessee came back to New Orleans to ask me to go live with him again," Rodriguez said. (LLI with Pancho Rodriguez, 1983, LLC.)

145 "Stanley (M.B.) like E.K.": Bosworth, Marlon Brando, p. 46.

145 "the lame duck in the line-up": Williams to Margo Jones, Oct. 1947, L2, p. 128.

145 "What we've got here is oysters": Peter Manso, *Brando: The Biography* (New York: Hyperion, 1994), p. 231.

145 "RIDE OUT BOY": Williams telegram to Marlon Brando, HRC.

145 "Streetcar opened last night": Williams to James Laughlin, Dec. 4, 1947, *L2*, pp. 133–34.

145 others and so on: Also at the opening night were Cary Grant, Paul Muni, Montgomery Clift, Edward G. Robinson, Olivia de Havilland, Lillian Hellman, Moss Hart, Ruth Gordon, Garson Kanin, and Josh Logan.

146 "the flag of beauty": Arthur Miller, "Introduction," in Tennessee Williams, *A Streetcar Named Desire* (New York: New Directions, 2004), p. xii.

146 "Southern genital-man": Alan Sinfield, *Out on Stage: Lesbian and Gay Theater in the 20th Century* (Bath, U.K.: Bath Press, 1999), p. 89.

146 "The play might well have been titled": *Theatre Book of the Year 1947–1948* (New York: Alfred A. Knopf, 1948), pp. 163–66.

146 "In 1947, when Marlon Brando appeared": Vidal, "Tennessee Williams," p. 61.

146 "Stanley Kowalski changed the concept of sex": JLI with Gore Vidal, 2000, JLC.

146 "He builds a hedonistic life": Elia Kazan, *An American Odyssey*, ed. Michel Ciment (London: Bloomsbury, 1988), p. 184.

146 "I am the king around here": LOA1, p. 537.

149 "Tenn, are you really happy?": *Life*, Dec. 15, 1948.

150 Williams won the Pulitzer Prize: Audrey Wood to Irene Selznick, May 3, 1947, ISC: "Dear Woman of the Year—'It's all beautiful and like a fairy tale. This is the way we both dreamt it could be and seeing a dream come true is more dramatic than the play itself. We are both so proud and happy you were chosen to be the mid-wife.'"

150 rumbled by most of the critics: "I am afraid Margo did a rather mediocre job," Williams wrote to Donald Windham. "Not inspired. Not vital, as Kazan would have been and as the play so dreadfully needed." (Oct. 19, 1948, *TWLDW*, p. 225.)

150 "the critics who gave us the two worst notices": Williams to Donald Windham, Oct. 19, 1948, *TWLDW*, p. 226.

150 "The party was really swell": Ibid., p. 225.

150 "I enjoyed the ride": Ibid., p. 226. Jane and Tony Smith, Sandy Campbell, Joanna Albus.

CHAPTER 3: THE EROTICS OF ABSENCE

151 Erotics of Absence: The phrase was coined by Christopher Bollas in *Hysteria*; it is used here with his permission.

151 "The desiring fingers": *RS*, pp. 70–71.

151 "My writing dealt with you": Franz Kafka, *Letter to His Father* (London: Oneworld, 2008), p. 56.

151 as an adult, and he was going solo: At seventeen, in 1928, Williams traveled for two months in Europe with his grandfather.

151 "I don't intend to get seriously involved": Williams to Oliver Evans, Feb. 11, 1948, *L2*, p. 165.

151 two thousand dollars a week in royalties: Tennessee Williams, "Night Passage" (unpublished), p. 11, LLC.

151 "My nights have been wild": Williams to Margo Jones, Dec. 31, 1947, *L2*, p. 141.

152 "a packing-bee": Ibid., p. 140.
152 "Sartre did not show up": Williams to Donald Windham, July 25, 1948, *TWLDW*, p. 223.
152 "cold, bad food": Williams to Donald Windham, Jan. 17, 1948, ibid., p. 205.
152 press interviews in his hotel bathtub: *M*, p. 140.
152 "I found nothing very good about Paris": Williams to Elia Kazan, Jan. 25, 1948, WUCA.
152 "The *sun*—glorious sun": *N*, Jan. 27, 1948, p. 469.
153 "the capitol of my heart": Williams to Oliver Evans, Jan. 31, 1948, *L2*, p. 155.
153 "Here in Italy": Williams to Carson McCullers, Feb. 8, 1948, ibid., p. 160.
153 "soft city": *RS*, p. 9.
153 "They do not hate Americans": Williams to Brooks Atkinson, Mar. 29, 1948, *L2*, p. 177.
153 "I haven't the slightest idea": Williams to Elia Kazan, Jan. 25, 1948, WUCA.
153 "under the moon of pause": *RS*, p. 51.
153 "Sometimes the lamp burns very low": Williams to Carson McCullers, Mar. 1, 1948, *L2*, p. 170.
153 "the trapeze of the flesh": Hart Crane, "The Bridge" (1930): "the empty trapeze of the flesh."
153 "You can't walk a block without being accosted": Williams to Donald Windham, Feb. 20, 1948, *TWLDW*, p. 207.
153 "In the evenings, very late": Williams to Jane Lawrence Smith, June 29, 1950, *L2*, p. 328.
153 "The nightingales busted their larynx!": Williams to Oliver Evans, Jan. 31, 1948, ibid., p. 155.
154 "turned into orgies": Williams to Donald Windham, Mar. 9, 1948, *TWLDW*, p. 210.
154 "that unhappy young egotist Gore Vidal": Williams to James Laughlin, May 18, 1948, *L2*, pp. 192–93.
154 "I shall remember all of them": Ibid.
155 "back under the dining-room table": John Updike, *Self-Consciousness* (New York: Alfred A. Knopf, 1989), pp. 252–53.
155 "Italy has been a real experience": Williams to James Laughlin, May 18, 1948, *L2*, p. 193.
155 "Being successful and famous": Williams to Audrey Wood, Dec. 5, 1948, ibid., p. 217.
155 "You know, then, that the public Somebody": "On a Streetcar Named Success," *New York Times*, Nov. 30, 1947, as quoted in *NSE*, p. 35. (The essay title was later changed to "The Catastrophe of Success.")
155 "as nervous as a cat": Williams to Carson McCullers, June 18, 1948, *L2*, p. 196.
155 "I am quite forlorn here": Williams to Donald Windham, July 9, 1948, *TWLDW*, p. 222.
155 "To really appreciate Italy fully": Williams to Donald Windham, June 22, 1948, ibid., p. 220.
156 "I don't want the beautiful effect": Sheridan Morley, *John Gielgud: The Authorized Biography* (New York: Simon & Schuster, 2002), p. 199.
156 "He is too English, too stylish": Williams to Audrey Wood, Apr. 24, 1948, *L2*, p. 185.
156 "frightfully nervous high-handed prima donna": Williams to Audrey Wood, June 13, 1948, ibid., p. 198.

156 "the Old One": Sheridan Morley, *John G: The Authorized Biography of John Gielgud* (London: Hodder & Stoughton, 2001), p. 199.

156 "John G. says I should *not* take a bow": Williams to Maria Britneva, July 18, 1948, *FOA*, p. 3.

156 "I want everybody to see": Helen Hayes, *My Life in Three Acts* (New York: Simon & Schuster, 1990), p. 168.

156 "She was everything I disliked": Ibid.

157 "She's spearing a shrimp": JLI with Gore Vidal, 2006, JLC.

157 "I do not altogether understand myself": Williams to Helen Hayes, July 30, 1948, *L2*, p. 205.

157 "compensations": Williams to Maria Britneva, July 30, 1948, *FOA*, p. 5.

157 "She scared people": John Lahr, "The Lady and Tennessee," *The New Yorker*, Dec. 19, 1994, p. 78.

157 "her spectacular velocity through time": Ibid.

157 "She was extraordinary": Ibid., p. 83.

157 "desperate grip": Kazan, quoted in *FOA*, p. ix.

157 "She is full of a good kind of mischief": Williams to Carson McCullers, June 18, 1949, *L2*, p. 256.

158 "I am quite incapable of learning": Williams to Audrey Wood, June 13, 1948, ibid., p. 199. Describing sharing the same room with his lover and Jones on a Jeep trip to Capri and Sorrento, Williams wrote about his Italian lover's bewilderment at Jones's apparent indifference to the Italian landscape. "'This donna molto strana. This donna like parlare, like mangiare, like drink, pero no like amore, no like poesia!' However this donna is very useful and obliging in such matters as packing for trips and making arrangements. We have our tickets and reservations straight through to London without my lifting a finger." (Williams to Donald Windham, June 7, 1948, *TWLDW*, p. 219.)

158 British reviews: "The press is the worst the play has ever been given anywhere in Europe," Williams wrote Britneva. (July 30, 1948, *FOA*, p. 4.)

158 "Somehow I cannot make plans": Williams to Maria Britneva, July 30, 1948, *FOA*, p. 5.

158 "my bosom was too big": Lahr, "Lady and Tennessee," p. 78.

159 "shot by the Soviets": Ibid.

159 revised or fabricated history: Ibid.

159 "I feel sorry for Maria": Williams to Donald Windham, May 8, 1949, *TWLDW*, p. 241.

159 "I felt I was in a state of grace": Lahr, "Lady and Tennessee," p. 80.

159 "When Edith Evans": Ibid., p. 79.

160 "She wasn't a good actress": Ibid.

160 "eighteen or nineteen": Ibid.

160 "I was invited to this wonderful party": Ibid.

160 "Maria ate and ate": Ibid.

160 "five o'clock angel": Feb. 2, 1952, *FOA*, p. 52.

160 "Word has reached here": Truman Capote to Donald Windham and Sandy Campbell, ca. Mar. 25, 1949, in Truman Capote, *Too Brief a Treat: Letters of Truman Capote*, ed. Gerald Clarke (New York: Random House, 2004), p. 69.

162 "savagely mordant sense of humor": *FOA*, p. xiv.

162 "You seem to say all the things": Williams to Maria Britneva, Feb. 7, 1949, ibid., p. 13.

162 "Tennessee, with a glint of malice": Ibid., p. 10.

162 "We were fighting": Williams to Brooks Atkinson, June 1954, *L2*, p. 533.

162 "Total autonomy": *Sweet Tornado: Margo Jones and the American Theater*, DVD, directed by A. Dean Bell, Kay Cattarulla, and Rob Trachin (KERA-TV, PBS, 2006).

162 "If you want to (*dare* to) bring up": Williams to Audrey Wood, Apr. 2, 1948, *L2*, p. 178.

163 "I expressed my doubts to Tennessee": *RBAW*, p. 157.

163 "did, as usual, the gentlemanly thing": Ibid.

163 "She was the con of cons": *Sweet Tornado*, DVD.

163 "The tragedy is that her performance": Williams to Brooks Atkinson, June 1954, *L2*, p. 533.

163 more removed proscenium: Four years later, José Quintero's production of *Summer and Smoke*, starring Geraldine Page, at New York's new Circle in the Square, redeemed the play's critical reputation. "Nothing more momentous has happened in the theatre in the last few years than the revival of *Summer and Smoke*," Atkinson wrote in the *New York Times*.

163 "began to have depressing premonitions": *M*, p. 153.

163 "the work of a dying man": Williams to Audrey Wood, Mar. 23, 1949, *L2*, p. 239.

163 "I had been ill at the time": Williams to Brooks Atkinson, June 1954, ibid., pp. 533–34.

163 "In my opinion Margo Jones": *M*, p. 153.

163 "I was onstage playing the scene": *Sweet Tornado*, DVD.

164 "Margo Jones's Farewell Address to the Troops": *RBAW*, p. 158.

164 "A pretentious and amateurish bore": Howard Barnes, *New York Herald Tribune*, Oct. 7, 1948.

164 "mawkish, murky": John Coleman, *New York Daily News*, Oct. 7, 1948.

164 "mediocre job": Williams to Donald Windham, Oct. 19, 1948, *TWLDW*, p. 225.

164 "Not inspired, not vital": Ibid. By the same time the following year, Williams's disappointment had turned to disgust over Jones's slapdash Chicago touring production of the play. "Very cross with Margo," he wrote to Britneva. "Two sticks could not be crosser. Her Chicago company which she praised so highly was a poor travesty of what it should have been." (Williams to Maria Britneva, Oct. 9, 1949, *FOA*, p. 27.)

164 "Something started or something stopped": *CP*, "Little Horse," pp. 75–76.

164 "He was enthusiastic about everything": JLI with Mary Henderson, 2001, JLC. Between 1979 and 1985, she was curator of the theater collection at the Museum of the City of New York. Among her books were *The City and the Theatre* and *Mielziner: Master of Modern Stage Design*.

165 "fleshed in a god's perfection": "A Separate Poem": "You put on the clothes of a god which was your naked body / and moved from window to window in a room made of windows, drawing, closing the curtains, your back / turned to me showing no sign that you knew that you were / building an island: then came to rest, fleshed, in a god's perfection beside me . . . " (*CP*, "A Separate Poem," pp. 80–81.)

165 swarthy complexion: "Perhaps Frankie will get into the movies," Capote wrote in 1949, referring to him as "that loathsome Merlo boy." "I understand all the old Lon Chaney movies are going to be remade, and by hiring him they'd save on makeup." (Truman Capote to Andrew Lyndon, Aug. 23, 1949, in Capote, *Too Brief*, p. 98.)

165 "change-of-life baby": JLI with Mary Henderson, 2001, JLC.

165 "He was far better read than Tennessee": JLI with Gore Vidal, 2006, 2001, JLC.

165 "I damn near got to know": Frank Merlo to Frank Gionataiso, Nov. 3, 1942, LLC.

165 "I had just witnessed": Ibid.

165 "The path was very narrow": Ibid.

166 "It's a very well set up book": Frank Merlo to Frank Gionataiso, Feb. 27, 1943, LLC.

166 "high brow": Frank Merlo to Frank Gionataiso, Feb. 3, 1943, LLC.

166 "Every symphony that has come to San Francisco": Ibid.

166 "When I do, watch out cousin": Frank Merlo to Frank Gionataiso, Apr. 8, 1942, LLC.

166 "In regards to travelling after the war": Frank Merlo to Frank Gionataiso, Feb. 27, 1943, LLC.

166 "I had intentions of marrying Lena": Frank Merlo to Frank Gionataiso, Feb. 3, 1943, LLC.

167 "who may soon be my future wife": Frank Merlo to Frank Gionataiso, Feb. 27, 1943, LLC.

167 "Tomorrow I have liberty": Frank Merlo to Frank Gionataiso, Feb. 27, 1943, JLC.

167 "He got a job in New York": JLI with Mary Henderson, 2001, JLC.

167 "My tongue, of late": Frank Merlo to Frank Gionataiso, Feb. 27, 1943, LLC.

167 lover of the Washington columnist Joseph Alsop: Gore Vidal, *Palimpsest: A Memoir* (New York: Random House, 1995), pp. 200–201.

169 "Pancho is in town": Audrey Wood to Irene Selznick, June 2, 1948, HRC.

169 "I thought you knew about Frankie": Oliver Evans to Marion Vaccaro, Jan. 30, 1950, THNOC. Evans, a poet and professor of English, was known to Williams as "The Clown"; Vaccaro, an heiress and another traveling companion, was dubbed "The Banana Queen."

169 "Frank was a warm, decent man": Donald Spoto, *The Kindness of Strangers: The Life of Tennessee Williams* (Boston: Little, Brown, 1985), p. 153.

169 "It is a small world": Williams to Carson McCullers, July 5, 1948, *L2*, p. 201.

169 "What do you do?": *CWTW*, p. 235.

169 "He gave me the connection": Ibid., p. 340.

169 "He kept his wig on": Spoto, *Kindness*, p. 153.

169 "the cleft in the rock": LOA1, p. 546.

170 "My sexual feeling for the boy": *M*, p. 159.

170 "the most charming ship": Ibid.

170 "Finit": *N*, Dec. 4, 1948, p. 487.

170 "She meant as an artist": Ibid., p. 489.

171 "The simple truth": Williams to Elia Kazan and Molly Day Thacher, July 12, 1949, *L2*, p. 261.

171 "GLADYS: Your son misses you": Tennessee Williams, "The Big Time Operators" (unpublished), HRC.

172 "It doesn't seem very like me": *N*, Dec. 5, 1948, p. 493.

172 "You are really washed up": Williams, "Big Time Operators," HRC.

172 "The trouble is that I am being bullied": *N*, Dec. 5, 1948, p. 493.

172 "the baleful sun of success": Ibid., July 22, 1950, p. 515.

172 "Talent died in me": Ibid., Dec. 5, 1948, p. 493.

172 "The trouble is that you can't make": Williams to Brooks Atkinson, June 1949, *L2*, pp. 258–59.

173   "gauze hung over gauze": *CP*, "The Soft City," p. 10. Williams sent off the poem in May. "And if there is something which is not soft in the city," he wrote "such as a cry too hard for the mouth to hold, God puts a soft stop to it. / Bending invisibly down, He breathes a narcosis / Over the panicky face upturned to entreat Him."

173   "slowly with great pomp": Williams to Audrey Wood, Feb. 15, 1949, *L2*, p. 234.

173   "one long blue and gold ribbon": Williams to James Laughlin, Apr. 10, 1949, ibid., p. 249.

173   "The fear that I am repeating myself": Williams to James Laughlin, Jan. 30, 1950, ibid., p. 297.

173   "There is no point in hiding": *N*, May 27, 1949, p. 501.

173   "I received today five complete sets": Williams to Audrey Wood, Feb. 15, 1949, *L2*, p. 234.

173   "the cornball department": "A disgrace to any name that is signed to it," Williams said of the screenplay, on whose front page he wrote, "A horrible thing! Certified as such by Tennessee Williams." (Williams to Audrey Wood, May 13, 1949, ibid., p. 245.) As early June 1949, he told his publisher Jay Laughlin, "It's a real abomination." (Williams to James Laughlin, June 3, 1949, ibid., p. 252.)

174   "ridiculous state of gloom": Williams to Brooks Atkinson, June 1949, ibid., p. 258.

174   "my little secretary": Williams to Audrey Wood, Feb. 15, 1949, ibid., p. 233.

174   "I do hope that I can manage": Ibid., p. 235.

174   "a sorry companion": Williams to Donald Windham, Mar. 23, 1949, *TWLDW*, p. 236.

174   "I am not alone": Williams to Carson McCullers, Mar. 23, 1949, *L2*, p. 240.

174   "latched onto us like barnacles": Truman Capote to Andrew Lyndon, Mar. 28, 1949, in Capote, *Too Brief*, p. 72. The noticeable strain Capote was referring to was the altercation that took place after he repeated Margo Jones's canard to the cast of *Summer and Smoke*: "This is the play of a dying man."

174   "He hates the dependence": Williams to Donald Windham, Mar. 23, 1949, *TWLDW*, p. 234.

174   "Frankie's passion is clothes": Williams to Donald Windham, Apr. 8, 1949, ibid., p. 238.

175   "Picked up Frank": *N*, May 23, 1949, p. 499.

175   "Violent (verbally) scene on the streets": Ibid., June 3, 1949, p. 505.

175   "Faint as leaf shadow does he fade": *CP*, "Faint as Leaf Shadow," pp. 8–9.

176   "When I see him enjoy so much": Williams to Donald Windham, Mar. 23, 1949, *TWLDW*, p. 236.

176   "Frank is possessive and destructive": *FOA*, July 11, 1949, p. 25.

176   "There is a curious listlessness": Ibid., June 10, 1949, p. 19.

176   titled "Stornello": Tennessee Williams, "Stornello: Brief Outline of Play in Progress," HRC.

176   "This may turn out to be foolish": Williams to James Laughlin, June 3, 1949, *L2*, p. 251.

176   "the drift": *RS*, p. 21.

176   "Eyre de Lanux is a woman": Williams to James Laughlin, June 3, 1949, *L2*, p. 252. De Lanux died in 1996 at the age of 102.

177   "stopped": *RS*, p. 37.

177   "Mrs. Stone *knew* it": Ibid., p. 85.

177   "you can't retire from an art": Ibid., p. 16.

178 "wounded gladiator": *N*, Dec. 5, 1948, p. 493.
178 "King On The Mountain": Williams to Donald Windham, Apr. 4, 1960, *TWLDW*, p. 298: "I gathered out of my father's fierce blood, the power to rise somehow. And how could that rise be gentle."
178 "Scrambling, pushing, kicking": *RS*, pp. 82–83.
178 "Security is a kind of death": *NSE*, p. 36.
178 "Being purposeless was like being drunk": *RS*, p. 34.
178 "She had been continually occupied": Ibid., pp. 86–87.
179 "could not bear to look at him": Ibid., p. 55.
179 "Their marriage, in its beginning": Ibid., pp. 67–68.
179 "they exchanged their eagerly denying smiles": Ibid., p. 71.
179 "Her effort to express a tenderness": Tentative play outline for *The Roman Spring of Mrs. Stone* (unpublished), HRC.
179 "What she felt, now, was desire": *RS*, p. 52.
179 "emotional anarchy": Ibid., p. 76.
179 "Mrs. Stone knew, as well as Paolo": Ibid., p. 29.
180 "I will call you in the morning": Ibid., p. 34.
180 "incontinent longings": Ibid., p. 51.
180 "When we're alone together": Ibid., p. 95.
180 "Frankie and I have been happy": *N*, May 30, 1949, p. 503.
180 "I love F.—deeply": Ibid., May 29, 1949, p. 501.
181 "somewhat taller than Paolo": *RS*, p. 36.
181 "to be waiting to receive a signal": Ibid., p. 10.
181 "Nothing could not be allowed": Ibid., p. 116.
181 "It was nothing that she had planned": Ibid.
181 "the occult reasons": Ibid., p. 64.
181 "does not need to be conscious knowing": Ibid., p. 40.
181 "It looked up at her": Ibid., p. 116.
181 "Yes, in a few minutes now": Ibid., pp. 116–17.
182 "I don't ask for your pity": LOA2, p. 236.
182 "wandered": Williams to Elia Kazan and Molly Day Thacher, July 12, 1949, *L2*, p. 261.
182 "idolizes": Tennessee Williams, "Stornello" (unpublished), HRC.
182 "To say she is fallen in love": Ibid.
182 kill herself with a butcher's knife: Rose Williams, in her dementia, according to *Memoirs* (p. 119), once "put a kitchen knife in her purse and started to leave for the psychiatrist's with apparent intent to murder." Edwina Williams, in her memoir, *Remember Me to Tom* (p. 85), writes, "One of the psychiatrists told Cornelius something I do not think he should have. He said to my husband, 'Rose is liable to go down and get a butcher knife one night and cut your throat.'"
182 "a young bull of a man": Williams, "Stornello," HRC.
183 "tremendously understanding": Ibid.
183 "crawls sobbing to the Madonna": Ibid.
183 "My efforts to make it sound": Williams to Elia Kazan and Molly Day Thacher, July 12, 1949, *L2*, p. 262.
183 "Honesty about failure": Williams to James Laughlin, Aug. 17, 1949, ibid., p. 266.
183 "Approaching a crisis": *N*, July 12, 1949, p. 507.
183 "illogical phantoms": Williams to Elia Kazan, Feb. 24, 1950, WUCA.
184 "Left F. at theatre": *N*, July 12 or 13, 1949, p. 509.

184 "Saw Frank only in morning": Ibid., July 16, 1949, p. 509.

184 "the nightingales sang": Ibid., Aug. 10, 1949, p. 511.

184 "They say they don't want a fairy-tale": Williams to James Laughlin, Aug. 17, 1949, *L2*, p. 266.

184 half a million dollars, plus a percentage: *RBAW*, p. 157.

185 "I always feel Tennessee is bound": Audrey Wood to George Cukor, Sept. 7, 1949, HRC.

185 "like a wet dream of Louella Parsons's": Williams to Elia Kazan, undated, *L2*, p. 269.

185 "who was arranging place cards": *RBAW*, p. 156.

185 "The deeper you go": Williams to Elia Kazan, undated, WUCA.

185 "They are all very nice": Ibid.

186 "The vulgarities have been eliminated": Williams to Walter Dakin, Edwina Williams, and Dakin Williams, Sept. 1949, *L2*, p. 268.

186 Gertrude Lawrence: Bette Davis, Tallulah Bankhead, Miriam Hopkins, Mildred Dunnock, Judith Anderson, and Ethel Barrymore had been considered for the role.

186 "dismal error": *L2*, p. 269. See note.

186 "amazingly good": Williams to Walter Dakin, Edwina Williams, and Dakin Williams, Sept. 1949, *L2*, p. 269.

186 "I brought her a corsage": Williams to Maria Britneva, Oct. 9, 1949, *FOA*, p. 26.

186 "in my heart the ending as it exists": Williams to Irving Rapper, Aug. 5, 1949, *L2*, p. 264.

186 "I think it is all right to suggest": Ibid.

186 "If we don't show that Laura changes": R. Barton Palmer and Williams Robert Bray, *Hollywood's Tennessee: The Williams Films and Postwar America* (Austin: University of Texas, 2009), p. 52.

187 "We have tagged on the ending": Ibid.

187 "quality of poetic mystery and beauty": Williams to Jack Warner, Jerry Wald, and Charles Feldman, May 6, 1950, *L2*, p. 316.

187 "Life isn't a bust": *Variety*, Sept. 19, 1950.

187 "'The Glass Menagerie' Reaches the Screen": Bosley Crowther, *New York Times*, Sept. 29, 1959.

187 "travesty": Ibid.

187 "Am surprised at Tennessee": Jack Warner to Mort Blumenstock, Apr. 29, 1950, in Palmer and Bray, *Hollywood's Tennessee*, p. 58.

187 "I can't impress upon you": Palmer and Bray, *Hollywood's Tennessee*, p. 58.

188 "In the picture there is less darkness": Ibid., p. 59.

188 Key West in November 1949: They arrived around November 12. See *L2*, p. 271.

188 "a sort of Tom Thumb mansion": Williams to Maria Britneva, Nov. 1949, *FOA*, p. 30.

188 "improvised poultry yard": Williams to Audrey Wood, Nov. 1949, *L2*, p. 272.

188 "magnificent black goat": Ibid.

188 "Life here is as dull as paradise": Williams to James Laughlin, Dec. 9, 1949, James Laughlin Papers, Houghton Library, Harvard University, Cambridge, Mass.

188 improved on his paradise: *CWTW*, p. 167.

188 "the water, the eternal turquoise": Williams to Carson McCullers, Apr. 1950, *L2*, p. 310.

188 "Frank is now happy here": Williams to Paul Bigelow, Dec. 4, 1949, ibid., p. 275.

188 "Grandfather is having the time": Williams to Margo Jones, Jan. 2, 1950, ibid., p. 280.

189   "pretending to be deaf": Williams to Donald Windham, Jan. 26, 1949, *TWLDW*, p. 230.

189   "Tom is so good to me": Rev. Walter Dakin to Audrey Wood, Jan. 30, 1949, LLC.

189   "A girl makes her best contacts": Williams to Paul Bigelow, Dec. 4, 1949, *L2*, p. 275.

189   "I feel somewhat rejuvenated": Williams to Margo Jones, Jan. 2, 1950, ibid., p. 280.

190   "five drinks a day": Williams to Carson McCullers, Dec. 6, 1949, ibid., p. 278.

190   "He will bring you good-luck": Ibid., p. 277.

190   "the nicest piece of jewelry": Williams to Jane Lawrence and Tony Smith, Jan. 5, 1950, ibid., p. 282.

190   "Frankie had lost weight at home": Williams to Jane Lawrence and Tony Smith, Jan. 5, 1950, *L2*, p. 282.

190   "We shall all be together again soon": Frank Merlo to Rev. Walter Dakin, July 6, 1950, LLC.

190   "kitchen sink version": In the note to this first draft, Williams writes, "I call this 'the kitchen sink draft' because I have thrown into it every dramatic implement I could think of. Perhaps all of them will work. Perhaps none of them will work. Probably a few of them will work." (See Williams to Paul Bigelow, Dec. 4, 1949, *L2*, p. 275.) For Williams, the completion of a play was always a moving goal. As late as February 2, 1950, he was writing to Windham about *The Rose Tattoo*: "I am pleased with the way I think it is going to be." (*TWLDW*, p. 254.)

190   "dark, blood-red translucent stone": Williams to Elia Kazan, June 16, 1950, *L2*, p. 324.

190   "During the past two years": Ibid., pp. 324–25.

190   "Well, this is your little friend": Tennessee Williams, "The Rose Tattoo" (unpublished kitchen-sink version), HRC.

190   "one of those Mediterranean types": Ibid.

190   "Humble Star": Williams to Paul Bowles, Feb. 23, 1950, HRC. This early draft was later published in a much-revised version as "Death Is High" without the dedication to Merlo.

192   "I want him to feel some independence": Williams to Audrey Wood, Mar. 27, 1950, *L2*, p. 300.

192   "in return for Sicily": LOA1, p. 246.

192   "I remember Frankie telling us": *FOA*, pp. 18–19.

192   "My approach to my work": Williams to Elia Kazan, June 16, 1950, *L2*, p. 325.

192   "Have I ever told you": Williams to Maria Britneva, Mar. 5, 1949, *FOA*, p. 16.

193   "the Dionysian element": *NSE*, p. 63.

193   "somewhere along the Gulf Coast": LOA1, p. 654.

193   "giant step forward": Audrey Wood to Williams, Mar. 5, 1950, HRC.

193   "the baffled look": Williams to Elia Kazan, June 16, 1950, *L2*, p. 324.

193   "tentative and mixed": Ibid.

193   "very optimistic": Williams to Audrey Wood, undated, LLC.

193   "that the script might be something": Williams to Elia Kazan, Feb. 24, 1950, *L2*, p. 289.

193   "I said I was still too nervous": Williams to Audrey Wood, Jan. 23, 1950, HRC.

193   "The play is probably too subjective": Williams to Paul Bigelow, Feb. 23, 1950, HRC.

193   "Audrey is sitting on the new script": Williams to Gore Vidal, Mar. 1, 1950, *L2*, p. 293.

194 "It is a kind of comic-grotesque Mass": Elia Kazan to Williams, undated, HRC.

194 Williams himself later adopted it: *NSE*, p. 63.

194 "Your letter about the play": Williams to Elia Kazan, Feb. 27, 1950, *L2*, p. 289.

194 "Kazan, Kazan": *KAL*, p. 223.

194 Gadg: "I despised my nickname," he wrote later. "It suggested an agreeable, ever-compliant little cuss, a 'good Joe' who worked hard and always followed orders." (*KAL*, p. 5.)

194 "I do not think the material": Elia Kazan to Williams, undated, HRC.

194 "Sometimes I can make a virtue": Williams to Elia Kazan, Feb. 24, 1950, *L2*, pp. 289–90.

195 "like a radio": As quoted in Williams to Elia Kazan and Molly Day Thacher, Mar. 23, 1950, WUCA.

195 "I think if you start much later": Kazan to Williams, undated, WUCA, permission granted.

195 "I'd cut out Rosario": In the final version, Rosario is an idea who never material- izes; earlier drafts had him out of sight, unseen behind rose-colored curtains, but not internalized in this way.

195 "Consider Gadg's approach with great care": Audrey Wood to Williams, Mar. 5, 1950, HRC.

196 "I have just now completed": Williams to Elia Kazan and Molly Day Thacher, Mar. 23, 1950, WUCA.

196 "The most violent see-saw of my life!": Williams to Audrey Wood, Apr. 3, 1950, HRC.

196 "Dame Selznick": Williams to Oliver Evans, Apr. 7, 1950, *L2*, p. 304.

196 "When I think about Irene": Williams to Audrey Wood, Apr. 11, 1950, ibid., p. 306.

196 "Woman of the Year": Audrey Wood to Irene Selznick, May 3, 1948, ISC. By 1950, Wood was singing a different tune. She wrote to Williams, "I am terribly and deeply concerned about Irene's approach on a second venture, not again as a measure of her functioning as a producer but greatly so as her functioning as a human being. I don't function well if compelled to work in what I would call a vacuum of acquiescence." (Audrey Wood to Williams, Apr. 10, 1950, HRC.)

196 "I place it, like Pilate": Williams to Irene Selznick, Feb. 1949, *L2*, p. 311.

196 lackluster but successful British-debut production: The production ran for 326 performances. Olivier rarely directed a contemporary play. Kenneth Tynan said that Olivier's production showed the way "in which a good play can be scarred by unsympathetic and clumsy direction."

196 "I simply had to have a play": Irene Selznick, *A Private View* (New York: Alfred A. Knopf, 1983), p. 329.

197 "be as devastatingly candid": Williams to Irene Selznick, Apr. 10, 1950, *L2*, p. 305.

197 "Just hope with me that I am dead wrong": Irene Selznick to Williams, Apr. 16, 1950, HRC.

197 "To me, this is not a play": Irene Selznick to Williams, Apr. 16, 1950, ISC.

197 "Your letter knocked the goddam bottom": Williams to Irene Selznick, Apr. 1950, *L2*, p. 311.

197 "eventually happens to most lyric talents": Ibid.

197 "For the first time since this draft": Williams to Irene Selznick, Apr. 1950, *L2*, p. 311.

197 "Were I to see rather than read": Irene Selznick to Williams, Apr. 16, 1950, HRC.

197 "fully documented and justified": Williams to Irene Selznick, Apr. 1950, *L2*, p. 313.

198 "The great advance I have made": Ibid.

198 Cheryl Crawford: A co-founder of the Actors Studio, Crawford, who produced her first play in 1931, was also a founding member of the Group Theatre, for which she had produced plays by Clifford Odets, Maxwell Anderson, and John Howard Lawson; she had also produced *Porgy and Bess*, *One Touch of Venus*, and *Brigadoon*, among many Broadway musicals.

198 "I don't know if you realize": Cheryl Crawford to Elia Kazan, Apr. 13, 1950, WUCA.

198 Thacher told Williams what she thought: Molly Day Thacher to Williams, May 9, 1950, WUCA.

199 "All-At-Sea, May, 1950": Williams to Elia Kazan, May 1950, WUCA.

199 "a grim, nihilistic mood": Williams to Elia Kazan, June 16, 1950, *L2*, p. 323.

199 ". . . I have never been anything with you": Williams to Elia Kazan, May 30, 1950, WUCA.

200 "clutching . . . for all it is worth": Williams to Elia Kazan, June 16, 1950, *L2*, pp. 323–24.

200 "Not very manly of me": Ibid., p. 322.

200 "My main concern, now": Ibid, p. 324.

201 "mixed feelings": Irwin Shaw to Elia Kazan, June 19, 1950, WUCA.

201 "Please keep after Gadg": Williams to Cheryl Crawford, June 26, 1950, *L2*, p. 329.

201 "Kazan is still not entirely sold on the play": Williams to Oliver Evans, June 20, 1950, ibid., p. 327.

201 "infinitely *wrong*": *N*, July 23, 1950, p. 515.

201 "like the battle front in Korea": Williams to Maria Britneva, Aug. 8, 1950, *FOA*, p. 34.

201 "Key West seems like heaven": *N*, July 23, 1950, p. 515.

201 "I have felt like a tired horse": Williams to Audrey Wood and Cheryl Crawford, Aug. 15, 1950, *L2*, p. 343.

202 "The play is hung like a tent": Williams to Cheryl Crawford, Aug. 11, 1950, ibid., p. 342.

202 "If we don't get Magnani": Audrey Wood to Williams, Mar. 5, 1950, HRC.

202 "Magnani told a friend of mine": Williams to Audrey Wood, July 1950, *L2*, p. 331.

202 "She has the warmth and vigor": Williams to Paul Bigelow, Aug. 3, 1950, ibid., p. 339.

202 "She was looking quite marvelous": Williams to Cheryl Crawford, Aug. 11, 1950, ibid., p. 342.

202 "For an actor": Quoted in Giancarlo Governi, *Nannarella: Il romanzo di Anna Magnani* (Rome: Minimum, Fax, 2008).

203 "almost complete control over everything": Williams to Cheryl Crawford, Aug. 11, 1950, *L2*, p. 342.

203 "it would be very easy": Ibid. In 1954, Magnani starred opposite Burt Lancaster in the Hal Wallis production of *The Rose Tattoo*.

203 "the long dalliance with Gadg": Williams to Robert Lewis, Oct. 10, 1950, *L2*, p. 352.

203 "Tell Tennessee how badly I feel": Elia Kazan to Audrey Wood, Aug. 12, 1950, HRC.

203   "If Gadg were available": Williams to Audrey Wood and Cheryl Crawford, Aug. 15, 1950, *L2*, p. 344.

203   "On the sea, returning": *N*, Sept. 1, 1950, p. 517.

203   "I still believe that the flat stretches": Williams to Audrey Wood and Cheryl Crawford, Aug. 15, 1950, *L2*, p. 344.

203   "very impressed with it": James Laughlin to Tennessee Williams, Nov. 3, 1950, Harvard.

204   "The heart should have a permanent harbor": Williams to Elia Kazan, Nov. 18, 1950, WUCA.

204   "You wild, wild crazy thing": LOA1, p. 687.

204   royal road to knowledge *was* sexuality: "I doubt that anything did me more good as a writer than the many years of loneliness, of cruising around, making sudden and deep acquaintances, one after another, each leaving a new and fresh imprint on me," Williams said. (As quoted in *KAL*, p. 496.)

205   "To me the big bed": LOA1, p. 696.

205   "a female ostrich": Ibid., p. 680.

205   "slovenly deshabille": Ibid., p. 685.

205   "Are you in there, Mama?": Ibid., p. 684.

205   "spectral rose": Williams, "Rose Tattoo," HRC.

205   instead of this external imposition of the ghostly: Also cut was the Parrott who mimics Rosario's voice.

205   "Each time is the first time": LOA1, p. 661.

205   "a pain like a needle": Ibid., p. 659.

205   "Serafina stares at the truck driver": Ibid., p. 702.

206   "I always cry": Ibid., p. 703.

207   "the grandson of the village idiot": Ibid., p. 712.

207   "Love and affection": Ibid., p. 711.

207   "You are simpatico, molto": Williams, "Stornello," HRC.

207   "I like everything": LOA1, p. 707.

207   "profound unconscious response": Ibid., p. 702.

207   Serafina: (*from inside the house*): "Aaaaaahhhhhhhh!": Ibid., p. 729.

207   "the scene should be played": Ibid., p. 733.

207   "*Che* bel-la, *che* bel-*la*!": Ibid., p. 734.

208   "like a great bird": Ibid.

208   "I don't know how he got in": Ibid., p. 736.

208   "abandoning all pretence": Ibid.

208   "How beautiful": Ibid., p. 737.

208   "I was very surprised": Elia Kazan to Williams, undated, WUCA.

208   "The urn is broken": Williams, "Stornello," HRC.

208   "quietly and gravely as two children": Ibid.

208   "It would be a comic Mass": Elia Kazan to Williams, undated, 1950, WUCA.

209   "might be read as a massive autobiography": *KAL*, p. 494.

209   "little cave of consciousness": Williams to Audrey Wood, Aug. 7, 1939, *L1*, p. 193.

209   "forever his": Gore Vidal, "Tennessee Williams: Someone to Laugh at the Squares With," in Gore Vidal, *Armageddon? Essays 1983–1987* (London: Andre Deutsch, 1987), p. 59.

209   "A man, when he burns": Williams, "Stornello," HRC.

209   "Holding the shirt above her head": LOA1, p. 738.

209   "Vengo, vengo, amore!": "I'm coming, I'm coming, my love!"

210 "something that is made to occupy": Vidal, "Tennessee Williams," p. 59.

210 "my love-play to the world": *M*, p. 162.

210 "terribly afraid of critical reactions": Williams to Cheryl Crawford, July 14, 1950, *L2*, p. 337.

210 "It comes at a point in my life": Williams to James Laughlin, Oct. 15, 1950, ibid., p. 353.

211 "Critical reactions to the novel": Williams to Audrey Wood, Nov. 26, 1950, HRC.

211 "at a crucial point": Williams to Cheryl Crawford, Mar. 3, 1951, *L2*, p. 374.

211 "a gigantic task": Audrey Wood to Williams, undated, HRC.

211 "He has your aliveness": Williams to Elia Kazan, undated, WUCA.

211 "'Mood' is 'doom' spelt backwards": Williams to James Laughlin, Nov. 7, 1950, *L2*, p. 357.

211 "Probably means that I shall have to put": Ibid.

211 "Would Maureen Stapleton be all right?": Williams to Cheryl Crawford, Aug. 11, 1950, ibid., p. 342.

211 "Maureen must have been a victim": Quoted in Maureen Stapleton and Jane Scovell, *A Hell of a Life* (New York: Simon & Schuster, 1995), p. 82.

212 "a World Series of readings": Ibid., p. 83. "It was I who found Maureen Stapleton for the part," Williams claimed in his *Memoirs* (p. 160).

212 "Finally, I assisted her": *M*, p. 162.

212 "They seemed to want more assurance": Arthur Gelb, "Frank Talk from an Actress," *New York Times*, Feb. 18, 1951.

212 "I don't care if she turns into a deaf mute": As quoted in Mike Steen, *A Look at Tennessee Williams* (New York: Hawthorn Books, 1969), p. 284.

212 "The girl playing the lead": Williams to Edwina Williams and Walter Dakin, Dec. 16, 1950, *L2*, p. 362.

212 "the desire of an artist": *NSE*, p. 63.

212 "the Caesarean delivery": Williams to Elia Kazan, Nov. 18, 1950, WUCA.

212 "It was the most miraculous opening": Ibid.

213 "For some time I have suspected": Ibid.

214 "Four days now": *N*, Jan. 30, 1951, p. 519.

CHAPTER 4: FUGITIVE MIND

215 "Once Kazan and I": Williams to Bill Barnes, Dec. 23, 1973, LLC.

215 "Now that the waiting is over": Williams to Brooks Atkinson, Feb. 5, 1951, *L2*, p. 369.

215 "intermittently satisfactory": Richard Watts Jr., "Mr. Williams among the Sicilians," *New York Post*, Feb. 5, 1951.

215 "Play Isn't Worthy of the Fine Acting": John McClain, "Play Isn't Worthy of the Fine Acting," *New York Journal-American*, Feb. 5, 1951.

215 "We believe that the world today": Robert Coleman, "'Rose Tattoo' Is Thorny, Much Too Earthy," *New York Daily Mirror*, Feb. 5, 1951.

215 "His folk comedy about a Sicilian family": Brooks Atkinson, "The Rose Tattoo," *New York Times*, Feb. 5, 1951.

215 "Behind the fury and uproar": Brooks Atkinson, "Tattooing," *New York Times*, June 3, 1951.

216 "If I keep working on it": Arthur Gelb, "Frank Talk from an Actress," *New York Times*, Feb. 18, 1951.

217 "Paw": Maureen Stapleton and Jane Scovell, *A Hell of a Life* (New York: Simon & Schuster, 1995), p. 86. In an opening-night note, Williams wrote to Stapleton, "Dearest Maureen, I do not say fuck the drama critics because fucking is too good for them. Love, Paw." (Ibid., p. 87.)

217 "improvements": Tennessee Williams to Maureen Stapleton, Feb. 19, 1951, HRC.

217 "You are good at public relations": Ibid.

217 "happiest experience in the theatre": Williams to Cheryl Crawford, Mar. 3, 1951, *L2*, pp. 373–74.

217 "the first time I have ever felt at home": Ibid.

217 "I am a little vexed": Williams to Audrey Wood, Mar. 14, 1951, *L2*, p. 375. The play closed on October 27, 1951, after 306 performances; two days later, the tour began with Stapleton and Wallach in the leads.

218 "This play *was* a radical departure": Williams to Brooks Atkinson, Feb. 5, 1951, *L2*, p. 369.

218 "Modern creative theatre": Williams to Theatre Musicians Union, Aug. 3, 1951, ibid., p. 393.

218 "only the barest glimpse": *NSE*, p. 206.

218 "Consequently many people missed": Ibid.

218 "If it had been a smash hit": Williams to Irene Selznick, Feb. 27, 1951, *L2*, p. 370.

219 "The big Chinese Red offensive": *CS*, "Two on a Party," p. 287.

219 "lit by lightning": LOA1, p. 465.

219 "Dakin, my brother's, number": Williams to Maureen Stapleton, Feb. 19, 1951, HRC.

219 "game": *KAL*, p. 454.

219 "It is part of Nixon's job": Williams to Elia Kazan, Aug. 23, 1952, WUCA.

220 "the bright idea of property": J. Hector St. John de Crèvecoeur, *Letters from an American Farmer* (Carlisle, Mass.: Applewood Books, 2007), p. 27.

220 increase in consumption: David Halberstam, *The Fifties* (New York: Villard, 1993), p. 186.

220 "Radio was abandoned": Fred Allen, *Treadmill to Oblivion* (Rockville, Md.: Wildside Press, 2009), p. 239.

221 "It was a bad time": Nora Sayre, *Previous Convictions: A Journey through the 1950s* (New Brunswick, N.J.: Rutgers University Press, 1995), p. 112.

221 "Do you realize": Williams to Margo Jones, Dec. 1950, *L2*, p. 363.

221 "A lizardic dormancy": Arthur Miller, "Many Writers, Few Plays," *New York Times*, Aug. 10, 1952.

221 "a never-ending contest": *CS*, "Two on a Party," p. 292.

221 "calling the pack to follow": *CP*, "Cried the Fox," p. 7.

221 "Nothing can kill the beauty": Williams to Oliver Evans, Mar. 31, 1951, *L2*, p. 378.

221 "One of the very few advantages": Ibid.

222 "a fermenting new world": Gore Vidal, *The Golden Age* (New York: Doubleday, 2000), p. 317.

222 "The town has changed much": Williams to Cheryl Crawford, Nov. 1950, *L2*, p. 359.

222 Strange things were happening: David Aaronovitch, *Voodoo Histories* (New York: Riverhead, 2010), p. 111.

222 "to investigate links": Sayre, *Previous Convictions*, p. 274.

222 "If you want to be against McCarthy": Halberstam, *Fifties*, p. 54.

222 "The anti-fag battalions": Gore Vidal, *The Essential Gore Vidal*, ed. Fred Kaplan (New York: Random House, 1999), p. 964.

222 "limp-wristers": Michael S. Sherry, *Gay Artists in Modern American Culture: An Imagined Conspiracy* (Chapel Hill: University of North Carolina Press, 2007), p. 29.

222 "time for TV": Ibid., p. 30.

222 "feminized": Ibid.

223 "was prudish enough": Halberstam, *Fifties*, p. 273.

223 Homophobia extended: Michael Paller, *Gentleman Callers: Tennessee Williams, Homosexuality, and Mid-Twentieth-Century Drama* (New York: Palgrave Macmillan, 2005), p. 62.

223 "Fortunately property values": Williams to Cheryl Crawford, Nov. 1950, *L2*, p. 359.

223 "You can't run a Puritan": Williams to Josephine Healy, Feb. 27, 1951, Columbia.

223 "the unmentionable article": Williams to Brooks Atkinson, June 12, 1951, *L2*, p. 384.

224 "I must tell you that I have lived": Williams to Brooks Atkinson, Apr. 3, 1953, ibid., pp. 469–70.

225 "Insensitivity": Mervyn Rothstein, "Remembering Tennessee Williams as a Gentle Genius of Empathy," *New York Times*, May 30, 1990.

225 "Oh Laura, Laura": LOA1, p. 465.

226 "the foul-minded and utterly stupid tyranny": Williams to Jack Warner, Jerry Wald, and Charles K. Feldman, May 6, 1950, *L2*, p. 317.

226 "to trace the visionary company of love": LOA1, p. 467.

226 "correct standards of life": R. Barton Palmer and William Robert Bray, *Hollywood's Tennessee: The Williams Films in Postwar America* (Austin: University of Texas Press, 2009), p. 64.

226 "sordid and morbid": *KAL*, p. 433.

226 "this story and this script": Palmer and Bray, *Hollywood's Tennessee*, p. 87.

226 "The device by which he proves himself": Ibid., p. 83.

226 "The results were highly unsatisfactory": Ibid.

227 "I only want to do": Ibid.

227 "If Mr. Kazan's solution was one": Ibid., p. 86.

227 "In effect, Breen was asking Kazan": Ibid.

227 "The rape of Blanche by Stanley": Williams to Joseph Ignatius Breen, Oct. 29, 1950, *L2*, pp. 355–56.

228 "The thing that makes this piece": Palmer and Bray, *Hollywood's Tennessee*, p. 87.

229 "Stanley would be 'punished'": Ibid., p. 84.

229 "Now, honey. Now, love": LOA1, p. 564.

229 "This game is seven-card stud": Ibid.

229 "Don't you touch me": Tennessee Williams, *A Streetcar Named Desire* (screenplay), HRC.

229 "the primacy of moral order": Palmer and Bray, *Hollywood's Tennessee*, p. 91.

230 "Joe, a very strange thing": Ibid.

230 Radio City Music Hall canceled: Elia Kazan, "Pressure Problem," *New York Times*, Oct. 21, 1951.

230 "When you speak of the primacy of moral values": Elia Kazan to Martin Quigley, Aug. 16, 1951, WUCA.

230 "You asked *whose* moral values": Martin Quigley to Elia Kazan, Aug. 20, 1951, WUCA.

231 "should take them at their word": Elia Kazan to Jack Warner, July 20, 1951, WUCA.

231 "They range from a trivial cut": Kazan, "Pressure Problem."

232 "My picture had been cut": *KAL*, p. 434. The article had been rewritten and tempered by Kazan's wife, Molly Day Thacher.

232 "The Legion of Decency had acted": Ibid., p. 437.

232 "Now an air of dissolution": Ibid., p. 438.

232 "It seems to me": Elia Kazan to Williams, ca. 1954–1955, as quoted in Elia Kazan, *An American Odyssey*, ed. Michel Ciment (London: Bloomsbury, 1988), p. 190.

233 "a sort of penumbra": Williams to Oliver Evans, Mar. 5, 1951, *L2*, p. 371.

233 "summer of wanderings": Williams to Audrey Wood, Aug. 23, 1951, ibid., p. 395.

233 "Yesterday was the first time in our lives": *N*, July 25, 1951, pp. 521–23.

233 "makes the foulest coffee": Williams to Konrad Hopkins, Dec. 22, 1952, LLC.

235 "He is not at all keen": *N*, July 25, 1951, p. 523.

235 "the summer of the long knives": Ibid., 1951, p. 532.

235 "I had been quite witless": Williams to Elia Kazan, 1951, LLC.

235 "About one hundred miles out of Rome": Williams to Audrey Wood, July 22, 1951, *L2*, pp. 390–91.

236 "almost panicky with depression": *N*, July 22, 1951, p. 521.

236 "be sweet to acquaintances": Ibid., July 30, 1951, p. 527.

236 "term in Purgatory": Ibid., July 29, 1951, p. 527.

236 "Southern Drinkers": The title of the first section of the original story.

236 "great vigor and promise": Tennessee Williams, "Three against Grenada," HRC.

236 published fifteen months later: Tennessee Williams, "Three Players of a Summer Game," *The New Yorker*, Nov. 1, 1952.

236 "No one noticed Mr. Brick Bishop": Williams, "Three against Grenada," HRC.

236 "The crustacean world for a while!": *N*, July 31, 1951, p. 529.

236 "drawing the sails of my heart": Ibid., July 25, 1951, p. 523.

236 "Just taken: 2 phenobarbs": Ibid., Aug. 29, 1951, p. 533.

236 "had not yet completely fallen": *CS*, "Three Players of a Summer Game," p. 305.

237 "I am telling you mostly what I saw": Williams, "Three against Grenada," HRC.

237 "couldn't get going": Williams to Brooks Atkinson, May 1952, *L2*, p. 425.

237 "working, working, working": Williams to Audrey Wood, Sept. 28, 1951, ibid., p. 403. Brick is symbolically hobbled after he sprains his ankle while drunkenly running the hurdles on the track.

237 "all the warmth and charm": *N*, Aug. 4, 1951, p. 529.

237 "I think the reason the Horse": Williams to Maria Britneva, Aug. 3, 1951, *FOA*, p. 44.

237 "*amitié amoureuse*": Ibid., p. 7.

238 "Thank God for Maria": *N*, Oct. 1, 1951, p. 539.

238 "good kind of mischief": Williams to Carson McCullers, June 18, 1949, *L2*, p. 256.

238 Hermione Baddeley: Britneva had introduced Williams to Baddeley as a possible Serafina in the English production of *The Rose Tattoo*; in 1962, she starred as Mrs. Goforth in *The Milk Train Doesn't Stop Here Anymore*.

238 "attractive in a wild sharp-toothed way": Entry dated Nov. 25, 1972, in Kenneth Tynan, *The Diaries of Kenneth Tynan*, ed. John Lahr (New York: Bloomsbury, 2001), p. 110.

238 "We entered a small living-room": Ibid., pp. 111–12.

240 "The queen spat in Maria's face": Williams to Frank Merlo, Aug. 29, 1951, *L2*, p. 401.

240 "the cool air of detachment": LOA1, p. 885.

240 "At times in life": *N*, Sept. 11, 1951, p. 537.

240 "I like being with Frank": *N*, Sept. 16, 1951, p. 537.

240 "The Horse is in bed": Williams to Maria Britneva, Sept. 18, 1951, *FOA*, p. 46.

240 "sexy, original and lively": Elia Kazan, undated, BRTC.

240 two scenes of which Kazan had workshopped: Kazan directed blocks 6 and 7.

241 "The prospect of another Kazan production": Williams to Elia Kazan, Oct. 8, 1951, WUCA.

241 "Do you think": Williams to Audrey Wood, Sept. 28, 1951, *L2*, pp. 403–4.

241 "It was a mysterious harmony": *KAL*, p. 334.

241 "I always had fun working with Kazan": *M*, p. 166.

241 "Some day you will know how much": Williams to Elia Kazan, 1959, *KOD*, p. ix.

241 "Life in America": *KAL*, p. 336.

241 "I come from a family of voyagers": *KAL*, pp. 190–91.

242 "We both felt vulnerable": Ibid., p. 495.

242 "disappearer": Ibid., p. 335.

242 "The one thing any ambitious outsider": Ibid., p. 71.

242 "The terror in the house lifted": Ibid., p. 10.

242 "was a man full of violence": Ibid., p. 357.

242 "good for nothing": Ibid., p. 25.

242 "hopeless case": Ibid., p. 317.

242 "We entered a secret life": Ibid., p. 24.

243 "I learned to mask my desires": Ibid., p. 29.

243 "would be opposed": Ibid.

243 "He hit her smack across the face": Ibid., p. 31.

243 "I knew what I was": Ibid., p. 41.

243 "I wanted what they had": Ibid., p. 44.

243 "'Fuck you all, big and small!'": Ibid., p. 138.

243 "Didn't you look in the mirror?": Ibid., p. 12.

243 "He didn't have the kind": JLI with Elizabeth Ashley, 2003, JLC.

244 "Women have always meant everything": *KAL*, p. 27.

244 "strong 'feminine' characteristics": Ibid.

244 "Baby, you know as well as I know": Williams to Elia Kazan, Jan. 21, 1952, *L2*, p. 415.

244 "Promiscuity for an artist": *KAL*, p. 178.

244 "the undisputed darling": "If a man has been his mother's undisputed darling," Freud wrote, "he retains throughout life the triumphant feeling, the confidence in success, which not seldom brings actual success along with it." (Sigmund Freud, *The Complete Psychological Works of Sigmund Freud*, vol. 17 (1917–1919): *An Infantile Neurosis and Other Works* (London: Vintage, 2001), pp. 145–46.)

244 "I wanted to be the source": *KAL*, p. 562.

244 "the hushed air of conspiracy": Arthur Miller, *Timebends: A Life* (London: Methuen, 1999), p. 273.

244 "grinned a lot": Miller, *Timebends*, p. 132.

244 "He would send one actor": Ibid., p. 273.

245 "He let the actors talk": Ibid., p. 132.

245 "You are a man of action": Williams to Elia Kazan, 1949, WUCA.

245 "I am very excited": Williams to Audrey Wood, Oct. 27, 1951, *L2*, p. 405.

245 "salvation lies only in new work": Williams to Elia Kazan, Jan. 21, 1952, ibid., p. 415.

246 "always to have had a slightly superstitious awe": Williams to Konrad Hopkins, Feb. 24, 1954, LLC.

246 "We laugh our heads off": Williams to Cheryl Crawford, Feb. 10, 1952, *L2*, p. 419.

246 "F. and Bigelow joined us": *N*, Feb. 1952, p. 547.

246 "Frank has found a crowd": Williams to Oliver Evans, Feb. 20, 1952, *L2*, p. 420.

246 "a gorgeous . . . Adonis": Williams to Oliver Evans, Jan. 18, 1952, ibid., p. 413.

247 "Frankie is having himself a ball": Williams to Cheryl Crawford, Apr. 5, 1952, ibid., p. 423.

247 "Coarse fabrics are the ones": Tennessee Williams, "A Moment in a Room" (unpublished), LLC.

248 "must fold away": *N*, p. 546.

248 "I decided to look the other way": *KAL*, p. 454.

248 "We made a clean sweep": Williams to Elia Kazan, Feb. 14, 1952, WUCA.

248 "with sufficient firmness": *KAL*, p. 451.

248 "everyone seems pleased": *N*, Mar. 7, 1952, p. 547.

248 "Warner's stalled us": Williams to Cheryl Crawford, Apr. 5, 1952, *L2*, p. 422.

248 "Almost immediately that put him": Williams to Maria Britneva, Mar. 29, 1952, *FOA*, p. 54.

249 "Gadg, Marlon and I": Williams to Cheryl Crawford, Apr. 5, 1953, *L2*, p. 422.

249 "I was afraid even to remove my flask": Ibid.

249 "I believed my days in that town": *KAL*, p. 456.

249 "desperate request": Ibid., p. 442.

250 "He is going through some curious phase": Williams to Maria Britneva, Mar. 29, 1951, *FOA*, pp. 54–55.

250 "I say 'we' as if I felt": Ibid., p. 54.

250 "She was madly in love with Tenn": John Lahr, "The Lady and Tennessee," *The New Yorker*, Dec. 19, 1994, p. 80.

250 "I do love Tennessee": Ibid.

251 "To go around saying": Ibid.

251 "She called me up and said": Ibid.

251 "There was no way I could go along": *KAL*, p. 449.

251 "There was a certain gloomy logic": Miller, *Timebends*, pp. 333–34.

252 ". . . I joined the Communist Party": Elia Kazan, "A Statement by Elia Kazan," *New York Times*, Apr. 12, 1952.

252 "A very sad comment on our Times": Williams to Audrey Wood, Apr. 14, 1952, *L2*, p. 424.

252 "I seemed to have crossed": *KAL*, p. 468.

253 "He was, on the whole": Irene Selznick, *A Private View* (New York: Alfred A. Knopf, 1983), p. 339.

253 "on a great social griddle and frying": *KAL*, p. 472.

253 "a passionate absolutist": Ibid., p. 194.

253 "Yes! You did a solid and brave thing": Molly Day Thacher to Elia Kazan, Aug. 18, 1952, WUCA.

253 "I take no attitude": Williams to Maria Britneva, May 27, 1952, *FOA*, p. 56.

253 "the most loyal and understanding friend": *KAL*, p. 495.

253 "Did some top-drawer work": Williams to Elia Kazan, Jan. 10, 1952, WUCA.

253 "treacherous": Williams to Maria Britneva, Dec. 22, 1951, *FOA*, p. 51. "I must confess that Gadg and the actors did a bad job on it. It was a good play. But it was over-produced. The scenes were played too hard and heavy, so that the simple truth was lost in a lot of highly virtuoso theatricality."

253 "There were tears and protestations": Ibid.

254 "Now to 'Camino'": Eli Wallach to Elia Kazan, Feb. 12, 1952, WUCA.

254 "an extension of the free and plastic turn": Williams to Audrey Wood, June 10, 1952, HRC.

254 "The Blue Guitar" or "The Guitar of Picasso": Williams to Audrey Wood, Feb. 27, 1946, HRC.

254 "To me the appeal of this work": LOA1, p. 743.

254 "spiritual purgation of that abyss": *NSE*, p. 108.

254 "In the middle of the journey": LOA1, p. 741.

254 "This play is possible": Williams to Elia Kazan, July 29, 1952, *L2*, p. 443.

254 "galloping into totalitarianism": Williams to Oliver Evans, Oct. 7, 1953, ibid., p. 500.

255 "the old pure music": LOA1, p. 797.

255 "If you people": Williams to Elia Kazan, July 29, 1952, *L2*, p. 442.

255 "the all-but-complete suppression": *NSE*, p. 202.

255 "The spring of humanity": LOA1, p. 751.

256 "It is they": Kazan script for *Camino Real*, WUCA.

256 "The people are nearly all archetypes": Williams to Elia Kazan, Nov. 11, 1949, WUCA.

256 "I was its unfortunate hero": *KAL*, pp. 495–97.

257 "Turn again, turn again": *CP*, "Carrousel Tune," p. 60.

257 punning pronunciation of the title: Camino *RE*al: the royal way; Camino Real: grim reality.

257 "traceable to the spirit": Williams to Brooks Atkinson, Apr. 3, 1953, *L2*, p. 469.

257 "In the direction of this thing": Kazan script for *Camino Real*, WUCA.

257 "I say that symbols": LOA1, p. 745.

257 "Conventions of dreams": Elia Kazan, "Notes on Camino Real," WUCA.

257 "literally got down on its knees": Williams to Brooks Atkinson, Apr. 3, 1953, *L2*, p. 469.

257 "The essential stylistic problem": Kazan script for *Camino Real*, WUCA.

258 "This play is moving to me": Elia Kazan to Williams, Nov. 17, 1952, HRC.

258 "My suit is pale yellow": LOA1, p. 772.

258 "I say, if the play IS about these people": Elia Kazan to Williams, Nov. 17, 1952, HRC. In the August 10, 1952, issue of the *New York Times*, in his essay "Many Writers, Few Plays," Arthur Miller called attention to the lack of daring in the arts community. "Is the knuckle-headedness of McCarthyism behind it all?" Miller asked about the weird cultural entropy. He went on, "Guardedness, suspicion, aloof circumspection, these are the strongest traits I see around me, and what did they ever have to do with the creative act. . . . Is it quixotic to say that a time comes for an artist—and for all those who want and love theatre—when the world must be left behind. When, like some Pilgrim, he must consult only his own heart and cleave to the truth it utters?"

258 "To the hard of hearing": Flannery O'Connor, "The Fiction Writer & His Coun-

try," in *Mystery and Manners: Occasional Prose*, ed. Sally and Robert Fitzgerald (New York: Farrar, Straus & Giroux, 1969), p. 34.

258 "Are you afraid": LOA1, p. 767.

258 "to put [it] away": *M*, p. 165.

258 "The script is only about 1/10": Williams to Elia Kazan, Apr. 12, 1954, WUCA.

259 "I was prepared for anything": Williams to Audrey Wood, June 22, 1952, *L2*, p. 433.

259 "I am *terribly stimulated*": Williams to Elia Kazan, July 29, 1952, ibid., p. 443.

259 "The Terrible Turk": Williams to Audrey Wood, June 22, 1952, ibid., p. 433.

259 "slippery customer": Williams to Audrey Wood, Sept. 28, 1951, ibid., p. 403.

259 "The important thing is to keep Gadg": Williams to Audrey Wood, June 22, 1952, ibid., p. 434.

259 "very likely my last": Williams to Elia Kazan, July 29, 1952, ibid., p. 443.

259 "We're fighting here for fun": Elia Kazan to Williams, undated, ca. Aug. 1952, WUCA.

260 "essentially a plastic poem": Williams to Cheryl Crawford, Feb. 10, 1952, *L2*, p. 419.

260 "felt like an ungrateful dog": Jo Mielziner to Williams, Aug. 26, 1952, HRC.

260 "hot light": Williams to Elia Kazan, July 14, 1952, *L2*, p. 438.

260 "This play ends with a sort": Ibid.

260 "I think it is remarkable": Williams to Elia Kazan, July 29, 1952, ibid., p. 442.

261 "a retrenchment": *N*, July 29, 1952, p. 555.

261 "Yesterday eve we read over the work": Ibid., Aug. 20, 1952, p. 557.

261 "I hate writing that is a parade": LOA1, p. 745.

261 "a chowder of archetypes": Ethan Mordden, *All That Glittered: The Golden Age of Drama on Broadway, 1919–1959* (New York: St. Martin's Press, 2007), p. 286.

261 "It's an almost super-human job": Williams to Maria Britneva, Feb. 11, 1953, *FOA*, p. 71.

261 "I am very, very disturbed": Williams to Elia Kazan, undated, 1952, LLC.

261 As Williams suspected: Williams to Elia Kazan, Oct. 1952, *L2*, p. 457.

261 "the self-appointed scourge of Bohemia": Williams to Paul Bowles, Jan. 1953, ibid., p. 460.

261 "About Tennessee": Elia Kazan to Molly Day Thacher, undated, WUCA.

262 "When you're sold, you just sell": Molly Day Thacher to Elia Kazan, Sept. 24, 1952, WUCA.

262 "Molly, to all extents and purposes": JLI with Nick Kazan, 2010, JLC.

262 "talisman of success": *KAL*, p. 54.

263 "I think you can help him": Molly Day Thacher to Elia Kazan, Aug. 22, 1952, WUCA.

263 "Never before with you": Molly Day Thacher to Williams, Dec. 9, 1952, WUCA.

263 "She is my bete-noir!": Williams to Maria Britneva, Dec. 19, 1952, *FOA*, p. 69.

263 "Catch-as-Catch-Can Kazan": Williams to Maria Britneva, Feb. 11, 1953, ibid., p. 71.

263 "Molly is a pain": Williams to Maria Britneva, Dec. 19, 1953, ibid., p. 69.

263 "to be accepted as their hero": *KAL*, p. 498.

263 "I have fallen off remarkably": *N*, Aug. 16, 1952, p. 557.

263 "It's awful how quickly": Williams to Carson McCullers, Aug. 1952, *L2*, p. 444.

264 "This play moves me": Elia Kazan to Williams, Nov. 17, 1952, HRC.

264 "God bless all con men": LOA1, p. 839.

265   preamble: Tennessee Williams, "Invocation to Possible Angels by Author," LLC.

265   "Where are we": Ibid. "Just reading it does very little good as most of its values are so plastic, pictorial and dynamic, that just listening to it or reading it is almost useless unless the listener or reader has a trained theatrical mind," Williams wrote to Maria Britneva. (Dec. 3, 1952, *FOA*, p. 67.)

265   "I screamed at her": Williams to Maria Britneva, Dec. 19, 1952, *FOA*, p. 69.

265   "This play is at least twenty minutes": Elia Kazan to Williams, Dec. 10, 1952, WUCA.

265   "Why stick to a conventional length?": Elia Kazan to Williams, Dec. 10, 1952, LLC.

265   "You also exercise": Molly Day Thacher to Williams, Dec. 9, 1952, WUCA.

266   "I'm not going to make": Elia Kazan to Williams, Dec. 10, 1952, HRC.

266   "from A to infinity": Elia Kazan to Williams, Dec. 2, 1952, LLC.

266   "I sat down one morning": Ibid.

266   "Just do that": Elia Kazan to Williams, Dec. 10, 1952, WUCA.

266   "like ladies running barefooted": Williams to Maria Britneva, Apr. 22, 1953, *FOA*, p. 75.

266   tinkling of glass pendants on the Japanese lantern: Ibid.

266   "perennial work-in-progress": Williams to Konrad Hopkins, Jan. 16, 1953, LLC.

267   "so beat!": Ibid.

267   "Kazan is still dissatisfied": Ibid.

267   "My dream-self betrays": Ibid.

267   "All of us in the cast": Eli Wallach, *The Good, the Bad, and Me: In My Anecdotage* (Boston: Houghton Mifflin Harcourt, 2005), pp. 151, 153.

267   "His air is one of unusual power": Seymour Milbert, "Stage Manager's Rehearsal Account," BRTC.

268   "Motto: No matter what you do": Kazan rehearsal script for *Camino Real*, WUCA.

268   "This is a profound, emotionally charged play": Milbert, "Stage Manager's Rehearsal Account," BRTC.

268   "Fantastic events are played simply": Ibid.

268   "Death is too real": Ibid.

268   "adjusted, make a living": Kazan rehearsal script for *Camino Real*, WUCA.

268   "behave absurdly": Ibid.

269   "Audience are his friends": Kazan, "Notes on Camino Real," WUCA.

269   "He is the eternal spiritual wanderer": Ibid.

269   "He is full of wonder": Kazan rehearsal script for *Camino Real*, WUCA.

269   "utterly unaware of his own tragedy": Ibid.

269   "The violets in the mountains": LOA1, p. 842.

269   "like mad": Milbert, "Stage Manager's Rehearsal Account," BRTC.

270   "During these sessions": Ibid.

270   "All day—Williams and Kazan": Ibid.

271   "Kilroy represents freedom to you": Ibid.

271   "You, Kilroy, you're really jazzed now": Ibid.

271   "You're alone and you're scared": Ibid.; Wallach, *Good, Bad*, p. 151.

271   "Profoundly depressing": *N*, Feb. 10, 1953, p. 563.

271   "I wanted a production": *KAL*, p. 497.

272   "It made the fantasies": Ibid.

272   "The rehearsals are shaping up": *N*, Feb. 20, 1953, p. 563.

272   "at least half of which were dancers": Williams to James Laughlin, Jan. 5, 1953, *L2*, p. 472.

272   "pro-and-confusion": Walter Winchell, "The Broadway Lights," *New York Daily Mirror*, Mar. 22, 1953.

272   "Some actually hiss it": Williams to Konrad Hopkins, Feb. 28, 1953, LLC.

272   "I'm not sure 'Camino Real'": Elia Kazan, "Playwright's 'Letter to the World,'" *New York Times*, Mar. 15, 1953.

273   "militant incomprehension": Williams to James Laughlin, Apr. 5, 1953, *L2*, p. 472.

273   "The worst play yet written": Walter Kerr, "Camino Real," *New York Herald Tribune*, Mar. 20, 1953.

273   "an enigmatic bore": Richard Watts Jr., "An Enigma by Tennessee Williams," *New York Post*, Mar. 20, 1953.

273   "overall bushwah": John Chapman, "Symbols Clash in 'Camino Real,'" *New York Daily News*, Mar. 20, 1953.

273   "Camino Unreal": Eric Bentley, *What Is Theatre? Incorporating the Dramatic Event and Other Reviews 1946–1967* (New York: Hill & Wang, 2000), p. 74.

273   "'Camino Real' is a serious failure": Louis Kronenberger, ed., *The Best Plays of 1952–1953* (New York: Dodd, Mead, 1953).

273   "You're heading toward the cerebral": Walter Kerr to Williams, Apr. 13, 1953, as quoted in Donald Spoto, *The Kindness of Strangers: The Life of Tennessee Williams* (Boston: Little, Brown, 1985), p. 188.

273   "the first real bop play": Robert Sylvester, "A Stroll along 'Camino Real,'" *New York Daily News*, Mar. 23, 1953.

273   "As theatre, *Camino Real*": Brooks Atkinson, "Camino Real," *New York Times*, Mar. 20, 1953.

273   "it surpassed its flaws": *M*, p. 167.

273   "I knew that I was doing": Ibid., p. 166.

273   "I was hardly conscious of anything": Williams to Konrad Hopkins, Apr. 14, 1953, LLC.

273   "a marvel of controlled cool empathy": *M*, p. 167.

274   "I've come out of the production": *KAL*, p. 497.

274   "How dare you": *M*, p. 167.

274   "I believe it to be a very great play": Letters to the Editor, LLC. Sitwell also wrote to the *New York Times*, Apr. 5, 1953: "I have long thought Mr. Williams a playwright of very great importance. I now believe him to be a very great playwright. . . . Why are people who can see a little deeper to be deprived of a work which throws a blinding light on the whole of our civilization? Verbally, intellectually, and visually (the décor is amazing) it is a most extraordinary work."

275   "What I would like to know": Williams to Walter Kerr, Mar. 31, 1953, *L2*, p. 464.

275   "A Statement in Behalf of a Poet": Signed letter by Jane and Paul Bowles, Lotte Lenya, Elaine and Willem de Kooning, John La Touche, and Gore Vidal, among others, sent to newspapers, Columbia.

275   "The controversy over 'Camino Real'": Walter Winchell, *New York Daily Mirror*, Apr. 6, 1953.

276   "Concerning Camino Real": "Concerning Camino Real," *New York Times*, Apr. 5, 1953.

276   *Post*'s "Sidewalks of New York": Carl Gaston, "Sidewalks of New York," *New York Post*, Apr. 23, 1953.

276   "The Talk of the Town, Indeed!": *New York Herald Tribune*, Apr. 15, 1953.

276   "Bloody but unbowed": *RMTT*, p. 206.

277 "I can't believe that you really think": Williams to Brooks Atkinson, Mar. 24, 1953, *L2*, p. 462.

277 "psychopathic bitterness": Brooks Atkinson, "Tennessee Williams Writes a Cosmic Fantasy Entitled 'Camino Real,'" *New York Times*, Mar. 20, 1953.

277 "Has this play alienated": Williams to Brooks Atkinson, Mar. 24, 1953, LLC.

277 "flood of correspondence": Williams to Brooks Atkinson, Apr. 3, 1953, *L2*, p. 468.

277 "You have no idea how much": Williams to Brooks Atkinson, Apr. 3, 1953, LLC.

277 "Of course soon as the notices": Williams to Maria Britneva, Apr. 22, 1953, *FOA*, p. 75.

277 "The work was done": Williams to Brooks Atkinson, Apr. 1953, *L2*, p. 474.

278 "long-exceeded": Williams to James Laughlin, Apr. 3, 1953, LLC.

278 play by Donald Windham: *The Starless Air* opened at the Playhouse Theatre in Houston, May 13, 1953. Williams had to ban Windham from the theater; their friendship never recovered. "I have a brand new appreciation of Gadg. I always loved and admired him, but when I consider how many times I 'blew my top' at poor Windham and how often Gadg must have wanted to scream at me, but never did, I feel a real awe of his composure or control." (Williams to Brooks Atkinson, June 25, 1952, BRTC.)

278 "with a little painting in oils": Williams to Maria Britneva, Apr. 22, 1953, *FOA*, p. 75.

278 "shut out": Williams to Brooks Atkinson, Apr. 3, 1953, *L2*, p. 468.

278 "I have nothing more to expect": Williams to James Laughlin, Apr. 5, 1953, ibid., p. 473.

CHAPTER 5: THUNDER OF DISINTEGRATION

279 "I believe I said": *N*, May 8, 1936, p. 33.

279 "If only I could realize": Ibid.

279 "thrombosed hemorrhoids": Williams to Gore Vidal, Jan. 27, 1954, *L2*, p. 514.

279 "Don't think I ever spent such a night of pain": *N*, Dec. 28, 1953, p. 609. The 1946 operation was the traumatic removal of his appendix and infected intestine in Taos, New Mexico, which was, he told Kenneth Tynan, "where the desperate time started." (Williams to Kenneth Tynan, July 27, 1955, *TWLDW*, p. 306.) Of his 1953 ailment, Williams wrote, "It is relentless, constant, burning, aching. Frightens & appals one to think what misery, what anguish, our bodies are capable of. And this one such a sordid one, too. It might at least be in a decent place." (*N*, Dec. 29, 1953, p. 609.)

279 "this pain eclipses thought": *N*, Dec. 28, 1953, p. 609.

279 "a great storm has stripped me bare": Ibid., Aug. 19, 1953, p. 583.

280 "pinkies": *N*, July 4, 1958, p. 713.

280 "All hell is descended on me": *N*, Dec. 29, 1953, p. 609.

280 "not auspiciously": Ibid., June 5, 1953, p. 567.

280 "These suspicions of mine": Ibid.

280 "One gets tired of begging": Ibid., July 1, 1953, p. 571.

280 "treated like a stupid, unsatisfactory whore": Ibid., July 10, 1953, p. 571.

280 "Conversation had fallen to the level of grunts": Williams to Elia Kazan, undated, WUCA; also quoted, *N*, p. 572.

280 "What a sorry companion I make": *N*, July 17, 1953, p. 575.

281 "'The Horse' and I never laugh": Ibid., p. 575.

281 "dreary": *N*, Aug. 24, 1953, p. 583.

281 "juvenile poetics": Williams to Audrey Wood, Oct. 14, 1953, *L2*, p. 502.

281 "on the one big thing": Williams to Kenneth Tynan, July 26, 1955, *TWLDW*, p. 307.

281 "work and worry over work": Williams to Donald Windham, Dec. 20, 1949, ibid., p. 249.

281 "physical deterioration and a mental fatigue": *N*, Aug. 19, 1953, p. 583.

281 "and they were not too good": Ibid., Dec. 4, 1953, p. 601.

281 "Audrey wrote me a devastatingly negative": Williams to Maria Britneva, Oct. 15, 1953, *FOA*, p. 79.

281 "Death has no sound or light in it": *N*, Oct. 20, 1953, p. 601.

282 "Was so disheartened": Ibid., Oct. 1953, p. 595.

282 "If anything goes wrong": Ibid., Dec. 29, 1953, p. 611.

282 "And on that morning": *CP*, "Cortege," pp. 30–33.

283 "I'm such a coward": *N*, Dec. 30, 1953, pp. 611–13.

283 "If I am ever even relatively well": Ibid., p. 615.

283 "whispered": Ibid.

283 "He says you should have an operation": Ibid., Jan. 1, 1954, p. 619.

283 "that old breast-beating": Ibid., Jan. 2, 1954, p. 621.

283 "to make no more incontinent demands": Ibid., Jan. 5, 1954, p. 623.

283 "Oh, how I long to be loose again": Ibid., Jan. 1, 1954, p. 619.

283 "I am doing what I dreamed": Ibid., Jan. 16, 1954, p. 627.

284 "all the emotional content": *M*, p. 109.

284 "get a grip on": Williams to Audrey Wood, Apr. 1, 1954, *L2*, p. 525.

284 "I'm . . . pulling together": Williams to Audrey Wood, Mar. 21, 1954, ibid., p. 541.

284 "I do think it has a terrible sort of truthfulness": Williams to Audrey Wood, Apr. 1, 1954, ibid., p. 525.

284 "work script": *RBAW*, p. 165.

284 "I was terribly excited": Ibid.

284 "passing through": Williams to Cheryl Crawford, June 1954, *L2*, p. 534.

284 "at just about the pit": *N*, June 9, 1954, p. 643.

284 "I'm just holding on": Ibid., June 3, 1954, p. 637.

285 "Am I worthy of it?": Ibid., Aug. 13, 1954, p. 653.

285 "my soul": Ibid., June 6, 1954, p. 639.

285 "begun to develop": Williams to Kenneth Tynan, July 26, 1955, *TWLDW*, p. 307.

285 "That's a very dangerous thing": Ibid.

285 "Once the heart is thoroughly insulated": Williams to Kenneth Tynan, July 26, 1955, *TWLDW*, p. 307.

285 "Maybe Frank can help": *N*, June 9, 1954, p. 643.

285 "the Delta's biggest cotton-planter": LOA1, p. 880.

285 "In this version": *RBAW*, p. 165.

285 "a synthesis of all my life": Williams to Elia Kazan, Nov. 31, 1954, *L2*, p. 558.

285 "A man can be scared and calm": *N*, Dec. 30, 1953, p. 615.

287 "This click that I get in my head": LOA1, p. 936.

287 "a cemetery of refusals": Masud Khan, *Hidden Selves: Between Theory and Practice in Psychoanalysis* (London: Karnac Books, 1989), p. 57. "Hysteria is not so much an illness as a technique of staying blank and absent from oneself, with symptoms as a substitute to screen this absence. The question arises: what has necessitated this need for blankness and caused this dread of psychic surrender

through the early mother-child relationship in the hysteric? Or to put it differently: why does the hysteric's inner life become a cemetery of refusals?"

287 "Born poor, raised poor": LOA1, pp. 911–12.

287 *"Skipper is dead!"*: Ibid., p. 91.

287 "But how in hell on earth": Ibid., p. 913.

287 "Did Brick love Maggie?": Williams, "About Evasions," *FOA*, p. 110.

288 "I've gone through this": LOA1, p. 890.

288 "I never could keep my finger": Ibid., p. 892.

288 "There is torment in this play": Williams to Cheryl Crawford, June 1954, *L2*, p. 536.

288 shift from self-dramatization to self-justification: *TWLDW*, p. 321.

288 "I'm not sure self-pity": Williams to Ted Kalem, ca. 1962, Columbia.

289 "When you're feelin sorry": Tennessee Williams, "Drinky-Pie" (unpublished poem), Harvard.

289 "It has gotten so bad": Williams to Cheryl Crawford, June 1954, *L2*, p. 535.

289 "For the New Year": Elia Kazan to Williams, Dec. 25, 1953, LLC.

290 "Of course I wrote it for you": Williams to Elia Kazan, Aug. 18, 1954, WUCA.

290 "Will return with 2 other plays": Williams to Elia Kazan, undated, 1954, HRC.

290 "I still wish it could be a full evening": Audrey Wood to Williams, July 19, 1954, HRC.

291 play was unfinished: "This play has tremendous potential, but it has to be finished," she told him. *RBAW*, pp. 165–66.

291 "To me the story is complete": Williams to Audrey Wood, Sept. 1954, *L2*, p. 543.

291 "I'm quite exhausted": Elia Kazan to Williams, undated, ibid., p. 548.

291 "both hot for it": Williams to Maria Britneva, Oct. 17, 1954, *FOA*, p. 101.

291 "The only thing I want is Kazan": Ibid.

291 "You are on the threshold": Williams to Elia Kazan, Sept. 16, 1954, WUCA.

292 "I've occasionally lied to playwrights": *KAL*, p. 73.

292 "a brilliant first draft": Elia Kazan to Williams, Oct. 20, 1954, WUCA.

292 "PLEASE PLEASE stop": Elia Kazan to Williams, Oct. 18, 1954, WUCA.

292 "I'm scared to death": Ibid.

292 "I have no good suggestions": Elia Kazan to Williams, Oct. 20, 1954, WUCA.

292 "the richest land": LOA1, p. 929.

292 "no-neck monsters": Ibid., p. 883.

292 *"From Manager to Owner"*: HRC.

293 "My father had a great gift for phrases": Donald Spoto, *The Kindness of Strangers: The Life of Tennessee Williams* (Boston: Little, Brown, 1985), p. 198.

293 "strikes the keynote of the play": Williams to Elia Kazan, Nov. 3, 1954, *L2*, p. 551.

293 "reached beyond": *M*, p. 168.

293 "a monster of fertility": LOA1, p. 942.

293 BIG DADDY: *(He snatches the glass from Brick's hand)*: Ibid.

294 "long drawn cry of agony and rage": First draft of *Cat on a Hot Tin Roof*, HRC.

294 This play is about what the second act is about": Elia Kazan to Williams, Oct. 18, 1954, WUCA.

295 "I am left at the end of Act II": Elia Kazan to Williams, Oct. 20, 1954, WUCA.

295 "to get what you want": Williams to Elia Kazan, Oct. 1954, *L2*, pp. 549–50.

295 "had committed himself (verbally)": Williams to Maria Britneva, Oct. 29, 1954, *FOA*, p. 103.

296 "More melody in your voice": *KAL*, p. 541.

296 "the core of the play very hard": Williams to Elia Kazan, Nov. 3, 1954, *L2*, pp. 551–52.

296 "This is a play about good bastards and good bitches": Ibid.

296 "Vitality is the hero of the play!": Williams to Elia Kazan, undated, LLC.

296 "and concentrating on the character of Margaret": Williams to Elia Kazan, undated, *N*, p. 658.

297 "Maggie the Cat": "Last week Margaret Lewis Powell died in a nursing home in North Carolina. . . . We all called her 'Maggie the Cat,' and indeed she was a survivor. Tennessee knew her and had heard all the stories from Paul [Bigelow] and me. . . . I do think Tennessee took the name from her. She was *very* beautiful." (Jordan Massie to Lyle Leverich, May 19, 1995, LLC.) "He seemed more interested in stories about Maggie than in her. That same summer he got to know Big Daddy. Obviously, the seeds were planted and subsequently grew into a major play in the Williams canon." (Jordan Massie to Lyle Leverich, June 5, 1995, LLC.)

297 "I think a lot of you": Williams to Maria Britneva, Nov. 7, 1954, *FOA*, p. 106.

297 "no-neck monsters": LOA1, p. 883.

297 "Honey! I'm writing about your spirit": *FOA*, p. 107.

297 "You can be young without money": LOA1, p. 908.

297 "always had to suck up to people": Ibid., p. 907.

297 "The dress I married you in": Drafts of *Cat on a Hot Tin Roof*, HRC.

298 "I introduced them": Williams to Audrey Wood, July 8, 1952, HRC.

298 "made me cry with happiness": James Laughlin, *The Way It Wasn't: From the Files of James Laughlin*, eds. Barbara Epler and Daniel Javitch (New York: New Directions, 2006), p. 184.

298 "Jamesie! A RUSSIAN!": Ibid., pp. 184–85.

298 "Darling!": Williams to Maria Britneva, Mar. 27, 1954, *FOA*, p. 90.

299 "My God!": *FOA*, p. 91.

299 "broken her engagement to a multimillionaire": John Lahr, "The Lady and Tennessee," *The New Yorker*, Dec. 19, 1994, p. 81.

299 "I think you are one of the world's": Ibid.

299 "She is so strong-willed": Ibid.

299 wandered around Europe: Williams to Audrey Wood, Aug. 5, 1954, *L2*, p. 538.

299 "Poor little Maria": Williams to Audrey Wood, undated, ibid., p. 540.

299 "All hell has broke loose here": Williams to Audrey Wood, Sept. 1954, ibid., p. 547.

300 "Maria and I are writing letters": Williams to Audrey Wood, July 10, 1954, HRC.

300 "an artist of outstanding merit": *FOA*, p. 112.

300 "The help she needs": Williams to James Laughlin, Dec. 3, 1954, James Laughlin Papers, Houghton Library, Harvard University, Cambridge, Mass.

300 "I don't think anyone has ever upset me": James Laughlin to Williams, Jan. 9, 1955, James Laughlin Papers.

301 "exciting ideas about the doomed heroine": *FOA*, p. 112.

301 "There is no point in pretending": Brooks Atkinson, "Williams Play Revived by Originals Only," *New York Times*, Mar. 4, 1955.

301 "He was in kind of strange shape": Lahr, "Lady and Tennessee," p. 82.

302 "He thought she could help him": Ibid., p. 81.

302 "Maria was living in a tiny, tiny flat": Ibid., p. 82.

302 "I am not at all sure": Williams to Audrey Wood, Nov. 23, 1954, *L2*, p. 554.

302 "He loved it": Ibid.

302 "Loathe every minute of it": *N*, Dec. 3, 1954, p. 663.

303 "the poem of the play": *L2*, p. 559. This phrase appears in a manuscript fragment held by HRC, which is mentioned in the *L2* source cited.

303 "I do get his point": *N*, Nov. 29, 1954, p. 663.

304 "I'm going to do the Williams play": Elia Kazan to Molly Day Thacher, undated, WUCA.

304 "I 'buy' a lot of your letter": Williams to Elia Kazan, Nov. 31, 1954, WUCA.

304 "the romantic world of adolescence": Ibid.

305 "Brick gives me a pain": Elia Kazan to Williams, Feb. 3, 1955, WUCA.

305 "Tenn, it's the job of the playwright": Elia Kazan to Williams, Feb. 11, 1955, WUCA.

305 "go a little further'": Elia Kazan to Williams, Jan. 5, 1955, WUCA.

305 "BIG DADDY: What did you say to him?": Ibid.

306 "BIG DADDY: You musta said": LOA1, p. 951.

306 "worried sick": Elia Kazan to Williams, Feb. 11, 1955, WUCA.

306 "Brick all thru!": Ibid.

306 "We see here": Ibid.

307 "It's only fair to put you on notice": Elia Kazan to Williams, Feb. 3, 1955, WUCA.

307 forgo the estate: Elia Kazan to Williams, Feb. 5, 1955, WUCA: "Mightn't this be a good spot for him to say to Gooper and Mae that they can have the fucking plantation . . . thus making Maggie's job harder?"

307 "Can we make him funny": Elia Kazan to Williams, Feb. 11, 1955, WUCA.

308 "Truth is something desperate": LOA1, p. 1004.

308 "a meaningless piece of chi-chi": *N*, Mar. 2, 1955, p. 667.

308 "acted like a stuffed turkey": Ibid., Feb. 26, 1955, p. 665.

308 "inadequate": Ibid., Feb. 22, 1955, p. 665.

308 "Already making plans": Ibid., Feb. 26, 1955, p. 665.

308 "I am being utterly sincere": Williams to Elia Kazan, Mar. 1, 1955, *L2*, p. 567.

308 "I didn't write, plan, or edit": *KAL*, p. 544.

308 Kazan had winkled out of Williams: Ibid., p. 546: "In my wish to make them 'mine,' I did overpower these two plays [*Cat on a Hot Tin Roof* and *Sweet Bird of Youth*]. A sort of distortion was going on. I remember I'd felt an irritable impatience as I'd worked on those plays and, with it, a need to speak for myself at last. Here was born, I must suppose, the resolve to stop forcing myself into another person's skin but rather to look for my own subjects and find, however inferior it must be to Tennessee's, my own voice."

308 "I told a lie to Big Daddy": LOA1, p. 1005.

308 "I'd phone ahead": Ibid.

310 "What do you say?": Ibid., p. 976.

310 "that he has it still in his power": Brian Parker, "Swinging a Cat," in Tennessee Williams, *Cat on a Hot Tin Roof* (New York: New Directions, 2004), p. 181.

310 he was agitated: *FOA*, p. 108.

310 "The New York opening of *Cat*": *M*, p. 169.

310 "was in such a state of anger": *RBAW*, p. 169.

311 "a failure, a distortion": *M*, p. 169.

311 one person he trusted: Williams to Audrey Wood, Aug. 9, 1955, *L2*, p. 592: "You're the only person that I trust in this world."

311 she had ruined his play: *FOA*, p. 108.

311 "The wait for the morning notices": Williams to Brooks Atkinson, Mar. 25, 1955, *L2*, p. 569.

311 Toffenetti's: The Italian restaurant occupied the corner where NASDAQ now stands.

311 "'Cat on a Hot Tin Roof' is Mr. Williams' finest drama": Brooks Atkinson, "Tennessee Williams' 'Cat,'" *New York Times*, Mar. 25, 1955.

311 "Mr. Williams is the man of our time": Walter Kerr, "Cat on a Hot Tin Roof," *New York Herald Tribune*, Mar. 25, 1955.

311 "enormous theatrical power": Richard Watts Jr., "The Impact of Tennessee Williams," *New York Post*, Mar. 25, 1955.

311 "He studiously refused to permit": *RBAW*, pp. 169–70.

311 "the shocking *duality*": Williams to Elia Kazan, Nov. 3, 1954, *L2*, p. 552.

311 "Now that you've written your lovely notice": Williams to Brooks Atkinson, Mar. 25, 1955, ibid., p. 569.

311 "invidious resentment of [William] Inge's great success": Inge interviewed Williams in 1944 for the *St. Louis Star-Times*; they became friends and briefly lovers. Williams introduced Inge to Wood and to Margo Jones, who produced Inge's first play, *Farther Off from Heaven* (1947).

312 "I wanted Kazan to direct the play": *LOA1*, p. 978.

312 "gave people generally the idea": Elia Kazan to Williams, Apr. 22, 1960, *KOD*, p. 136.

312 "a success when I had given up thought": Williams to Elia Kazan, Aug. 1955, *L2*, p. 588.

312 half a million dollars: The fee was the equivalent in today's purchasing power of four million dollars.

312 "Figures stagger imagination": Williams to Audrey Wood, July 2, 1955, *L2*, p. 576.

312 "You and I have come to know how difficult": Audrey Wood to Williams, Aug. 3, 1955, HRC.

313 "I think he [Kazan] cheapened": Williams to Audrey Wood, July 28, 1955, *L2*, p. 586.

313 "I was terribly distressed": *CWTW*, p. 72.

313 "You never stated that in your preface": Elia Kazan to Williams, Apr. 22, 1960, *KOD*, pp. 136–37.

313 "One's enemy is always part of oneself": Williams to Maria Britneva, Jan. 10, 1956, *FOA*, p. 131.

313 "A failure reaches fewer people": *LOA1*, p. 978.

314 "a sort of a lunar personality": *N*, June 24, 1955, p. 675.

314 "I am running away from something": Williams to Audrey Wood, July 11, 1955, *L2*, p. 574.

314 died, at ninety-seven: The Reverend Walter Dakin died February 14, 1955. "Your presence in the city [New York] would be a great joy and comfort as well as bringing good luck." (Williams to Rev. Walter Dakin, Sept. 13, 1950, HRC.) "Why is luck so resolutely against me. Did it die with grandfather?" (*N*, Mar. 2, 1955, p. 667.)

314 praise the quality of the dialogue and the atmosphere: Dan Isaac, ed., "Introduction," in Tennessee Williams, *Spring Storm* (New York: New Directions, 1999), p. xv.

314 "The reaper is not only grim": Williams to Audrey Wood, Aug. 1955, *L2*, p. 591.

314 "the drugged state of semi-oblivion": Williams to Audrey Wood, July 21, 1956, ibid., p. 620.

315 "an examination of what is really corrupt": Spoto, *Kindness*, p. 206.

315 "I believe very strongly in the existence": *New York Herald Tribune*, 1957.

315 "Oh, Lady, wrap me": First draft of "The Enemy: Time," HRC.

315 "It is hard for me to like any playwright": Williams to Audrey Wood, Sept. 1955, *L2*, p. 592.

315 "It's much easier to give money than love": Williams to Maria Britneva, Apr. 27, 1955, *FOA*, p. 113.

315 "Magnani is outspokenly puzzled": Williams to Audrey Wood, July 11, 1955, *L2*, p. 574.

315 "I am determined to express just me": Williams to Audrey Wood, Nov. 18, 1955, ibid., p. 594.

317 "Have to finish the film-script": Williams to Maria Britneva, June 20, 1955, *FOA*, p. 117.

317 "Insert Somewhere": *KAL*, p. 562.

317 Williams took full screen credit: Williams to Audrey Wood, June 1955, *L2*, p. 574. Williams had suggested co-billing: "Screenplay by me. Adaptation by Elia Kazan."

317 "Those people chased me": Spoto, *Kindness*, p. 204.

317 "God damn it": Ibid.

317 "under the supervision of Tennessee Williams": Sandy Campbell, *B: Twenty-Nine Letters from Coconut Grove* (Campagnola di Zevio, Italy: Stamperia Valdonega, 1974), p. 47.

317 "Now I was without an author": *KAL*, p. 562.

318 "There is one small element here": Elia Kazan to Williams, Dec. 18, 1955, WUCA.

319 "both tragic and funny": Elia Kazan to Williams, Dec. 18, 1955, WUCA.

319 "I simply can't believe": Williams to Elia Kazan, Jan. 1956, *L2*, p. 597.

319 "Not false to the country": Williams to Elia Kazan, Jan. 1959, ibid., p. 597.

320 "No one showboats anymore": R. Barton Palmer and Williams Robert Bray, *Hollywood's Tennessee: The Williams Films and Postwar America* (Austin: University of Texas, 2009), p. 130.

320 "a very cute movie": Richard Schickel, *Elia Kazan: A Biography* (New York: HarperCollins, 2005), p. 332.

320 "took to the pulpit of St. Patrick's Cathedral": This was only the third time that Spellman had taken to the pulpit; the other two were to attack Communism and the imprisonment of Cardinal Joseph Mindszenty by the Hungarian Communists.

320 "I exhort Catholic people to refrain": Schickel, *Elia Kazan*, p. 333.

320 pay the Church twenty-five dollars: *Knoxville Sentinel*, Mar. 31, 1956.

320 "'BABY DOLL' IN NEW ROW": *New York Post*, Dec. 17, 1956.

320 "a harrowing experience": Williams to Maria Britneva, Jan. 3, 1957, *FOA*, p. 141.

320 "I cannot believe that an ancient and august branch": *New York Post*, Dec. 17, 1956.

320 "I am outraged by the charge": Ibid.

320 "This is the greatest idea": Palmer and Bray, *Hollywood's Tennessee*, p. 130.

321 made news and money: *Variety*, May 29, 1957: "According to Kazan, 'Baby Doll,' which cost $1,200,000, will have a worldwide gross of $5,000,000, of which $3,000,000 is already in the till. Kazan's own company, Newtown Productions, will make more than $1,000,000 on the picture, he stated."

321 "The Crass Menagerie": Palmer and Bray, *Hollywood's Tennessee*, p. 147.

321 "Just possibly the dirtiest": Ibid., p. 148.

321 "the high priest of *merde*": Robert E. Fitch, "The Mystique of Merde," *New Republic*, Sept. 3, 1956, pp. 17–18.

321 another half-million dollars for his new play: Williams to Audrey Wood, July 21, 1956, *L2*, p. 620.

322 "She is the bitch of all time": Williams to Audrey Wood, Jan. 1, 1956, HRC.

322 "From the moment Miss Bankhead saw Maria": Campbell, *B*, p. 10.

322 "Tenn is licking his lips": Ibid.

322 "Tallulah this is the way": Ibid., p. 32.

322 "in a voice all nearby": Ibid., p. 35.

323 "Batten the hatches!": Williams to Paul Bigelow, undated postcard, 1956, LLC.

323 "probably the most heroic accomplishment": *New York Times*, Mar. 4, 1956.

324 "Mr. Williams' talents as a playwright": Campbell, *B*, p. 58.

324 "Tenn, you and I": Paul Taylor, "Tennessee Williams: A Tormented Playwright Who Unzipped His Heart," *Independent*, Dec. 13, 2013.

324 "Let's face it": Campbell, *B*, p. 40.

324 "a regular stop": Williams to Edwina Williams, Mar. 18, 1956, *L2*, p. 608.

324 "the worst I can remember": Williams to Lady St. Just, Jan. 3, 1957, *FOA*, pp. 139–41.

324 "lost decency": *N*, Aug. 6, 1956, p. 691.

324 "Living on Miltowns": Williams to Christopher Isherwood and Don Bachardy, May 12, 1956, *L2*, p. 613.

324 "an almost unbroken decline": *N*, July 28, 1956, p. 689.

324 "I didn't feel the presence of God": Ibid., Sept. 27, 1956, p. 693.

325 "perhaps the most charming man": Françoise Sagan, *With Fondest Regards* (New York: Dutton, 1985), pp. 46, 49.

325 "She did not even laugh": Ibid., pp. 52–53.

325 "The Horse gave me a very bad time": Williams to Maria Britneva, Sept. 4, 1955, *FOA*, p. 126.

325 "I don't think my company": Williams to Audrey Wood, July 28, 1955, *L2*, p. 586.

326 "He would be a trial": *RMTT*, p. 152.

326 "To know me is not to love me": *M*, p. 131.

326 "He is haunted continually": Williams to Audrey Wood, July 28, 1955, *L2*, p. 586.

326 "We don't have to worry": Williams to Frank Merlo, July 22, 1955, ibid., pp. 581–82.

326 "This is the first time in years": Williams to Audrey Wood, Mar. 16, 1956, ibid., p. 605.

327 "'Attention must be paid to this man'": Williams to Audrey Wood, July 28, 1955, ibid., p. 587.

327 "They were having troubles": Spoto, *Kindness*, p. 205.

327 "For the first time since I've known him": Williams to Maria Britneva, Apr. 20, 1956, *FOA*, p. 133.

328 "How Can I Tell You?": *N*, p. 690.

328 "He has changed a great deal": Williams to Lady St. Just, Aug. 27, 1957, *FOA*, p. 149.

328 "another big row with F.": *N*, Aug. 6, 1956, p. 691.

328 "bad, nearly disastrous, quarrel": Ibid., Feb. 19, 1957, p. 701.

329 "streak of savagery": Brooks Atkinson, "Early Williams," *New York Times*, Nov. 22, 1956.

329 "If something is wrong at the top": "Stairs to the Roof" story, HRC.

329 "that to desire a thing": *NSE*, p. 94.

329   "a boy who hungered for something": Williams to Audrey Wood, Dec. 1939, *L1*, p. 220.

329   "fighting his own descent": *Miami Herald*, Jan. 22, 1956.

329   "trapeze of the flesh": Hart Crane, "The Bridge" (1930).

329   "we persist, like the cactus": *N*, Sept. 27, 1956, p. 693.

330   "Unfortunately in 1940": Williams to Audrey Wood, Oct. 14, 1953, *L2*, p. 502. William Liebling was equally unimpressed with *Orpheus Descending*; as late as 1956, he insulted Williams by suggesting that he liquidate the play as a financial asset by selling it to the movies. "I worked, God, what a long, long time on that script as a play. As a *PLAY!* It stung me terribly to have it proposed that I send it to the glue-factory," Williams wrote him. (Williams to William Liebling, July 21, 1956, HRC.)

330   "For the first time I think I may stay away": Williams to Lady St. Just, Jan. 3, 1957, *FOA*, p. 141.

330   "recapture some of my earlier warmth": Williams to Elia Kazan, Apr. 3, 1957, *L2*, p. 646.

330   "He is still trapped in his corruption": *CWTW*, p. 209.

330   "I felt like my whole life": *The Fugitive Kind* (1959), screenplay by Tennessee Williams and Meade Roberts, directed by Sidney Lumet. Essentially a monologue, played directly to the camera, the opening scene, with Marlon Brando as Val, makes it clear that he has survived by selling sex, not songs. These first five minutes represent one of Brando's finest, and least-known, screen moments.

331   "streaked with moisture and cobwebbed": LOA2, p. 9.

331   "shadowy and poetic": Ibid.

331   "she's not a Dago for nothin'!": LOA1, p. 701.

331   "coarsened, even brutalized": Williams to Audrey Wood, Oct. 14, 1953, *L2*, p. 501.

331   "Corruption—rots men's hearts": LOA2, p. 58.

331   "from seats down front": Ibid., p. 59.

331   "Heavy drinking and smoking the weed": Ibid., p. 24.

331   "I'm not young any more ": Ibid.

331   "a Wop bootlegger": Ibid., p. 34.

332   "He bought her": Ibid., p. 11.

332   "He is death's self": Ibid., p. 95.

332   "How come the shoe department's": Ibid., p. 25.

332   "Tomorrow I'll get me some niggers": Ibid., p. 26.

332   "You do whatever you want to": Ibid.

332   "I wanted death after that": Ibid., p. 54.

332   "What else can you do?": Ibid., p. 34.

332   "in sudden friendly laughter": Ibid., p. 37.

332   "I'm through with the life": Ibid., p. 34.

333   "My feet took a walk in heavenly grass": *CP*, "Heavenly Grass," p. 63.

333   "disgusted": LOA2, p. 38.

333   "off-stage guitar music fades in": Tennessee Williams, *Orpheus Descending* (New York: Dramatists Play Service, 1959), p. 29.

333   "VAL: You know they's a kind of bird": LOA2, p. 39.

334   "Ask me how it felt to be coupled": Ibid., p. 91.

334   "Everything Death's scraped": Ibid.

334   "Electric moon": Ibid., p. 83.

334   "To—be *not defeated!*": Ibid., p. 87.

335   "Didn't I marry a live one": Ibid., p. 74.

335   "Lady, you been a lunatic": Ibid., p. 90.

335   "I was made to commit a *murder*": Ibid., p. 87.

335   "You can't open a night-place": Ibid.

335   "LADY: You bet your sweet life I'm *going* to!": Ibid.

335   "a true love": Ibid., p. 89.

335   "Oh, don't talk about love": Ibid.

335   "You've given me life": Ibid., p. 94.

336   "in a sort of delirium": Ibid., p. 95.

336   "Oh, God, what did I do?": Williams, *Orpheus Descending*, p. 77. In LOA2, p. 95, Lady moans, "Oh, God, oh—God."

336   "The show is over": LOA2, p. 96.

336   "the Tigress of the Tiber": Tennessee Williams, "Anna Magnani: Tigress of the Tiber," *New York Herald Tribune*, Dec. 11, 1955.

336   "a woman who met with emotional disaster": LOA2, p. 24.

336   "The only important thing in life": Anna Magnani to Martin Juro, Sept. 11, 1955, LLC.

336   "She was beyond convention": *M*, p. 165.

336   "the intermediary between my reserve": Ibid., p. 163.

337   "Forget that bit about her being nervous": Williams to Elia Kazan, undated, WUCA.

337   "incomparable sense of truth": Williams, "Anna Magnani."

337   "like a mackerel sky": Ibid.

337   "surpasses mine but is more excusable": Williams to Audrey Wood, June 29, 1956, *L2*, p. 616.

337   "Ciao, Tenn. What is the program": *M*, pp. 163–64.

337   "I know how to write for that boy": Williams to Audrey Wood, June 1955, *L2*, p. 573.

337   ghostwriting mash notes: *TWIB*, p. 227.

337   "She has a genius": Williams to Maria Britneva, Sept. 29, 1954, *FOA*, p. 104.

337   "This news gave me a great joy": Anna Magnani to Audrey Wood, undated, HRC.

337   "I know that Brando is very much interested": Anna Magnani to Audrey Wood, November 3, 1955, HRC. About Brando, Magnani goes on to say, "As far as I am concerned I am not interested in him as a person, he only remains the perfect actor for the role of Val. That's about all. For the rest I don't give a damn."

339   "You wrote your funky ass off": Marlon Brando to Williams, undated, Columbia.

339   "When you play with her": Quotation from undated letter from Marlon Brando reproduced by permission of Brando Enterprises, L.P.

340   "The money wasn't nearly as much a problem": JLI with Sidney Lumet, 2011, JLC.

340   "After we had some meetings": Marlon Brando with Robert Lindsey, *Brando: Songs My Mother Taught Me* (New York: Random House, 1994), p. 262.

341   "The essence of Anna?": JLI with Sidney Lumet, 2011, JLC.

341   "It completely ruined my staging": Ibid.

341   "sputters more often": Review of *The Fugitive Kind*, *Variety*, Dec. 31, 1959.

341   "throbbing and feeling staggered": Bosley Crowther, "2 Theatres Show Film from Williams Play," *New York Times*, Apr. 5, 1960.

341   "the first time I saw the rushes": JLI with Sidney Lumet, 2011, JLC.

342   offered to mount one of Williams's one-act plays: Williams to Audrey Wood, Feb.

7, 1940, *L1*, p. 230: "Clurman took long play [*Battle of Angels*] to Boston with him. . . . *Clurman* says he may do 1-acts if Odets play is successful—this spring— Afraid the '*if*' clause is a big one."

342 "It is the 'peculiar people'": Harold Clurman, "Introduction," in Tennessee Williams, *Tennessee Williams: Eight Plays* (Garden City, N.Y.: Nelson Doubleday, 1979).

342 "dear man and fine critic": *M*, p. 172.

342 "Harold's rehearsals": *KAL*, pp. 121–22.

342 "I know that Anna would break": Williams to Audrey Wood, July 28, 1955, *L2*, p. 587.

342 "under-directed": *M*, p. 172.

342 "For your own sake, honey": Williams to Cheryl Crawford, Dec. 1956, *L2*, p. 641.

343 "a truly shattering setback": *M*, p. 172.

343 "one of Mr. Williams's pleasantest plays": Brooks Atkinson, "Theatre: Rural Orpheus," *New York Times*, Mar. 22, 1957.

343 "something missing": "Only the Flashes," *Newsweek*, Jan. 1, 1957.

343 "a drama of notable power": Richard Watts Jr., "The World of Tennessee Williams," *New York Post*, Mar. 22, 1957.

343 "The trouble with Tennessee Williams's new play": Wolcott Gibbs, "Well, Descending, Anyway," *The New Yorker*, Mar. 30, 1957.

343 "put it down with a vengeance": *M*, p. 173.

343 "There was an emotional shock": Williams to Donald Windham, *TWLDW*, June 13, 1957, p. 293.

343 "If he ever refers to my sister": CC Williams to Audrey Wood, Feb. 8, 1950, *L2*, p. 274.

343 "a flop": *Knoxville News-Sentinel*, Mar. 28, 1957, LLC.

343 "my desperate old father": *N*, June 6, 1954, p. 639.

343 "I've stopped hating my father": Williams to Kenneth Tynan, July 26, 1955, *TWLDW*, p. 302.

344 "So a tragic situation works itself out": Williams to Paul Bigelow, Jan. 7, 1948, *L2*, p. 143.

344 "My father was really quite an embarrassment": LLI with Dakin Williams, 1985, LLC.

344 "I was surprised that Tennessee came": Ibid.

344 "Dakin told me": *RMTT*, p. 202.

344 both Dakin and Tennessee cried over their father: *TWIB*, p. 212; see also Gilbert Maxwell, *Tennessee Williams and Friends: An Informal Biography* (Cleveland: World Publishing, 1965), p. 222.

344 "The Williams family was not one": *TWIB*, p. 150.

344 "I wonder if he knew": *CS*, "The Man in the Overstuffed Chair," p. xvii.

345 as "an exceptionally beautiful service": Williams to Audrey Wood, Jan. 5, 1957, LLC.

345 "Am I wrong in thinking": Williams to Elia Kazan, Apr. 31, 1957, *L2*, p. 646. The previous month Kazan had written Williams his critique of the production of *Orpheus Descending*. "I think you should have gotten more of a fight from somebody; a tougher, a keener, or possibly more unpleasant collaborator, telling you more objectively what was wrong with the script, where it was unclear, where it was too sudden, where it appeared unmotivated and abrupt. In fact, you needed someone to take the chance that I took in CAT. To take the chance that you would be resentful later and feel that you had been too strongly influenced. . . .

You might have written another preface saying, 'I didn't really mean that version you saw on the Broadway stage,' but still I think all in all you would have been happier now." (Elia Kazan to Williams, Mar. 27, 1957, *The Selected Letters of Elia Kazan*, ed. Albert J Devlin with Marlene J. Devlin [New York: Alfred A. Knopf, 2014], p. 350.)

345 "Tenn became a terrific hypochondriac": Spoto, *Kindness*, p. 215.

345 "a certain stop": Williams to Brooks Atkinson, Mar. 24, 1957, *L2*, p. 644.

345 "Since the failure of 'Orpheus'": Williams to Lady St. Just, June 7, 1957, *FOA*, p. 147.

345 "What a season we've been having": Williams to Audrey Wood, Apr. 24, 1957, HRC.

345 "I can't be the better part": Williams to Sandy Campbell, Jan. 5, 1957, *TWLDW*, p. 292.

345 "The moment has certainly come": *N*, Mar. 31, 1957, p. 701.

CHAPTER 6: BEANSTALK COUNTRY

346 "Who am I": *CP*, "You and I," p. 123.

346 hard-drinking poet Gilbert Maxwell: "I saw Gilbert throw his drink squarely iTenn's face more than once; when he was in a particularly bitchy mood he'd call Tennessee 'Ta-ness-a,'" the director George Keathley said. (Keathley, unpublished Ms., JLC.)

346 biographical album about his life: Richard Leavitt's album was *The World of Tennessee Williams*. He also published *Tennessee Williams and the South*, with Kenneth Holditch, in 2002.

346 "I announced that I was retiring": *N*, Apr. 1, 1957, p. 703.

346 "He reminded me of Thomas Wolfe": Eugene B. Brody, "Introduction," in Lawrence S. Kubie, *Symbol and Neurosis: Selected Papers of Lawrence S. Kubie* (Madison, Conn.: International Universities Press, 1978), p. 6.

348 "The tree of psychoanalytic theory": *N*, Apr. 1, 1957, p. 703.

348 Kubie was the man: In a 1966 survey that asked 490 of the country's leading psychiatrists to list the outstanding living psychiatrists, Kubie came in fifth, ahead of such renowned clinicians as the Menningers. See Norman Cousins, *Memorial* (privately published), p. 237.

348 history of the place: Lawrence Kubie, *The Riggs Story: The Development of the Austen Riggs Center for the Study and Treatment of the Neuroses* (New York: Paul B. Hoeber, 1960).

349 "What is cut off": Lawrence Kubie, *Practical and Theoretical Aspects of Psychoanalysis* (Madison, Conn.: International Universities Press, 1950), p. 129.

349 "a good team-player": Gore Vidal, "Tennessee Williams: Someone to Laugh at the Squares With," in Gore Vidal, *Armageddon? Essays 1983–1987* (London: Andre Deutsch, 1987), p. 54.

349 The psychoanalyst": Kubie, *Practical and Theoretical Aspects*, p. 131.

349 "I don't think I can stand much": *N*, June 3, 1957, p. 705.

349 "salvation": Ibid., June 7, 1957, p. 705.

349 "my favorite city in the Americas": Williams to Elia Kazan, June 10, 1957, WUCA.

349 "goofed": *N*, June 13, 1957, p. 707.

349 "With the plane trip as an excuse": Ibid., June 11, 1957, p. 707.

349 "rarely take[s] more than one goofball": Williams to Elia Kazan, June 10, 1957, WUCA.

349 "The swimming and the fucking": Ibid.

350 "I am going on with my work": He was working on *The Loss of a Teardrop Diamond*, which was made into a film in 2008.

350 "had knocked me out so completely": Williams to Frank Merlo, June 1957, THNOC.

350 had nightmares: Williams to Lady St. Just, June 17, 1957, *FOA*, p. 148.

350 "a plush-lined loony-bin": Ibid.

350 "a Christian Retreat": Williams to Audrey Wood, June 19, 1957, HRC.

350 "I stayed only five minutes": Williams to Edwina Williams, June 28, 1957, *N*, p. 706.

350 "My analyst is very anxious": Williams to Paul Bowles, June 1957, HRC.

351 "Analysis is very upsetting at first": Williams to Lady St. Just, Aug. 27, 1957, *FOA*, p. 149.

351 "into a swinging honky-tonk": Williams to Oliver Evans, undated, Harvard.

352 "I've been wanting to try it": Williams to Edwina Williams, June 28, 1957, *N*, p. 704.

352 "With Kubie I have worked": Williams to Elia Kazan, June 28, 1958, WUCA.

352 "If only we could turn up something": Williams to Lady St. Just, Oct. 30, 1957, *FOA*, p. 150.

352 "Kubie would imitate my father": *CWTW*, p. 245.

352 "wasn't really that bad": Robert Rice, "A Man Named Tennessee," *New York Post*, May 4, 1958.

352 "terrible light": *New York Post*, May 4, 1958.

353 "Iron Man": Tennessee Williams, "Iron Man" (unpublished poem), ca. 1935–1939, Harvard.

353 "A psychiatrist once said to me": *CS*, "The Man in the Overstuffed Chair," p. xv.

354 "I think it was the constraint of working": Williams to Lucy Freeman, undated (ca. July 1962), LLC.

354 "My mother would scream": *CWTW*, p. 169.

354 "a rather pathetically regular life": *RMTT*, p. 202.

354 "Oh, no, I can't make peace": *N*, June 17, 1942, p. 291.

354 "Happily, the Bird's anarchy": Vidal, "Tennessee Williams," p. 54.

354 "WALLACE: Richard Watts, whom I know": *CWTW*, p. 54.

356 "I was bored not working": *Miami Herald*, Dec. 21, 1958.

356 "extraordinary power": Williams to Elia Kazan, July 5, 1980, Harvard.

356 "much of the beautiful": As quoted in Geoffrey Galt Harpham, *On the Grotesque* (Princeton, N.J.: Princeton University Press, 1982), p. 181.

356 "a well-groomed jungle": LOA2, p. 100.

356 "that string of pearls": Ibid., p. 138.

357 "I was PROCURING": Ibid., p. 141.

357 "It wasn't *folie de grandeur*": Ibid., p. 111.

357 "Really I was actually the only one": Ibid., p. 110.

357 "After the operation": Ibid., p. 147.

357 "*Do you want to bore a hole*": Ibid., p. 127.

357 "Now that it's over": Edwina Williams to Williams, Jan. 20, 1943, in Lyle Leverich, *Tom: The Unknown Tennessee Williams* (New York: W. W. Norton, 1995), p. 480.

357 "What kind of operation was it": Williams to Edwina Williams, Jan. 25, 1943, *L1*, p. 481.

359 "had given up on Rose": Leverich, *Tom*, p. 481.

359 "The psychiatrists convinced Cornelius": *RMTT*, p. 85. Dr. Emmett Hoctor, the

superintendent of Farmington State Hospital, had suggested the operation, which was carried out by Dr. Paul Schrader with Dr. Hoctor in attendance. "He was perfectly lovely to me and inspired me with confidence that he will do the right thing by her. He is of fine moral & Christian character also a Roman Catholic," Edwina wrote. (Leverich, *Tom*, p. 224.)

359 "only hope": "She is now in the State Hospital in Farmington. Cornelius had her taken there on Saturday," Edwina wrote to her parents. "She became violently insane just after you left and they placed her in a room off from the rest and told me they would advise insulin immediately as the only hope for her. . . . They all agree that this is the only hope and that Farmington is the best place, so there was nothing for me to do but consent." (Leverich, *Tom*, p. 223.)

359 "Does no work": Leverich, *Tom*, p. 335.

359 "has been eccentric most of his life": Ibid., p. 247.

359 "Any of the normal hugging or kissing": Ibid.

359 "I remember her stalking": Williams to Oliver Evans, July 1971, Harvard.

360 "Let's all die together": Leverich, *Tom*, p. 149.

360 "with refugees": Ibid., p. 199.

360 "Cornelius . . . lost his temper": Ibid., pp. 199–200.

360 "Rose was like a wild animal": *TWIB*, p. 63.

360 "both of her parents had lost their minds": "Psychiatric Summary": Farmington State Hospital, Dr. CC Ault, Dec. 16, 1937, LLC.

361 "Valediction": *N*, p. 82.

361 "Horrible, Horrible!": *N*, Dec. 20, 1939, p. 177.

361 "tragically mistaken": *M*, p. 251.

361 "was essentially more psychotic": *CWTW*, p. 327.

362 "dearest brother": Rose Williams to Williams, July 8, 1944, HRC.

362 "Probably the best thing I've done": *M*, p. 127.

363 "She and Tennessee sang carols": John Lahr, "The Belle of Bethel," Talk of the Town, *The New Yorker*, Sept. 23, 1996, p. 34.

363 "She moved among her subjects": Ibid.

363 "the Windsor Wave": Ibid.

363 "I am the Queen": Ibid.

363 visited Rose with unusual frequency: Donald Spoto, *The Kindness of Strangers: The Life of Tennessee Williams* (Boston: Little, Brown, 1985), p. 219.

363 "I've seen Rose four times": *RMTT*, p. 233.

365 "just a body": Williams to Cheryl Crawford, Oct. 1956, *L2*, p. 634.

365 "Oh, Laura, Laura": *LOA1*, p. 465.

365 "Rose in one of her neurotic sprees": *N*, Oct. 7, 1936, p. 59.

365 "God forgive me for this!": Ibid.

365 "We passed each other on the landing": *M*, p. 122.

366 "I think of Rose": *N*, Oct. 9, 1937, p. 109.

366 "poor mad creature": Ibid., Dec. 20, 1939, p. 177.

366 "Rose, my dear little sister": Ibid., July 10, 1939, p. 159.

366 "I seldom think of Rose anymore": Ibid., Sept. 16, 1939, p. 159.

366 "the most shocking experience": Ibid., Jan. 14, 1943, p. 343.

366 "my lack of feeling": Ibid., Mar. 22, 1943, p. 359.

366 "Rose. Her head cut open": Ibid., Mar. 24, 1943, p. 361.

366 "depend upon a feverish animation": *LOA1*, p. 13.

367 "You—you *disgust* me. . . . !": Ibid., p. 79.

367 "It was because": Ibid., p. 528.

367 "a band of frightfully thin and dark naked children": LOA2, p. 142.

367 "The madness is still present": Williams to Paul Bigelow, Apr. 10, 1943, *N*, p. 362.

367 "what a dark and bewildering thing": Williams to Donald Windham, Apr. 1943, *TWLDW*, p. 57.

367 his lifetime dedication to memorializing her: Williams based a character on Rose in more than fifteen plays, at least eight poems are dedicated to her, and a dozen plays deal with mental illness and lobotomies. (See *N*, p. 40.)

368 "best-liked": *CS*, "Portrait of a Girl in Glass," p. 114.

368 "the others had now begun to smile": Ibid., p. 118.

368 "Laura was the first to speak": Ibid.

368 "I think the petals of her mind": Ibid., p. 112.

368 "pop out with something": Ibid., p. 119.

369 "unceremoniously outed": Tony Kushner, "Introduction: Notes on *The Glass Menagerie*," in Tennessee Williams, *The Glass Menagerie* (Centennial Edition) (New York: New Directions, 2011), p. 27.

369 "I suppose this means the end": Williams to Paul Bowles, Dec. 1957, HRC.

369 *Suddenly Last Summer*: *Suddenly Last Summer* was produced with *Something Unspoken*, under the collective title *Garden District*.

369 "Apparently, judging from some of the reviews": Katherine Anne Porter to Williams, Jan. 28, 1958, Maryland.

369 "An impressive and genuinely shocking play": Wolcott Gibbs, "Oddities, Domestic and Imported," *The New Yorker*, Jan. 18, 1958.

369 "An exercise in the necromancy": Brooks Atkinson, "2 By Williams," *New York Times*, Jan. 8, 1958.

369 "I don't think I've ever been quite": Williams to Brooks Atkinson, Jan. 9, 1958, BRTC.

370 "a big white-paper-wrapped bunch": LOA2, p. 147.

370 "*He!—accepted—all!*": Ibid., p. 145.

370 "Even though he knew": Ibid.

370 "emotionally stirred": Lawrence S. Kubie to Williams, Jan. 13, 1958, Columbia.

370 "Doctor—Cu?—Cu?": LOA2, p. 102.

370 "Of all the many portrayals": Lawrence S. Kubie to Williams, Jan. 13, 1958, Columbia.

371 "I am a realist": Katherine Anne Porter to Williams, Jan. 28, 1958, Maryland.

371 "Life is cannibalistic": Whitney Bolton, "Williams Talks on Violence," *Philadelphia Inquirer*, Feb. 1, 1959.

371 "I think we ought at least to consider": LOA2, p. 148.

371 "I remember a couple of years ago": *New York Post*, May 2, 1958.

371 "I'll tell you a new 'bit'": Elia Kazan to Williams, undated, WUCA.

372 "'Just this second'": Elia Kazan to Williams, Jan. 10, 1958, WUCA.

372 "Kubie has said for me": Williams to Elia Kazan, June 4, 1958, WUCA.

372 "passing through purgatory": Williams to Lady St. Just, Apr. 23, 1958, *FOA*, p. 151.

372 "But instead of posting it": Ibid.

372 "It turned into a contest of wills": Williams to Elia Kazan, June 27, 1958, WUCA.

373 "He is a strange and interesting phenomenon": Lawrence Kubie to Lucie Freeman, undated, LLC.

373 "I had to defy my analyst": Williams to Elia Kazan, June 4, 1958, *N*, p. 711.

373 "I resented him telling me": Williams to Audrey Wood, July 9, 1958, ibid., p. 716.
     In the same letter, he complained, "I feel that he has been stubbornly obtuse
     about the need to continue my work when there's nothing to put in its place, and
     when I feel so strongly that I have so little time left in which to complete it."

373 "seems to have set the keynote": N, Aug. 1958, p. 719.

374 "Another day without coffee": Ibid., July 18, 1958, p. 717. "I am planning to
     return to the States sooner than I had expected to facilitate this collaboration [on
     Sweet Bird] and also because I think I must resume my analysis, maybe not with
     Kubie, maybe with a younger man with fresher ideas or with a woman, more
     inclined to the school of Jung." (Williams to Audrey Wood, July 9, 1958, HRC.)

374 "grave error": Williams to Audrey Wood, July 9, 1958, LLC.

374 "The truth of the play": Williams to Audrey Wood, June 6, 1958, HRC.

374 "Frank and I never get along": Williams to Jo Mielziner, Aug. 5, 1958, HRC.

374 "I'm drunk enough to write you": Williams to Frank Merlo, Spring 1959, Har-
     vard.

375 his unfulfillable emotional demands: "I am too ready, too quick, to condemn a
     person I love because I can't believe that the love is returned," he confessed to
     Wood. "And [I'm] such a great egotist that no matter how little attention I am
     able to give to other people, I want a whole lot given me." (Williams to Audrey
     Wood, Sept. 27, 1959, HRC.)

375 "outlived legend": LOA2, p. 230.

376 "2 by 4 situation": Ibid., p. 417.

376 "gnaws off its own foot": Ibid., p. 236.

376 "There's nowhere else to retire to": Ibid., p. 172.

376 "In a life like mine": Ibid., p. 182.

376 "monster": Tennessee Williams, "Anna Magnani: Tigress of the Tiber," *New York
     Herald Tribune*, Dec. 11, 1955.

377 "I am a monster": Williams to Elia Kazan, Dec. 23, 1958, WUCA.

377 "I wasn't always this monster": LOA2, p. 230.

377 "Kubie said I can't believe anyone": Williams to Audrey Wood, July 9, 1958,
     HRC.

377 "I came to discover": Williams to Oliver Evans, Nov. 15, 1958, HRC.

377 "Kubie didn't seem to understand": Williams to Elia Kazan, June 28, 1958,
     WUCA.

377 "A writer is always two beings": Williams to Ted Kalem, undated, Columbia.

378 "It's the work": Williams to Brooks Atkinson, Sept. 2, 1959, BRTC.

378 "I think the arias": Elia Kazan to Williams, May 20, 1958, WUCA.

378 "the potential of being a character": Ibid.

378 "I think this is the most truly autobiographical play": Elia Kazan to Jo Mielziner,
     Sept. 9, 1958, WUCA.

378 "The play is an expression": Molly Day Thacher to Elia Kazan, May 29, 1958,
     WUCA.

379 "The PLOT of the play": Ibid.

379 "He is surrounded by murderous forces": Elia Kazan to Jo Mielziner, Sept. 9,
     1958, WUCA.

379 "There, if ever I saw one": Ibid.

380 "subjective scenery": Ibid.

381 "Chance, you've got to help me": LOA2, p. 217.

381 "PRINCESS: . . . I seem to be standing": Ibid., p. 230.

381 "Grown, did you say?": Ibid., p. 232.

381 "You've just been using me": Ibid., p. 233.

381 "Frank . . . is so pitifully": Williams to Audrey Wood, Sept. 27, 1959, HRC.

382 "the huddling-together": LOA2, p. 235.

383 "the home of my heart": Ibid., p. 207.

383 "Something's got to mean something": Ibid., p. 234.

383 "I don't ask for your pity": Ibid.

383 "big deal gamble": Williams to Audrey Wood, May 7, 1958, HRC.

383 "if you want to wait": Elia Kazan to Williams, May 20, 1958, *KOD*, p. 118.

383 "the most important thing": Williams to Audrey Wood, June 6, 1958, LLC.

383 "Please help me not to be seduced": Williams to Audrey Wood, June 6, 1958, HRC.

383 "what happens to Chance": Sept. 2, 1958, *KOD*, p. 119.

384 "attention to his presence in town": May 20, 1958, ibid., p. 117.

384 "the camera cutting from enormous close-ups": Elia Kazan to Williams, Aug. 28, 1958, WUCA.

384 "stunt": *KAL*, p. 544.

384 "I can't think of any other director": Williams to Audrey Wood, July 26, 1958, HRC.

384 "I am out": Elia Kazan to Audrey Wood, Aug. 28, 1958, Columbia.

384 "I don't really make deals with agents": Elia Kazan to Williams, Aug. 28, 1958, Columbia.

384 "I do think he's probably entitled": Williams to Audrey Wood, July 26, 1958, HRC.

385 "I feel that this play needs him": Williams to Cheryl Crawford, Sept. 4, 1958, HRC.

385 "He mustn't try to screw me": Williams to Audrey Wood, Aug. 31, 1958, HRC.

385 "for the inner qualities": *KAL*, p. 545.

385 "Miss Page is not the kind of actress": José Quintero, *If You Don't Dance They Beat You* (Boston: Little, Brown, 1974), p. 113.

385 "I think it may demand more power": Williams to Cheryl Crawford, Aug. 13, 1958, HRC.

385 "The Princess is a pretty cosmopolitan character": Williams to Audrey Wood, July 24, 1958, HRC.

385 "consanguinity": Ibid.

386 "an air of great vulnerability": Mike Steen, *A Look at Tennessee Williams* (New York: Hawthorn Books, 1969), p. 229.

386 "If Miss Page": *RBAW*, p. 177.

386 "Stop it, stop it!": *M*, p. 174.

386 "*temporary* obfuscation": LOA2, p. 271.

386 "She was convinced": *KAL*, p. 545.

387 "sweetly and genially smiling": *M*, p. 174.

387 "now dreadfully ashamed": Ibid.

387 "He doubted his own play": *KAL*, p. 545.

387 "I think we have to go for broke": Williams to Elia Kazan, Feb. 18, 1959, WUCA.

387 "You get the impression": Steen, *Look*, p. 242.

388 "a close, undisturbed working relationship": Williams to Elia Kazan, undated, Harvard.

388 "brought in to rewrite my work": *M*, p. 174.

388 "rightful place": Ibid.

388 "O.K. I'll play it cool": Williams to Elia Kazan, undated, Harvard.

388 "correct": Ibid.

388 "The sick fury": Ibid.

390 "You know how suspicious": Williams to Elia Kazan, undated, Columbia.

390 "A sort of distortion was going on": *KAL*, p. 546.

390 "the most truly powerful and moving scene in the play": Williams to Elia Kazan, undated, 1959, LLC.

390 "A director of your skill": Ibid.

391 "was more moving": Elia Kazan to Williams, undated, Columbia.

391 "shallow": Elia Kazan to Williams, undated, 1959, LLC.

392 "If this be blockbustering": Walter Kerr, "Sweet Bird of Youth," *New York Herald Tribune*, Mar. 11, 1959.

392 "One of his finest dramas": Brooks Atkinson, "Portrait of Corruption," *New York Times*, Mar. 11, 1959.

392 "A play of overwhelming force": Richard Watts Jr., *New York Post*, Mar. 11, 1959.

392 "a tigress with the voice of a trumpet": Kerr, "Sweet Bird of Youth."

392 "Kazan was marvelous": Williams to Brooks Atkinson, Mar. 27, 1959, BRTC.

392 "He thought the writing": Williams to Elia Kazan and Jo Mielziner, Nov. 16, 1958, WUCA.

393 "Pride and dignity": Williams to Kenneth Tynan, undated, HRC.

393 "None of Mr. Williams' other plays": Kenneth Tynan, "Ireland and Points West," *The New Yorker*, Mar. 21, 1959, pp. 97–102.

393 "My complaint is that you didn't listen": Williams to Kenneth Tynan, undated, LLC.

393 "dismayed and alarmed": Tynan, "Ireland and Points West."

393 "to be somebody—anybody—else": Kenneth Tynan, *The Diaries of Kenneth Tynan*, ed. John Lahr (London: Bloomsbury, 2001), p. 9.

393 "Something always blocks me": LOA2, p. 175.

394 "Still a non-smoker": Tynan, *Diaries*, p. 15.

394 "Big Daddy rewritten": Williams to Kenneth Tynan, undated, 1959, LLC.

394 "You were obviously totally alienated": Williams to Kenneth Tynan, undated, 1959, LLC.

394 "As an artist grows older": Williams to Max Learner, undated, 1959, Harvard. About his critics, Williams continued to Lerner, "I think these detractors, so curiously impassioned in their attacks, far more impassioned than they could be if provoked by dullness, tedium, by that which is ordinary or pedantic—don't really know what they want. They pay homage to foreign theatre, mostly French. But when you examine their reviews even of Giraudoux, Camus and Anouilh, you are disturbed by a response which is more intellectual than emotional. And isn't theatre always addressed, first of all, to that part of us, wherever, whatever it is, that is capable of warm feeling?"

394 "You are tired": Williams to Elia Kazan, undated, WUCA.

394 "the rule of the straight line": Williams to Elia Kazan, undated, WUCA.

395 "back alone up the beanstalk": LOA2, p. 233.

395 "Are you driven and compelled": Williams to Elia Kazan, Mar. 28, 1959, WUCA.

395 "You are giving me the same advice": Williams to Elia Kazan, undated, WUCA.

395 "freedom from pressure": Williams to Audrey Wood, May 7, 1959, HRC.

395 "She has the Barrymore madness": Williams to Lady St. Just, July 8, 1959, *FOA*, pp. 161–62.

396 "like crazy": Williams to Audrey Wood, Oct. 30, 1959, HRC.

396 "Something suddenly triggers my nerves": Williams to Lilla Van Saher, Oct. 20, 1959, HRC.

396 "Oh, God, Gadg, I don't know": Williams to Elia Kazan, undated, HRC.

CHAPTER 7: KOOKHOOD

397 "Perhaps my heart has died in me": Williams to Hermione Baddeley, 1963, HRC.

397 "She had great honesty": "Playwrights: Unbeastly Williams," *Newsweek*, June 27, 1960. According to Gilbert Maxwell, Williams seemed discombobulated by Barrymore's death: he arrived in snowy New York wearing cotton slacks and no jacket, and he forgot the keys to his New York apartment, which had to be retrieved from his maid in Harlem. (Gilbert Maxwell, *Tennessee Williams and Friends: An Informal Biography* (Cleveland: World Publishing, 1965), p. 276.)

397 "Personality Deb No. 1": Mervin Block, "The Diana Barrymore Tragedy," *Chicago Tribune*, Jan. 26, 1960.

397 "Any time she wants to stop fooling around": Brooks Atkinson, "*Ivory Branch* Opens at the Provincetown," *New York Times*, May 25, 1956.

397 "I repeat my vow": Diana Barrymore and Gerold Frank, *Too Much, Too Soon* (London: Muller, 1957), p. 303.

398 "I don't mean this in a sacrilegious way": Dakin Williams, "Last Days," LLC.

398 "You can make a career": Beatrice Washburn, "D. B.: Bewitching," *Miami Herald*, June 1, 1959.

399 *The Poem of Two*: Williams to the Editors of *Time*, Feb. 10, 1960, HRC. The material resurfaced years later in *The Red Devil Battery Sign*.

399 "1960 is *our* year": Maxwell, *Tennessee Williams and Friends*, p. 264.

399 "Not knowing anything": D. Williams, "Last Days," LLC.

399 "She flashed it everywhere": George Keathley, unpublished Ms., JLC.

399 "held no surprise": *M*, p. 177.

399 "I thought Diana": Ibid., pp. 176–77.

399 "She read the part with a violence": Williams to Lucy Freeman, Feb. 27, 1963, LLC.

399 "the most heart-breaking point": D. Williams, "Last Days," LLC.

399 "My hatred for Kazan burns black": Ibid.

400 "The only strong men I had met": Barrymore and Frank, *Too Much*, p. 301.

400 "Just your brother matters to me": D. Williams, "Last Days," LLC.

400 two other friends: Marion Vaccaro and Dr. Hugh Hyatt.

400 "It was an idyll": D. Williams, "Last Days," LLC.

400 "If you don't watch out": Maxwell, *Tennessee Williams and Friends*, p. 283.

400 "sympathetic attachment": Williams to Brooks Atkinson, Mar. 1960, BRTC.

400 "Tom and I have talked of many things": D. Williams, "Last Days," LLC.

401 "I remember her wearing": *M*, p. 177.

401 "Diana loved me as a writer": Williams to Lucy Freeman, undated, LLC.

401 "deeply disturbed": *M*, p. 177.

401 "I didn't think she would take it so badly": Ibid.

401 "The two of them": Maxwell, *Tennessee Williams and Friends*, p. 266.

401 "It was half in jest": Ibid.

402 "sinking into [a cavern] gradually": LOA2, p. 272. Williams wrote to his then agent Bill Barnes about his memoirs: "I have a new title for them. 'Flee, Flee This Sad Hotel'—it's a quote from a poem by Anne Sexton, who borrowed it from

Rimbaud. Of course a hotel is a metaphor for my life, and flight from it—if not an impulse—at least an imminence." (Williams to Bill Barnes, May 31, 1973, HRC.)

402   "The human heart would never pass": LOA2, p. 322.

402   "isn't my best": Williams to Cheryl Crawford, undated, BRTC.

402   "to cast a kinder shadow": "Playwrights: Unbeastly Williams."

402   "the nightmare merchant of Broadway": Ted Kalem, "The Angel of the Odd," *Time*, Mar. 9, 1962.

402   "only violent melodramas": Ibid.

402   "After my analysis": David Levin, "Desperation," *World-Telegram and Sun*, Aug. 20, 1960.

402   "what have been called my 'black' plays": "Playwrights: Unbeastly Williams."

402   "more belief in the truth": Williams to Elia Kazan, undated, WUCA.

403   "We all have to be smart and lucky": LOA2, p. 321. *"Period of Adjustment* is so far below Mr. Williams's standard that it proves nothing one way or another," Brooks Atkinson wrote in the *New York Times Book Review* (Nov. 26, 1961). "His heart is not in this mediocre jest."

403   "one of those rare people": LOA2, p. 240.

403   "a girl with no looks": Ibid., p. 312.

403   "unintentionally unfair": Williams to Elia Kazan, Mar. 1963, WUCA.

403   "very often . . . misjudge Frank": Audrey Wood to Williams, June 11, 1963, HRC.

403   "It becomes difficult to distinguish": Charlotte Chandler, *The Girl Who Walked Home Alone: Bette Davis* (New York: Simon & Schuster, 2006), p. 233.

403   "he was an angel all during rehearsals": Williams to Elia Kazan, June 1959, WUCA.

403   "Frank made it clear": Ibid.

403   "I think Frank would be reluctantly willing": Williams to Christopher Isherwood, Dec. 27, 1959, Huntington.

404   "in voices turned softer": *CP*, "A Separate Poem," pp. 80–81.

404   "When we speak to each other": Ibid.

404   "The Horse is on pills": Williams to Lady St. Just, August 10, 1960, *FOA*, p. 165.

405   "of passing out stoned": Williams to Robert MacGregor, 1963, LLC.

405   "To beg a question": Frank Merlo, unpublished poem, 1960, THNOC.

405   "looking rather shaky": Arthur Gelb, "Williams and Kazan and the Big Walk-Out," *New York Times*, May 1, 1960.

405   most important theatrical collaboration: Only Lloyd Richards's collaboration with August Wilson approaches the depth and import of Williams and Kazan's.

406   "sight unseen and unread": Audrey Wood to Tennessee Williams, Oct. 16, 1959, HRC.

406   "I tried my best": Arthur Gelb, "Williams and Kazan and the Big Walk-Out," *New York Times*, May 1, 1960. "I offered to do the play when I was through with my movie, but Tennessee was not willing to wait till then," Kazan told the *New York Times*.

406   "signal that I preferred working with Inge": *KAL*, p. 595. "In my heart it is hard for me to like any playwright who is still writing plays. Miller, yes! Inge, sometimes . . . an ugly effect of the competitive system. They have to stun me with splendor that drives vanity out!" (Williams to Audrey Wood, Aug. 1955, *L2*, p. 592.)

406   "Tennessee had shown me": *RBAW*, p. 222.

406   "I did promise to do your play": Elia Kazan to Williams, Apr. 22, 1960, *KOD*, pp. 134–35.

406 "I'm furious at the way": Ibid., p. 134.

408 "You haven't a right in the world": Ibid., pp. 134–35.

408 "a very charged man": Whitney Bolton, "Williams Talks on Violence," *Philadelphia Inquirer*, Feb. 1, 1959.

408 "Frankly, it appears to me": Elia Kazan to Williams, Apr. 22, 1960, *KOD*, pp. 135–36.

408 "The first and in part third are authentic Williams": Claudia Cassidy, "Some Heady Virtuosity Even Tho Williams' 'Bird' Flies Half Mast," *Chicago Tribune*, Apr. 26, 1959.

409 "prostitution": *CWTW*, p. 72.

409 "Kazan's ending": See *KAL*, p. 544. Also, see "Note of Explanation," "Act Three (Broadway Version)," in Tennessee Williams, *Cat on a Hot Tin Roof and Other Plays* (London: Penguin Classics, 1976), p. 107.

409 "I was surprised to find": Elia Kazan to Williams, undated, Columbia.

409 "The charge that Kazan has forced me": Gelb, "Williams and Kazan."

409 "I thought": Elia Kazan to Williams, Apr. 22, 1960, *KOD*, p. 137.

410 "I wanted to be the unchallenged source": *KAL*, p. 660.

410 "I no longer gave a damn": Ibid., p. 596.

410 "Something has happened to me": Elia Kazan to Williams, undated, WUCA.

410 "vowed not to look back": *KAL*, p. 596.

410 "just as brilliant as Kazan": Gelb, "Williams and Kazan."

410 "I want you back": Williams to Elia Kazan, undated, WUCA.

410 "Please stay with me in spirit": Williams to Elia Kazan, undated, WUCA.

410 "I think our friendship will survive": Elia Kazan to Williams, undated, Columbia.

411 "I don't know": Williams to Elia Kazan, undated, Harvard.

412 "We young directors": Williams to Cheryl Crawford, 1961, LLC.

412 "You monster": Williams to Elia Kazan, undated, Harvard. In 1962, when Kazan became co-artistic director of the newly formed Repertory Theater of Lincoln Center, intended, in the early fizzy months of the Kennedy presidency, to be a national theater, Williams was one of two living American playwrights Kazan asked to inaugurate the enterprise. "We really need your relationship, BADLY," Kazan wrote to him. "It won't be much of a repertory-theatre-aspiring-to-be–a-National Theatre if we don't do your plays. And we just must do one the very first season, straight off number one or number two. . . . We want to make Lincoln Center, among other things, a place where a Williams play can be seen every year, the 'successes' and the most far-out things you can write, a place where these pieces live by being constantly played. . . . It would be a stunning blow to us, to me, if we don't get some of your new plays and all of your old ones. . . . We'll do right by them." (Elia Kazan to Williams, Apr. 25, 1962, Columbia.) Williams declined. "What I'm doing now is a reflection of how I am now, which is so far from well," he wrote back. (Williams to Elia Kazan, undated, Harvard.) Arthur Miller accepted; his play *After the Fall* opened the theater.

412 "on more than the pumpkins": Williams to Lady St. Just, Dec. 25, 1960, *FOA*, p. 169.

412 "I crept around like that man": Ibid.

412 "a turbid stew of immiscible ingredients": John McCarten, "Tennessee Tries a Tender Pitch," *The New Yorker*, Nov. 19, 1960.

412 a movie sale: Released by MGM in 1962, directed by George Roy Hill, and starring Jane Fonda and Tony Franciosa.

412   "I figure that I have had my day": Williams to Lady St. Just, Dec. 25, 1960, *FOA*, p. 169.

412   "would have saved": Williams to Audrey Wood, undated, HRC.

412   no longer sufficient: JLI with Frank Corsaro, 2011, JLC.

413   " 'Your friend—' ": *CS*, "The Night of the Iguana," p. 243.

413   "the strangling rope of her loneliness": Ibid., p. 229.

413   "a bit of a louse": JLI with Frank Corsaro, 2011, JLC.

413   "As we're talking": Ibid.

413   "an expression of my present": Williams to Frank Corsaro, May 13, 1960, Morgan.

413   "more of a dramatic poem": *CWTW*, p. 86.

414   "a football squad of old maids": LOA2, p. 331.

414   "the underworlds of all places": Ibid., p. 397.

414   "man of God, on vacation": Ibid., p. 378.

414   "how to live beyond despair": *CWTW*, p. 104.

414   "Ethereal, almost ghostly": LOA2, p. 338.

414   "a dainty teapot": *CS*, "Night of the Iguana," p. 230.

414   "the oldest living": LOA2, p. 377.

414   "a sense of really having a home": Williams to Katharine Hepburn, Feb. 16, 1961, Delaware.

414   "When he died": Ibid.

414   "When the old keep serenity": Williams to Frank Corsaro, undated fragment, LLC.

415   "dedicated to the memory": Tennessee Williams, "Three Acts of Grace," HRC.

415   carnal: The young writer ejaculates on Edith. "She felt a wing-like throbbing against her belly, and then a scalding wetness. Then he let go of her altogether." Later, she lies on her bed reflecting on the incident. "Just before falling asleep she remembered and felt again the spot of dampness, now turning cool but still adhering to the flesh of her belly as a light but persistent kiss. Her fingers approached it timidly. They expected to draw back with revulsion but were not so affected. They touched it curiously and even pityingly and did not draw back for a while. *Ah, Life,* she thought to herself and was about to smile at the originality of this thought when darkness lapped over the outward gaze of her mind." (*CS*, "Night of the Iguana," pp. 244–45.)

415   "See? The iguana?": LOA2, p. 421.

415   "It's horrible": Ibid., p. 387.

415   "My life has cracked up on me": Ibid., p. 343.

415   "I am a little bit in the condition": Williams to Frank Corsaro, Mar. 13, 1960, Morgan.

415   "We—live on two levels": LOA2, p. 380.

415   "Don't ask me why": Williams to Audrey Wood, Oct. 30, 1959, HRC.

416   "Hannah is not a loser": Williams to Frank Corsaro, Aug. 17, 1960, Morgan.

416   "She is profoundly understanding": Ibid.

416   "Passion Play performance": LOA2, p. 403.

416   "understanding and kindness": Williams to Lilla Van Saher, Oct. 20, 1959, HRC.

416   "As we were working": JLI with Frank Corsaro, 2011, JLC.

416   "I'm tired, the energy's low": Williams to Brooks Atkinson, Sept. 2, 1959, BRTC.

417   "I think the play for Spoleto": Williams to Audrey Wood, May 7, 1959, HRC.

417   "Tenn dear, you're right": Anna Magnani to Williams, Nov. 23, 1961, Columbia.

417   Brooks Atkinson, who retired: "I'm almost inclined to follow you into retirement," Williams wrote to Atkinson (June 3, 1960, BRTC).

417 "In all the letters and phone-calls and talks": Williams to Audrey Wood, undated, HRC.

417 "Dear Horse: or Saint Francis": Williams to Frank Merlo, Jan. 2, 1961, Columbia.

418 "I set myself down at our patio table": *M*, pp. 184–85.

418 "When people I care for turn violent": Gore Vidal, *Palimpsest: A Memoir* (New York: Random House, 1995), p. 405.

418 "There was no use in saying": Ibid.

418 "declined to eat": *M*, pp. 185–86.

419 "Are you going to leave me": Ibid., p. 186.

419 "I'm not any longer": Williams to Audrey Wood, Mar. 13, 1961, HRC.

420 "I have never stopped loving": Ibid.

420 Marion Vaccaro: Williams first met and became friends with Marion Vaccaro in 1941 when her mother allowed him to stay in slave quarters at the back of "Tradewinds," her 125-year-old mansion in Key West. Vaccaro, who had been expensively educated at the Hewlett School and Rosemary Hall, and who had attended both the University of Michigan and Smith College, was lively and charming, with an interest in the arts. For a time, before marrying Regis Vaccaro, the heir to the Standard Fruit and Steamship Company—thus her nickname "The Banana Queen"—she worked for the impresario Florenz Ziegfeld and his wife, the actress Billie Burke, as a tutor to their daughter. Williams kept a photo of Vaccaro from these early days by his Key West bedside. Hard drinking and high loving, she was the model of Cora in his short-story "Two on a Party." She remained a close and big-hearted friend to Williams up to her death in 1970. (See Philip C. Kolin, "Tenn and the Banana Queen: The Correspondence of Tennessee Williams and Marion Black Vaccaro," *Tennessee Williams Annual Review*, no. 8 (2006), available at www.tennesseewilliamsstudies.org/archives/2006/07kolin.htm.)

420 "Perhaps I will meet": Williams to Robert MacGregor, Apr. 30, 1960, LLC.

420 "terrific waves of loneliness": Williams to Audrey Wood, undated, THNOC.

420 "the dreadful facts of my life": Ibid.

420 "I gave my love": Ibid.

420 "the answering party said": Williams to Audrey Wood, Apr. 1961, THNOC.

420 "I suppose he is so revolted": Williams to Robert MacGregor, Apr. 30, 1961, LLC.

420 "Sic Transit Gloria Swanson": Williams to Audrey Wood, Apr. 29, 1961, HRC.

420 "I've always tried to respect his pride": Williams to Audrey Wood, May 7, 1961, HRC.

421 "Magnani says": Williams to Frank Corsaro and Charles Bowden, May 19, 1961, Morgan.

421 "Don't! Break!": LOA2, p. 346.

421 "I think of a home": Ibid., p. 414.

421 "The Horse has done just about all": Williams to Lady St. Just, undated (ca. 1961), *FOA*, p. 175.

422 "In Iguana you can have your finest play": Cheryl Crawford to Williams, Aug. 6, 1960, Houston. After the Actors Studio workshop, Crawford reported to Wood, "Sunday night Ten saw Iguana and was so overcome he cried." (Cheryl Crawford to Audrey Wood, May 31, 1960, HRC.)

422 "During the intermission": Cheryl Crawford, *One Naked Individual: My Fifty Years in the Theatre* (Indianapolis: Bobbs-Merrill, 1977), pp. 197–98.

422 "This play is a dramatic poem": Ibid., p. 199.

422 "I never thought that you really wanted": Ibid.

422   "I want to be around for the staging": Williams to Charles Bowden, Sept. 28, 1960, HRC.

422   "a terrifically dynamic man": Bowden with H. Ridgely Bullock, his producing partner at the time, had mounted *Hotel Paradiso*, *Caligula*, *Season of Choice*, and a revival of *Fallen Angels*. "He truly 'digs' the play and will stop at nothing to give it the finest possible production. He doesn't just call Hepburn and send her re-writes, he flies out to see her, for instance, and he is still operating, I understand, without a signed contract, which makes it all the more touching and impressive." (Williams to Audrey Wood, Mar. 13, 1961, HRC.)

423   "silly putty—a silly person": JLI with Frank Corsaro, 2011, JLC.

423   "My scripts at this stage": Williams to Charles Bowden, undated, HRC.

423   "The revisions extended certain areas": JLI with Frank Corsaro, 2011, JLC.

423   "undigested" scraps from a dung hill: Shannon: "Then she noticed, and I noticed too, a pair of very old natives of this nameless country, practically naked expect for a few filthy rags, creeping and crawling about this mound of . . . and . . . occasionally stopping to pick something out of it, and pop it in their mouths." (LOA2, p. 422.)

423   "I said, 'What do I do with them?' ": JLI with Frank Corsaro, 2011, JLC.

423   "Despite your talent": Williams to Frank Corsaro, July 1960, HRC.

424   "aristocracy of spirit": Williams to Katharine Hepburn, Feb. 15, 1961, Delaware.

424   "I wrote the part of Hannah for Hepburn": Williams to Elia Kazan, undated, Harvard.

424   "absolutely impossible": Williams to Katharine Hepburn, Jan. 5, 1961, Delaware.

424   "You're a hustler": LOA2, p. 371.

424   "pitch": Williams to Katharine Hepburn, Jan. 5, 1961, Delaware.

424   "an abortion": Ibid.

424   "I don't mean to put down": Ibid.

424   "Yes, I know, I'm coming on": Williams to Katharine Hepburn, Feb. 16, 1961, Delaware.

425   "Bit by bit": Ibid.

425   "You must understand something!": Dan Isaac, "Love in Its Purest Terms: Williams, Hepburn and Night of the Iguana," *Village Voice*, May 14, 1996.

425   "She won't give us more time": Ibid.

425   "that wonderful old bitch": Williams to Oliver Evans, 1961, HRC.

425   highest-paid woman in America: James Spada, *More Than a Woman: An Intimate Biography of Bette Davis* (New York: Warner Books, 1994), p. 361.

425   "Granted she is a name": Williams to Audrey Wood, Mar. 13, 1961, HRC.

425   "living definition of nature": Williams to Bette Davis, undated, *FOA*, p. 176.

426   "the play wasn't completely finished": JLI with Frank Corsaro, 2011, JLC.

426   "when she discovers": Ibid.

426   "I love the play": Williams to Charles Bowden, Oct. 4, 1961, HRC.

426   "longest and most appalling tour": *M*, p. 180.

426   "over made-up like a mailbox": John Maxtone-Graham, "Production Notes," Sewanee.

426   "No one was to go near": JLI with Frank Corsaro, 2011, JLC.

426   "We don't have to be friends": Ibid.

426   "a piece of superb one-upsmanship": Maxtone-Graham, "Production Notes," Sewanee.

426   "She was frightened to death": JLI with Frank Corsaro, 2011, JLC.

426 "she came up behind me": Ibid.

427 "I'm sick of this Actors Studio *shit"*: Maxtone-Graham, "Production Notes," Sewanee.

427 "When she is on a rampage": Ibid.

427 "This was the sight": JLI with Frank Corsaro, 2011, JLC.

427 "that she had an *artistic* difference": Maxtone-Graham, "Production Notes," Sewanee.

427 "a little red-rimmed around the eyes": Ibid.

428 "a wild comedy": JLI with Frank Corsaro, 2011, JLC.

428 "suffering from a wrenched knee": Barbara Leaming, *Bette Davis: A Biography* (London: Penguin Books, 1993), p. 230.

428 "She was only good on opening night": JLI with Frank Corsaro, 2011, JLC.

428 "She was really very disruptive": Spada, *More Than a Woman*, p. 482.

428 "La Davis": Leaming, *Bette Davis*, p. 229.

428 "Jessica Dragonet": Maxtone-Graham, "Production Notes," Sewanee.

428 "She was asking for rewrites": JLI with Frank Corsaro, 2011, JLC.

428 "I'm sorry to have to agree": Ibid.

428 "perfidy galore": Ibid.

428 "I can't help feeling": Maxtone-Graham, "Production Notes," Sewanee.

428 "IGUANA LIMPS INTO DETROIT": JLI with Frank Corsaro, 2011, JLC.

429 "Overlong, dreadfully overlong": Maxtone-Graham, "Production Notes," Sewanee.

429 "Frank is not a bad boy": Williams to Audrey Wood, Mar. 13, 1961, HRC.

429 "really didn't feel well": LLI with Charles Bowden and Paula Laurence, 1996, LLC.

429 "It's over between us!": JLI with Frank Corsaro, 2011, JLC.

429 "He is a handy thing": Williams to Oliver Evans, Nov. 1961, LLC.

429 seven stitches in Marion Vaccaro's hand: Ibid.

429 "He used to sit in front of me": *M*, p. 180.

431 "like a guardian": Ibid.

431 "He was starting for my throat": Ibid.

431 "had swollen up": Ibid., p. 181.

431 his rampaging paranoia: Donald Spoto, *The Kindness of Strangers: The Life of Tennessee Williams* (Boston: Little, Brown, 1985), p. 247.

431 "I'll have a drink": LLI with Charles Bowden and Paula Laurence, 1996, LLC.

431 "Frankie had dealt so well": JLI with Maureen Stapleton, 2005, JLC.

431 "a pharmacology of the lost": Mary F. Lux, "Tenn among the Lotus-Eaters: Drugs in the Life of Tennessee Williams," *Southern Quarterly* (Fall 1999), p. 117.

432 "I hope to get through this": Williams to Robert MacGregor, Apr. 30, 1961, LLC.

432 "I don't care if it's horse piss": Richard Reeves, *President Kennedy: Profile of Power* (New York: Simon & Schuster, 1993), p. 147.

432 revocation of Jacobson's medical license: Boyce Rensberger, "Amphetamines Used by a Physician to Lift Moods of Famous Patients," *New York Times*, Dec. 4, 1972.

432 Mellaril: *M*, p. 209. Besides the Mellaril, his daily cocktail of drugs included liquor, two Doriden tablets, and barbiturates.

432 "the Goforth Syndrome": Williams to Joseph Losey, Nov. 11, 1966, HRC.

432 "I felt as if a concrete sarcophagus": *M*, p. 208.

432 "Would you like to try it?": JLI with Frank Corsaro, 2011, JLC.

432 "EVEN FOR A MAN OF LESS TALENT": Claudia Cassidy, "Even for a Man of

Less Talent This Would Be a Bankrupt Play," On the Aisle, *Chicago Tribune*, Nov. 22, 1961.

433 "What is rather pathetic": John Maxtone-Graham, "Production Notes," Sewanee.

433 "punch-drunk with new pages": Mike Steen, *A Look at Tennessee Williams* (New York: Hawthorn Books, 1969), p. 67.

433 "Flushed with whisky": Maxtone-Graham, "Production Notes," Sewanee.

433 "I can't": JLI with Frank Corsaro, 2011, JLC.

433 "It was insane": Spada, *More Than a Woman*, pp. 486–87.

433 "that rather hysterical": Maxtone-Graham, "Production Notes," Sewanee.

434 "I can't agree with you": Williams to Bette Davis, Jan. 1962, BDC.

434 "Where have you been?": JLI with Frank Corsaro, 2011, JLC.

434 "You filthy *cunt!*": Ibid.

435 "I can feel vibrations": Maxtone-Graham, "Production Notes," Sewanee.

435 "He was a frazzled man": JLI with Frank Corsaro, 2011, JLC.

435 "We now have no director": Maxtone-Graham, "Production Notes," Sewanee.

435 "He told Williams": JLI with Frank Corsaro, 2011, JLC.

435 "unabashed disregard": Leaming, *Bette Davis*, p. 234.

435 "I think this creation of Maxine": Williams to Bette Davis, undated, BDC.

436 "giving color and visual poetry": Williams to Bette Davis, undated, BDC.

436 "It is made apparent that": Williams to Bette Davis, undated, BDC.

436 "she's ready for a night swim": Williams to Bette Davis, undated, BDC.

436 "I thought Maggie Leighton's final bit": Elia Kazan to Williams, Feb. 12, 1962, Columbia.

436 "Mr. Williams is the most gifted": Brooks Atkinson, "His Bizarre Images Can't Be Denied," *New York Times*, Nov. 26, 1961.

437 changed its theater critic: Ted Kalem (1961–1965) took over from Louis Kronenberger (1938–1961).

437 "in his best dramatic form": Ted Kalem, "The Angel of the Odd," *Time*, Mar. 9, 1962.

437 "I fell down": JLI with Frank Corsaro, 2011, JLC.

437 "allowed": Ibid.

437 "greeted by a flat, dead house ": Spada, *More Than a Woman*, p. 489.

437 "tattered and forlorn splendor": Walter Kerr, "First Night Report: 'The Night of the Iguana,'" *New York Herald Tribune*, Dec. 30, 1961.

437 "The day I left New York": Williams to Bette Davis, Jan. 1962, BDC.

437 "I want to tell you": Ibid.

438 "It is hard to say which was worse": Williams to Lady St. Just, Apr. 15, 1962, *FOA*, pp. 179–80. "All is chaos. La Winters has a fifth of Jack Daniel's Tennessee sour mash whiskey in her dressing room and nips all through the show. She never enters on cue."

438 "I'm *so* happy": Spada, *More Than a Woman*, p. 492.

438 "Thirty years experience as an actress": *Variety*, Sept. 21, 1962.

438 "We would sit there": JLI with Frank Corsaro, 2011, JLC.

438 "I turned around": Ibid.

438 "a minor league poet": LOA2, p. 379.

439 "the earth's obscene, corrupting love": Ibid., p. 424.

439 "beings of a golden kind": Ibid., p. 425.

439 "in a loud exalted voice": Ibid., p. 426.

439 "my . . . brain's going out now": Ibid., p. 423. "I am convinced the mind wears out more rapidly than the body." (Williams to Oliver Evans, 1962, LLC.)

439 "The play may seem meaningless": Harold Clurman, "Theatre," *Nation*, Jan. 27, 1962.

439 "writing at the top of his form": Howard Taubman, "'Night of the Iguana' Opens," *New York Times*, Dec. 29, 1961.

439 "at his poetic, moving best": John Chapman, "Williams Is at His Poetic, Moving Best with 'Night of the Iguana,'" *New York Daily News*, Dec. 29, 1961.

439 "perhaps the wisest play he has written": Kalem, "Angel of the Odd."

439 "one of [his] saddest, darkest": Richard Watts Jr., "Reveries of Tennessee Williams," *New York Post*, Dec. 29, 1961.

440 "I can make it down the hill": LOA2, p. 427.

440 "half leading half supporting him": Ibid.

440 "chuckles happily": Ibid.

440 "a dream of immobility": Walter Kerr, "Iguana: True Tone," *New York Herald Tribune*, Jan. 7, 1962.

440 "Shannon has given up": Leaming, *Bette Davis*, p. 235.

440 "Oh, God, can't we stop now?": LOA2, p. 427.

440 "I'm sorry you're not feeling well": Elia Kazan to Williams, 1962, Columbia.

440 "I think my kind of literary": *CWTW*, p. 99.

441 "I want to tell you tonight": "An Evening with Nichols and May" ran for 306 performances from Oct. 8, 1960, to July 1, 1961, at the John Golden Theatre. A record of the show, *An Evening with Mike Nichols and Elaine May* (directed by Arthur Penn, for Mercury Records, 1960), won the Grammy for Best Comedy performance in 1961.

441 "I didn't and don't blame him": Mike Nichols to John Lahr, Aug. 23, 2011, JLC.

441 "I'm so tired": Williams to Herbert Machiz, Oct. 1962, Columbia. Albee's play opened on October 13, 1962.

441 "one of those works": Ibid.

441 "astringency": Williams to Joseph Losey, Mar. 5, 1967, HRC.

441 "crazy with jealousy": *CWTW*, p. 98.

442 "While I'm in the theatre": Ibid.

442 "my answer to the school of Ionesco": Williams to James Laughlin, Sept. 24, 1962, JLC.

442 "They're not just funny": Ibid.

442 "dying monster": LOA2, p. 512.

442 "a poem of death": Williams to Herbert Machiz, Oct. 1962, Columbia.

442 "Ahhhhhhhh, meeeeeeeeee!": LOA2, p. 496.

442 "Which brings us to Mr. Williams' own predicament": Walter Kerr, "Williams' Reworked 'Milk Train' Is Back," *New York Herald Tribune*, Jan. 2, 1964.

442 "Courageous title, by the way": John Hancock to John Lahr, Nov. 11, 2011, JLC. When Jules Irving and Herbert Blau left the San Francisco Actor's Workshop to run the Vivian Beaumont Theater at Lincoln Center in New York, Hancock became then the youngest-ever American director of a repertory theater.

443 "'the daid Mistuh William'": Williams to John Hancock, undated, 1965, Harvard.

443 most difficult of his plays to write: Henry Hewes, *Best Plays of 1964–1965* (New York: Dodd, Mead, 1965).

443 "a golden griffin": LOA2, p. 495.

443 "Consume my heart away": Williams to Hermione Baddeley, undated, LLC.

443 "a portrait": Williams to John Hancock, undated (ca. 1965), Harvard.

443 "swamp-bitch": LOA2, p. 555.

443 "demented memoirs": Ibid., p. 512.

443 "We're working against time": Ibid., p. 497.

443 scattershot ramblings about her six husbands: Mrs. Goforth seems unclear about how many husbands she's had. Sometimes it's four, sometimes it's six.

443 "apparently never thought": Ibid., p. 512.

443 "A legend in my own lifetime": Ibid., p. 541.

444 "I beg you to play the broken queen": Williams to Hermione Baddeley, undated, LLC.

444 "death angel": LOA2, p. 549.

444 "a guest desperately wanted": Williams to Hermione Baddeley, Jan. 1963, HRC.

444 "Sometimes, once in a while": LOA2, p. 576.

444 "I can't explain Chris": Williams to John Hancock, undated, Harvard.

445 "There's the element of the con man": *CWTW*, p. 288.

445 "Everything about him": LOA2, p. 529.

445 "We don't all live in the same world": Ibid., p. 543.

445 "And one person's sense of reality": For the first Broadway staging, Kabuki-style screens turned the stage into a dreamy, disorienting world and reinforced the sense of separation between realms.

445 "It sounds like something religious": LOA2, p. 518.

446 "You have the distinction": Ibid., p. 575.

446 "You need somebody or something": Ibid., p. 576.

446 "Once the heart is thoroughly insulated": Williams to Kenneth Tynan, July 26, 1955, *TWLDW*, p. 307.

446 "Grab, fight, or go hungry": LOA2, p. 555.

446 "a shell of bone round my heart": Ibid., p. 579.

446 "Here's where the whole show started": Ibid., p. 563.

446 "burning me up like a house on fire": Ibid., p. 572.

447 "In my own writing": Williams to David Lobdell, Apr. 17, 1967, HRC.

447 "Anything solid takes the edge": LOA2, p. 545.

447 "One long-ago meeting between us": Ibid., p. 547.

447 "panicky when I": Ibid.

447 "can't stand the smell of food": Ibid., p. 554.

447 "*Chris opens the milk bottle*": Ibid., p. 571.

447 "We're all of us living in a house": Ibid., p. 548.

448 "That's what it means": Ibid., p. 582.

448 "the sound of shock": Harry Medved and Michael Medved, *The Hollywood Hall of Shame: The Most Expensive Flops in Movie History* (New York: Perigee Books, 1984), p. 107.

448 Joseph Losey's 1968 film adaptation *Boom!*: The film starred Elizabeth Taylor and Richard Burton. "You don't call something 'Boom!' (since 1945) and imply that one of the characters is an angel of death without having something nuclear in mind," John Hancock said. (JLI with John Hancock, 2012, JLC.)

448 "much better written than the play": *CWTW*, p. 288.

448 "*Don't leave me alone*": LOA2, p. 581.

448 "fierce life": Ibid.

449 "clothed in a god's perfection": Ibid., p. 501.

449 "You put on the clothes of a god": Ibid.

449 "Blackie, the boss is sorry": Ibid., p. 500.

449 "just barely marching": Williams to Marion Vaccaro, June 28, 1962, LLC.

449 "Angel": *M*, p. 188.

449   "He's a desperate young man": Williams to Robert MacGregor, Aug. 1, 1967, LLC.

449   "I was stacking books": LLI with Frederick Nicklaus, 1983, LLC.

449   "I have engaged a very gentle": Williams to Lilla Van Saher, Aug. 1962, HRC.

449   "soul-searching": LLI with Frederick Nicklaus, 1986, LLC.

450   "villa": Robert Hines to Nancy Tischler, undated, LLC.

450   "The 'fireworks' started immediately": Robert Hines to Nancy Tischler, June 2, 1996, LLC.

451   "Robert, Sir, do me the honor": Robert Hines to Nancy Tischler, undated, LLC.

451   "Frankie was hurt and stunned": Ibid.

451   "All quiet": Ibid.

451   "Tenn took to baiting Frankie": Robert Hines to Nancy Tischler, June 2, 1996, LLC.

451   "who understands life so well": Tennessee Williams, "Intimations of Mortality," THNOC. "Closing Time" is handwritten over the typed original title, "Intimations of Mortality" (an early one-act play with later revisions).

452   "It has, or seems to have": Williams to Andreas Brown, Feb. 23, 1962, HRC.

452   "has lost so much weight": Williams to Elia Kazan, Mar. 19, 1962, WUCA.

452   "I feel that if we didn't have to share": Williams to Lady St. Just, Apr. 15, 1962, *FOA*, p. 180.

452   "I may not be in the apartment": Williams to Frederick Nicklaus, May 6, 1962, LLC.

452   "I was as frightened to see him": *M*, p. 188.

452   "Frankie was on his best behavior": Ibid.

453   "I remained curiously resolute": Ibid.

453   "My young companion": *CP*, "Tangiers: The Speechless Summer," p. 139.

453   poem dedicated to "T.W.": Frederick Nicklaus, *The Man Who Bit the Sun* (New York: New Directions, 1964), p. 29.

453   ". . . You woke in the night": Frederick Nicklaus, "Tangier 1," in ibid., pp. 29–30.

453   "inept at anything of a practical nature": Williams to Andreas Brown, 1962, LLC.

454   "like a flea": Williams to Robert Hines, undated, LLC.

454   "The beauty of my companion": *M*, p. 187.

454   "internal bleeding": Williams to Lilla Van Saher, Aug. 16, 1962, HRC.

454   "I am still able to do my morning's work": Ibid.

454   "the Merlo situation": Williams to Robert MacGregor, Summer 1962, LLC.

454   contemplated pulling up stakes: Williams to Robert Hines, Sept. 1962, LLC.

454   "I'm still desperately looking": Williams to Andreas Brown, Sept. 17, 1962, THNOC.

454   "Get on your knees and pray": Williams to Herbert Machiz, Nov. 1962, Columbia.

454   "There was just too much double-talk": Williams to Hermione Baddeley, undated, HRC.

455   "Unless a miracle happens in Philly": Williams to Audrey Wood, undated, HRC.

455   "Mistuh Williams, He Dead": Richard Gilman, "Mistuh Williams, He Dead," *Commonweal*, Feb. 8, 1963.

455   "Why, rather than be banal": Ibid.

455   "The truth I guess": Williams to John Hancock, undated, Harvard.

455   "swollen up like a pumpkin": Williams to Robert MacGregor, Mar. 27, 1963, LLC.

455   "Suspect following circumstances: lung cancer": Ibid.

CHAPTER 8: WAVING *and* DROWNING

456 "Nobody heard him": Stevie Smith, "Not Waving but Drowning," in Stevie Smith, *Selected Poems*, ed. James MacGibbon (London: Penguin Books, 1978), p. 167.

456 "waiting shakily": Williams to Elia Kazan, Sept. 9, 1963, WUCA.

456 Key West doctors had attributed Merlo's exhaustion: Donald Spoto, *The Kindness of Strangers: The Life of Tennessee Williams* (Boston: Little, Brown, 1985), p. 255.

457 "the cumulative effect of passing 14 years": Williams to Lady St. Just, Apr. 15, 1962, *FOA*, p. 179. Although Merlo was a four-packs-a-day man, neither the doctors nor Williams made any connection between his smoking and the likelihood of cancer.

457 "I was stricken with remorse": *M*, p. 189.

457 "He was quite matter-of-fact": Ibid.

457 "I hung up": Ibid.

457 writer James Leo Herlihy: LLI with Frederick Nicklaus, 1985, LLC.

457 "Frankie was quite unaware": *M*, p. 190.

457 "the sudden and shocking illness of Frank": Williams to Edwina Williams, Feb. 25, 1963, LLC.

458 "I saw a white dove in a tree": *CP*, "Morgenlied," p. 143.

458 "waiting to take over the house": Williams to Lady St. Just, Apr. 5, 1963, *FOA*, p. 182.

459 "Tennessee got Frank a television set": LLI with Frederick Nicklaus, 1985, LLC.

459 "We pulled up to the house": Ibid.

459 When Merlo moved back: *M*, p. 190.

459 "I think Tennessee's and my relationship": LLI with Frederick Nicklaus, 1983, LLC.

459 "seemed annoyed that I remained": *M*, p. 191.

459 "swimmingly": LLI with Frederick Nicklaus, 1985, LLC.

459 "Tennessee was ready to go to bed": Ibid.

460 "the worst crisis in our relationship": LLI with Frederick Nicklaus, 1983, LLC.

460 "the air is as stimulating": Williams to Marion Vaccaro, undated, THNOC.

460 "Although he made no reference to it": Williams to Marian Vaccaro, 1963, THNOC.

460 "He has seen me through an intolerable period": Williams to Paul Bowles, June 13, 1963, LLC.

460 "All this, the cutting short": Williams to Marion Vaccaro, undated, THNOC. In *The Kindness of Strangers* (p. 251), Spoto contends that a telegram from Audrey Wood summoned Williams back to Key West, but there is nothing in Wood's memoir or her archive or in any Williams letter to support this claim. Williams's honorable instinct, it seems, was his own.

460 "I'd rather bear the heat of New York": Williams to Audrey Wood, ca. July 1963, Harvard.

460 "We do very little": Williams to Lady St. Just, Aug. 5, 1963, *FOA*, p. 184.

460 "Each night": *M*, p. 191.

460 "a little Hercules": Ibid., p. 193.

460 "It was a nightmare": Ibid.

460 "I remember seeing Frank": JLI with Alan U. Schwartz, 2009, JLC.

460 "had been in and out of Memorial": *M*, p. 193.

461 "my dear buddy": Maureen Stapleton and Jane Scovell, *A Hell of a Life* (New York: Simon & Schuster, 1995), p. 86.

461 "I said, 'He'll die this Thursday'": *M*, p. 193.

461 "like a hooked fish": Ibid., p. 194.

462 "You sat up in the chair next to mine": Tennessee Williams, "The Final Day of Your Life" (unpublished poem), THNOC.

462 "dreadful vigil": Ibid.

462 "Frankie, try to lie still": *M*, p. 193.

462 "pretended to sleep": Williams, "Final Day of Your Life," THNOC. In his memoirs, Williams says that Merlo "lay there silently." (*M*, p. 194.)

462 "The statement of habituation": *M*, p. 194.

462 "My name for him is Little Horse": *CP*, "Little Horse," p. 76.

462 "told him rather hysterically": *M*, p. 194.

462 "Tennessee just couldn't stand it anymore": LLI with Richard Leavitt, 1983, LLC.

462 "friends that were mine": Williams, "Final Day of Your Life," THNOC.

462 "quite drunk": Ibid.

462 "I usually answered the phone": LLI with Frederick Nicklaus, 1983, LLC.

463 "I am just beginning": Williams to Lady St. Just, Sept. 23, 1963, *FOA*, pp. 185–87.

463 "a recollection": Gilbert Maxwell, *Tennessee Williams and Friends: An Informal Biography* (Cleveland: World Publishing, 1965), p. 322.

463 "He was a man of honor": Ibid., pp. 322–24.

465 cemetery: Merlo is buried in Rosedale & Rosehill Cemetery in Linden, New Jersey. The birth year on Merlo's tombstone was intentionally misdated. As his niece, Josephine DePetris, explained, "The year he was born was 1922. When he was 15 years old he enlisted in the US Navy, lied about his age and changed his birth certificate (you had to be at least 16 years old to enlist then). . . . When he passed away the family continued to list his year of birth as 1921 thinking they would get in trouble with the military if the truth came out." (Josephine DePetris to John Lahr, July 4, 2013.)

465 "He was pacing the floor": LLI with Elaine Steinbeck, 1985, LLC.

465 "When Frankie was dying": Spoto, *Kindness*, pp. 258–59.

465 "made the talk somewhat dull": Alan U. Schwartz, "Mr. Williams and His Monkey" (unpublished), 2005.

465 "I don't know why this creature": *M*, p. 190.

465 "Tenn, your monkey": Schwartz, "Mr. Williams and His Monkey."

466 "My heart is heavy": Williams to Marion Vaccaro, Oct. 1963, THNOC.

466 "I have been very depressed": Williams to Dakin Williams and Edwina Williams, Nov. 14, 1963, LLC.

466 "Things were never the same": LLI with Frederick Nicklaus, 1983, LLC.

466 "The house, in fact the whole island": Williams to Audrey Wood, undated, 1963, LLC.

466 "almost a miracle": Williams to Audrey Wood, Oct. 31, 1963, LLC.

467 "to conclude my Broadway career": Ibid.

467 "I have no more illusions": Williams to Audrey Wood, July 18, 1963, LLC.

467 "one of your best": David Merrick to Williams, May 3, 1963, LLC.

467 "liked writers in the way": John Heilpern, *John Osborne: A Patriot for Us* (New York: Vintage, 2007), p. 203.

467 "Tony is a man of genius": Williams to Audrey Wood, undated, LLC.

467 "Every good female part": Brendan Gill, *Tallulah* (New York: Holt McDougal, 1972), pp. 83–84.

467 "more than slightly right": Tennessee Williams, "T. Williams's View of T. Bankhead," *New York Times*, Dec. 29, 1963.

467 "Tennessee has written a play": Gill, *Tallulah*, p. 84.

468 "It was an occasion when I might have lied": Williams, "T. Williams's View of T. Bankhead."

468 "Well, dahling, that's all right": Gill, *Tallulah*, p. 84.

468 "I saw exactly what Tennessee meant": Tony Richardson, *The Long-Distance Runner: A Memoir* (London: Faber & Faber, 1993), p. 145.

468 "It was either Tallulah": Ibid., p. 146.

468 "I have spent a sleepless night": Williams to Audrey Wood, undated, LLC.

469 Henry Willson: A gay agent credited with creating "his boys": Rock Hudson, Rory Calhoun, Guy Madison, and Tab Hunter.

469 "your beneficent witch-craft": Williams to Audrey Wood, Oct. 31, 1963, LLC.

469 "Everyone who mentions the production": Ibid.

470 "YOUR PERFORMANCE": Tab Hunter with Eddie Muller, *Tab Hunter Confidential: The Making of a Movie Star* (Chapel Hill, N.C.: Algonquin Books, 2006), p. 254.

470 "Fuck you!": Ibid., p. 247.

470 "Tallulah was the most unpleasant person": Richardson, *Long-Distance Runner*, p. 147.

470 "though they really couldn't be called that": Ibid.

470 "On the way to rehearsal": Ibid., p. 149.

470 "Loud or soft": Ibid., p. 147.

470 "Then, like a hideous old vulture": Ibid.

471 "Don't worry, darling": Ibid.

471 "Why the *fuck* don't you shut up!": Hunter, *Tab Hunter Confidential*, p. 251.

471 "So that's what the bitch": Richardson, *Long-Distance Runner*, p. 148.

471 "In the middle of this": Ibid.

471 "The second Milk Train": Williams to Herbert Machiz, undated, Columbia.

471 "There was no way": Richardson, *Long-Distance Runner*, p. 148.

471 "He showed a strange indifference": *M*, p. 199.

472 "I don't think you're insane": Ibid. Williams added parenthetically, "Which was true at the time he said it, if not quite always."

472 "I think it would kill Tallulah": Ibid., p. 200.

472 "desertion": Williams to Herbert Machiz, undated, 1964, LLC.

472 "Half the seats": Hunter, *Tab Hunter Confidential*, p. 253.

472 "For the kind of playgoer": "Tallulah and Tennessee," *Newsweek*, Jan. 13, 1964.

472 "Miss Bankhead was hoarse": John McCarten, "Durable Dame," *The New Yorker*, Jan. 11, 1964.

472 "not a performance": Walter Kerr, "Williams' Play Revamp 'Worse Than Original,'" *New York Herald Tribune*, Jan. 2, 1964.

472 an "appearance": After Bankhead was passed over to star in the film adaptation, *Boom!*—a part she felt she had "originated"—she stopped speaking to Williams. Shortly before she died, in 1968, she happened to be in Miami when *Boom!* was playing. She hired a car to take her to Williams's Key West home, and then she walked up to the front door in a mink coat. "I shouted, 'Tallu, baby! Come in,'" Williams told Dotson Rader, who reported the conversation in *Tennessee: Cry of*

the Heart. "She didn't move. She just stood there glaring at me like a mongoose at a snake. And then she said . . . 'Mr. Williams, I have come to tell you that I have just seen that *dreadful* movie they made of your *terrible* play!' And that was the last time I ever saw her." (Dotson Rader, *Tennessee: Cry of the Heart* (Garden City, N.Y.: Doubleday, 1985), p. 172.)

472 "I felt very badly about leaving New York": Williams to Dakin Williams, Feb. 29, 1964, LLC.

472 "Stoned Age": *M*, p. 212.

472 "It occurred in protracted stages": Ibid., p. 203.

472 "The colored lights": Williams to Audrey Wood, Mar. 4, 1944, *L1*, p. 516.

473 "I work but I have no faith left": Williams to Sidney Lanier, Jan. 21, 1964, THNOC.

473 "I am floundering": Williams to Frederick Nicklaus, Apr. 15, 1964, Columbia.

473 "an extended visit to Grant's Tomb": Marion Vaccaro to Charles Bowden, May 1964, LLC.

473 "I came for a weekend": Ibid.

473 "I have been hoping each day": Charles Bowden to Marion Vaccaro, June 18, 1964, LLC.

474 "He was in such a depressed condition": Marion Vaccaro to Henry Field, Sept. 9, 1964, LLC.

474 "bitten by the culture bug": Williams to Paul Bowles, Sept. 1964, LLC.

474 "He calls me": Ibid.

474 "To believe in pills": Williams to Paul Bowles, Sept. 18, 1964, LLC.

474 "Tom came here to dinner": Paula Laurence to Marion Vaccaro, Sept. 17, 1964, LLC.

475 "I am going into rehearsal": Williams to Lady St. Just, Jan. 20, 1965, *FOA*, p. 190.

475 lost his audience: "I don't have an audience, you see. I had one once, but I lost it in the 60's." Williams, *Topeka Daily Capital*, Sept. 10, 1971.

475 "We are not soft people": Williams to Mary Hunter, Apr. 1943, *L1*, p. 439.

475 "matriculating in a school for the blind": LOA1, p. 400.

476 "We are on the verge of Armageddon": Harold Clurman, "The New Drama," *Nation,* Jan. 16, 1967.

476 "thrilling alienation": Arthur Miller, *Timebends: A Life* (London: Methuen, 1999), p. 542.

476 "Once again we were looking almost completely": Ibid.

476 "The new theatre is lunging": Stefan Kanfer, "White Dwarf's Tragic Fade-Out," *Life*, June 13, 1969.

476 "The permission that Williams helped create": JLI with Tony Kushner, 2011, JLC.

477 "Why pick on me?": Geoffrey Wansell, *Terence Rattigan: A Biography* (London: Oberon Books, 2009), p. 365.

477 "the Broadway audience has changed": Robert Brustein, "A Question of Identity," *New Republic*, Mar. 16, 1966.

477 "fits people and societies going a bit mad": *CWTW*, p. 218.

477 "It's harder as you get older": Ibid., p. 120.

478 "I decided they were right": Ibid., p. 157.

478 "Everything's southernmost here": Tennessee Williams, *The Gnadiges Fraulein* (New York: Dramatists Play Service, 1967), p. 6.

478 "You'd go a long way out of your way": Ibid., p. 10.

478   "with Caribbean blue eyes": Ibid., p. 4.

479   "POLLY: HOW": Ibid., p. 20.

479   Cubist parody of Southern Gothic: Williams called the play "a gothic comedy."

479   "Picasso designed it": Williams, *Gnadiges Fraulein*, p. 4.

479   symbolic triumph of the pratfall: "We'd enter a restaurant and before Tenn had
        had even one drink, he'd fall down," Maureen Stapleton recalled. "After a while
        he was always falling down." (Spoto, *Kindness*, p. 264.)

479   "gunfire dialogue": *CWTW*, p. 98.

479   blind in one eye: Alleane Hale, "The Gnadiges Fraulein: Tennessee Williams's
        Clown Show," in Philip C. Kolin, ed., *The Undiscovered Country: The Later
        Plays of Tennessee Williams* (New York: Peter Lang, 2002), p. 43.

479   "would not be out of place": Williams, *Gnadiges Fraulein*, p. 13.

479   "Her scroll has been charged": Ibid., p. 12.

479   "Having passed and long passed the zenith": Ibid., p. 18.

480   "Three fish a day": Ibid., p. 19.

480   "the competish": Ibid., p. 20.

480   "assumes the starting position": Ibid., p. 35.

480   "The Disunited Mistakes": Ibid., p. 5.

480   "incomprehensible evil": Spoto, *Kindness*, p. 265.

480   "didn't have a clue": Zoe Caldwell, *I Will Be Cleopatra: An Actress's Journey*
        (New York: W. W. Norton, 2001), p. 190.

480   Schneider confessed as much: Hale, "Gnadiges Fraulein," p. 42.

480   "who followed the printed script": Mike Steen, *A Look at Tennessee Williams*
        (New York: Hawthorn Books, 1969), p. 70.

480   "I had my arm in a sling": Ibid.

481   "*I doubt the audience will see*": Caldwell, *I Will Be Cleopatra*, p. 190. Caldwell
        also writes, "Three years later, in 1969, I went to Key West and there were the
        little gray clapboard houses blown at a slant by the gulf winds with two weathered
        rocking chairs on the veranda. There were the pelicans down at the dock compet-
        ing for fish. There were hippies dressed as Indians, and the sailors still had those
        tight bums. And inside the bars, there were quite a few leftover ladies with dyed
        hair, red lips, bright eye shadow, and shoes that belong to another time or some-
        one else—and, because of the heat, a lot of white powder was caked on their
        faces. Sad clowns. I realized that, like all great artists, Tennessee didn't write lies.
        . . . Artists make us stop and look."

482   "marvelous": Steen, *Look*, p. 120.

482   "The press hit me with all the ammo": *M*, p. 212.

482   "A brilliant talent is sleeping": Stanley Kauffmann, "Tennessee Williams Returns,"
        New York Times, Feb. 23, 1966.

482   "savage slapstick": Walter Kerr, "Kerr Reviews Two by Tennessee Williams," *New
        York Herald Tribune*, Feb. 23, 1966.

482   "Walter Kerr dismissed 'Gnadiges Fraulein'": *CWTW*, p. 235.

482   "they might have gained considerable esteem": Harold Clurman, "Slapstick Trag-
        edy," *Nation*, Mar. 14, 1966.

482   derisory reviews: "Pointless, pompous nightmare" (*Newsweek*); "an ordeal of
        tedium" (*Hollywood Reporter*); "pretentious . . . ludicrous. Why was 'Boom!' ever
        filmed in the first place?" (*Los Angeles Herald-Examiner*). Quoted in Harry Med-
        ved and Michael Medved, *The Hollywood Hall of Shame: The Most Expensive
        Flops in Movie History* (New York: Perigee Books, 1984), p. 109.

482 "I want to die": *RBAW*, p. 192.

482 "I would fall down often": *M*, p. 211.

483 "I was abandoned by friends": *CWTW*, p. 235.

483 "zombie": *M*, p. 210.

483 Carson McCullers: "To have known a person of Carson's spiritual purity and magnitude has been one of the great graces of my life." (Williams to Virginia Spencer Carr, Aug. 18, 1970, Delaware.)

483 "I did not pick him up": JLI with John Hancock, 2012, JLC.

483 "He confessed that he'd been furious": Ibid.

483 "in quite imminent danger": Murray Schumach, "Tennessee Williams Expresses Fear for Life in Note to Brother," *New York Times*, June 29, 1968.

483 "If anything of a violent nature": Ibid.

483 "Please check up on my son": Edwina Williams to Marion Vaccaro, Dec. 10, 1968, LLC.

483 "the life bit": Williams to David Lobdell, Aug. 22, 1965, LLC.

483 "I wrote it": *Courier-Journal and Louisville Times*, June 6, 1971.

483 "To play with fear": Tennessee Williams, *The Two-Character Play* (New York: New Directions, 1979), p. 2. All quotes from *The Two-Character Play* are from this edition.

483 "incomplete interior": Ibid., p. 1.

483 "insane": Ibid., p. 14.

483 "a play within a play within a play": Tom Buckley, "Tennessee Williams Survives," *Atlantic Monthly*, Nov. 1970, p. 164.

483 "So it's a prison": Williams, *Two-Character Play*, p. 59.

483   "If we can imagine summer": Ibid.

483 *"Do it while you still can!"*: Ibid., p. 63.

485 "Mishima told me then": Williams to Oliver Evans, undated, Harvard.

485 "been ravaged, without Vaseline": Williams to James Laughlin, Mar. 10, 1968, LLC.

485 "I am in a state of panic": Williams to David Lobdell, Jan. 1968, LLC.

485 "I don't believe God is dead": Williams to Robert MacGregor, Apr. 1968, LLC.

485 "He still is not taking care": Audrey Wood to Lady St. Just, July 16, 1968, *FOA*, p. 196.

485 "Everyday I work slowly": Williams to James Laughlin and Robert MacGregor, July 5, 1968, LLC.

485 "an artist's one-ness": Williams to Herbert Machiz, undated, THNOC.

486 "The Negative": Tennessee Williams, "The Negative" (unpublished poem), undated, Harvard.

486 "the constant unbearable": "MARK: The constant unbearable of. MIRIAM: *Mine*! MARK: *Mine! . . .*" Tennessee Williams, *In the Bar of a Tokyo Hotel* (New York: Dramatists Play Service, 1969), p. 23.

487 "total collapse of the nervous system": Ibid., p. 10.

487 "He is mad": Ibid., p. 30.

487 "adventure": Ibid., p. 22.

487 "crock": Ibid., p. 28.

487 "He's gone through drip": Ibid., p. 32.

487 finish each other's sentences: Walter Kerr's review contended that Williams "made a fetish of the unfinished sentence." (Walter Kerr, "The Facts Don't Add Up to Faces," *New York Times*, May 25, 1969.) "My incompleted sentences are

quite deliberate," Williams wrote back to Kerr. "I feel they give a quality of urgency to dialogue, even to monologues." (Williams to Walter Kerr, May 30, 1969, Wisconsin.)

487 "MIRIAM—Are we two people": Williams, *In the Bar of a Tokyo Hotel*, p. 24.

487 "MARK: For the first time": Ibid., p. 14.

488 "I don't complete many sentences": *CWTW*, p. 136.

488 "peculiarly humiliating doom": Williams to Herbert Machiz, Apr. 29, 1969, THNOC.

488 "but stumbles to his knees": Williams, *In the Bar of a Tokyo Hotel*, p. 12.

488 "Too soon after work": Ibid., p. 15.

488 "shaking, unbathed, unshaved": Ibid.

488 "demanding what I can't give": Ibid., p. 16.

488 "MIRIAM: You'll return to the States": Ibid., p. 23.

488 "I'll tell you something": Ibid., p. 36.

488 "be back in ten minutes": Ibid., p. 38.

489 letter to Herbert Machiz: On May 14, 1969, part of the letter was later reproduced in an ad in the *New York Times*.

489 "As Mark truthfully says": Williams to Herbert Machiz, May 14, 1969, LLC.

489 "MIRIAM: I have clipped flowers": Williams, *In the Bar of a Tokyo Hotel*, p. 23.

490 "I have, under my own name": Ibid., p. 30.

490 "Miriam appears to see": Ibid., p. 38.

490 "Released!": Ibid.

490 "Animation": Ibid., p. 39.

490 "What are your actual plans?": Ibid., p. 40.

490 "With abrupt violence": Ibid.

490 "He thought that he could create": Ibid.

491 "At this moment": *TWIB*, p. 285.

491 "broad hints in person and in print": Ted Kalem, "The Angel of the Odd," *Time*, Mar. 9, 1962.

491 "weakened by the flu": *Miami Herald*, Jan. 11, 1969.

491 "I also received the last rites": Williams to Robert MacGregor, Mar. 9, 1969, LLC. After his conversion, at night in Key West when he'd turn out his reading light, Williams told a friend, "I'd feel the presence of Our Lady sitting by my bed. Sad to think it was only two Doridens and a 100 milligram Mellaril tablet taking effect, I suppose. *Mais! Je suis une religieuse loute la meme vraiment dans ma coeur sacre violee.*" (Williams to Andrew Lyndon, Nov. 4, 1969, Harvard.)

491 "Salty Author Williams Takes Catholic Vows": *Miami Herald*, Jan. 11, 1969.

491 "Dear Father Joe": Williams to Ruth Guttman, Nov. 7, 1969, Harvard. "My conversion to The Roman Catholic Church was altogether sincere and remains so."

491 "He didn't understand": "Salty Author Williams Takes Catholic Vows," *Miami Herald*, Jan. 11, 1969. According to a letter written from the Archdiocese of Miami to the executive director of the Bishop's Committee for Ecumenical and Interreligious Affairs, Williams's baptism was a mistake. "Mr. Williams had previously been an Episcopalian and had been baptized. However, he insisted that Father LeRoy, S.J. of Key West baptize him, explaining that he wanted 'the full spiritual benefit of being received into the Catholic faith.' Father LeRoy did baptize him conditionally and admits and regrets his mistake. Father LeRoy is new in Key West and in the Archdiocese of Miami and perhaps had not seen the guidelines." (Rev. James D. Enright to Rev. Bernard F. Law, Feb. 6, 1969, LLC.)

491 "get my goodness back": *TWIB*, p. 285.

491 "Tenn thinks his conversion": *Miami Herald*, Jan. 18, 1969.

491 "the eventual, unavoidable doom": Williams to Herbert Machiz, Apr. 2, 1969, THNOC.

492 "He seemed to be interested only in stage movement": Williams to James Laughlin, May 4, 1969, LLC.

492 "Anne Meacham as Mark's wife": Harold Clurman, "Theatre," *Nation*, June 2, 1969.

492 "In the age of the heartless avant-garde": Jack Kroll, "Life Is a Bitch," *Newsweek*, May 26, 1969.

492 "almost too personal": Clive Barnes, "Williams Play Explores Decay of an Artist," *New York Times*, May 12, 1969.

492 "more deserving of a coroner's report": "New Plays," *Time*, May 23, 1969.

492 "Tennessee Williams appears to be": Stefan Kanfer, "White Dwarf's Tragic Fade-Out," *Life*, June 13, 1969.

492 "Tom, it's time for you": *M*, p. 213.

492 "Whatever the exact price was": *RBAW*, p. 197.

492 "Played out?": *New York Times*, June 10, 1969.

492 "I really began to crack": *M*, p. 216.

493 "I had an evening with very sad Tennessee": Yukio Mishima to Robert MacGregor, July 3, 1969, HRC.

494 "My condition had so deteriorated": Williams to Oliver Evans, undated, 1971, LLC.

494 "rollicking nature": *M*, p. 210.

494 "an almost suspect glamour": Ibid., p. 208.

494 "Tennessee always preferred someone": LLI with William Gray, 1986, LLC.

494 "He didn't look after him": LLI with Robert Hines and Jack Fricks, 1986, LLC.

494 "would get Tennessee knocked out": Ibid.

494 "There's a limit to what anybody": LLI with Dakin Williams, 1985, LLC.

494 "elected to be a zombie": *M*, p. 210.

495 "shooting up with Dr. Feelgood's amphetamines": LLI with Charles Bowden, 1996, LLC.

495 "very attractive to ladies": *M*, p. 210.

495 "perhaps . . . closest": Ibid., p. 208.

495 "During our nearly five years together": Ibid., p. 210.

495 "Tennessee made impossible demands": LLI with Dakin Williams, 1988, LLC.

495 "Tennessee, how do you dare live": *M*, p. 211.

495 "being a madman": Ibid.

495 "[Glavin] probably started": Ibid.

495 "three favorite modern plays": Williams to William Glavin, ca. Mar. 20, 1971, LLC.

495 "It isn't so much my life": Ibid. "It took a high level of desperate delusion to assign Glavin 'The Dance of Death.' The idea that he would've been able to read it and appreciate it in any way is crazy. He was actually kind of creepy to have around. I never heard Tennessee relate to him in any way about intellectual matters. The Tool Box, yes, Strindberg no." (John Hancock to John Lahr, May 17, 2012, JLC.)

496 "Old men go mad at night": *CP*, "Old Men Go Mad at Night," p. 85.

497 "He never knew where he was": *TWIB*, p. 290.

497 "He insisted someone": Spoto, *Kindness*, p. 283.

497 "The rest is not a blur": Williams to Andrew Lyndon, Nov. 4, 1969, Harvard.

497 "Dakin, an attempt will be made on my life": "Salty Author Williams Takes Catholic Vows," *Miami Herald*, Jan. 11, 1969.

499 "Queeny Towers": *CWTW*, p. 173.

499 "I thought Shirley was making": Spoto, *Kindness*, p. 283.

499 "thought he was in full control": LLI with Dakin Williams, 1985, LLC.

499 "a little Prussian officer in drag": *M*, p. 219.

499 "There was now, quite clearly": Ibid.

500 "He told me that I could sign a letter": LLI with Dakin Williams, 1985, LLC.

500 "by a wheel-chair with straps": *M*, p. 220.

500 "fainting as Tennessee was being wheeled": LLI with Dakin Williams, 1985, LLC.

500 running for the U.S. Senate: Dakin's campaign poster (in Tennessee Williams Papers at Harvard) read:

   DAKIN WILLIAMS FOR U.S. SENATOR
   Peace & Love Join GO-DAKE (Gun Owners for America; Stop Abortion Vote Dakin)

500 "Who are you?": *TWIB*, p. 293.

500 "It wasn't voluntary at all": Williams to Andrew Lyndon, Nov. 10, 1969, Harvard.

501 "a 2 by 4 situation": LOA1, p. 417.

501 "Where am I?": LLI with Dakin Williams, 1985, LLC. Williams disputed the story.

501 "every half hour by an intern": Williams to William Glavin, undated, LLC.

501 "Spooksville": Williams to Audrey Wood, Nov. 4, 1969, LLC.

501 "nightmare alley": Williams to William Glavin, undated, LLC.

501 "Upset the card table": LLI with Dakin Williams, 1985, LLC.

501 "I am a completely disenfranchised citizen": Williams to William Glavin, undated, LLC.

501 "convulsive seizures": Williams to Andreas Brown, Nov. 4, 1969, HRC.

501 seizures escalated to "heart attacks": *CWTW*, p. 175.

501 "The circumstances under which I was treated": Williams to Robert MacGregor, Aug. 19, 1970, Harvard.

502 "De Profundis 200,502": Williams to Audrey Wood, Nov. 4, 1969, LLC.

502 "I'm afraid I bear him malice": Williams to Paul Bowles, Dec. 23, 1969, Delaware.

502 "sort of a Quixote": Williams to Andrew Lyndon, Dec. 7, 1967, LLC.

502 "Brother Cain": Williams to Andrew Lyndon, Nov. 1969, Harvard.

502 "legalized fratricide": Williams to Robert MacGregor, Aug. 19, 1970, LLC.

502 "I know that you never intended": Williams to Dakin Williams, Nov. 11, 1970, LLC.

503 "Redemption from what?": *M*, p. 220.

503 "How terribly I've abused myself": Williams to James Laughlin and Robert MacGregor, Nov. 10, 1969, Harvard.

503 "'You say you do not sleep well'": *CP*, "What's Next on the Agenda, Mr. Williams?," p. 152.

504 "was fully aware of who Tennessee was": LLI with Dakin Williams, 1985, LLC.

505 "The worst may be over": Williams to William Glavin, undated, LLC.

506 "I was obviously quite ill": Williams to Audrey Wood, Oct. 29, 1969, HRC.

506 "Today, for the first time": Ibid.

506 "I'd planned to get a couple of suits": Williams to David Lobdell, Nov. 12, 1969, LLC.

507 "sprung": Williams to Andrew Lyndon, Nov. 1969, Harvard.

507 "The prospect of early release": Ibid.

507 "My mind is quite clear": Williams to Andrew Lyndon, Nov. 10, 1969, Harvard.

507 "Perhaps that's for the best": Williams to Paul Bowles, Dec. 11, 1969, LLC.

507 "to ship Glavin off": Williams to Audrey Wood, Feb. 1970, LLC.

507 "With his facile Irish charm": Ibid.

508 "without my knowledge or authorization": Williams to Dakin Williams, Feb. 4, 1970, LLC.

508 "at best, he's pitiable": Williams to Jo Mielziner, Mar. 20, 1971, Harvard.

508 "Nobody knows the true desolation": Ibid. Williams's disenchantment with "the Charming Irishman," as he began to refer to Glavin in letters, was compounded in February 1970 when Glavin didn't come to Williams's aid in an unprovoked bar fight during which Williams was thrown against a wall and the right side of his head was badly bruised. "A vicious-looking ape of a man at a bar began glaring at me. He got up and said, 'Will you step outside?' I said: 'Why not?' and followed him out," Williams explained to Wood. "Glavin remained in the bar, sitting, until two strangers drove the man away from me. They then took me home." Williams added, "He is not only a con-man of the first water, but a dangerous one, and one that is clever as the 'Heathen Chinee.'" (Williams to Audrey Wood, Feb. 1970, HRC.)

508 "Tennessee wanted out": JLI with Dotson Rader, 2013, JLC.

508 "most of the stuff": Williams to Audrey Wood, Nov. 4, 1969, LLC.

508 "Dear, dear Tenn": Audrey Wood to Williams, Nov. 9, 1969, HRC.

508 "On to the future": Ibid.

CHAPTER 9: THE LONG FAREWELL

509 "Time betrays us": LOA1, p. 809.

509 "was choppy as hell": George Keathley, unpublished Ms., JLC.

509 "Tennessee had been obstreperous": Ibid.

509 "sort of like Sister Elizabeth": Williams to Cheryl Crawford and Paul Bigelow, May 29, 1971, Columbia.

509 "petrified": Williams to Oliver Evans, May 21, 1971, LLC.

510 "It's a cold world without you": Williams to Lady St. Just, Dec. 2, 1970, FOA, p. 221.

510 "The results were awful": Keathley, unpublished Ms., JLC.

511 "He could not respond": Ibid.

511 "We should not again make the mistake": Audrey Wood to Williams, Nov. 11, 1970, LLC.

511 "In one of our arguments": Keathley, unpublished Ms., JLC.

511 "Did you notice how Audrey was?": FOA, p. 231.

511 "an uncanny sense": NSE, p.132.

511 "Tennessee, I have a thought": Keathley, unpublished Ms., JLC.

512 "will to manage": NSE, p. 131.

512 "too much domination": Ibid.

512 "Now Williams whirled on her": Keathley, unpublished Ms., JLC.

512   "I became a sort of madman": *M*, p. 228.

512   "quiet ferocity": Ibid.

512   screaming hysterically: Williams acknowledged as much to St. Just a few weeks later, when he recounted another outburst, which he referred to as "one of my really apocalyptic rages the sort usually reserved for 'the Widow' [Wood]." (Williams to Lady St. Just, July 23, 1971, *FOA*, p. 232.)

512   "And you, you bitch": Keathley, unpublished Ms., JLC.

512   "No one knew what to say": Ibid.

512   "For the first time in all our years together": *RBAW*, p. 200.

512   "to get the hell out of there": Ibid.

512   "That bitch!": Ibid.

512   "After such a trauma": Ibid.

513   "I have been through similar Williams scenes": Ibid., pp. 200–201.

513   "'Don't come'": JLI with Alan U. Schwartz, 2009, JLC.

513   "Dear, dear Maria": Audrey Wood to Maria St. Just, Aug. 6, 1963, Columbia. Wood was proprietary about Williams and quick to scuttle loose talk about any rift. To the *New York Daily News*'s columnist Charles McHarry, who alleged in an item that her relationship with Williams's might "be over," she wrote, "I don't know where you picked up this bit of misinformation, but I am happy to say that Mr. Williams and I have been working together since 1937 and the relationship has continued for all these years through eleven full-length plays. It would be fine one day if you would run a correction, if you please." (Audrey Wood to Charles McHarry, Mar. 19, 1962, HRC.)

513   "DEAREST AUDREY": Williams to Audrey Wood, Mar. 28, 1963, HRC.

514   "Tenn's defection": James Laughlin to Audrey Wood, Aug. 21, 1971, HRC.

514   "I wonder what part": James Laughlin to Audrey Wood, Oct. 1, 1971, HRC.

514   "I don't believe": Dotson Rader, *Tennessee: Cry of the Heart* (Garden City, N.Y.: Doubleday, 1985), p. 42. Rader adds in a letter, "Peter Glenville, who directed 'Out Cry' on Broadway in 1973, told me that Maria was the one behind the sacking of Audrey. Milton Goldman, the head of theatre department of ICM, agreed with that assessment." (Dotson Rader to John Lahr, Oct. 1, 1971, JLC.)

514   "she could share": Williams to Ardis Blackburn and Oliver Evans, July 26, 1971, LLC.

514   "I find myself thinking of you": Williams to Audrey Wood, Mar. 1970, HRC.

514   "I had stupidly feared": Williams to Lady St. Just, Mar. 16, 1970, *FOA*, p. 199.

515   It had gone undelivered: *FOA*, p. 198.

515   unavailable to Williams: "You haven't heard from me by mail in any detail primarily because each time you have written me you have indicated you were going on to another address and when you gave your next stop there was no reference to any hotel or how I can reach you. So please understand it has not been negligence on my part," Wood wrote to Williams. (Audrey Wood to Williams, Nov. 11, 1970, HRC.)

515   "little faith left in my own judgment": Williams to Audrey Wood, July 1970, LLC.

515   "My agent Audrey Wood": *CWTW*, p. 190.

515   "You have written a poem of extreme": Williams to Lady St. Just, May 31, 1971, *FOA*, p. 227.

515   "TENNESSEE WILLIAMS UNFAIR TO HIS BROTHER": JLI with Dotson Rader, 2013, JLC.

515   "I'll never understand": Williams to Audrey Wood, Sept. 25, 1970, LLC.

515   "in on the conspiracy": Williams to Lady St. Just, Nov. 9, 1970, *FOA*, p. 218.

515 "I have a suspicion": Williams to Audrey Wood, May 26, 1970, HRC.

515 "Once she got the inkling": John Lahr, "The Lady and Tennessee," *The New Yorker*, Dec. 19, 1994, p. 85.

515 "Obviously Audrey has a pair of wire clippers": Lady St. Just to Williams, Aug. 1, 1970, *FOA*, p. 206.

515 *"amitié amoureuse"*: *FOA*, p. 7.

516 "Remember me as one of your clients": Williams to Audrey Wood, July 7, 1970, LLC.

516 "I knocked Audrey's little hat": Williams to Lady St. Just, Aug. 14, 1970, *FOA*, p. 206.

516 "DO NOT BE CONCERNED": Williams to Frank Roberts, Aug. 25, 1970, Columbia.

516 "a forsaken creature": Williams to Audrey Wood, Sept. 25, 1970, LLC.

516 "It appears for all practical purposes": Williams to Lady St. Just, Sept. 29, 1970, *FOA*, p. 209.

516 "Naturally, I never took the fifteen percent": *FOA*, p. 211.

516 "one of her Old Testament furies": Williams to Lady St. Just, Sept. 24, 1970, ibid., p. 208.

517 "Somehow we must circumvent": Williams to Lady St. Just, Jan. 15, 1971, ibid., p. 222.

517 "by hook or crook": Williams to Audrey Wood, July 7, 1970, HRC.

517 "for the 94th time": Williams to Audrey Wood, Nov. 11, 1970, HRC.

517 "I would like *you* to act": Williams to Alan U. Schwartz, Jan. 27, 1971, LLC.

517 "Audrey informed me on the phone": Ibid.

517 "He is an ethical idiot": Williams to Audrey Wood, Oct. 2, 1970, LLC.

517 "Why didn't anyone tell me?": Williams to Audrey Wood, Oct. 2, 1970, HRC.

518 "Tennessee was adamant": Rader, *Tennessee*, p. 74.

518 "To quote a line now deleted": Williams to Audrey Wood, undated (ca. July 1971), HRC.

519 "a temporary holding action": JLI with Dotson Rader, 2012, JLC. "I had a rather turbulent break-up with Audrey Wood in Chicago," Williams wrote to his mother. "This had been developing for a long time, at least ten years, as she has not been helping at all. Now I have a new agent who is much more attentive to my professional matters and also much more agreeable." (Williams to Edwina Williams, Nov. 5, 1971, LLC.)

519 "Then something happened": *RBAW*, p. 202.

519 "There was no way": JLI with Arthur Kopit, 2012, JLC.

519 "She was way more than an agent": Ibid.

519 "weird tribe": David Lobdell to Patricia Lobdell Hepplewhite, Dec. 6, 1970, LLC.

520 "There is much about her": *NSE*, p. 131.

520 obligation to be great: "My need for success is different now. It's really more a case of acceptance than success. I don't even think anything I do is a masterpiece anymore. You either get by with it or you don't." Craig Zadan, "Tennessee Williams: The Revitalization of a Great Dramatist," *Show*, May 1972.

520 "She found it quite easy": Williams to Floria Lasky, Sept. 5, 1971, LLC.

520 "the Dixie Buzz Bomb": Williams to unknown, Oct. 1972, THNOC.

520 "I feel that since we've met": Williams to Bill Barnes, Apr. 14, 1971, THNOC.

520 "He is a thoroughly dangerous": Charles Bowden to Lady St. Just, May 21, 1972, HRC.

520 "I need the fact": Williams to Bill Barnes, Apr. 14, 1971, THNOC.

520 "boiling with something": Williams to Floria Lasky, Sept. 5, 1971, LLC.

520 "I am making a number of changes": Ibid.

521 "just this side of final": Williams to William Hunt, Dec. 24, 1971, LLC.

521 "minor": Williams to James Laughlin, ca. July 1972, LLC.

521 "I have no intention": Williams to William Hunt, Dec. 24, 1971, LLC.

521 "The thing you mustn't lose in life": Mel Gussow, "Williams Looking to Play's Opening," *New York Times*, Mar. 31, 1972.

521 "it repeats the mood and mode": Harold Clurman, "Small Craft Warnings," *Nation*, Apr. 24, 1972.

521 "I don't want to be involved": *CWTW*, p. 146.

521 "not a person dedicated": Ibid., p. 132.

521 "Young people were the world": John Weisman, "Sweet Bird of Youth at 60," *Detroit Free Press*, Feb. 20, 1972.

522 "the only thing at this point in my life": Williams to William Hunt, Dec. 24, 1971, LLC.

522 "I am too ornery": Williams to Dotson Rader, Aug. 2, 1971, Columbia.

522 "indispensable": Ibid.

522 "You gave me charm": Williams to Dotson Rader, Dec. 21, 1972, Columbia.

523 "We both seemed much older": Rader, *Tennessee*, p. 23.

523 "I want to meet your underground friends": Williams to Dotson Rader, Aug. 2, 1971, Columbia.

523 "How liberating that was!": JLI with Dotson Rader, 2012, JLC.

523 "In a night, we'd go to dinner": Ibid.

523 "Being places where respectable people": Rader, *Tennessee*, p. 9.

523 "For you . . . being part": Williams to Dotson Rader, undated, Columbia.

524 "was the fact that young people": Rader, *Tennessee*, p. 85.

524 "My bringing Tennessee": JLI with Dotson Rader, 2012, JLC.

524 "drifting almost willfully": *NSE*, p. 165.

525 "pure revolutionaries": Williams to Dotson Rader, undated, Columbia.

525 Williams chose Fire Island: Williams to Dotson Rader, Aug. 12, 1972, Columbia.

525 "It is impossible to overstate": JLI with Dotson Rader, 2012, JLC.

525 "It becomes very easy": Williams to Dotson Rader, undated, Columbia.

526 "to subvert the media image of protesters": Dotson Rader to John Lahr, June 29, 1971, JLC.

526 "I must be rehabilitated": Williams to Dotson Rader, undated, Columbia.

526 "pig-dom": Tennessee Williams, "We Are Dissenters Now," *Harper's Bazaar*, Jan. 1972.

527 "IF WE DO NOT ACT": Dotson Rader to Williams, undated, Columbia.

527 "I am certainly in favor": Williams to William Hunt, Nov. 23, 1971, LLC.

527 "I am too old to march anymore": Dotson Rader, *Blood Dues* (New York: Alfred A. Knopf, 1973), p. 97.

527 "Suddenly 'The Movement' was unmasked": "Statement to be Presented to Knopf Publishers" (relating to Rader's *Blood Dues*), Oct. 1, 1972, LLC.

527 "probably the most shocking": Williams to Dotson Rader, Dec. 21, 1972, Columbia.

528 "I avoided all affiliations": Ibid. Williams wrote this in response to Rader's "The Day the Movement Died," *Esquire*, Dec. 1972.

528 "to be conducted by my revolutionary comrades": Williams, "Last Will and Testament," June 21, 1972, LLC.

528 "this ambience of continual dreadfulness": Williams to Dotson Rader, July 16, 1972, Columbia.

528 "I was thinking last night": Ibid.

528 "a quality of sexlessness": LOA2, p. 727.

528 "the finest writing I've done": William Glover, "Interview with Tennessee Williams: Playwright Subdues His Demons," Associated Press, June 16, 1972.

528 "QUENTIN: . . . There's a coarseness": LOA2, p. 744.

529 "can do no harm": Williams to Bill Barnes, Jan. 1, 1972, LLC. During rehearsals, Williams ran into Gore Vidal at the bar of the Plaza Hotel. "He assured me that it was no longer possible for me to get good notices on a play because of all 'the awful personal publicity,'" Williams wrote to Oliver Evans, adding, "Gore's invidious attitude toward other writers has become a real sickness. And I am sick of it." (Williams to Oliver Evans, Mar. 23, 1972, LLC.)

529 "I certainly had no desire": Tennessee Williams, *Moise and the World of Reason* (London: Brilliance Books, 1984), p. 42.

530 "metaphor for posterity": Williams to Bill Barnes, Jan. 9, 1972, THNOC.

530 "They'll say the Resurrection": Mel Gussow, "Williams Looking to Play's Opening," *New York Times*, Mar. 31, 1972.

530 "The critics in New York": Williams to Lady St. Just, Apr. 14, 1972, *FOA*, p. 256.

530 "The Revitalization of a Great Dramatist": Zadan, "Tennessee Williams."

530 "may survive better than some": Clive Barnes, "Williams Accepting Life As Is," *New York Times*, Apr. 3, 1972.

530 "a five-finger exercise": Ted Kalem, "Clinging to a Spar," *Time*, Apr. 17, 1972.

530 "Surely you meant": Williams to Ted Kalem, Apr. 27, 1972, HRC.

530 "Goddam it, no": Williams to Lady St. Just, June 9, 1972, *FOA*, p. 263.

530 "A star is born": Ibid.

530 "He never shut up": JLI with Peg Murray, 2012, JLC. Murray also starred in *A House Not Meant to Stand* and *A Lovely Sunday for Creve Coeur.*

531 "Just watch his lips": Ibid.

531 "he was wonderful in the part": Ibid.

531 "a pair of jerks imitating": Williams to Lady St. Just, Sept. 18, 1972, *FOA*, p. 272.

531 "A synonym for a manager": Ibid.

532 "Not as bad as they'll go": Williams to Oliver Evans, Sept. 20, 1972, Harvard.

532 "We were all terrified": JLI with Peg Murray, 2012, JLC.

532 "I was belting out every line": Williams to Oliver Evans, Sept. 20, 1972, Harvard.

532 "Tennessee, look": "An Open Letter to Tennessee Williams," by Mike Silverstein, as quoted in Kaila Jay and Allen Young, eds., *Out of the Closet: Voices of Gay Liberation* (New York: New York University Press, 1992), p. 69.

532 "the 'freed' generation": Lee Barton, "Why Do Homosexual Playwrights Hide Their Homosexuality?," *New York Times*, Jan. 23, 1972.

533 "I feel sorry for the author": Arthur Bell, "Tennessee Williams: 'I've Never Faked It,'" *Village Voice*, Feb. 24, 1972.

533 *Gay Sunshine* review of Williams's *Memoirs*: Andrew Dvosin, "Outcast as Success," *Gay Sunshine*, Summer/Fall 1976.

533 "shocking misapprehension of my work": Tennessee Williams, "A Reply to a Review," *Gay Sunshine*, Winter 1977.

533 "founding father": Ibid.

533 "Now, surely, Mr. Dvosin": Ibid.

534 "There are a great many people in this town": David Lobdell to Patricia Lobdell Hepplewhite, Dec. 6, 1970, LLC.

534 "Certain people on the streets": Ibid.

534 "My name is Tennessee Williams!": Rader, *Tennessee*, p. 194.

534 Williams had stood his ground: On the Key West police blotter for Jan. 28, 1979, Williams is quoted as saying, "They were just punks. It happened quickly. There was no injury sustained. A lens fell out of my glasses." Asked later, why the attack hadn't bothered him, he said, "Because, baby, I don't allow it to." (See *N*, p. 742.)

534 "to whom my heart is committed": Williams, *Moise*, p. 139.

534 "relentless thing called time": Williams to Bill Barnes, Jan. 1, 1972, THNOC.

534 "I feel so OLD": William A. Raidy, *St. Louis Globe-Democrat*, Apr. 15, 1972.

534 "At sixty-one": *CWTW*, p. 219.

535 "Time had interred his looks": Truman Capote, *Answered Prayers* (London: Penguin Books, 1988), p. 59.

535 "Perhaps I'll have a face-lift": *N*, "Mes Cahiers Noirs," Spring 1979, p. 737.

535 "eye-lift": Ibid. In 1978, at the suggestion of "Texas" Kate Moldawer, Williams had cosmetic surgery.

535 "an aging man's almost continual scuttling": *M*, p. xviii.

535 "My best work was always done": *CWTW*, p. 220.

535 "the charm of the Orientals": Williams to Oliver Evans, Oct. 18, 1972, Harvard.

535 "I was comforted greatly": Williams to Edmund Perret, Sept. 20, 1972, THNOC. Perret, who was from an aristocratic New Orleans family, graduated from St. John Fisher College, then got his MA at Duquesne University. At Brown University and Catholic University he did doctoral studies. He became an executive director of the Contact Lens Association of Ophthalmologists. He met Williams in 1972, while still a student, and became a close friend. "I always thought if he and I had been born in the same year or a few years apart it would have been the greatest gay love affair that ever existed. He knew that. That's why he said, 'Baby, we missed the boat,'" Perret told Lyle Leverich in a 1983 interview. "He was my platonic lover. It was never consummated."

535 "Robert was very, very, very quiet": JLI with Dotson Rader, 2012, JLC.

535 "He drives well": Williams to Oliver Evans, Oct. 18, 1972, Harvard.

536 "he alternates in moods": Williams to Bill Barnes, May 31, 1973, THNOC.

537 "Tennessee would touch him": JLI with Dotson Rader, 2012, JLC.

537 "There was something about him": Ibid.

537 "My young writer friend": Williams to Lady St. Just, Dec. 4, 1972, *FOA*, p. 279.

537 "a disastrous and destructive liaison": *FOA*, p. 292.

537 "a nature I know": Williams to Robert Carroll, Dec. 29, 1978, HRC.

537 "Traveller, stranger": Williams to Robert Carroll, Jan. 13, 1977, HRC.

537 "a beautiful dream": Williams to Edmund Perret, Oct. 1972, LLC.

537 work of Carson McCullers: "The best I've known personally since McCullers," he said. (Williams to Oliver Evans, Oct. 5, 1972, Harvard.)

537 "My name for him": *CP*, "Little Horse," pp. 75–76.

538 "cryin' all the time": "Hound Dog" written by Doc Pomus/Mort Shuman. Famously recorded by Elvis Presley.

538 "Where is Robert?": Tennessee Williams, "Robert" (unpublished), undated, Harvard.

538 "He got himself": Williams to Edmund Perret, Oct. 31, 1972, LLC.

538 "He has a young": Williams to Harry Rasky, Oct. 20, 1972, Harvard.

538 documentary: *Tennessee Williams's South*, DVD, written and directed by Harry
     Rasky (Canadian Broadcasting Corporation, 1972).

538 "I did not complain": Williams to Harry Rasky, Oct. 20, 1972, Harvard.

539 "All rights, moral, or in writing": June 1972, *FOA*, p. 264. St. Just kept the copy-
     right, however, when Williams deeded it to her.

539 "Glenville's abortion": Williams to Lady St. Just, Oct. 1973, *FOA*, p. 303.

539 "You don't recover": Williams to Lady St. Just, May 8, 1973, ibid., p. 291.

539 "great sweetness to me": Williams to Lady St. Just, May 26, 1973, ibid., p. 292.

539 "hired companion": Williams to Bill Barnes, May 31, 1973, LLC.

539 "just lay there chain-smoking": *N*, p. 738.

540 "the Twerp": Williams to Andrew Lyndon, Dec. 18, 1976, Harvard. The feeling
     was mutual. "Robert called her a cunt to her face," Rader said. (JLI with Dotson
     Rader, 2013, JLC.)

540 "That 'grass' he smokes": Williams to Lady St. Just, Dec. 4, 1972, *FOA*, p. 279.

540 "I said: 'You find me intolerable' ": Williams to Lady St. Just, Apr. 18, 1973, ibid.,
     p. 289.

540 "was talking persistently": Williams to Lady St. Just, May 31, 1973, ibid., p. 294.

540 "The co-habitation with Carroll": Williams to Bill Barnes, June 13, 1973, THNOC.

540 "It turned out that 'enigmatic' ": Williams to Oliver Evans, June 22, 1973, Har-
     vard.

540 "The West Virginia Kid": Williams to Lady St. Just, Feb. 5, 1974, *FOA*, p. 309.

541 "abruptly decided he wouldn't leave": Williams to Andrew Lyndon, Dec. 18,
     1976, Harvard.

541 "When Tenn was with Robert": JLI with Dotson Rader, 2012, JLC.

541 "You see, you had laid": Williams to Robert Carroll, Jan. 13, 1977, HRC.

541 "Robert seemed to be going through": Williams to Bruce Cook, Feb. 23, 1978,
     Harvard.

542 "My beloved Genius": Pancho Rodriguez to Andreas Brown, Nov. 2, 1978,
     THNOC.

542 "I hope to see you some day": Williams to Robert Carroll, undated, HRC.

542 "Robert was far more confident": JLI with Dotson Rader, 2012, JLC.

544 "The banishment of Frank": Ibid.

544 "There are not many readers": Williams to Robert Carroll, Feb. 2, 1980, HRC.

544 "Take care": Williams to Robert Carroll, July 14, 1980, HRC.

544 "It is true that my charms": Williams to Bill Barnes, July 15, 1973, THNOC.

545 "I have a conviction": Williams to Bill Barnes, Apr. 10, 1973, JLC.

545 "a kind of autobiographical peep show": Michael Korda, "That's It, Baby," *The
     New Yorker*, Mar. 22, 1999. In the same article, Korda said, "I thought it coura-
     geous of Tennessee to have tried his hand at a novel, particularly one that cele-
     brated the decline of the characters' sexual and artistic powers."

545 "If he hasn't exactly opened his heart": Allean Hale, "Afterword," in Tennessee
     Williams, *Memoirs* (New York: New Directions, 2006), p. 253.

545 "I am knocking it out": Williams to Lady St. Just, July 30, 1972, *FOA*, p. 270. St.
     Just was so offended by the book's sexual explicitness that she threw her copy
     away.

545 "I don't plan": Williams to Kate Medina, July 16, 1972, HRC.

545 "I feel that the project": Williams to Kate Medina, Feb. 1973, HRC.

546 "You impressed me": Williams to Thomas Congdon, Apr. 4, 1973, HRC.

546 "I feel I've been had": *San Francisco Chronicle*, Mar. 25, 1976.

546 full power of his romantic connection: Williams wrote, "Donald Windham had suggested the dramatization of this story [*You Touched Me!*] but it was I who had secured the rights to dramatize it from Lawrence's widow. . . . Unhappily it is also true that Donald's contribution to this adaptation is not hugely under-estimated by the word minimal. . . . Donald Windham was already, in my opinion, a precociously gifted writer of prose-fiction, but he had not learned to write dialogue that actors could comfortably employ on a professional stage nor even off . . . ." (As quoted in an unpublished essay, "The Flowers of Friendship Fade the Flowers of Friendship," LLC.)

546 "amusing and well-written": *N*, Spring 1979, p. 749.

546 given permission to Windham: In a disingenuous letter to the *New York Times*, answering Williams's complaints about Robert Brustein's review of the book, Windham wrote, "The first agreement was signed January 6, 1976. . . . This letter asked him, if he agreed, to give the accompanying rough-drafted document to his lawyer to draw up an agreement between us. It was because TW signed this rough draft that evening when he came to dinner, saying that there was no need for his lawyer to be involved, that I went to a lawyer and had the second agreement prepared to make everything legally clear between us. TW was given this second agreement after he returned to New York, on Feb. 17, 1976, at a restaurant where he was having lunch with his sister and friends and had asked me to join him. He signed it in front of his five guests, after reading it and making a handwritten addition on it, as he had made on the first agreement." (*New York Times*, Jan. 15, 1978.)

546 "insulting and damaging": Williams to Floria Lasky, Nov. 21, 1976, LLC.

546 "What makes a Windham?": *N*, Spring 1979, p. 749.

547 "The love that previously dared not speak": Robert Brustein, "The Perfect Friend," *New York Times*, Nov. 20, 1977.

547 "*I can't live in a professional vacuum*": Williams to Hillard Elkins, June 18, 1974, LLC.

547 Kennedy assassination: "I think the panic and rot of our present era really did first manifest itself in full when those murders of JFK and Oswald took place in Dallas; it was the elevation of that red devil battery sign," Williams wrote to Barnes. (Williams to Bill Barnes, Oct. 19, 1973, THNOC.)

547 "Did I die by my own hand": *N*, Spring 1979, p. 739.

547 "one big hell-hollering *death grin*": Tennessee Williams, *The Red Devil Battery Sign* (New York: New Directions, 1984), p. 25.

547 "Oh, they trusted me": Ibid., p. 24.

548 "Tonight?": Ibid., p. 38.

549 "grief and disease receive little pity": Herbert Kretzmer, "High Level Plot That Is Hatched in Hell," *London Daily Express*, June 9, 1977, cited in William Prosser, *The Late Plays of Tennessee Williams* (New York: Scarecrow Press, 2009), p. 145.

549 "Dreams necessary": Williams, *Red Devil Battery Sign*, p. 90.

549 "outlaws in appearance": Ibid., p. 92.

549 "They seem to explode": Ibid., p. 84.

549 "He's just 32": Williams to David Merrick, Nov. 3, 1973, LLC.

549 "In the old days": Williams to Bill Barnes, undated, THNOC.

550 declare him "dead": John Simon, in his review of *Creve Coeur* in *New York*, for instance, wrote, "The kindest thing to assume is that Williams died shortly after completing *Sweet Bird of Youth*." (Cited in Prosser, *Late Plays*, p. 157.)

550   "If the play has not your confidence": Williams to David Merrick, Nov. 23, 1973, LLC.

550   "I sensed that you were seriously interested": Williams to Elia Kazan, Dec. 1973, LLC.

550   "What's the matter, David?": Howard Kissel, *David Merrick: The Abominable Showman* (New York: Applause Books, 1993), p. 426.

550   after Merrick's option lapsed: Ed Sherin, "A View from inside the Storm" (unpublished), ESC.

551   "None of us wanted to be involved": Tennessee Williams, "The Curious History of This Play and Plans for the Future," LLC.

551   "one of the most important works": Sherin, "View," ESC.

551   "were paranoid": Ibid.

551   "I fancy this": Williams to Lady St. Just, May 4, 1975, *FOA*, p. 326.

551   "another actress be found": Sherin, "View," ESC.

551   "As I live and breathe": Williams to Lady St. Just, Apr. 1975, *FOA*, p. 325.

551   "amateurish": Sherin, "View," ESC.

551   "a mess": Prosser, *Late Plays*, p. vi.

551   "cause for rejoicing": Ibid.

551   "beginning to emerge": Sherin, "View," ESC.

553   "I stood in disbelief": Ibid.

553   "He gave me this shocking report": Williams memo, undated, LLC.

553   "Tennessee Williams": Kissel, *David Merrick*, p. 429.

553   "the very forces in our society": Sherin, "View," ESC.

553   "It's not closing for good": Kissel, *David Merrick*, p. 429.

553   "Burn, burn, burn": Prosser, *Late Plays*, p. 144.

553   "one of the most thrilling tragedies": Ibid.

554   "a blazing torch": Ibid.

554   "coup-de-disgrace": Williams to Bill Barnes, undated, LLC.

554   "I am like some old opera star": *Leicester Mercury*, May 11, 1978.

554   "Aside from you": Williams to Walter Kerr, Mar. 10, 1978, LLC.

554   "Why, Roger": Teddy Vaughn, *Washington Star*, Dec. 2, 1979.

554   "I am widely regarded": Tennessee Williams, "I Am Widely Regarded as the Ghost of a Writer," *New York Times*, May 8, 1977. In his "Epitaph for Tennessee Williams," included in *Writing in Restaurants*, David Mamet wrote "his life and view of life became less immediately accessible, and our gratitude was changed to distant reverence for a man whom we felt obliged—if we were to continue in our happy feelings toward him—to consider already dead."

554   "imminently posthumous": Williams, interview by Dick Cavett, *The Dick Cavett Show*, May 16, 1979.

554   "Help!": Prosser, *Late Plays*, p. xvi.

554   "I phoned Tennessee": Ibid.

555   "so they might hear": *FOA*, p. 333. The leading lady and the director were Ruth Brinkmann and Franz Schafranek. "Ruth took it very badly and screamed at Tennessee. . . . Franz fell to his knees and apologized for her outburst."

555   "The lady who produced my new play": Peter Hall, *Peter Hall's Diaries: The Story of a Dramatic Battle*, ed. John Goodwin (London: Oberon Books, 2555), p. 274.

555   "Tenn used death": JLI with Dotson Rader, 2012, JLC.

555   "I saw him use it most in places": Ibid.

555 "inordinately possessed of the past": Richard F. Leavitt, *The World of Tennessee Williams* (New York: G. P. Putnam's Sons, 1978), p. x.

555 plays teemed with apparitions: *Vieux Carré*; *Stopped Rocking*; *Something Cloudy, Something Clear*; *Clothes for a Summer Hotel*; *Will Mr. Merriweather Return from Memphis?*; *The Chalky White Substance*.

556 "alternate projects": Williams to Bill Barnes, Nov. 18, 1974, THNOC.

556 "spectral country": Tennessee Williams, *Stopped Rocking and Other Screenplays* (New York: New Directions, 1984), p. 382.

556 "No, not alone": Ibid.

556 "No more Sunday visits": Ibid., p. 377.

556 "utterly peaceful": Ibid., p. 384.

556 "stone outside and in": Williams, *Stopped Rocking*, p. 327. Rose Williams haunts *Stopped Rocking*—Farmington, the state institution to which Janet is being transferred, is the name of the state hospital where Rose spent nineteen years. Williams, like Olaf, was also increasingly haunted by his own sense of deadness and hardening heart.

557 "he told me ruefully": JLI with John Hancock, 2012, JLC.

557 "calamari fritti": Ibid.

557 "had written another": Ibid.

557 "skimpy": Ibid.

557 "I knew we were in trouble": Ibid.

558 "The actors were stunned": Ibid.

558 "Tennessee stirred": Ibid.

558 "a passionate will to create": Opening stage direction, original Ms. of *Vieux Carré*, Harvard.

558 "Once this house was alive": Tennessee Williams, *Vieux Carré* (New York: New Directions, 1979), p. 5.

558 "(*As he first draws the door open*": Ibid., p. 116.

559 "Old cats know how to fall": Early draft of *Vieux Carré*, HRC; lines appear later in Tennessee Williams, *The Magic Tower and Other One-Act Plays* (New York: New Directions, 2011), p. 236.

559 "None of us saw Tennessee": Donald Spoto, *The Kindness of Strangers: The Life of Tennessee Williams* (Boston: Little, Brown, 1985), p. 324.

559 "I am as frightened as ever": Williams to Arthur Seidelman, May 1977, LLC.

559 "It developed that the backers": Williams to Andrew Lyndon, May 22, 1977, LLC.

560 "Tennessee Williams's voice": Walter Kerr, "A Touch of the Poet Isn't Enough to Sustain Williams's Latest Play," *New York Times*, May 22, 1977.

560 "body snatching": Brendan Gill, "Body Snatching," *The New Yorker*, Apr. 7, 1980.

560 "We are simply being told": Walter Kerr, "The Stage: 'Clothes for a Summer Hotel'; People Out of Books," *New York Times*, Mar. 27, 1980.

560 "In a sense all plays are ghost plays": Tennessee Williams, *Clothes for a Summer Hotel: A Ghost Play* (New York: New Directions, 1983), p. 84.

561 "Zelda is the type": Michiko Kakutani, "'Ghosts' of the Fitzgeralds Rehearsing under the Watchful Eye of Williams," *New York Times*, Jan. 8, 1980.

561 "the brutality of the unconscious": As quoted in Tennessee Williams, "In Masks Outrageous and Austere" (unpublished), JLC.

561 "In Tennessee's work": Kakutani, "'Ghosts,'" Jan. 8, 1980.

561 "Scott used Zelda's life": Ibid. Walter Kerr on Geraldine Page's Zelda: "She looks

like a gypsy moth that's been put through a shredder, leaving only her pink ballet dancing slippers more or less intact." (*New York Times*, Mar. 27, 1980.)

561 "Is that really you, Scott?": Williams, *Clothes for a Summer Hotel*, p. 9.

561 "*What was important to you*": Ibid., p. 11.

561 "Mr. Fitzgerald . . . seems to believe": Charles E. Shain, *F. Scott Fitzgerald* (St Paul: University of Minnesota Press, 1961), p. 31.

562 "The will to cry out remains": Williams, *Clothes for a Summer Hotel*, p. 50.

562 "Call it a ring of": Ibid., p. 12.

562 "ZELDA:—I'm approaching him": Ibid., p. 48.

563 "The gates are iron": Ibid., p. 77.

563 appropriation of Fitzgerald's life for his own short stories: In *The Notebook of Trigorin*, Williams's free adaptation of Chekhov's *The Seagull*, which was commissioned by the University of British Columbia, in Vancouver, and staged there in 1981, Williams continued his meditation on self-destruction and the appropriation of others for art. As Williams's retitled play implies, the famed Trigorin makes a myth of writing—"A writer's a madman—probationally released," he says—and is a testament to the smug brutality of the artistic temperament. (Williams, *The Notebook of Trigorin* (New York: New Directions, 1997), p. 45.) He uses his literary legend to seduce and to betray the aspiring young actress, Nina. Trigorin's obsessive need to write drains his experience of all meaning. Trigorin doesn't understand his brutality; Williams did. The year that *Trigorin* was staged, Williams was interviewed by Studs Terkel, who started to define his talents in the following exchange (from a transcribed tape):
Terkel: Lyricist, poet, storywriter, playwright.
Williams: Playwright, yes. Is it all right to say son-of-bitch? (Laughs)
Terkel: I suppose that's an art form in itself, isn't it?
Williams: It's something you learn in show business.

563 "You see, I can betray": Williams, *Clothes for a Summer Hotel*, pp. 67–68.

564 "write yourself a new book": Ibid., p. 77.

564 "He said he wanted to fly away": JLI with Dotson Rader, 2011, JLC.

564 "hung on for ten years": Ibid.

566 "He seemed nervous": Dotson Rader, *Tennessee: Cry of the Heart* (Garden City, N.Y.: Doubleday, 1985), p. 333.

566 "Eli was the first to grab him": Dotson Rader to John Lahr, Sept. 8, 2012, JLC.

566 "I have had it all my life": Rader, *Tennessee*, p. 336.

566 "Slender Is the Night": Jack Kroll, "Slender Is the Night," *Newsweek*, Apr. 7, 1980.

566 " 'Clothes' Needs Some Tailoring": Clive Barnes, " 'Clothes' Needs Some Tailoring," *New York Post*, Mar. 27, 1980.

567 "There is nothing necessary": John Simon, "Damsels Inducing Distress," *New York*, Apr. 7, 1980.

567 "The action is set in the 1940s": Robert Brustein, "Advice for Broadway," *New Republic*, May 3, 1980.

567 "This is an evening at the morgue": Rex Reed, *New York Daily News*, Mar. 27, 1980.

567 " 'Clothes' was a victim": Williams to Elia Kazan, July 5, 1980, Harvard.

567 "Couldn't the son of a bitch": Bruce Smith, *Costly Performances: Tennessee Williams: The Last Stage: A Personal Memoir* (St. Paul, Minn.: Paragon House, 1990), p. 158.

567 "critical homicide": Earl Wilson, 1980, LLC.

567 induction to the American Academy of Arts and Letters: Williams took Chair 19 vacated by the death of the sculptor Alexander Calder.

567 "a playwright in the way": Elia Kazan, Kennedy Center Honors speech, 1979, WUCA.

567 "shaped the history": President Jimmy Carter, "Presidential Medal of Freedom Remarks at the Presentation Ceremony," Jan. 9, 1980, The American Presidency Project, www.presidency.ucsb.edu/ws/?pid=45389#axzz2ikgS3SEj.

568 "I will never recover": Williams to Mitch Douglas, Apr. 14, 1980, LLC. "UNSPEAKABLEY DISGUSTED AND APPALLED!" Williams wrote to Christopher Isherwood and Don Bachardy about the critical reception of *Clothes*. (Williams to Christopher Isherwood and Don Bachardy, Mar. 29, 1979, LLC.)

568 "Tennessee was difficult": JLI with Mitch Douglas, 2012, JLC.

568 "Well, that would be difficult": Ibid.

568 "Mitch, the windows are filthy": Ibid.

568 "You guys play so fucking good": Ibid.

569 "time runs short": Michiko Kakutani, "Tennessee Williams: 'I Keep Writing. Sometimes I Am Pleased,'" *New York Times*, Sept. 23, 1981.

569 "level with each other": Williams to Mitch Douglas, undated, Harvard.

569 "Let's do": Mitch Douglas to Williams, July 27, 1981, Harvard.

569 "You've been quoted in the press": Ibid.

571 "I wish you luck": Williams to Mitch Douglas, Aug. 1981, LLC. In the same letter, Williams added, "Mitch, I'm winding things up and not with too much regret. I mean the career side of my life. . . . I like you. I admire you. I respect you. But I have entered a stage in my life that you should not have to cope with."

571 "Can you place me in the hands": Williams to Milton Goldman, Dec. 18, 1981, LLC.

571 "I will not again open an envelope": Ibid.

571 his review of *Clothes*: Harold Clurman, "Theatre," *Nation*, Apr. 19, 1980.

571 "There are periods in life": Williams to Oliver Evans, Jan. 12, 1981, Harvard.

571 "that stands for 'The Beast of the Apocalypse'": Williams to Elia Kazan, July 5, 1980, Harvard.

571 hung over her bed: JLI with Mitch Douglas, 2012, JLC.

571 "a long, long stretch of desolation": *N*, Spring 1979, p. 739.

572 "When I am very ill": Williams to Oliver Evans, Jan. 12, 1981, Harvard.

572 "There's an explosive center": Frank Rich, "Play: Adapted Memoirs of Tennessee Williams," *New York Times*, Sept. 11, 1981.

572 "spook sonata": Tennessee Williams, *A House Not Meant to Stand* (New York: New Directions, 2008), p. 100.

572 "Never, never, never stop laughing!": Williams to Truman Capote, July 2, 1978, LLC.

573 "I don't compete with Joe Orton": *CWTW*, p. 341.

573 "panicky disarray": Tennessee Williams, *A House Not Meant to Stand: A Gothic Comedy* (New York: New Directions, 2008), p. 3.

573 "to produce a shock of disbelief": Ibid.

573 "a large mantel clock": Ibid.

573 "ticks rather loudly": Ibid.

573 "a metaphor for the state of society": Ibid.

573 "Things fall apart": William Butler Yeats, *The Collected Works of W. B. Yeats*, vol. 1: *The Poems*, rev. 2nd ed. (New York: Simon & Schuster, 2010), p. 187.

573 "sinister times": Williams, *House Not Meant to Stand*, p. 48.

575 "I don't respect tears": Ibid., p. 35.

575 "Miss Nancy": *NSE*, p. 93.

575 "I remember when": Williams, *House Not Meant to Stand*, p. 22.

575 "CORNELIUS: You encouraged it": Ibid., p. 7.

575 "No one whom I have discussed": Williams to Edwina Williams, Mar. 3, 1972, LLC.

576 "Dancie money": Williams, *House Not Meant to Stand*, p. 18.

576 "lunacy runs rampant": Ibid., p. 17.

576 "alarming incidences": *M*, p. 116.

577 "CHARLIE: Mom?": Williams, *House Not Meant to Stand*, p. 21.

577 "Bella should be presented": Thomas Keith, "Introduction: A Mississippi Fun House," in ibid., p. xxi.

577 "My eyes keep clouding over": Williams, *House Not Meant to Stand*, p. 35.

577 "CORNELIUS: [*half-rising and freezing in position*]": Ibid., p. 6.

577 "Little Joanie": Ibid., p. 72.

577 "All I had was a little nervous break down": Ibid., p. 71.

578 "Blow out your candles, Laura": LOA1, p. 465.

578 "Ghostly outcries of children": Williams, *House Not Meant to Stand*, p. 82.

578 "enchanting lost lyricism of childhood": Ibid., p. 85.

578 "VOICE OF YOUNG CHIPS:—*Dark!*": Ibid.

578 "Chips—will you say": Ibid., p. 86.

578 "We can't say grace": LOA1, p. 401.

578 "Ceremonially the ghost children rise": Williams, *House Not Meant to Stand*, p. 86.

578 "to glance back at their mother": Ibid.

579 "When I hear [the critics] say": *N*, Nov. 24, 1981, p. 764.

579 "the best thing Williams has written": Gerald Clarke, "Show Business: Sweating It out in Miami," *Time*, June 28, 1982.

579 "My God, that's Mother Teresa": Primus V, "Blessed Unexpectedly," *Harvard Magazine*, Jan.–Feb. 2013.

580 "It was an Underwood typewriter": Spoto, *Kindness*, p. 363.

580 "He looked old": LLI with John Uecker, 1985, LLC.

580 "That's the end of the performance": Ibid.

580 "I don't understand my life": Williams to Kate Moldawer, May 31, 1982, LLC.

580 spent several days recovering: Peter Hoffman, "The Last Days of Tennessee Williams," *New York*, July 25, 1983.

580 "He just wouldn't have it": LLI with John Uecker, 1983, LLC.

580 toyed with the idea of renting: "Ask him if he knows how I can dispose of this old shambles of a house. For this summer at least. If I do return to it (improbably) it will be with a little, warm-hearted Sicilian," he wrote to Moldawer. (Williams to Kate Moldawer, May 31, 1982, LLC.)

580 "I won't ever be coming home again": Rader, *Tennessee*, p. 339.

580 "Before Mr. Tom went away": Ibid.

582 "It was James Laughlin in the beginning": Williams on James Laughlin, Jan. 1983, LLC.

582 "I know that it is the poetry": Ibid.

582 "I've gone from good reviews": JLI with Dotson Rader, 2011, JLC.

582 "To us": *RBAW*, p. 325.

582 "*I, I, I!*—a burden to be surrendered": *N*, p. 729.

CHAPTER 10: THE SUDDEN SUBWAY

583   "The Sudden Subway": Unless otherwise noted, material in this chapter is drawn from John Lahr, "The Lady and Tennessee," *The New Yorker*, Dec. 19, 1994.

583   "Tennessee called death the sudden subway": James Laughlin, "Tennessee," in James Laughlin, Peter Glassgold, and Elizabeth Harper, *New Directions 47: An International Anthology of Poetry and Prose* (New York: New Directions, 1983), p. 180.

583   "He wrote his own life": JLI with John Uecker, 2010, JLC.

583   when the police arrived at Williams's room: Office of the Chief Medical Examiner, Report of Death, Case M83-1568.

583   "I run, cried the fox, in circles": *CP*, "Cried the Fox," pp. 6–7.

584   "I knew he was dealing": LLI with John Uecker, 2010, JLC.

584   "deathly afraid of institutions": Tennessee Williams, *The One Exception*, Jan. 1983, LLC.

584   "retreated to her room": Ibid.

584   "She dreads any encounter": Ibid.

584   "She used to have periods of depression": Ibid.

584   "I—can't talk much": Ibid.

584   "I wonder if it wouldn't be better": Ibid.

584   "nods with a senseless look": Ibid.

584   "Kyra takes a few hesitant steps": Ibid.

585   "Tennessee begged me": JLI with John Uecker, 2010, JLC.

585   "I most certainly will not": LLI with John Uecker, 1985, LLC.

585   "Every time I'd go in the room": JLI with John Uecker, 2010, JLC.

585   "right-hand bower": LOA1, p. 419.

585   "I can't write": JLI with John Uecker, 2010, JLC.

585   "I have faced the fact": Ibid.

585   "I said, 'What if he should take the whole bottle?'": LLI with John Uecker, 1983, LLC.

586   "He just seemed to be in dreamland": JLI with John Uecker, 2010, JLC.

586   "It was bad": JLI with John Uecker, 2011, JLC.

586   "My next thought": JLI with John Uecker, 2010, JLC.

586   "Water witches crowned with reeds": Thomas Chatterton, "Minstrel Song" from *Aella*: The final verse reads, "Water-witches, crowned with reytes, / Bear me to your lethal tide. / I die! I come! My true-love waits . . . / Thus the damsel spake, and died."

587   "There were so many people": JLI with John Uecker, 2011, JLC.

587   "I've got to see him!": JLI with John Uecker, 2010, JLC.

587   "The cause of death": Suzanne Daley, "Williams Choked on a Bottle Cap: No Evidence of Foul Play Seen by the Medical Examiner," *New York Times*, Feb. 27, 1983.

587   "was not wide enough": Michael M. Baden with Judith Adler Hennessee, *Unnatural Death: Confessions of a Medical Examiner* (New York: Ballantine, 2005), p. 73.

588   official public story about his death: Daley, "Williams Choked on a Bottle Cap."

588   "an autopsy was performed": Ibid.

588   "Gross told me": Philip Shenon, "Broad Deterioration in Coroner's Office Charged," *New York Times*, Jan. 30, 1985.

588   "apparently the overcap": LLI with John Uecker, 1984, LLC.

588   toxicology report: The report from the toxicology laboratory shows the break-down of secobarbital in Williams's body. Blood: 1.8 mg%; Brain: 2.6 mg%; Stomach content: 96 mg/85 ml; Liver: 5.5 mg%; Kidney: 3.7%; Urine: 0.4%. Certified by Dr. Milton Lessa Bastos, April 6, 1983. (Copy of report, LLC.)

588   "sad group noises": Letter from Elia Kazan, Mar. 25, 1983, LLC.

588   "The man lived a very good life": Ibid.

589   "In order to negotiate life": Michiko Kakutani, "The Legacy of Tennessee Williams," New York Times, Mar. 6, 1983.

589   "For a while the theater loved him": "Williams Dies Alone in Midtown Hotel: Literary, Theater Greats Mourn a Towering Talent," New York Post, Feb. 26, 1983.

589   "the Orthodox Jewish coffin": Peter Hoffman, "The Last Days of Tennessee Williams," New York, July 25, 1983, p. 41.

589   "It is a time of reconciliation": Sara Rimer, "Fans Give Williams Last Review," Miami Herald, Mar. 3, 1983.

589   "I'm to be borne out to sea": Tennessee Williams' South, DVD, directed by Harry Rasky (Canadian Broadcasting Corporation, 1972).

590   "If he had to die": David Richards, "The Long Shadow of Tennessee," Washington Post, Mar. 15, 1983.

590   "Suddenly out of obscurity": Ibid.

590   "Parisian outfit": Hoffman, "Last Days of Tennessee Williams," p. 42.

590   "The milk train doesn't stop": Margaria Fichtner, "Another Williams: Dakin for President," Miami Herald, June 9, 1983.

590   "I'm sure he'd disapprove": New Orleans Times-Picayune, Mar. 6, 1983.

590   "Dakin planned a concession stand": JLI with Dotson Rader, 2011, JLC.

591   Dakin could make him pay in death: Robert Bray, the Williams scholar who knew Dakin and interviewed him, recalled other schemes to exploit the Williams franchise: "Dakin's idea of digging up the coffin in St. Louis and repatriating TW back to New Orleans, in order to establish a TW theme park. He'd say, 'You know, we could have Brick hobbling around on a crutch, Amanda strolling about with her jonquils, Shannon looking for a drink.' " (JLI with Robert Bray, 2012, JLC.)

591   the city he called "St. Pollution": CWTW, p. 180.

591   "Tennessee's two great loves": Lahr, "Lady and Tennessee," p. 88.

591   her own obituaries: Maria St. Just died February 15, 1994.

591   "THE ARISTOCRATIC HELLCAT": Lahr, "Lady and Tennessee," p. 88.

591   "She was Williams's closest woman friend": Ibid.

592   "an occasional actress": M, p. 149.

592   "I will write more about Maria later": Ibid.

592   "The lady is afflicted": Ibid., p. 215.

592   "In the American edition of my memoirs": Lahr, "Lady and Tennessee," p. 86.

592   "The answer is no": Ibid.

592   "I suppose in a way he had": Ibid.

592   "My last request is a last command": Ibid., p. 96.

593   throws himself in the Thames: Ibid.

593   "He knew that she had exaggerated": Ibid.

593   "weaning himself away from her": Ibid.

593   "Maria was very much a presence": Ibid.

593   "he was a procrastinator": Ibid., p. 92.

593   "She was always whining": Ibid., p. 88.

594 "Ultimately, money": Ibid.

594 percentage of the royalties: Edwina got 50 percent of the royalties from *The Glass Menagerie*, which was returned to Williams on her death. Merlo also got a percentage of *The Rose Tattoo*; however, much to Williams's annoyance, Merlo's royalties were not assigned back to him by the family after Merlo's death.

594 "second best bed": William Shakespeare's Last Will and Testament (1616) contains this stipulation: "Item, I give unto my wife my second best bed with the furniture."

594 "Suppose both Peter and Tenn were terminally ill?": Lahr, "Lady and Tennessee," p. 86.

594 "What do you think?": Ibid.

595 "'Tell her I'm asleep'": Ibid., p. 92.

595 "I knew that *she* was the one": Ibid.

595 "BANG, BANG, BANG": Ibid., p. 90.

595 "the oubliette": Ibid.

595 "She was engaged in vigorous battles": Ibid., p. 86.

596 "Maria was the greatest cheerleader": Ibid., p. 92.

596 "Eastman is perfectly willing": Ibid.

596 "These are the people": Ibid., p. 88.

596 "Denying this group of users": Ibid., p. 89.

596 "Maria wasn't really interested": Ibid., p. 96.

597 St. Just wrote: Lady St. Just to Ed Sherin, Mar. 27, 1983, ESC.

597 "I wanted to name": Lahr, "Lady and Tennessee," p. 93.

597 disliked because it was "homosexual": Ibid., p. 89.

597 "She said, 'The play is not doable'": Ibid., p. 95.

597 "She pretended an awful lot": Ibid., p. 94.

598 "His personal image": Ibid., p. 89.

598 "I explained to her": Ibid.

598 Many biographers were called: A. Scott Berg, Judith Thurman, Virginia Spencer Carr, John Lahr.

598 "She definitely wanted to vet the manuscript": Lahr, "Lady and Tennessee," p. 89.

598 "I would never trust you with him": Ibid.

598 "You have ruined Tennessee Williams!": Ibid.

598 "full access to my private correspondence and journals": Ibid., p. 90.

599 "Baby, you write it!": Ibid.

599 "pirate book": Ibid.

599 "fit into Maria's plans": Ibid., p. 91.

600 "I admired the depth of its research": Ibid.

600 "As I recall": Ibid.

600 "The answer is spelled blackmail": Ibid.

600 "I must remain friends": Ibid.

600 "I've denounced her": Ibid.

600 "submit for your review and comment": Ibid.

600 "Maria wreaked havoc": Ibid.

601 allowed Leverich's biography to proceed to publication: *The Late Plays of Tennessee Williams*, by the director and theater professor William Prosser, set aside in 1991 because of St. Just's diktats, was also posthumously published, in 2009.

601 In 2000: The figures were provided and confirmed by the University of the South, which owns the Williams copyrights.

601 ". . . this much will be clear": *CP*, "Part of a Hero," p. 34.

601 "I have always depended": LOA1, p. 563.

601 "Sometimes—there's God": Ibid., p. 529.

601 "Nowadays the world is lit": Ibid., p. 465.

601 *"Make voyages!"*: LOA1, p. 797.

601 "fatal need": Gilbert Maxwell, *Tennessee Williams and Friends: An Informal Biography* (Cleveland: World Publishing, 1965), p. 20.

602 "the tragic division of the human spirit": Williams to Jessica Tandy, undated, as quoted in Mike Steen, *A Look at Tennessee Williams* (New York: Hawthorn Books, 1969), p. 181.

602 "I want to get my goodness back": Lahr, "Lady and Tennessee," p. 91.

602 "What implements have we but words": *NSE*, p. 188.

Sources

ARCHIVES AND SPECIAL COLLECTIONS

Betty Davis Collection, Howard Gotlieb Archival Research Center, Boston University, Boston, Mass.

Billy Rose Theatre Collection, New York Public Library for the Performing Arts, Lincoln Center, New York, N.Y.

Carson McCullers Papers, David M. Rubenstein Rare Book and Manuscript Library, Duke University, Durham, N.C.

Carter Burden Collection of American Literature, Morgan Library and Museum, New York, N.Y.

Cheryl Crawford Collection, Courtesy of Special Collections, University of Houston Libraries, Houston, Tex.

Chicago Theater Collection, Harold Washington Library Center, Chicago Public Library, Chicago, Ill.

Columbia University Center for Oral History Collection, New York, N.Y.

Elia Kazan Collection, Cinema Archives, Wesleyan University, Middletown, Conn.

Fred W. Todd Tennessee Williams Collection, Williams Research Center, The Historic New Orleans Collection, New Orleans, La.

Irene Mayer Selznick Collection, Howard Gotlieb Archival Research Center, Boston University, Boston, Mass.

James Laughlin Papers, Houghton Library, Harvard University, Cambridge, Mass.

John Lahr Collection, Howard Gotlieb Archival Research Center, Boston University, Boston, Mass.

Katherine Anne Porter Collection, University of Maryland Libraries, College Park, Md.

Lyle Leverich Collection, attached to the John Lahr Collection, Howard Gotlieb Archival Research Center, Boston University, Boston, Mass.

Manuscripts Department, Huntington Library, San Marino, Calif.

Papers of the Rev. Walter Dakin, Archives of the University of the South, Sewanee, Tenn.

Tennessee Williams Collection, Archives of the University of the South, Sewanee, Tenn.

Tennessee Williams Collection, Harry Ransom Center, University of Texas at Austin, Tex.

Tennessee Williams Collection, Special Collections, University of Delaware Library, Newark, Del.

Tennessee Williams Papers, Harvard Theatre Collection, Houghton Library, Harvard University, Cambridge, Mass.

Tennessee Williams Papers, Rare Book and Manuscript Library, Columbia University, New York, N.Y.

Wisconsin Center for Film and Theater Research, Wisconsin Historical Society, Madison, Wisc.

MANUSCRIPTS, BOOKS, AND ESSAYS

Aaronovitch, David. *Voodoo Histories*. New York: Riverhead, 2010.

Baden, Michael M., with Judith Adler Hennessee. *Unnatural Death: Confessions of a Medical Examiner*. New York: Ballantine, 2005.

Barrymore, Diana, and Gerold Frank. *Too Much, Too Soon*. London: Muller, 1957.

Bollas, Christopher. *Hysteria*. New York: Routledge, 1999.

Bosworth, Patricia. *Marlon Brando*. New York: Viking, 2001.

Brando, Marlon, with Robert Lindsey. *Brando: Songs My Mother Taught Me*. New York: Random House, 1994.

Brody, Eugene B. "Introduction." In Lawrence S. Kubie, *Symbol and Neurosis: Selected Papers of Lawrence S. Kubie*. Madison, Conn.: International Universities Press, 1978.

Caldwell, Zoe. *I Will Be Cleopatra: An Actress's Journey*. New York: W. W. Norton, 2001.

Campbell, Sandy. *B: Twenty-Nine Letters from Coconut Grove*. Campagnola di Zevio, Italy: Stamperia Valdonega, 1974.

Capote, Truman. *Too Brief a Treat: Letters of Truman Capote*. Edited by Gerald Clarke. New York: Random House, 2004.

Carr, Virginia Spencer. *The Lonely Hunter: A Biography of Carson McCullers*. New York: Doubleday, 1975.

Chandler, Charlotte. *The Girl Who Walked Home Alone: Bette Davis*. New York: Simon & Schuster, 2006.

Clurman, Harold. "Introduction." In Tennessee Williams, *Tennessee Williams: Eight Plays*. Garden City, N.Y.: Nelson Doubleday, 1979.

Courtney, Marguerite. *Laurette: The Intimate Biography of Laurette Taylor*. New York: Limelight Editions, 1984.

Crawford, Cheryl. *One Naked Individual: My Fifty Years in the Theatre*. Indianapolis: Bobbs-Merrill, 1977.

Devlin, Albert J., ed. *Conversations with Tennessee Williams*. Jackson: University Press of Mississippi, 1986.

Dowling, Eddie. "The Reminiscences of Eddie Dowling" (unpublished). Columbia University Center for Oral History Collection, New York.

Evans, Harold. *The American Century*. New York: Alfred A. Knopf, 2000.

Foote, Horton. *Beginnings: A Memoir.* New York: Scribner, 2001.

Freud, Anna. *The Writings of Anna Freud*. Vol. 2: *Ego and the Mechanisms of Defense*. Madison, Conn.: International Universities Press, 1936.

Frommer, Myrna Katz, and Harvey Frommer, eds. *It Happened on Broadway: An Oral History of the Great White Way*. New York: Harcourt Brace, 1998.

Gill, Brendan. *Tallulah*. New York: Holt McDougal, 1972.

Governi, Giancarlo. *Nannarella: Il romanzo di Anna Magnani*. Rome: Minimum Fax, 2008.

Halberstam, David. *The Fifties*. New York: Villard, 1993.

Hale, Alleane. "The Gnadiges Fraulein: Tennessee Williams's Clown Show." In Philip C. Kolin, ed., *The Undiscovered Country: The Later Plays of Tennessee Williams*. New York: Peter Lang, 2002.

Hall, Peter. *Peter Hall's Diaries: The Story of a Dramatic Battle*. Edited by John Goodwin. London: Oberon Books, 2000.

Harpham, Geoffrey Galt. *On the Grotesque*. Princeton, N.J.: Princeton University Press, 1982.

Heilpern, John. *John Osborne: A Patriot for Us*. New York: Vintage, 2007.

Hewes, Henry. *Best Plays of 1964–1965*. New York: Dodd, Mead, 1965.

Hunter, Tab, with Eddie Muller. *Tab Hunter Confidential: The Making of a Movie Star*. Chapel Hill, N.C.: Algonquin Books, 2006.

Isaac, Dan, ed. "Introduction." In Tennessee Williams, *Spring Storm*. New York: New Directions, 1999.

Jay, Kaila, and Allen Young, eds. *Out of the Closet: Voices of Gay Liberation*. New York: New York University Press, 1992.

Kazan, Elia. *An American Odyssey*. Edited by Michel Ciment. London: Bloomsbury, 1988.

———. *Elia Kazan: Interviews*. Edited by William Baer. Jackson: University Press of Mississippi, 2000.

———. *Kazan on Directing*. New York: Alfred A. Knopf, 2009.

———. *A Life*. New York: Alfred A. Knopf, 1988.

Keathley, George. Unpublished, untitled manuscript. John Lahr Collection, Howard Gotlieb Archival Research Center, Boston University, Boston, Mass.

Keith, Thomas. "Introduction: A Mississippi Fun House." In Tennessee Williams, *A House Not Meant to Stand*. New York: New Directions, 2008.

Khan, Masud. *Hidden Selves: Between Theory and Practice in Psychoanalysis*. London: Karnac Books, 1989.

Kissel, Howard. *David Merrick: The Abominable Showman*. New York: Applause Books, 1993.

Kubie, Lawrence. *Practical and Theoretical Aspects of Psychoanalysis*. Madison, Conn.: International Universities Press, 1950.

Kushner, Tony. "Introduction: Notes on *The Glass Menagerie*." In Tennessee Williams, *The Glass Menagerie* (Centennial Edition). New York: New Directions, 2011.

Lahr, John. "The Lady and Tennessee." *The New Yorker*, December 19, 1994.

———. *Show and Tell: New Yorker Profiles*. Woodstock, N.Y.: Overlook Press, 2000.

Laughlin, James. *The Way It Wasn't: From the Files of James Laughlin*. Edited by Barbara Epler and Daniel Javitch. New York: New Directions, 2006.

Leaming, Barbara. *Bette Davis: A Biography*. London: Penguin Books, 1993.

Leavitt, Richard F. *The World of Tennessee Williams*. New York: G. P. Putnam's Sons, 1978.

Leverich, Lyle. *Tom: The Unknown Tennessee Williams*. New York: W. W. Norton, 1995.

Manso, Peter. *Brando: The Biography*. New York: Hyperion, 1994.

Maxtone-Graham, John. Production Notes for *Night of the Iguana* (audiotape diary). Tennessee Williams Collection, Archives of the University of the South. Sewanee, Tenn.

Maxwell, Gilbert. *Tennessee Williams and Friends: An Informal Biography*. Cleveland: World Publishing, 1965.

Medved, Harry, and Michael Medved. *The Hollywood Hall of Shame: The Most Expensive Flops in Movie History*. New York: Perigee Books, 1984.

Milbert, Seymour. "Stage Manager's Rehearsal Account" (unpublished) of *Camino Real*. Billy Rose Theatre Collection, New York Public Library for the Performing Arts, Lincoln Center, New York, N.Y.

Miller, Arthur. "Introduction." In Tennessee Williams, *A Streetcar Named Desire*. New York: New Directions, 2004.

———. "Tennessee Williams' Legacy: An Eloquence and Amplitude of Feeling." In Arthur Miller, *Echoes Down the Corridor: Collected Essays: 1944–2000*. New York: Penguin Books, 2000.

———. *Timebends: A Life*. London: Methuen, 1999.

Morley, Sheridan. *John Gielgud: The Authorized Biography*. New York: Simon & Schuster, 2002.

Murphy, Brenda. *Tennessee Williams and Elia Kazan: A Collaboration in the Theatre*. Cambridge, U.K.: Cambridge University Press, 1992.

Nicklaus, Frederick. *The Man Who Bit the Sun*. New York: New Directions, 1964.

Odets, Clifford. *The Time Is Ripe: The 1940 Journal of Clifford Odets*. New York: Grove Press, 1988.

Paller, Michael. *Gentlemen Callers: Tennessee Williams, Homosexuality, and Mid-Twentieth-Century Drama*. New York: Palgrave Macmillan, 2005.

Palmer, R. Barton, and William Robert Bray. *Hollywood's Tennessee: The Williams Films in Postwar America*. Austin: University of Texas Press, 2009.

Parker, Brian. "Swinging a Cat." In Tennessee Williams, *Cat on a Hot Tin Roof*. New York: New Directions, 2004.

Prosser, William. *The Late Plays of Tennessee Williams*. New York: Scarecrow Press, 2009.

Quintero, José. *If You Don't Dance They Beat You*. Boston: Little, Brown, 1974.

Rader, Dotson. *Blood Dues*. New York: Alfred A. Knopf, 1973.

———. *Tennessee: Cry of the Heart*. Garden City, N.Y.: Doubleday, 1985.

Reeves, Richard. *President Kennedy: Profile of Power*. New York: Simon & Schuster, 1993.

Richardson, Tony. *The Long-Distance Runner: A Memoir*. London: Faber & Faber, 1993.

Sagan, Françoise. *With Fondest Regards*. New York: Dutton, 1985.

Sayre, Nora. *Previous Convictions: A Journey through the 1950s.* New Brunswick, N.J.: Rutgers University Press, 1995.

Schickel, Richard. *Elia Kazan: A Biography.* New York: HarperCollins, 2005.

Selznick, Irene. *A Private View.* New York: Alfred A. Knopf, 1983.

Sherry, Michael S. *Gay Artists in Modern American Culture: An Imagined Conspiracy.* Chapel Hill: University of North Carolina Press, 2007.

Smith, Bruce. *Costly Performances: Tennessee Williams: The Last Stage: A Personal Memoir.* St. Paul, Minn.: Paragon House, 1990.

Spada, James. *More Than a Woman: An Intimate Biography of Bette Davis.* New York: Warner Books, 1994.

Spoto, Donald. *The Kindness of Strangers: The Life of Tennessee Williams.* Boston: Little, Brown, 1985.

Staggs, Sam. *When Blanche Met Brando: The Scandalous Story of "A Streetcar Named Desire."* New York: St. Martin's Press, 2005.

Stapleton, Maureen, and Jane Scovell. *A Hell of a Life.* New York: Simon & Schuster, 1995.

Steen, Mike. *A Look at Tennessee Williams.* New York: Hawthorn Books, 1969.

Sweet Tornado: Margo Jones and the American Theater. DVD, directed by A. Dean Bell, Kay Cattarulla, and Rob Trachin. KERA-TV, PBS, 2006.

Tennessee Williams' South. DVD, directed by Harry Rasky. Canadian Broadcasting Corporation, 1972.

Tynan, Kenneth. *The Diaries of Kenneth Tynan.* Edited by John Lahr. New York: Bloomsbury, 2001.

Updike, John. *Self-Consciousness.* New York: Alfred A. Knopf, 1989.

Vidal, Gore. *The Essential Gore Vidal.* Edited by Fred Kaplan. New York: Random House, 1999.

———. *The Golden Age.* New York: Doubleday, 2000.

———. *Palimpsest: A Memoir.* New York: Random House, 1995.

———. "Tennessee Williams: Someone to Laugh at the Squares With." In Gore Vidal, *Armageddon? Essays 1983–1987.* London: Andre Deutsch, 1987.

Wallach, Eli. *The Good, the Bad, and Me: In My Anecdotage.* Boston: Houghton Mifflin Harcourt, 2005.

Webster, Margaret. *Don't Put Your Daughter on the Stage.* New York: Alfred A. Knopf, 1972.

Williams, Dakin. "The Last Days of Diana Barrymore" (unpublished). Lyle Leverich Collection, attached to the John Lahr Collection, Howard Gotlieb Archival Research Center. Boston University, Boston, Mass.

Williams, Dakin, and Shepherd Mead. *Tennessee Williams: An Intimate Biography.* New York: Arbor House, 1983.

Williams, Edwina Dakin, as told to Lucy Freeman. *Remember Me to Tom.* New York: G. P. Putnam's Sons, 1963.

Williams, Tennessee. "The Big Time Operators" (unpublished). Tennessee Williams Collection, Harry Ransom Center, University of Texas at Austin.

———. *The Collected Poems of Tennessee Williams.* Edited by David Roessel and Nicholas Moschovakis. New York: New Directions, 2002.

————. *Collected Stories*. New York: New Directions, 1985.

————. *Five O'Clock Angel: Letters of Tennessee Williams to Maria St. Just, 1948–1982*. With commentary by Maria St. Just. New York: Alfred A. Knopf, 1990.

————. *Memoirs*. New York: Doubleday, 1975.

————. "Memoirs" (unpublished manuscript). Lyle Leverich Collection, attached to the John Lahr Collection, Howard Gotlieb Archival Research Center, Boston University, Boston, Mass.

————. *Moise and the World of Reason*. London: Brilliance Books, 1984.

————. *New Selected Essays: Where I Live*. Edited by John S. Bak. New York: New Directions, 2009.

————. "Night Passage" (unpublished). Lyle Leverich Collection, attached to the John Lahr Collection, Howard Gotlieb Archival Research Center, Boston University, Boston, Mass.

————. *Notebooks: Tennessee Williams*. Edited by Margaret Bradham Thornton. New Haven, Conn.: Yale University Press, 2006.

————. "The Primary Colors" (unpublished). Tennessee Williams Collection, Harry Ransom Center, University of Texas at Austin.

————. *The Roman Spring of Mrs. Stone*. London: Vintage Classic, 1999.

————. *The Selected Letters of Tennessee Williams*. Vol. 1: *1920–1945*. Edited by Albert J. Devlin and Nancy M. Tischler. New York: New Directions, 2000.

————. *The Selected Letters of Tennessee Williams*. Vol. 2: *1945–1957*. Edited by Albert J. Devlin, co-edited by Nancy M. Tischler. New York: New Directions, 2004.

————. *Tennessee Williams' Letters to Donald Windham, 1940–1965*. Edited and with comments by Donald Windham. New York: Holt, Rinehart & Winston, 1977.

————. *Tennessee Williams: Plays 1937–1955*. New York: Library of America, 2000.

————. *Tennessee Williams: Plays 1957–1980*. New York: Library of America, 2000.

Williams, Tennessee, and Donald Windham. *You Touched Me!* New York: Samuel French, 2010.

Windham, Donald. *As If: A Personal View of Tennessee Williams*. Verona, N.Y.: Privately published, 1985.

Wood, Audrey, with Max Wilk. *Represented by Audrey Wood*. Garden City, N.Y.: Doubleday, 1981.

Young, Jeff. *Kazan: The Master Director Discusses His Films*. New York: Newmarket Press, 1999.

Credits

147 © Eileen Darby Images, Inc.
148 By Martin Harris, PIX International, The Museum of the City of New York.
149 By Jo Healy, Courtesy Erin Clermont.
154 By Jo Healy, Courtesy Erin Clermont.
161 Tennessee Williams Papers, Rare Book and Manuscript Library, Columbia University.
168 Tennessee Williams Papers, Rare Book and Manuscript Library, Columbia University.
170 © Herbert List/Magnum Photos.
177 Culver Pictures Inc.
189 By John Vachon, *Look* Magazine Photograph Collection, Library of Congress, Prints and Photographs Division.
206 Personal Collection of Maureen Stapleton.
213 By John Vachon, *Look* Magazine Photograph Collection, Library of Congress, Prints and Photographs Division.
216 By Arnold Newman/Getty Images.
220 Tennessee Williams Papers, Rare Book and Manuscript Library, Columbia University.
224 Tennessee Williams Papers, Rare Book and Manuscript Library, Columbia University.
228 Photofest.
234 By Clifford Coffin/Condé Nast Archive.
260 World-Telegram Photo, Library of Congress, Prints and Photographs Division, New York World-Telegram & Sun Photograph Collection.
270 By Alfredo Valente/Billy Rose Theatre Division, the New York Public Library for the Performing Arts, Astor, Lenox and Tilden Foundations.
274 Photofest.
286 MSThr550(52), Harvard Theatre Collection, Harvard University.
303 The Museum of the City of New York.
309 © Genevieve Naylor/Corbis.
316 Photofest.
318 Warner Bros./Photofest.
321 © Bettmann/Corbis.
323 By Stan Wayman/Photofest.
327 © Ray Fisher/Tennessee Williams Papers, Rare Book and Manuscript Library, Columbia University.
338 Photofest.
340 Photofest.
347 Collection of Daniel L. Rabinowitz.
358 © Burt Glinn/Magnum Photos.
364 Tennessee Williams Papers, Rare Book and Manuscript Library, Columbia University.
382 By Fred Fehl/Courtesy of Gabriel Pinski.
398 Tennessee Williams Literary File, Photography Collection, Harry Ransom Center, the University of Texas at Austin.
407 Collection of the Begner Family.
419 By Sam Anderson. Tennessee Williams Literary File, Photography Collection, Harry Ransom Center, the University of Texas at Austin.
430 By Friedman-Abeles/ © Billy Rose Theatre Division, the New York Public Library for the Performing Arts.

445 By Friedman-Abeles/© Billy Rose Theatre Division, the New York Public Library for the Performing Arts.

450 Box 3, Frederick Nicklaus Papers, Manuscript Division, Library of Congress, Washington, D.C.

464 By Fuller, Tennessee Williams Papers, Rare Book and Manuscript Library, Columbia University.

469 United Press Photo, Tennessee Williams Literary File, Photography Collection, Harry Ransom Center, the University of Texas at Austin.

481 By Friedman-Abeles/© Billy Rose Theatre Division, the New York Public Library for the Performing Arts.

486 Photofest.

493 Photofest.

498 Tennessee Williams, playwright, the Algonquin Hotel, New York, August 26, 1969. Photograph by Richard Avedon © The Richard Avedon Foundation.

510 By John Vachon, *Look* Magazine Photograph Collection, Library of Congress, Prints and Photographs Division.

524 By Christopher Makos/Makostudio.com.

531 AP/Press Association Images.

536 By Dotson Rader.

543 Pancho Rodriguez Collection.

548 © Philippe Halsman/Magnum Photos.

552 By Sam Shaw © 2014 Sam Shaw Inc., licensed by Shaw Family Archives, www.shawfamilyarchives.com.

565 Photofest.

572 Tennessee Williams (Art), Harry Ransom Center, the University of Texas at Austin.

574 By Kevin Horan/Photofest.

576 AP/Press Association Images.

581 Courtesy of Robert Kiely.

INSERT 1

1. By Karl Bissinger/Karl Bissinger Papers, University of Delaware Library, Courtesy of David Fechheimer.

2. By George Karger/Time & Life Pictures/Getty Images.

3. Photofest.

4. © Ruth Orkin.

5. By Eliot Elisofon/Time & Life Pictures/Getty Images.

6. By W. Eugene Smith/Time & Life Pictures/Getty Images.

7. By Karl Bissinger/Karl Bissinger Papers, University of Delaware Library, Courtesy of David Fechheimer.

8. By Jim Parrott, Tennessee Williams Literary File, Photography Collection, Harry Ransom Center, the University of Texas at Austin.

INSERT 2

1. By Cecil Beaton/Cecil Beaton Studio Archive at Sotheby's.

2. Tennessee Williams Literary File, Photography Collection, Harry Ransom Center, the University of Texas at Austin.

3. By John Vachon, Look Magazine Photograph Collection, Library of Congress, Prints and Photographs Division.
4. Photofest.
5. By Sanford H. Roth/Photofest.
6. By Friedman-Abeles/© Billy Rose Theatre Division, the New York Public Library for the Performing Arts.
7. © Annie Leibovitz/Contact Press images.
8. By Bill Viggiano, Rare Book and Manuscript Library, Columbia University.
9. By Nancy Ellison/Polaris Images.
10. © Scavullo, reprinted by permission of the Francesco Scavullo Foundation, In., and Francesco Scavullo Estate.

TEXT CREDITS

Quotation from undated letter from Marlon Brando reproduced by permission of Brando Enterprises, L.P.
Excerpt from *Brando: Songs My Mother Taught Me* by Marlon Brando and Robert Lindsey © 1994 by Random House.
Brief extracts from four letters of Paul Bigelow to Jordan Massie reprinted by permission of Hank Schwartz.
Excerpt from letters of Cheryl Crawford used courtesy of Special Collections, University of Houston Libraries.
Excerpt from Mitch Douglas's letter to Tennessee Williams (July 1981) reprinted by permission of Mitch Douglas.
Reminiscences of Eddie Dowling reprinted courtesy of Columbia University Center for Oral History Collection.
Extract "Young people who pass through the kind of ascetic phase . . . any sort of external restrictions" from *The Writings of Anna Freud*, by permission of the Marsh Agency Ltd on behalf of the Estate of Anna Freud.
Excerpt of a poem Ruth Gordon sent to Laurette Taylor used by permission of Jerrold B. Gold, executor to the estate of Garson Kanin.
Excerpt from Masud Khan's *Hidden Selves*, © 1989 by Karnac Books.
George Keathley's unpublished reminiscence of Tennessee Williams used by permission of Stanley Klimczyk.
Excerpt from two letters written by Lawrence Kubie used by permission of Ann Kubie Rabinowitz.
Quote from *A Life* by Elia Kazan, © 1988 by Knopf Publishing.
All quotes from the letters, diaries, notebooks, and papers of Elia Kazan used by permission of Frances Kazan.
Excerpts from letters by James Laughlin used by permission of James Laughlin.
Letters from Tennessee Williams to David Lobdell used by permission of the estate of Tennessee Williams.
Excerpts from letters written by Anna Magnani used by permission of Luca Magnani.
Excerpts of a letter from Yukio Mishima to Robert McGregor used by permission of the heirs of Yukio Mishima.
Excerpt from John Maxtone-Graham's stage manager's account of the out-of-town tryout of *Night of the Iguana* used by permission of John Maxtone-Graham.
Excerpts of Seymour Milbert's unpublished account of the rehearsals of the

original production of Tennessee Williams's *Camino Real* used by permission of Katherine Glass.

Excerpts from *Timebends: A Life* by Arthur Miller, copyright © 1987 by Arthur Miller. Used by permission of Grove/Atlantic, Inc. Any third party use of this material, outside of this publication, is prohibited. Excerpts from *Timebends: A Life* by Arthur Miller, copyright © 1987, 1995, used by permission of the Wylie Agency (UK) Limited.

"Love and the Rind of Time" from *The Mortgaged Heart* by Carson McCullers. Copyright © 1971 by Floria V. Lasky, Executrix of the Estate of Carson McCullers. Reprinted by permission of Houghton Mifflin Harcourt Publishing Company. All rights reserved.

Frank Merlo's letters and his poem "To Beg a Question" used by permission of Josephine dePetris.

Excerpt from a letter describing the arrival of Williams in New Orleans in the 1970s used by permission of Zulema Loup.

Quote from Clifford Odets's *The Time Is Ripe* used by permission of Walt Odets.

Excerpt from *The Long-Distance Runner* by Tony Richardson, © 1993 by William Morrow & Co.

Excerpts from *Tennessee: Cry of the Heart*, © 1985 by Dotson Rader, used by permission of Dotson Rader.

Excerpt from "Not Waving but Drowing" by Stevie Smith, © 1957 by Stevie Smith. Used by permission of New Directions Publishing Corporation.

An unpublished letter by Irwin Shaw to Elia Kazan, © Irwin Shaw, reprinted by kind permission of the Estate of Irwin Shaw and the Sayle Literary Agency.

Excerpts from the letters and telegrams of Irene Selznick in the Howard Gottlieb Archival Research Center at Boston University used by permission of Robert Gottlieb.

Excerpts from "A View from inside the Storm" used by permission of Ed Sherin.

A few sentences spoken to John Lahr by Alan Schwartz about a dead monkey quoted with the permission of Alan Schwartz.

Quotes from *Laurette: The Intimate Biography of Laurette Taylor*, © 1984 by Marguerite Courtney, used by permission of Meg Courtney.

Excerpt from *The Diaries of Kenneth Tynan*, © 2001 by Kenneth Tynan and John Lahr. Used by permission of Bloomsbury Publishing.

Excerpt from *Palimpsest: A Memoir*, © 1995 by Gore Vidal/Random House Publishing.

Excerpts from the letters of Marion Vaccaro reprinted by permission of Historic New Orleans Collection. Every effort has been made to locate an heir for Ms. Vaccaro, without success.

Excerpts from Eli Wallach's letters to Elia Kazan used by permission of Eli Wallach.

Excerpt from "Represented by Audrey Wood" by Audrey Wood and Max Wilk used by permission of David Wilk.

Excerpts from letters of Audrey Wood to Tennessee Williams used by permission of Jerold Couture and the Dramatists Guild Fund.

Excerpt from *A House Not Meant to Stand* by Tennessee Williams © 2008 by the University of the South. Reprinted by permission of New Directions Publishing Corp.

Excerpt from *A Streetcar Named Desire* by Tennessee Williams, © 1947 by the University of the South. Reprinted by permission of New Directions Publishing Corp.

Index

Page numbers in *italics* refer to illustrations.